THE
ESSENTIAL
C. S. LEWIS

THE
ESSENTIAL
C. S. LEWIS

Edited and with an introduction by

LYLE W. DORSETT

COLLIER BOOKS

MACMILLAN PUBLISHING COMPANY

NEW YORK

Collier Books
Macmillan Publishing Company
866 Third Avenue, New York, NY 10022

Library of Congress Cataloging-in-Publication Data
Lewis, C. S. (Clive Staples), 1898–1963.
The essential C. S. Lewis.
Bibliography: p.
I. Dorsett, Lyle W. II. Title.
[PR6023.E926A6   1988b]   823'.912   88-11882
ISBN 0-02-019550-8 (pbk.)

Macmillan books are available at special discounts for bulk purchases
for sales promotions, premiums, fund-raising, or educational use.
For details, contact:

Special Sales Director
Macmillan Publishing Company
866 Third Avenue
New York, NY 10022

10 9 8 7 6 5 4 3 2 1

Designed by Jack Meserole

The Essential C. S. Lewis is also available in a hardcover edition
from Macmillan Publishing Company.

PRINTED IN THE UNITED STATES OF AMERICA

The Editor gratefully acknowledges permissions granted by the following sources to reprint material in their control:

THE BODLEY HEAD for *Perelandra*, copyright © 1944 by C. S. Lewis Pte. Ltd.;

CAMBRIDGE UNIVERSITY PRESS for material from *An Experiment in Criticism*, copyright © 1961 by Cambridge University Press, and from *Studies in Words*, copyright © 1960, 1967 by Cambridge University Press;

CURTIS BROWN LTD., London, for material from *God in the Dock*, copyright © 1970 by C. S. Lewis Pte. Ltd., for "Remember Joy Davidman," copyright © 1979 by C. S. Lewis Pte. Ltd., and for "De Descriptione Temporum" from *They Asked for a Paper*, copyright © 1962 by C. S. Lewis Pte. Ltd.;

WILLIAM COLLINS SONS & COMPANY LTD. for *The Abolition of Man*, copyright © 1947 by Macmillan Publishing Company, a division of Macmillan, Inc., for *The Lion, the Witch and the Wardrobe*, copyright © 1950 by C. S. Lewis Pte. Ltd., for material from *Mere Christianity*, copyright © 1943, 1945, 1952 by Macmillan Publishing Company, a division of Macmillan, Inc., from *The Screwtape Letters*, copyright © 1961 by C. S. Lewis Pte. Ltd., and from *The Weight of Glory*, copyright © 1975, 1980 by C. S. Lewis Pte. Ltd., copyright © 1949 by Macmillan Publishing Company, a division of Macmillan, Inc., copyright © 1962, 1965 by C. S. Lewis Pte. Ltd.;

WM. B. EERDMANS PUBLISHING COMPANY for material from *Christian Reflections*, copyright © 1967 by C. S. Lewis Pte. Ltd., from *Letters to an American Lady*, copyright © 1967 by Wm. B. Eerdmans Publishing Company, and from *The Pilgrim's Regress*, copyright 1933, 1943 by C. S. Lewis Pte. Ltd.;

HARCOURT BRACE JOVANOVICH, INC., for material from *Letters of C. S. Lewis*, copyright © 1966 by W. H. Lewis and C. S. Lewis Pte. Ltd., from *Letters to Malcolm: Chiefly on Prayer*, copyright © 1963, 1964 by C. S. Lewis Pte. Ltd., from *On Stories and Other Essays on Literature*, copyright © 1982 by C. S. Lewis Pte. Ltd., from *Poems*, copyright © 1964 by C. S. Lewis Pte. Ltd., from *Reflections on the Psalms*, copyright © 1958 by C. S. Lewis Pte. Ltd., from *Surprised by Joy*, copyright © 1958 by C. S. Lewis Pte. Ltd., and from *The World's Last Night*, copyright © 1952, 1955, 1958, 1959, 1960 by C. S. Lewis Pte. Ltd.;

MACMILLAN PUBLISHING COMPANY, a division of Macmillan, Inc., for material from *C. S. Lewis Letters to Children*, copyright © 1985 by C. S. Lewis Pte. Ltd., and from *They Stand Together: The Letters of C. S. Lewis to Arthur Greeves*, copyright © 1979 by C. S. Lewis Pte. Ltd.;

OXFORD UNIVERSITY PRESS for material from *The Allegory of Love*, copyright © 1936 by Oxford University Press, from *English Literature in the Sixteenth Century*, copyright © 1954 by Oxford University Press, and for "Edmund Spenser" from *Fifteen Poets*, copyright © 1941 by Oxford University Press.

CONTENTS

PREFACE

This anthology is designed to meet an ever-growing need. It is an introduction to C. S. Lewis and his writing for the person who hears him quoted and sees numerous references to his books. Such men and women are aware of Lewis's reputation and importance, they desire to become acquainted with his work, yet they have no idea where to begin. It is also for those who have read one or two of his books, but have no idea what to read next. Finally, this volume attempts to represent the essential Lewis for those whose time or resources are limited.

As director of the Marion E. Wade Center at Wheaton College, Illinois, I meet many people who are drawn by the extraordinary collection of Lewisiana. On hand are all of Lewis's published writings, hundreds of unpublished letters, an enormous collection of secondary literature, some of his furniture (writing desk and chair, wardrobe, table), and many items of memorabilia. Our museum and study center attract hundreds of visitors annually. Besides the people who come to Wheaton, I meet others when I travel and lecture on Lewis and his work. Among the people I encounter are many who say "I have read very little of C. S. Lewis. I want to get into his writing in more depth, but I don't know where to begin. What do you suggest?"

In brief, this collection is designed to introduce readers to the man and the fields or genres in which he wrote. Once you have familiarized yourself with his titles, learned something about the scope and purpose of his work, and read portions of his wide-ranging fare, then it will be easier to go to your bookstore or library and choose from Lewis's writings the works that most appeal to your needs and tastes.

A few words must be said about the selections in this volume. Because this is an introduction for the general reader, I have chosen extracts from each of the seven genres Lewis wrote in: children's fiction, adult fiction, Christian topics, poetry, philosophy, literary history and criticism, and autobiography. An eighth category—letters—is added because Lewis wrote many important letters which are now available in book form. These epistles comprise some of his best work, and the newcomer to Lewis studies will want to be aware of them.

In making selections I have attempted to include as many complete works as possible. For example, an entire children's book, one adult novel, all of *The Abolition of Man,* an entire, if brief, essay on Edmund Spenser rather than portions of a larger piece, are presented. When portions of books are of necessity included, I have sought to use entire chapters where possible. In all cases, I have avoided rearranging and reducing C. S. Lewis's work to suit my tastes or simply to conform to space limitations. I know he would have deplored too much meddling.

Finally, the reader should know that every selection included here has been published, and most of it is still in print. Consequently you can go from these excerpts directly to your local library or bookstore and read the complete text of everything found here.

ACKNOWLEDGMENTS

I am indebted to four colleagues at Wheaton College, Illinois, for careful and critical readings of the Introduction: Mary H. Dorsett, Wayne Martindale, Marjorie Mead, and Mark Noll.

I am grateful, also, to my editor Stephen Wilburn, for all the help he has given me along the way on this and other projects.

A CHRONOLOGY OF SOME IMPORTANT EVENTS IN THE LIFE OF C. S. LEWIS

1898   Born on 29 November in Belfast, Ireland.

1905   The family moves to "Little Lea" on the outskirts of Belfast.

1908   His mother, Florence Lewis, dies of cancer on 23 August. In September he is sent to school at Wynyard in Watford, Hertfordshire, England.

1910   He attends Campbell College in Ireland.

1911   Returns to England and attends school at Cherbourg House, Malvern, beginning in January.

1913   Enters Malvern College, a university preparatory school, in September.

1914   Moves to Surrey and is tutored by W. T. Kirkpatrick ("The Great Knock").

1916   Reads George MacDonald's *Phantastes*. This book, he wrote, "baptized" his imagination. MacDonald, he later claimed, was quoted in every book he subsequently published.

1917   Begins his studies at University College, Oxford, in April; commissioned a second lieutenant in the Somerset Light Infantry in September; goes to the front in November.

1918   Wounded in action in April.

1919   Returns to University College; publishes *Spirits in Bondage* under the pseudonym Clive Hamilton.

1920   Takes a First in Honour Moderations (midway examinations).

1922   Takes a First in Greats (classics and philosophy), and awarded the B. A.

1923   Takes a First in English Language and Literature in the Honour School.

1924   Assumes duties as tutor at University College.

1925 Elected Fellow in English Language and Literature at Magdalen College, Oxford.

1926 Publishes *Dymer* under the pseudonym Clive Hamilton.

1929 His father, Albert J. Lewis, dies in Belfast; becomes a theist but not a Christian.

1931 Confesses belief in Jesus Christ as the Son of God and becomes a regular communicant in the Church of England.

1933 Publishes *The Pilgrim's Regress: An Allegorical Apology for Christianity, Reason and Romanticism* under his own name, dropping the Clive Hamilton pseudonym forever.

1936 Publishes *The Allegory of Love: A Study in Medieval Tradition.*

1938 Publishes *Out of the Silent Planet.*

1939 Publishes *The Personal Heresy: A Controversy*, with E. M. W. Tillyard; publishes *Rehabilitations and Other Essays.*

1940 Publishes *The Problem of Pain;* begins lectures on Christianity to members of the Royal Air Force.

1941 Begins a series of over twenty talks on the British Broadcasting Corporation radio.

1942 Publishes *Broadcast Talks,* a small book based on his 1941 and 1942 BBC radio lectures; publishes *The Screwtape Letters* and *A Preface to "Paradise Lost".*

1943 Publishes *Perelandra, The Abolition of Man,* and the BBC radio lectures entitled *Christian Behaviour.*

1944 Publishes *Beyond Personality* from his BBC talks.

1945 Publishes *The Great Divorce* and *That Hideous Strength.*

1946 Edits *George MacDonald: An Anthology.*

1947 Publishes *Miracles: A Preliminary Study;* edits with others *Essays Presented to Charles Williams.*

1948 Publishes *Arthurian Torso.*

1949 Publishes *Transposition and Other Addresses.*

1950 Receives his first letter from Joy Davidman; publishes *The Lion, the Witch and the Wardrobe.*

1951 Publishes *Prince Caspian: The Return to Narnia*

1952 Meets Joy Davidman; publishes *Mere Christianity,* which includes *Broadcast Talks, Christian Behaviour,* and *Beyond Personality,* all in revised form; publishes *The Voyage of the "Dawn Treader."*

1953 Publishes *The Silver Chair.*

1954   Publishes *The Horse and His Boy* and *English Literature in the Sixteenth Century, Excluding Drama.*

1955   Assumes the position of Professor of Medieval and Renaissance Literature at Magdalene College, Cambridge. His inaugural address is *"De Descriptione Temporum";* publishes *Surprised by Joy: The Shape of My Early Life* and *The Magician's Nephew.*

1956   Marries Joy Davidman in a civil ceremony in April; publishes *The Last Battle* and *Till We Have Faces: A Myth Retold.*

1957   Marries Joy Davidman in an Anglican ceremony in January.

1958   Publishes *Reflections on the Psalms.*

1960   Publishes *The Four Loves, Studies in Words,* and *The World's Last Night and Other Essays.* His wife, Joy, dies on 13 July.

1961   Publishes *A Grief Observed* and *An Experiment in Criticism.*

1962   Publishes *They Asked for a Paper.*

1963   Dies on 22 November, the same day Aldous Huxley and John F. Kennedy died.

1964   *Letters to Malcolm: Chiefly on Prayer,* which he finished in 1963, is published.

PART I

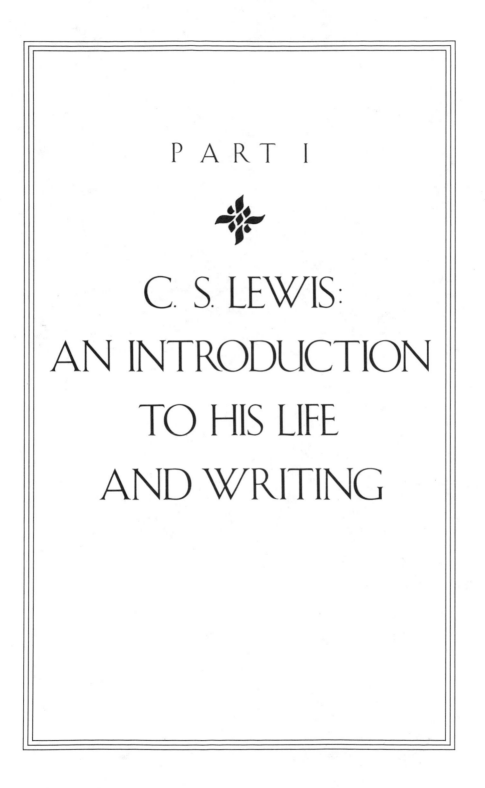

C. S. LEWIS:
AN INTRODUCTION
TO HIS LIFE
AND WRITING

A PORTRAIT of C. S. Lewis appeared on the September 8, 1947, cover of *Time* magazine, focusing national attention on a British Christian who was not yet forty-nine years old and who had been a believer only sixteen years. Lewis's recent conversion and his relatively young age notwithstanding, he was already one of the most popular Christian authors in America and Great Britain.

The passage of over forty years has not diminished C. S. Lewis's popularity. Indeed, over three dozen of his titles are available, with over forty million copies in print. He is one of the best-selling authors of all time and his works are available in many languages.

This man whose books have opened the minds and imaginations of so many people was born in Belfast, Ireland, on November 29, 1898. Baptized into the Church of Ireland a few days later, Clive Staples Lewis, or Jack as his family and friends knew him, was brought up in a Christian home. His one brother, Warren, called Warnie, had been born in 1894. His parents, Albert and Flora, possessed first-rate minds and eclectic reading tastes. They consistently bought and read a wide range of books, taught Jack and Warnie to read at an early age, and encouraged the boys to make use of the family library. Looking back on his youth in their big house named "Little Lea," C. S. Lewis remembered "endless books." He noted in his autobiography that "there were books in the study, books in the drawing-room, books in the cloakroom, books (two deep) in the great bookcase on the landing, books in a bedroom, books piled high as my shoulder in the cistern attic, books of all kinds. . . ."

This world of books became a home within a home to the youngest Lewis. Because he was neither athletically inclined nor given to hunting and fishing, he spent countless days inside, especially during those long Irish months of wind, mist, and rain. Those days at home were usually spent alone once ten-year-old Warnie had been sent off to school in England. Their parting left Jack with books as companions and such authors as Conan Doyle, E. Nesbit, Henry Wadsworth Longfellow, and Mark Twain as his closest friends.

If young C. S. Lewis was often alone, he was not unhappy. His father, a busy lawyer who worked hard and earned a comfortable living for the family, took little time for his children. Nevertheless, Jack enjoyed his mother and his books, and he felt secure in their handsome house near the coast of northeastern Ireland. The boy's world collapsed in August 1908 when his mother was stricken with cancer. A massive tumor was surgically removed at home, but she lived only a few days longer. Upon her death, Lewis recalled, "all settled happiness, all that was tranquil and reliable, disappeared from my life. There was to be much fun, many pleasures, many stabs of Joy; but no more of the old security."

Mrs. Lewis evidently anticipated the boys' loneliness, because she rallied long enough to give each of them a parting gift that would, she prayed, offer solace and guidance. Just before her death she presented them with Bibles signed "From Mommy, with Fondest Love, August 1908." The desired effect would be slow in coming. C. S. Lewis grew angry with God about his mother's death and he concluded that God was either cruel or a vague abstraction. By 1911 or 1912 he had become a confirmed atheist, apparently helped along this path by a strange and spiritually unorthodox teacher at Campbell College, the preparatory school he attended near Little Lea.

Without God or his mother, C. S. Lewis drifted unhappily through the next few years. Following Flora's death, his father sent him off to a school which he greatly disliked. The only thing that made the experience palatable was that Warnie was there too. However, the bond was broken the next year when Warnie was sent to a different school in Malvern, England. Consequently the brothers, who were always the closest of friends, were separated. For the remainder of their school years they saw one another only over holidays.

Young C. S. Lewis was not only separated from his brother for long intervals of time after 1910, he never developed a close relationship with his father. The widower never sufficiently recovered from his grief to be a close companion or guide. A significant change took place in C. S. Lewis's life in autumn 1914. In September he was sent to Great Bookham, Surrey, in southern England, for tutoring by a brilliant former headmaster and family friend, William T. Kirkpatrick. "The Great Knock," as the Lewises dubbed Kirkpatrick, became a father substitute for the bright young pupil, thereby giving him a role model and stability over the next three years. Lewis lived in the Kirkpatrick home, where Mrs. Kirkpatrick fed him and "The Great Knock" introduced him to the classics in Greek, Latin, and Italian literature. Young Jack Lewis also made a start in German. Kirkpatrick not only pushed the teenaged Ulster lad to read great literature in the original languages, he taught him to think critically and analytically as well as how to express himself logically and clearly.

After nearly three years with Kirkpatrick, C. S. Lewis was widely read and rather tough-minded. From the perspective of nearly forty years Lewis looked back and wrote, "My debt to him is very great, my reverence to this day undiminished." His debt was indeed massive. His aged Scotch-Irish tutor had helped him prepare for scholarship examinations at Oxford. Certainly this demanding mentor played a key role in Lewis's exceptional performance at University College, where he took highest honors in Honour Moderations (midway examinations), Greats (classics and philosophy), and English in 1920, 1922, and 1923, respectively.

"The Great Knock" taught C. S. Lewis more than how to think and read intelligently. An atheist, rationalist, and pessimist, the retired schoolmaster reinforced his pupil's already well-formed disdain for people who could believe in the existence and goodness of God without palpable evidence. Truth, as C. S. Lewis learned, is eminently worth pursuing. But the teaching he received insisted that the pathway to truth came only through reason.

Kirkpatrick's teachings left permanent marks on C. S. Lewis. The writer's clear language, careful thoughts, meticulous logic, and persuasive evidence reflect the old teacher's care in developing a brilliant young mind. The Great Knock's imprint notwithstanding, other influences entered the young man's life and left their traces as well. In spring 1916 something happened that rivalled going to Great Bookham for Lewis. In his spare time—of which he had an ample supply since W. T. Kirkpatrick encouraged Jack to pursue his own reading interests— Lewis picked up a copy of George MacDonald's *Phantastes*. Originally published in 1858, this faerie romance fascinated the young reader, who immediately wrote to his friend, Arthur Greeves, and urged him to drop whatever he was reading and get into *Phantastes*.

The impact of this book on Lewis was profound. In retrospect the Belfast-born author recalled that although he had read many other works of romanticism, this little volume touched a deep need in his life. Nothing was at that time further from his thoughts than Christianity. Nevertheless he was aware of a strange "new world"—one that was "also homely and humble." If it was only a dream, it was one "in which one at least felt strongly vigilant; that the whole book had about it a sort of cool, morning innocence, and also, quite unmistakenly, a certain quality of Death, *good* Death." Lewis subsequently recalled that this book "was to convert, even to baptise (that was where the Death came in) my imagination." In his introduction to *George MacDonald: An Anthology* (1946) Lewis said that in 1916 *Phantastes* did nothing to his intellect or conscience. This would come later and with the help of other books and people. "But when the process was complete—by which, of course, I mean 'when it had *really* begun'—I found that I was still with MacDonald and that he had accompanied me all the way and that I was now at last ready to hear from him much that he could not have told me at that first meeting." Lewis admitted that what MacDonald eventually revealed to him was what he had been saying to him already in *Phantastes*— that what enchanted him in the romance and the other imaginative literature "turned out to be the quality of the real universe, the divine, magical, terrifying, and ecstatic reality in which we all live."

C. S. Lewis never overthrew the rationalist baggage he collected from William T. Kirkpatrick, but George MacDonald helped him see that the pursuit of truth is more complicated than he had been taught. MacDonald, however, was not alone in causing Lewis to adopt new angles of vision. The ancient academic community of Oxford itself provided the location and atmosphere for subsequent influences and changes. Ever since his mother died and his father withdrew into himself, Jack had been looking for a home and a family. The Kirkpatricks sufficed at a crucial time, but that influence, while prodigious, could not go on much longer. For a few years Mrs. Kirkpatrick gave the young man a home while her husband prepared his mind for a new one.

The new home was Oxford, where the nineteen-year-old scholar went in 1917. Entering University College that year, Lewis was so happy in Oxford that he never left. Except for a stint of combat in France from 1917 to 1919, he seldom ventured from the academic community of aged buildings, archaic streets, and old books except for brief visits to his Irish birthplace or to take walking holidays with his closest Oxford companions. Even after thirty years as a Fellow in English language and literature at Magdalen College, when Lewis accepted a professorship at Cambridge University in 1955, he maintained his Headington residence, The Kilns, on the eastern edge of Oxford and commuted between the two cities on weekends. He lived there until he died in 1963 and his remains are interred in the Anglican churchyard just a short walk away.

During his early Oxford years Lewis began to assemble a family around himself. After his friend E. F. C. "Paddy" Moore was killed in World War I, motherless Lewis began to look after his deceased friend's mother and little sister. Indeed, by 1921 Jack Lewis moved into an Oxford house with Mrs. Janie King Moore and her child, Maureen. Although Maureen eventually married and moved away, Lewis virtually adopted Mrs. Moore as a mother. They lived together (Warnie joined them in 1930) in Oxford until the surrogate mother was placed in a nursing home in 1950. She died in 1951.

Lewis gained more than a new home and family in Oxford; he discovered new authors and found a circle of friends who influenced his thinking. In the intellectually stimulating world of drafty lecture halls, smoke-filled pubs, and book-lined tutorial rooms, Lewis feasted on a rich fare of books, ideas, and conversation. Among the authors Lewis imbibed was G. K. Chesterton. It was this Cockney man's *Orthodoxy* and *The Everlasting Man* that helped stimulate the Ulster man's spirituality and raised serious questions about his Surrey-bred philosophic materialism.

While MacDonald and Chesterton were stirring Lewis's thoughts, a new friend, Owen Barfield, began to assault his atheism and rationalistic assumptions. Probably no single person besides Kirkpatrick exerted so much influence on C. S. Lewis's mind as Owen Barfield. Born in England in 1898, Barfield was the same age as Lewis and they were destined to be friends for life. They first met during their undergraduate days at Oxford. Both men fought in the world war and returned to Oxford where they began what they called their own "Great War" through conversation and correspondence. In the dedication to his first major scholarly book, *The Allegory of Love* (1936), Lewis labels Barfield the "wisest and best of my unofficial teachers." In their debates about philosophy Lewis rejected Barfield's theory of "evolution of consciousness" and the idea system of anthroposophy that Barfield acquired and built on from Rudolph Steiner. However, Lewis did learn from Barfield that two aspects of his own thought were myopic. Lewis admitted that Barfield "made short work of . . . my 'chronological snobbery,' the uncritical acceptance of the intellectual climate common to our age . . ."—the assumption that whatever is "out of date is on that account discredited." This freed Lewis to take seriously the writings of the Middle Ages and Renaissance. Exercising this freedom also caused him to reexamine the supernatural world he had encountered through the books of George MacDonald. Secondly, Barfield, who by this time had become a theist, also convinced Lewis that realism, or the world of the senses "as rock bottom" reality, did not go far enough to explain logic, ethics, and aesthetics. In short, through hours, months, and eventually years of argumentation, Barfield, the brilliant combatant, finally convinced Lewis of the existence of "The Absolute."

Several other factors spurred Lewis farther down the pathway toward Christianity. First, his father died in autumn 1929, causing Lewis to meditate on eternal issues. Then in May 1931 Warnie returned to the Christian faith he had deserted many years before. Three months later the two brothers returned to Ireland, making their first sentimental journey there since their father's death. Most certainly Warren spoke with Jack of his newly found faith, and it is tempting to see the men discussing what their father's life and death had to do with their own view of God. It is significant, too, that the brothers went to church together in Ireland in August 1931, resuming a ritual they had discontinued many years before.

In mid-September two friends, Hugo Dyson, who had studied English at Oxford and lectured both there and at Reading, and J. R. R. Tolkien, Professor of Anglo-Saxon at Oxford, engaged Lewis in what he immediately recalled "was really a memorable walk [and discussion] . . . on metaphor and myth." A few days later Lewis wrote, "I have just passed on from believing in God to definitely believing in Christ." Dyson and Tolkien had helped him see that pagan myths of dying and reviving gods did not prove that the Christ story is false. On the contrary, these ancient myths show us how pagan peoples had a glimpse of the Truth that was going to happen and in fact did happen two thousand years ago.

Changing his mind about the veracity of the Christ story marked a watershed in C. S. Lewis's life. The light by which he newly walked illuminated all things in a fresh way and this was nowhere more apparent than in his writing. Prior to his conversion in 1931, Lewis had written two books of poems: *Spirits in Bondage* (1919) and *Dymer* (1926). Both volumes were written under the pseudonym Clive Hamilton, and both received tepid acclaim and limited readership. Nevertheless, Lewis had a burning desire to express himself in writing; yet he, even more than the critics, recognized the limitations of his poetry. An artist in search of a medium, he desperately needed a focus or a muse.

His new faith in Christ apparently ended his agony; at least it propelled him forward and gave his life and writing a new direction. His primary medium became prose, much of it inspired by his religion. Looking back from the vantage point of more than a quarter century after returning to his childhood faith, Lewis emphatically maintained that "most of my books are evangelistic. . . ." Reason and imagination were no longer at loggerheads in C. S. Lewis's mind. He saw both avenues leading to the Christian God, and he eagerly communicated his discovery to anyone of any age who would listen.

An early manifestation of his purposeful life came in 1933 with the publication of *The Pilgrims Regress: An Allegorical Apology for Christianity, Reason and Romanticism.* Published by Dent in London, the book received favorable reviews, but fewer than 700 copies out of a 1,500-printing were sold. Nevertheless, the zealous believer was undaunted. He had received his calling, he put his hand to the plow, and he never looked back. With *The Pilgrim's Regress* Lewis began a lifelong avocation of publishing the fruits of his reason and imagination regarding Christianity. For the next three decades, until his death in 1963, Lewis produced an enormous list of books embracing Christian fantasy, apologetics, and discipleship. He became what can only be described as a literary evangelist. Indeed, most of his colleagues in academia, as well as some of his closest friends, found this zealous element in his writing to be irritating, if not embarrassing.

To the dismay of some Oxford aesthetes Lewis exclaimed that "the salvation of a single soul is more important than the production or preservation of all the epics and tragedies in the world. . . ." But this position notwithstanding, the Oxford scholar continued to admire great literature, and he made a decision to study, critically analyze, and teach it as well. His vocation, after all, was college teaching. He never considered any other career. No doubt Kirkpatrick helped him make this choice because the old schoolmaster wrote Jack's father that "you may make a writer or a scholar of him, but you'll not make anything else. You may make up your mind to *that.*"

C. S. Lewis pursued his academic calling with enthusiasm. Former pupils testify that he was a superb teacher—one who packed the lecture hall to capacity and kept the eager and voluntary listeners enthralled. His tutorials, if demanding, were nevertheless rewarding. Most survivors praised his skill in teaching them to think and write effectively, and they applauded his ability to reveal the hidden as well as the obvious threads of English literary history. The vigorous pedagogical style of "The Great Knock" helped shape Lewis's own teaching. Pupils eager to learn flourished on it; the laggards and unusually sensitive wilted under the strain.

Lewis excelled as an academician in more places than the lecture hall and tutorial room. A productive scholar, he made original and lasting contributions to the fields of Medieval and Renaissance literary history and criticism. Never neglecting his professional calling for popular literature and theology, he maintained a long and consistent record of scholarly publications. Besides his popular work, he produced more books (well-received ones at that) than most of his colleagues.

The pattern of this prolific writer's publishing history suggests that he was always writing, and usually worked on more than one book at a time. He must have found it helpful to work on a religious theme as well as a scholarly subject, refreshing himself by alternating from one to the other. Whatever the impetus for his pattern, he produced both academic books and popular theology with astonishing frequency.

Soon after the publication of his first apologetical work, *The Pilgrim's Regress,* Lewis prepared his first book-length venture in literary history and criticism, *The Allegory of Love: A Study in Medieval Tradition* (1936). Published by the Oxford University Press, this original contribution to the scholarship of Medieval literature received outstanding critical acclaim and it is still hailed as a classic in the field. While working on this 366-page monograph, Lewis's far-ranging mind, vivid imagination, and profound need to communicate the reality of his faith to others, prompted him to a first-time experience of writing fiction. In 1938 the published poet and literary historian wrote his first novel, *Out of the Silent Planet.* Written for people who would never read the Bible or enter a church, this tale of fantasy was designed to draw unsuspecting materialists into a story that would tempt them to contemplate spiritual realities and the struggle between good and evil. For Lewis this initial excursion into a new genre proved to be rewarding and successful. People read the book and clamored for more. They were eventually treated to two more volumes of what became his popular space trilogy, *Perelandra* (1943) and *That Hideous Strength* (1945).

As World War II engulfed the British Isles and all of Europe, many ordinary enterprises halted. But for C. S. Lewis it was writing as usual with the only noticeable alterations being a shortage of paper, which forced him to economize by using what would have been scrap paper in the pre-war years. During the international conflict he published *Rehabilitations and Other Essays* (1939), a book of essays in defense of several unpopular causes, among them Romanticism, the English Studies program at Oxford, popular literature, and Anglo-Saxon poetry.

While younger Britishers and his older brother went on active service against the Germans and Japanese, C. S. Lewis stayed at home and battled evil, promoted Christianity, and encouraged the armed forces in an aptly named volume, *The Problem of Pain* (1940). He told the nation about God's love in the midst of turmoil. This book attracted much attention from a wounded nation, but it did not prove as popular as *The Screwtape Letters* (1942), which introduced the reading public to Screwtape and Wormwood, Lewis's fictional depictions of one of Satan's personnel managers and his young trainee.

The increasingly famous author agreed to do a series of lectures on BBC radio. Fashioned to explain and defend Christianity in laymen's language to millions of people who had lost their moorings, these well-received talks were hurried into print in 1942, 1943, and 1944 as *Broadcast Talks, Christian Behaviour,* and *Beyond Personality,* respectively.

Lewis not only wrote novels and performed radio broadcasts during the war, he gave a series of talks on the faith to Royal Air Force crews who were flying regular missions over the military and industrial centers of Germany. This would have been enough activity to keep most people completely occupied, but the apparently indefatigable Lewis found time to preach sermons and write several other books during World War II. A debate on literary-critical theory, with E. M. W. Tillyard, was published early in the war as *The Personal Heresy: A Controversy* (1939) and then came *The Abolition of Man: Reflections on Education with Special Reference to the Teaching of English in the Upper Forms of Schools* (1943). This slender book was initially delivered as a series of lectures at the University of Durham. It is a classic essay on educational and moral philosophy that probes the place of education in moral development.

An ancient proverb reminds us that "iron sharpeneth iron; so a man sharpeneth the countenance of his friend." During the war this saying applied to C. S. Lewis and an informal group called the "Inklings." For years prior to World War II a number of Oxford intellectuals met regularly, reading aloud from their books or essays in progress. Spirited discussion followed as the assembled Inklings applauded or criticized the efforts of their fellows. The attendance at these literary gatherings varied, but C. S. Lewis, J. R. R. Tolkien, and Neville Coghill were usually present. Warren Lewis came if he could, Owen Barfield occasionally ventured up from London (he had a law practice there), and R. E. Havard participated as often as his medical practice allowed. Oxford fellows and tutors Hugo Dyson, Colin Hardie, and a dozen or so others appeared from time to time.

In 1939 a newcomer named Charles William joined the Inklings. He was a member of the Oxford University Press editorial staff and when the press relocated from London to Oxford to escape the Nazi air raids, Williams entered the circle of Inklings as a regular attender until his unexpected death in 1945.

At first glance Charles Williams appeared an unlikely member of the Oxford group. Although comprised of singular characters who displayed little in common besides a love for books, ideas, and conversation about both, they all had a vaguely academic look and seemed uniformly at home in tweed jackets, slouch hats, and corduroy or wool trousers rounded at the knees. While this motley group looked like professors and artists, Williams more closely resembled a big city banker. A bespectacled and slender man with piercing eyes, Charles Williams wore neatly pressed conservative-colored suits, fashionable shirts and ties, and carefully polished shoes. These obvious differences notwithstanding, Williams realized numerous benefits from the Inklings, and he gave them much in return. A poet, critic, playwright, novelist, and biographer, Williams profited from the critiques of his work. And while he had never received the formal schooling his new associates enjoyed, it was their influence that won him an honorary Master of Arts degree from Oxford in 1943.

Williams certainly gave as much to the Inklings as he received. He possessed an animated and original mind, and his contributions enlivened the meetings. He published some of his new colleagues' manuscripts and helped launch a monograph series with Lewis and Tolkien as general editors. Certainly the writers among the Inklings, such as Tolkien and Warren H. Lewis, profited from his critiques, but probably no one found Williams as stimulating as C. S. Lewis. For several years Lewis had been lecturing on John Milton, and in Williams he found a kindred spirit who shared his deep attraction to the poet and who spent many hours helping him hone his insights on the meaning of seventeenth-century literature. One of the manifestations of Lewis's relationship with Charles Williams was A Preface to "Paradise Lost" (1942), published by Oxford University Press. Dedicated to Williams, this book criticized modern interpretations of Paradise Lost and attempted to "restore the belief that Milton may, after all, have hated what he displays as hateful."

If Charles Williams influenced the writing of A Preface to "Paradise Lost," George MacDonald's books (he died in 1905) became the impetus for Lewis's last World War II vintage book, The Great Divorce (1945). Published at the end of the war, this fantasy presents a powerful tale about heaven, hell, and the ultimate effects of our free choices. Like The Screwtape Letters, The Great Divorce was serialized in a weekly newspaper, the Guardian, before it appeared in book form. Similar to the BBC radio broadcasts and most of Lewis's popular literary efforts, The Great Divorce pointed the way to the Christian faith. What he wrote about his radio talks he could have said about his religious books: "Mine are praeparatio evangelica rather than evangelism, an attempt to convince people that there is a moral law, that we disobey it, and that the existence of a Lawgiver is at least very probable and also (unless you add the Christian doctrine of the Atonement) that this imparts despair rather than comfort."

The Great Divorce fulfilled its purpose well. One of the people touched by this book and The Screwtape Letters was Joy Davidman Gresham of New York City. A Jewess of Communist rather than religious persuasion, Joy Davidman was a published poet, novelist, and film critic. She became a baptized Christian in 1947 at age thirty-two, the same year Lewis published Miracles: A Preliminary Study. The slender volume of just over two hundred pages had a profound impact on Joy Davidman Gresham as she grew in her faith during the late 1940s, but neither she nor Lewis could know the profound impact she was destined to have on his life and work during the last decade of his life.

By the end of the decade of the 1940s, most of Lewis's writing focused on Christianity. A volume of sermons and essays, Transpositions and Other Essays, appeared in 1949. In all he had published eight volumes of non-fiction on the faith, one work of social theory marked with Christian overtones, and three novels arising from his Christ-inspired imagination. Yet he had neither forgotten nor neglected his academic responsibilities. In 1948 Oxford University Press brought out *Arthurian Torso*. This book included Charles Williams's unfinished prose study on Arthurian legend called "The Figure of Arthur." Lewis made this important piece of Williams's work available to the public, and he published with it an extended and indispensable commentary on the late author's Arthurian poetry.

The decade of the 1950s brought prodigious change to Lewis's life. He was already well known, but when he launched a series of seven children's books in as many years, his fame soared to new heights. "The Chronicles of Narnia" delighted youngsters and the young at heart and they sold extremely well. These fantasies were intended to awaken youthful imaginations and bring young and old alike to an awareness of spiritual reality. The seven books in the series are: *The Lion, the Witch and the Wardrobe* (1950); *Prince Caspian* (1951); *The Voyage of the "Dawn Treader"* (1952); *The Silver Chair* (1953); *The Horse and His Boy* (1954); *The Magician's Nephew* (1955); *The Last Battle* (1956).

If these books made C. S. Lewis famous throughout the English-speaking world, they also encouraged a flood of criticism at home. As a champion of such unpopular causes as Christian orthodoxy and literary romanticism, he had already made numerous enemies. Now an even larger group of critics emerged. A sizeable body of Oxford faculty shunned him; others criticized him to his face; some did so behind his back. There was jealousy, to be sure, because of his popularity; there was also disdain for an academician without ordination or training in theology who presumed to write outside of his academic field. Finally, many colleagues saw him as hopelessly misguided because he wasted his time writing fiction for children instead of spending all of his efforts producing solid scholarship for the academic community.

C. S. Lewis considered the charge of short-changing his professional field absurd. He continued to write highly original works for the scholarly world. During the years that the Narnian books appeared he published an important volume for *The Oxford History of English Literature* series entitled *English Literature in the Sixteenth Century, Excluding Drama* (1954). This erudite tome of nearly seven hundred pages of small print stands as a model of its kind and it is still required reading for serious students of the early modern period.

With the notoriety surrounding the publication of "The Chronicles of Narnia" came a torrent of mail from fans throughout the United States and the United Kingdom. Answering the scores of letters that arrived each week—and Lewis believed it was his personal responsibility to respond—changed his life significantly. He devoted two or three hours a day, several days a week, to answering his correspondents of all ages.

The outpouring of royalties from his British and American publishers rivalled the tidal wave of fan mail. This development further complicated Lewis's life because he believed these monies should be placed in a fund and carefully distributed to worthy causes, and this took time. Continually upgrading his standard of living neither suited Lewis's lifestyle nor his calling. He saw himself as God's steward and felt responsible for the careful expenditure and distribution of everything the Heavenly Father provided.

Stewardship of money, like answering piles of mail, took time away from writing and increased the pressures of life, but nothing complicated Lewis's life like his marriage to Joy Davidman Gresham. Born in New York City in 1915, Joy Davidman was exceptionally intelligent. Everyone who knew her remembered her photographic mind, unbounded energy, voracious appetite for books, and sometimes abrasive disposition. Physically attractive until she was stricken with cancer in the mid-1950s, the dark-haired, dark-eyed, and shapely Joy Davidman began writing to C. S. Lewis about matters of Christian faith in the late 1940s. In 1952 they met for the first time when she took a holiday in England. There this American sought Lewis's help in finding a British publisher for a book she had just finished on the Ten Commandments entitled *Smoke on the Mountain.* Lewis became her unofficial agent, spiritual advisor, confidant, and friend. In the meantime, however, Joy's husband abandoned her for another woman, and soon thereafter she relocated to London with David and Douglas, her two pre-teen sons.

Trouble plagued the American divorcée from the outset. Her mother, father, and brother took a dim view of her conversion, her boys disliked England, and her ex-husband, William Lindsay Gresham, seldom paid child support. Although she had several books in print, they did not sell well. Only C. S. Lewis's generosity paid the rent and allowed the boys to attend a good school.

A deep friendship grew from charity and common interests in literature and religion; but eventually *agape* was accompanied by *eros*. Although Joy was sixteen years Lewis's junior, they were married in 1956 and began a happy life together. Lewis wrote to one of his friends soon after their marriage that "it's funny having at 59 the sort of happiness most men have in their twenties. . . . 'Thou hast kept the good wine til now.' "

The new wine was heady but it flowed briefly. On July 13, 1960, Mrs. C. S. Lewis died from cancer. She was only forty-five years old. Her sudden invasion of Lewis's life—complete with an instant family of two active boys—brought novelty if not disorder to the bachelor's home. Joy's illness, which struck hard, retreated into remission, and then lashed out once more with a fatal blow, added to the tension.

C. S. Lewis's unexpected marriage to a divorced Jewish American with a Communist Party past won even less approval in Oxford than the Narnian books. With only a few exceptions, Jack Lewis's friends and colleagues disliked Mrs. Lewis and made every effort to avoid her company. Social ostracism and the problems of parenting, complicated by his wife's deteriorating health, did not promote life as usual at The Kilns. Nevertheless, the new family seems to have been a blessing to the aging bachelor. The boys reminded Jack of his own childhood and his delight in youthful activities. Also, his election to a professor-

ship at Cambridge freed him from many responsibilities, thereby allowing him
more time for his new family. Furthermore, Joy became a source of inspiration
to her new husband. She encouraged him to continue writing religious books. In
particular she urged him to write *Reflections on the Psalms* (1958). Likewise, her
influence was so great on what Lewis considered his best book, *Till We Have
Faces: A Myth Retold* (1956), that he told one close friend she was actually his
co-author.

Not only did Joy encourage him to write *Reflections on the Psalms* and *Till
We Have Faces*, she most certainly helped inspire a book on biblical concepts
of love (affection, friendship, *eros*, charity) entitled *The Four Loves* (1960). And
if she did not directly influence his next two books she was, as usual, his most
severe and helpful critic. The year she died he published *Studies in Words* and
The World's Last Night and Other Essays, as well as *The Four Loves*.

Joy's death in 1960 retarded but did not halt Lewis's writing. He published
An Experiment in Criticism in 1961 and followed it the next year with a journal
he kept that chronicled his spiritual development during this time of bereavement and loneliness. Lewis published the slender volume, entitled *A Grief Observed*, under the pseudonym N. W. Clerk. Today it sells under the name of
C. S. Lewis, as does a book of addresses on literary and religious topics published
in 1962 and called *They Asked for a Paper*.

This incredibly productive author had two more books in press when he died
in 1963. Like his publications of years before, they demonstrated his continued
commitment to writing more than one book at a time. Published posthumously
in 1964 these last two finalize and symbolize that recurring pattern of dividing
his time between literary history and popular religion. *Letters to Malcolm: Chiefly
on Prayer* tackles difficult questions related to prayer and the believer's relationship with God. *The Discarded Image: An Introduction to Medieval and Renaissance Literature* represents Lewis's last teaching effort. Here he mapped out the
literature of this era by developing the problem of a culture's world image upon
the mind.

After this celebrated intellectual's death many books of his own words have
been edited and published. Among these are several volumes of letters: Warren
Hamilton Lewis, ed., *Letters of C. S. Lewis* (1966); Clyde S. Kilby, ed., *Letters
to an American Lady* (1967); Walter Hooper, ed., *They Stand Together: The
Letters of C. S. Lewis to Arthur Greeves, 1914–1963* (1979); Lyle W. Dorsett
and Marjorie Lamp Mead, eds., *C. S. Lewis Letters to Children* (1985). Some
other notable books of Lewis's writings, edited by Walter Hooper, are: *Poems*
(1964); *Studies in Medieval and Renaissance Literature* (1966); *Of Other
Worlds: Essays and Stories* (1966); *Christian Reflections* (1967); *Narrative
Poems* (1969); *Selected Literary Essays* (1969); *God in the Dock: Essays on
Theology and Ethics* (1970); *Fern-Seed and Elephants: And Other Essays on
Christianity* (1974); *The Dark Tower and Other Stories* (1977); and *Present
Concerns: Ethical Essays* (1986). Perhaps J. R. R. Tolkien only half jested when

he commented that C. S. Lewis was the only author who published more after he died than before.

Interest in the late Cambridge professor continues to grow. Indeed annual sales of Lewis's books have nearly quadrupled since his death. There are many reasons for Lewis's popularity, not the least of them the fact that Christianity has enjoyed few articulate English-speaking defenders since the death of G. K. Chesterton in 1936. Throughout much of this century, orthodox Christianity has been bereft of leadership; proponents of the faith have been on the defensive. The growing tide of secularism, manifested in philosophic materialism, religious liberalism, Freudianism, logical positivism, and mass consumerism has benefitted from a large share of intelligent writers, whereas historic creedal Christianity has had few able spokesmen.

If the intellectual elite eschewed orthodox Christianity, many of the mainstream laity and clergy looked for a defender to champion their cause. Beginning his writing in the 1930s and carrying on unabated until his death in 1963, Lewis intelligently and articulately took up the cause. He came to believe that Christianity—complete with Scripture and creed—was true, and he told the world about it. He fearlessly and aggressively went on the offensive, taking the secularists to task by attacking their assumptions and poking holes in their logic. He likewise made a concerted effort to communicate the Christian story to a post-Christian culture by dropping the stained-glass language of a bygone era and using in its place earthy illustrations easily grasped by the public. Through his books and essays he gave less articulate clergy words to illuminate their religious doctrine, and he also opened the eyes of many secular seekers to the spiritual dimension of their own experiences. Books such as *Mere Christianity, The Problem of Pain,* and *Miracles,* were excellent volumes for those who sought a rational and didactic exposition of historic Christianity. These seekers—and there turned out to be thousands of them on both sides of the Atlantic—revelled in Lewis's sharply written prose. They joined together in study groups and clubs to discuss his works, and they passed out copies to sideline skeptics who said Christianity was not a religion for thoughtful people.

C. S. Lewis won an even larger following when he branched out into fiction. Many readers in the United Kingdom and America had no taste for transparently Christian topics or books on religion in any form. By writing the space trilogy, the Narnian Chronicles, and other works, Lewis awakened the imaginations of readers of all ages. Through his other books like *The Screwtape Letters, The Great Divorce,* and *Till We Have Faces,* Lewis confronted secular people with questions about spiritual realities that they might never have encountered in another format.

If Lewis's works of fantasy touched sympathetic chords in people who would never enter a church or pick up a Bible, many of his writings took the place of textbooks or study guides for Christians who sought instruction. Countless churchgoers looked in vain for sound teaching on Christian doctrine, morals, and ethics. Consequently, Lewis became a spiritual guide and tutor in absentia.

Lewis's persistent popularity is partially explained by his refusal to sidestep the difficult questions of the faith—the questions he had and instinctively knew others wrestled with as well. A man who had seen his mother die at an early age, who also experienced the mass carnage of a European war, did not easily shy away from questions about suffering, evil, heaven, and hell. While many religious leaders seemed to dodge the toughest questions most people asked, Lewis tackled them head on in such volumes as *The Problem of Pain* and *A Grief Observed*. Likewise, he hammered through the knotty issues of prayer, forthrightly asking if our petitions change things or make no difference at all. *Letters to Malcolm: Chiefly on Prayer* confronted this subject, as did the essays "The Efficacy of Prayer," in the *Atlantic Monthly* (January 1959), and "Scraps," in *God in the Dock*.

Certainly Lewis's following was larger than most writers because he served up age-old themes in formats suitable for everyone. Almost any topic he covered in prose can be found in his fiction and poetry as well. Indeed, this unusually versatile writer frequently presented his thoughts in one genre and then reiterated the theme in one or two other types of literature. For example, the complexity of love can be found first in the novel *Till We Have Faces*, and then reappears didactically in *The Four Loves*. The fall of man is in much of Lewis's writing but it is a major theme in fictional *Perelandra* and the scholarly literary criticism of *A Preface to "Paradise Lost"*. In the same vein, grief and suffering are central to his teaching in *The Problem of Pain* as well as to his autobiographical essay *A Grief Observed*.

Something Evelyn Underhill wrote suggests another reason for C. S. Lewis's popularity. According to Underhill everyone has three deep cravings: "The first is the craving which makes him a pilgrim and a wanderer. It is the longing to go out from his normal world in search of a lost home, a 'better country,' an Eldorado, a Sarras, a Heavenly Syon. The next is the craving of heart for heart, or the Soul for its perfect mate, which makes him a lover. The third is the craving for inward purity and perfection, which makes him an ascetic, and in the last resort a saint." Perhaps C. S. Lewis's frequent preoccupation with pilgrimage and longing (or joy) explains why, for example, the Narnian Chronicles, *Surprised by Joy* and *The Pilgrims Regress* are so widely read that they are now being labelled classics.

Despite the Christian appeal of his books, Lewis has a large audience of readers who may or may not be Christians. The Belfast-born writer, who from childhood loved to explore other worlds through books, developed a historian's passion to introduce other people to past cultures and ideas. His desire to communicate Christianity to a post-Christian world doubtlessly reflected this need, but it went even further. In his volumes of literary history and criticism such as *The Discarded Image*, *The Allegory of Love*, and *English Literature in the Sixteenth Century, Excluding Drama*, we find the teacher at his best. These books continue to impart to younger scholars important insights into the ideas and culture of the Middle Ages.

C. S. Lewis, of course, had his limitations. Many critics remind readers of his neglect of social and political issues, the sexism in his early writing, his philosophical inconsistencies regarding reason and imagination in his apologetics, as well as his too pat "either-or" approach to complicated theological problems. Some Catholic and Protestant sacramentalists criticize Lewis's neglect of the sacraments in his "mere" or "basic Christianity," and some Roman Catholics deplore his disregard for the Magisterium in the same way.

Lewis's critics notwithstanding, his books still sell in record numbers; a growing list of books and articles, as well as masters' and doctoral theses are based on his works, and formal courses on his literature appear on class schedules in many colleges and seminaries. Perhaps his writing continues to attract readers because he is so often witty, fervent, non-sectarian, and apolitical. Certainly his style accounts for much of the popularity. His writing is replete with simple sentences, and his prose is highly visual. His habitual use of analogy, particularly his skill in explaining the unfamiliar in terms of the familiar, captivates the mind of the reader.

In the last analysis, Lewis's works live because of his confident and enthusiastic focus on Christianity and the way it gives meaning to everything we think, crave, are, and do. To Lewis orthodox Christianity explains everything. This ancient faith—both what it is and what it means—is the unifying theme of his most popular books. To him, Christianity is more than true, it explains all truth. For C. S. Lewis and many of his readers this is a declaration of liberation.

PART II

AUTOBIOGRAPHY

C. S. LEWIS enjoyed writing, and like most authors he hoped his books would be widely read. Nevertheless, he did not seek public scrutiny or personal acclaim. When this personal reticence is added to his distrust of self-analysis, it is not surprising that his autobiographical writing is sparse. His first book of prose, *The Pilgrim's Regress: An Allegorical Apology for Christianity, Reason and Romanticism* (1933), is essentially autobiographical. Anyone who wants to understand Lewis should read it, but they should know that ten years after publication he admitted that the book was unnecessarily obscure and uncharitable in tone. A clear rationale of Lewis's personal and spiritual development can be found in the preface to the third edition of this allegory.

Surprised by Joy: The Shape of My Early Life (1955) provides the key to his early life and spiritual journey. He wrote this not to put himself on public display but, as he phrased it in the preface, "partly in answer to requests that I would tell how I passed from Atheism to Christianity and partly to correct one or two false notions that seem to have got about."

The excerpts reprinted here from his autobiography demonstrate some of the profound influences on his life.

Although Lewis wrote only one autobiography of limited scope, he did reveal the nature of his marriage to Joy Davidman in *A Grief Observed* (1961). In this small book he chronicles his battle with grief over her pain and untimely death. A few literary critics argue that this book, first published under the pseudonym of N. W. Clerk, is fictional rather than autobiographical. However, his close friends Owen Barfield and Roger Lancelyn Green have convinced me that *A Grief Observed* belongs in the category of autobiography.

No portion of *A Grief Observed* is reproduced here, but some particularly revealing letters are taken from *They Stand Together: The Letters of C. S. Lewis to Arthur Greeves, 1914–1963* (1979), edited by Walter Hooper. Arthur Greeves was one of Lewis's dearest friends. The letters included in this chapter illuminate the events surrounding a watershed in Lewis's life.

The First Years

In ADDITION TO good parents, good food, and a garden (which then seemed large) to play in, I began life with two other blessings. One was our nurse, Lizzie Endicott, in whom even the exacting memory of childhood can discover no flaw—nothing but kindness, gaiety, and good sense. There was no nonsense about "lady nurses" in those days. Through Lizzie we struck our roots into the peasantry of County Down. We were thus free of two very different social worlds. To this I owe my lifelong immunity from the false identification which some people make of refinement with virtue. From before I can remember I had understood that certain jokes could be shared with Lizzie which were impossible in the drawing room; and also that Lizzie was, as nearly as a human can be, simply good.

The other blessing was my brother. Though three years my senior, he never seemed to be an elder brother; we were allies, not to say confederates, from the first. Yet we were very different. Our earliest pictures (and I can remember no time when we were not incessantly drawing) reveal it. His were of ships and trains and battles; mine, when not imitated from his, were of what we both called "dressed animals"—the anthropomorphized beasts of nursery literature. His earliest story—as my elder he preceded me in the transition from drawing to writing—was called *The Young Rajah*. He had already made India "his country"; Animal-Land was mine. I do not think any of the surviving drawings date from the first six years of my life which I am now describing, but I have plenty of them that cannot be much later. From them it appears to me that I had the better talent. From a very early age I could draw movement—figures that looked as if they were really running or fighting—and the perspective is good. But nowhere, either in my brother's work or my own, is there a single line drawn in obedience to an idea, however crude, of beauty. There is action, comedy, invention; but there is not even the germ of a feeling for design, and there is a shocking ignorance of natural form. Trees appear as balls of cotton wool stuck on posts, and there is nothing to show that either of us knew the shape of any leaf in the garden where we played almost daily. This absence of beauty, now that I come to think of it, is characteristic of our childhood. No picture on the walls of my father's house ever attracted—and indeed none deserved—our attention. We never saw a beautiful building nor imagined that a building could be beautiful. My earliest aesthetic experiences, if indeed they were aesthetic, were not of that kind; they were already incurably romantic, not formal. Once in those very early days my brother brought into the nursery the lid of a biscuit tin which he had covered with moss and garnished with twigs and flowers so as to make it a toy garden or a toy forest. That was the first beauty I ever knew. What the real garden had failed to do, the toy garden did. It made me aware of nature—not, indeed, as a storehouse of forms and colors but as something cool, dewy, fresh, exuberant. I do not think the impression was very important at the moment, but it soon became important in memory. As long as I live my imagination of Paradise will retain something of my brother's toy garden. And every day there were what we called "the Green Hills"; that is, the low line of the Castlereagh Hills which we saw from the nursery windows. They were not very far off but they were, to children, quite unattainable. They taught me longing—*Sehnsucht;* made me for good or ill, and before I was six years old, a votary of the Blue Flower.

If aesthetic experiences were rare, religious experiences did not occur at all. Some people have got the impression from my books that I was brought up in strict and vivid Puritanism, but this is quite untrue. I was taught the usual things and made to say my prayers and in due time taken to church. I naturally accepted what I was told but I cannot remember feeling much interest in it. My father, far from being specially Puritanical, was, by nineteenth-century and Church of Ireland standards, rather "high," and his approach to religion, as to literature, was at the opposite pole from what later became my own. The charm of tradition and the verbal beauty of Bible and Prayer Book (all of them for me late and acquired tastes) were his natural delight, and it would have been hard to find an equally intelligent man who cared so little for metaphysics. Of my mother's religion I can say almost nothing from my own memory. My childhood, at all events, was not in the least other-worldly. Except for the toy garden and the Green Hills it was not even imaginative; it lives in my memory mainly as a period of humdrum, prosaic happiness and awakes none of the poignant nostalgia with which I look back on my much less happy boyhood. It is not settled happiness but momentary joy that glorifies the past.

In 1905, my seventh year, the first great change in my life took place. We moved house. My father, growing, I suppose, in prosperity, decided to leave the semidetached villa in which I had been born and build himself a much larger house, further out into what was then the country. The "New House," as we continued for years to call it, was a large one even by my present standards; to a child it seemed less like a house than a city. My father, who had more capacity for being cheated than any man I have ever known, was badly cheated by his builders; the drains were wrong, the chimneys were wrong, and there was a draft in every room. None of this, however, mattered to a child. To me, the important thing about the move was that the background of my life became larger. The New House is almost a major character in my story. I am a product of long corridors, empty sunlit rooms, upstairs indoor silences, attics explored in solitude, distant noises of gurgling cisterns and pipes, and the noise of wind under the tiles. Also, of endless books. My father bought all the books he read and never got rid of any of them. There were books in the study, books in the drawing room, books in the cloakroom, books (two deep) in the great bookcase on the landing, books in a bedroom, books piled as high as my shoulder in the cistern attic, books of all kinds reflecting every transient stage of my parents' interest, books readable and unreadable, books suitable for a child and books most emphatically not. Nothing was forbidden me. In the seemingly endless rainy afternoons I took volume after volume from the shelves. I had always the same certainty of finding a book that was new to me as a man who walks into a field has of finding a new blade of grass. Where all these books had been before we came to the New House is a problem that never occurred to me until I began writing this paragraph. I have no idea of the answer.

It will be clear that at this time—at the age of six, seven, and eight—I was living almost entirely in my imagination; or at least that the imaginative experience of those years now seems to me more important than anything else. Thus I pass over a holiday in Normandy (of which, nevertheless, I retain very clear memories) as a thing of no account; if it could be cut out of my past I should still be almost exactly the man I am. But imagination is a vague word and I must make some distinctions. It may mean the world of reverie, daydream, wish-fulfilling fantasy. Of that I knew more than enough. I often pictured myself cutting a fine figure. But I must insist that this was a totally different activity from the invention of Animal-Land. Animal-Land was not (in that sense) a fantasy at all. I was not one of the characters it contained. I was its creator, not a candidate for admission to it. Invention is essentially different from reverie; if some fail to recognize the difference that is because they have not themselves experienced both. Anyone who has will understand me. In my day-dreams I was training myself to be a fool; in mapping and chronicling Animal-Land I was training myself to be a novelist. Note well, a novelist; not a poet. My invented world was full (for me) of interest, bustle, humor, and character; but there was no poetry, even no romance, in it. It was almost astonishingly prosaic.[1] Thus if we use the word imagination in a third sense, and the highest sense of all, this invented world was not imaginative. But certain other experiences were, and I will now try to record them. The thing has been much better done by Traherne and Wordsworth, but every man must tell his own tale.

The first is itself the memory of a memory. As I stood beside a flowering currant bush on a summer day there suddenly arose in me without warning, and as if from a depth not of years but of centuries, the memory of that earlier morning at the Old House when my brother had brought his toy garden into the nursery. It is difficult to find words strong enough for the sensation which came over me; Milton's "enormous bliss" of Eden (giving the full, ancient meaning to "enormous") comes somewhere near it. It was a sensation, of course, of desire; but desire for what? not, certainly, for a biscuit tin filled with moss, nor even (though that came into it) for my own past. 'Ιοῦλίανποθῶ[2]—and before I knew what I desired, the desire itself was gone, the whole glimpse withdrawn, the world turned commonplace again, or only stirred by a longing for the longing that had just ceased. It had taken only a moment of time; and in a certain sense everything else that had ever happened to me was insignificant in comparison.

The second glimpse came through *Squirrel Nutkin;* through it only, though I loved all the Beatrix Potter books. But the rest of them were merely entertaining; it administered the shock, it was a trouble. It troubled me with what I can only describe as the Idea of Autumn. It sounds fantastic to say that one can be enamored of a season, but that is something like what happened; and, as before, the experience was one of intense desire. And one went back to the book, not to gratify the desire (that was impossible—how can one *possess* Autumn?) but to reawake it. And in this experience also there was the same surprise and the same sense of incalculable importance. It was something quite different from ordinary life and even from ordinary pleasure; something, as they would now say, "in another dimension."

The third glimpse came through poetry. I had become fond of Longfellow's *Saga of King Olaf:* fond of it in a casual, shallow way for its story and its vigorous rhythms. But then, and quite different from such pleasures, and like a voice from far more distant regions, there came a moment when I idly turned the pages of the book and found the unrhymed translation of *Tegner's Drapa* and read

[1] For readers of my children's books, the best way of putting this would be to say that Animal-Land had nothing whatever in common with Narnia except the anthropomorphic beasts. Animal-Land, by its whole quality, excluded the least hint of wonder.

[2] Oh, I desire too much.

> I heard a voice that cried,
> Balder the beautiful
> Is dead, is dead—

I knew nothing about Balder; but instantly I was uplifted into huge regions of northern sky, I desired with almost sickening intensity something never to be described (except that it is cold, spacious, severe, pale, and remote) and then, as in the other examples, found myself at the very same moment already falling out of that desire and wishing I were back in it.

The reader who finds these three episodes of no interest need read this book no further, for in a sense the central story of my life is about nothing else. For those who are still disposed to proceed I will only underline the quality common to the three experiences; it is that of an unsatisfied desire which is itself more desirable than any other satisfaction. I call it Joy, which is here a technical term and must be sharply distinguished both from Happiness and from Pleasure. Joy (in my sense) has indeed one characteristic, and one only, in common with them; the fact that anyone who has experienced it will want it again. Apart from that, and considered only in its quality, it might almost equally well be called a particular kind of unhappiness or grief. But then it is a kind we want. I doubt whether anyone who has tasted it would ever, if both were in his power, exchange it for all the pleasures in the world. But then Joy is never in our power and pleasure often is.

I cannot be absolutely sure whether the things I have just been speaking of happened before or after the great loss which befell our family and to which I must now turn. There came a night when I was ill and crying both with headache and toothache and distressed because my mother did not come to me. That was because she was ill too; and what was odd was that there were several doctors in her room, and voices and comings and goings all over the house and doors shutting and opening. It seemed to last for hours. And then my father, in tears, came into my room and began to try to convey to my terrified mind things it had never conceived before. It was in fact cancer and followed the usual course; an operation (they operated in the patient's house in those days), an apparent convalescence, a return of the disease, increasing pain, and death. My father never fully recovered from this loss.

Children suffer not (I think) less than their elders, but differently. For us boys the real bereavement had happened before our mother died. We lost her gradually as she was gradually withdrawn from our life into the hands of nurses and delirium and morphia, and as our whole existence changed into something alien and menacing, as the house became full of strange smells and midnight noises and sinister whispered conversations. This had two further results, one very evil and one very good. It divided us from our father as well as our mother. They say that a shared sorrow draws people closer together; I can hardly believe that it often has that effect when those who share it are of widely different ages. If I may trust my own experience, the sight of adult misery and adult terror has an effect on children which is merely paralyzing and alienating. Perhaps it was our fault. Perhaps if we had been better children we might have lightened our father's sufferings at this time. We certainly did not. His nerves had never been of the steadiest and his emotions had always been uncontrolled. Under the pressure of anxiety his temper became incalculable; he spoke wildly and acted unjustly. Thus by a peculiar cruelty of fate, during those months the unfortunate man, had he but known it, was really losing his sons as well as his wife. We were coming, my brother and I, to rely more and more exclusively on each other for all that made life bearable; to have confidence only in each other. I expect that we (or at any rate I) were already learning to lie to him. Everything that had made the house a home had failed us; everything except one another. We drew daily closer together (that was the good result)—two frightened urchins huddled for warmth in a bleak world.

Grief in childhood is complicated with many other miseries. I was taken into the bedroom where my mother lay dead; as they said, "to see her," in reality, as I at once knew, "to see it." There was nothing that a grown-up would call disfigurement—except for that total disfigurement which is death itself. Grief was overwhelmed in terror. To this day I do not know what they mean when they call dead bodies beautiful. The ugliest man alive is an angel of beauty compared with the loveliest of the dead. Against all the subsequent paraphernalia of coffin, flowers, hearse, and funeral I reacted with horror. I even lectured one of my aunts on the absurdity of mourning clothes in a style which would have seemed to most adults both heartless and precocious; but this was our dear Aunt Annie, my maternal uncle's Canadian wife, a woman almost as sensible and sunny as my mother herself. To my hatred for what I already felt to be all the fuss and flummery of the funeral I may perhaps trace something in me which I now recognize as a defect but which I have never fully overcome—a distaste for all that is public, all that belongs to the collective; a boorish inaptitude for formality.

My mother's death was the occasion of what some (but not I) might regard as my first religious experience. When her case was pronounced hopeless I remembered what I had been taught; that prayers offered in faith would be granted. I accordingly set myself to produce by will power a firm belief that my prayers for her recovery would be successful; and, as I thought, I achieved it. When nevertheless she died I shifted my ground and worked myself into a belief that there was to be a miracle. The interesting thing is that my disappointment produced no results beyond itself. The thing hadn't worked, but I was used to things not working, and I thought no more about it. I think the truth is that the belief into which I had hypnotized myself was itself too irreligious for its failure to cause any religious revolution. I had approached God, or my idea of God, without love, without awe, even without fear. He was, in my mental picture of this miracle, to appear neither as Savior nor as Judge, but merely as a magician; and when He had done what was required of Him I supposed He would simply— well, go away. It never crossed my mind that the tremendous contact which I solicited should have any consequences beyond restoring the *status quo*. I imagine that a "faith" of this kind is often generated in children and that its disappointment is of no religious importance; just as the things believed in, if they could happen and be only as the child pictures them, would be of no religious importance either.

With my mother's death all settled happiness, all that was tranquil and reliable, disappeared from my life. There was to be much fun, many pleasures, many stabs of Joy; but no more of the old security. It was sea and islands now; the great continent had sunk like Atlantis.

The Great Knock

You will often meet with characters in nature so extravagant
that a discreet poet would not venture to set them upon the
stage.

LORD CHESTERFIELD

ON A SEPTEMBER DAY, having crossed to Liverpool and reached London,
I made my way to Waterloo and ran down to Great Bookham. I had been told
that Surrey was "suburban," and the landscape that actually flitted past the
windows astonished me. I saw steep little hills, watered valleys, and wooded
commons which ranked by my Wyvernian and Irish standards as forest; bracken
everywhere; a world of red and russet and yellowish greens. Even the sprinkling
of suburban villas (much rarer then than now) delighted me. These timbered and
red-tiled houses, embosomed in trees, were wholly unlike the stuccoed monstrosities which formed the suburbs of Belfast. Where I had expected gravel drives and
iron gates and interminable laurels and monkey puzzlers, I saw crooked paths
running up or down hill from wicket gates, between fruit trees and birches. By
a severer taste than mine these houses would all be mocked perhaps; yet I cannot
help thinking that those who designed them and their gardens achieved their
object, which was to suggest Happiness. They filled me with a desire for that
domesticity which, in its full development, I had never known; they set one
thinking of tea trays.

At Bookham I was met by my new teacher—"Kirk" or "Knock" or the Great
Knock as my father, my brother, and I all called him. We had heard about him
all our lives and I therefore had a very clear impression of what I was in for. I
came prepared to endure a perpetual lukewarm shower bath of sentimentality.
That was the price I was ready to pay for the infinite blessedness of escaping
school; but a heavy price. One story of my father's, in particular, gave me the
most embarrassing forebodings. He had loved to tell how once at Lurgan, when
he was in some kind of trouble or difficulty, the Old Knock, or the dear Old
Knock, had drawn him aside and there "quietly and naturally" slid his arm round
him and rubbed his dear old whiskers against my father's youthful cheek and
whispered a few words of comfort. . . . And here was Bookham at last, and there
was the arch-sentimentalist himself waiting to meet me.

He was over six feet tall, very shabbily dressed (like a gardener, I thought),
lean as a rake, and immensely muscular. His wrinkled face seemed to consist
entirely of muscles, so far as it was visible; for he wore mustache and side whiskers
with a clean-shaven chin like the Emperor Franz Joseph. The whiskers, you will
understand, concerned me very much at that moment. My cheek already tingled
in anticipation. Would he begin at once? There would be tears for certain;
perhaps worse things. It is one of my lifelong weaknesses that I never could

endure the embrace or kiss of my own sex. (An unmanly weakness, by the way; Aeneas, Beowulf, Roland, Launcelot, Johnson, and Nelson knew nothing of it.)

Apparently, however, the old man was holding his fire. We shook hands, and though his grip was like iron pincers it was not lingering. A few minutes later we were walking away from the station.

"You are now," said Kirk, "proceeding along the principal artery between Great and Little Bookham."

I stole a glance at him. Was this geographical exordium a heavy joke? Or was he trying to conceal his emotions? His face, however, showed only an inflexible gravity. I began to "make conversation" in the deplorable manner which I had acquired at those evening parties and indeed found increasingly necessary to use with my father. I said I was surprised at the "scenery" of Surrey; it was much "wilder" than I had expected.

"Stop!" shouted Kirk with a suddenness that made me jump. "What do you mean by wildness and what grounds had you for not expecting it?"

I replied I don't know what, still "making conversation." As answer after answer was torn to shreds it at last dawned upon me that he really wanted to know. He was not making conversation, nor joking, nor snubbing me; he wanted to know. I was stung into attempting a real answer. A few passes sufficed to show that I had no clear and distinct idea corresponding to the word "wildness," and that, in so far as I had any idea at all, "wildness" was a singularly inept word. "Do you not see, then," concluded the Great Knock, "that your remark was meaningless?" I prepared to sulk a little, assuming that the subject would now be dropped. Never was I more mistaken in my life. Having analyzed my terms, Kirk was proceeding to deal with my proposition as a whole. On what had I based (but he pronounced it *baized*) my expectations about the Flora and Geology of Surrey? Was it maps, or photographs, or books? I could produce none. It had, heaven help me, never occurred to me that what I called my thoughts needed to be "baized" on anything. Kirk once more drew a conclusion—without the slightest sign of emotion, but equally without the slightest concession to what I thought good manners: "Do you not see, then, that you had no right to have any opinion whatever on the subject?"

By this time our acquaintance had lasted about three and a half minutes; but the tone set by this first conversation was preserved without a single break during all the years I spent at Bookham. Anything more grotesquely unlike the "dear Old Knock" of my father's reminiscences could not be conceived. Knowing my father's invariable intention of veracity and also knowing what strange transformations every truth underwent when once it entered his mind, I am sure he did not mean to deceive us. But if Kirk at any time of his life took a boy aside and there "quietly and naturally" rubbed the boy's face with his whiskers, I shall as easily believe that he sometimes varied the treatment by quietly and naturally standing on his venerable and egg-bald head.

If ever a man came near to being a purely logical entity, that man was Kirk. Born a little later, he would have been a Logical Positivist. The idea that human

beings should exercise their vocal organs for any purpose except that of communicating or discovering truth was to him preposterous. The most casual remark
was taken as a summons to disputation. I soon came to know the differing values
of his three openings. The loud cry of "Stop!" was flung in to arrest a torrent
of verbiage which could not be endured a moment longer; not because it fretted
his patience (he never thought of that) but because it was wasting time, darkening
counsel. The hastier and quieter "Excuse!" (*i.e.*, "Excuse me") ushered in a
correction or distinction merely parenthetical and betokened that, thus set right,
your remark might still, without absurdity, be allowed to reach completion. The
most encouraging of all was, "I hear you." This meant that your remark was
significant and only required refutation; it had risen to the dignity of error.
Refutation (when we got so far) always followed the same lines. Had I read this?
Had I studied that? Had I any statistical evidence? Had I any evidence in my
own experience? And so to the almost inevitable conclusion, "Do you not see
then that you had no right, etc."

Some boys would not have liked it; to me it was red beef and strong beer.
I had taken it for granted that my leisure hours at Bookham would be passed in
"grown-up conversation." And that, as you know already, I had no taste for. In
my experience it meant conversation about politics, money, deaths, and digestion. I assumed that a taste for it, as for eating mustard or reading newspapers,
would develop in me when I grew older (so far, all three expectations have been
disappointed). The only two kinds of talk I wanted were the almost purely
imaginative and the almost purely rational; such talk as I had about Boxen with
my brother or about Valhalla with Arthur, on the one hand, or such talk as I had
had with my uncle Gussie about astronomy on the other. I could never have gone
far in any science because on the path of every science the lion Mathematics lies
in wait for you. Even in Mathematics, whatever could be done by mere reasoning
(as in simple geometry) I did with delight; but the moment calculation came in
I was helpless. I grasped the principles but my answers were always wrong. Yet
though I could never have been a scientist, I had scientific as well as imaginative
impulses, and I loved ratiocination. Kirk excited and satisfied one side of me. Here
was talk that was really about something. Here was a man who thought not about
you but about what you said. No doubt I snorted and bridled a little at some of
my tossings; but, taking it all in all, I loved the treatment. After being knocked
down sufficiently often I began to know a few guards and blows, and to put on
intellectual muscle. In the end, unless I flatter myself, I became a not contemptible sparring partner. It was a great day when the man who had so long been
engaged in exposing my vagueness at last cautioned me against the dangers of
excessive subtlety.

If Kirk's ruthless dialectic had been merely a pedagogic instrument I might
have resented it. But he knew no other way of talking. No age or sex was spared
the elenchus. It was a continuous astonishment to him that anyone should not
desire to be clarified or corrected. When a very dignified neighbor, in the course
of a Sunday call, observed with an air of finality, "Well, well, Mr. Kirkpatrick,

it takes all sorts to make a world. You are a Liberal and I am a Conservative; we naturally look at the facts from different angles," Kirk replied, "What do you mean? Are you asking me to picture Liberals and Conservatives playing peep-bo at a rectangular Fact from opposite sides of a table?" If an unwary visitor, hoping to waive a subject, observed, "Of course, I know opinions differ—" Kirk would raise both his hands and exclaim, "Good heavens! I have no *opinions* on any subject whatsoever." A favorite maxim was, "You can have enlightenment for ninepence but you prefer ignorance." The commonest metaphors would be questioned till some bitter truth had been forced from its hiding place. "These fiendish German atrocities—" "But are not fiends a figment of the imagination?"—"Very well, then; these brutal atrocities—" "But none of the brutes does anything of the kind!"—"Well, what am I to call them?" "Is it not plain that we must call them simply *Human?*" What excited his supreme contempt was the conversation of other Headmasters, which he had sometimes had to endure at conferences when he himself was Head of Lurgan. "They would come and ask me, 'What attitude do you adopt to a boy who does so-and-so?' Good Heavens! As if I ever adopted an attitude to anybody or anything!" Sometimes, but rarely, he was driven to irony. On such occasions his voice became even weightier than usual and only the distention of his nostrils betrayed the secret to those who knew him. It was in such fashion that he produced his *dictum*, "The Master of Balliol is one of the most important beings in the universe."

It will be imagined that Mrs. Kirkpatrick led a somewhat uneasy life: witness the occasion on which her husband by some strange error found himself in the drawing room at the beginning of what his lady had intended to be a bridge party. About half an hour later she was observed to leave the room with a remarkable expression on her face; and many hours later still the Great Knock was discovered sitting on a stool in the midst of seven elderly ladies ("ful drery was hire chere") begging them to clarify their terms.

I have said that he was almost wholly logical; but not quite. He had been a Presbyterian and was now an Atheist. He spent Sunday, as he spent most of his time on weekdays, working in his garden. But one curious trait from his Presbyterian youth survived. He always, on Sundays, gardened in a different, and slightly more respectable, suit. An Ulster Scot may come to disbelieve in God, but not to wear his weekday clothes on the Sabbath.

Having said that he was an Atheist, I hasten to add that he was a "Rationalist" of the old, high and dry nineteenth-century type. For Atheism has come down in the world since those days, and mixed itself with politics and learned to dabble in dirt. The anonymous donor who now sends me anti-God magazines hopes, no doubt, to hurt the Christian in me; he really hurts the ex-Atheist. I am ashamed that my old mates and (which matters much more) Kirk's old mates should have sunk to what they are now. It was different then; even McCabe wrote like a man. At the time when I knew him, the fuel of Kirk's Atheism was chiefly of the anthropological and pessimistic kind. He was great on *The Golden Bough* and Schopenhauer.

The reader will remember that my own Atheism and Pessimism were fully formed before I went to Bookham. What I got there was merely fresh ammunition for the defense of a position already chosen. Even this I got indirectly from the tone of his mind or independently from reading his books. He never attacked religion in my presence. It is the sort of fact that no one would infer from an outside knowledge of my life, but it is a fact.

I arrived at Gastons (so the Knock's house was called) on a Saturday, and he announced that we would begin Homer on Monday. I explained that I had never read a word in any dialect but the Attic, assuming that when he knew this he would approach Homer through some preliminary lessons on the Epic language. He replied merely with a sound very frequent in his conversation which I can only spell "Huh." I found this rather disquieting; and I woke on Monday saying to myself, "Now for Homer. Golly!" The name struck awe into my soul. At nine o'clock we sat down to work in the little upstairs study which soon became so familiar to me. It contained a sofa (on which we sat side by side when he was working with me), a table and chair (which I used when I was alone), a bookcase, a gas stove, and a framed photograph of Mr. Gladstone. We opened our books at *Iliad*, Book I. Without a word of introduction Knock read aloud the first twenty lines or so in the "new" pronunciation, which I had never heard before. Like Smewgy, he was a chanter; less mellow in voice, yet full gutturals and rolling r's and more varied vowels seemed to suit the Bronze Age epic as well as Smewgy's honey tongue had suited Horace. For Kirk, even after years of residence in England, spoke the purest Ulster. He then translated, with a few, a very few explanations, about a hundred lines. I had never seen a classical author taken in such large gulps before. When he had finished he handed me over Crusius' *Lexicon* and, having told me to go through again as much as I could of what he had done, left the room. It seems an odd method of teaching, but it worked. At first I could travel only a very short way along the trail he had blazed, but every day I could travel further. Presently I could travel the whole way. Then I could go a line or two beyond his furthest North. Then it became a kind of game to see how far beyond. He appeared at this stage to value speed more than absolute accuracy. The great gain was that I very soon became able to understand a great deal without (even mentally) translating it; I was beginning to think in Greek. That is the great Rubicon to cross in learning any language. Those in whom the Greek word lives only while they are hunting for it in the lexicon, and who then substitute the English word for it, are not reading the Greek at all; they are only solving a puzzle. The very formula, *"Naus* means a ship," is wrong. *Naus* and *ship* both mean a thing, they do not mean one another. Behind *Naus,* as behind *navis* or *naca,* we want to have a picture of a dark, slender mass with sail or oars, climbing the ridges, with no officious English word intruding.

We now settled into a routine which has ever since served in my mind as an archetype, so that what I still mean when I speak of a "normal" day (and lament that normal days are so rare) is a day of the Bookham pattern. For if I could please myself I would always live as I lived there. I would choose always to breakfast at exactly eight and to be at my desk by nine, there to read or write till one. If a cup of good tea or coffee could be brought me about eleven, so much the better. A step or so out of doors for a pint of beer would not do quite so well; for a man does not want to drink alone and if you meet a friend in the taproom the break is likely to be extended beyond its ten minutes. At one precisely lunch should be on the table; and by two at the latest I would be on the road. Not, except at rare intervals, with a friend. Walking and talking are two very great pleasures, but it is a mistake to combine them. Our own noise blots out the sounds and silences of the outdoor world; and talking leads almost inevitably to smoking, and then farewell to nature as far as one of our senses is concerned. The only friend to walk with is one (such as I found, during the holidays, in Arthur) who so exactly shares your taste for each mood of the countryside that a glance, a halt, or at most a nudge, is enough to assure us that the pleasure is shared. The return from the walk, and the arrival of tea, should be exactly coincident, and not later than a quarter past four. Tea should be taken in solitude, as I took it at Bookham on those (happily numerous) occasions when Mrs. Kirkpatrick was out; the Knock himself disdained this meal. For eating and reading are two pleasures that combine admirably. Of course not all books are suitable for mealtime reading. It would be a kind of blasphemy to read poetry at table. What one wants is a gossipy, formless book which can be opened anywhere. The ones I learned so to use at Bookham were Boswell, and a translation of Herodotus, and Lang's *History of English Literature. Tristram Shandy, Elia* and the *Anatomy of Melancholy* are all good for the same purpose. At five a man should be at work again, and at it till seven. Then, at the evening meal and after, comes the time for talk, or, failing that, for lighter reading; and unless you are making a night of it with your cronies (and at Bookham I had none) there is no reason why you should ever be in bed later than eleven. But when is a man to write his letters? You forget that I am describing the happy life I led with Kirk or the ideal life I would live now if I could. And it is an essential of the happy life that a man would have almost no mail and never dread the postman's knock. In those blessed days I received, and answered, only two letters a week; one from my father, which was a matter of duty, and one from Arthur which was the high light of the week, for we poured out to each other on paper all the delight that was intoxicating us both. Letters from my brother, now on active service, were longer and rarer, and so were my replies.

Such is my ideal, and such then (almost) was the reality, of "settled, calm, Epicurean life." It is no doubt for my own good that I have been so generally prevented from leading it, for it is a life almost entirely selfish. Selfish, not self-centered: for in such a life my mind would be directed toward a thousand things, not one of which is myself. The distinction is not unimportant. One of the happiest men and most pleasing companions I have ever known was intensely selfish. On the other hand I have known people capable of real sacrifice whose lives were nevertheless a misery to themselves and to others, because self-concern and self-pity filled all their thoughts. Either condition will destroy the soul in the end. But till the end, give me the man who takes the best of everything (even at my expense) and then talks of other things, rather than the man who serves me and talks of himself, and whose very kindnesses are a continual reproach, a continual demand for pity, gratitude, and admiration.

Kirk did not, of course, make me read nothing but Homer. The Two Great Bores (Demosthenes and Cicero) could not be avoided. There were (oh glory!) Lucretius, Catullus, Tacitus, Herodotus. There was Virgil, for whom I still had no true taste. There were Greek and Latin compositions. (It is a strange thing that I have contrived to reach my late fifties without ever reading one word of Caesar.) There were Euripides, Sophocles, Aeschylus. In the evenings there was French with Mrs. Kirkpatrick, treated much as her husband treated Homer. We got through a great many good novels in this way and I was soon buying French books on my own. I had hoped there would be English essays, but whether because he felt he could not endure mine or because he soon guessed that I was already only too proficient in that art (which he almost certainly despised) Kirk never set me one. For the first week or so he gave me directions about my English reading, but when he discovered that, left to myself, I was not likely to waste my time, he gave me absolute freedom. Later in my career we branched out into German and Italian. Here his methods were the same. After the very briefest contact with Grammars and Exercises I was plunged into *Faust* and the *Inferno*. In Italian we succeeded. In German I have little doubt that we should equally have succeeded if I had stayed with him a little longer. But I left too soon and my German has remained all my life that of a schoolboy. Whenever I have set about rectifying this, some other and more urgent task has always interrupted me.

But Homer came first. Day after day and month after month we drove gloriously onward, tearing the whole *Achilleid* out of the *Iliad* and tossing the rest on one side, and then reading the *Odyssey* entire, till the music of the thing and the clear, bitter brightness that lives in almost every formula had become part of me. Of course my appreciation was very romanticized—the appreciation of a boy soaked in William Morris. But this slight error saved me from that far deeper error of "classicism" with which the Humanists have hoodwinked half the world. I cannot therefore deeply regret the days when I called Circe a "wise-wife" and every marriage a "high-tide." That has all burned itself out and left no snuff, and I can now enjoy the *Odyssey* in a maturer way. The wanderings mean as much as ever they did; the great moment of "eucatastrophe" (as Professor Tolkien would call it) when Odysseus strips off his rags and bends the bow, means more; and perhaps what now pleases me best of all is those exquisite, Charlotte M. Yonge families at Pylos and elsewhere. How rightly Sir Maurice Powicke says, "There have been civilised people in all ages." And let us add, "In all ages they have been surrounded by barbarism."

Meanwhile, on afternoons and on Sundays, Surrey lay open to me. County Down in the holidays and Surrey in the term—it was an excellent contrast. Perhaps, since their beauties were such that even a fool could not force them into competition, this cured me once and for all of the pernicious tendency to compare and to prefer—an operation that does little good even when we are dealing with works of art and endless harm when we are dealing with nature. Total surrender is the first step toward the fruition of either. Shut your mouth; open your eyes and ears. Take in what is there and give no thought to what might have been there or what is somewhere else. That can come later, if it must come at all. (And notice here how the true training for anything whatever that is good always prefigures and, if submitted to, will always help us in, the true training for the Christian life. That is a school where they can always use your previous work whatever subject it was on.) What delighted me in Surrey was its intricacy. My Irish walks commanded large horizons and the general lie of land and sea could be taken in at a glance; I will try to speak of them later. But in Surrey the contours were so tortuous, the little valleys so narrow, there was so much timber, so many villages concealed in woods or hollows, so many field paths, sunk lanes, dingles, copses, such an unpredictable variety of cottage, farmhouse, villa, and country seat, that the whole thing could never lie clearly in my mind, and to walk in it daily gave one the same sort of pleasure that there is in the labyrinthine complexity of Malory or the *Faerie Queene*. Even where the prospect was tolerably open, as when I sat looking down on the Leatherhead and Dorking valley from Polesdan Lacey, it always lacked the classic comprehensibility of the Wyvern landscape. The valley twisted away southward into another valley, a train thudded past invisible in a wooded cutting, the opposite ridge concealed its bays and promontories. This, even on a summer morning. But I remember more dearly autumn afternoons in bottoms that lay intensely silent under old and great trees, and especially the moment, near Friday Street, when our party (that time I was not alone) suddenly discovered, from recognizing a curiously shaped stump, that we had traveled round in a circle for the last half-hour; or one frosty sunset over the Hog's Back at Guildford. On a Saturday afternoon in winter, when nose and fingers might be pinched enough to give an added relish to the anticipation of tea and fireside, and the whole weekend's reading lay ahead, I suppose I reached as much happiness as is ever to be reached on earth. And especially if there were some new, long-coveted book awaiting me.

For I had forgotten. When I spoke of the post I forgot to tell you that it brought parcels as well as letters. Every man of my age has had in his youth one blessing for which our juniors may well envy him: we grew up in a world of cheap and abundant books. Your *Everyman* was then a bare shilling, and, what is more, always in stock; your *World's Classic, Muses' Library, Home University Library, Temple Classic,* Nelson's French series, Bohn, and Longman's Pocket Library, at proportionate prices. All the money I could spare went in postal orders to Messrs. Denny of the Strand. No days, even at Bookham, were happier than those on which the afternoon post brought me a neat little parcel in dark gray paper. Milton, Spenser, Malory, *The High History of the Holy Grail,* the *Laxdale Saga,* Ronsard, Chénier, Voltaire, *Beowulf* and *Gawain and the Green Knight* (both in translations), Apuleius, the *Kalevala,* Herrick, Walton, Sir John Mandeville, Sidney's *Arcadia,* and nearly all of Morris, came volume by volume into my hands. Some of my purchases proved disappointments and some went beyond my hopes, but the undoing of the parcel always remained a delicious moment. On my rare visits to London I looked at Mcssrs. Denny in the Strand with a kind of awe; so much pleasure had come from it.

Smewgy and Kirk were my two greatest teachers. Roughly, one might say (in medieval language) that Smewgy taught me Grammar and Rhetoric and Kirk taught me Dialectic. Each had, and gave me, what the other lacked. Kirk had none of Smewgy's graciousness or delicacy, and Smewgy had less humor than Kirk. It was a saturnine humor. Indeed he was very like Saturn—not the dispossessed King of Italian legend, but grim old Cronos, Father Time himself with scythe and hourglass. The bitterest, and also funniest, things came out when he had risen abruptly from table (always before the rest of us) and stood ferreting in a villainous old tobacco jar on the mantelpiece for the dottles of former pipes which it was his frugal habit to use again. My debt to him is very great, my reverence to this day undiminished.

The New Look

For barfield's conversion to Anthroposophy marked the beginning of what I can only describe as the Great War between him and me. It was never, thank God, a quarrel, though it could have become one in a moment if he had used to me anything like the violence I allowed myself to him. But it was an almost incessant disputation, sometimes by letter and sometimes face to face, which lasted for years. And this Great War was one of the turning points of my life.

Barfield never made me an Anthroposophist, but his counterattacks destroyed forever two elements in my own thought. In the first place he made short work of what I have called my "chronological snobbery," the uncritical acceptance of the intellectual climate common to our own age and the assumption that whatever has gone out of date is on that account discredited. You must find why it went out of date. Was it ever refuted (and if so by whom, where, and how conclusively) or did it merely die away as fashions do? If the latter, this tells us nothing about its truth or falsehood. From seeing this, one passes to the realization that our own age is also "a period," and certainly has, like all periods, its own characteristic illusions. They are likeliest to lurk in those widespread assumptions which are so ingrained in the age that no one dares to attack or feels it necessary to defend them. In the second place he convinced me that the positions we had hitherto held left no room for any satisfactory theory of knowledge. We had been, in the technical sense of the term, "realists"; that is, we accepted as rock-bottom reality the universe revealed by the senses. But at the same time we continued to make for certain phenomena of consciousness all the claims that really went with a theistic or idealistic view. We maintained that abstract thought (if obedient to logical rules) gave indisputable truth, that our moral judgment was "valid," and our aesthetic experience not merely pleasing but "valuable." The view was, I think, common at the time; it runs through Bridges' *Testament of Beauty*, the work of Gilbert Murray, and Lord Russell's "Worship of a Free Man." Barfield convinced me that it was inconsistent. If thought were a purely subjective event, these claims for it would have to be abandoned. If one kept (as rock-bottom reality) the universe of the senses, aided by instruments and co-ordinated so as to form "science," then one would have to go much further—as many have since gone—and adopt a Behavioristic theory of logic, ethics, and aesthetics. But such a theory was, and is, unbelievable to me. I am using the word "unbelievable," which many use to mean "improbable" or even "undesirable," in a quite literal sense. I mean that the act of believing what the behaviorist believes is one that my mind simply will not perform. I cannot force my thought into that shape any more than I can scratch my ear with my big toe or pour wine out of a bottle into the cavity at the base of that same bottle. It is as final as a physical impossibility. I was therefore compelled to give up realism. I had been trying to defend it ever since I began reading philosophy. Partly, no doubt, this was mere "cussedness." Idealism was then the dominant philosophy at Oxford and I was by nature "against Government." But partly, too, realism satisfied an emotional need. I wanted Nature to be quite independent of our observation; something other, indifferent, self-existing. (This went with the Jenkinian zest for rubbing one's nose in the mere quiddity.) But now, it seemed to me, I had to give that up. Unless I were to accept an unbelievable alternative, I must admit that mind was no late-come epiphenomenon; that the whole universe was, in the last resort, mental; that our logic was participation in a cosmic *Logos*.

It is astonishing (at this time of day) that I could regard this position as something quite distinct from Theism. I suspect there was some willful blindness. But there were in those days all sorts of blankets, insulators, and insurances which enabled one to get all the conveniences of Theism, without believing in God. The English Hegelians, writers like T. H. Green, Bradley, and Bosanquet (then mighty names), dealt in precisely such wares. The Absolute Mind—better still, the Absolute—was impersonal, or it knew itself (but not us?) only in us, and it was so absolute that it wasn't really much more like a mind than anything else. And anyway, the more muddled one got about it and the more contradictions one committed, the more this proved that our discursive thought moved only on the level of "Appearance," and "Reality" must be somewhere else. And where else but, of course, in the Absolute? There, not here, was "the fuller splendor" behind the "sensuous curtain." The emotion that went with all this was certainly religious. But this was a religion that cost nothing. We could talk religiously about the Absolute: but there was no danger of Its doing anything about us. It was "there"; safely and immovably "there." It would never come "here," never (to be blunt) make a nuisance of Itself. This quasi-religion was all a one-way street; all *eros* (as Dr. Nygren would say) steaming up, but no *agape* darting down. There was nothing to fear; better still, nothing to obey.

Yet there was one really wholesome element in it. The Absolute was "there," and that "there" contained the reconciliation of all contraries, the transcendence of all finitude, the hidden glory which was the only perfectly real thing there is. In fact, it had much of the quality of Heaven. But it was a Heaven none of us could ever get to. For we are appearances. To be "there" is, by definition, not to be we. All who embrace such a philosophy live, like Dante's virtuous Pagans, "in desire without hope." Or like Spinoza they so love their God as to be unable even to wish that He should love them in return. I should be very sorry not to have passed through that experience. I think it is more religious than many experiences that have been called Christian. What I learned from the Idealists (and still most strongly hold) is this maxim: it is more important that Heaven should exist than that any of us should reach it.

And so the great Angler played His fish and I never dreamed that the hook was in my tongue. But two great advances had been made. Bergson had showed me necessary existence; and from Idealism I had come one step nearer to understanding the words, "We give thanks to thee for thy great glory." The Norse gods had given me the first hint of it; but then I didn't believe in them, and I did believe (so far as one can believe an *Unding*) in the Absolute.

Checkmate

The one principle of hell is—"I am my own."
GEORGE MACDONALD

In THE SUMMER OF 1922 I finished Greats. As there were no philo-sophical posts going, or none that I could get, my long-suffering father offered me a fourth year at Oxford during which I read English so as to get a second string to my bow. The Great War with Barfield had, I think, begun at this time.

No sooner had I entered the English School than I went to George Gordon's discussion class. And there I made a new friend. The very first words he spoke marked him out from the ten or twelve others who were present; a man after my own heart, and that too at an age when the instantaneous friendships of earlier youth were becoming rather rare events. His name was Nevill Coghill. I soon had the shock of discovering that he—clearly the most intelligent and best-informed man in that class—was a Christian and a thorough-going supernaturalist. There were other traits that I liked but found (for I was still very much a modern) oddly archaic; chivalry, honor, courtesy, "freedom," and "gentillesse." One could imag-ine him fighting a duel. He spoke much "ribaldry" but never "villeinye." Barfield was beginning to overthrow my chronological snobbery; Coghill gave it another blow. Had something really dropped out of our lives? Was the archaic simply the civilized, and the modern simply the barbaric? It will seem strange to many of my critics who regard me as a typical *laudator temporis acti* that this question should have arisen so comparatively late in my life. But then the key to my books is Donne's maxim, "The heresies that men leave are hated most." The things I assert most vigorously are those that I resisted long and accepted late.

These disturbing factors in Coghill ranged themselves with a wider distur-bance which was now threatening my whole earlier outlook. All the books were beginning to turn against me. Indeed, I must have been as blind as a bat not to have seen, long before, the ludicrous contradiction between my theory of life and my actual experiences as a reader. George MacDonald had done more to me than any other writer; of course it was a pity he had that bee in his bonnet about Christianity. He was good *in spite of it*. Chesterton had more sense than all the other moderns put together; bating, of course, his Christianity. Johnson was one of the few authors whom I felt I could trust utterly; curiously enough, he had the same kink. Spenser and Milton by a strange coincidence had it too. Even among ancient authors the same paradox was to be found. The most religious (Plato, Aeschylus, Virgil) were clearly those on whom I could really feed. On the other hand, those writers who did not suffer from religion and with whom in theory my sympathy ought to have been complete—Shaw and Wells and Mill and Gibbon and Voltaire—all seemed a little thin; what as boys we called "tinny." It wasn't that I didn't like them. They were all (especially Gibbon) entertaining; but hardly more. There seemed to be no depth in them. They were too simple. The roughness and density of life did not appear in their books.

Now that I was reading more English, the paradox began to be aggravated. I was deeply moved by the *Dream of the Rood;* more deeply still by Langland; intoxicated (for a time) by Donne; deeply and lastingly satisfied by Thomas Browne. But the most alarming of all was George Herbert. Here was a man who seemed to me to excel all the authors I had ever read in conveying the very quality of life as we actually live it from moment to moment; but the wretched fellow, instead of doing it all directly, insisted on mediating it through what I would still have called "the Christian mythology." On the other hand most of the authors who might be claimed as precursors of modern enlightenment seemed to me very small beer and bored me cruelly. I thought Bacon (to speak frankly) a solemn, pretentious ass, yawned my way through Restoration Comedy, and, having manfully struggled on to the last line of *Don Juan,* wrote on the end leaf "Never again." The only non-Christians who seemed to me really to know anything were the Romantics; and a good many of them were dangerously tinged with something like religion, even at times with Christianity. The upshot of it all could nearly be expressed in a perversion of Roland's great line in the *Chanson*—

Christians are wrong, but all the rest are bores.

The natural step would have been to inquire a little more closely whether the Christians were, after all, wrong. But I did not take it. I thought I could explain their superiority without that hypothesis. Absurdly (yet many Absolute Idealists have shared this absurdity) I thought that "the Christian myth" conveyed to unphilosophic minds as much of the truth, that is of Absolute Idealism, as they were capable of grasping, and that even that much put them above the irreligious. Those who could not rise to the notion of the Absolute would come nearer to the truth by belief in "a God" than by disbelief. Those who could not understand how, as Reasoners, we participated in a timeless and therefore deathless world, would get a symbolic shadow of the truth by believing in a life after death. The implication—that something which I and most other undergraduates could master without extraordinary pains would have been too hard for Plato, Dante, Hooker, and Pascal—did not yet strike me as absurd. I hope this is because I never looked it squarely in the face.

As the plot quickens and thickens toward its end, I leave out more and more of such matters as would go into a full autobiography. My father's death, with all the fortitude (even playfulness) which he displayed in his last illness, does not really come into the story I am telling. My brother was at that time in Shanghai. Nor would it be relevant to tell in detail how I became a temporary lecturer at Univ for a year and was elected a fellow of Magdalen in 1925. The worst is that I must leave undescribed many men whom I love and to whom I am deeply in debt; G. H. Stevenson and E. F. Carritt, my tutors, the Fark (but who could paint him anyway?), and five great Magdalen men who enlarged my very idea of what a learned life should be—P. V. M. Benecke, C. C. J. Webb, J. A. Smith, F. E.

Brightman, and C. T. Onions. Except for Oldie, I have always been blessed both in my official and my unofficial teachers. In my earlier years at Magdalen I inhabited a world where hardly anything I wanted to know needed to be found out by my own unaided efforts. One or other of these could always give you a clue. ("You'll find something about it in Alanus. . . ."—"Macrobius would be the man to try. . . ."—"Doesn't Comparetti mention it?" . . . "Have you looked for it in Du Cange?") I found, as always, that the ripest are kindest to the raw and the most studious have most time to spare. When I began teaching for the English Faculty, I made two other friends, both Christians (these queer people seemed now to pop up on every side) who were later to give me much help in getting over the last stile. They were H. V. V. Dyson (then of Reading) and J. R. R. Tolkien. Friendship with the latter marked the breakdown of two old prejudices. At my first coming into the world I had been (implicitly) warned never to trust a Papist, and at my first coming into the English Faculty (explicitly) never to trust a philologist. Tolkien was both.

Realism had been abandoned; the New Look was somewhat damaged; and chronological snobbery was seriously shaken. All over the board my pieces were in the most disadvantageous positions. Soon I could no longer cherish even the illusion that the initiative lay with me. My Adversary began to make His final moves.

The first Move annihilated the last remains of the New Look. I was suddenly impelled to reread (which was certainly no business of mine at the moment) the *Hippolytus* of Euripides. In one chorus all that world's end imagery which I had rejected when I assumed my New Look rose before me. I liked, but did not yield; I tried to patronize it. But next day I was overwhelmed. There was a transitional moment of delicious uneasiness, and then—instantaneously—the long inhibition was over, the dry desert lay behind, I was off once more into the land of longing, my heart at once broken and exalted as it had never been since the old days at Bookham. There was nothing whatever to do about it; no question of returning to the desert. I had simply been ordered—or, rather, compelled—to "take that look off my face." And never to resume it either.

The next Move was intellectual, and consolidated the first Move. I read in Alexander's *Space Time and Deity* his theory of "Enjoyment" and "Contemplation." These are technical terms in Alexander's philosophy; "Enjoyment" has nothing to do with pleasure, nor "Contemplation" with the contemplative life. When you see a table you "enjoy" the act of seeing and "contemplate" the table. Later, if you took up Optics and thought about Seeing itself, you would be contemplating the seeing and enjoying the thought. In bereavement you contemplate the beloved and the beloved's death and, in Alexander's sense, "enjoy" the loneliness and grief; but a psychologist, if he were considering you as a case of melancholia, would be contemplating your grief and enjoying psychology. We do not "think a thought" in the same sense in which we "think that Herodotus is unreliable." When we think a thought, "thought" is a cognate accusative (like "blow" in "strike a blow"). We enjoy the thought (that Herodotus is unreliable) and, in so doing, contemplate the unreliability of Herodotus.

I accepted this distinction at once and have ever since regarded it as an indispensable tool of thought. A moment later its consequences—for me quite catastrophic—began to appear. It seemed to me self-evident that one essential property of love, hate, fear, hope, or desire was attention to their object. To cease thinking about or attending to the woman is, so far, to cease loving; to cease thinking about or attending to the dreaded thing is, so far, to cease being afraid. But to attend to your own love or fear is to cease attending to the loved or dreaded object. In other words the enjoyment and the contemplation of our inner activities are incompatible. You cannot hope and also think about hoping at the same moment; for in hope we look to hope's object and we interrupt this by (so to speak) turning round to look at the hope itself. Of course the two activities can and do alternate with great rapidity; but they are distinct and incompatible. This was not merely a logical result of Alexander's analysis, but could be verified in daily and hourly experience. The surest means of disarming an anger or a lust was to turn your attention from the girl or the insult and start examining the passion itself. The surest way of spoiling a pleasure was to start examining your satisfaction. But if so, it followed that all introspection is in one respect misleading. In introspection we try to look "inside ourselves" and see what is going on. But nearly everything that was going on a moment before is stopped by the very act of our turning to look at it. Unfortunately this does not mean that introspection finds nothing. On the contrary, it finds precisely what is left behind by the suspension of all our normal activities; and what is left behind is mainly mental images and physical sensations. The great error is to mistake this mere sediment or track or by-product for the activities themselves. That is how men may come to believe that thought is only unspoken words, or the appreciation of poetry only a collection of mental pictures, when these in reality are what the thought or the appreciation, when interrupted, leave behind—like the swell at sea, working after the wind has dropped. Not, of course, that these activities, before we stopped them by introspection, were unconscious. We do not love, fear, or think without knowing it. Instead of the two-fold division into Conscious and Unconscious, we need a threefold division: the Unconscious, the Enjoyed, and the Contemplated.

This discovery flashed a new light back on my whole life. I saw that all my waitings and watchings for Joy, all my vain hopes to find some mental content on which I could, so to speak, lay my finger and say, "This is it," had been a futile attempt to contemplate the enjoyed. All that such watching and waiting ever *could* find would be either an image (Asgard, the Western Garden, or what not) or a quiver in the diaphragm. I should never have to bother again about these images or sensations. I knew now that they were merely the mental track left by the passage of Joy—not the wave but the wave's imprint on the sand. The inherent dialectic of desire itself had in a way already shown me this; for all

images and sensations, if idolatrously mistaken for Joy itself, soon honestly confessed themselves inadequate. All said, in the last resort, "It is not I. I am only
a reminder. Look! Look! What do I remind you of?"

So far, so good. But it is at the next step that awe overtakes me. There was
no doubt that Joy was a desire (and, in so far as it was also simultaneously a good,
it was also a kind of love). But a desire is turned not to itself but to its object.
Not only that, but it owes all its character to its object. Erotic love is not like
desire for food, nay, a love for one woman differs from a love for another woman
in the very same way and the very same degree as the two women differ from
one another. Even our desire for one wine differs in tone from our desire for
another. Our intellectual desire (curiosity) to know the true answer to a question
is quite different from our desire to find that one answer, rather than another,
is true. The form of the desired is in the desire. It is the object which makes the
desire harsh or sweet, coarse or choice, "high" or "low." It is the object that
makes the desire itself desirable or hateful. I perceived (and this was a wonder
of wonders) that just as I had been wrong in supposing that I really desired the
Garden of the Hesperides, so also I had been equally wrong in supposing that
I desired Joy itself. Joy itself, considered simply as an event in my own mind,
turned out to be of no value at all. All the value lay in that of which Joy was the
desiring. And that object, quite clearly, was no state of my own mind or body
at all. In a way, I had proved this by elimination. I had tried everything in my
own mind and body; as it were, asking myself, "Is it this you want? Is it this?"
Last of all I had asked if Joy itself was what I wanted; and, labelling it "aesthetic
experience," had pretended I could answer Yes. But that answer too had broken
down. Inexorably Joy proclaimed, "You want—I myself am your want of—
something other, outside, not you nor any state of you." I did not yet ask, Who
is the desired? only What is it? But this brought me already into the region of
awe, for I thus understood that in deepest solitude there is a road right out of
the self, a commerce with something which, by refusing to identify itself with
any object of the senses, or anything whereof we have biological or social need,
or anything imagined, or any state of our own minds, proclaims itself sheerly
objective. Far more objective than bodies, for it is not, like them, clothed in our
senses; the naked Other, imageless (though our imagination salutes it with a
hundred images), unknown, undefined, desired.

That was the second Move; equivalent, perhaps, to the loss of one's last
remaining bishop. The third Move did not seem to me dangerous at the time.
It consisted merely in linking up this new *éclaircissement* about Joy with my
idealistic philosophy. I saw that Joy, as I now understood it, would fit in. We
mortals, seen as the sciences see us and as we commonly see one another, are mere
"appearances." But appearances of the Absolute. In so far as we really are at all
(which isn't saying much) we have, so to speak, a root in the Absolute, which
is the utter reality. And that is why we experience Joy: we yearn, rightly, for that
unity which we can never reach except by ceasing to be the separate phenomenal
beings called "we." Joy was not a deception. Its visitations were rather the

moments of clearest consciousness we had, when we became aware of our fragmentary and phantasmal nature and ached for that impossible reunion which would annihilate us or that self-contradictory waking which would reveal, not that we had had, but that we *were,* a dream. This seemed quite satisfactory intellectually. Even emotionally too; for it matters more that Heaven should exist than that we should ever get there. What I did not notice was that I had passed an important milestone. Up till now my thoughts had been centrifugal; now the centripetal movement had begun. Considerations arising from quite different parts of my experience were beginning to come together with a click. This new dovetailing of my desire-life with my philosophy foreshadowed the day, now fast approaching, when I should be forced to take my "philosophy" more seriously than I ever intended. I did not foresee this. I was like a man who has lost "merely a pawn" and never dreams that this (in that state of the game) means mate in a few moves.

The fourth Move was more alarming. I was now teaching philosophy (I suspect very badly) as well as English. And my watered Hegelianism wouldn't serve for tutorial purposes.[1] A tutor must make things clear. Now the Absolute cannot be made clear. Do you mean Nobody-knows-what, or do you mean a superhuman mind and therefore (we may as well admit) a Person? After all, did Hegel and Bradley and all the rest of them ever do more than add mystifications to the simple, workable, theistic idealism of Berkeley? I thought not. And didn't Berkeley's "God" do all the same work as the Absolute, with the added advantage that we had at least some notion of what we meant by Him? I thought He did. So I was driven back into something like Berkeleyanism; but Berkeleyanism with a few top dressings of my own. I distinguished this philosophical "God" very sharply (or so I said) from "the God of popular religion." There was, I explained, no possibility of being in a personal relation with Him. For I thought He projected us as a dramatist projects his characters, and I could no more "meet" Him, than Hamlet could meet Shakespeare. I didn't call Him "God" either; I called Him "Spirit." One fights for one's remaining comforts.

Then I read Chesterton's *Everlasting Man* and for the first time saw the whole Christian outline of history set out in a form that seemed to me to make sense. Somehow I contrived not to be too badly shaken. You will remember that I already thought Chesterton the most sensible man alive "apart from his Christianity." Now, I veritably believe, I thought—I didn't of course *say;* words would have revealed the nonsense—that Christianity itself was very sensible "apart from its Christianity." But I hardly remember, for I had not long finished *The Everlasting Man* when something far more alarming happened to me. Early in 1926 the hardest boiled of all the atheists I ever knew sat in my room on the other side of the fire and remarked that the evidence for the historicity of the Gospels was really surprisingly good. "Rum thing," he went on. "All that stuff of Frazer's

[1]Not, of course, that I thought it a tutor's business to make converts to his own philosophy. But I found I needed a position of my own as a basis from which to criticize my pupils' essays.

about the Dying God. Rum thing. It almost looks as if it had really happened once." To understand the shattering impact of it, you would need to know the man (who has certainly never since shown any interest in Christianity). If he, the cynic of cynics, the toughest of the toughs, were not—as I would still have put it—"safe," where could I turn? Was there then no escape?

The odd thing was that before God closed in on me, I was in fact offered what now appears a moment of wholly free choice. In a sense. I was going up Headington Hill on the top of a bus. Without words and (I think) almost without images, a fact about myself was somehow presented to me. I became aware that I was holding something at bay, or shutting something out. Or, if you like, that I was wearing some stiff clothing, like corsets, or even a suit of armor, as if I were a lobster. I felt myself being, there and then, given a free choice. I could open the door or keep it shut; I could unbuckle the armor or keep it on. Neither choice was presented as a duty; no threat or promise was attached to either, though I knew that to open the door or to take off the corslet meant the incalculable. The choice appeared to be momentous but it was also strangely unemotional. I was moved by no desires or fears. In a sense I was not moved by anything. I chose to open, to unbuckle, to loosen the rein. I say, "I chose," yet it did not really seem possible to do the opposite. On the other hand, I was aware of no motives. You could argue that I was not a free agent, but I am more inclined to think that this came nearer to being a perfectly free act than most that I have ever done. Necessity may not be the opposite of freedom, and perhaps a man is most free when, instead of producing motives, he could only say, "I am what I do." Then came the repercussion on the imaginative level. I felt as if I were a man of snow at long last beginning to melt. The melting was starting in my back—drip-drip and presently trickle-trickle. I rather disliked the feeling.

The fox had been dislodged from Hegelian Wood and was now running in the open, "with all the wo in the world," bedraggled and weary, hounds barely a field behind. And nearly everyone was now (one way or another) in the pack; Plato, Dante, MacDonald, Herbert, Barfield, Tolkien, Dyson, Joy itself. Everyone and everything had joined the other side. Even my own pupil Griffiths—now Dom Bede Griffiths—though not yet himself a believer, did his share. Once, when he and Barfield were lunching in my room, I happened to refer to philosophy as "a subject." "It wasn't a *subject* to Plato," said Barfield, "it was a *way*." The quiet but fervent agreement of Griffiths, and the quick glance of understanding between these two, revealed to me my own frivolity. Enough had been thought, and said, and felt, and imagined. It was about time that something should be done.

For of course there had long been an ethic (theoretically) attached to my Idealism. I thought the business of us finite and half-unreal souls was to multiply the consciousness of Spirit by seeing the world from different positions while yet remaining qualitatively the same as Spirit; to be tied to a particular time and place and set of circumstances, yet there to will and think as Spirit itself does. This was hard; for the very act whereby Spirit projected souls and a world gave those souls different and competitive interests, so that there was a temptation to selfishness. But I thought each of us had it in his power to discount the emotional perspective produced by his own particular selfhood, just as we discount the optical perspective produced by our position in space. To prefer my own happiness to my neighbor's was like thinking that the nearest telegraph post was really the largest. The way to recover, and act upon, this universal and objective vision was daily and hourly to remember our true nature, to reascend or return into that Spirit which, in so far as we really were at all, we still were. Yes; but I now felt I had better try to do it. I faced at last (in MacDonald's words) "some thing to be neither more nor less nor other than *done.*" An attempt at complete virtue must be made.

Really, a young Atheist cannot guard his faith too carefully. Dangers lie in wait for him on every side. You must not do, you must not even try to do, the will of the Father unless you are prepared to "know of the doctrine." All my acts, desires, and thoughts were to be brought into harmony with universal Spirit. For the first time I examined myself with a seriously practical purpose. And there I found what appalled me; a zoo of lusts, a bedlam of ambitions, a nursery of fears, a harem of fondled hatreds. My name was legion.

Of course I could do nothing—I could not last out one hour—without continual conscious recourse to what I called Spirit. But the fine, philosophical distinction between this and what ordinary people call "prayer to God" breaks down as soon as you start doing it in earnest. Idealism can be talked, and even felt; it cannot be lived. It became patently absurd to go on thinking of "Spirit" as either ignorant of, or passive to, my approaches. Even if my own philosophy were true, how could the initiative lie on my side? My own analogy, as I now first perceived, suggested the opposite: if Shakespeare and Hamlet could ever meet, it must be Shakespeare's doing.[1] Hamlet could initiate nothing. Perhaps, even now, my Absolute Spirit still differed in some way from the God of religion. The real issue was not, or not yet, there. The real terror was that if you seriously believed in even such a "God" or "Spirit" as I admitted, a wholly new situation developed. As the dry bones shook and came together in that dreadful valley of Ezekiel's, so now a philosophical theorem, cerebrally entertained, began to stir and heave and throw off its gravecloths, and stood upright and became a living presence. I was to be allowed to play at philosophy no longer. It might, as I say, still be true that my "Spirit" differed in some way from "the God of popular religion." My Adversary waived the point. It sank into utter unimportance. He would not argue about it. He only said, "I am the Lord"; "I am that I am"; "I am."

People who are naturally religious find difficulty in understanding the horror of such a revelation. Amiable agnostics will talk cheerfully about "man's search

---

[1] *I.e.*, Shakespeare could, in principle, make himself appear as Author within the play, and write a dialogue between Hamlet and himself. The "Shakespeare" within the play would of course be at once Shakespeare and one of Shakespeare's creatures. It would bear some analogy to Incarnation.

for God." To me, as I then was, they might as well have talked about the mouse's search for the cat. The best image of my predicament is the meeting of Mime and Wotan in the first act of *Siegfried; hier brauch' ich nicht Spärer noch Späher, Einsam will ich.* . . . (I've no use for spies and snoopers. I would be private. . . .)

Remember, I had always wanted, above all things, not to be "interfered with." I had wanted (mad wish) "to call my soul my own." I had been far more anxious to avoid suffering than to achieve delight. I had always aimed at limited liabilities. The supernatural itself had been to me, first, an illicit dram, and then, as by a drunkard's reaction, nauseous. Even my recent attempt to live my philosophy had secretly (I now knew) been hedged round by all sorts of reservations. I had pretty well known that my ideal of virtue would never be allowed to lead me into anything intolerably painful; I would be "reasonable." But now what had been an ideal became a command; and what might not be expected of one? Doubtless, by definition, God was Reason itself. But would He also be "reasonable" in that other, more comfortable, sense? Not the slightest assurance on that score was offered me. Total surrender, the absolute leap in the dark, were demanded. The reality with which no treaty can be made was upon me. The demand was not even "All or nothing." I think that stage had been passed, on the bus top when I unbuckled my armor and the snowman started to melt. Now, the demand was simply "All."

You must picture me alone in that room in Magdalen, night after night, feeling, whenever my mind lifted even for a second from my work, the steady, unrelenting approach of Him whom I so earnestly desired not to meet. That which I greatly feared had at last come upon me. In the Trinity Term of 1929 I gave in, and admitted that God was God, and knelt and prayed: perhaps, that night, the most dejected and reluctant convert in all England. I did not then see what is now the most shining and obvious thing; the Divine humility which will accept a convert even on such terms. The Prodigal Son at least walked home on his own feet. But who can duly adore that Love which will open the high gates to a prodigal who is brought in kicking, struggling, resentful, and darting his eyes in every direction for a chance of escape? The words *compelle intrare,* compel them to come in, have been so abused by wicked men that we shudder at them; but, properly understood, they plumb the depth of the Divine mercy. The hardness of God is kinder than the softness of men, and His compulsion is our liberation.

FROM

The Letters of C. S. Lewis to Arthur Greeves

MY DEAR ARTHUR,

Thanks for your letter of the 11th. I couldn't write to you last Sunday because I had a week end guest—a man called Dyson who teaches English at Reading University. I meet him I suppose about four or five times a year and am beginning to regard him as one of my friends of the 2nd class—i.e. not in the same rank as yourself or Barfield, but on a level with Tolkien or Macfarlane.

He stayed the night with me in College—I sleeping in in order to be able to talk far into the night as one cd. hardly do out here. Tolkien came too, and did not leave till 3 in the morning: and after seeing him out by the little postern on Magdalen bridge Dyson and I found still more to say to one another, strolling up and down the cloister of New Building, so that we did not get to bed till 4. It was really a memorable talk. We began (in Addison's walk just after dinner) on metaphor and myth—interrupted by a rush of wind which came so suddenly on the still, warm evening and sent so many leaves pattering down that we thought it was raining. We all held our breath, the other two appreciating the ecstasy of such a thing almost as you would. We continued (in my room) on Christianity: a good long satisfying talk in which I learned a lot: then discussed the difference between love and friendship—then finally drifted back to poetry and books.

On Sunday he came out here for lunch and Maureen and Minto and I (and

Tykes) all motored him to Reading—a very delightful drive with some lovely villages, and the autumn colours are here now.

I am so glad you have really enjoyed a Morris again. I had the same feeling about it as you, in a way, with this proviso—that I don't think Morris was conscious of the meaning either here or in any of his works, except *Love is Enough* where the flame actually breaks through the smoke so to speak. I feel more and more that Morris has taught me things he did not understand himself. These hauntingly beautiful lands which somehow never satisfy,—this passion to escape from death *plus* the certainty that life owes all its charm to mortality— these push you on to the real thing because they fill you with desire and yet prove absolutely clearly that in Morris's world that desire cannot be satisfied.

The Macdonald conception of death—or, to speak more correctly, St Paul's—is really the answer to Morris: but I don't think I should have understood it without going through Morris. He is an unwilling witness to the truth. He shows you *just how far* you can go without knowing God, and that is far enough to force you (tho' not poor Morris himself) to go further. If ever you feel inclined to relapse into the mundane point of view—to feel that your book and pipe and chair are enough for happiness—it only needs a page or two of Morris to sting you wide awake into uncontrollable longing and to make you feel that everything is worthless except the hope of finding one of his countries. But if you read any of his romances through you will find the country dull before the end. All he has done is to rouse the desire: but so strongly that you *must* find the real satisfaction. And then you realise that *death* is at the root of the whole matter, and why he chose the subject of the Earthly Paradise, and how the true solution is one he never saw.

I have finished the Taylor, and enjoyed it much from the purely literary point of view. As a religious writer I put him low and still think as I did when I last wrote.

I have been studying Hamlet very intensively, and never enjoyed it more. I have been reading all the innumerable theories about him, and don't despise that sort of thing in the least: but each time I turn back to the play itself I am more delighted than ever with the mere atmosphere of it—an atmosphere hard to describe and made up equally of the prevalent sense of death, solitude, & horror and of the extraordinary graciousness and lovableness of H. himself. Have you read it at all lately? If not, do: and just surrender yourself to the magic, regarding it as a poem or a romance. . . .

It is perfect autumn here—splashes of yellow on every other tree and delicious smells. We have been up in the wood clipping all afternoon. . . .

Yrs
Jack

Oct. 1st/31

My dear Arthur,

Very many thanks for the letter and enclosure that arrived this morning. Now, as to their return. I confess that I had not supposed you often read them, and had in view merely an *ultimate* return when W. had finished his editing, that is, in about 4 years' time. If however you want them at once, they are of course your property and will be returned by registered post whenever you wish. I shall follow absolutely your directions. In the meantime you can feel quite confident about their safe keeping. I have spent this morning on them and established a pretty good order for all except about eight. (How maddening my habit of not dating them now becomes! And how ridiculous the arguments by wh. I defended it!)

All the ones that deal with what we used to call 'It' I am suppressing and will return to you in a day or two. I am surprised to find what a very large percentage of the whole they are. I am now inclined to agree with you in *not* regretting that we confided in each other even on this subject, because it has done no harm in the long run—and how could young adolescents really be friends without it? At the same time, the letters give away some of your secrets as well as mine: and I do not wish to recall things of that sort to W's mind, so that in every way they had better be kept out of the final collection. I am also sending back some others in which my replies to you imply that you have said foolish things—you will see what I mean when I return them. Finally, I am suppressing (i.e. sending back at once and keeping from W.—that is what the word 'suppressing' means throughout) all letters that refer to my pretended assignation with the Belgian. I am not at all sure that if J. Taylor were at my elbow he would not tell me that my repentance for that folly was incomplete if I did not submit to the 'mortification' of having them typed and laid open to posterity. I hope, however, this is not really necessary in the case of a sin so old and (I hope) so fully abandoned.

Thanks for all you say about the letters in general. You see mine with too friendly eyes. To me, as I re-read them, the most striking thing is their egotism: sometimes in the form of priggery, intellectual and even social: often in the form of downright affectation (I seem to be posturing and showing off in every letter): and always in the form of complete absorption in ourselves. I have you to thank that it was at least 'ourselves' and not wholly 'myself'. I can now honestly say that I envy you the much more artless letters you were writing me in those days: they all had at least the grace of humility and of affection. How ironical that the very things wh. I was proud of in my letters then should make the reading of them a humiliation to me now!

Don't suppose from this that I have not enjoyed the other aspect of them— the glorious memories they call up. I think I have got over *wishing* for the past back again. I look at it this way. The delights of those days were given to lure us into the world of the Spirit, as sexual rapture is there to lead to offspring and family life. They were nuptial ardours. To ask that they should return, or should remain, is like wishing to prolong the honeymoon at an age when a man should rather be interested in the careers of his growing sons. They have done their work, those days and led on to better things. All the 'homeliness' (wh. was your chief lesson to me) was the introduction to the Christian virtue of charity or love. I sometimes manage now to get into a state in wh. I think of all my enemies and can honestly say that I find something lovable (even if it is only an oddity) in them all: and your conception of 'homeliness' is largely the route by wh. I have reached this. On the other hand, all the 'strangeness' (wh. was my lesson to you) has turned out to be only the first step in far deeper mysteries.

How deep I am just now beginning to see: for I have just passed on from believing in God to definitely believing in Christ—in Christianity. I will try to explain this another time. My long night talk with Dyson and Tolkien had a good deal to do with it.

I am so glad you liked the *Seasons.* I agree with you that some parts are frankly boring, and some (e.g. the bathing episode in *Summer*) are in a false taste. I don't myself think that any of it is as good as the opening of *The Castle of Indolence:* the second canto everyone gives up as hopeless. It is delightful to hear of your thinking of having another try at Spenser. I have read nothing that would interest you since my last letter and am engaged on the Poetical Works of [John] Skelton (XVIth century)—a very bad poet except for the half dozen good things I knew already.

W. and I are busy still clearing the undergrowth in the top wood. This place gets more beautiful every day at present, with yellow leaves and crimson leaves and a more and more autumnal smell. I do hope you will some time make an opportunity of visiting it in winter.

Did it strike you in reading those letters how completely *both* of us were wrong in most of our controversies, or rather in the great standing controversy about 'sentiment' wh. was the root of most of our quarrels? If anyone had said 'There is good feeling and bad: you can't have too much of the first, and you can't have too little of the second' it wd. have blown the gaff on the whole argument. But we blundered along—my indiscriminate hardness only provoking you into a more profound self pity (wh. is the root of all bad sentiment) and that bad sentiment in return making me harder and more willing to hurt.

Term begins next Friday.

Yours
Jack

P.S. I have just finished *The Epistle to the Romans,* the first Pauline epistle I have ever seriously read through. It contains many difficult and some horrible things, but the essential idea of Death (the Macdonald idea) is there alright. What I meant about the Earthly Paradise was simply that the whole story turns on a number of people setting out to look for a country where you don't die.

Oct. 18th 1931

My dear Arthur,

I must have expressed myself rather confusedly about the letters. When I asked you for them I did not think that you would want them back except 'ultimately'—that is, the question of *time* was not seriously in my mind at all. Besides this, as people usually do in such circumstances, I was half consciously fooling myself about the length of time W. had still here. You know how 'He's not going just yet' leads one to plan and feel as if there was a month more when there is really 10 days. Then came your letter, showing your wish (a very flattering one to me) to have the letters back quite soon: and on top of that the *fact* (now unconcealable) that W. was actually packing and wd. be off in a day or two. It was therefore impossible that he should finish his editing of the family letters and get them all typed before he went: if I had known that you wanted them back soon, and if I had faced the real date of his departure, I would not have raised the question of the letters with you till after his return, 3 years hence. That indeed is what I ought to have done.

As things are, the four years I mentioned consist of 1 year's editing preceded by 3 years during wh. W. will be in China and the letters will be lying neatly in a drawer—safe, but idle. You see what a fool I have made of myself! The matter is now entirely in your hands, for of course they are your property not mine. If you want them seriously I will send them back: if you don't, they will be perfectly safe where they are, and safer indeed without the risk of a second postal journey. Still, the next move is to you and I will obey any orders you give.

This has filled up nearly a page so that I don't know whether I should now start to try and explain what I meant about Christianity. For one thing, reading your reply, I began to feel that perhaps I had said too much in my previous letter, that perhaps I was not nearly as clear on the subject as I had led you to think. But I certainly have moved *a bit,* even if it turns out to be a less bit than I thought.

What has been holding me back (at any rate for the last year or so) has not been so much a difficulty in believing as a difficulty in knowing what the doctrine *meant:* you can't believe a thing while you are ignorant *what* the thing is. My puzzle was the whole doctrine of Redemption: in what sense the life and death of Christ 'saved' or 'opened salvation to' the world. I could see how miraculous salvation might be necessary: one could see from ordinary experience how sin (e.g. the case of a drunkard) could get a man to such a point that he was bound to reach Hell (i.e. complete degradation and misery) in this life unless something quite beyond mere natural help or effort stepped in. And I could well imagine a whole world being in the same state and similarly in need of miracle. What I couldn't see was how the life and death of Someone Else (whoever he was) 2000 years ago could help us here and now—except in so far as his *example* helped us. And the example business, tho' true and important, is not Christianity: right in the centre of Christianity, in the Gospels and St Paul, you keep on getting

something quite different and very mysterious expressed in those phrases I have
so often ridiculed ('propitiation'—'sacrifice'—'the blood of the Lamb')—expressions wh. I cd. only interpret in senses that seemed to me either silly or shocking.

Now what Dyson and Tolkien showed me was this: that if I met the idea of
sacrifice in a Pagan story I didn't mind it at all: again, that if I met the idea of
a god sacrificing himself to himself (cf. the quotation opposite the title page of
Dymer) I liked it very much and was mysteriously moved by it: again, that the
idea of the dying and reviving god (Balder, Adonis, Bacchus) similarly moved me
provided I met it anywhere *except* in the Gospels. The reason was that in Pagan
stories I was prepared to feel the myth as profound and suggestive of meanings
beyond my grasp even tho' I could not say in cold prose 'what it meant'.

Now the story of Christ is simply a true myth: a myth working on us in the
same way as the others, but with this tremendous difference that *it really happened:* and one must be content to accept it in the same way, remembering that
it is God's myth where the others are men's myths: i.e. the Pagan stories are God
expressing Himself through the minds of poets, using such images as He found
there, while Christianity is God expressing Himself through what we call 'real
things'. Therefore it is *true*, not in the sense of being a 'description' of God (that
no finite mind could take in) but in the sense of being the way in which God
chooses to (or can) appear to our faculties. The 'doctrines' we get *out of* the true
myth are of course *less* true: they are translations into our *concepts* and *ideas*
of that wh. God has already expressed in a language more adequate, namely the
actual incarnation, crucifixion, and resurrection. Does this amount to a belief in
Christianity? At any rate I am now certain (a) That this Christian story is to be
approached, in a sense, as I approach the other myths. (b) That it is the most
important and full of meaning. I am also *nearly* certain that it really happened.

No time for more now. I hope to have some literary chat in my next letter.

Yours
Jack

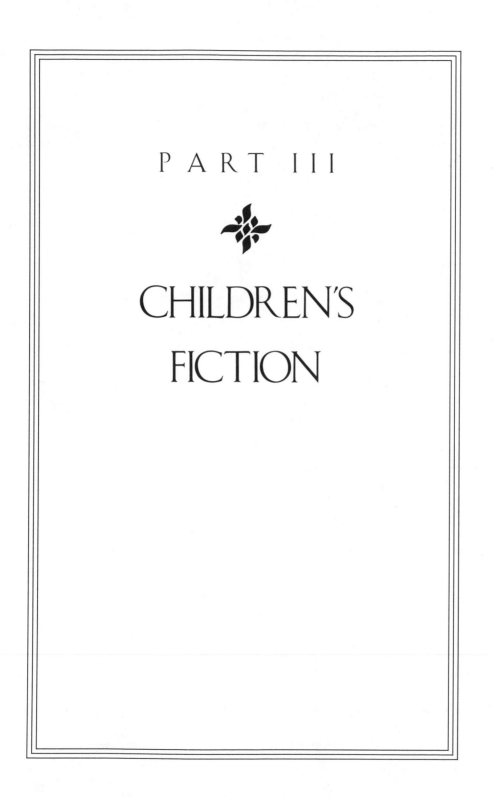

PART III

CHILDREN'S
FICTION

W HEN LEWIS was a child he enjoyed fairy tales. Reading fantasies about dressed and talking animals, knights in armour, witches, fairies, and the search for distant lands, engrossed his youthful imagination. As he grew into young adulthood this world of romance dimmed. Indeed, with budding manhood came a devotion to different things of the mind—in particular the world of reason and observable phenomena. By mid-life, however, Lewis experienced a resurgence of his youthful heart. Once again the lure of the far country and fascination with imaginary worlds occupied his thoughts.

By the late 1940s at least two things conspired to prompt Lewis to write children's books. First, images of such things as a faun with an umbrella, a magnificent talking lion, and a queen on a sleigh, increasingly filled his mind. Second, many of his friends had children and he was called into service as a godfather. Because it was Lewis's habit to write about things that were important to him, he ventured to write a fairy tale to entertain his godchild Lucy, the daughter of his friend Owen Barfield.

Lewis insisted that the writing of his first children's book, *The Lion, the Witch and the Wardrobe* (1950), began with animal pictures in his mind. The Christian imagery came in "of its own accord." Initially he had no intention of writing a full-blown series of seven books called "The Chronicles of Narnia." Each volume came to him, unplanned, during the seven years from 1950 to 1956.

There is a chronological order to these seven fairy stories, according to

Narnian time: *The Magician's Nephew, The Lion, the Witch and the Wardrobe, The Horse and His Boy, Prince Caspian, The Voyage of the "Dawn Treader," The Silver Chair,* and *The Last Battle.* However, the tales first appeared in a different order, with *The Lion, the Witch and the Wardrobe* introducing the series in 1950.

Lewis himself said it makes no difference in what order you read these books. Some of his readers disagree. In any case the entire book, *The Lion, The Witch and the Wardrobe,* is included here because it was the first Narnian Chronicle he wrote, and it is an excellent place to begin the adventure.

The Lion, the Witch and the Wardrobe

CONTENTS

I

Lucy Looks into a Wardrobe

ONCE there were four children whose names were Peter, Susan, Edmund and Lucy. This story is about something that happened to them when they were sent away from London during the war because of the air-raids. They were sent to the house of an old Professor who lived in the heart of the country, ten miles from the nearest railway station and two miles from the nearest post office. He had no wife and he lived in a very large house with a housekeeper called Mrs. Macready and three servants. (Their names were Ivy, Margaret and Betty, but they do not come into the story much.) He himself was a very old man with shaggy white hair, which grew over most of his face as well as on his head, and they liked him almost at once; but on the first evening when he came out to meet them at the front door he was so odd-looking that Lucy (who was the youngest) was a little afraid of him, and Edmund (who was the next youngest) wanted to laugh and had to keep on pretending he was blowing his nose to hide it.

As soon as they had said good night to the Professor and gone upstairs on the first night, the boys came into the girls' room and they all talked it over.

"We've fallen on our feet and no mistake," said Peter. "This is going to be perfectly splendid. That old chap will let us do anything we like."

"I think he's an old dear," said Susan.

"Oh, come off it!" said Edmund, who was tired and pretending not to be tired, which always made him bad-tempered. "Don't go on talking like that."

"Like what?" said Susan; "and anyway, it's time you were in bed."

"Trying to talk like Mother," said Edmund. "And who are you to say when I'm to go to bed? Go to bed yourself."

"Hadn't we all better go to bed?" said Lucy. "There's sure to be a row if we're heard talking here."

"No there won't," said Peter. "I tell you this is the sort of house where no one's going to mind what we do. Anyway, they won't hear us. It's about ten minutes' walk from here down to that dining room, and any amount of stairs and passages in between."

"What's that noise?" said Lucy suddenly. It was a far larger house than she had ever been in before and the thought of all those long passages and rows of doors leading into empty rooms was beginning to make her feel a little creepy.

"It's only a bird, silly," said Edmund.

"It's an owl," said Peter. "This is going to be a wonderful place for birds. I shall go to bed now. I say, let's go and explore to-morrow. You might find anything in a place like this. Did you see those mountains as we came along? And the woods? There might be eagles. There might be stags. There'll be hawks."

"Badgers!" said Lucy.

"Snakes!" said Edmund.

"Foxes!" said Susan.

But when next morning came, there was a steady rain falling, so thick that when you looked out of the window you could see neither the mountains nor the woods nor even the stream in the garden.

"Of course it *would* be raining!" said Edmund. They had just finished breakfast with the Professor and were upstairs in the room he had set apart for them—a long, low room with two windows looking out in one direction and two in another.

"Do stop grumbling, Ed," said Susan. "Ten to one it'll clear up in an hour or so. And in the meantime we're pretty well off. There's a wireless and lots of books."

"Not for me," said Peter, "I'm going to explore in the house."

Everyone agreed to this and that was how the adventures began. It was the sort of house that you never seem to come to the end of, and it was full of unexpected places. The first few doors they tried led only into spare bedrooms, as everyone had expected that they would; but soon they came to a very long room full of pictures and there they found a suit of armour; and after that was a room all hung with green, with a harp in one corner; and then came three steps down and five steps up, and then a kind of little upstairs hall and a door that led out onto a balcony, and then a whole series of rooms that led into each other and were lined with books—most of them very old books and some bigger than a Bible in a church. And shortly after that they looked into a room that was quite empty except for one big wardrobe; the sort that has a looking-glass in the door. There was nothing else in the room at all except a dead blue-bottle on the window-sill.

"Nothing there!" said Peter, and they all trooped out again—all except Lucy. She stayed behind because she thought it would be worth while trying the door of the wardrobe, even though she felt almost sure that it would be locked. To her surprise it opened quite easily, and two moth-balls dropped out.

Looking into the inside, she saw several coats hanging up—mostly long fur coats. There was nothing Lucy liked so much as the smell and feel of fur. She immediately stepped into the wardrobe and got in among the coats and rubbed her face against them, leaving the door open, of course, because she knew that it is very foolish to shut oneself into any wardrobe. Soon she went further in and found that there was a second row of coats hanging up behind the first one. It was almost quite dark in there and she kept her arms stretched out in front of her so as not to bump her face into the back of the wardrobe. She took a step further in—then two or three steps—always expecting to feel woodwork against the tips of her fingers. But she could not feel it.

"This must be a simply enormous wardrobe!" thought Lucy, going still further in and pushing the soft folds of the coats aside to make room for her. Then she noticed that there was something crunching under her feet. "I wonder is that more moth-balls?" she thought, stooping down to feel it with her hands. But instead of feeling the hard, smooth wood of the floor of the wardrobe, she felt something soft and powdery and extremely cold. "This is very queer," she said, and went on a step or two further.

Next moment she found that what was rubbing against her face and hands was no longer soft fur but something hard and rough and even prickly. "Why, it is just like branches of trees!" exclaimed Lucy. And then she saw that there was a light ahead of her; not a few inches away where the back of the wardrobe ought to have been, but a long way off. Something cold and soft was falling on her. A moment later she found that she was standing in the middle of a wood at night-time with snow under her feet and snowflakes falling through the air.

Lucy felt a little frightened, but she felt very inquisitive and excited as well. She looked back over her shoulder and there, between the dark tree-trunks, she could still see the open doorway of the wardrobe and even catch a glimpse of the empty room from which she had set out. (She had, of course, left the door open, for she knew that it is a very silly thing to shut oneself into a wardrobe.) It seemed to be still daylight there. "I can always get back if anything goes wrong," thought Lucy. She began to walk forward, *crunch-crunch*, over the snow and through the wood towards the other light.

In about ten minutes she reached it and found that it was a lamp-post. As she stood looking at it, wondering why there was a lamp-post in the middle of a wood and wondering what to do next, she heard a pitter patter of feet coming towards her. And soon after that a very strange person stepped out from among the trees into the light of the lamp-post.

He was only a little taller than Lucy herself and he carried over his head an umbrella, white with snow. From the waist upwards he was like a man, but his legs were shaped like a goat's (the hair on them was glossy black) and instead of feet he had goat's hoofs. He also had a tail, but Lucy did not notice this at first because it was neatly caught up over the arm that held the umbrella so as to keep it from trailing in the snow. He had a red woollen muffler round his neck and his skin was rather reddish too. He had a strange, but pleasant little face with a short pointed beard and curly hair, and out of the hair there stuck two horns, one on each side of his forehead. One of his hands, as I have said, held the umbrella: in the other arm he carried several brown paper parcels. What with the parcels and the snow it looked just as if he had been doing his Christmas shopping. He was a Faun. And when he saw Lucy he gave such a start of surprise that he dropped all his parcels.

"Goodness gracious me!" exclaimed the Faun.

II

What Lucy Found There

"GOOD EVENING," said Lucy. But the Faun was so busy picking up his parcels that at first he did not reply. When he had finished he made her a little bow.

"Good evening, good evening," said the Faun. "Excuse me—I don't want to be inquisitive—but should I be right in thinking that you are a Daughter of Eve?"

"My name's Lucy," said she, not quite understanding him.

"But you are—forgive me—you are what they call a girl?" asked the Faun.

"Of course I'm a girl," said Lucy.

"You are in fact Human?"

"Of course I'm human," said Lucy, still a little puzzled.

"To be sure, to be sure," said the Faun. "How stupid of me! But I've never seen a Son of Adam or a Daughter of Eve before. I am delighted. That is to say—" and then he stopped as if he had been going to say something he had not intended but had remembered in time. "Delighted, delighted," he went on "Allow me to introduce myself. My name is Tumnus."

"I am very pleased to meet you, Mr. Tumnus," said Lucy.

"And may I ask, O Lucy, Daughter of Eve," said Mr. Tumnus, "how you have come into Narnia?"

"Narnia? What's that?" said Lucy.

"This is the land of Narnia," said the Faun, "where we are now; all that lies between the lamp-post and the great castle of Cair Paravel on the eastern sea. And you—you have come from the wild woods of the west?"

"I—I got in through the wardrobe in the spare room," said Lucy.

"Ah!" said Mr. Tumnus in a rather melancholy voice, "if only I had worked harder at geography when I was a little Faun, I should no doubt know all about those strange countries. It is too late now."

"But they aren't countries at all," said Lucy, almost laughing. "It's only just back there—at least—I'm not sure. It is summer there."

"Meanwhile," said Mr. Tumnus, "it is winter in Narnia, and has been for ever so long, and we shall both catch cold if we stand here talking in the snow. Daughter of Eve from the far land of Spare Oom where eternal summer reigns around the bright city of War Drobe, how would it be if you came and had tea with me?"

"Thank you very much, Mr. Tumnus," said Lucy. "But I was wondering whether I ought to be getting back."

"It's only just round the corner," said the Faun, "and there'll be a roaring fire—and toast—and sardines—and cake."

"Well, it's very kind of you," said Lucy. "But I shan't be able to stay long."

"If you will take my arm, Daughter of Eve," said Mr. Tumnus, "I shall be able to hold the umbrella over both of us. That's the way. Now—off we go."

And so Lucy found herself walking through the wood arm in arm with this strange creature as if they had known one another all their lives.

They had not gone far before they came to a place where the ground became rough and there were rocks all about and little hills up and little hills down. At the bottom of one small valley Mr. Tumnus turned suddenly aside as if he were going to walk straight into an unusually large rock, but at the last moment Lucy found he was leading her into the entrance of a cave. As soon as they were inside she found herself blinking in the light of a wood fire. Then Mr. Tumnus stooped and took a flaming piece of wood out of the fire with a neat little pair of tongs, and lit a lamp. "Now we shan't be long," he said, and immediately put a kettle on.

Lucy thought she had never been in a nicer place. It was a little, dry, clean cave of reddish stone with a carpet on the floor and two little chairs ("one for me and one for a friend," said Mr. Tumnus) and a table and a dresser and a mantelpiece over the fire and above that a picture of an old Faun with a grey beard. In one corner there was a door which Lucy thought must lead to Mr. Tumnus' bedroom, and on one wall was a shelf full of books. Lucy looked at these while he was setting out the tea things. They had titles like *The Life and Letters of Silenus* or *Nymphs and Their Ways* or *Men, Monks and Gamekeepers; a Study in Popular Legend* or *Is Man a Myth?*

"Now, Daughter of Eve!" said the Faun.

And really it was a wonderful tea. There was a nice brown egg, lightly boiled, for each of them, and then sardines on toast, and then buttered toast, and then toast with honey, and then a sugar-topped cake. And when Lucy was tired of eating the Faun began to talk. He had wonderful tales to tell of life in the forest. He told about the midnight dances and how the Nymphs who lived in the wells and the Dryads who lived in the trees came out to dance with the Fauns; about long hunting parties after the milk-white Stag who could give you wishes if you caught him; about feasting and treasure-seeking with the wild Red Dwarfs in deep mines and caverns far beneath the forest floor; and then about summer when the woods were green and old Silenus on his fat donkey would come to visit them, and sometimes Bacchus himself, and then the streams would run with wine instead of water and the whole forest would give itself up to jollification for weeks on end. "Not that it isn't always winter now," he added gloomily. Then to cheer himself up he took out from its case on the dresser a strange little flute that looked as if it were made of straw and began to play. And the tune he played made Lucy want to cry and laugh and dance and go to sleep all at the same time. It must have been hours later when she shook herself and said,

"Oh Mr. Tumnus—I'm so sorry to stop you, and I do love that tune—but really, I must go home. I only meant to stay for a few minutes."

"It's no good *now*, you know," said the Faun, laying down his flute and shaking his head at her very sorrowfully.

"No good?" said Lucy, jumping up and feeling rather frightened. "What do you mean? I've got to go home at once. The others will be wondering what has happened to me." But a moment later she asked, "Mr. Tumnus! Whatever is the matter?" for the Faun's brown eyes had filled with tears and then the tears began trickling down his cheeks, and soon they were running off the end of his nose; and at last he covered his face with his hands and began to howl.

"Mr. Tumnus! Mr. Tumnus!" said Lucy in great distress. "Don't! Don't! What is the matter? Aren't you well? Dear Mr. Tumnus, do tell me what is wrong." But the Faun continued sobbing as if his heart would break. And even when Lucy went over and put her arms round him and lent him her handkerchief, he did not stop. He merely took the handkerchief and kept on using it, wringing it out with both hands whenever it got too wet to be any more use, so that presently Lucy was standing in a damp patch.

"Mr. Tumnus!" bawled Lucy in his ear, shaking him. "Do stop. Stop it at once! You ought to be ashamed of yourself, a great big Faun like you. What on earth are you crying about?"

"Oh—oh—oh!" sobbed Mr. Tumnus, "I'm crying because I'm such a bad Faun."

"I don't think you're a bad Faun at all," said Lucy. "I think you are a very good Faun. You are the nicest Faun I've ever met."

"Oh—oh—you wouldn't say that if you knew," replied Mr. Tumnus between his sobs. "No, I'm a bad Faun. I don't suppose there ever was a worse Faun since the beginning of the world."

"But what have you done?" asked Lucy.

"My old father, now," said Mr. Tumnus, "that's his picture over the mantelpiece. He would never have done a thing like this."

"A thing like what?" said Lucy.

"Like what I've done," said the Faun. "Taken service under the White Witch. That's what I am. I'm in the pay of the White Witch."

"The White Witch? Who is she?"

"Why, it is she that has got all Narnia under her thumb. It's she that makes it always winter. Always winter and never Christmas; think of that!"

"How awful!" said Lucy. "But what does she pay *you* for?"

"That's the worst of it," said Mr. Tumnus with a deep groan. "I'm a kidnapper for her, that's what I am. Look at me, Daughter of Eve. Would you believe that I'm the sort of Faun to meet a poor innocent child in the wood, one that had never done me any harm, and pretend to be friendly with it, and invite it home to my cave, all for the sake of lulling it asleep and then handing it over to the White Witch?"

"No," said Lucy. "I'm sure you wouldn't do anything of the sort."

"But I have," said the Faun.

"Well," said Lucy rather slowly (for she wanted to be truthful and yet not to be too hard on him), "well, that was pretty bad. But you're so sorry for it that I'm sure you will never do it again."

"Daughter of Eve, don't you understand?" said the Faun. "It isn't something I *have* done. I'm doing it now, this very moment."

"What do you mean?" cried Lucy, turning very white.

"You are the child," said Mr. Tumnus. "I had orders from the White Witch that if ever I saw a Son of Adam or a Daughter of Eve in the wood, I was to catch them and hand them over to her. And you are the first I ever met. And I've pretended to be your friend and asked you to tea, and all the time I've been meaning to wait till you were asleep and then go and tell *her.*"

"Oh but you won't, Mr. Tumnus," said Lucy. "You won't, will you? Indeed, indeed you really mustn't."

"And if I don't," said he, beginning to cry again, "she's sure to find out. And she'll have my tail cut off, and my horns sawn off, and my beard plucked out, and she'll wave her wand over my beautiful cloven hoofs and turn them into horrid solid hoofs like a wretched horse's. And if she is extra and specially angry she'll turn me into stone and I shall be only a statue of a Faun in her horrible house until the four thrones at Cair Paravel are filled—and goodness knows when that will happen, or whether it will ever happen at all."

"I'm very sorry, Mr. Tumnus," said Lucy. "But please let me go home."

"Of course I will," said the Faun. "Of course I've got to. I see that now. I hadn't known what Humans were like before I met you. Of course I can't give you up to the Witch; not now that I know you. But we must be off at once. I'll see you back to the lamp-post. I suppose you can find your own way from there back to Spare Oom and War Drobe?"

"I'm sure I can," said Lucy.

"We must go as quietly as we can," said Mr. Tumnus. "The whole wood is full of *her* spies. Even some of the trees are on her side."

They both got up and left the tea things on the table, and Mr. Tumnus once more put up his umbrella and gave Lucy his arm, and they went out into the snow. The journey back was not at all like the journey to the Faun's cave; they stole along as quickly as they could, without speaking a word, and Mr. Tumnus kept to the darkest places. Lucy was relieved when they reached the lamp-post again.

"Do you know your way from here, Daughter of Eve?" said Tumnus.

Lucy looked very hard between the trees and could just see in the distance a patch of light that looked like daylight. "Yes," she said, "I can see the wardrobe door."

"Then be off home as quick as you can," said the Faun, "and—c-can you ever forgive me for what I meant to do?"

"Why, of course I can," said Lucy, shaking him heartily by the hand. "And I do hope you won't get into dreadful trouble on my account."

"Farewell, Daughter of Eve," said he. "Perhaps I may keep the handker-chief?"

"Rather!" said Lucy, and then ran towards the far-off patch of daylight as quickly as her legs would carry her. And presently instead of rough branches brushing past her she felt coats, and instead of crunching snow under her feet she felt wooden boards, and all at once she found herself jumping out of the wardrobe into the same empty room from which the whole adventure had started. She shut the wardrobe door tightly behind her and looked around, panting for breath. It was still raining and she could hear the voices of the others in the passage.

"I'm here," she shouted. "I'm here. I've come back, I'm all right."

III

Edmund and the Wardrobe

L<small>UCY</small> ran out of the empty room into the passage and found the other three.

"It's all right," she repeated, "I've come back."

"What on earth are you talking about, Lucy?" asked Susan.

"Why?" said Lucy in amazement, "haven't you all been wondering where I was?"

"So you've been hiding, have you?" said Peter. "Poor old Lu, hiding and nobody noticed! You'll have to hide longer than that if you want people to start looking for you."

"But I've been away for hours and hours," said Lucy.

The others all stared at one another.

"Batty!" said Edmund tapping his head. "Quite batty."

"What do you mean, Lu?" asked Peter.

"What I said," answered Lucy. "It was just after breakfast when I went into the wardrobe, and I've been away for hours and hours, and had tea, and all sorts of things have happened."

"Don't be silly, Lucy," said Susan. "We've only just come out of that room a moment ago, and you were there then."

"She's not being silly at all," said Peter, "she's just making up a story for fun, aren't you, Lu? And why shouldn't she?"

"No, Peter, I'm not," she said. "It's—it's a magic wardrobe. There's a wood inside it, and it's snowing, and there's a Faun and a witch and it's called Narnia; come and see."

The others did not know what to think, but Lucy was so excited that they all went back with her into the room. She rushed ahead of them, flung open the door of the wardrobe and cried, "Now! go in and see for yourselves."

"Why, you goose," said Susan, putting her head inside and pulling the fur coats apart, "it's just an ordinary wardrobe, look! there's the back of it."

Then everyone looked in and pulled the coats apart; and they all saw—Lucy herself saw—a perfectly ordinary wardrobe. There was no wood and no snow, only the back of the wardrobe, with hooks on it. Peter went in and rapped his knuckles on it to make sure that it was solid.

"A jolly good hoax, Lu," he said as he came out again, "you have really taken us in, I must admit. We half believed you."

"But it wasn't a hoax at all," said Lucy, "really and truly. It was all different a moment ago. Honestly it was. I promise."

"Come, Lu," said Peter, "that's going a bit far. You've had your joke. Hadn't you better drop it now?"

Lucy grew very red in the face and tried to say something, though she hardly knew what she was trying to say, and burst into tears.

For the next few days she was very miserable. She could have made it up with the others quite easily at any moment if she could have brought herself to say that the whole thing was only a story made up for fun. But Lucy was a very truthful girl and she knew that she was really in the right; and she could not bring herself to say this. The others who thought she was telling a lie, and a silly lie too, made her very unhappy. The two elder ones did this without meaning to do it, but Edmund could be spiteful, and on this occasion he was spiteful. He sneered and jeered at Lucy and kept on asking her if she'd found any other new countries in other cupboards all over the house. What made it worse was that these days ought to have been delightful. The weather was fine and they were out of doors from morning to night, bathing, fishing, climbing trees, birds' nesting, and lying in the heather. But Lucy could not properly enjoy any of it. And so things went on until the next wet day.

That day, when it came to the afternoon and there was still no sign of a break in the weather, they decided to play hide-and-seek. Susan was "It" and as soon as the others scattered to hide, Lucy went to the room where the wardrobe was. She did not mean to hide in the wardrobe, because she knew that would only set the others talking again about the whole wretched business. But she did want to have one more look inside it; for by this time she was beginning to wonder herself whether Narnia and the Faun had not been a dream. The house was so large and complicated and full of hiding places that she thought she would have time to have one look into the wardrobe and then hide somewhere else. But as soon as she reached it she heard steps in the passage outside, and then there was nothing for it but to jump into the wardrobe and hold the door closed behind her. She did not shut it properly because she knew that it is very silly to shut oneself into a wardrobe, even if it is not a magic one.

Now the steps she had heard were those of Edmund; and he came into the room just in time to see Lucy vanishing into the wardrobe. He at once decided to get into it himself—not because he thought it a particularly good place to hide but because he wanted to go on teasing her about her imaginary country. He opened the door. There were the coats hanging up as usual, and a smell of moth-balls, and darkness and silence, and no sign of Lucy. "She thinks I'm Susan come to catch her," said Edmund to himself, "and so she's keeping very quiet in at the back." He jumped in and shut the door, forgetting what a very foolish thing this is to do. Then he began feeling about for Lucy in the dark. He had expected to find her in a few seconds and was very surprised when he did not. He decided to open the door again and let in some light. But he could not find the door either. He didn't like this at all and began groping wildly in every direction; he even shouted out, "Lucy! Lu! Where are you? I know you're here."

There was no answer and Edmund noticed that his own voice had a curious sound—not the sound you expect in a cupboard but a kind of open-air sound. He also noticed that he was unexpectedly cold; and then he saw a light.

"Thank goodness," said Edmund, "the door must have swung open of its own accord." He forgot all about Lucy and went towards the light which he thought

was the open door of the wardrobe. But instead of finding himself stepping out
into the spare room he found himself stepping out from the shadow of some thick
dark fir trees into an open place in the middle of a wood.

There was crisp, dry snow under his feet and more snow lying on the branches
of the trees. Overhead there was a pale blue sky, the sort of sky one sees on a
fine winter day in the morning. Straight ahead of him he saw between the tree
trunks the sun, just rising, very red and clear. Everything was perfectly still, as
if he were the only living creature in that country. There was not even a robin
or a squirrel among the trees, and the wood stretched as far as he could see in
every direction. He shivered.

He now remembered that he had been looking for Lucy; and also how
unpleasant he had been to her about her "imaginary country" which now turned
out not to have been imaginary at all. He thought that she must be somewhere
quite close and so he shouted, "Lucy! Lucy! I'm here too—Edmund."

There was no answer.

"She's angry about all the things I've been saying lately," thought Edmund.
And though he did not like to admit that he had been wrong, he also did not
much like being alone in this strange, cold, quiet place; so he shouted again.

"I say, Lu! I'm sorry I didn't believe you. I see now you were right all along.
Do come out. Make it Pax."

Still there was no answer.

"Just like a girl," said Edmund to himself, "sulking somewhere, and won't
accept an apology." He looked round him again and decided he did not much
like this place, and had almost made up his mind to go home, when he heard,
very far off in the wood, a sound of bells. He listened and the sound came nearer
and nearer and at last there swept into sight a sledge drawn by two reindeer.

The reindeer were about the size of Shetland ponies and their hair was so
white that even the snow hardly looked white compared with them; their branching horns were gilded and shone like something on fire when the sunrise caught
them. Their harness was of scarlet leather and covered with bells. On the sledge,
driving the reindeer, sat a fat dwarf who would have been about three feet high
if he had been standing. He was dressed in polar bear's fur and on his head he
wore a red hood with a long gold tassel hanging down from its point; his huge
beard covered his knees and served him instead of a rug. But behind him, on a
much higher seat in the middle of the sledge sat a very different person—a great
lady, taller than any woman that Edmund had ever seen. She also was covered
in white fur up to her throat and held a long straight golden wand in her right
hand and wore a golden crown on her head. Her face was white—not merely pale,
but white like snow or paper or icing sugar, except for her very red mouth. It was
a beautiful face in other respects, but proud and cold and stern.

The sledge was a fine sight as it came sweeping towards Edmund with the
bells jingling and the Dwarf cracking his whip and the snow flying up on each
side of it.

"Stop!" said the Lady, and the Dwarf pulled the reindeer up so sharp that they almost sat down. Then they recovered themselves and stood champing their bits and blowing. In the frosty air the breath coming out of their nostrils looked like smoke.

"And what, pray, are you?" said the Lady, looking hard at Edmund.

"I'm—I'm—my name's Edmund," said Edmund rather awkwardly. He did not like the way she looked at him.

The Lady frowned. "Is that how you address a Queen?" she asked, looking sterner than ever.

"I beg your pardon, your Majesty, I didn't know," said Edmund.

"Not know the Queen of Narnia?" cried she. "Ha! You shall know us better hereafter. But I repeat—what are you?"

"Please, your Majesty," said Edmund, "I don't know what you mean. I'm at school—at least I was—it's the holidays now."

IV

Turkish Delight

"But what *are* you?" said the Queen again. "Are you a great overgrown dwarf that has cut off its beard?"

"No, your Majesty," said Edmund, "I never had a beard, I'm a boy."

"A boy!" said she. "Do you mean you are a Son of Adam?"

Edmund stood still, saying nothing. He was too confused by this time to understand what the question meant.

"I see you are an idiot, whatever else you may be," said the Queen. "Answer me, once and for all, or I shall lose my patience. Are you human?"

"Yes, your Majesty," said Edmund.

"And how, pray, did you come to enter my dominions?"

"Please, your Majesty, I came in through a wardrobe."

"A wardrobe? What do you mean?"

"I—I opened a door and just found myself here, your Majesty," said Edmund.

"Ha!" said the Queen, speaking more to herself than to him. "A door. A door from the world of men! I have heard of such things. This may wreck all. But he is only one, and he is easily dealt with." As she spoke these words she rose from her seat and looked Edmund full in the face, her eyes flaming; at the same moment she raised her wand. Edmund felt sure that she was going to do something dreadful but he seemed unable to move. Then, just as he gave himself up for lost, she appeared to change her mind.

"My poor child," she said in quite a different voice, "how cold you look! Come and sit with me here on the sledge and I will put my mantle around you and we will talk."

Edmund did not like this arrangement at all but he dared not disobey; he stepped on to the sledge and sat at her feet, and she put a fold of her fur mantle around him and tucked it well in.

"Perhaps something hot to drink?" said the Queen. "Should you like that?"

"Yes please, your Majesty," said Edmund, whose teeth were chattering.

The Queen took from somewhere among her wrappings a very small bottle which looked as if it were made of copper. Then, holding out her arm, she let one drop fall from it on to the snow beside the sledge. Edmund saw the drop for a second in mid-air, shining like a diamond. But the moment it touched the snow there was a hissing sound and there stood a jewelled cup full of something that steamed. The Dwarf immediately took this and handed it to Edmund with a bow and a smile; not a very nice smile. Edmund felt much better as he began to sip the hot drink. It was something he had never tasted before, very sweet and foamy and creamy, and it warmed him right down to his toes.

"It is dull, Son of Adam, to drink without eating," said the Queen presently. "What would you like best to eat?"

74

"Turkish Delight, please, your Majesty," said Edmund.

The Queen let another drop fall from her bottle on to the snow, and instantly there appeared a round box, tied with green silk ribbon, which, when opened, turned out to contain several pounds of the best Turkish Delight. Each piece was sweet and light to the very centre and Edmund had never tasted anything more delicious. He was quite warm now, and very comfortable.

While he was eating the Queen kept asking him questions. At first Edmund tried to remember that it is rude to speak with one's mouth full, but soon he forgot about this and thought only of trying to shovel down as much Turkish Delight as he could, and the more he ate the more he wanted to eat, and he never asked himself why the Queen should be so inquisitive. She got him to tell her that he had one brother and two sisters, and that one of his sisters had already been in Narnia and had met a Faun there, and that no one except himself and his brother and his sisters knew anything about Narnia. She seemed especially interested in the fact that there were four of them, and kept on coming back to it. "You are sure there are just four of you?" she asked. "Two Sons of Adam and two Daughters of Eve, neither more nor less?" and Edmund, with his mouth full of Turkish Delight, kept on saying, "Yes, I told you that before," and forgetting to call her "Your Majesty" but she didn't seem to mind now.

At last the Turkish Delight was all finished and Edmund was looking very hard at the empty box and wishing that she would ask him whether he would like some more. Probably the Queen knew quite well what he was thinking; for she knew, though Edmund did not, that this was enchanted Turkish Delight and that anyone who had once tasted it would want more and more of it, and would even, if they were allowed, go on eating it till they killed themselves. But she did not offer him any more. Instead, she said to him,

"Son of Adam, I should so much like to see your brother and your two sisters. Will you bring them to me?"

"I'll try," said Edmund, still looking at the empty box.

"Because, if you did come again—bringing them with you of course—I'd be able to give you some more Turkish Delight. I can't do it now, the magic will only work once. In my own house it would be another matter."

"Why can't we go to your house now?" said Edmund. When he had first got on to the sledge he had been afraid that she might drive away with him to some unknown place from which he would not be able to get back, but he had forgotten about that fear now.

"It is a lovely place, my house," said the Queen. "I am sure you would like it. There are whole rooms full of Turkish Delight, and what's more, I have no children of my own. I want a nice boy whom I could bring up as a Prince and who would be King of Narnia when I am gone. While he was Prince he would wear a gold crown and eat Turkish Delight all day long; and you are much the cleverest and handsomest young man I've ever met. I think I would like to make you the Prince—some day, when you bring the others to visit me."

"Why not now?" said Edmund. His face had become very red and his mouth and fingers were sticky. He did not look either clever or handsome whatever the Queen might say.

"Oh, but if I took you there now," said she, "I shouldn't see your brother and your sisters. I very much want to know your charming relations. You are to be the Prince and—later on—the King; that is understood. But you must have courtiers and nobles. I will make your brother a Duke and your sisters Duchesses."

"There's nothing special about *them,*" said Edmund, "and, anyway, I could always bring them some other time."

"Ah, but once you were in my house," said the Queen, "you might forget all about them. You would be enjoying yourself so much that you wouldn't want the bother of going to fetch them. No. You must go back to your own country now and come to me another day, *with them,* you understand. It is no good coming without them."

"But I don't even know the way back to my own country," pleaded Edmund.

"That's easy," answered the Queen. "Do you see that lamp?" She pointed with her wand and Edmund turned and saw the same lamp-post under which Lucy had met the Faun. "Straight on, beyond that, is the way to the World of Men. And now look the other way"—here she pointed in the opposite direction—"and tell me if you can see two little hills rising above the trees."

"I think I can," said Edmund.

"Well my house is between those two hills. So next time you come you have only to find the lamp-post and look for those two hills and walk through the wood till you reach my house. You had better keep the river on your right when you get to it. But remember—you must bring the others with you. I might have to be very angry with you if you came alone."

"I'll do my best," said Edmund.

"And, by the way," said the Queen, "you needn't tell them about me. It would be fun to keep it a secret between us two, wouldn't it? Make it a surprise for them. Just bring them along to the two hills—a clever boy like you will easily think of some excuse for doing that—and when you come to my house you could just say 'Let's see who lives here' or something like that. I am sure that would be best. If your sister has met one of the Fauns, she may have heard strange stories about me—nasty stories that might make her afraid to come to me. Fauns will say anything, you know, and now—"

"Please, please," said Edmund suddenly, "please couldn't I have just one piece of Turkish Delight to eat on the way home?"

"No, no," said the Queen with a laugh, "you must wait till next time." While she spoke, she signalled to the Dwarf to drive on, but as the sledge swept away out of sight, the Queen waved to Edmund calling out, "Next time! Next time! Don't forget. Come soon."

Edmund was still staring after the sledge when he heard someone calling his own name, and looking round he saw Lucy coming towards him from another part of the wood.

"Oh, Edmund!" she cried. "So you've got in too! Isn't it wonderful, and now—"

"All right," said Edmund, "I see you were right and it is a magic wardrobe after all. I'll say I'm sorry if you like. But where on earth have you been all this time? I've been looking for you everywhere."

"If I'd known you had got in I'd have waited for you," said Lucy who was too happy and excited to notice how snappishly Edmund spoke or how flushed and strange his face was. "I've been having lunch with dear Mr. Tumnus, the Faun, and he's very well and the White Witch has done nothing to him for letting me go, so he thinks she can't have found out and perhaps everything is going to be all right after all."

"The White Witch?" said Edmund, "who's she?"

"She is a perfectly terrible person," said Lucy. "She calls herself the Queen of Narnia though she has no right to be queen at all, and all the Fauns and Dryads and Naiads and dwarfs and animals—at least all the good ones—simply hate her. And she can turn people into stone and do all kinds of horrible things. And she has made a magic so that it is always winter in Narnia—always winter, but it never gets to be Christmas. And she drives about on a sledge, drawn by a reindeer, with her wand in her hand and a crown on her head."

Edmund was already feeling uncomfortable from having eaten too many sweets, and when he heard that the Lady he had made friends with was a dangerous witch he felt even more uncomfortable. But he still wanted to taste that Turkish Delight again more than he wanted anything else.

"Who told you all that stuff about the White Witch?" he asked.

"Mr. Tumnus, the Faun," said Lucy.

"You can't always believe what Fauns say," said Edmund, trying to sound as if he knew far more about them than Lucy.

"Who said so?" asked Lucy.

"Everyone knows it," said Edmund, "ask anybody you like. But it's pretty poor sport standing here in the snow. Let's go home."

"Yes, let's," said Lucy. "Oh Edmund, I *am* glad you've got in too. The others will have to believe in Narnia now that both of us have been there. What fun it will be."

But Edmund secretly thought that it would not be as good fun for him as for her. He would have to admit that Lucy had been right, before all the others, and he felt sure the others would all be on the side of the Fauns and the animals; but he was already more than half on the side of the Witch. He did not know what he would say, or how he would keep his secret once they were all talking about Narnia.

By this time they had walked a good way. Then suddenly they felt coats around them instead of branches and next moment they were both standing outside the wardrobe in the empty room.

"I say," said Lucy, "you do look awful, Edmund. Don't you feel well?"

"I'm all right," said Edmund, but this was not true. He was feeling very sick.

"Come on then," said Lucy, "let's find the others. What a lot we shall have to tell them! And what wonderful adventures we shall have now that we're all in it together."

V

Back on This Side of the Door

BECAUSE the game of hide-and-seek was still going on, it took Edmund and Lucy some time to find the others. But when at last they were all together (which happened in the long room, where the suit of armour was) Lucy burst out,

"Peter! Susan! It's all true. Edmund has seen it too. There *is* a country you can get to through the wardrobe. Edmund and I both got in. We met one another in there, in the wood. Go on, Edmund; tell them all about it."

"What's all this about, Ed?" said Peter.

And now we come to one of the nastiest things in this story. Up to that moment Edmund had been feeling sick, and sulky, and annoyed with Lucy for being right, but he hadn't made up his mind what to do. When Peter suddenly asked him the question he decided all at once to do the meanest and most spiteful thing he could think of. He decided to let Lucy down.

"Tell us, Ed," said Susan.

And Edmund gave a very superior look as if he were far older than Lucy (there was really only a year's difference) and then a little snigger and said, "Oh, yes, Lucy and I have been playing—pretending that all her story about a country in the wardrobe is true. Just for fun, of course. There's nothing there really."

Poor Lucy gave Edmund one look and rushed out of the room.

Edmund, who was becoming a nastier person every minute, thought that he had scored a great success, and went on at once to say, "There she goes again. What's the matter with her? That's the worst of young kids, they always—"

"Look here," said Peter turning on him savagely, "shut up! You've been perfectly beastly to Lu ever since she started this nonsense about the wardrobe and now you go playing games with her about it and setting her off again. I believe you did it simply out of spite."

"But it's all nonsense," said Edmund, very taken aback.

"Of course it's all nonsense," said Peter, "that's just the point. Lu was perfectly all right when we left home, but since we've been down here she seems to be either going queer in the head or else turning into a most frightful liar. But whichever it is, what good do you think you'll do by jeering and nagging at her one day and encouraging her the next?"

"I thought—I thought," said Edmund; but he couldn't think of anything to say.

"You didn't think anything at all," said Peter, "it's just spite. You've always liked being beastly to anyone smaller than yourself; we've seen that at school before now."

"Do stop it," said Susan; "it won't make things any better having a row between you two. Let's go and find Lucy."

It was not surprising that when they found Lucy, a good deal later, everyone could see that she had been crying. Nothing they could say to her made any difference. She stuck to her story and said:

"I don't care what you think, and I don't care what you say. You can tell the Professor or you can write to Mother or you can do anything you like. I know I've met a Faun in there and—I wish I'd stayed there and you are all beasts, beasts."

It was an unpleasant evening. Lucy was miserable and Edmund was beginning to feel that his plan wasn't working as well as he had expected. The two older ones were really beginning to think that Lucy was out of her mind. They stood in the passage talking about it in whispers long after she had gone to bed.

The result was that next morning they decided that they really would go and tell the whole thing to the Professor. "He'll write to Father if he thinks there is really something wrong with Lu," said Peter; "it's getting beyond us." So they went and knocked at the study door, and the Professor said "Come in," and got up and found chairs for them and said he was quite at their disposal. Then he sat listening to them with the tips of his fingers pressed together and never interrupting, till they had finished the whole story. After that he said nothing for quite a long time. Then he cleared his throat and said the last thing either of them expected.

"How do you know?" he asked, "that your sister's story is not true?"

"Oh, but—" began Susan, and then stopped. Anyone could see from the old man's face that he was perfectly serious. Then Susan pulled herself together and said, "But Edmund said they had only been pretending."

"That is a point," said the Professor, "which certainly deserves consideration; very careful consideration. For instance—if you will excuse me for asking the question—does your experience lead you to regard your brother or your sister as the more reliable? I mean, which is the more truthful?"

"That's just the funny thing about it, Sir," said Peter. "Up till now, I'd have said Lucy every time."

"And what do you think, my dear?" said the Professor, turning to Susan.

"Well," said Susan, "in general, I'd say the same as Peter, but this couldn't be true—all this about the wood and the Faun."

"That is more than I know," said the Professor, "and a charge of lying against someone whom you have always found truthful is a very serious thing; a very serious thing indeed."

"We were afraid it mightn't even be lying," said Susan. "We thought there might be something wrong with Lucy."

"Madness, you mean?" said the Professor quite coolly. "Oh, you can make your minds easy about that. One has only to look at her and talk to her to see that she is not mad."

"But then," said Susan and stopped. She had never dreamed that a grown-up would talk like the Professor and didn't know what to think.

"Logic!" said the Professor half to himself. "Why don't they teach logic at these schools? There are only three possibilities. Either your sister is telling lies, or she is mad, or she is telling the truth. You know she doesn't tell lies and it is obvious that she is not mad. For the moment then and unless any further evidence turns up, we must assume that she is telling the truth."

Susan looked at him very hard and was quite sure from the expression on his face that he was not making fun of them.

"But how could it be true, Sir?" said Peter.

"Why do you say that?" asked the Professor.

"Well, for one thing," said Peter, "if it was real why doesn't everyone find this country every time they go to the wardrobe? I mean, there was nothing there when we looked; even Lucy didn't pretend there was."

"What has that to do with it?" said the Professor.

"Well, Sir, if things are real, they're there all the time."

"Are they?" said the Professor; and Peter did not know quite what to say.

"But there was no time," said Susan, "Lucy had had no time to have gone anywhere, even if there was such a place. She came running after us the very moment we were out of the room. It was less than a minute, and she pretended to have been away for hours."

"That is the very thing that makes her story so likely to be true," said the Professor. "If there really is a door in this house that leads to some other world (and I should warn you that this is a very strange house, and even I know very little about it)—if, I say, she had got into another world, I should not be at all surprised to find that that other world had a separate time of its own; so that however long you stayed there it would never take up any of *our* time. On the other hand, I don't think many girls of her age would invent that idea for themselves. If she had been pretending, she would have hidden for a reasonable time before coming out and telling her story."

"But do you really mean, Sir," said Peter, "that there could be other worlds— all over the place, just round the corner—like that?"

"Nothing is more probable," said the Professor, taking off his spectacles and beginning to polish them, while he muttered to himself, "I wonder what they *do* teach them at these schools."

"But what are we to do?" said Susan. She felt that the conversation was beginning to get off the point.

"My dear young lady," said the Professor, suddenly looking up with a very sharp expression at both of them, "there is one plan which no one has yet suggested and which is well worth trying."

"What's that?" said Susan.

"We might all try minding our own business," said he. And that was the end of that conversation.

After this things were a good deal better for Lucy. Peter saw to it that Edmund stopped jeering at her, and neither she nor anyone else felt inclined to talk about the wardrobe at all. It had become a rather alarming subject. And so for a time it looked as if all the adventures were coming to an end; but that was not to be.

This house of the Professor's—which even he knew so little about—was so old and famous that people from all over England used to come and ask permission to see over it. It was the sort of house that is mentioned in guide books and even in histories; and well it might be, for all manner of stories were told about it, some of them even stranger than the one I am telling you now. And when parties of sight-seers arrived and asked to see the house, the Professor always gave them permission, and Mrs. Macready, the housekeeper, showed them around, telling them about the pictures and the armour, and the rare books in the library. Mrs. Macready was not fond of children, and did not like to be interrupted when she was telling visitors all the things she knew. She had said to Susan and Peter almost on the first morning (along with a good many other instructions) "And please remember you're to keep out of the way whenever I'm taking a party over the house."

"Just as if any of us would *want* to waste half the morning trailing round with a crowd of strange grown-ups!" said Edmund, and the other three thought the same. That was how the adventures began for the second time.

A few mornings later Peter and Edmund were looking at the suit of armour and wondering if they could take it to bits when the two girls rushed into the room and said, "Look out! Here comes the Macready and a whole gang with her."

"Sharp's the word," said Peter, and all four made off through the door at the far end of the room. But when they had got out into the Green Room and beyond it, into the library, they suddenly heard voices ahead of them, and realised that Mrs. Macready must be bringing her party of sight-seers up the back stairs— instead of up the front stairs as they had expected. And after that—whether it was that they lost their heads, or that Mrs. Macready was trying to catch them, or that some magic in the house had come to life and was chasing them into Narnia—they seemed to find themselves being followed everywhere, until at last Susan said, "Oh bother those trippers! Here—let's get into the Wardrobe Room till they've passed. No one will follow us in there." But the moment they were inside they heard voices in the passage—and then someone fumbling at the door—and then they saw the handle turning.

"Quick!" said Peter, "there's nowhere else," and flung open the wardrobe. All four of them bundled inside it and sat there, panting, in the dark. Peter held the door closed but did not shut it; for, of course, he remembered, as every sensible person does, that you should never shut yourself up in a wardrobe.

VI

Into the Forest

"I wish the Macready would hurry up and take all these people away," said Susan presently, "I'm getting horribly cramped."

"And what a filthy smell of camphor!" said Edmund.

"I expect the pockets of these coats are full of it," said Susan, "to keep away moths."

"There's something sticking into my back," said Peter.

"And isn't it cold?" said Susan.

"Now that you mention it, it is cold," said Peter, "and hang it all, it's wet too. What's the matter with this place? I'm sitting on something wet. It's getting wetter every minute." He struggled to his feet.

"Let's get out," said Edmund, "they've gone."

"O-o-oh!" said Susan suddenly. And everyone asked her what was the matter.

"I'm sitting against a tree," said Susan, "and look! It's getting lighter—over there."

"By jove, you're right," said Peter, "and look there—and there. It's trees all round. And this wet stuff is snow. Why, I do believe we've got into Lucy's wood after all."

And now there was no mistaking it and all four children stood blinking in the daylight of a winter day. Behind them were coats hanging on pegs, in front of them were snow-covered trees.

Peter turned at once to Lucy.

"I apologise for not believing you," he said, "I'm sorry. Will you shake hands?"

"Of course," said Lucy, and did.

"And now," said Susan, "what do we do next?"

"Do?" said Peter, "why, go and explore the wood, of course."

"Ugh!" said Susan, stamping her feet, "it's pretty cold. What about putting on some of these coats?"

"They're not ours," said Peter doubtfully.

"I am sure nobody would mind" said Susan. "It isn't as if we wanted to take them out of the house; we shan't take them even out of the wardrobe."

"I never thought of that, Su," said Peter. "Of course, now you put it that way, I see. No one could say you had bagged a coat as long as you leave it in the wardrobe where you found it. And I suppose this whole country is in the wardrobe."

They immediately carried out Susan's very sensible plan. The coats were rather too big for them so that they came down to their heels and looked more like royal robes than coats when they had put them on. But they all felt a good deal warmer and each thought the others looked better in their new get-up and more suitable to the landscape.

"We can pretend we are Arctic explorers," said Lucy.

"This is going to be exciting enough without any pretending," said Peter, as he began leading the way forward into the forest. There were heavy darkish clouds overhead and it looked as if there might be more snow before night.

"I say," began Edmund presently, "oughtn't we to be bearing a bit more to the left, that is, if we are aiming for the lamp-post." He had forgotten for the moment that he must pretend never to have been in the wood before. The moment the words were out of his mouth he realised that he had given himself away. Everyone stopped; everyone stared at him. Peter whistled.

"So you really were here," he said, "that time Lu said she'd met you in here—and you made out she was telling lies."

There was a dead silence. "Well, of all the poisonous little beasts—" said Peter and shrugged his shoulders and said no more. There seemed, indeed, no more to say and presently the four resumed their journey; but Edmund was saying to himself, "I'll pay you all out for this, you pack of stuck-up, self-satisfied prigs."

"Where *are* we going anyway?" said Susan, chiefly for the sake of changing the subject.

"I think Lu ought to be the leader," said Peter, "goodness knows she deserves it. Where will you take us, Lu?"

"What about going to see Mr. Tumnus?" said Lucy. "He's the nice Faun I told you about."

Everyone agreed to this and off they went, walking briskly and stamping their feet. Lucy proved a good leader. At first she wondered whether she would be able to find the way, but she recognised an odd-looking tree in one place and a stump in another and brought them on to where the ground became uneven and into the little valley and at last to the very door of Mr. Tumnus' cave. But there a terrible surprise awaited them.

The door had been wrenched off its hinges and broken to bits. Inside, the cave was dark and cold and had the damp feel and smell of a place that had not been lived in for several days. Snow had drifted in from the doorway and was heaped on the floor, mixed with something black, which turned out to be the charred sticks and ashes from the fire. Someone had apparently flung it about the room and then stamped it out. The crockery lay smashed on the floor and the picture of the Faun's father had been slashed into shreds with a knife.

"This is a pretty good wash-out," said Edmund, "not much good coming here."

"What's this?" said Peter, stooping down. He had just noticed a piece of paper which had been nailed through the carpet to the floor.

"Is there anything written on it?" asked Susan.

"Yes, I think there is," answered Peter, "but I can't read it in this light. Let's get out into the open air."

They all went out in the daylight and crowded round Peter as he read out the following words:—

The former occupant of these premises, Faun Tumnus, is under arrest and awaiting his trial on a charge of High Treason against her Imperial Majesty Jadis, Queen of Narnia, Chatelaine of Cair Paravel, Empress of the Lone Islands, etc., also of comforting her said Majesty's enemies, harbouring spies and fraternising with Humans.

Signed FENRIS ULF,
Captain of the Secret Police,

LONG LIVE THE QUEEN!

The children stared at each other.

"I don't know that I'm going to like this place after all," said Susan.

"Who is this Queen, Lu?" said Peter. "Do you know anything about her?"

"She isn't a real queen at all," answered Lucy, "she's a horrible witch, the White Witch. Everyone—all the wood people—hate her. She has made an enchantment over the whole country so that it is always winter here and never Christmas."

"I—I wonder if there's any point in going on," said Susan. "I mean, it doesn't seem particularly safe here and it looks as if it won't be much fun either. And it's getting colder every minute, and we've brought nothing to eat. What about just going home?"

"Oh, but we can't, we can't," said Lucy suddenly. "Don't you see? We can't just go home, not after this. It is all on my account that the poor Faun has got into this trouble. He hid me from the Witch and showed me the way back. That's what it means by comforting the Queen's enemies and fraternising with Humans. We simply must try to rescue him."

"A lot *we* could do!" said Edmund, "when we haven't even got anything to eat!"

"Shut up—you!" said Peter, who was still very angry with Edmund. "What do you think, Susan?"

"I've a horrid feeling that Lu is right," said Susan. "I don't want to go a step further and I wish we'd never come. But I think we must try to do something for Mr. Whatever-his-name is—I mean the Faun."

"That's what I feel too," said Peter. "I'm worried about having no food with us. I'd vote for going back and getting something from the larder, only there doesn't seem to be any certainty of getting into this country again when once you've got out of it. I think we'll have to go on."

"So do I," said both the girls.

"If only we knew where the poor chap was imprisoned!" said Peter.

They were all still, wondering what to do next, when Lucy said, "Look! There's a robin, with such a red breast. It's the first bird I've seen here. I say!—I wonder can birds talk in Narnia? It almost looks as if it wanted to say something to us." Then she turned to the Robin and said, "Please, can you tell us where

Tumnus the Faun has been taken to?" As she said this she took a step towards the bird. It at once hopped away but only as far as to the next tree. There it perched and looked at them very hard as if it understood all they had been saying. Almost without noticing that they had done so, the four children went a step or two nearer to it. At this the Robin flew away again to the next tree and once more looked at them very hard. (You couldn't have found a robin with a redder chest or a brighter eye.)

"Do you know," said Lucy, "I really believe he means us to follow him."

"I've an idea he does," said Susan, "what do you think, Peter?"

"Well, we might as well try it," answered Peter.

The Robin appeared to understand the matter thoroughly. It kept going from tree to tree, always a few yards ahead of them but always so near that they could easily follow it. In this way it led them on, slightly down hill. Wherever the Robin alighted a little shower of snow would fall off the branch. Presently the clouds parted overhead and the winter sun came out and the snow all around them grew dazzlingly bright. They had been travelling in this way for about half an hour, with the two girls in front, when Edmund said to Peter, "If you're not still too high and mighty to talk to me, I've something to say which you'd better listen to."

"What is it?" asked Peter.

"Hush! Not so loud," said Edmund, "there's no good frightening the girls. But have you realised what we're doing?"

"What?" said Peter, lowering his voice to a whisper.

"We're following a guide we know nothing about. How do we know which side that bird is on? Why shouldn't it be leading us into a trap?"

"That's a nasty idea. Still—a robin you know. They're good birds in all the stories I've ever read. I'm sure a robin wouldn't be on the wrong side."

"If it comes to that, which *is* the right side? How do we know that the fauns are in the right and the Queen (yes, I know we've been *told* she's a witch) is in the wrong? We don't really know anything about either."

"The Faun saved Lucy."

"He *said* he did. But how do we know? And there's another thing too. Has anyone the least idea of the way home from here?"

"Great Scott!" said Peter, "I hadn't thought of that."

"And no chance of dinner either," said Edmund.

VII

A Day with the Beavers

WHILE the two boys were whispering behind, both the girls suddenly cried "Oh!" and stopped. "The robin!" cried Lucy, "the robin. It's flown away." And so it had—right out of sight.

"And now what are we to do?" said Edmund, giving Peter a look which was as much as to say "What did I tell you?"

"Sh! Look!" said Susan.

"What?" said Peter.

"There's something moving among the trees—over there to the left."

They all stared as hard as they could, and no one felt very comfortable.

"There it goes again," said Susan presently.

"I saw it that time too," said Peter. "It's still there. It's just gone behind that big tree."

"What is it?" asked Lucy, trying very hard not to sound nervous.

"Whatever it is," said Peter, "it's dodging us. It's something that doesn't want to be seen."

"Let's go home," said Susan. And then, though nobody said it out loud, everyone suddenly realised the same fact that Edmund had whispered to Peter at the end of the last chapter. They were lost.

"What's it like?" said Lucy.

"It's—it's a kind of animal," said Susan; and then, "Look! Look! Quick! There it is."

They all saw it this time, a whiskered furry face which had looked out at them from behind a tree. But this time it didn't immediately draw back. Instead, the animal put its paw against its mouth just as humans put their finger on their lips when they are signalling to you to be quiet. Then it disappeared again. The children all stood holding their breaths.

A moment later the stranger came out from behind the tree, glanced all round as if it were afraid someone was watching, said "Hush," made signs to them to join it in the thicker bit of wood where it was standing, and then once more disappeared.

"I know what it is," said Peter, "it's a beaver. I saw the tail."

"It wants us to go to it," said Susan, "and it is warning us not to make a noise."

"I know," said Peter. "The question is are we to go to it or not? What do you think, Lu?"

"I think it's a nice beaver," said Lucy.

"Yes, but how do we *know?*" said Edmund.

"Shan't we have to risk it?" said Susan. "I mean, it's no good just standing here and I feel I want some dinner."

At this moment the Beaver again popped its head out from behind the tree and beckoned earnestly to them.

"Come on," said Peter, "let's give it a try. All keep close together. We ought to be a match for one beaver if it turns out to be an enemy."

So the children all got close together and walked up to the tree and in behind it, and there, sure enough, they found the Beaver; but it still drew back, saying to them in a hoarse throaty whisper, "Further in, come further in. Right in here. We're not safe in the open!" Only when it had led them into a dark spot where four trees grew so close together that their boughs met and the brown earth and pine needles could be seen underfoot because no snow had been able to fall there, did it begin to talk to them.

"Are you the Sons of Adam and the Daughters of Eve?" it said.

"We're some of them," said Peter.

"S-s-s-sh!" said the Beaver, "not so loud please. We're not safe even here."

"Why, who are you afraid of?" said Peter. "There's no one here but ourselves."

"There are the trees," said the Beaver. "They're always listening. Most of them are on our side, but there *are* trees that would betray us to *her;* you know who I mean," and it nodded its head several times.

"If it comes to talking about sides," said Edmund, "how do we know you're a friend?"

"Not meaning to be rude, Mr. Beaver," added Peter, "but you see, we're strangers."

"Quite right, quite right," said the Beaver. "Here is my token." With these words it held up to them a little white object. They all looked at it in surprise, till suddenly Lucy said, "Oh, of course. It's my handkerchief—the one I gave to poor Mr. Tumnus."

"That's right," said the Beaver. "Poor fellow, he got wind of the arrest before it actually happened and handed this over to me. He said that if anything happened to him I must meet you here and take you on to—" Here the Beaver's voice sank into silence and it gave one or two very mysterious nods. Then signalling to the children to stand as close around it as they possibly could, so that their faces were actually tickled by its whiskers, it added in a low whisper—

"They say Aslan is on the move—perhaps has already landed."

And now a very curious thing happened. None of the children knew who Aslan was any more than you do; but the moment the Beaver had spoken these words everyone felt quite different. Perhaps it has sometimes happened to you in a dream that someone says something which you don't understand but in the dream it feels as if it had some enormous meaning—either a terrifying one which turns the whole dream into a nightmare or else a lovely meaning too lovely to put into words, which makes the dream so beautiful that you remember it all your life and are always wishing you could get into that dream again. It was like that now. At the name of Aslan each one of the children felt something jump in his inside. Edmund felt a sensation of mysterious horror. Peter felt suddenly brave and adventurous. Susan felt as if some delicious smell or some delightful strain of music had just floated by her. And Lucy got the feeling you have when you wake up in the morning and realise that it is the beginning of the holidays or the beginning of summer.

"And what about Mr. Tumnus," said Lucy; "where is he?"

"S-s-s-sh," said the Beaver, "not here. I must bring you where we can have a real talk and also dinner."

No one except Edmund felt any difficulty about trusting the Beaver now and everyone, including Edmund, was very glad to hear the word "dinner." They therefore all hurried along behind their new friend who led them at a surprisingly quick pace, and always in the thickest parts of the forest, for over an hour. Everyone was feeling very tired and very hungry when suddenly the trees began to get thinner in front of them and the ground to fall steeply down hill. A minute later they came out under the open sky (the sun was still shining) and found themselves looking down on a fine sight.

They were standing on the edge of a steep, narrow valley at the bottom of which ran—at least it would have been running if it hadn't been frozen—a fairly large river. Just below them a dam had been built across this river; and when they saw it everyone suddenly remembered that of course beavers are always making dams and felt quite sure that Mr. Beaver had made this one. They also noticed that he now had a sort of modest expression on his face—the sort of look people have when you are visiting a garden they've made or reading a story they've written. So it was only common politeness when Susan said, "What a lovely dam!" And Mr. Beaver didn't say "Hush" this time but "Merely a trifle! Merely a trifle! And it isn't really finished!"

Above the dam there was what ought to have been a deep pool but was now of course a level floor of dark green ice. And below the dam, much lower down, was more ice, but instead of being smooth this was all frozen into the foamy and wavy shapes in which the water had been rushing along at the very moment when the frost came. And where the water had been trickling over and spurting through the dam there was now a glittering wall of icicles, as if the side of the dam had been covered all over with flowers and wreaths and festoons of the purest sugar. And out in the middle, and partly on the top of the dam, was a funny little house shaped rather like an enormous bee-hive and from a hole in the roof smoke was going up, so that when you saw it (especially if you were hungry) you at once thought of cooking and became hungrier than you were before.

That was what the others chiefly noticed, but Edmund noticed something else. A little lower down the river there was another small river which came down another small valley to join it. And looking up that valley, Edmund could see two small hills, and he was almost sure they were the two hills which the White Witch had pointed out to him when he parted from her at the lamp-post that other day. And then between them, he thought, must be her palace, only a mile off or less. And he thought about Turkish Delight and about being a King ("And I wonder how Peter will like that?" he asked himself) and horrible ideas came into his head.

"Here we are," said Mr. Beaver, "and it looks as if Mrs. Beaver is expecting us. I'll lead the way. But be careful and don't slip."

The top of the dam was wide enough to walk on, though not (for humans) a very nice place to walk because it was covered with ice, and though the frozen pool was level with it on one side, there was a nasty drop to the lower river on the other. Along this route Mr. Beaver led them in single file right out to the middle where they could look a long way up the river and a long way down it. And when they had reached the middle they were at the door of the house.

"Here we are, Mrs. Beaver," said Mr. Beaver, "I've found them. Here are the Sons and Daughters of Adam and Eve"—and they all went in.

The first thing Lucy noticed as she went in was a burring sound, and the first thing she saw was a kind-looking old she-beaver sitting in the corner with a thread in her mouth working busily at her sewing machine and it was from it that the sound came. She stopped her work and got up as soon as the children came in.

"So you've come at last!" she said, holding out both her wrinkled old paws. "At last! To think that ever I should live to see this day! The potatoes are on boiling and the kettle's singing and I daresay, Mr. Beaver, you'll get us some fish."

"That I will," said Mr. Beaver and he went out of the house (Peter went with him) and across the ice of the deep pool to where he had a little hole in the ice which he kept open every day with his hatchet. They took a pail with them, Mr. Beaver sat down quietly at the edge of the hole (he didn't seem to mind it's being so chilly), looked hard into it, then suddenly shot in his paw, and before you could say Jack Robinson had whisked out a beautiful trout. Then he did it all over again until they had a fine catch of fish.

Meanwhile the girls were helping Mrs. Beaver to fill the kettle and lay the table and cut the bread and put the plates in the oven to heat and draw a huge jug of beer for Mr. Beaver from a barrel which stood in one corner of the house, and to put on the frying pan and get the dripping hot. Lucy thought the Beavers had a very snug little home though it was not at all like Mr. Tumnus's cave. There were no books or pictures and instead of beds there were bunks, like on board ship, built into the wall. And there were hams and strings of onions hanging from the roof and against the walls were gum boots and oilskins and hatchets and pairs of shears and spades and trowels and things for carrying mortar in and fishing rods and fishing nets and sacks. And the cloth on the table tho' very clean was very rough.

Just as the frying pan was nicely hissing Peter and Mr. Beaver came in with the fish which Mr. Beaver had already opened with his knife and cleaned out in the open air. You can think how good the new-caught fish smelled while they were frying and how the hungry children longed for them to be done and how very much hungrier still they had become before Mrs. Beaver said, "Now we're nearly ready." Susan drained the potatoes and then put them all back in the empty pot to dry on the side of the range while Lucy was helping Mrs. Beaver to dish up the trout, so that in a very few minutes everyone was drawing up stools (it was all three-legged stools in the Beavers' house except for Mrs. Beaver's own special rocking chair beside the fire) and preparing to enjoy themselves. There was a jug of creamy milk for the children (Mr. Beaver stuck to beer) and a great big lump of deep yellow butter in the middle of the table from which everyone took as much as he wanted to go with his potatoes and all the children thought—and I agree with them—that there's nothing to beat good freshwater fish if you eat it when it has been alive half an hour ago and has come out of the pan half a minute ago. And when they had finished the fish Mrs. Beaver brought unexpectedly out of the oven a great and gloriously sticky marmalade roll, steaming hot, and at the same time moved the kettle on to the fire, so that when they had finished the marmalade roll the tea was made and ready to be poured out. And when each person had got his (or her) cup of tea, each person shoved back his (or her) stool so as to be able to lean against the wall and gave a long sigh of contentment.

"And now," said Mr. Beaver pushing away his empty beer mug and pulling his cup of tea towards him, "if you'll just wait till I've got my pipe lit up and going nicely—why, now we can get to business. It's snowing again," he added, cocking his eye at the window. "That's all the better, because it means we shan't have any visitors; and if anyone should have been trying to follow you, why he won't find any tracks."

VIII

What Happened After Dinner

"And now," said Lucy, "do please tell us what's happened to Mr. Tumnus."

"Ah, that's bad," said Mr. Beaver shaking his head. "That's a very, very bad business. There's no doubt he was taken off by the police. I got that from a bird who saw it done."

"But where's he been taken to?" asked Lucy.

"Well, they were heading northwards when they were last seen and we all know what that means."

"No, *we* don't," said Susan. But Mr. Beaver shook his head in a very gloomy fashion.

"I'm afraid it means they were taking him to her house," said Mr. Beaver.

"But what'll they do to him, Mr. Beaver?" gasped Lucy.

"Well," said Mr. Beaver, "you can't exactly say for sure. But there's not many taken in there that ever comes out again. Statues. All full of statues they say it is—in the courtyard and up the stairs and in the hall. People she's turned—" (he paused and shuddered) "turned into stone."

"But, Mr. Beaver," said Lucy, "can't we—I mean we *must* do something to save him. It's too dreadful and it's all on my account."

"I don't doubt you'd save him if you could, dearie," said Mrs. Beaver, "but you've no chance of getting into that House against her will and ever coming out alive."

"Couldn't we have some stratagem?" said Peter. "I mean couldn't we dress up as something, or pretend to be—oh, pedlars or anything—or watch till she was gone out—or—oh, hang it all, there must be *some* way. This Faun saved my sister at his own risk, Mr. Beaver. We can't just leave him to be—to be—to have that done to him."

"It's no good, Son of Adam," said Mr. Beaver, "no good *your* trying, of all people. But now that Aslan is on the move—"

"Oh, yes! Tell us about Aslan!" said several voices at once; for once again that strange feeling—like the first signs of spring, like good news, had come over them.

"Who is Aslan?" asked Susan.

"Aslan?" said Mr. Beaver, "Why don't you know? He's the King. He's the Lord of the whole wood, but not often here, you understand. Never in my time or my father's time. But the word has reached us that he has come back. He is in Narnia at this moment. He'll settle the White Queen all right. It is he, not you, that will save Mr. Tumnus."

"She won't turn him into stone too?" said Edmund.

"Lord love you, Son of Adam, what a simple thing to say!" answered Mr. Beaver with a great laugh. "Turn *him* into stone? If she can stand on her two feet and look him in the face it'll be the most she can do and more than I expect of her. No, no. He'll put all to rights as it says in an old rhyme in these parts:—

> Wrong will be right, when Aslan comes in sight,
> At the sound of his roar, sorrows will be no more,
> When he bares his teeth, winter meets its death
> And when he shakes his mane, we shall have spring again.

You'll understand when you see him."

"But shall we see him?" asked Susan.

"Why, Daughter of Eve, that's what I brought you here for. I'm to lead you where you shall meet him," said Mr. Beaver.

"Is—is he a man?" asked Lucy.

"Aslan a man!" said Mr. Beaver sternly. "Certainly not. I tell you he is the King of the wood and the son of the great Emperor-Beyond-the-Sea. Don't you know who is the King of Beasts? Aslan is a lion—*the* Lion, the great Lion."

"Ooh!" said Susan, "I'd thought he was a man. Is he—quite safe? I shall feel rather nervous about meeting a lion."

"That you will, dearie, and no mistake," said Mrs. Beaver, "if there's anyone who can appear before Aslan without their knees knocking, they're either braver than most or else just silly."

"Then he isn't safe?" said Lucy.

"Safe?" said Mr. Beaver. "Don't you hear what Mrs. Beaver tells you? Who said anything about safe? 'Course he isn't safe. But he's good. He's the King, I tell you."

"I'm longing to see him," said Peter, "even if I do feel frightened when it comes to the point."

"That's right, Son of Adam," said Mr. Beaver bringing his paw down on the table with a crash that made all the cups and saucers rattle. "And so you shall. Word has been sent that you *are* to meet him, tomorrow if you can, at the Stone Table."

"Where's that?" said Lucy.

"I'll show you," said Mr. Beaver. "It's down the river, a good step from here. I'll take you to it!"

"But meanwhile what about poor Mr. Tumnus?" said Lucy.

"The quickest way you can help him is by going to meet Aslan," said Mr. Beaver, "once he's with us, then we can begin doing things. Not that we don't need you too. For that's another of the old rhymes:—

> When Adam's flesh and Adam's bone
> Sits at Cair Paravel in throne,
> The evil time will be over and done.

So things must be drawing near their end now he's come and you've come. We've heard of Aslan coming into these parts before—long ago, nobody can say when. But there's never been any of your race here before."

"That's what I don't understand, Mr. Beaver," said Peter, "I mean isn't the Witch herself human?"

"She'd like us to believe it," said Mr. Beaver, "and it's on that that she bases her claim to be Queen. But she's no Daughter of Eve. She comes of your father Adam's—" (here Mr. Beaver bowed) "your father Adam's first wife, her they called Lilith. And she was one of the Jinn. That's what she comes from on one side. And on the other she comes of the giants. No, no, there isn't a drop of real Human blood in the Witch."

"That's why she's bad all through, Mr. Beaver," said Mrs. Beaver.

"True enough, Mrs. Beaver," replied he, "there may be two views about Humans (meaning no offence to the present company). But there's no two views about things that look like Humans and aren't."

"I've known good dwarfs," said Mrs. Beaver.

"So've I, now you come to speak of it," said her husband, "but precious few, and they were the ones least like men. But in general, take my advice, when you meet anything that's going to be Human and isn't yet, or used to be Human once and isn't now, or ought to be Human and isn't, you keep your eyes on it and feel for your hatchet. And that's why the Witch is always on the lookout for any Humans in Narnia. She's been watching for you this many a year, and if she knew there were four of you she'd be more dangerous still."

"What's that to do with it?" asked Peter.

"Because of another prophecy," said Mr. Beaver. "Down at Cair Paravel— that's the castle on the sea coast down at the mouth of this river which ought to be the capital of the whole country if all was as it should be—down at Cair Paravel there are four thrones and it's a saying in Narnia time out of mind that when two Sons of Adam and two Daughters of Eve sit in those four thrones, then it will be the end not only of the White Witch's reign but of her life, and that is why we had to be so cautious as we came along, for if she knew about you four, your lives wouldn't be worth a shake of my whiskers!"

All the children had been attending so hard to what Mr. Beaver was telling them that they had noticed nothing else for a long time. Then during the moment of silence that followed his last remark, Lucy suddenly said:

"I say—where's Edmund?"

There was a dreadful pause, and then everyone began asking "Who saw him last? How long has he been missing? Is he outside?" And then all rushed to the door and looked out. The snow was falling thickly and steadily, the green ice of the pool had vanished under a thick white blanket, and from where the little house stood in the centre of the dam you could hardly see either bank. Out they went, plunging well over their ankles into the soft new snow, and went round the house in every direction. "Edmund! Edmund!" they called till they were hoarse. But the silently falling snow seemed to muffle their voices and there was not even an echo in answer.

"How perfectly dreadful!" said Susan as they at last came back in despair. "Oh, how I wish we'd never come."

"What on earth are we to do, Mr. Beaver?" said Peter.

"Do?" said Mr. Beaver who was already putting on his snow boots, "do? We must be off at once. We haven't a moment to spare!"

"We'd better divide into four search parties," said Peter, "and all go in different directions. Whoever finds him must come back here at once and—"

"Search parties, Son of Adam?" said Mr. Beaver; "what for?"

"Why, to look for Edmund of course!"

"There's no point in looking for him," said Mr. Beaver.

"What do you mean?" said Susan, "he can't be far away yet. And we've got to find him. What do you mean when you say there's no use looking for him?"

"The reason there's no use looking," said Mr. Beaver, "is that we know already where he's gone!" Everyone stared in amazement. "Don't you understand?" said Mr. Beaver. "He's gone to *her*, to the White Witch. He has betrayed us all."

"Oh surely—oh really!" said Susan, "he can't have done that."

"Can't he?" said Mr. Beaver looking very hard at the three children, and everything they wanted to say died on their lips for each felt suddenly quite certain inside that this was exactly what Edmund had done.

"But will he know the way?" said Peter.

"Has he been in this country before?" asked Mr. Beaver, "has he ever been here alone?"

"Yes," said Lucy almost in a whisper, "I'm afraid he has."

"And did he tell you what he'd done or who he'd met?"

"Well, no, he didn't," said Peter.

"Then mark my words," said Mr. Beaver, "he has already met the White Witch and joined her side, and been told where she lives. I didn't like to mention it before (he being your brother and all) but the moment I set eyes on that brother of yours I said to myself 'Treacherous.' He had the look of one who has been with the Witch and eaten her food. You can always tell them if you've lived long in Narnia, something about their eyes."

"All the same," said Peter in a rather choking sort of voice, "we'll still have to go and look for him. He is our brother after all, even if he is rather a little beast, and he's only a kid."

"Go to the Witch's house?" said Mrs. Beaver. "Don't you see that the only chance of saving either him or yourselves is to keep away from her?"

"How do you mean?" said Lucy.

"Why all she wants is to get all four of you (she's thinking all the time of those four thrones at Cair Paravel). Once you were all four inside her house her job would be done—and there'd be four new statues in her collection before you'd had time to speak. But she'll keep him alive as long as he's the only one she's got, because she'll want to use him as a decoy; as bait to catch the rest of you with."

"Oh, can *no* one help us?" wailed Lucy.

"Only Aslan," said Mr. Beaver, "we must go and meet him. That's our only chance now."

"It seems to me, my dears," said Mrs. Beaver, "that it is very important to know just *when* he slipped away. How much he can tell her depends on how much he heard. For instance, had we started talking of Aslan before he left? If not, then we may do very well, for she won't know that Aslan has come to Narnia, or that we are meeting him and will be quite off her guard as far as *that* is concerned."

"I don't remember his being here when we were talking about Aslan—" began Peter, but Lucy interrupted him.

"Oh yes, he was," she said miserably; "don't you remember, it was he who asked whether the Witch couldn't turn Aslan into stone too?"

"So he did, by Jove," said Peter, "just the sort of thing he would say, too!"

"Worse and worse," said Mr. Beaver, "and the next thing is this. Was he still here when I told you that the place for meeting Aslan was the Stone Table?"

And of course no one knew the answer to this question.

"Because, if he was," continued Mr. Beaver, "then she'll simply sledge down in that direction and get between us and the Stone Table and catch us on our way down. In fact we shall be cut off from Aslan."

"But that isn't what she'll do first," said Mrs. Beaver, "not if I know her. The moment that Edmund tells her that we're all here she'll set out to catch us this very night, and if he's been gone about half an hour, she'll be here in about another twenty minutes."

"You're right, Mrs. Beaver," said her husband, "we must all get away from here. There's not a moment to lose."

IX

In the Witch's House

AND NOW of course you want to know what had happened to Edmund. He had eaten his share of the dinner, but he hadn't really enjoyed it because he was thinking all the time about Turkish Delight—and there's nothing that spoils the taste of good ordinary food half so much as the memory of bad magic food. And he had heard the conversation and hadn't enjoyed it much either, because he kept on thinking that the others were taking no notice of him and trying to give him the cold shoulder. They weren't, but he imagined it. And then he had listened until Mr. Beaver told them about Aslan and until he had heard the whole arrangement for meeting Aslan at the Stone Table. It was then that he began very quietly to edge himself under the curtain which hung over the door. For the mention of Aslan gave him a mysterious and horrible feeling just as it gave the others a mysterious and lovely feeling.

Just as Mr. Beaver had been repeating the rhyme about *Adam's flesh and Adam's bone* Edmund had been very quietly turning the door handle; and just before Mr. Beaver had begun telling them that the White Witch wasn't really human at all but half a Jinn and half a giantess, Edmund had got outside into the snow and cautiously closed the door behind him.

You mustn't think that even now Edmund was quite so bad that he actually wanted his brother and sisters to be turned into stone. He did want Turkish Delight and to be a Prince (and later a King) and to pay Peter out for calling him a beast. As for what the Witch would do with the others, he didn't want her to be particularly nice to them—certainly not to put them on the same level as himself—but he managed to believe, or to pretend he believed, that she wouldn't do anything very bad to them, "Because," he said to himself, "all these people who say nasty things about her are her enemies and probably half of it isn't true. She was jolly nice to me, anyway, much nicer than they are. I expect she is the rightful Queen really. Anyway, she'll be better than that awful Aslan!" At least, that was the excuse he made in his own mind for what he was doing. It wasn't a very good excuse, however, for deep down inside him he really knew that the White Witch was bad and cruel.

The first thing he realised when he got outside and found the snow falling all around him, was that he had left his coat behind in the Beavers' house. And of course there was no chance of going back to get it now. The next thing he realised was that the daylight was almost gone, for it had been nearly three o'clock when they sat down to dinner and the winter days were short. He hadn't reckoned on this; but he had to make the best of it. So he turned up his collar and shuffled across the top of the dam (luckily it wasn't so slippery since the snow had fallen) to the far side of the river.

It was pretty bad when he reached the far side. It was growing darker every minute and what with that and the snowflakes swirling all round him he could hardly see three feet ahead. And then too there was no road. He kept slipping into deep drifts of snow, and skidding on frozen puddles, and tripping over fallen treetrunks, and sliding down steep banks, and barking his shins against rocks, till he was wet and cold and bruised all over. The silence and the loneliness were dreadful. In fact I really think he might have given up the whole plan and gone back and owned up and made friends with the others, if he hadn't happened to say to himself, "When I'm King of Narnia the first thing I shall do will be to make some decent roads." And of course that set him off thinking about being a King and all the other things he would do and this cheered him up a good deal. He had just settled in his mind what sort of palace he would have and how many cars and all about his private cinema and where the principal railways would run and what laws he would make against beavers and dams and was putting the finishing touches to some schemes for keeping Peter in his place, when the weather changed. First the snow stopped. Then a wind sprang up and it became freezing cold. Finally, the clouds rolled away and the moon came out. It was a full moon and, shining on all that snow, it made everything almost as bright as day—only the shadows were rather confusing.

He would never have found his way if the moon hadn't come out by the time he got to the other river—you remember he had seen (when they first arrived at the Beavers') a smaller river flowing into the great one lower down. He now reached this and turned to follow it up. But the little valley down which it came was much steeper and rockier than the one he had just left and much overgrown with bushes, so that he could not have managed it at all in the dark. Even as it was, he got wet through for he had to stoop to go under branches and great loads of snow came sliding off on to his back. And every time this happened he thought more and more how he hated Peter—just as if all this had been Peter's fault.

But at last he came to a part where it was more level and the valley opened out. And there, on the other side of the river, quite close to him, in the middle of a little plain between two hills, he saw what must be the White Witch's house. And the moon was shining brighter than ever. The house was really a small castle. It seemed to be all towers; little towers with long pointed spires on them, sharp as needles. They looked like huge dunce's caps or sorcerer's caps. And they shone in the moonlight and their long shadows looked strange on the snow! Edmund began to be afraid of the house.

But it was too late to think of turning back now. He crossed the river on the ice and walked up to the house. There was nothing stirring; not the slightest sound anywhere. Even his own feet made no noise on the deep newly fallen snow. He walked on and on, past corner after corner of the house, and past turret after turret to find the door. He had to go right round to the far side before he found it. It was a huge arch but the great iron gates stood wide open.

Edmund crept up to the arch and looked inside into the courtyard, and there he saw a sight that nearly made his heart stop beating. Just inside the gate, with the moonlight shining on it, stood an enormous lion crouched as if it was ready to spring. And Edmund stood in the shadow of the arch, afraid to go on and afraid to go back, with his knees knocking together. He stood there so long that his teeth would have been chattering with cold even if they had not been chattering with fear. How long this really lasted I don't know, but it seemed to Edmund to last for hours.

Then at last he began to wonder why the lion was standing so still—for it hadn't moved one inch since he first set eyes on it. Edmund now ventured a little nearer, still keeping in the shadow of the arch as much as he could. He now saw from the way the lion was standing that it couldn't have been looking at him at all. ("But supposing it turns its head?" thought Edmund.) In fact it was staring at something else—namely a little dwarf who stood with his back to it about four feet away. "Aha!" thought Edmund. "When it springs at the dwarf then will be my chance to escape." But still the lion never moved, nor did the dwarf. And now at last Edmund remembered what the others had said about the White Witch turning people into stone. Perhaps this was only a stone lion. And as soon as he had thought of that he noticed that the lion's back and the top of its head were covered with snow. Of course it must be only a statue! No living animal would have let itself get covered with snow. Then very slowly and with his heart beating as if it would burst, Edmund ventured to go up to the lion. Even now he hardly dared to touch it, but at last he put out his hand, very quickly, and did. It was cold stone. He had been frightened of a mere statue!

The relief which Edmund felt was so great that in spite of the cold he suddenly got warm all over right down to his toes, and at the same time there came into his head what seemed a perfectly lovely idea. "Probably," he thought, "this is the great Lion Aslan that they were all talking about. She's caught him already and turned him into stone. So *that's* the end of all their fine ideas about him! Pooh! Who's afraid of Aslan?"

And he stood there gloating over the stone lion, and presently he did something very silly and childish. He took a stump of lead pencil out of his pocket and scribbled a moustache on the lion's upper lip and then a pair of spectacles on its eyes. Then he said, "Yah! Silly old Aslan! How do you like being a stone? You thought yourself mighty fine, didn't you?" But in spite of the scribbles on it the face of the great stone beast still looked so terrible, and sad, and noble, staring up in the moonlight that Edmund didn't really get any fun out of jeering at it. He turned away and began to cross the courtyard.

As he got into the middle of it he saw that there were dozens of statues all about—standing here and there rather as the pieces stand on a chess board when it is half way through the game. There were stone satyrs, and stone wolves, and bears and foxes and cat-a-mountains of stone. There were lovely stone shapes that looked like women but who were really the spirits of trees. There was the great shape of a centaur and a winged horse and a long lithe creature that Edmund took to be a dragon. They all looked so strange standing there perfectly lifelike and also perfectly still, in the bright cold moonlight, that it was eerie work crossing the courtyard. Right in the very middle stood a huge shape like a man, but as tall as a tree, with a fierce face and a shaggy beard and a great club in its right hand. Even though he knew that it was only a stone giant and not a live one, Edmund did not like going past it.

He now saw that there was a dim light showing from a doorway on the far side of the courtyard. He went to it, there was a flight of stone steps going up to an open door. Edmund went up them. Across the threshold lay a great wolf:

"It's all right, it's all right," he kept saying to himself, "it's only a stone wolf. It can't hurt me," and he raised his leg to step over it. Instantly the huge creature rose, with all the hair bristling along its back, opened a great, red mouth and said in a growling voice,

"Who's there? Who's there? Stand still, stranger, and tell me who you are."

"If you please, Sir," said Edmund, trembling so that he could hardly speak, "my name is Edmund, and I'm the Son of Adam that Her Majesty met in the wood the other day and I've come to bring her the news that my brother and sisters are now in Narnia—quite close, in the Beavers' house. She—she wanted to see them."

"I will tell Her Majesty," said the Wolf. "Meanwhile, stand still on the threshold, as you value your life." Then it vanished into the house.

Edmund stood and waited, his fingers aching with cold and his heart pounding in his chest, and presently the grey Wolf, Fenris Ulf, the Chief of the Witch's Secret Police, came bounding back and said, "Come in! Come in! Fortunate favourite of the Queen—or else not so fortunate."

And Edmund went in, taking great care not to tread on the Wolf's paws.

He found himself in a long gloomy hall with many pillars, full, as the courtyard had been, of statues. The one nearest the door was a little Faun with a very sad expression on its face, and Edmund couldn't help wondering if this might be Lucy's friend. The only light came from a single lamp and close behind this sat the White Witch.

"I'm come, your Majesty," said Edmund rushing eagerly forward.

"How dare you come alone?" said the Witch in a terrible voice. "Did I not tell you to bring the others with you?"

"Please, your Majesty," said Edmund, "I've done the best I can. I've brought them quite close. They're in the little house on top of the dam just up the river—with Mr. and Mrs. Beaver."

A slow cruel smile came over the Witch's face.

"Is this all your news?" she asked.

"No, your Majesty," said Edmund, and proceeded to tell her all he had heard before leaving the Beavers' house.

"What! Aslan?" cried the Queen, "Aslan! Is this true? If I find you have lied to me—"

"Please, I'm only repeating what they said," stammered Edmund.

But the Queen, who was no longer attending to him, clapped her hands. Instantly the same dwarf whom Edmund had seen with her before appeared.

"Make ready our sledge," ordered the Witch, "and use the harness without bells."

X

The Spell Begins to Break

Now we must go back to Mr. and Mrs. Beaver and the three other children. As soon as Mr. Beaver said "There's no time to lose" everyone began bundling themselves into coats, except Mrs. Beaver who started picking up sacks and laying them on the table and said: "Now, Mr. Beaver, just reach down that ham. And here's a packet of tea, and there's sugar, and some matches. And if someone will get two or three loaves out of the crock over there in the corner."

"What *are* you doing, Mrs. Beaver?" exclaimed Susan.

"Packing a load for each of us, dearie," said Mrs. Beaver very coolly. "You didn't think we'd set out on a journey with nothing to eat, did you?"

"But we haven't time!" said Susan, buttoning the collar of her coat. "She may be here any minute."

"That's what I say," chimed in Mr. Beaver.

"Get along with you all," said his wife. "Think it over, Mr. Beaver. She can't be here for a quarter of an hour at least."

"But don't we want as big a start as we can possibly get," said Peter, "if we're to reach the Stone Table before her?"

"You've got to remember *that*, Mrs. Beaver," said Susan. "As soon as she has looked in here and finds we're gone she'll be off at top speed."

"That she will," said Mrs. Beaver. "But we can't get there before her whatever we do, for she'll be on a sledge and we'll be walking."

"Then—have we no hope?" said Susan.

"Now don't you get fussing, there's a dear," said Mrs. Beaver, "but just get half a dozen clean handkerchiefs out of that drawer. 'Course we've got a hope. We can't get there *before* her but we can keep under cover and go by ways she won't expect and perhaps we'll get through."

"That's true enough, Mrs. Beaver," said her husband. "But it's time we were out of this."

"And don't *you* start fussing either, Mr. Beaver," said his wife. "There. That's better. There's four loads and the smallest for the smallest of us: that's you, my dear," she added looking at Lucy.

"Oh, do please come on," said Lucy.

"Well, I'm nearly ready now," answered Mrs. Beaver at last allowing her husband to help her into her snow boots. "I suppose the sewing machine's too heavy to bring?"

"Yes. It *is,*" said Mr. Beaver. "A great deal too heavy. And you don't think you'll be able to use it while we're on the run, I suppose?"

"I can't abide the thought of that Witch fiddling with it," said Mrs. Beaver, "and breaking it or stealing it, as likely as not."

"Oh, please, please, please, do hurry!" said the three children. And so at last they all got outside and Mr. Beaver locked the door ("It'll delay her a bit," he said) and they set off, all carrying their loads over their shoulders.

The snow had stopped and the moon had come out when they began their journey. They went in single file—first Mr. Beaver, then Lucy, then Peter, then Susan, and Mrs. Beaver last of all. Mr. Beaver led them across the dam and onto the right bank of the river and then along a very rough sort of path among the trees right down by the river-bank. The sides of the valley, shining in the moonlight, towered up far above them on either hand. "Best keep down here as much as possible," he said. "She'll have to keep to the top, for you couldn't bring a sledge down here."

It would have been a pretty enough scene to look at it through a window from a comfortable armchair; and even as things were, Lucy enjoyed it at first. But as they went on walking—and walking—and as the sack she was carrying felt heavier and heavier, she began to wonder how she was going to keep up at all. And she stopped looking at the dazzling brightness of the frozen river with all its waterfalls of ice and at the white masses of the tree-tops and the great glaring moon and the countless stars and could only watch the little short legs of Mr. Beaver going pad-pad-pad-pad through the snow in front of her as if they were never going to stop. Then the moon disappeared and the snow began to fall once more. And at last Lucy was so tired that she was almost asleep and walking at the same time when suddenly she found that Mr. Beaver had turned away from the river bank to the right and was leading them steeply uphill into the very thickest bushes. And then as she came fully awake she found that Mr. Beaver was just vanishing into a little hole in the bank which had been almost hidden under the bushes until you were quite on top of it. In fact, by the time she realised what was happening, only his short flat tail was showing.

Lucy immediately stooped down and crawled in after him. Then she heard noises of scrambling and puffing and panting behind her and in a moment all five of them were inside.

"Wherever is this?" said Peter's voice, sounding tired and pale in the darkness. (I hope you know what I mean by a voice sounding pale.)

"It's an old hiding-place for beavers in bad times," said Mr. Beaver, "and a great secret. It's not much of a place but we must get a few hours' sleep."

"If you hadn't all been in such a plaguey fuss when we were starting, I'd have brought some pillows," said Mrs. Beaver.

It wasn't nearly such a nice cave as Mr. Tumnus's, Lucy thought—just a hole in the ground but dry and earthy. It was very small so that when they all lay down they were all a bundle of fur and clothes together, and what with that and being warmed up by their long walk they were really rather snug. If only the floor of the cave had been a little smoother! Then Mrs. Beaver handed round in the dark a little flask out of which everyone drank something—it made one cough and splutter a little and stung the throat but it also made you feel deliciously warm after you'd swallowed it—and everyone went straight to sleep.

It seemed to Lucy only the next minute (though really it was hours and hours later) when she woke up feeling a little cold and dreadfully stiff and thinking how she would like a hot bath. Then she felt a set of long whiskers tickling her cheek and saw the cold daylight coming in through the mouth of the cave. But immediately after that she was very wide awake indeed, and so was everyone else. In fact they were all sitting up with their mouths and eyes wide open, listening to a sound which was the very sound they'd all been thinking of (and sometimes imagining they heard) during their walk last night. It was a sound of jingling bells.

Mr. Beaver was out of the cave like a flash the moment he heard it. Perhaps you think, as Lucy thought for a moment, that this was a very silly thing for him to do? But it was really a very sensible one. He knew he could scramble to the top of the bank among bushes and brambles without being seen; and he wanted above all things to see which way the Witch's sledge went. The others all sat in the cave waiting and wondering. They waited nearly five minutes. Then they heard something that frightened them very much. They heard voices. "Oh," thought Lucy, "he's been seen. She's caught him!"

Great was their surprise when, a little later, they heard Mr. Beaver's voice calling to them from just outside the cave.

"It's all right," he was shouting. "Come out, Mrs. Beaver. Come out, Sons and Daughters of Adam and Eve. It's all right! It isn't *her!*" This was bad grammar of course, but that is how beavers talk when they are excited; I mean, in Narnia—in our world they usually don't talk at all.

So Mrs. Beaver and the children came bundling out of the cave, all blinking in the daylight, and with earth all over them, and looking very frowsty and unbrushed and uncombed and with the sleep in their eyes.

"Come on!" cried Mr. Beaver, who was almost dancing with delight. "Come and see! This is a nasty knock for the Witch! It looks as if her power was already crumbling."

"What *do* you mean, Mr. Beaver?" panted Peter as they all scrambled up the steep bank of the valley together.

"Didn't I tell you," answered Mr. Beaver, "that she'd made it always winter and never Christmas? Didn't I tell you? Well, just come and see!"

And then they were all at the top and did see.

It *was* a sledge, and it *was* reindeer with bells on their harness. But they were far bigger than the Witch's reindeer, and they were not white but brown. And on the sledge sat a person whom everyone knew the moment they set eyes on him. He was a huge man in a bright red robe (bright as holly-berries) with a hood that had fur inside it and a great white beard that fell like a foamy waterfall over his chest. Everyone knew him because, though you see people of his sort only in Narnia, you see pictures of them and hear them talked about even in our world—the world on this side of the wardrobe door. But when you really see them in Narnia it is rather different. Some of the pictures of Father Christmas in our world make him look only funny and jolly. But now that the children actually stood looking at him they didn't find it quite like that. He was so big, and so glad, and so real, that they all became quite still. They felt very glad, but also solemn.

"I've come at last," said he. "She has kept me out for a long time, but I have got in at last. Aslan is on the move. The Witch's magic is weakening."

And Lucy felt running through her that deep shiver of gladness which you only get if you are being solemn and still.

"And now," said Father Christmas, "for your presents. There is a new and better sewing machine for you, Mrs. Beaver. I will drop it in your house as I pass."

"If you please, sir," said Mrs. Beaver, making a curtsey. "It's locked up."

"Locks and bolts make no difference to me," said Father Christmas. "And as for you, Mr. Beaver, when you get home you will find your dam finished and mended and all the leaks stopped and a new sluice gate fitted."

Mr. Beaver was so pleased that he opened his mouth very wide and then found he couldn't say anything at all.

"Peter, Adam's Son," said Father Christmas.

"Here, Sir," said Peter.

"These are your presents," was the answer, "and they are tools not toys. The time to use them is perhaps near at hand. Bear them well." With these words he handed to Peter a shield and a sword. The shield was the colour of silver and across it there ramped a red lion, as bright as a ripe strawberry at the moment when you pick it. The hilt of the sword was of gold and it had a sheath and a sword belt and everything it needed, and it was just the right size and weight for Peter to use. Peter was silent and solemn as he received these gifts for he felt they were a very serious kind of present.

"Susan, Eve's Daughter," said Father Christmas. "These are for you," and he handed her a bow and a quiver full of arrows and a little ivory horn. "You must use the bow only in great need," he said, "for I do not mean you to fight in the battle. It does not easily miss. And when you put this horn to your lips and blow it, then, wherever you are, I think help of some kind will come to you."

Last of all he said, "Lucy, Eve's Daughter," and Lucy came forward. He gave her a little bottle of what looked like glass (but people said afterwards that it was made of diamond) and a small dagger. "In this bottle," he said, "there is a cordial made of the juice of one of the fire-flowers that grow in the mountains of the sun. If you or any of your friends are hurt, a few drops of this will restore you. And the dagger is to defend yourself at great need. For you also are not to be in the battle."

"Why, Sir," said Lucy. "I think—I don't know—but I think I could be brave enough."

"That is not the point," he said. "But battles are ugly when women fight. And now"—here he suddenly looked less grave—"here is something for the moment for you all!" and he brought out (I suppose from the big bag at his back, but nobody quite saw him do it) a large tray containing five cups and saucers, a bowl of lump sugar, a jug of cream, and a great big teapot all sizzling and piping hot. Then he cried out "A Merry Christmas! Long live the true King!" and cracked his whip and he and the reindeer and the sledge and all were out of sight before anyone realised that they had started.

Peter had just drawn his sword out of its sheath and was showing it to Mr. Beaver when Mrs. Beaver said:

"Now then, now then! Don't stand talking there till the tea's got cold. Just like men. Come and help to carry the tray down and we'll have breakfast. What a mercy I thought of bringing the bread-knife."

So down the steep bank they went and back to the cave, and Mr. Beaver cut some of the bread and ham into sandwiches and Mrs. Beaver poured out the tea and everyone enjoyed himself. But long before they had finished enjoying themselves Mr. Beaver said, "Time to be moving on now."

XI

Aslan Is Nearer

EDMUND meanwhile had been having a most disappointing time. When the Dwarf had gone to get the sledge ready he expected that the Witch would start being nice to him, as she had been at their last meeting. But she said nothing at all. And when at last Edmund plucked up his courage to say, "Please, your Majesty, could I have some Turkish Delight? You—you—said—" she answered, "Silence, fool!" Then she appeared to change her mind and said, as if to herself, "And yet it will not do to have the brat fainting on the way," and once more clapped her hands. Another dwarf appeared.

"Bring the human creature food and drink," she said.

The Dwarf went away and presently returned bringing an iron bowl with some water in it and an iron plate with a hunk of dry bread on it. He grinned in a repulsive manner as he set them down on the floor beside Edmund and said:

"Turkish Delight for the little Prince. Ha! Ha! Ha!"

"Take it away," said Edmund sulkily. "I don't want dry bread." But the Witch suddenly turned on him with such a terrible expression on her face that he apologised and began to nibble at the bread, though it was so stale he could hardly get it down.

"You may be glad enough of it before you taste bread again," said the Witch.

While he was still chewing away the first dwarf came back and announced that the sledge was ready. The White Witch rose and went out, ordering Edmund to go with her. The snow was again falling as they came into the courtyard but she took no notice of that and made Edmund sit beside her on the sledge. But before they drove off she called Fenris Ulf and he came bounding like an enormous dog to the side of the sledge.

"Take with you the swiftest of your wolves and go at once to the house of the Beavers," said the Witch, "and kill whatever you find there. If they are already gone, then make all speed to the Stone Table, but do not be seen. Wait for me there in hiding. I meanwhile must go many miles to the West before I find a place where I can drive across the river. You may overtake these humans before they reach the Stone Table. You will know what to do if you find them!"

"I hear and obey, O Queen," growled the Wolf; and immediately he shot away into the snow and darkness, as quickly as a horse can gallop. In a few minutes he had called another wolf and was with him down on the dam and sniffing at the Beavers' house. But of course they found it empty. It would have been a dreadful thing for the Beavers and the children if the night had remained fine, for the wolves would then have been able to follow their trail—and ten to one would have overtaken them before they had got to the cave. But now that the snow had begun again the scent was cold and even the footprints were covered up.

Meanwhile the Dwarf whipped up the reindeer and the Witch and Edmund drove out under the archway and on and away into the darkness and the cold. This was a terrible journey for Edmund who had no coat. Before they had been going a quarter of an hour all the front of him was covered with snow—he soon stopped trying to shake it off because, as quickly as he did that, a new lot gathered, and he was so tired. Soon he was wet to the skin. And oh, how miserable he was. It didn't look now as if the Witch intended to make him a King! All the things he had said to make himself believe that she was good and kind and that her side was really the right side sounded to him silly now. He would have given anything to meet the others at this moment—even Peter! The only way to comfort himself now was to try to believe that the whole thing was a dream and that he might wake up at any moment. And as they went on, hour after hour, it did come to seem like a dream.

This lasted longer than I could describe even if I wrote pages and pages about it. But I will skip on to the time when the snow had stopped and the morning had come and they were racing along in the daylight. And still they went on and on, with no sound but the everlasting swish of the snow and the creaking of the reindeer's harness. And then at last the Witch said, "What have we here? Stop!" and they did.

How Edmund hoped she was going to say something about breakfast! But she had stopped for quite a different reason. A little way off at the foot of a tree sat a merry party, a squirrel and his wife with their children and two satyrs and a dwarf and an old dog-fox, all on stools round a table. Edmund couldn't quite see what they were eating, but it smelled lovely and there seemed to be decorations of holly and he wasn't at all sure that he didn't see something like a plum pudding. At the moment when the sledge stopped, the Fox, who was obviously the oldest person present, had just risen to its feet, holding a glass in its right paw as if it was going to say something. But when the whole party saw the sledge stopping and who was in it, all the gaiety went out of their faces. The father squirrel stopped eating with his fork half-way to his mouth and one of the satyrs stopped with its fork actually in its mouth, and the baby squirrels squealed with terror.

"What is the meaning of this?" asked the Witch Queen. Nobody answered.

"Speak, vermin!" she said again. "Or do you want my dwarf to find you a tongue with his whip? What is the meaning of all this gluttony, this waste, this self indulgence? Where did you get all these things?"

"Please, your Majesty," said the Fox, "we were given them. And if I might make so bold as to drink your Majesty's very good health—"

"Who gave them to you?" said the Witch.

"F-F-F-Father Christmas," stammered the Fox.

"What?" roared the Witch, springing from the sledge and taking a few strides nearer to the terrified animals. "He has not been here! He cannot have been here! How dare you—but no. Say you have been lying and you shall even now be forgiven."

At that moment one of the young squirrels lost its head completely.

"He has—he has—he has!" it squeaked beating its little spoon on the table. Edmund saw the Witch bite her lips so that a drop of blood appeared on her white cheek. Then she raised her wand. "Oh don't, don't, please don't," shouted Edmund, but even while he was shouting she had waved her wand and instantly where the merry party had been there were only statues of creatures (one with its stone fork fixed forever half-way to its stone mouth) seated round a stone table on which there were stone plates and a stone plum pudding.

"As for you," said the Witch, giving Edmund a stunning blow on the face as she re-mounted the sledge, "let that teach you to ask favour for spies and traitors. Drive on!" And Edmund for the first time in this story felt sorry for someone besides himself. It seemed so pitiful to think of those little stone figures sitting there all the silent days and all the dark nights, year after year, till the moss grew on them and at last even their faces crumbled away.

Now they were steadily racing on again. And soon Edmund noticed that the snow which splashed against them as they rushed through it was much wetter than it had been all last night. At the same time he noticed that he was feeling much less cold. It was also becoming foggy. In fact every minute it grew both foggier and warmer. And the sledge was not running nearly as well as it had been running up till now. At first he thought this was because the reindeer were tired, but soon he saw that that couldn't be the real reason. The sledge jerked, and skidded, and kept on jolting as if it had struck against stones. And however the Dwarf whipped the poor reindeer the sledge went slower and slower. There also seemed to be a curious noise all round them but the noise of their driving and jolting and the Dwarf's shouting at the reindeer prevented Edmund from hearing what it was, until suddenly the sledge stuck so fast that it wouldn't go on at all. When that happened there was a moment's silence. And in that silence Edmund could at last listen to the other noise properly. A strange, sweet, rustling, chattering noise—and yet not so strange, for he knew he'd heard it before—if only he could remember where! Then all at once he did remember. It was the noise of running water. All round them, though out of sight, there were streams chattering, murmuring, bubbling, splashing and even (in the distance) roaring And his heart gave a great leap (though he hardly knew why) when he realised that the frost was over. And much nearer there was a drip-drip-drip from the branches of all the trees. And then, as he looked at one tree he saw a great load of snow slide off it and for the first time since he had entered Narnia he saw the dark green of a fir tree. But he hadn't time to listen or watch any longer for the Witch said:

"Don't sit staring, fool! Get out and help."

And of course Edmund had to obey. He stepped out into the snow—but it was really only slush by now—and began helping the Dwarf to get the sledge out of the muddy hole it had got into. They got it out in the end, and by being very cruel to the reindeer the Dwarf managed to get it on the move again, and they drove a little further. And now the snow was really melting in earnest and patches of green grass were beginning to appear in every direction. Unless you have looked at a world of snow as long as Edmund had been looking at it, you will hardly be able to imagine what a relief those green patches were after the endless white. Then the sledge stopped again.

"It's no good, your Majesty," said the Dwarf. "We can't sledge in this thaw."

"Then we must walk," said the Witch.

"We shall never overtake them walking," growled the Dwarf. "Not with the start they've got."

"Are you my councillor or my slave?" said the Witch. "Do as you're told. Tie the hands of the human creature behind it and keep hold of the end of the rope. And take your whip. And cut the harness of the reindeer; they'll find their own way home."

The Dwarf obeyed, and in a few minutes Edmund found himself being forced to walk as fast as he could with his hands tied behind him. He kept on slipping in the slush and mud and wet grass, and every time he slipped the Dwarf gave him a curse and sometimes a flick with the whip. The Witch walked behind the dwarf and kept on saying, "Faster! Faster!"

Every moment the patches of green grew bigger and the patches of snow grew smaller. Every moment more and more of the trees shook off their robes of snow. Soon, wherever you looked, instead of white shapes you saw the dark green of firs or the black prickly branches of bare oaks and beeches and elms. Then the mist turned from white to gold and presently cleared away altogether. Shafts of delicious sunlight struck down onto the forest floor and overhead you could see a blue sky between the tree-tops.

Soon there were more wonderful things happening. Coming suddenly round a corner into a glade of silver birch trees Edmund saw the ground covered in all directions with little yellow flowers—celandines. The noise of water grew louder. Presently they actually crossed a stream. Beyond it they found snowdrops growing.

"Mind your own business!" said the Dwarf when he saw that Edmund had turned his head to look at them; and he gave the rope a vicious jerk.

But of course this didn't prevent Edmund from seeing. Only five minutes later he noticed a dozen crocuses growing round the foot of an old tree—gold and purple and white. Then came a sound even more delicious than the sound of the water. Close beside the path they were following a bird suddenly chirped from the branch of a tree. It was answered by the chuckle of another bird a little further off. And then, as if that had been a signal, there was chattering and chirruping in every direction, and then a moment of full song, and within five minutes the whole wood was ringing with birds' music, and wherever Edmund's eyes turned he saw birds alighting on branches, or sailing overhead or having their little quarrels.

"Faster! Faster!" said the Witch.

There was no trace of the fog now. The sky became bluer and bluer and now there were white clouds hurrying across it from time to time. In the wide glades there were primroses. A light breeze sprang up which scattered drops of moisture from the swaying branches and carried cool, delicious scents against the faces of the travellers. The trees began to come fully alive. The larches and birches were covered with green, the laburnums with gold. Soon the beech trees had put forth their delicate, transparent leaves. As the travellers walked under them the light also became green. A bee buzzed across their path.

"This is no thaw," said the Dwarf, suddenly stopping. "This is *spring*. What are we to do? Your winter has been destroyed, I tell you! This is Aslan's doing."

"If either of you mention that name again," said the Witch, "he shall instantly be killed."

XII

Peter's First Battle

Wh ile the Dwarf and the White Witch were saying this, miles away the Beaver and the children were walking on hour after hour into what seemed a delicious dream. Long ago they had left the coats behind them. And by now they had even stopped saying to one another, "Look! There's a kingfisher!" or "I say, bluebells!" or "What was that lovely smell?" or "Just listen to that thrush!" They walked on in silence drinking it all in, passing through patches of warm sunlight into cool, green thickets and out again into wide mossy glades where tall elms raised the leafy roof far overhead, and then into dense masses of flowering currant and among hawthorn bushes where the sweet smell was almost overpowering.

They had been just as surprised as Edmund when they saw the winter vanishing and the whole wood passing in a few hours or so from January to May. They hadn't even known for certain (as the Witch did) that this was what would happen when Aslan came to Narnia. But they all knew that it was her spells which had produced the endless winter; and therefore they all knew when this magic spring began that something had gone wrong, and badly wrong, with the Witch's schemes. And after the thaw had been going on for some time they all realised that the Witch would no longer be able to use her sledge. After that they didn't hurry so much and they allowed themselves more rests and longer ones. They were pretty tired by now of course; but not what I'd call bitterly tired—only slow and feeling very dreamy and quiet inside as one does when one is coming to the end of a long day in the open. Susan had a slight blister on one heel.

They had left the course of the big river some time ago; for one had to turn a little to the right (that meant a little to the South) to reach the place of the Stone Table. Even if this had not been their way, they couldn't have kept to the river valley once the thaw began, for with all that melting snow the river was soon in flood—a wonderful, roaring, thundering yellow flood—and their path would have been under water.

And now the sun got low and the light got redder and the shadows got longer and the flowers began to think about closing.

"Not long now," said Mr. Beaver, and began leading them uphill across some very deep, springy moss (it felt nice under their tired feet) in a place where only tall trees grew, very wide apart. The climb, coming at the end of the long day, made them all pant and blow. And just as Lucy was wondering whether she could really get to the top without another long rest, suddenly they *were* at the top. And this is what they saw.

They were on a green open space from which you could look down on the forest spreading as far as one could see in every direction—except right ahead. There, far to the East, was something twinkling and moving. "By gum!" whispered Peter to Susan. "The sea!" In the very middle of this open hilltop was the Stone Table. It was a great grim slab of grey stone supported on four upright stones. It looked very old; and it was cut all over with strange lines and figures that might be the letters of an unknown language. They gave you a curious feeling when you looked at them. The next thing they saw was a pavilion pitched on one side of the open place. A wonderful pavilion it was—and especially now when the light of the setting sun fell upon it—with sides of what looked like yellow silk and cords of crimson and tent-pegs of ivory; and high above it on a pole a banner, which bore a red rampant lion, fluttered in the breeze which was blowing in their faces from the far-off sea. While they were looking at this they heard a sound of music on their right; and turning in that direction they saw what they had come to see.

Aslan stood in the centre of a crowd of creatures who had grouped themselves around him in the shape of a half-moon. There were Tree-Women there and Well-Women (Dryads and Naiads as they used to be called in our world) who had stringed instruments; it was they who had made the music. There were four great centaurs. The horse part of them was like huge English farm horses, and the man part was like stern but beautiful giants. There was also a unicorn, and a bull with the head of a man, and a pelican, and an eagle, and a great dog. And next to Aslan stood two leopards of whom one carried his crown and the other his standard.

But as for Aslan himself, the Beavers and the children didn't know what to do or say when they saw him. People who have not been in Narnia sometimes think that a thing cannot be good and terrible at the same time. If the children had ever thought so, they were cured of it now. For when they tried to look at Aslan's face they just caught a glimpse of the golden mane and the great, royal, solemn, overwhelming eyes; and then they found they couldn't look at him and went all trembly.

"Go on," whispered Mr. Beaver.

"No," whispered Peter, "you first."

"No, Sons of Adam before animals," whispered Mr. Beaver back again.

"Susan," whispered Peter, "what about you? Ladies first."

"No, you're the eldest," whispered Susan. And of course the longer they went on doing this the more awkward they felt. Then at last Peter realised that it was up to him. He drew his sword and raised it to the salute and hastily saying to the others "Come on. Pull yourselves together," he advanced to the Lion and said:

"We have come—Aslan."

"Welcome, Peter, Son of Adam," said Aslan. "Welcome, Susan and Lucy, Daughters of Eve. Welcome He-Beaver and She-Beaver."

His voice was deep and rich and somehow took the fidgets out of them. They now felt glad and quiet and it didn't seem awkward to them to stand and say nothing.

"But where is the fourth?" asked Aslan.

"He has tried to betray them and joined the White Witch, O Aslan," said Mr. Beaver. And then something made Peter say:

"That was partly my fault, Aslan. I was angry with him and I think that helped him to go wrong."

And Aslan said nothing either to excuse Peter or to blame him but merely stood looking at him with his great golden eyes. And it seemed to all of them that there was nothing to be said.

"Please—Aslan," said Lucy, "can anything be done to save Edmund?"

"All shall be done," said Aslan. "But it may be harder than you think." And then he was silent again for some time. Up to that moment Lucy had been thinking how royal and strong and peaceful his face looked; now it suddenly came into her head that he looked sad as well. But next minute that expression was quite gone. The Lion shook his mane and clapped his paws together ("Terrible paws," thought Lucy, "if he didn't know how to velvet them!") and said:

"Meanwhile, let the feast be prepared. Ladies, take these Daughters of Eve to the pavilion and minister to them."

When the girls had gone Aslan laid his paw—and though it was velveted it was very heavy—on Peter's shoulder and said, "Come, Son of Adam, and I will show you a far-off sight of the castle where you are to be King."

And Peter with his sword still drawn in his hand went with the Lion to the eastern edge of the hill-top. There a beautiful sight met their eyes. The sun was setting behind their backs. That meant that the whole country below them lay in the evening light—forest and hills and valleys and, winding away like a silver snake, the lower part of the great river. And beyond all this, miles away, was the sea, and beyond the sea the sky, full of clouds which were just turning rose colour with the reflection of the sunset. But just where the land of Narnia met the sea—in fact, at the mouth of the great river—there was something on a little hill, shining. It was shining because it was a castle and of course the sunlight was reflected from all the windows which looked towards Peter and the sunset; but to Peter it looked like a great star resting on the seashore.

"That, O Man," said Aslan, "is Cair Paravel of the four thrones, in one of which you must sit as King. I show it to you because you are the first-born and you will be High King over all the rest."

And once more Peter said nothing, for at that moment a strange noise woke the silence suddenly. It was like a bugle, but richer.

"It is your sister's horn," said Aslan to Peter in a low voice; so low as to be almost a purr, if it is not disrespectful to think of a lion purring.

For a moment Peter did not understand. Then, when he saw all the other creatures start forward and heard Aslan say with a wave of his paw, "Back! Let the Prince win his spurs," he did understand, and set off running as hard as he could to the pavilion. And there he saw a dreadful sight.

The Naiads and Dryads were scattering in every direction. Lucy was running towards him as fast as her short legs would carry her and her face was as white as paper. Then he saw Susan make a dash for a tree, and swing herself up, followed by a huge grey beast. At first Peter thought it was a bear. Then he saw that it looked like an Alsatian, though it was far too big to be a dog. Then he realised that it was a wolf—a wolf standing on its hind legs, with its front paws against the tree-trunk snapping and snarling. All the hair on its back stood up on end. Susan had not been able to get higher than the second big branch. One of her legs hung down so that her foot was only an inch or two above the snapping teeth. Peter wondered why she did not get higher or at least take a better grip; then he realised that she was just going to faint and that if she fainted she would fall off.

Peter did not feel very brave; indeed, he felt he was going to be sick. But that made no difference to what he had to do. He rushed straight up to the monster and aimed a slash of his sword at its side. That stroke never reached the Wolf. Quick as lightning it turned round, its eyes flaming, and its mouth wide open in a howl of anger. If it had not been so angry that it simply had to howl it would have got him by the throat at once. As it was—though all this happened too quickly for Peter to think at all—he had just time to duck down and plunge his sword, as hard as he could, between the brute's forelegs into its heart. Then came a horrible, confused moment like something in a nightmare. He was tugging and pulling and the Wolf seemed neither alive nor dead, and its bared teeth knocked against his forehead, and everything was blood and heat and hair. A moment later he found that the monster lay dead and he had drawn his sword out of it and was straightening his back and rubbing the sweat off his face and out of his eyes. He felt tired all over.

Then, after a bit, Susan came down the tree. She and Peter felt pretty shaky when they met and I won't say there wasn't kissing and crying on both sides. But in Narnia no one thinks any the worse of you for that.

"Quick! Quick!" shouted the voice of Aslan, "Centaurs! Eagles! I see another wolf in the thickets. There—behind you. He has just darted away. After him, all of you! He will be going to his mistress. Now is your chance to find the Witch and rescue the fourth Son of Adam." And instantly with a thunder of hoofs and a beating of wings a dozen or so of the swiftest creatures disappeared into the gathering darkness.

Peter, still out of breath, turned and saw Aslan close at hand.

"You have forgotten to clean your sword," said Aslan.

It was true. Peter blushed when he looked at the bright blade and saw it all smeared with the Wolf's hair and blood. He stooped down and wiped it quite clean on the grass, and then wiped it quite dry on his coat.

"Hand it to me and kneel, Son of Adam," said Aslan. And when Peter had done so he struck him with the flat of the blade and said, "Rise up, Sir Peter Fenris-Bane. And, whatever happens, never forget to wipe your sword."

XIII

Deep Magic from the Dawn of Time

Now we must go back to Edmund. When he had been made to walk far further than he had ever known that anybody *could* walk, the Witch at last halted in a dark valley all overshadowed with fir trees and yew trees. Edmund simply sank down and lay on his face, doing nothing at all and not even caring what was going to happen next provided they would let him lie still. He was too tired even to notice how hungry and thirsty he was. The Witch and the Dwarf were talking close beside him in low tones.

"No," said the Dwarf, "it is no use now, O Queen. They must have reached the Stone Table by now."

"Perhaps the Wolf will smell us out and bring us news," said the Witch.

"It cannot be good news if he does," said the Dwarf.

"Four thrones in Cair Paravel," said the Witch. "How if only three were filled? That would not fulfil the prophecy."

"What difference would that make now that *he* is here?" said the Dwarf. He did not dare, even now, to mention the name of Aslan to his mistress.

"He may not stay long. And then—we would fall upon the three at Cair."

"Yet it might be better," said the Dwarf, "to keep this one" (here he kicked Edmund) "for bargaining with."

"Yes! And have him rescued," said the Witch scornfully.

"Then," said the Dwarf, "we had better do what we have to do at once."

"I would like to have done it on the Stone Table itself," said the Witch. "That is the proper place. That is where it has always been done before."

"It will be a long time now before the Stone Table can again be put to its proper use," said the Dwarf.

"True," said the Witch; and then, "Well, I will begin."

At that moment with a rush and a snarl a Wolf rushed up to them.

"I have seen them. They are all at the Stone Table, with *him*. They have killed my captain, Fenris Ulf. I was hidden in the thickets and saw it all. One of the Sons of Adam killed him. Fly! Fly!"

"No," said the Witch. "There need be no flying. Go quickly. Summon all our people to meet me here as speedily as they can. Call out the giants and the werewolves and the spirits of those trees who are on our side. Call the Ghouls, and the Boggles, the Ogres and the Minotaurs. Call the Cruels, the Hags, the Spectres, and the people of the Toadstools. We will fight. What? Have I not still my wand? Will not their ranks turn into stone even as they come on? Be off quickly, I have a little thing to finish here while you are away."

The great brute bowed its head, turned, and galloped away.

"Now!" said she, "we have no table—let me see. We had better put it against the trunk of a tree."

Edmund found himself being roughly forced to his feet. Then the Dwarf set him with his back against a tree and bound him fast. He saw the Witch take off her outer mantle. Her arms were bare underneath it and terribly white. Because they were so very white he could not see much else, it was so dark in this valley under the dark trees.

"Prepare the victim," said the Witch. And the Dwarf undid Edmund's collar and folded back his shirt at the neck. Then he took Edmund's hair and pulled his head back so that he had to raise his chin. After that Edmund heard a strange noise—whizz—whizz—whizz. For a moment he couldn't think what it was. Then he realised. It was the sound of a knife being sharpened!

At that very moment he heard loud shouts from every direction—a drumming of hoofs and a beating of wings—a scream from the Witch—confusion all round him. And then he found he was being untied. Strong arms were round him and he heard big, kind voices saying things like "Let him lie down—give him some wine—drink this—steady now—you'll be all right in a minute."

Then he heard the voices of people who were talking not to him but to one another. And they were saying things like "Who's got the Witch?—I thought you had her—I didn't see her after I knocked the knife out of her hand—I was after the Dwarf—Do you mean to say she's escaped?—A chap can't mind everything at once—What's that? Oh sorry it's only an old stump!" But just at this point Edmund went off in a dead faint.

Presently the centaurs and unicorns and deer and birds (they were of course the rescue party which Aslan had sent in the last chapter) all set off to go back to the Stone Table, carrying Edmund with them. But if they could have seen what happened in that valley after they had gone, I think they might have been surprised.

It was perfectly still and presently the moon grew bright, if you had been there you would have seen the moonlight shining on an old tree-stump and on a fair sized boulder. But if you had gone on looking you would gradually have begun to think there was something odd about both the stump and the boulder. And next you would have thought that the stump did look really remarkably like a little fat man crouching on the ground. And if you had watched long enough you would have seen the stump walk across to the boulder and the boulder sit up and begin talking to the stump; for in reality the stump and the boulder were simply the Witch and the Dwarf. For it was part of her magic that she could make things look like what they weren't, and she had the presence of mind to do so at the very moment when the knife was knocked out of her hand. She had kept hold of her wand also, so it had been kept safe, too.

When the other children woke up next morning (they had been sleeping on piles of cushions in the pavilion) the first thing they heard—from Mrs. Beaver—was that their brother had been rescued and brought into camp late last night; and was at that moment with Aslan. As soon as they had breakfasted they all went out, and there they saw Aslan and Edmund walking together in the dewy grass, apart from the rest of the court. There is no need to tell you (and no one ever heard) what Aslan was saying but it was a conversation which Edmund never forgot. As the others drew nearer Aslan turned to meet them bringing Edmund with him.

"Here is your brother," he said, "and—there is no need to talk to him about what is past."

Edmund shook hands with each of the others and said to each of them in turn, "I'm sorry," and everyone said, "That's all right." And then everyone wanted very hard to say something which would make it quite clear that they were all friends with him again—something ordinary and natural—and of course no one could think of anything in the world to say. But before they had time to feel really awkward one of the leopards approached Aslan and said:

"Sire, there is a messenger from the enemy who craves audience."

"Let him approach," said Aslan.

The leopard went away and soon returned leading the Witch's Dwarf.

"What is your message, Son of Earth?" asked Aslan.

"The Queen of Narnia and Empress of the Lone Islands desires a safe conduct to come and speak with you," said the Dwarf, "on a matter which is as much to your advantage as to hers."

"Queen of Narnia, indeed!" said Mr. Beaver. "Of all the cheek—"

"Peace, Beaver," said Aslan. "All names will soon be restored to their proper owners. In the meantime we will not dispute about noises. Tell your mistress, Son of Earth, that I grant her safe conduct on condition that she leaves her wand behind her at that great oak."

This was agreed to and two leopards went back with the Dwarf to see that the conditions were properly carried out. "But supposing she turns the two leopards into stone?" whispered Lucy to Peter. I think the same idea had occurred to the leopards themselves; at any rate, as they walked off their fur was all standing up on their backs and their tails were bristling—like a cat's when it sees a strange dog.

"It'll be all right," whispered Peter in reply. "He wouldn't send them if it weren't."

A few minutes later the Witch herself walked out on to the top of the hill and came straight across and stood before Aslan. The three children, who had not seen her before, felt shudders running down their backs at the sight of her face; and there were low growls among all the animals present. Though it was bright sunshine everyone felt suddenly cold. The only two people present who seemed to be quite at their ease were Aslan and the Witch herself. It was the oddest thing to see those two faces—the golden face and the dead-white face—so close together. Not that the Witch looked Aslan exactly in his eyes; Mrs. Beaver particularly noticed this.

"You have a traitor there, Aslan," said the Witch. Of course everyone present knew that she meant Edmund. But Edmund had got past thinking about himself after all he'd been through and after the talk he'd had that morning. He just went on looking at Aslan. It didn't seem to matter what the Witch said.

"Well," said Aslan. "His offence was not against you."

"Have you forgotten the Deep Magic?" asked the Witch.

"Let us say I have forgotten it," answered Aslan gravely. "Tell us of this Deep Magic."

"Tell you?" said the Witch, her voice growing suddenly shriller. "Tell you what is written on that very Table of Stone which stands beside us? Tell you what is written in letters deep as a spear is long on the trunk of the World Ash Tree? Tell you what is engraved on the sceptre of the Emperor-Beyond-the-Sea? You at least know the magic which the Emperor put into Narnia at the very beginning. You know that every traitor belongs to me as my lawful prey and that for every treachery I have a right to a kill."

"Oh," said Mr. Beaver. "So *that's* how you came to imagine yourself a Queen—because you were the Emperor's hangman. I see."

"Peace, Beaver," said Aslan, with a very low growl.

"And so," continued the Witch, "that human creature is mine. His life is forfeit to me. His blood is my property."

"Come and take it then," said the Bull with the man's head in a great bellowing voice.

"Fool," said the Witch with a savage smile that was almost a snarl, "do you really think your master can rob me of my rights by mere force? He knows the Deep Magic better than that. He knows that unless I have blood as the Law says all Narnia will be overturned and perish in fire and water."

"It is very true," said Aslan; "I do not deny it."

"Oh, Aslan!" whispered Susan in the Lion's ear, "can't we—I mean, you won't, will you? Can't we do something about the Deep Magic? Isn't there something you can work against it?"

"Work against the Emperor's magic?" said Aslan turning to her with something like a frown on his face. And nobody ever made that suggestion to him again.

Edmund was on the other side of Aslan, looking all the time at Aslan's face. He felt a choking feeling and wondered if he ought to say something; but a moment later he felt that he was not expected to do anything except to wait, and do what he was told.

"Fall back, all of you," said Aslan, "and I will talk to the Witch alone."

They all obeyed. It was a terrible time this—waiting and wondering while the Lion and the Witch talked earnestly together in low voices. Lucy said, "Oh, Edmund!" and began to cry. Peter stood with his back to the others looking out at the distant sea. The Beavers stood holding each other's paws with their heads bowed. The centaurs stamped uneasily with their hoofs. But everyone became perfectly still in the end, so that you noticed even small sounds like a bumble bee flying past, or the birds in the forest down below them, or the wind rustling the leaves. And still the talk between Aslan and the White Witch went on.

At last they heard Aslan's voice. "You can all come back," he said. "I have settled the matter. She has renounced the claim on your brother's blood." And all over the hill there was a noise as if everyone had been holding his breath and had now begun breathing again, and then a murmur of talk. They began to come back to Aslan's throne.

The Witch was just turning away with a look of fierce joy on her face when she stopped and said,

"But how do I know this promise will be kept?"

"Wow!" roared Aslan half rising from his throne; and his great mouth opened wider and wider and the roar grew louder and louder, and the Witch, after staring for a moment with her lips wide apart, picked up her skirts and fairly ran for her life.

XIV

The Triumph of the Witch

As soon as the Witch had gone Aslan said, "We must move from this place at once, it will be wanted for other purposes. We shall encamp tonight at the Fords of Beruna."

Of course everyone was dying to ask him how he had arranged matters with the Witch; but his face was stern and everyone's ears were still ringing with the sound of his roar and so nobody dared.

After a meal, which was taken in the open air on the hill-top (for the sun had got strong by now and dried the grass) they were busy for a while taking the pavilion down and packing things up. Before two o'clock they were on the march and set off in a North-Westerly direction, walking at an easy pace for they had not far to go.

During the first part of the journey Aslan explained to Peter his plan of campaign. "As soon as she has finished her business in these parts," he said, "the Witch and her crew will almost certainly fall back to her house and prepare for a siege. You may or may not be able to cut her off and prevent her from reaching it." He then went on to outline two plans of battle—one for fighting the Witch and her people in the wood and another for assaulting her castle. And all the time he was advising Peter how to conduct the operations, saying things like, "You must put your centaurs in such and such a place" or "You must post scouts to see that she doesn't do so-and-so," till at last Peter said,

"But you will be there yourself, Aslan."

"I can give you no promise of that," answered the Lion. And he continued giving Peter his instructions.

For the last part of the journey it was Susan and Lucy who saw most of him. He did not talk very much and seemed to them to be sad.

It was still afternoon when they came down to a place where the river valley had widened out and the river was broad and shallow. This was the Fords of Beruna and Aslan gave orders to halt on this side of the water. But Peter said,

"Wouldn't it be better to camp on the far side—for fear she should try a night attack or anything?"

Aslan who seemed to have been thinking about something else roused himself with a shake of his magnificent mane and said, "Eh? What's that?" Peter said it all over again.

"No," said Aslan in a dull voice, as if it didn't matter. "No. She will not make an attack to-night." And then he sighed deeply. But presently he added, "All the same it was well thought of. That is how a soldier ought to think. But it doesn't really matter." So they proceeded to pitch their camp.

Aslan's mood affected everyone that evening. Peter was feeling uncomfortable too at the idea of fighting the battle on his own; the news that Aslan might not be there had come as a great shock to him. Supper that evening was a quiet meal. Everyone felt how different it had been last night or even that morning. It was as if the good times, having just begun, were already drawing to their end.

The feeling affected Susan so much that she couldn't get to sleep when she went to bed. And after she had lain counting sheep and turning over and over she heard Lucy give a long sigh and turn over just beside her in the darkness.

"Can't you get to sleep either?" said Susan.

"No," said Lucy. "I thought you were asleep. I say, Susan?"

"What?"

"I've a most horrible feeling—as if something were hanging over us."

"Have you? Because, as a matter of fact, so have I."

"Something about Aslan," said Lucy. "Either some dreadful thing that is going to happen to him, or something dreadful that he's going to do."

"There's been something wrong with him all afternoon," said Susan. "Lucy! What was that he said about not being with us at the battle? You don't think he could be stealing away and leaving us to-night, do you?"

"Where is he now?" said Lucy. "Is he here in the pavilion?"

"I don't think so."

"Susan! Let's go outside and have a look round. We might see him."

"All right. Let's," said Susan, "we might just as well be doing that as lying awake here."

Very quietly the two girls groped their way among the other sleepers and crept out of the tent. The moonlight was bright and everything was quite still except for the noise of the river chattering over the stones. Then Susan suddenly caught Lucy's arm and said, "Look!" On the far side of the camping ground, just where the trees began, they saw the Lion slowly walking away from them into the wood. Without a word they both followed him.

He led them up the steep slope out of the river valley and then slightly to the left—apparently by the very same route which they had used that afternoon in coming from the Hill of the Stone Table. On and on he led them, into dark shadows and out into pale moonlight, getting their feet wet with the heavy dew. He looked somehow different from the Aslan they knew. His tail and his head hung low and he walked slowly as if he were very, very tired. Then, when they were crossing a wide open place where there were no shadows for them to hide in, he stopped and looked round. It was no good trying to run away so they came towards him. When they were closer he said,

"Oh, children, children, why are you following me?"

"We couldn't sleep," said Lucy—and then felt sure that she need say no more and that Aslan knew all they had been thinking.

"Please, may we come with you—wherever you're going?" said Susan.

"Well—" said Aslan and seemed to be thinking. Then he said, "I should be glad of company to-night. Yes, you may come, if you will promise to stop when I tell you, and after that leave me to go on alone."

"Oh, thank you, thank you. And we will," said the two girls.

Forward they went again and one of the girls walked on each side of the Lion. But how slowly he walked! And his great, royal head drooped so that his nose nearly touched the grass. Presently he stumbled and gave a low moan.

"Aslan! Dear Aslan!" said Lucy, "what is wrong? Can't you tell us?"

"Are you ill, dear Aslan?" asked Susan.

"No," said Aslan. "I am sad and lonely. Lay your hands on my mane so that I can feel you are there and let us walk like that."

And so the girls did what they would never have dared to do without his permission but what they had longed to do ever since they first saw him—buried their cold hands in the beautiful sea of fur and stroked it and, so doing, walked with him. And presently they saw that they were going with him up the slope of the hill on which the Stone Table stood. They went up at the side where the trees came furthest up, and when they got to the last tree (it was one that had some bushes about it) Aslan stopped and said,

"Oh, children, children. Here you must stop. And whatever happens, do not let yourselves be seen. Farewell."

And both the girls cried bitterly (though they hardly knew why) and clung to the Lion and kissed his mane and his nose and his paws and his great, sad eyes. Then he turned from them and walked out onto the top of the hill. And Lucy and Susan, crouching in the bushes, looked after him and this is what they saw.

A great crowd of people were standing all round the Stone Table and though the moon was shining many of them carried torches which burned with evil-looking red flames and black smoke. But such people! Ogres with monstrous teeth, and wolves, and bull-headed men; spirits of evil trees and poisonous plants; and other creatures whom I won't describe because if I did the grown-ups would probably not let you read this book—Cruels and Hags and Incubuses, Wraiths, Horrors, Efreets, Sprites, Orknies, Wooses, and Ettins. In fact here were all those who were on the Witch's side and whom the Wolf had summoned at her command. And right in the middle, standing by the Table, was the Witch herself.

A howl and a gibber of dismay went up from the creatures when they first saw the great Lion pacing towards them, and for a moment the Witch herself seemed to be struck with fear. Then she recovered herself and gave a wild, fierce laugh.

"The fool!" she cried. "The fool has come. Bind him fast."

Lucy and Susan held their breaths waiting for Aslan's roar and his spring upon his enemies. But it never came. Four hags, grinning and leering, yet also (at first) hanging back and half afraid of what they had to do, had approached him. "Bind him, I say!" repeated the White Witch. The hags made a dart at him and shrieked with triumph when they found that he made no resistance at all. Then others—evil dwarfs and apes—rushed in to help them and between them they rolled the huge Lion round on his back and tied all his four paws together, shouting and cheering as if they had done something brave, though, had the Lion chosen, one of those paws could have been the death of them all. But he made no noise, even when the enemies, straining and tugging, pulled the cords so tight that they cut into his flesh. Then they began to drag him towards the Stone Table.

"Stop!" said the Witch. "Let him first be shaved."

Another roar of mean laughter went up from her followers as an ogre with a pair of shears came forward and squatted down by Aslan's head. Snip-snip-snip went the shears and masses of curling gold began to fall to the ground. Then the ogre stood back and the children, watching from their hiding-place, could see the face of Aslan looking all small and different without its mane. The enemies also saw the difference.

"Why, he's only a great cat after all!" cried one.

"Is *that* what we were afraid of?" said another.

And they surged round Aslan jeering at him, saying things like "Puss, Puss! Poor Pussy," and "How many mice have you caught to-day, Cat?" and "Would you like a saucer of milk, Pussums?"

"Oh how *can* they?" said Lucy, tears streaming down her cheeks. "The brutes, the brutes!" for now that the first shock was over the shorn face of Aslan looked to her braver, and more beautiful, and more patient than ever.

"Muzzle him!" said the Witch. And even now, as they worked about his face putting on the muzzle, one bite from his jaws would have cost two or three of them their hands. But he never moved. And this seemed to enrage all that rabble. Everyone was at him now. Those who had been afraid to come near him even after he was bound began to find their courage, and for a few minutes the two girls could not even see him—so thickly was he surrounded by the whole crowd of creatures kicking him, hitting him, spitting on him, jeering at him.

At last the rabble had had enough of this. They began to drag the bound and muzzled Lion to the Stone Table, some pulling and some pushing. He was so huge that even when they got him there it took all their efforts to hoist him onto the surface of it. Then there was more tying and tightening of cords.

"The cowards! The cowards!" sobbed Susan. "Are they *still* afraid of him, even now?"

When once Aslan had been tied (and tied so that he was really a mass of cords) on the flat stone, a hush fell on the crowd. Four Hags, holding four torches, stood at the corners of the Table. The Witch bared her arms as she had bared them the previous night when it had been Edmund instead of Aslan. Then she began to whet her knife. It looked to the children, when the gleam of the torchlight fell on it, as if the knife were made of stone not of steel and it was of a strange and evil shape.

At last she drew near. She stood by Aslan's head. Her face was working and twitching with passion, but his looked up at the sky, still quiet, neither angry nor afraid, but a little sad. Then, just before she gave the blow, she stooped down and said in a quivering voice,

"And now, who has won? Fool, did you think that by all this you would save the human traitor? Now I will kill you instead of him as our pact was and so the

Deep Magic will be appeased. But when you are dead what will prevent me from killing him as well? And who will take him out of my hand *then?* Understand that you have given me Narnia forever, you have lost your own life and you have not saved his. In that knowledge, despair and die."

The children did not see the actual moment of the killing. They couldn't bear to look and had covered their eyes.

XV

Deeper Magic from *Before* the Dawn of Time

W<small>HILE</small> the two girls still crouched in the bushes with their hands over their faces, they heard the voice of the Witch calling out.

"Now! Follow me all and we will set about what remains of this war! It will not take us long to crush the human vermin and the traitors now that the great Fool, the great Cat, lies dead."

At this moment the children were for a few seconds in very great danger. For with wild cries and a noise of skirling pipes and shrill horns blowing, the whole of that vile rabble came sweeping off the hill-top and down the slope right past their hiding-place. They felt the Spectres go by them like a cold wind and they felt the ground shake beneath them under the galloping feet of the Minotaurs; and overhead there went a flurry of foul wings and a blackness of vultures and giant bats. At any other time they would have trembled with fear; but now the sadness and shame and horror of Aslan's death so filled their minds that they hardly thought of it.

As soon as the wood was silent again Susan and Lucy crept out into the open hill-top. The moon was getting low and thin clouds were passing across her, but still they could see the shape of the great Lion lying dead in his bonds. And down they both knelt in the wet grass and kissed his cold face and stroked his beautiful fur—what was left of it—and cried till they could cry no more. And then they looked at each other and held each other's hands for mere loneliness and cried again; and then again were silent. At last Lucy said,

"I can't bear the look of that horrible muzzle. I wonder could we take it off?"

So they tried. And after a lot of working at it (for their fingers were cold and it was now the darkest part of the night) they succeeded. And when they saw his face without it they burst out crying again and kissed it and fondled it and wiped away the blood and the foam as well as they could. And it was all more lonely and hopeless and horrid than I know how to describe.

"I wonder could we untie him as well?" said Susan presently. But the enemies, out of pure spitefulness had drawn the cords so tight that the girls could make nothing of the knots.

I hope no one who reads this book has been quite as miserable as Susan and Lucy were that night; but if you have been—if you've been up all night and cried till you have no more tears left in you—you will know that there comes in the end a sort of quietness. You feel as if nothing was ever going to happen again. At any rate that was how it felt to these two. Hours and hours seemed to go by in this dead calm, and they hardly noticed that they were getting colder and colder. But at last Lucy noticed two other things. One was that the sky on the East side of the hill was a little less dark than it had been an hour ago. The other was some tiny movement going on in the grass at her feet. At first she took no interest in this. What did it matter? Nothing mattered now! But at last she saw that whatever-it-was had begun to move up the upright stones of the Stone Table. And now whatever-they-were were moving about on Aslan's body. She peered closer. They were little grey things.

"Ugh!" said Susan from the other side of the Table. "How beastly! There are horrid little mice crawling over him. Go away, you little beasts." And she raised her hand to frighten them away.

"Wait!" said Lucy who had been looking at them more closely still. "Can you see what they're doing?"

Both girls bent down and stared.

"I do believe!" said Susan. "But how queer. They're nibbling away at the cords!"

"That's what I thought," said Lucy. "I think they're friendly mice. Poor little things—they don't realise he's dead. They think it'll do some good untying him."

It was quite definitely lighter by now. Each of the girls noticed for the first time the white face of the other. They could see the mice nibbling away; dozens and dozens, even hundreds, of little field mice. And at last, one by one, the ropes were all gnawed through.

The sky in the East was whitish by now and the stars were getting fainter—all except one very big one low down on the Eastern horizon. They felt colder than they had been all night. The mice crept away again.

The girls cleared away the remains of the gnawed ropes. Aslan looked more like himself without them. Every moment his dead face looked nobler, as the light grew and they could see it better.

In the wood behind them a bird gave a chuckling sound. It had been so still for hours and hours that it startled them. Then another bird answered it. Soon there were birds singing all over the place.

It was quite definitely early morning now, not late night.

"I'm so cold," said Lucy.

"So am I," said Susan. "Let's walk about a bit."

They walked to the Eastern edge of the hill and looked down. The one big star had almost disappeared. The country all looked dark grey, but beyond, at the very end of the world, the sea showed pale. The sky began to turn red. They walked to and fro more times than they could count between the dead Aslan and the Eastern ridge, trying to keep warm; and oh, how tired their legs felt. Then at last, as they stood for a moment looking out towards the sea and Cair Paravel (which they could now just make out) the red turned to gold along the line where the sea and the sky met and very slowly up came the edge of the sun. At that moment they heard from behind them a loud noise—a great cracking, deafening noise as if a giant had broken a giant's plate.

"What's that?" said Lucy, clutching Susan's arm.

"I—I feel afraid to turn round," said Susan; "something awful is happening."

"They're doing something worse to *him*," said Lucy. "Come on!" And she turned, pulling Susan round with her.

The rising of the sun had made everything look so different—all the colours and shadows were changed—that for a moment they didn't see the important thing. Then they did. The Stone Table was broken into two pieces by a great crack that ran down it from end to end; and there was no Aslan.

"Oh, oh, oh!" cried the two girls rushing back to the Table.

"Oh, it's *too* bad," sobbed Lucy; "they might have left the body alone."

"Who's done it?" cried Susan. "What does it mean? Is it more magic?"

"Yes!" said a great voice behind their backs. "It is more magic." They looked round. There, shining in the sunrise, larger than they had seen him before, shaking his mane (for it had apparently grown again) stood Aslan himself.

"Oh, Aslan!" cried both the children, staring up at him, almost as much frightened as they were glad.

"Aren't you dead then, dear Aslan?" said Lucy.

"Not now," said Aslan.

"You're not—not a—?" asked Susan in a shaky voice. She couldn't bring herself to say the word *ghost*.

Aslan stooped his golden head and licked her forehead. The warmth of his breath and a rich sort of smell that seemed to hang about his hair came all over her.

"Do I look it?" he said.

"Oh, you're real, you're real! Oh, Aslan!" cried Lucy and both girls flung themselves upon him and covered him with kisses.

"But what does it all mean?" asked Susan when they were somewhat calmer.

"It means," said Aslan, "that though the Witch knew the Deep Magic, there is a magic deeper still which she did not know. Her knowledge goes back only to the dawn of Time. But if she could have looked a little further back, into the stillness and the darkness before Time dawned, she would have read there a different incantation. She would have known that when a willing victim who had committed no treachery was killed in a traitor's stead, the Table would crack and Death itself would start working backwards. And now—"

"Oh yes. Now?" said Lucy jumping up and clapping her hands.

"Oh, children," said the Lion, "I feel my strength coming back to me. Oh, children, catch me if you can!" He stood for a second, his eyes very bright, his limbs quivering, lashing himself with his tail. Then he made a leap high over their heads and landed on the other side of the Table. Laughing, though she didn't know why, Lucy scrambled over it to reach him. Aslan leaped again. A mad chase began. Round and round the hill-top he led them, now hopelessly out of their reach, now letting them almost catch his tail, now diving between them, now tossing them in the air with his huge and beautifully velveted paws and catching them again, and now stopping unexpectedly so that all three of them rolled over together in a happy laughing heap of fur and arms and legs.

It was such a romp as no one has ever had except in Narnia; and whether it was more like playing with a thunderstorm or playing with a kitten Lucy could never make up her mind. And the funny thing was that when all three finally lay together panting in the sun the girls no longer felt in the least tired or hungry or thirsty.

"And now," said Aslan presently, "to business. I feel I am going to roar. You had better put your fingers in your ears."

And they did. And Aslan stood up and when he opened his mouth to roar his face became so terrible that they did not dare to look at it. And they saw all the trees in front of him bend before the blast of his roaring as grass bends in a meadow before the wind. Then he said,

"We have a long journey to go. You must ride on me." And he crouched down and the children climbed onto his warm, golden back and Susan sat first holding on tightly to his mane and Lucy sat behind holding on tightly to Susan. And with a great heave he rose underneath them and then shot off, faster than any horse could go, downhill and into the thick of the forest.

That ride was perhaps the most wonderful thing that happened to them in Narnia. Have you ever had a gallop on a horse? Think of that; and then take away the heavy noise of the hoofs and the jingle of the harness and imagine instead the almost noiseless padding of the great paws. Then imagine instead of the black or grey or chestnut back of the horse the soft roughness of golden fur, and the mane flying back in the wind. And then imagine you are going about twice as fast as the fastest racehorse. But this is a mount that doesn't need to be guided and never grows tired. He rushes on and on, never missing his footing, never hesitating, threading his way with perfect skill between tree-trunks, jumping over bush and briar and the smaller streams, wading the larger, swimming the largest of all. And you are riding not on a road nor in a park nor even on the downs but right across Narnia, in spring, down solemn avenues of beech and across sunny glades of oak, through wild orchards of snow-white cherry trees, past roaring waterfalls and mossy rocks and echoing caverns, up windy slopes alight with gorse bushes and across the shoulders of heathery mountains and along giddy ridges and down, down, down again into wild valleys and out into acres of blue flowers.

It was nearly mid-day when they found themselves looking down a steep hillside at a castle—a little toy castle it looked from where they stood—which seemed to be all pointed towers. But the Lion was rushing down at such a speed that it grew larger every moment and before they had time even to ask themselves what it was they were already on a level with it. And now it no longer looked like a toy castle but rose frowning in front of them. No face looked over the battlements and the gates were fast shut. And Aslan, not at all slacking his pace, rushed straight as a bullet towards it.

"The Witch's home!" he cried. "Now, children, hold tight."

Next moment the whole world seemed to turn upside down, and the children felt as if they had left their insides behind them; for the Lion had gathered himself together for a greater leap than any he had yet made and jumped—or you may call it flying rather than jumping—right over the castle wall. The two girls, breathless but unhurt, found themselves tumbling off his back in the middle of a wide stone courtyard full of statues.

XVI

What Happened About the Statues

"WHAT an extraordinary place!" cried Lucy. "All those stone animals—and people too! It's—it's like a museum."

"Hush," said Susan, "Aslan's doing something."

He was indeed. He had bounded up to the stone lion and breathed on him. Then without waiting a moment he whisked round—almost as if he had been a cat chasing its tail—and breathed also on the stone dwarf, which (as you remember) was standing a few feet from the lion with his back to it. Then he pounced on a tall stone Dryad which stood beyond the dwarf, turned rapidly aside to deal with a stone rabbit on his right, and rushed on to two centaurs. But at that moment Lucy said,

"Oh, Susan! Look! Look at the lion."

I expect you've seen someone put a lighted match to a bit of newspaper which is propped up in a grate against an unlit fire. And for a second nothing seems to have happened; and then you notice a tiny streak of flame creeping along the edge of the newspaper. It was like that now. For a second after Aslan had breathed upon him the stone lion looked just the same. Then a tiny streak of gold began to run along his white marble back—then it spread—then the colour seemed to lick all over him as the flame licks all over a bit of paper—then, while his hind-quarters were still obviously stone the lion shook his mane and all the heavy, stony folds rippled into living hair. Then he opened a great red mouth, warm and living, and gave a prodigious yawn. And now his hind legs had come to life. He lifted one of them and scratched himself. Then, having caught sight of Aslan, he went bounding after him and frisking round him whimpering with delight and jumping up to lick his face.

Of course the children's eyes turned to follow the lion; but the sight they saw was so wonderful that they soon forgot about *him*. Everywhere the statues were coming to life. The courtyard looked no longer like a museum; it looked more like a zoo. Creatures were running after Aslan and dancing round him till he was almost hidden in the crowd. Instead of all that deadly white the courtyard was now a blaze of colours; glossy chestnut sides of centaurs, indigo horns of unicorns, dazzling plumage of birds, reddy-brown of foxes, dogs, and satyrs, yellow stockings and crimson hoods of dwarfs; and the birch-girls in silver, and the beech-girls in fresh, transparent green, and the larch-girls in green so bright that it was almost yellow. And instead of the deadly silence the whole place rang with the sound of happy roarings, brayings, yelpings, barkings, squealings, cooings, neighings, stampings, shouts, hurrahs, songs and laughter.

"Ooh!" said Susan in a different tone. "Look! I wonder—I mean, is it safe?"

Lucy looked and saw that Aslan had just breathed on the feet of the stone giant.

"It's all right!" shouted Aslan joyously. "Once the feet are put right, all the rest of him will follow."

"That wasn't exactly what I meant," whispered Susan to Lucy. But it was too late to do anything about it now even if Aslan would have listened to her. The change was already creeping up the Giant's legs. Now he was moving his feet. A moment later he lifted the club off his shoulder, rubbed his eyes and said,

"Bless me! I must have been asleep. Now! Where's that dratted little Witch that was running about on the ground. Somewhere just by my feet it was." But when everyone had shouted up to him to explain what had really happened, and when the Giant had put his hand to his ear and got them to repeat it all again so that at last he understood, then he bowed down till his head was no further off than the top of a haystack and touched his cap repeatedly to Aslan, beaming all over his honest ugly face. (Giants of any sort are now so rare in England and so few giants are good tempered that ten to one you have never seen a giant when his face is beaming. It's a sight well worth looking at.)

"Now for the inside of this house!" said Aslan. "Look alive, everyone. Up stairs and down stairs and in my lady's chamber! Leave no corner unsearched. You never know where some poor prisoner may be concealed."

And into the interior they all rushed and for several minutes the whole of that dark, horrible, fusty old castle echoed with the opening of windows and with everyone's voices crying out at once "Don't forget the dungeons—Give us a hand with this door!—Here's another little winding stair—Oh! I say. Here's a poor little kangaroo. Call Aslan—Phew! How it smells in here—Look out for trap-doors—Up here! There are a whole lot more on the landing!" But the best of all was when Lucy came rushing upstairs shouting out,

"Aslan! Aslan! I've found Mr. Tumnus. Oh, do come quick."

A moment later Lucy and the little Faun were holding one another by both hands and dancing round and round for joy. The little chap was none the worse for having been a statue and was of course very interested in all she had to tell him.

But at last the ransacking of the Witch's fortress was ended. The whole castle stood empty with every door and window open and the light and the sweet spring air flooding in to all the dark and evil places which needed them so badly. The whole crowd of liberated statues surged back into the courtyard. And it was then that someone (Tummus, I think) first said,

"But how are we going to get out?" for Aslan had got in by a jump and the gates were still locked.

"That'll be all right," said Aslan; and then, rising on his hind-legs, he bawled up at the Giant. "Hi! You up there," he roared. "What's your name?"

"Giant Rumblebuffin if it please your honour," said the Giant, once more touching his cap.

"Well then, Giant Rumblebuffin," said Aslan, "just let us out of this, will you?"

"Certainly, your honour. It will be a pleasure," said Giant Rumblebuffin.

"Stand well away from the gates, all you little 'uns." Then he strode to the gate himself and bang—bang—bang—went his huge club. The gates creaked at the first blow, cracked at the second, and shivered at the third. Then he tackled the towers on each side of them and after a few minutes of crashing and thudding both the towers and a good bit of the wall on each side went thundering down in a mass of hopeless rubble; and when the dust cleared it was odd, standing in that dry, grim, stony yard, to see through the gap all the grass and waving trees and sparkling streams of the forest, and the blue hills beyond that and beyond them the sky.

"Blowed if I ain't all in a muck sweat," said the Giant puffing like the largest railway engine. "Comes of being out of condition. I suppose neither of you young ladies has such a thing as a pocket-handkerchee about you?"

"Yes, I have," said Lucy standing on tiptoes and holding her handkerchief up as far as she could reach.

"Thank you, Missie," said Giant Rumblebuffin stooping down. Next moment Lucy got rather a fright for she found herself caught up in mid-air between the Giant's finger and thumb. But just as she was getting near his face he suddenly started and then put her gently back on the ground muttering, "Bless me! I've picked up the little girl instead. I beg your pardon, Missie, I thought you *was* the handkerchee!"

"No, no," said Lucy laughing, "here it is!" This time he managed to get it but it was only about the same size to him that a saccharine tablet would be to you, so that when she saw him solemnly rubbing it to and fro across his great red face, she said, "I'm afraid it's not much use to you, Mr. Rumblebuffin."

"Not at all. Not at all," said the Giant politely. "Never met a nicer handker-chee. So fine, so handy. So—I don't know how to describe it."

"What a nice giant he is!" said Lucy to Mr. Tumnus.

"Oh yes," replied the Faun. "All the Buffins always were. One of the most respected of all the giant families in Narnia. Not very clever, perhaps (I never knew a giant that was) but an old family. With traditions, you know. If he'd been the other sort she'd never have turned him into stone."

At this point Aslan clapped his paws together and called for silence.

"Our day's work is not yet over," he said, "and if the Witch is to be finally defeated before bed-time we must find the battle at once."

"And join in I hope, Sir!" added the largest of the centaurs.

"Of course," said Aslan. "And now! Those who can't keep up—that is, children, dwarfs, and small animals—must ride on the backs of those who can— that is, lions, centaurs, unicorns, horses, giants and eagles. Those who are good with their noses must come in the front with us lions to smell out where the battle is. Look lively and sort yourselves.

And with a great deal of bustle and cheering they did. The most pleased of the lot was the other lion, who kept running about everywhere pretending to be very busy but really in order to say to everyone he met, "Did you hear what he said? *Us lions.* That means him and me. *Us lions.* That's what I like about Aslan.

No side, no stand-off-ishness. *Us lions.* That meant him and me." At least he went on saying this till Aslan had loaded him up with three dwarfs, one Dryad, two rabbits, and a hedgehog. That steadied him a bit.

When all were ready (it was a big sheep-dog who actually helped Aslan most in getting them sorted into their proper order) they set out through the gap in the castle wall. At first the lions and dogs went nosing about in all directions. But then suddenly one great hound picked up the scent and gave a bay. There was no time lost after that. Soon all the dogs and lions and wolves and other hunting animals were going at full speed with their noses to the ground, and all the others, streaked out for about half a mile behind them, were following as fast as they could. The noise was like an English fox-hunt only better because every now and then with the music of the hounds was mixed the roar of the other lion and sometimes the far deeper and more awful roar of Aslan himself. Faster and faster they went as the scent became easier and easier to follow. And then, just as they came to the last curve in a narrow, winding valley, Lucy heard above all these noises another noise—a different one, which gave her a queer feeling inside. It was a noise of shouts and shrieks and of the clashing of metal against metal.

Then they came out of the narrow valley and at once she saw the reason. There stood Peter and Edmund and all the rest of Aslan's army fighting desperately against the crowd of horrible creatures whom she had seen last night; only now, in the daylight, they looked even stranger and more evil and more deformed. There also seemed to be far more of them. Aslan's army—which had their backs to her—looked terribly few. And there were statues dotted all over the battlefield, so apparently the Witch had been using her wand. But she did not seem to be using it now. She was fighting with her stone knife. It was Peter she was fighting—both of them going at it so hard that Lucy could hardly make out what was happening; she only saw the stone knife and Peter's sword flashing so quickly that they looked like three knives and three swords. That pair were in the centre. On each side the line stretched out. Horrible things were happening wherever she looked.

"Off my back, children," shouted Aslan. And they both tumbled off. Then with a roar that shook all Narnia from the Western lamppost to the shores of the Eastern sea the great beast flung himself upon the White Witch. Lucy saw her face lifted towards him for one second with an expression of terror and amazement. Then Lion and Witch had rolled over together but with the Witch underneath; and at the same moment all war-like creatures whom Aslan had led from the Witch's house rushed madly on the enemy's line, dwarfs with their battle-axes, dogs with teeth, the giant with his club (and his feet also crushed dozens of the foe), unicorns with their horns, centaurs with swords and hoofs. And Peter's tired army cheered, and the newcomers roared, and the enemy squealed and gibbered till the wood re-echoed with the din of that onset.

XVII

The Hunting of the White Stag

THE BATTLE was all over a few minutes after their arrival. Most of the enemy had been killed in the first charge of Aslan and his companions; and when those who were still living saw that the Witch was dead they either gave themselves up or took to flight. The next thing that Lucy knew was that Peter and Aslan were shaking hands. It was strange to her to see Peter looking as he looked now—his face was so pale and stern and he seemed so much older.

"It was all Edmund's doing, Aslan," Peter was saying. "We'd have been beaten if it hadn't been for him. The Witch was turning our troops into stone right and left. But nothing would stop him. He fought his way through three ogres to where she was just turning one of your leopards into a statue. And when he reached her he had the sense to bring his sword smashing down on her wand instead of trying to go for her directly and simply getting made a statue himself for his pains. That was the mistake all the rest were making. Once her wand was broken we began to have some chance—if we hadn't lost so many already. He was terribly wounded. We must go and see him."

They found Edmund in charge of Mrs. Beaver a little way back from the fighting line. He was covered with blood, his mouth was open, and his face a nasty green colour.

"Quick, Lucy," said Aslan.

And then, almost for the first time, Lucy remembered the precious cordial that had been given her for a Christmas present. Her hands trembled so much that she could hardly undo the stopper, but she managed it in the end and poured a few drops into her brother's mouth.

"There are other people wounded," said Aslan while she was still looking eagerly into Edmund's pale face and wondering if the cordial would have any result.

"Yes, I know," said Lucy crossly. "Wait a minute."

"Daughter of Eve," said Aslan in a graver voice, "others also are at the point of death. Must *more* people die for Edmund?"

"I'm sorry, Aslan," said Lucy getting up and going with him. And for the next half hour they were busy—she attending to the wounded while he restored those who had been turned into stone. When at last she was free to come back to Edmund she found him standing on his feet and not only healed of his wounds but looking better than she had seen him look—oh, for ages; in fact ever since his first term at that horrid school which was where he had begun to go wrong. He had become his real old self again and could look you in the face. And there on the field of battle Aslan made him a Knight.

"Does he know," whispered Lucy to Susan, "what Aslan did for him? Does he know what the arrangement with the Witch really was?"

"Hush! No. Of course not," said Susan.

"Oughtn't he to be told?" said Lucy.

"Oh, surely not," said Susan. "It would be too awful for him. Think how you'd feel if you were he."

"All the same I think he ought to know," said Lucy. But at that moment they were interrupted.

That night they slept where they were. How Aslan provided food for them all I don't know; but somehow or other they found themselves all sitting down on the grass to a fine high tea at about eight o'clock. Next day they began marching Eastward down the side of the great river. And the next day after that, at about teatime, they actually reached the mouth. The castle of Cair Paravel on its little hill towered up above them; before them were the sands, with rocks and little pools of salt water, and sea weed, and the smell of the sea, and long miles of bluish-green waves breaking forever and ever on the beach. And, oh, the cry of the sea gulls! Have you heard it? Can you remember?

That evening after tea the four children all managed to get down to the beach again and get their shoes and stockings off and feel the sand between their toes. But next day was more solemn. For then, in the Great Hall of Cair Paravel—that wonderful hall with the ivory roof and the west door all hung with peacock's feathers and the eastern door which opens right onto the sea, in the presence of all their friends and to the sound of trumpets, Aslan solemnly crowned them and led them onto the four thrones amid deafening shouts of, "Long Live King Peter! Long Live Queen Susan! Long Live King Edmund! Long Live Queen Lucy!"

"Once a king or queen in Narnia, always a king or queen. Bear it well, Sons of Adam! Bear it well, Daughters of Eve!" said Aslan.

And through the Eastern door, which was wide open, came the voices of the mermen and the mermaids swimming close to the castle steps and singing in honour of their new Kings and Queens.

So the children sat in their thrones and sceptres were put into their hands and they gave rewards and honours to all their friends, to Tumnus the Faun, and to the Beavers, and Giant Rumblebuffin, to the leopards, and the good centaurs and the good dwarfs, and to the lion. And that night there was a great feast in Cair Paravel, and revelry and dancing, and gold flashed and wine flowed, and answering to the music inside, but stranger, sweeter, and more piercing, came the music of the sea people.

But amidst all these rejoicings Aslan himself quietly slipped away. And when the Kings and Queens noticed that he wasn't there they said nothing about it. For Mr. Beaver had warned them, "He'll be coming and going," he had said. "One day you'll see him and another you won't. He doesn't like being tied down—and of course he has other countries to attend to. It's quite all right. He'll often drop in. Only you mustn't press him. He's wild, you know. Not like a *tame* lion."

And now, as you see, this story is nearly (but not quite) at an end. These two Kings and two Queens governed Narnia well and long and happy was their reign.

At first much of their time was spent in seeking out the remnants of the White Witch's army and destroying them, and indeed for a long time there would be news of evil things lurking in the wilder parts of the forest—a haunting here and a killing there, a glimpse of a werewolf one month and a rumour of a hag the next. But in the end all that foul brood was stamped out. And they made good laws and kept the peace and saved good trees from being unnecessarily cut down, and liberated young dwarfs and young satyrs from being sent to school, and generally stopped busybodies and interferers and encouraged ordinary people who wanted to live and let live. And they drove back the fierce giants (quite a different sort from Giant Rumblebuffin) on the North of Narnia when these ventured across the frontier. And they entered into friendship and alliance with countries beyond the sea and paid them visits of state and received visits of state from them. And they themselves grew and changed as the years passed over them. And Peter became a tall and deep chested man and a great warrior, and he was called King Peter the Magnificent. And Susan grew into a tall and gracious woman with black hair that fell almost to her feet and the Kings of the countries beyond the sea began to send ambassadors asking for her hand in marriage. And she was called Queen Susan the Gentle. Edmund was a graver and quieter man than Peter, and great in council and judgement. He was called King Edmund the Just. But as for Lucy, she was always gay and golden haired, and all Princes in those parts desired her to be their Queen, and her own people called her Queen Lucy the Valiant.

So they lived in great joy and if ever they remembered their life in this world it was only as one remembers a dream. And one year it fell out that Tumnus (who was a middle-aged Faun by now and beginning to be stout) came down river and brought them news that the White Stag had once more appeared in his parts— the White Stag who would give you wishes if you caught him. So these two Kings and two Queens with the principal members of their court, rode a-hunting with horns and hounds in the Western Woods to follow the White Stag. And they had not hunted long before they had a sight of him. And he led them a great pace over rough and smooth and through thick and thin, till the horses of all the courtiers were tired out and only these four were still following. And they saw the stag enter into a thicket where their horses could not follow. Then said King Peter (for they talked in quite a different style now, having been Kings and Queens for so long) "Fair Consorts, let us now alight from our horses and follow this beast into the thicket; for in all my days I never hunted a nobler quarry."

"Sir," said the others, "even so let us do."

So they alighted and tied their horses to trees and went on into the thick wood on foot. And as soon as they had entered it Queen Susan said,

"Fair friends, here is a great marvel, for I seem to see a tree of iron."

"Madam," said King Edmund, "if you look well upon it you shall see it is a pillar of iron with a lantern set on the top thereof."

"Marry, a strange device," said King Peter, "to set a lantern here where the trees cluster so thick about it and so high above it that if it were lit it should give light to no man!"

"Sir," said Queen Lucy. "By likelihood when this post and this lamp were set here there were smaller trees in the place, or fewer, or none. For this is a young wood and the iron post is old." And they stood looking upon it. Then said King Edmund,

"I know not how it is, but this lamp on the post worketh upon me strangely. It runs in my mind that I have seen the like before; as it were a dream, or in the dream of a dream."

"Sir," answered they all, "it is even so with us also."

"And more," said Queen Lucy, "for it will not go out of my mind that if we pass this post and lantern, either we shall find strange adventures or else some great change of our fortunes."

"Madam," said King Edmund, "the like foreboding stirreth in my heart also."

"And in mine, fair brother," said King Peter.

"And in mine too," said Queen Susan. "Wherefore by my council we shall lightly return to our horses and follow this White Stag no further."

"Madam," said King Peter, "therein I pray thee to have me excused. For never since we four were Kings and Queens in Narnia have we set our hands to any high matter, as battles, quests, feats of arms, acts of justice, and the like, and then given over; but always what we have taken in hand, the same we have achieved."

"Sister," said Queen Lucy, "my royal brother speaks rightly. And it seems to me we should be shamed if for any fearing or foreboding we turned back from following so noble a beast as now we have in chase."

"And so say I," said King Edmund. "And I have such desire to find the signification of this thing that I would not by my good will turn back for the richest jewel in all Narnia and all the islands."

"Then in the name of Aslan," said Queen Susan, "if ye will all have it so, let us go on and take the adventure that shall fall to us."

So these Kings and Queens entered the thicket, and before they had gone a score of paces they all remembered that the thing they had seen was called a lamp-post, and before they had gone twenty more, they noticed that they were making their way not through branches but through coats. And next moment they all came tumbling out of a wardrobe door into the empty room, and they were no longer Kings and Queens in their hunting array but just Peter, Susan, Edmund and Lucy in their old clothes. It was the same day and the same hour of the day on which they had all gone into the wardrobe to hide. Mrs. Macready and the visitors were still talking in the passage; but luckily they never came into the empty room and so the children weren't caught.

And that would have been the very end of the story if it hadn't been that they felt they really must explain to the Professor why four of the coats out of his wardrobe were missing. And the Professor, who was a very remarkable man, didn't tell them not to be silly or not to tell lies, but believed the whole story. "No," he said, "I don't think it will be any good trying to go back through the wardrobe door to get the coats. You won't get into Narnia again by *that* route.

Nor would the coats be much use by now if you did! Eh? What's that? Yes, of course you'll get back to Narnia again some day. Once a King in Narnia, always a King in Narnia. But don't go trying to use the same route twice. Indeed, don't *try* to get there at all. It'll happen when you're not looking for it. And don't talk too much about it even among yourselves. And don't mention it to anyone else unless you find that they've had adventures of the same sort themselves. What's that? How will you know? Oh, you'll *know* all right. Odd things, they say—even their looks—will let the secret out. Keep your eyes open. Bless me, what *do* they teach them at these schools?"

And that is the very end of the adventures of the wardrobe. But if the Professor was right it was only the beginning of the adventures of Narnia.

The End

PART IV

ADULT

FICTION

C. S. LEWIS'S first effort at publishing prose came to fruition in *The Pilgrim's Regress* (1933). This is a book that is at once autobiographical and patterned on John Bunyan's *Pilgrim's Progress*. The adult fiction genre suited Lewis well and he eventually wrote seven novels communicating spiritual truths as he perceived them. His angle of vision apparently coincides with the insight of many other people because all of his novels are still in print.

Any thoughtful contemporary reader will detect spiritual themes in Lewis's fiction. Among the most prominent are the struggle between good and evil and the consequences of rebellion against God's laws. However, not all of today's readers will be familiar with the overarching themes that emerge, in one form or another, in all of his fiction. Lewis was a careful student of the Bible, and the entire biblical drama of creation, the fall, judgment, redemption, and the hope for a renewed creation and eternal life, is manifested in his fiction.

This drama unfolds in his space trilogy: *Out of the Silent Planet* (1938), *Perelandra* (1943) and *That Hideous Strength* (1945). Different aspects of the overall theme are presented in his fantasy on heaven and hell, *The Great Divorce* (1945), and we find the hellish consequences of selfishness masquerading as love in *Till We Have Faces: A Myth Retold* (1956).

Lewis long believed *Perelandra* to be his artistically best work. He did not change his mind until he bestowed the honor on *Till We Have Faces*, a novel he published seven years before he died. Because this latter novel, a retelling of the myth of Psyche and Cupid, is often difficult for the beginning reader to understand, the unabridged *Perelandra* is reprinted here.

In the twilight of his career Lewis grew less pleased with his fictional account of Screwtape, a secretary to the High Command of Hell, who continually wrote letters of instruction, admonition and reprimand to his young nephew Wormwood, a newcomer to the corps of tempters. The reading public, however, has not shared Lewis's disillusionment. *The Screwtape Letters* is still one of the author's best-selling and most influential books. Four epistles from that popular work are reproduced here.

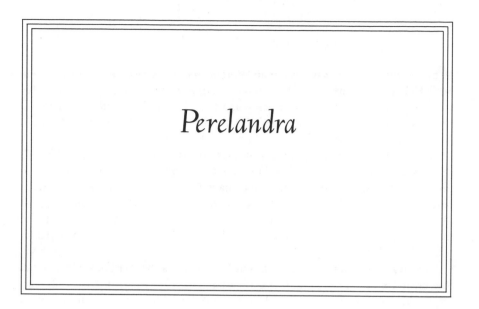

Perelandra

PREFACE

THIS STORY can be read by itself but is also a sequel to *Out of the Silent Planet* in which some account was given of Ransom's adventures in Mars—or, as its inhabitants call it, *Malacandra*. All the human characters in this book are purely fictitious and none of them is allegorical.

C. S. L.

1

As i left the railway station at Worchester and set out on the three-mile walk to Ransom's cottage, I reflected that no one on that platform could possibly guess the truth about the man I was going to visit. The flat heath which spread out before me (for the village lies all behind and to the north of the station) looked an ordinary heath. The gloomy five-o'clock sky was such as you might see on any autumn afternoon. The few houses and the clumps of red or yellowish trees were in no way remarkable. Who could imagine that a little farther on in that quiet landscape I should meet and shake by the hand a man who had lived and eaten and drunk in a world forty million miles distant from London, who had seen this Earth from where it looks like a mere point of green fire, and who had spoken face to face with a creature whose life began before our own planet was inhabitable?

For Ransom had met other things in Mars besides the Martians. He had met the creatures called *eldila,* and specially that great eldil who is the ruler of Mars or, in their speech, the *Oyarsa* of *Malacandra.* The eldila are very different from any planetary creatures. Their physical organism, if organism it can be called, is quite unlike either the human or the Martian. They do not eat, breed, breathe, or suffer natural death, and to that extent resemble thinking minerals more than they resemble anything we should recognise as an animal. Though they appear on planets and may even seem to our senses to be sometimes resident in them, the precise spatial location of an eldil at any moment presents great problems. They themselves regard space (or "Deep Heaven") as their true habitat, and the planets are to them not closed worlds but merely moving points—perhaps even interruptions—in what we know as the Solar System and they as the Field of Arbol.

At present I was going to see Ransom in answer to a wire which had said "Come down Thursday if possible. Business." I guessed what sort of business he meant, and that was why I kept on telling myself that it would be perfectly delightful to spend a night with Ransom and also kept on feeling that I was not enjoying the prospect as much as I ought to. It was the eldila that were my trouble. I could just get used to the fact that Ransom had been to Mars . . . but to have met an eldil, to have spoken with something whose life appeared to be practically unending. . . . Even the journey to Mars was bad enough. A man who has been in another world does not come back unchanged. One can't put the difference into words. When the man is a friend it may become painful: the old footing is not easy to recover. But much worse my growing conviction that, since his return, the eldila were not leaving him alone. Little things in his conversation, little mannerisms, accidental allusions which he made and then drew back with an awkward apology, all suggested that he was keeping strange company; that there were—well, Visitors—at that cottage.

As I plodded along the empty, unfenced road which runs across the middle of Worchester Common I tried to dispel my growing sense of *malaise* by analysing it. What, after all, was I afraid of? The moment I had put this question I regretted it. I was shocked to find that I had mentally used the word "afraid." Up till then I had tried to pretend that I was feeling only distaste, or embarrassment, or even boredom. But the mere word *afraid* had let the cat out of the bag. I realised now that my emotion was neither more, nor less, nor other, than Fear. And I realised that I was afraid of two things—afraid that sooner or later I myself might meet an eldil, and afraid that I might get "drawn in." I suppose every one knows this fear of getting "drawn in"—the moment at which a man realises that what had seemed mere speculations are on the point of landing him in the Communist Party or the Christian Church—the sense that a door has just slammed and left him on the inside. The thing was such sheer bad luck. Ransom himself had been taken to Mars (or Malacandra) against his will and almost by accident, and I had become connected with his affair by another accident. Yet here we were both getting more and more involved in what I could only describe as inter-planetary politics. As to my intense wish never to come into contact with the eldila myself, I am not sure whether I can make you understand it. It was something more than a prudent desire to avoid creatures alien in kind, very powerful, and very intelligent. The truth was that all I heard about them served to connect two things which one's mind tends to keep separate, and that connecting gave one a sort of shock. We tend to think about non-human intelligences in two distinct categories which we label "scientific" and "supernatural" respectively. We think, in one mood, of Mr. Wells' Martians (very unlike the real Malacandrians, by the bye), or his Selenites. In quite a different mood we let our minds loose on the possibility of angels, ghosts, fairies, and the like. But the very moment we are compelled to recognise a creature in either class as *real* the distinction begins to get blurred: and when it is a creature like an eldil the distinction vanishes altogether. These things were not animals—to that extent one had to classify them with the second group; but they had some kind of material vehicle whose presence could (in principle) be scientifically verified. To that extent they belonged to the first group. The distinction between natural and supernatural, in fact, broke down; and when it had done so, one realised how great a comfort it had been—how it had eased the burden of intolerable strangeness which this universe imposes on us by dividing it into two halves and encouraging the mind never to think of both in the same context. What price we may have paid for this comfort in the way of false security and accepted confusion of thought is another matter.

"This is a long, dreary road," I thought to myself. "Thank goodness I haven't anything to carry." And then, with a start of realisation, I remembered that I ought to be carrying a pack, containing my things for the night. I swore to myself. I must have left the thing in the train. Will you believe me when I say that my immediate impulse was to turn back to the station and "do something about it"?

Of course there was nothing to be done which could not equally well be done by ringing up from the cottage. That train, with my pack in it, must by this time be miles away.

I realise that now as clearly as you do. But at the moment it seemed perfectly obvious that I must retrace my steps, and I had indeed begun to do so before reason or conscience awoke and set me once more plodding forwards. In doing this I discovered more clearly than before how very little I wanted to do it. It was such hard work that I felt as if I were walking against a headwind; but in fact it was one of those still, dead evenings when no twig stirs, and beginning to be a little foggy.

The farther I went the more impossible I found it to think about anything except these eldila. What, after all, did Ransom really know about them? By his own account the sorts which he had met did not usually visit our own planet—or had only begun to do so since his return from Mars. We had eldila of our own, he said, Tellurian eldils, but they were of a different kind and mostly hostile to man. That, in fact, was why our world was cut off from communication with the other planets. He described us as being in a state of siege, as being, in fact, an enemy-occupied territory, held down by eldils who were at war both with us and with the eldils of "Deep Heaven," or "space." Like the bacteria on the microscopic level, so these co-inhabiting pests on the macroscopic permeate our whole life invisibly and are the real explanation of that fatal bent which is the main lesson of history. If all this were true, then, of course, we should welcome the fact that eldila of a better kind had at last broken the frontier (it is, they say, at the Moon's orbit) and were beginning to visit us. Always assuming that Ransom's account was the correct one.

A nasty idea occurred to me. Why should not Ransom be a dupe? If something from outer space were trying to invade our planet, what better smoke-screen could it put up than this very story of Ransom's? Was there the slightest evidence, after all, for the existence of the supposed maleficent eldils on this earth? How if my friend were the unwitting bridge, the Trojan Horse, whereby some possible invader were effecting its landing on Tellus? And then once more, just as when I had discovered that I had no pack, the impulse to go no farther returned to me. "Go back, go back," it whispered to me, "send him a wire, tell him you were ill, say you'll come some other time—anything." The strength of the feeling astonished me. I stood still for a few moments telling myself not to be a fool, and when I finally resumed my walk I was wondering whether this might be the beginning of a nervous breakdown. No sooner had this idea occurred to me than it also became a new reason for not visiting Ransom. Obviously, I wasn't fit for any such jumpy "business" as his telegram almost certainly referred to. I wasn't even fit to spend an ordinary week-end away from home. My only sensible course was to turn back at once and get safe home, before I lost my memory or became hysterical, and to put myself in the hands of a doctor. It was sheer madness to go on.

I was now coming to the end of the heath and going down a small hill, with a copse on my left and some apparently deserted industrial buildings on my right. At the bottom the evening mist was partly thick. "They call it a Breakdown *at first,*" I thought. Wasn't there some mental disease in which quite ordinary objects looked to the patient unbelievably ominous? . . . looked, in fact, just as that abandoned factory looks to me now? Great bulbous shapes of cement, strange brickwork bogeys, glowered at me over dry scrubby grass pock-marked with grey pools and intersected with the remains of a light railway. I was reminded of things which Ransom had seen in that other world: only there, they were people. Long spindle-like giants whom he called Sorns. What made it worse was that he regarded them as good people—very much nicer, in fact, than our own race. He was in league with them! How did I know he was even a dupe? He might be something worse . . . and again I came to a standstill.

The reader, not knowing Ransom, will not understand how contrary to all reason this idea was. The rational part of my mind, even at that moment, knew perfectly well that even if the whole universe were crazy and hostile, Ransom was sane and wholesome and honest. And this part of my mind in the end sent me forward—but with a reluctance and a difficulty I can hardly put into words. What enabled me to go on was the knowledge (deep down inside me) that I was getting nearer at every stride to the one friend: but I *felt* that I was getting nearer to the one enemy—the traitor, the sorcerer, the man in league with "them" . . . walking into the trap with my eyes open, like a fool. "They call it a breakdown at first," said my mind, "and send you to a nursing home; later on they move you to an asylum."

I was past the dead factory now, down in the fog, where it was very cold. Then came a moment—the first one—of absolute terror and I had to bite my lips to keep myself from screaming. It was only a cat that had run across the road, but I found myself completely unnerved. "Soon you will really be screaming," said my inner tormentor, "running round and round, screaming, and you won't be able to stop it."

There was a little empty house by the side of the road, with most of the windows boarded up and one staring like the eye of a dead fish. Please understand that at ordinary times the idea of a "haunted house" means no more to me than it does to you. No more; but also, no less. At that moment it was nothing so definite as the thought of a ghost that came to me. It was just the *word* "haunted." "Haunted" . . . "haunting" . . . what a quality there is in that first syllable! Would not a child who had never heard the word before and did not know its meaning shudder at the mere sound if, as the day was closing in, it heard one of its elders say to another "This house is haunted"?

At last I came to the cross-roads by the little Wesleyan chapel where I had to turn to the left under the beech trees. I ought to be seeing the lights from Ransom's windows by now—or was it past black-out time? My watch had stopped, and I didn't know. It was dark enough but that might be due to the fog and the trees. It wasn't the dark I was afraid of, you understand. We have all known times when inanimate objects seemed to have almost a facial expression, and it was the expression of this bit of road which I did not like. "It's not true," said my mind, "that people who are really going mad never think they're going mad." Suppose that real insanity had chosen this place in which to begin? In that case, of course, the black enmity of those dripping trees—their horrible expectancy—would be a hallucination. But that did not make it any better. To think that the spectre you see is an illusion does not rob him of his terrors: it simply adds the further terror of madness itself—and then on top of that the horrible surmise that those whom the rest call mad have, all along, been the only people who see the world as it really is.

This was upon me now. I staggered on into the cold and the darkness, already half convinced that I must be entering what is called Madness. But each moment my opinion about sanity changed. Had it ever been more than a convention—a comfortable set of blinkers, an agreed mode of wishful thinking, which excluded from our view the full strangeness and malevolence of the universe we are compelled to inhabit? The things I had begun to know during the last few months of my acquaintance with Ransom already amounted to more than "sanity" would admit; but I had come much too far to dismiss them as unreal. I doubted his interpretation, or his good faith. I did not doubt the existence of the things he had met in Mars—the Pfifltriggi, the Hrossa, and the Sorns—nor of these interplanetary eldila. I did not even doubt the reality of that mysterious being whom the eldila call Maleldil and to whom they appear to give a total obedience such as no Tellurian dictator can command. I knew what Ransom supposed Maleldil to be.

Surely that was the cottage. It was very well blacked-out. A childish, whining thought arose on my mind: why was he not out at the gate to welcome me? An even more childish thought followed it. Perhaps he *was* in the garden waiting for me, hiding. Perhaps he would jump on me from behind. Perhaps I should see a figure that looked like Ransom standing with its back to me and when I spoke to it, it would turn round and show a face that was not human at all. . . .

I have naturally no wish to enlarge on this phase of my story. The state of mind I was in was one which I look back on with humiliation. I would have passed it over if I did not think that some account of it was necessary for a full understanding of what follows—and, perhaps, of some other things at well. At all events, I *can't* really describe how I reached the front door of the cottage. Somehow or other, despite the loathing and dismay that pulled me back and a sort of invisible wall of resistance that met me in the face, fighting for each step, and almost shrieking as a harmless spray of the hedge touched my face, I managed to get through the gate and up the little path. And there I was, drumming on the door and wringing the handle and shouting to him to let me in as if my life depended on it.

There was no reply—not a sound except the echo of the sounds I had been making myself. There was only something white fluttering on the knocker. I guessed, of course, that it was a note. In striking a match to read it by, I discovered how very shaky my hands had become; and when the match went out I realised how dark the evening had grown. After several attempts I read the thing. "Sorry. Had to go up to Cambridge. Shan't be back till the late train. Eatables in larder and bed made up in your usual room. Don't wait supper for me unless you feel like it—E. R." And immediately the impulse to retreat, which had already assailed me several times, leaped upon me with a sort of demoniac violence. Here was my retreat left open, positively inviting me. Now was my chance. If anyone expected me to go into that house and sit there alone for several hours, they were mistaken! But then, as the thought of the return journey began to take shape in my mind, I faltered. The idea of setting out to traverse the avenue of beech trees again (it was really dark now) with this house behind me (one had the absurd feeling that it could follow one) was not attractive. And then, I hope, something better came into my mind—some rag of sanity and some reluctance to let Ransom down. At least I could try the door to see if it were really unlocked. I did. And it was. Next moment, I hardly know how, I found myself inside and let it slam behind me.

It was quite dark, and warm. I groped a few paces forward, hit my shin violently against something, and fell. I sat still for a few seconds nursing my leg. I thought I knew the layout of Ransom's hall-sitting-room pretty well and couldn't imagine what I had blundered into. Presently I groped in my pocket, got out my matches, and tried to strike a light. The head of the match flew off. I stamped on it and sniffed to make sure it was not smouldering on the carpet. As soon as I sniffed I became aware of a strange smell in the room. I could not for the life of me make out what it was. It had an unlikeness to ordinary domestic smells as great as that of some chemicals, but it was not a chemical kind of smell at all. Then I struck another match. It flickered and went out almost at once—not unnaturally, since I was sitting on the door-mat and there are few front doors even in better built houses than Ransom's country cottage which do not admit a draught. I had seen nothing by it except the palm of my own hand hollowed in an attempt to guard the flame. Obviously I must get away from the door. I rose gingerly and felt my way forward. I came at once to an obstacle—something smooth and very cold that rose a little higher than my knees. As I touched it I realised that it was the source of the smell. I groped my way along this to the left and finally came to the end of it. It seemed to present several surfaces and I couldn't picture the shape. It was not a table, for it had no top. One's hand groped along the rim of a kind of low wall—the thumb on the outside and the fingers down inside the enclosed space. If it had felt like wood I should have supposed it to be a large packing-case. But it was not wood. I thought for a moment that it was wet, but soon decided that I was mistaking coldness for moisture. When I reached the end of it I struck my third match.

I saw something white and semi-transparent—rather like ice. A great big thing, very long: a kind of box, an open box: and of a disquieting shape which

I did not immediately recognize. It was big enough to put a man into. Then I took a step back, lifting the lighted match higher to get a more comprehensive view, and instantly tripped over something behind me. I found myself sprawling in darkness, not on the carpet, but on more of the cold substance with the odd smell. How many of the infernal things were there?

I was just preparing to rise again and hunt systematically round the room for a candle when I heard Ransom's name pronounced; and almost, but not quite, simultaneously I saw the thing I had feared so long to see. I heard Ransom's name pronounced: but I should not like to say I heard a voice pronounce it. The sound was quite astonishingly unlike a voice. It was perfectly articulate: it was even, I suppose, rather beautiful. But it was, if you understand me, inorganic. We feel the difference between animal voices (including those of the human animal) and all other noises pretty clearly, I fancy, though it is hard to define. Blood and lungs and the warm, moist cavity of the mouth are somehow indicated in every Voice. Here they were not. The two syllables sounded more as if they were played on an instrument than as if they were spoken: and yet they did not sound mechanical either. A machine is something we make out of natural materials; this was more as if rock or crystal or light had spoken of itself. And it went through me from chest to groin like the thrill that goes through you when you think you have lost your hold while climbing a cliff.

That was what I heard. What I saw was simply a very faint rod or pillar of light. I don't think it made a circle of light either on the floor or the ceiling, but I am not sure of this. It certainly had very little power of illuminating its surroundings. So far, all is plain sailing. But it had two other characteristics which are less easy to grasp. One was its colour. Since I saw the thing I must obviously have seen it either white or coloured; but no efforts of my memory can conjure up the faintest image of what that colour was. I try blue, and gold, and violet, and red, but none of them will fit. How it is possible to have a visual experience which immediately and ever after becomes impossible to remember, I do not attempt to explain. The other was its angle. It was not at right angles to the floor. But as soon as I have said this, I hasten to add that this way of putting it is a later reconstruction. What one actually felt at the moment was that the column of light was vertical but the floor was not horizontal—the whole room seemed to have heeled over as if it were on board ship. The impression, however produced, was that this creature had reference to some horizontal, to some whole system of directions, based outside the Earth, and that its mere presence imposed that alien system on me and abolished the terrestrial horizontal.

I had no doubt at all that I was seeing an eldil, and little doubt that I was seeing the archon of Mars, the Oyarsa of Malacandra. And now that the thing had happened I was no longer in a condition of abject panic. My sensations were, it is true, in some ways very unpleasant. The fact that it was quite obviously not organic—the knowledge that intelligence was somehow located in this homogeneous cylinder of light but not related to it as our consciousness is related to our brains and nerves—was profoundly disturbing.[1] It would not fit into our categories. The response which we ordinarily make to a living creature and that which we make to an inanimate object were here both equally inappropriate. On the other hand, all those doubts which I had felt before I entered the cottage as to whether these creatures were friend or foe, and whether Ransom were a pioneer or a dupe, had for the moment vanished. My fear was now of another kind. I felt sure that the creature was what we call "good," but I wasn't sure whether I liked "goodness" so much as I had supposed. This is a very terrible experience. As long as what you are afraid of is something evil, you may still hope that the good may come to your rescue. But suppose you struggle through to the good and find that it also is dreadful? How if food itself turns out to be the very thing you can't eat, and home the very place you can't live, and your very comforter the person who makes you uncomfortable? Then, indeed, there is no rescue possible: the last card has been played. For a second or two I was nearly in that condition. Here at last was a bit of that world from beyond the world, which I had always supposed that I loved and desired, breaking through and appearing to my senses: and I didn't like it, I wanted it to go away. I wanted every possible distance, gulf, curtain, blanket, and barrier to be placed between it and me. But I did not fall quite into the gulf. Oddly enough my very sense of helplessness saved me and steadied me. For now I was quite obviously "drawn in." The struggle was over. The next decision did not lie with me.

Then, like a noise from a different world, came the opening of the door and the sound of boots on the door-mat, and I saw, silhouetted against the greyness of the night in the open doorway, a figure which I recognized as Ransom. The speaking which was not a voice came again out of the rod of light, and Ransom, instead of moving, stood still and answered it. Both speeches were in a strange polysyllabic language which I had not heard before. I make no attempt to excuse the feelings which awoke in me when I heard the unhuman sound addressing my friend and my friend answering it in the unhuman language. They are, in fact, inexcusable, but if you think they are improbable at such a

---

[1] In the text I naturally keep to what I thought and felt at the time, since this alone is first-hand evidence: but there is obviously room for much further speculation about the form in which *eldila* appear to our senses. The only serious considerations of the problem so far are to be sought in the early seventeenth century. As a starting point for future investigation I recommend the following from Natvilcius (*De Aethereo at aerio Corpore*, Basel, 1627, II. xii.); *liquet simplicem flammam sensibus nostris subjectam non esse corpus proprie dictum angeli vel daemonis, sed potius aut illius corporis sensorium aut superficiem corporis in coelesti dispositione locorum supra cogitationes humanas existentis* ("It appears that the homogeneous flame perceived by our senses is not the body, properly so called, of an angel or daemon, but rather either the sensorium of that body or the surface of a body which exists after a manner beyond our conception in the celestial frame of special references."). By the "celestial frame of references" I take him to mean what we should now call "multi-dimensional space." Not, of course, that Natvilcius knew anything about multi-dimensional geometry, but that he had reached empirically what mathematics has since reached on theoretical grounds.

juncture, I must tell you plainly that you have read neither history nor your own heart to much effect. They were feelings of resentment, horror, and jealousy. It was in my mind to shout out, "Leave your familiar alone, you damned magician, and attend to Me."

What I actually said was, "Oh, Ransom. Thank God you've come."

2

THE DOOR was slammed (for the second time that night) and after a moment's groping Ransom had found and lit a candle. I glanced quickly round and could see no one but ourselves. The most noticeable thing in the room was the big white object. I recognized the shape well enough this time. It was a large coffin-shaped casket, open. On the floor beside it lay its lid, and it was doubtless this that I had tripped over. Both were made of the same white material, like ice, but more cloudy and less shining.

"By Jove, I'm glad to see you," said Ransom, advancing and shaking hands with me. "I'd hoped to be able to meet you at the station, but everything has had to be arranged in such a hurry and I found at the last moment that I'd got to go up to Cambridge. I never intended to leave you to make *that* journey alone." Then, seeing, I suppose, that I was still staring at him rather stupidly, he added, "I say—you're *all right*, aren't you? You got through the barrage without any damage?"

"The barrage?—I don't understand."

"I was thinking you would have met some difficulties in getting here."

"Oh, *that!*" said I. "You mean it wasn't just my nerves? There really was something in the way?"

"Yes. They didn't want you to get here. I was afraid something of the sort might happen but there was no time to do anything about it. I was pretty sure you'd get through somehow."

"By *they* you mean the others—our own eldila?"

"Of course. They've got wind of what's on hand. . . ."

I interrupted him. "To tell you the truth, Ransom," I said, "I'm getting more worried every day about the whole business. It came into my head as I was on my way here———"

"Oh, they'll put all sorts of things into your head if you let them," said Ransom lightly. "The best plan is to take no notice and keep straight on. Don't try to answer them. They like drawing you into an interminable argument."

"But, look here," said I. "This isn't child's play. Are you quite certain that this Dark Lord, this depraved Oyarsa of Tellus, really exists? Do you know for certain either that there are two sides, or which side is ours?"

He fixed me suddenly with one of his mild, but strangely formidable, glances.

"You are in *real* doubt about either, are you?" he asked.

"No," said I, after a pause, and felt rather ashamed.

"That's all right, then," said Ransom cheerfully. "Now let's get some supper and I'll explain as we go along."

"What's that coffin affair?" I asked as we moved into the kitchen.

"That is what I'm to travel in."

"Ransom!" I exclaimed. "He—it—the eldil—is not going to take you back to Malacandra?"

"Don't!" said he. "Oh, Lewis, you don't understand. Take me back to Malacandra? If only he would! I'd give anything I possess . . . just to look down one of those gorges again and see the blue, blue water winding in and out among the woods. Or to be up on top—to see a Sorn go gliding along the slopes. Or to be back there of an evening when Jupiter was rising, too bright to look at, and all the asteroids like a Milky Way, with each star in it as bright as Venus looks from Earth! And the smells! It is hardly ever out of my mind. You'd expect it to be worse at night when Malacandra is up and I can actually see it. But it isn't then that I get the real twinge. It's on hot summer days—looking up at the deep blue and that thinking that *in there*, millions of miles deep where I can never, never get back to it, there's a place I know, and flowers at that very moment growing over Meldilorn, and friends of mine, going about their business, who would welcome me back. No. No such luck. It's not Malacandra I'm being sent to. It's Perelandra."

"That's what we call Venus, isn't it?"

"Yes."

"And you say you're being sent."

"Yes. If you remember, before I left Malacandra the Oyarsa hinted to me that my going there at all might be the beginning of a whole new phase in the life of the Solar System—the Field of Arbol. It might mean, he said, that the isolation of our world, the siege, was beginning to draw to an end."

"Yes. I remember."

"Well, it really does look as if something of the sort were afoot. For one thing, the two sides, as you call them, have begun to appear much more clearly, much less mixed, here on Earth, in our own human affairs—to show in something a little more like their true colours."

"I see that all right."

"The other thing is this. The black archon—our own bent Oyarsa—is meditating some sort of attack on Perelandra."

"But is he at large like that in the Solar System? Can he get there?"

"That's just the point. He can't get there in his own person, in his own photosome or whatever we should call it. As you know, he was driven back within these bounds centuries before any human life existed on our planet. If he ventured to show himself outside the Moon's orbit he'd be driven back again—by main force. That would be a different kind of war. You or I could contribute no more to it than a flea could contribute to the defence of Moscow. No. He must be attempting Perelandra in some different way."

"And where do you come in?"

"Well—simply I've been ordered there."

"By the—by Oyarsa, you mean?"

"No. The order comes from much higher up. They all do, you know, in the long run."

"And what have you got to do when you get there?"

"I haven't been told."

"You are just part of the Oyarsa's *entourage?*"

"Oh, no. He isn't going to be there. He is to transport me to Venus—to deliver me there. After that, as far as I know, I shall be alone."

"But, look here, Ransom—I mean . . ." my voice trailed away.

"I know!" said he with one of his singularly disarming smiles. "You are feeling the absurdity of it. Dr. Elwin Ransom setting out single-handed to combat powers and principalities. You may even be wondering if I've got megalomania."

"I didn't mean that quite," said I.

"Oh, but I think you did. At any rate that is what I have been feeling myself ever since that thing was sprung on me. But when you come to think of it, is it odder than what all of us have to do every day? When the Bible used that very expression about fighting with principalities and powers and depraved hyper-somatic beings at great heights (our translation is very misleading at that point, by the way) it meant that quite ordinary people were to do the fighting."

"Oh, I dare say," said I. "But that's rather different. That refers to a moral conflict."

Ransom threw back his head and laughed. "Oh, Lewis, Lewis," he said, "you are inimitable, simply inimitable!"

"Say what you like, Ransom, there *is* a difference."

"Yes. There is. But not a difference that makes it megalomania to think that any of us might have to fight either way. I'll tell you how I look at it. Haven't you noticed how in our own little war here on earth, there are different phases, and while any one phase is going on people get into the habit of thinking and behaving as if it was going to be permanent? But really the thing is changing under your hands all the time, and neither your assets nor your dangers this year are the same as the year before. Now your idea that ordinary people will never have to meet the Dark Eldila in any form except a psychological or moral form—as temptations or the like—is simply an idea that held good for a certain phase of the cosmic war: the phase of the great siege, the phase which gave to our planet its name of Thulcandra, the *silent* planet. But supposing that phase is passing? In the next phase it may be anyone's job to meet them . . . well, in some quite different mode."

"I see."

"Don't imagine I've been selected to go to Perelandra because I'm anyone in particular. One never can see, or not till long afterwards, why *any* one was selected for *any* job. And when one does, it is usually some reason that leaves no room for vanity. Certainly, it is never for what the man himself would have regarded as his chief qualifications. I rather fancy I am being sent because those two blackguards who kidnapped me and took me to Malacandra, did something which they never intended: namely, gave a human being a chance to learn that language."

"What language do you mean?"

"*Hressa-Hlab,* of course. The language I learned in Malacandra."

"But surely you don't imagine they will speak the same language on Venus?"

"Didn't I tell you about that?" said Ransom, leaning forward. We were now at table and had nearly finished our cold meat and beer and tea. "I'm surprised I didn't, for I found out two or three months ago, and scientifically it is one of the most interesting things about the whole affair. It appears we were quite mistaken in thinking *Hressa-Hlab* the peculiar speech of Mars. It is really what may be called Old Solar, *Hlab-Eribol-ef-Cordi.*"

"What on earth do you mean?"

"I mean that there was originally a common speech for all rational creatures inhabiting the planets of our system: those that were ever inhabited, I mean— what the eldils call the Low Worlds. Most of them, of course, have never been inhabited and never will be. At least not what we'd call inhabited. That original speech was lost on Thulcandra, our own world, when our whole tragedy took place. No human language now known in the world is descended from it."

"But what about the other two languages on Mars?"

"I admit I don't understand about them. One thing I do know, and I believe I could prove it on purely philological grounds. They are incomparably less ancient than *Hressa-Hlab,* specially *Surnibur,* the speech of the Sorns. I believe it could be shown that *Surnibur* is, by Malacandrian standards, quite a modern development. I doubt if its birth can be put further back than a date which would fall within our Cambrian Period."

"And you think you will find *Hressa-Hlab,* or Old Solar, spoken on Venus?"

"Yes. I shall arrive knowing the language. It saves a lot of trouble—though, as a philologist I find it rather disappointing."

"But you've no idea what you are to do, or what conditions you will find?"

"No idea at all what I'm to do. There are jobs, you know, where it is essential that one should *not* know too much beforehand . . . things one might have to say which one couldn't say effectively if one had prepared them. As to conditions, well, I don't know much. It will be warm: I'm to go naked. Our astronomers don't know anything about the surface of Perelandra at all. The outer layer of her atmosphere is too thick. The main problem, apparently, is whether she revolves on her own axis or not, and at what speed. There are two schools of thought. There's a man called Schiaparelli who thinks she revolves once on herself in the same time it takes her to go once round Arbol—I mean, the Sun. The other people think she revolves on her own axis once in every twenty-three hours. That's one of the things I shall find out."

"If Schiaparelli is right there'd be perpetual day on one side of her and perpetual night on the other?"

He nodded, musing. "It'd be a funny frontier," he said presently. "Just think of it. You'd come to a county of eternal twilight, getting colder and darker every mile you went. And then presently you wouldn't be able to go further because there'd be no more air. I wonder can you stand in the day, just on the right side of the frontier, and look *into* the night which you can never reach? And perhaps see a star or two—the only place you *could* see them, for of course in the Day-Lands they would never be visible. . . . Of course if they have a scientific civilisation they may have diving-suits or things like submarines on wheels for going into the Night."

His eyes sparkled, and even I who had been mainly thinking of how I should miss him and wondering what chances there were of my ever seeing him again, felt a vicarious thrill of wonder and of longing to know. Presently he spoke again.

"You haven't yet asked me where *you* come in," he said.

"Do you mean I'm to go too?" said I, with a thrill of exactly the opposite kind.

"Not at all. I mean you are to pack me up, and to stand by to unpack me when I return—if all goes well."

"Pack you? Oh, I'd forgotten about that coffin affair. Ransom, how on earth are you going to travel in that thing? What's the motive power? What about air—and food—and water? There's only just room for you to lie in it."

"The Oyarsa of Malacandra himself will be the motive power. He will simply move it to Venus. Don't ask me how. I have no idea what organs or instruments they use. But a creature who has kept a planet in its orbit for several billions of years will be able to manage a packing-case!"

"But what will you eat? How will you breathe?"

"He tells me I shall need to do neither. I shall be in some state of suspended animation, as far as I can make out. I can't understand him when he tries to describe it. But that's his affair."

"Do you feel quite happy about it?" said I, for a sort of horror was beginning once more to creep over me.

"If you mean, Does my reason accept the view that he will (accidents apart) deliver me safe on the surface of Perelandra?—the answer is Yes," said Ransom. "If you mean, Do my nerves and my imagination respond to this view?—I'm afraid the answer is No. One can believe in anæsthetics and yet feel in a panic when they actually put the mask over your face. I think I feel as a man who believes in the future life feels when he is taken out to face a firing party. Perhaps it's good practice."

"And I'm to pack you into that accursed thing?" said I.

"Yes," said Ransom. "That's the first step. We must get out into the garden as soon as the sun is up and point it so that there are no trees or buildings in the way. Across the cabbage bed will do. Then I get in—with a bandage across my eyes, for those walls won't keep out all the sunlight once I'm beyond the air—and you screw me down. After that, I think you'll just see it glide off."

"And then?"

"Well, then comes the difficult part. You must hold yourself in readiness to come down here again the moment you are summoned, to take off the lid and let me out when I return."

"When do you expect to return?"

"Nobody can say. Six months—a year—twenty years. That's the trouble. I'm afraid I'm laying a pretty heavy burden on you."

"I might be dead."

"I know. I'm afraid part of your burden is to select a successor: at once, too. There are four or five people whom we can trust."

"What will the summons be?"

"Oyarsa will give it. It won't be mistakable for anything else. You needn't bother about that side of it. One other point. I've no particular reason to suppose I shall come back wounded. But just in case—if you can find a doctor whom we can let into the secret, it might be just as well to bring him with you when you come down to let me out."

"Would Humphrey do?"

"The very man. And now for some more personal matters. I've had to leave you out of my will, and I'd like you to know why."

"My dear chap, I never thought about your will till this moment."

"Of course not. But I'd like to have left you something. The reason I haven't, is this. I'm going to disappear. It is possible I may not come back. It's just conceivable there might be a murder trial, and if so one can't be too careful. I mean, for your sake. And now for one or two other private arrangements."

We laid our heads together and for a long time we talked about those matters which one usually discusses with relatives and not with friends. I got to know a lot more about Ransom than I had known before, and from the number of odd people whom he recommended to my care, "If ever I happened to be able to do anything," I came to realise the extent and intimacy of his charities. With every sentence the shadow of approaching separation and a kind of graveyard gloom began to settle more emphatically upon us. I found myself noticing and loving all sorts of little mannerisms and expressions in him such as we notice always in a woman we love, but notice in a man only as the last hours of his leave run out or the date of the probably fatal operation draws near. I felt our nature's incurable incredulity; and could hardly believe that what was now so close, so tangible and (in a sense) so much at my command, would in a few hours be wholly inaccessible, an image—soon, even an elusive image—in my memory. And finally a sort of shyness fell between us because each knew what the other was feeling. It had got very cold.

"We must be going soon," said Ransom.

"Not till he—the Oyarsa—comes back," said I—though, indeed, now that the thing was so near I wished it to be over.

"He has never left us," said Ransom, "he has been in the cottage all the time."

"You mean he has been waiting in the next room all these hours?"

"Not waiting. They never have that experience. You and I are conscious of waiting, because we have a body that grows tired or restless, and therefore a sense of cumulative duration. Also we can distinguish duties and spare time and therefore have a conception of leisure. It is not like that with him. He has been here all this time, but you can no more call it *waiting* than you can call the whole of his existence *waiting*. You might as well say that a tree in a wood was waiting, or the sunlight waiting on the side of a hill." Ransom yawned. "I'm tired," he said, "and so are you. I shall sleep well in that coffin of mine. Come. Let us lug it out."

We went in to the next room and I was made to stand before the featureless flame which did not wait but just was, and there, with Ransom as our interpreter, I was in some fashion presented and with my own tongue sworn in to this great business. Then we took down the blackout and let in the grey, comfortless morning. Between us we carried out the casket and the lid, so cold they seemed to burn our fingers. There was a heavy dew on the grass and my feet were soaked through at once. The eldil was with us, outside there, on the little lawn; hardly visible to my eyes at all in the daylight. Ransom showed me the clasps of the lid and how it was to be fastened on, and then there was some miserable hanging about, and then the final moment when he went back into the house and reappeared, naked; a tall, white, shivering, weary scarecrow of a man at that pale, raw hour. When he had got into the hideous box he made me tie a thick black bandage round his eyes and head. Then he lay down. I had no thoughts of the planet Venus now and no real belief that I should see him again. If I had dared I would have gone back on the whole scheme: but the other thing—the creature that did not wait—was there, and the fear of it was upon me. With feelings that have since often returned to me in nightmare I fastened the cold lid down on top of the living man and stood back. Next moment I was alone. I didn't see how it went. I went back indoors and was sick. A few hours later I shut up the cottage and returned to Oxford.

Then the months went past and grew to a year and a little more than a year, and we had raids and bad news and hopes deferred and all the earth became full of darkness and cruel habitations, till the night when Oyarsa came to me again. After that there was a journey in haste for Humphrey and me, standings in crowded corridors and waitings at small hours on windy platforms, and finally the moment when we stood in clear early sunlight in the little wilderness of deep weeds which Ransom's garden had now become and saw a black speck against the sunrise and then, almost silently, the casket had glided down between us. We flung ourselves upon it and had the lid off in about a minute and a half.

"Good God! All smashed to bits," I cried at my first glance of the interior.

"Wait a moment," said Humphrey. And as he spoke the figure in the coffin began to stir and then sat up, shaking off as it did so a mass of red things which had covered its head and shoulders and which I had momentarily mistaken for ruin and blood. As they streamed off him and were caught in the wind I perceived them to be flowers. He blinked for a second or so, then called us by our names, gave each of us a hand, and stepped out on the grass.

"How are you both?" he said. "You're looking rather knocked up."

I was silent for a moment, astonished at the form which had risen from that narrow house—almost a new Ransom, glowing with health and rounded with muscle and seemingly ten years younger. In the old days he had been beginning to show a few grey hairs; but now the beard which swept his chest was pure gold.

"Hullo, you've cut your foot," said Humphrey: and I saw now that Ransom was bleeding from the heel.

"Ugh, it's cold down here," said Ransom. "I hope you've got the boiler going and some hot water—and some clothes."

"Yes," said I, as we followed him into the house. "Humphrey thought of all that. I'm afraid I shouldn't have."

Ransom was now in the bathroom, with the door open, veiled in clouds of steam, and Humphrey and I were talking to him from the landing. Our questions were more numerous than he could answer.

"That idea of Schiaparelli's is all wrong," he shouted. "They have an ordinary day and night there," and "No, my heel doesn't hurt—or, at least, it's only just begun to," and "Thanks, any old clothes. Leave them on the chair" and "No thanks. I don't somehow feel like bacon or eggs or anything of that kind. No fruit, you say? Oh well, no matter. Bread or porridge or something" and "I'll be down in five minutes now."

He kept on asking if we were really all right and seemed to think we looked ill. I went down to get the breakfast, and Humphrey said he would stay and examine and dress the cut on Ransom's heel. When he rejoined me I was looking at one of the red petals which had come in the casket.

"That's rather a beautiful flower," said I, handing it to him.

"Yes," said Humphrey, studying it with the hands and eyes of a scientist. "What extraordinary delicacy! It makes an English violet seem like a coarse weed."

"Let's put some of them in water."

"Not much good. Look—it's withered already."

"How do you think he is?"

"Tip-top general. But I don't quite like that heel. He says the hæmorrhage has been going on for a long time."

Ransom joined us, fully dressed, and I poured out the tea. And all that day and far into the night he told us the story that follows.

3

W HAT IT IS LIKE to travel in a celestial coffin was a thing that Ransom never described. He said he couldn't. But odd hints about that journey have come out at one time or another when he was talking of quite different matters.

According to his own account he was not what we call conscious, and yet at the same time the experience was a very positive one with a quality of its own. On one occasion, someone had been talking about "seeing life" in the popular sense of knocking about the world and getting to know people, and B. who was present (and who is an Anthroposophist) said something I can't quite remember about "seeing life" in a very different sense. I think he was referring to some system of meditation which claimed to make "the form of Life itself" visible to the inner eye. At any rate Ransom let himself in for a long cross-examination by failing to conceal the fact that he attached some very definite idea to this. He even went so far—under extreme pressure—as to say that life appeared to him, in that condition, as a "coloured shape." Asked "what colour," he gave a curious look and could only say "what colours! yes, what colours!" But then he spoiled it all by adding, "of course it wasn't colour at all really. I mean, not what we'd call colour," and shutting up completely for the rest of the evening. Another hint came out when a sceptical friend of ours called McPhee was arguing against the Christian doctrine of the resurrection of the human body. I was his victim at the moment and he was pressing on me in his Scots way with such questions as "So you think you're going to have guts and palate for ever in a world where there'll be no eating, and genital organs in a world without copulation? Man, ye'll have a grand time of it!" when Ransom suddenly burst out with great excitement, "Oh, don't you see, you ass, that there's a difference between a trans-sensuous life and a non-sensuous life?" That, of course, directed McPhee's fire to him. What emerged was that in Ransom's opinion the present functions and appetites of the body would disappear, not because they were atrophied but because they were, as he said "engulfed." He used the word "trans-sexual" I remember and began to hunt about for some similar words to apply to eating (after rejecting "trans-gastronomic"), and since he was not the only philologist present, that diverted the conversation into different channels. But I am pretty sure he was thinking of something he had experienced on his voyage to Venus. But perhaps the most mysterious thing he ever said about it was this. I was questioning him on the subject—which he doesn't often allow—and had incautiously said, "Of course I realise it's all rather too vague for you to put into words," when he took me up rather sharply, for such a patient man, by saying, "On the contrary, it is words that are vague. The reason why the thing can't be expressed is that it's too *definite* for language." And that is about all I can tell you of his journey. One thing is certain, that he came back from Venus even more changed than he had come back from Mars. But of course that may have been because of what happened to him after his landing.

To that landing, as Ransom narrated it to me, I will now proceed. He seems to have been awakened (if that is the right word) from his indescribable celestial state by the sensation of falling—in other words, when he was near enough to Venus to feel Venus as something in the downward direction. The next thing he noticed was that he was very warm on one side and very cold on the other, though neither sensation was so extreme as to be really painful. Anyway, both were soon swallowed up in the prodigious white light from below which began to penetrate through the semi-opaque walls of the casket. This steadily increased and became distressing in spite of the fact that his eyes were protected. There is no doubt this was the *albedo,* the outer veil of very dense atmosphere with which Venus is surrounded and which reflects the sun's rays with intense power. For some obscure reason he was not conscious, as he had been on his approach to Mars, of his own rapidly increasing weight. When the white light was just about to become unbearable, it disappeared altogether, and very soon after the cold on his left side and the heat on his right began to decrease and to be replaced by an equable warmth. I take it he was now in the outer layer of the Perelandrian atmosphere—at first in a pale, and later in a tinted, twilight. The prevailing colour, as far as he could see through the sides of the casket, was golden or coppery. By this time he must have been very near the surface of the planet, with the length of the casket at right angles to that surface—falling feet downwards like a man in a lift. The sensation of falling—helpless as he was and unable to move his arms—became frightening. Then suddenly there came a great green darkness, an unidentifiable noise—the first message from the new world—and a marked drop in temperature. He seemed now to have assumed a horizontal position and also, to his great surprise, to be moving not downwards but upwards; though, at the moment, he judged this to be an illusion. All this time he must have been making faint, unconscious efforts to move his limbs, for now he suddenly found that the sides of his prison-house yielded to pressure. He *was* moving his limbs, encumbered with some viscous substance. Where was the casket? His sensations were very confused. Sometimes he seemed to be falling, sometimes to be soaring upwards, and then again to be moving in the horizontal plane. The viscous substance was white. There seemed to be less of it every moment . . . white, cloudy stuff just like the casket, only not solid. With a horrible shock he realized that it *was* the casket, the casket melting, dissolving away, giving place to an indescribable confusion of colour—a rich, varied world in which nothing, for the moment, seemed palpable. There was no casket now. He was turned out—deposited—solitary. He was in Perelandra.

His first impression was of nothing more definite than of something slanted— as though he were looking at a photograph which had been taken when the camera was not held level. And even this lasted only for an instant. The slant was replaced by a different slant; then two slants rushed together and made a peak, and the peak flattened suddenly into a horizontal line, and the horizontal line tilted and became the edge of a vast gleaming slope which rushed furiously towards him. At the same moment he felt that he was being lifted. Up and up he soared till it seemed as if he must reach the burning dome of gold that hung above him instead of a sky. Then he was at a summit; but almost before his glance had taken in a huge valley that yawned beneath him—shining green like glass and marbled with streaks of scummy white—he was rushing down into that valley at perhaps thirty miles an hour. And now he realised that there was a delicious coolness over every part of him except his head, that his feet rested on nothing, and that he had for some time been performing unconsciously the actions of a swimmer. He was riding the foamless swell of an ocean, fresh and cool after the fierce temperatures of Heaven, but warm by earthly standards—as warm as a shallow bay with sandy bottom in a sub-tropical climate. As he rushed smoothly up the great convex hillside of the next wave he got a mouthful of the water. It was hardly at all flavoured with salt; it was drinkable—like fresh water and only, by an infinitesimal degree, less insipid. Though he had not been aware of thirst till now, his drink gave him a quite astonishing pleasure. It was almost like meeting Pleasure itself for the first time. He buried his flushed face in the green translucence, and when he withdrew it, found himself once more on the top of a wave.

There was no land in sight. The sky was pure, flat gold like the background of a medieval picture. It looked very distant—as far off as a cirrhus cloud looks from earth. The ocean was gold too, in the offing, flecked with innumerable shadows. The nearer waves, though golden where their summits caught the light, were green on their slopes: first emerald, and lower down a lustrous bottle green, deepening to blue where they passed beneath the shadow of other waves.

All this he saw in a flash; then he was speeding down once more into the trough. He had somehow turned on his back. He saw the golden roof of that world quivering with a rapid variation of paler lights as a ceiling quivers at the reflected sunlight from the bath-water when you step into your bath on a summer morning. He guessed that this was the reflection of the waves wherein he swam. It is a phenomenon observable three days out of five in the planet of love. The queen of those seas views herself continually in a celestial mirror.

Up again to the crest, and still no sight of land. Something that looked like clouds—or could it be ships?—far away on his left. Then down, down, down—he thought he would never reach the end of it . . . this time he noticed how dim the light was. Such tepid revelry in water—such glorious bathing, as one would have called it on earth, suggested as its natural accompaniment a blazing sun. But here there was no such thing. The water gleamed, the sky burned with gold, but all was rich and dim, and his eyes fed upon it undazzled and unaching. The very names of green and gold, which he used perforce in describing the scene, are too harsh for the tenderness, the muted iridescence, of that warm, maternal, delicately gorgeous world. It was mild to look upon as evening, warm like summer noon, gentle and winning like early dawn. It was altogether pleasurable. He sighed.

There was a wave ahead of him now so high that it was dreadful. We speak idly in our own world of seas mountain high when they are not much more than mast high. But this was the real thing. If the huge shape had been a hill of land and not of water he might have spent a whole forenoon or longer walking the slope before he reached the summit. It gathered him into itself and hurled him up to that elevation in a matter of seconds. But before he reached the top, he almost cried out in terror. For this wave had not a smooth top like the others. A horrible crest appeared; jagged and billowy and fantastic shapes, unnatural, even unliquid, in appearance, sprouted from the ridge. Rocks? Foam? Beasts? The question hardly had time to flash through his mind before the thing was upon him. Involuntarily he shut his eyes. Then he found himself once more rushing downhill. Whatever it was, it had gone past him. But it had been something. He had been struck in the face. Dabbing with his hands he found no blood. He had been struck by something soft which did him no harm but merely stung like a lash because of the speed at which he met it. He turned round on his back again—already, as he did so, soaring thousands of feet aloft to the high water of the next ridge. Far down below him in a vast momentary valley he saw the thing that had missed him. It was an irregularly shaped object with many curves and reentrants. It was variegated in colours like a patch-work quilt—flame-colour, ultramarine, crimson, orange, gamboge, and violet. He could not say more about it for the whole glimpse lasted so short a time. Whatever the thing was, it was floating, for it rushed up the slope of the opposite wave and over the summit and out of sight. It sat to the water like a skin, curving as the water curved. It took the wave's shape at the top, so that for a moment half of it was already out of sight beyond the ridge and the other half still lying on the hither slope. It behaved rather like a mat of weeds on a river—a mat of weeds that takes on every contour of the little ripples you make by rowing past it—but on a very different scale. This thing might have been thirty acres or more in area.

Words are slow. You must not lose sight of the fact that his whole life on Venus up till now had lasted less than five minutes. He was not in the least tired, and not yet seriously alarmed as to his power of surviving in such a world. He had confidence in those who had sent him there, and for the meantime the coolness of the water and the freedom of his limbs were still a novelty and a delight; but more than all these was something else at which I have already hinted and which can hardly be put into words—the strange sense of excessive pleasure which seemed somehow to be communicated to him through all his senses at once. I use the word "excessive" because Ransom himself could only describe it by saying that for his first few days on Perelandra he was haunted, not by a feeling of guilt, but by surprise that he had no such feeling. There was an exuberance or prodigality of sweetness about the mere act of living which our race finds it difficult not to associate with forbidden and extravagant actions. Yet it is a violent world too. Hardly had he lost sight of the floating object when his eyes were stabbed by an unendurable light. A grading, blue-to-violet illumination made the golden sky seem dark by comparison and in a moment of time revealed more of the new planet than he had yet seen. He saw the waste of waves spread illimitably before him, and far away, at the very end of the world, against the sky, a single smooth column of ghastly green standing up, the one thing fixed and vertical in this universe of shifting slopes. Then the rich twilight rushed back (now seeming almost darkness) and he heard thunder. But it has a different *timbre* from terrestrial thunder, more resonance, and even, when distant, a kind of tinkling. It is the laugh, rather than the roar, of heaven. Another flash followed, and another, and then the storm was all about him. Enormous purple clouds came driving between him and the golden sky, and with no preliminary drops a rain such as he never experienced began to fall. There were no lines in it; the water above him seemed only less continuous than the sea, and he found it difficult to breathe. The flashes were incessant. In between them, when he looked in any direction except that of the clouds, he saw a completely changed world. It was like being at the centre of a rainbow, or in a cloud of multi-coloured steam. The water which now filled the air was turning sea and sky into a bedlam of flaming and writhing transparencies. He was dazzled and now for the first time a little frightened. In the flashes he saw, as before, only the endless sea and the still green column at the end of the world. No land anywhere—not the suggestion of a shore from one horizon to the other.

The thunder was ear-splitting and it was difficult to get enough air. All sorts of things seemed to be coming down in the rain—living things apparently. They looked like preternaturally airy and graceful frogs—sublimated frogs—and had the colour of dragon-flies, but he was in no plight to make careful observations. He was beginning to feel the first symptoms of exhaustion and was completely confused by the riot of colours in the atmosphere. How long this state of affairs lasted he could not say, but the next thing that he remembers noticing with any accuracy was that the swell was decreasing. He got the impression of being near the end of a range of water-mountains and looking down into lower country. For a long time he never reached this lower country; what had seemed, by comparison with the seas which he had met on his first arrival, to be calm water, always turned out to be only slightly smaller waves when he rushed down into them. There seemed to be a good many of the big floating objects about. And these, again, from some distance looked like an archipelago, but always, as he drew nearer and found the roughness of the water they were riding, they became more like a fleet. But in the end there was no doubt that the swell was subsiding. The rain stopped. The waves were merely of Atlantic height. The rainbow colours grew fainter and more transparent and the golden sky first showed timidly through them and then established itself again from horizon to horizon. The waves grew smaller still. He began to breathe freely. But he was now really tired, and beginning to find leisure to be afraid.

One of the great patches of floating stuff was sidling down a wave not more than a few hundred yards away. He eyed it eagerly, wondering whether he could climb on to one of these things for rest. He strongly suspected that they would prove mere mats of weed, or the topmost branches of submarine forests, incapable of supporting him. But while he thought this, the particular one on which his eyes were fixed crept up a wave and came between him and the sky. It was not flat. From its tawny surface a whole series of feathery and billowy shapes arose, very unequal in height; they looked darkish against the dim glow of the golden roof. Then they all tilted one way as the thing which carried them curled over the crown of the water and dipped out of sight. But here was another, not thirty yards away and bearing down on him. He struck out towards it, noticing as he did so how sore and feeble his arms were and feeling his first thrill of true fear. As he approached it he saw that it ended in a fringe of undoubtedly vegetable matter; it trailed, in fact, a dark red skirt of tubes and strings and bladders. He grabbed at them and found he was not yet near enough. He began swimming desperately, for the thing was gliding past him at some ten miles an hour. He grabbed again and got a handful of whip-like red strings, but they pulled out of his hand and almost cut him. Then he thrust himself right in among them, snatching wildly straight before him. For one second he was in a kind of vegetable broth of gurgling tubes and exploding bladders; next moment his hands caught something firmer ahead, something almost like very soft wood. Then, with the breath nearly knocked out of him and a bruised knee, he found himself lying face downward on a resistant surface. He pulled himself an inch or so further. Yes—there was no doubt now; one did not go through; it was something one could lie on.

It seems that he must have remained lying on his face, doing nothing and thinking nothing for a very long time. When he next began to take any notice of his surroundings he was, at all events, well rested. His first discovery was that he lay on a dry surface, which on examination turned out to consist of something very like heather, except for the colour which was coppery. Burrowing idly with his fingers he found something friable like dry soil, but very little of it, for almost at once he came upon a base of tough interlocked fibres. Then he rolled round on his back, and in doing so discovered the extreme resilience of the surface on which he lay. It was something much more than the pliancy of the heatherlike vegetation, and felt more as if the whole floating island beneath the vegetation were a kind of mattress. He turned and looked "inland"—if that is the right word—and for one instant what he saw looked very like a country. He was looking up a long lonely valley with a copper-coloured floor bordered on each side by gentle slopes clothed in a kind of many-coloured forest. But even as he took this in, it became a long copper-coloured ridge with the forest sloping *down* on each side of it. Of course he ought to have been prepared for this, but he says that it gave him an almost sickening shock. The thing had looked, in that first glance, so like a real country that he had forgotten it was floating—an island if you like, with hills and valleys, but hills and valleys which changed places every minute so that only a cinematograph could make a contour map of it. And that is the nature of the floating islands of Perelandra. A photograph, omitting the colours and the perpetual variation of shape, would make them look deceptively like landscapes in our own world, but the reality is very different; for they are dry and fruitful like land but their only shape is the inconstant shape of the water beneath them. Yet the land-like appearance proved hard to resist. Although he had now grasped with his brain what was happening, Ransom had not yet grasped it with his muscles and nerves. He rose to take a few paces inland—and downhill, as it was at the moment of his rising—and immediately found himself flung down on his face, unhurt because of the softness of the weed. He scrambled to his feet—saw that he now had a steep slope to ascend—and fell a second time. A blessed relaxation of the strain in which he had been living since his arrival dissolved him into weak laughter. He rolled to and fro on the soft fragrant surface in a real schoolboy fit of the giggles.

This passed. And then for the next hour or two he was teaching himself to walk. It was much harder than getting your sea-legs on a ship, for whatever the sea is doing the deck of the ship remains a plane. But this was like learning to walk on water itself. It took him several hours to get a hundred years away from the edge, or coast, of the floating island; and he was proud when he could go five paces without a fall, arms outstretched, knees bent in readiness for sudden change of balance, his whole body swaying and tense like that of one who is learning to walk the tightrope. Perhaps he would have learned more quickly if his falls had not been so soft, if it had not been so pleasant, having fallen, to lie still and gaze at the golden roof and hear the endless soothing noise of the water and breathe in the curiously delightful smell of the herbage. And then, too, it was so strange, after rolling head over heels down into some little dell, to open his eyes and find himself seated on the central mountain peak of the whole island looking down like Robinson Crusoe on field and forest to the shores in every direction, that a man could hardly help sitting there a few minutes longer—and then being detained again because, even as he made to rise, mountain and valley alike had been obliterated and the whole island had become a level plain.

At long last he reached the wooded part. There was an undergrowth of feathery vegetation, about the height of gooseberry bushes, coloured like sea anemones. Above this were the taller growths—strange trees with tube-like trunks of grey and purple spreading rich canopies above his head, in which orange, silver, and blue were the predominant colours. Here, with the aid of the tree trunks, he could keep his feet more easily. The smells in the forest were beyond all that he had ever conceived. To say that they made him feel hungry and thirsty would be misleading; almost, they created a new kind of hunger and thirst, a longing that seemed to flow over from the body into the soul and which was a heaven to feel. Again and again he stood still, clinging to some branch to steady himself, and breathed it all in, as if breathing had become a kind of ritual. And at the same time the forest landscape furnished what would have been a dozen landscapes on earth—now level wood with trees as vertical as towers, now a deep bottom where it was surprising not to find a stream, now a wood growing on a hillside, and now again, a hilltop whence one looked down through slanted boles at the distant sea. Save for the inorganic sound of waves there was utter silence about him. The sense of his solitude became intense without becoming at all painful—only adding, as it were, a last touch of wildness to the unearthly pleasures that surrounded him. If he had any fear now, it was a faint apprehension that his reason might be in danger. There was something in Perelandra that might overload a human brain.

Now he had come to a part of the wood where great globes of yellow fruit hung from the trees—clustered as toy-balloons are clustered on the back of the balloon-man and about the same size. He picked one of them and turned it over and over. The rind was smooth and firm and seemed impossible to tear open. Then by accident one of his fingers punctured it and went through into coldness. After a moment's hesitation he put the little aperture to his lips. He had meant to extract the smallest, experimental sip, but the first taste put his caution all to flight. It was, of course, a taste, just as his thirst and hunger had been thirst and hunger. But then it was so different from every other taste that it seemed mere pedantry to call it a taste at all. It was like the discovery of a totally new *genus* of pleasures, something unheard of among men, out of all reckoning, beyond all covenant. For one draught of this on earth wars would be fought and nations betrayed. It could not be classified. He could never tell us, when he came back to the world of men, whether it was sharp or sweet, savoury or voluptuous, creamy or piercing. "Not like that" was all he could ever say to such inquiries. As he let the empty gourd fall from his hand and was about to pluck a second one, it came into his head that he was now neither hungry nor thirsty. And yet to repeat a pleasure so intense and almost so spiritual seemed an obvious thing to do. His reason, or what we commonly take to be reason in our own world, was all in favour of tasting this miracle again; the childlike innocence of fruit, the labours he had undergone, the uncertainty of the future, all seemed to commend the action. Yet something seemed opposed to this "reason." It is difficult to suppose that this opposition came from desire, for what desire would turn from so much deliciousness? But for whatever cause, it appeared to him better not to taste again. Perhaps the experience had been so complete that repetition would be a vulgarity—like asking to hear the same symphony twice in a day.

As he stood pondering over this and wondering how often in his life on earth he had reiterated pleasures not through desire, but in the teeth of desire and in obedience to a spurious rationalism, he noticed that the light was changing. It was darker behind him than it had been; ahead, the sky and sea shone through the wood with a changed intensity. To step out of the forest would have been a minute's work on earth; on this undulating island it took him longer, and when he finally emerged into the open an extraordinary spectacle met his eyes. All day there had been no variation at any point in the golden roof to mark the sun's position, but now the whole of one half-heaven revealed it. The orb itself remained invisible, but on the rim of the sea rested an arc of green so luminous that he could not look at it, and beyond that, spreading almost to the zenith, a great fan of colour like a peacock's tail. Looking over his shoulder he saw the whole island ablaze with blue, and across it and beyond it, even to the ends of the world, his own enormous shadow. The sea, far calmer now than he had yet seen it, smoked towards heaven in huge dolomites and elephants of blue and purple vapour, and a light wind, full of sweetness, lifted the hair on his forehead.

The day was burning to death. Each moment the waters grew more level; something not far removed from silence began to be felt. He sat down cross-legged on the edge of the island, the desolate lord, it seemed, of this solemnity. For the first time it crossed his mind that he might have been sent to an uninhabited world, and the terror added, as it were, a razor-edge to all that profusion of pleasure.

Once more, a phenomenon which reason might have anticipated took him by surprise. To be naked yet warm, to wander among summer fruits and lie in sweet heather—all this had led him to count on a twilit night, a mild midsummer greyness. But before the great apocalyptic colours had died out in the west, the eastern heaven was black. A few moments, and the blackness had reached the western horizon. A little reddish light lingered at the zenith for a time, during which he crawled back to the woods. It was already, in common parlance, "too dark to see your way." But before he had lain down among the trees the real night had come—seamless darkness, not like night but like being in a coal-cellar, darkness in which his own hand held before his face was totally invisible. Absolute blackness, the undimensioned, the impenetrable, pressed on his eyeballs. There is no moon in that land, no star pierces the golden roof. But the darkness was warm. Sweet new scents came stealing out of it. The world had no size now. Its boundaries were the length and breadth of his own body and the little patch of soft fragrance which made his hammock, swaying ever more and more gently. Night covered him like a blanket and kept all loneliness from him. The blackness might have been his own room. Sleep came like a fruit which falls into the hand almost before you have touched the stem.

4

AT RANSOM'S WAKING something happened to him which perhaps never happens to a man until he is out of his own world: he saw reality, and thought it was a dream. He opened his eyes and saw a strange heraldically coloured tree loaded with yellow fruits and silver leaves. Round the base of the indigo stem was coiled a small dragon covered with scales of red gold. He recognized the garden of the Hesperides at once. "This is the most vivid dream I have ever had," he thought. By some means or other he then realised that he was awake; but extreme comfort and some trance-like quality, both in the sleep which had just left him and in the experience to which he had awaked, kept him lying motionless. He remembered how in the very different world called Malacandra—that cold, archaic world, as it now seemed to him—he had met the original of the Cyclops, a giant in a cave and a shepherd. Were all the things which appeared as mythology on earth scattered through other worlds as realities? Then the realisation came to him "You are in an unknown planet, naked and alone, and that may be a dangerous animal." But he was not badly frightened. He knew that the ferocity of terrestrial animals was, by cosmic standards, an exception, and had found kindness in stranger creatures than this. But he lay quiet a little longer and looked at it. It was a creature of the lizard type, about the size of a St. Bernard dog, with a serrated back. Its eyes were open.

Presently he ventured to rise on one elbow. The creature went on looking at him. He noticed that the island was perfectly level. He sat up and saw, between the stems of the trees, that they were in calm water. The sea looked like gilded glass. He resumed his study of the dragon. Could this be a rational animal—a *hnau* as they said in Malacandra—and the very thing he had been sent there to meet? It did not look like one, but it was worth trying. Speaking in the Old Solar tongue he formed his first sentence—and his own voice sounded to him unfamiliar.

"Stranger," he said, "I have been sent to your world through the Heaven by the servants of Maleldil. Do you give me welcome?"

The thing looked at him very hard and perhaps very wisely. Then, for the first time, it shut its eyes. This seemed an unpromising start. Ransom decided to rise to his feet. The dragon reopened its eyes. He stood looking at it while you could count twenty, very uncertain how to proceed. Then he saw that it was beginning to uncoil itself. By a great effort of will he stood his ground; whether the thing were rational or irrational, flight could hardly help him for long. It detached itself from the tree, gave itself a shake, and opened two shining reptilian wings—bluish gold and bat-like. When it had shaken these and closed them again, it gave Ransom another long stare, and at last, half waddling and half crawling, made its way to the edge of the island and buried its long metallic-looking snout in the water. When it had drunk it raised its head and gave a kind of croaking bleat which was not entirely unmusical. Then it turned, looked yet again at Ransom, and finally approached him. "It's madness to *wait* for it," said the false reason, but Ransom set his teeth and stood. It came right up and began nudging him with its cold snout about his knees. He was in great perplexity. Was it rational and was this how it talked. Was it irrational but friendly—and if so, how should he respond? You could hardly stroke a creature with scales! Or was it merely scratching itself against him? At that moment, with a suddenness which convinced him it was only a beast, it seemed to forget all about him, turned away, and began tearing up the herbage with great avidity. Feeling that honour was now satisfied, he also turned away back to the woods.

There were trees near him loaded with the fruit which he had already tasted, but his attention was diverted by a strange appearance a little farther off. Amid the darker foliage of a greenish-grey thicket something seemed to be sparkling. The impression, caught out of the corner of his eye, had been that of a greenhouse roof with the sun on it. Now that he looked at it squarely it still suggested glass, but glass in perpetual motion. Light seemed to be coming and going in a spasmodic fashion. Just as he was moving to investigate this phenomenon he was startled by a touch on his left leg. The beast had followed him. It was once more nosing and nudging. Ransom quickened his pace. So did the dragon. He stopped; so did it. When he went on again it accompanied him so closely that its side pressed against his thighs and sometimes its cold, hard, heavy foot descended on his. The arrangement was so little to his satisfaction that he was beginning to wonder seriously how he could put an end to it when suddenly his whole attention was attracted by something else. Over his head there hung from a hairy tube-like branch a great spherical object, almost transparent, and shining. It held an area of reflected light in it and at one place a suggestion of rainbow colouring. So this was the explanation of the glass-like appearance in the wood. And looking round he perceived innumerable shimmering globes of the same kind in every direction. He began to examine the nearest one attentively. At first he thought it was moving, then he thought it was not. Moved by a natural impulse he put out his hand to touch it. Immediately his head, face, and shoulders were drenched with what seemed (in that warm world) an ice-cold shower bath, and his nostrils filled with a sharp, shrill, exquisite scent that somehow brought to his mind the verse in Pope, "die of a rose in aromatic pain." Such was the refreshment that he seemed to himself to have been, till now, but half awake. When he opened his eyes—which had closed involuntarily at the shock of moisture—all the colours about him seemed richer and the dimness of that world seemed clarified. A re-enchantment fell upon him. The golden beast at his side seemed no longer either a danger or a nuisance. If a naked man and a wise dragon were indeed the sole inhabitants of this floating paradise, then this also was fitting, for at that moment he had a sensation not of following an adventure but of enacting a myth. To be the figure that he was in this unearthly pattern appeared sufficient.

He turned again to the tree. The thing that had drenched him was quite vanished. The tube or branch, deprived of its pendent globe, now ended in a little quivering orifice from which there hung a bead of crystal moisture. He looked round in some bewilderment. The grove was still full of its iridescent fruit but now he perceived that there was a slow continual movement. A second later he had mastered the phenomenon. Each of the bright spheres was very gradually increasing in size, and each, on reaching a certain dimension, vanished with a faint noise, and in its place there was a momentary dampness on the soil and a soon-fading, delicious fragrance and coldness in the air. In fact, the things were not fruit at all but bubbles. The trees (he christened them at that moment) were bubble-trees. Their life, apparently, consisted in drawing up water from the ocean and then expelling it in this form, but enriched by its short sojourn in their sappy inwards. He sat down to feed his eyes upon the spectacle. Now that he knew the secret he could explain to himself why this wood looked and felt so different from every other part of the island. Each bubble, looked at individually, could be seen to emerge from its parent-branch as a mere bead, the size of a pea, and swell and burst; but looking at the wood as a whole, one was conscious only of a continual faint disturbance of light, an elusive interference with the prevailing Perelandrian silence, an unusual coolness in the air, and a fresher quality in the perfume. To a man born in our world it felt a more out-door place than the open parts of the island, or even the sea. Looking at a fine cluster of the bubbles which hung above his head he thought how easy it would be to get up and plunge oneself through the whole lot of them and to feel, all at once, that magical refreshment multiplied tenfold. But he was restrained by the same sort of feeling which had restrained him over-night from tasting a second gourd. He had always disliked the people who encored a favourite air in the opera—"That just spoils it" had been his comment. But this now appeared to him as a principle of far wider application and deeper moment. This itch to have things over again, as if life were a film that could be unrolled twice or even made to work backwards . . . was it possibly the root of all evil? No: of course the love of money was called that. But money itself—perhaps one valued it chiefly as a defence against chance, a security for being able to have things over again, a means of arresting the unrolling of the film.

He was startled from his meditation by the physical discomfort of some weight on his knees. The dragon had lain down and deposited its long, heavy head across them. "Do you know," he said to it in English, "that you are a considerable nuisance?" It never moved. He decided that he had better try and make friends with it. He stroked the hard dry head, but the creature took no notice. Then his hand passed lower down and found softer surface, or even a chink in the mail. Ah . . . that was where it liked being tickled. It grunted and shot out a long cylindrical slate-coloured tongue to lick him. It rolled round on its back revealing an almost white belly, which Ransom kneaded with his toes. His acquaintance with the dragon prospered exceedingly. In the end it went to sleep.

He rose and got a second shower from a bubble-tree. This made him feel so fresh and alert that he began to think of food. He had forgotten whereabouts on the island the yellow gourds were to be found, and so as he set out to look for them he discovered that it was difficult to walk. For a moment he wondered whether the liquid in the bubbles had some intoxicating quality, but a glance around assured him of the real reason. The plain of copper-coloured heather before him, even as he watched, swelled into a low hill and the low hill moved in his direction. Spellbound anew at the sight of land rolling towards him, like water, in a wave, he forgot to adjust himself to the movement and lost his feet. Picking himself up, he proceeded more carefully. This time there was no doubt about it. The sea was rising. Where two neighbouring woods made a vista to the edge of this living raft he could see troubled water, and the warm wind was now strong enough to ruffle his hair. He made his way gingerly towards the coast, but before he reached it he passed some bushes which carried a rich crop of oval green berries, about three times the size of almonds. He picked one and broke it in two. The flesh was dryish and bread-like, something of the same kind as a banana. It turned out to be good to eat. It did not give the orgiastic and almost alarming pleasure of the gourds, but rather the specific pleasure of plain food—the delight of munching and being nourished, a "Sober certainty of waking bliss." A man, or at least a man like Ransom, felt he ought to say grace over it; and so he presently did. The gourds would have required rather an oratorio or a mystical meditation. But the meal had its unexpected high lights. Every now and then one struck a berry which had a bright red centre: and these were so savoury, so memorable among a thousand tastes, that he would have begun to look for them and to feed on them only, but that he was once more forbidden by that same inner adviser which had already spoken to him twice since he came to Perelandra. "Now on earth," thought Ransom, "they'd soon discover how to breed these redhearts, and they'd cost a great deal more than the others." Money, in fact, would provide the means of saying *encore* in a voice that could not be disobeyed.

When he had finished his meal he went down to the water's edge to drink, but before he arrived there it was already "up" to the water's edge. The island at that moment was a little valley of bright land nestling between hills of green water, and as he lay on his belly to drink he had the extraordinary experience of dipping his mouth in a sea that was higher than the shore. Then he sat upright for a bit with his legs dangling over the edge among the red weeds that fringed this little country. His solitude became a more persistent element in his consciousness. What had he been brought here to do? A wild fancy came into his head that this empty world had been waiting for him as for its first inhabitant, that he was singled out to be the founder, the beginner. It was strange that the utter loneliness through all these hours had not troubled him so much as one night of it on Malacandra. He thought the difference lay in this, that mere chance, or what he took for chance, had turned him adrift in Mars, but here he knew that he was part of a plan. He was no longer unattached, no longer on the outside.

As his country climbed the smooth mountains of dimly lustrous water he had frequent opportunity to see that many other islands were close at hand. They varied from his own island and from one another in their colouring more than he would have thought possible. It was a wonder to see these big mats or carpets of land tossing all around him like yachts in harbour on a rough day—their trees each moment at a different angle just as the masts of the yachts would be. It was a wonder to see some edge of vivid green or velvety crimson come creeping over the top of a wave far above him and then wait till the whole country unrolled itself down the wave's side for him to study. Sometimes his own land and a neighbouring land would be on opposite slopes of a trough, with only a narrow strait of water between them; and then, for the moment, you were cheated with the semblance of a terrestrial landscape. It looked exactly as though you were in a well-wooded valley with a river at the bottom of it. But while you watched, that seeming river did the impossible. It thrust itself up so that the land on either side sloped downwards from it; and then up farther still and shouldered half the landscape out of sight beyond its ridge; and became a huge greeny-gold hog's back of water hanging in the sky and threatening to engulf your own land, which now was concave and reeled backwards to the next roller, and rushing upwards, became convex again.

A clanging, whirring noise startled him. For a moment he fancied he was in Europe and that a plane was flying low over his head. Then he recognized his friend the dragon. Its tail was streaked out straight behind it so that it looked like a flying worm, and it was heading for an island about half a mile away. Following its course with his eyes, he saw two long lines of winged objects, dark against the gold firmament, approaching the same island from the left and the right. But they were not bat-winged reptiles. Peering hard into the distance, he decided that they were birds, and a musical chattering noise, presently wafted to him by a change of the wind, confirmed this belief. They must have been a little larger than swans. Their steady approach to the same island for which the dragon was heading fixed his attention and filled him with a vague feeling of expectation. What followed next raised this to positive excitement. He became aware of some creamily foamed disturbance in the water, much nearer, and making for the same island. A whole fleet of objects was moving in formation. He rose to his feet. Then the lift of a wave cut them off from his sight. Next moment they were visible again, hundreds of feet below him. Silver-coloured objects, all alive with circling and frisking movements . . . he lost them again, and swore. In such a very uneventful world they had become important. Ah . . . ! here they were again. Fish certainly. Very large, obese, dolphin-like fish, two long lines together, some of them spouting columns of rainbow-coloured water from their noses, and one leader. There was something queer about the leader, some sort of projection or malformation on the back. If only the things would remain visible for more than fifty seconds at a time! They had almost reached that other island now, and the birds were all descending to meet them at its edge. There was the leader again, with his hump or pillar on his back. A moment of wild incredulity followed, and then Ransom was balanced, with legs wide apart, on the utmost fringe of his own island and shouting for all he was worth. For at the very moment when the leading fish had reached that neighbouring land, the land had risen up on a wave between him and the sky; and he had seen, in perfect and unmistakable silhouette, the thing on the fish's back reveal itself as a human form—a human form which stepped ashore, turned with a slight inclination of its body towards the fish and then vanished from sight as the whole island slid over the shoulder of the billow. With beating heart Ransom waited till it was in view again. This time it was not between him and the sky. For a second or so the human figure was undiscoverable. A stab of something like despair pierced him. Then he picked it out again—a tiny darkish shape moving slowly between him and a patch of blue vegetation. He waved and gesticulated and shouted till his throat was hoarse, but it took no notice of him. Every now and then he lost sight of it. Even when he found it again, he sometimes doubted whether it were not an optical illusion—some chance figuration of foliage which his intense desire had assimilated to the shape of a man. But always, just before he had despaired, it would become unmistakable again. Then his eyes began to grow tired and he knew that the longer he looked the less he would see. But he went on looking none the less.

At last, from mere exhaustion, he sat down. The solitude, which up till now had been scarcely painful, had become a horror. Any return to it was a possibility he dared not face. The drugging and entrancing beauty had vanished from his surroundings; take that one human form away and all the rest of this world was now pure nightmare, a horrible cell or trap in which he was imprisoned. The suspicion that he was beginning to suffer from hallucinations crossed his mind. He had a picture of living for ever and ever on this hideous island, always really alone but always haunted by the phantoms of human beings, who would come up to him with smiles and outstretched hands, and then fade away as he approached them. Bowing his head on his knees, he set his teeth and endeavoured to restore some order in his mind. At first he found he was merely listening to his own breathing and counting the beats of his heart; but he tried again and presently succeeded. And then, like revelation, came the very simple idea that if he wished to attract the attention of this man-like creature he must wait till he was on the crest of a wave and then stand up so that it would see him outlined against the sky.

Three times he waited till the shore whereon he stood became a ridge, and rose, swaying to the movement of his strange country, gesticulating. The fourth time he succeeded. The neighbouring island was, of course, lying for the moment beneath him like a valley. Quite unmistakably the small dark figure waved back. It detached itself from a confusing background of greenish vegetation and began running towards him—that is, towards the nearer coast of its own island—across an orange-coloured field. It ran easily: the heaving surface of the field did not seem to trouble it. Then his own land reeled downwards and backwards and a great wall of water pushed its way up between the two countries and cut each off from sight of the other. A moment later, and Ransom, from the valley in which he now stood, saw the orange-coloured land pouring itself like a moving hillside down the slightly convex slope of a wave far above him. The creature was still running. The width of water between the two islands was about thirty feet, and the creature was less than a hundred yards away from him. He knew now that it was not merely man-like, but a man—a green man on an orange field, green like the beautifully coloured green beetle in an English garden, running downhill towards him with easy strides and very swiftly. Then the seas lifted his own land and the green man became a foreshortened figure far below him, like an actor seen from the gallery at Covent Garden. Ransom stood on the very brink of his island, straining his body forward and shouting. The green man looked up. He was apparently shouting too, with his hands arched about his mouth; but the roar of the seas smothered the noise and the next moment Ransom's island dropped into the trough of the wave and the high green ridge of sea cut off his view. It was maddening. He was tortured with the fear that the distance between the islands might be increasing. Thank God: here came the orange land over the crest following him down into the pit. And there was the stranger, now on the very shore, face to face with him. For one second the alien eyes looked at his full of love and welcome. Then the whole face changed: a shock as of disappointment and astonishment passed over it. Ransom realised, not without a disappointment of his own, that he had been mistaken for someone else. The running, the waving, the shouts, had not been intended for him. And the green man was not a man at all, but a woman.

It is difficult to say why this surprised him so. Granted the human form, he was presumably as likely to meet a female as a male. But it did surprise him, so that only when the two islands once more began to fall apart into separate wave-valleys did he realise that he had said nothing to her, but stood staring like a fool. And now that she was out of sight he found his brain on fire with doubts. Was *this* what he had been sent to meet? He had been expecting wonders, had been prepared for wonders, but not prepared for a goddess carved apparently out of green stone, yet alive. And then it flashed across his mind—he had not noticed it while the scene was before him—that she had been strangely accompanied. She had stood up amidst a throng of beasts and birds as a tall sapling stands among bushes—big pigeon-coloured birds and flame-coloured birds, and dragons, and beaver-like creatures about the size of rats, and heraldic-looking fish in the sea at her feet. Or had he imagined that? Was this the beginning of the hallucinations he had feared? Or another myth coming out into the world of fact—perhaps a more terrible myth, of Circe or Alcina? And the expression on her face . . . what had she expected to find that made the finding of him such a disappointment?

The other island became visible again. He had been right about the animals. They surrounded her ten or twenty deep, all facing her, most of them motionless, but some of them finding their places, as at a ceremony, with delicate noiseless movements. The birds were in long lines and more of them seemed to be alighting on the island every moment and joining these lines. From a wood of bubble-trees behind her half a dozen creatures like very short-legged and elongated pigs—the dachshunds of the pig world—were waddling up to join the assembly. Tiny frog-like beasts, like those he had seen falling in the rain, kept leaping about her, sometimes higher than her head, sometimes alighting on her shoulders; their colours were so vivid that at first he mistook them for kingfishers. Amidst all this she stood looking at him; her feet together, her arms hanging at her sides, her stare level and unafraid, communicating nothing. Ransom determined to speak, using the Old Solar tongue. "I am from another world," he began and then stopped. The Green Lady had done something for which he was quite unprepared. She raised her arm and pointed at him: not as in menace, but as though inviting the other creatures to behold him. At the same moment her face changed again, and for a second he thought she was going to cry. Instead she burst into laughter—peal upon peal of laughter till her whole body shook with it, till she bent almost double, with her hands resting on her knees, still laughing and repeatedly pointing at him. The animals, like our own dogs in similar circumstances, dimly understood that there was merriment afoot; all manner of gambolling, wing-clapping, snorting, and standing upon hind legs began to be displayed. And still the Green Lady laughed till yet again the wave divided them and she was out of sight.

Ransom was thunderstruck. Had the eldila sent him to meet an idiot? Or an evil spirit that mocked men? Or was it after all a hallucination?—for this was just how a hallucination might be expected to behave. Then an idea occurred to him which would have taken much longer, perhaps, to occur to me or you. It might not be she who was mad but he who was ridiculous. He glanced down at himself. Certainly his legs presented an odd spectacle, for one was brownish-red (like the flanks of a Titian satyr) and the other was white—by comparison, almost a leprous white. As far as self-inspection could go, he had the same parti-coloured appearance all over—no unnatural result of his one-sided exposure to the sun during the voyage. Had this been the joke? He felt a momentary impatience with the creature who could mar the meeting of two worlds with laughter at such a triviality. Then he smiled in spite of himself at the very undistinguished career he was having on Perelandra. For dangers he had been prepared; but to be first a disappointment and then an absurdity . . . Hullo! Here were the Lady and her island in sight again.

She had recovered from her laughter and sat with her legs trailing in the sea, half unconsciously caressing a gazelle-like creature which had thrust its soft nose under her arm. It was difficult to believe that she had ever laughed, ever done anything but sit on the shore of her floating isle. Never had Ransom seen a face so calm, and so unearthly, despite the full humanity of every feature. He decided afterwards that the unearthly quality was due to the complete absence of that element of resignation which mixes, in however slight a degree, with all profound stillness in terrestrial faces. This was a calm which no storm had ever preceded. It might be idiocy, it might be immortality, it might be some condition of mind to which terrestrial experience offered no clue at all. A curious and rather horrifying sensation crept over him. On the ancient planet Malacandra he had met creatures who were not even remotely human in form but who had turned out, on further acquaintance, to be rational and friendly. Under an alien exterior he had discovered a heart like his own. Was he now to have the reverse experience?

For now he realised that the word "human" refers to something more than the bodily form or even to the rational mind. It refers also to that community of blood and experience which unites all men and women on the Earth. But this creature was not of his race; no windings, however intricate, of any genealogical tree, could ever establish a connection between himself and her. In that sense, not one drop in her veins was "human." The universe had produced her species and his quite independently.

All this passed through his mind very quickly, and was speedily interrupted by his consciousness that the light was changing. At first he thought that the green Creature had, of herself, begun to turn bluish and to shine with a strange electric radiance. Then he noticed that the whole landscape was a blaze of blue and purple—and almost at the same time that the two islands were not so close together as they had been. He glanced at the sky. The many-coloured furnace of the short-lived evening was kindled all about him. In a few minutes it would be pitch black . . . and the islands were drifting apart. Speaking slowly in that ancient language, he cried out to her, "I am a stranger. I come in peace. Is it your will that I swim over to your land?"

The Green Lady looked quickly at him with an expression of curiosity.

"What is 'peace'?" she asked.

Ransom could have danced with impatience. Already it was visibly darker and there was no doubt now that the distance between the islands was increasing. Just as he was about to speak again a wave rose between them and once more she was out of sight; and as that wave hung above him, shining purple in the light of the sunset, he noticed how dark the sky beyond it had become. It was already through a kind of twilight that he looked down from the next ridge upon the other island far below him. He flung himself into the water. For some seconds he found a difficulty in getting clear of the shore. Then he seemed to succeed and struck out. Almost at once he found himself back again among the red weeds and bladders. A moment or two of violent struggling followed and then he was free—and swimming steadily—and then, almost without warning, swimming in total darkness. He swam on, but despair of finding the other land, or even of saving his life, now gripped him. The perpetual change of the great swell abolished all sense of direction. It could only be by chance that he would land anywhere. Indeed, he judged from the time he had already been in the water that he must have been swimming *along* the space between the islands instead of across it. He tried to alter his course; then doubted the wisdom of this, tried to return to his original course, and became so confused that he could not be sure he had done either. He kept on telling himself that he must keep his head. He was beginning to be tired. He gave up all attempts to guide himself. Suddenly, a long time after, he felt vegetation sliding past him. He gripped and pulled. Delicious smells of fruit and flowers came to him out of the darkness. He pulled harder still on his aching arms. Finally, he found himself, safe and panting, on the dry, sweet-scented, undulating surface of an island.

5

Ransom must have fallen asleep almost as soon as he landed, for he remembered nothing more till what seemed the song of a bird broke in upon his dreams. Opening his eyes, he saw that it was a bird indeed, a long-legged bird like a very small stork, singing rather like a canary. Full daylight—or what passes for such in Perelandra—was all about him, and in his heart such a premonition of good adventure as made him sit up forthwith and brought him, a moment later, to his feet. He stretched his arms and looked around. He was not on the orange-coloured island, but on the same island which had been his home ever since he came to this planet. He was floating in a dead calm and therefore had no difficulty in making his way to the shore. And there he stopped in astonishment. The Lady's island was floating beside his, divided only by five feet or so of water. The whole look of the world had changed. There was no expanse of sea now visible—only a flat wooded landscape as far as the eye could reach in every direction. Some ten or twelve of the islands, in fact, were here lying together and making a short-lived continent. And there walking before him, as if on the other side of a brook, was the Lady herself—walking with her head a little bowed and her hands occupied in plaiting together some blue flowers. She was singing to herself in a low voice but stopped and turned as he hailed her and looked him full in the face.

"I was young yesterday," she began, but he did not hear the rest of her speech. The meeting, now that it had actually come about, proved overwhelming. You must not misunderstand the story at this point. What overwhelmed him was not in the least the fact that she, like himself, was totally naked. Embarrassment and desire were both a thousand miles away from his experience: and if he was a little ashamed of his own body, that was a shame which had nothing to do with difference of sex and turned only on the fact that he knew his body to be a little ugly and a little ridiculous. Still less was her colour a source of horror to him. In her own world that green was beautiful and fitting; it was his pasty white and angry sunburn which were the monstrosity. It was neither of these; but he found himself unnerved. He had to ask her presently to repeat what she had been saying.

"I was young yesterday," she said. "When I laughed at you. Now I know that the people in your world do not like to be laughed at."

"You say you were young?"

"Yes."

"Are you not young to-day also?"

She appeared to be thinking for a few moments, so intently that the flowers dropped, unregarded, from her hand.

"I see it now," she said presently. "It is very strange to say one is young at the moment one is speaking. But to-morrow I shall be older. And then I shall say I was young to-day. You are quite right. This is great wisdom you are bringing, O Piebald Man."

"What do you mean?"

"This looking backward and forward along the line and seeing how a day has one appearance as it comes to you, and another when you are in it, and a third when it has gone past. Like the waves."

"But you are very little older than yesterday."

"How do you know that?"

"I mean," said Ransom, "a night is not a very long time."

She thought again, and then spoke suddenly, her face lightening. "I see it now," she said. "You think times have lengths. A night is always a night whatever you do in it, as from this tree to that is always so many paces whether you take them quickly or slowly. I suppose that is true in a way. But the waves do not always come at equal distances. I see that you come from a wise world . . . if this is wise. I have never done it before—stepping out of life into the Alongside and looking at oneself living as if one were not alive. Do they all do that in your world, Piebald?"

"What do you know about other worlds?" said Ransom.

"I know this. Beyond the roof it is all Deep Heaven, the high place. And the low is not really spread out as it seems to be" (here she indicated the whole landscape) "but is rolled up into little balls: little lumps of the low swimming in the high. And the oldest and greatest of them have on them that which we have never seen nor heard and cannot at all understand. But on the younger Maleldil has made to grow the things like us, that breathe and breed."

"How have you found all this out? Your roof is so dense that your people cannot see through into Deep Heaven and look at the other worlds."

Up till now her face had been grave. At this point she clapped her hands and a smile such as Ransom had never seen changed her. One does not see that smile here except in children, but there was nothing of the child about it there.

"Oh, I see it," she said. "I am older now. Your world has no roof. You look right out into the high place and see the great dance with your own eyes. You live always in that terror and that delight, and what we must only believe you can behold. Is not this a wonderful invention of Maleldil's? When I was young I could imagine no beauty but this of our own world. But He can think of all, and all different."

"That is one of the things that is bewildering me," said Ransom. "That you are not different. You are shaped like the women of my own kind. I had not expected that. I have been in one other world beside my own. But the creatures there are not at all like you and me."

"What is bewildering about it?"

"I do not see why different worlds should bring forth like creatures. Do different trees bring forth like fruit?"

"But that other world was older than yours," she said.

"How do you know that?" asked Ransom in amazement.

"Maleldil is telling me," answered the woman. And as she spoke the landscape had become different, though with a difference none of the senses would identify. The light was dim, the air gentle, and all Ransom's body was bathed in bliss, but the garden world where he stood seemed to be packed quite full, and as if an unendurable pressure had been laid upon his shoulders, his legs failed him and he half sank, half fell, into a sitting position.

"It all comes into my mind now," she continued. "I see the big furry creatures, and the white giants—what is it you called them?—the Sorns, and the blue rivers. Oh, what a strong pleasure it would be to see them with my outward eyes, to touch them, and the stronger because there are no more of that kind to come. It is only in the ancient worlds they linger yet."

"Why?" said Ransom in a whisper, looking up at her.

"You must know that better than I," she said. "For was it not in your own world that all this happened?"

"All what?"

"I thought it would be you who would tell me of it," said the woman, now in her turn bewildered.

"What are you talking about?" said Ransom.

"I mean," said she, "that in your world Maleldil first took Himself this form, the form of your race and mine."

"You know that?" said Ransom sharply. Those who have had a dream which is very beautiful but from which, nevertheless, they have ardently desired to awake, will understand his sensations.

"Yes, I know that Maleldil has made me older to that amount since we began speaking." The expression on her face was such as he had never seen, and could not steadily look at. The whole of this adventure seemed to be slipping out of his hands. There was a long silence. He stooped down to the water and drank before he spoke again.

"Oh, my Lady," he said, "why do you say that such creatures linger only in the ancient worlds?"

"Are you so young?" she answered. "How could they come again? Since our Beloved became a man, how should Reason in any world take on another form? Do you not understand? That is all over. Among times there is a time that turns a corner and everything this side of it is new. Times do not go backward."

"And can one little world like mine be the corner?"

"I do not understand. Corner with us is not the name of a size."

"And do you," said Ransom with some hesitation—"and do you know *why* He came thus to my world?"

All through this part of the conversation he found it difficult to look higher than her feet, so that her answer was merely a voice in the air above him. "Yes," said the voice. "I know the reason. But it is not the reason you know. There was more than one reason, and there is one I know and cannot tell to you, and another that you know and cannot tell to me."

"And after this," said Ransom, "it will all be men."

"You say it as if you were sorry."

"I think," said Ransom, "I have no more understanding than a beast. I do not well know what I am saying. But I loved the furry people whom I met in Malacandra, that old world. Are they to be swept away? Are they only rubbish in the Deep Heaven?"

"I do not know what *rubbish* means," she answered, "nor what you are saying. You do not mean they are worse because they come early in the history and do not come again? They are their own part of the history and not another. We are on this side of the wave and they on the far side. All is new."

One of Ransom's difficulties was an inability to be quite sure who was speaking at any moment in this conversation. It may (or may not) have been due to the fact that he could not look long at her face. And now he wanted the conversation to end. He had "had enough"—not in the half-comic sense whereby we use those words to mean that a man has had too much, but in the plain sense. He had had his fill, like a man who has slept or eaten enough. Even an hour ago, he would have found it difficult to express this quite bluntly; but now it came naturally to him to say:

"I do not wish to talk any more. But I would like to come over to your island so that we may meet again when we wish."

"Which do you call my island?" said the Lady.

"The one you are on," said Ransom. "What else?"

"Come," she said, with a gesture that made that whole world a house and her a hostess. He slid into the water and scrambled out beside her. Then he bowed, a little clumsily as all modern men do, and walked away from her into a neighbouring wood. He found his legs unsteady and they ached a little; in fact a curious physical exhaustion possessed him. He sat down to rest for a few minutes and fell immediately into dreamless sleep.

He awoke completely refreshed but with a sense of insecurity. This had nothing to do with the fact that he found himself, on waking, strangely attended. At his feet, and with its snout partially resting upon them, lay the dragon; it had one eye shut and one open. As he rose on his elbow and looked about him he found that he had another custodian at his head: a furred animal something like a wallaby but yellow. It was the yellowest thing he had ever seen. As soon as he moved both beasts began nudging him. They would not leave him alone till he rose, and when he had risen they would not let him walk in any direction but one. The dragon was much too heavy for him to shove it out of the way, and the yellow beast danced round him in a fashion that headed him off every direction but the one it wanted him to go. He yielded to their pressure and allowed himself to be shepherded, first through a wood of higher and browner trees than he had yet seen and then across a small open space and into a kind of alley of bubble trees and beyond that into large fields of silver flowers that grew waist-high. And then he saw that they had been bringing him to be shown to their mistress. She was standing a few yards away, motionless but not apparently disengaged—doing something with her mind, perhaps even with her muscles, that he did not understand. It was the first time he had looked steadily at her, himself unobserved, and she seemed more strange to him than before. There was no category in the terrestrial mind which would fit her. Opposites met in her and were fused in a fashion for which we have no images. One way of putting it would be to say that neither our sacred nor our profane art could make her portrait. Beautiful, naked, shameless, young—she was obviously a goddess: but then the face, the face so calm that it escaped insipidity by the very concentration of its mildness, the face that was like the sudden coldness and stillness of a church when we enter it from a hot street—that made her a Madonna. The alert, inner silence which looked out from those eyes overawed him; yet at any moment she might laugh like a child, or run like Artemis or dance like a Mænad. All this against the golden sky which looked as if it were only an arm's length above her head. The beasts raced forward to greet her, and as they rushed through the feathery vegetation they startled from it masses of the frogs, so that it looked as if huge drops of vividly coloured dew were being tossed in the air. She turned as they approached her and welcomed them, and once again the picture was half like many earthly scenes but in its total effect unlike them all. It was not really like a woman making much of a horse, nor yet a child playing with a puppy. There was in her face an authority, in her caresses a condescension, which by taking seriously the inferiority of her adorers made them somehow less inferior—raised them from the status of pets to that of slaves. As Ransom reached her she stooped and whispered something in the ear of the yellow creature, and then, addressing the dragon, bleated to it almost in its own voice. Both of them, having received their congé, darted back into the woods.

"The beasts in your world seem almost rational," said Ransom.

"We make them older every day," she answered. "Is not that what it means to be a beast?"

But Ransom clung to her use of the word *we.*

"That is what I have come to speak to you about," he said. "Maleldil has sent me to your world for some purpose. Do you know what it is?"

She stood for a moment almost like one listening and then answered "No."

"Then you must take me to your home and show me to your people."

"People? I do not know what you are saying."

"Your kindred—the others of your kind."

"Do you mean the King?"

"Yes. If you have a King, I had better be brought before him."

"I cannot do that," she answered. "I do not know where to find him."

"To your own home then."

"What is *home?*"

"The place where people live together and have their possessions and bring up their children."

She spread out her hands to indicate all that was in sight. "This is my home," she said.

"Do you live here alone?" asked Ransom.

"What is *alone?*"

Ransom tried a fresh start. "Bring me where I shall meet others of our kind."

"If you mean the King, I have already told you I do not know where he is. When we were young—many days ago—we were leaping from island to island, and when he was on one and I was on another the waves rose and we were driven apart."

"But can you take me to some other of your kind? The King cannot be the only one."

"He is the only one. Did you not know?"

"But there must be others of your kind—your brothers and sisters, your kindred, your friends."

"I do not know what these words mean."

"Who is this King?" said Ransom in desperation.

"He is himself, he is the King," said she. "How can one answer such a question?"

"Look here," said Ransom. "You must have had a mother. Is she alive? Where is she? When did you see her last?"

"I have a mother?" said the Green Lady, looking full at him with eyes of untroubled wonder. "What do you mean? I *am* the Mother." And once again there fell upon Ransom the feeling that it was not she, or not she only, who had spoken. No other sound came to his ears, for the sea and the air were still, but a phantom sense of vast choral music was all about him. The awe which her apparently witless replies had been dissipating for the last few minutes returned upon him.

"I do not understand," he said.

"Nor I," answered the Lady. "Only my spirit praises Maleldil who comes down from Deep Heaven into this lowness and will make me to be blessed by all the times that are rolling towards us. It is He who is strong and makes me strong and fills empty worlds with good creatures."

"If you are a mother, where are your children?"

"Not yet," she answered.

"Who will be their father?"

"The King—who else?"

"But the King—had he no father?"

"He *is* the Father."

"You mean," said Ransom slowly, "that you and he are the only two of your kind in the whole world?"

"Of course." Then presently her face changed. "Oh, how young I have been," she said. "I see it now. I had known that there were many creatures in that ancient world of the Hrossa and the Sorns. But I had forgotten that yours also was an older world than ours. I see—there are many of you by now. I had been thinking that of you also there were only two. I thought you were the King and Father of your world. But there are children of children of children by now, and you perhaps are one of these."

"Yes," said Ransom.

"Greet your Lady and Mother well from me when you return to your own world," said the Green Woman. And now for the first time there was a note of deliberate courtesy, even of ceremony, in her speech. Ransom understood. She knew now at last that she was not addressing an equal. She was a queen sending a message to a queen through a commoner, and her manner to him was henceforward more gracious. He found it difficult to make his next answer.

"Our Mother and Lady is dead," he said.

"What is *dead?*"

"With us they go away after a time. Maleldil takes the soul out of them and puts it somewhere else—in Deep Heaven, we hope. They call it death."

"Do not wonder, O Piebald Man, that your world should have been chosen for time's corner. You live looking out always on heaven itself, and as if this were not enough Maleldil takes you all thither in the end. You are favoured beyond all worlds."

Ransom shook his head. "No. It is not like that," he said.

"I wonder," said the woman, "if you were sent here to teach us *death.*"

"You don't understand," he said. "It is not like that. It is horrible. It has a foul smell. Maleldil Himself wept when He saw it." Both his voice and his facial expression were apparently something new to her. He saw the shock, not of horror, but of utter bewilderment, on her face for one instant and then, without effort, the ocean of her peace swallowed it up as if it had never been, and she asked him what he meant.

"You could never understand, Lady," he replied. "But in our world not all events are pleasing or welcome. There may be such a thing that you would cut off both your arms and your legs to prevent it happening—and yet it happens: with us."

"But how can one wish any of those waves not to reach us which Maleldil is rolling towards us?"

Against his better judgment Ransom found himself goaded into argument.

"But even you," he said, "when you first saw me, I know now you were expecting and hoping that I was the King. When you found I was not, your face changed. Was *that* event not unwelcome? Did you not wish it to be otherwise?"

"Oh," said the Lady. She turned aside with her head bowed and her hands clasped in an intensity of thought. She looked up and said, "You make me grow older more quickly than I can bear," and walked a little farther off. Ransom wondered what he had done. It was suddenly borne in upon him that her purity and peace were not, as they had seemed, things settled and inevitable like the purity and peace of an animal—that they were alive and therefore breakable, a balance maintained by a mind and therefore, at least in theory, able to be lost. There is no reason why a man on a smooth road should lose his balance on a bicycle; but he could. There was no reason why she should step out of her happiness into the psychology of our own race; but neither was there any wall between to prevent her doing so. The sense of precariousness terrified him: but when she looked at him again he changed that word to Adventure, and then all words died out of his mind. Once more he could not look steadily at her. He knew now what the old painters were trying to represent when they invented the halo. Gaiety and gravity together, a splendour as of martyrdom yet with no pain in it at all, seemed to pour from her countenance. Yet when she spoke her words were a disappointment.

"I have been so young till this moment that all my life now seems to have been a kind of sleep. I have thought that I was being carried, and behold, I was walking."

Ransom asked what she meant.

"What you have made me see," answered the Lady, "is as plain as the sky, but I never saw it before. Yet it has happened every day. One goes into the forest to pick food and already the thought of one fruit rather than another has grown up in one's mind. Then, it may be, one finds a different fruit and not the fruit one thought of. One joy was expected and another is given. But this I had never noticed before—that the very moment of the finding there is in the mind a kind of thrusting back, or setting aside. The picture of the fruit you have *not* found is still, for a moment, before you. And if you wished—if it were possible to wish—you could keep it there. You could send your soul after the good you had expected, instead of turning it to the good you had got. You could refuse the real good; you could make the real fruit taste insipid by thinking of the other."

Ransom interrupted. "That is hardly the same thing as finding a stranger when you wanted your husband."

"Oh, that is how I came to understand the whole thing. You and the King differ more than two kinds of fruit. The joy of finding him again and the joy of all the new knowledge I have had from you are more unlike than two tastes; and when the difference is as great as that, and each of the two things so great, then the first picture does stay in the mind quite a long time—many beats of the heart—after the other good has come. And this, O Piebald, is the glory and wonder you have made me see; that it is I, I myself, who turn from the good expected to the given good. Out of my own heart I do it. One can conceive a heart which did not: which clung to the good it had first thought of and turned the good which was given it into no good."

"I don't see the wonder and the glory of it," said Ransom.

Her eyes flashed upon him such a triumphant flight above his thoughts as would have been scorn in earthly eyes; but in that world it was not scorn.

"I thought," she said, "that I was carried in the will of Him I love, but now I see that I walk with it. I thought that the good things He sent me drew me into them as the waves lift the islands; but now I see that it is I who plunge into them with my own legs and arms, as when we go swimming. I feel as if I were living in that roofless world of yours where men walk undefended beneath naked heaven. It is a delight with terror in it! One's own self to be walking from one good to another, walking beside Him as Himself may walk, not even holding hands. How has He made me so separate from Himself? How did it enter His mind to conceive such a thing? The world is so much larger than I thought. I thought we went along paths—but it seems there are no paths. The going itself is the path."

"And have you no fear," said Ransom, "that it will ever be hard to turn your heart from the thing you wanted to the thing Maleldil sends?"

"I see," said the Lady presently. "The wave you plunge into may be very swift and great. You may need all your force to swim into it. You mean, He might send me a good like that?"

"Yes—or like a wave so swift and great that all your force was too little."

"It often happens that way in swimming," said the Lady. "Is not that part of the delight?"

"But are you happy without the King? Do you not *want* the King?"

"Want him?" she said. "How could there be anything I did not want?"

There was something in her replies that began to repel Ransom. "You can't want him very much if you are happy without him," he said: and was immediately surprised at the sulkiness of his own voice.

"Why?" asked the Lady. "And why, O Piebald, are you making little hills and valleys in your forehead and why do you give a little lift of your shoulders? Are these the signs of something in your world?"

"They mean nothing," said Ransom hastily. It was a small lie; but there it would not do. It tore him as he uttered it, like a vomit. It became of infinite importance. The silver meadow and the golden sky seemed to fling it back at him. As if stunned by some measureless anger in the very air he stammered an emendation: "They mean nothing I could explain to you." The Lady was looking at him with a new and more judicial expression. Perhaps in the presence of the first mother's son she had ever seen, she was already dimly forecasting the problems that might arise when she had children of her own.

"We have talked enough now," she said at last. At first he thought she was going to turn away and leave him. Then, when she did not move, he bowed and drew back a step or two. She still said nothing and seemed to have forgotten about him. He turned and retraced his way through the deep vegetation until they were out of sight of each other. The audience was at an end.

6

As soon as the Lady was out of sight Ransom's first impulse was to run his hands through his hair, to expel the breath from his lungs in a long whistle, to light a cigarette, to put his hands in his pockets, and in general, to go through all that ritual of relaxation which a man performs on finding himself alone after a rather trying interview. But he had no cigarettes and no pockets: nor indeed did he feel himself alone. That sense of being in Someone's Presence which had descended on him with such unbearable pressure during the very first moments of his conversation with the Lady did not disappear when he had left her. It was, if anything, increased. Her society had been, in some degree, a protection against it, and her absence left him not to solitude but to a more formidable kind of privacy. At first it was almost intolerable; as he put it to us, in telling the story, "There seemed no *room.*" But later on, he discovered that it was intolerable only at certain moments—at just those moments in fact (symbolised by his impulse to smoke and to put his hands in his pockets) when a man asserts his independence and feels that now at last he's on his own. When you felt like that, then the very air seemed too crowded to breathe; a complete fulness seemed to be excluding you from a place which, nevertheless, you were unable to leave. But when you gave in to the thing, gave yourself up to it, there was no burden to be borne. It became not a load but a medium, a sort of splendour as of eatable, drinkable, breathable gold, which fed and carried you and not only poured into you but out from you as well. Taken the wrong way, it suffocated; taken the right way, it made terrestrial life seem, by comparison, a vacuum. At first, of course, the wrong moments occurred pretty often. But like a man who has a wound that hurts him in certain positions and who gradually learns to avoid those positions, Ransom learned not to make that inner gesture. His day became better and better as the hours passed.

During the course of the day he explored the island pretty thoroughly. The sea was still calm and it would have been possible in many directions to have reached neighbouring islands by a mere jump. He was placed, however, at the edge of this temporary archipelago, and from one shore he found himself looking out on the open sea. They were lying, or else very slowly drifting, in the neighbourhood of the huge green column which he had seen a few moments after his arrival in Perelandra. He had an excellent view of this object at about a mile's distance. It was clearly a mountainous island. The column turned out to be really a cluster of columns—that is, of crags much higher than they were broad, rather like exaggerated dolomites, but smoother; so much smoother in fact that it might be truer to describe them as pillars from the Giant's Causeway magnified to the height of mountains. This huge upright mass did not, however, rise directly from the sea. The island had a base of rough country, but with smoother land at the coast, and a hint of valleys with vegetation in them between the ridges, and even of steeper and narrower valleys which ran some way up between the central crags.

It was certainly land, real fixed land with its roots in the solid surface of the planet. He could dimly make out the texture of true rock from where he sat. Some of it was inhabitable land. He felt a great desire to explore it. It looked as if a landing would present no difficulties, and even the great mountain itself might turn out to be climbable.

He did not see the Lady again that day. Early next morning, after he had amused himself by swimming for a little and eaten his first meal, he was again seated on the shore looking out towards the Fixed Land. Suddenly he heard her voice behind him and looked around. She had come forth from the woods with some beasts, as usual, following her. Her words had been words of greeting, but she showed no disposition to talk. She came and stood on the edge of the floating island beside him and looked with him towards the Fixed Land.

"I will go there," she said at last.

"May I go with you?" asked Ransom.

"If you will," said the Lady. "But you see it is the Fixed Land."

"That is why I wish to tread on it," said Ransom. "In my world all the lands are fixed, and it would give me pleasure to walk in such a land again."

She gave a sudden exclamation of surprise and stared at him.

"Where, then, do you live in your world?" she asked.

"On the lands."

"But you said they are all fixed."

"Yes. We live on the fixed lands."

For the first time since they had met, something not quite unlike an expression of horror or disgust passed over her face.

"But what do you do during the nights?"

"During the nights?" said Ransom in bewilderment. "Why, we sleep, of course."

"But where?"

"Where we live. On the land."

She remained in deep thought so long that Ransom feared she was never going to speak again. When she did, her voice was hushed and once more tranquil, though the note of joy had not yet returned to it.

"He has never bidden you not to," she said, less as a question than as a statement.

"No," said Ransom.

"There can, then, be different laws in different worlds."

"Is there a law in your world not to sleep in a Fixed Land?"

"Yes," said the Lady. "He does not wish us to dwell there. We may land on them and walk on them, for the world is ours. But to stay there—to sleep and awake there . . ." she ended with a shudder.

"You couldn't have that law in our world," said Ransom. "There *are* no floating lands with us."

"How many of you are there?" asked the Lady suddenly.

Ransom found that he didn't know the population of the Earth, but contrived to give her some idea of many millions. He had expected her to be astonished, but it appeared that numbers did not interest her. "How do you all find room on your Fixed Land?" she asked.

"There is not one fixed land, but many," he answered. "And they are big: almost as big as the sea."

"How do you endure it?" she burst out. "Almost half your world empty and dead. Loads and loads of land, all tied down. Does not the very thought of it crush you?"

"Not at all," said Ransom. "The very thought of a world which was all sea like yours would make my people unhappy and afraid."

"Where will this end?" said the Lady, speaking more to herself than to him. "I have grown so old in these last few hours that all my life before seems only like the stem of a tree, and now I am like the branches shooting out in every direction. They are getting so wide apart that I can hardly bear it. First to have learned that I walk from good to good with my own feet . . . that was a stretch enough. But now it seems that good is not the same in all worlds; that Maleldil has forbidden in one what He allows in another."

"Perhaps my world is wrong about this," said Ransom rather feebly, for he was dismayed at what he had done.

"It is not so," said she. "Maleldil Himself has told me now. And it could not be so, if your world has no floating lands. But He is not telling me why He has forbidden it to us."

"There's probably some good reason," began Ransom, when he was interrupted by her sudden laughter.

"Oh, Piebald, Piebald," she said, still laughing. "How often the people of your race speak!"

"I'm sorry," said Ransom, a little put out.

"What are you sorry for?"

"I am sorry if you think I talk too much."

"Too much? How can I tell what would be too much for you to talk?"

"In our world when they say a man talks much they mean they wish him to be silent."

"If that is what they mean, why do they not say it?"

"What made you laugh?" asked Ransom, finding her question too hard.

"I laughed, Piebald, because you were wondering, as I was, about this law which Maleldil has made for one world and not for another. And you had nothing to say about it and yet made the nothing up into words."

"I *had* something to say, though," said Ransom almost under his breath. "At least," he added in a louder voice, "this forbidding is no hardship in such a world as yours."

"That also is a strange thing to say," replied the Lady. "Who thought of its being hard? The beasts would not think it hard if I told them to walk on their heads. It would become their delight to walk on their heads. I am His beast, and all His biddings are joys. It is not that which makes me thoughtful. But it was coming into my mind to wonder whether there are two kinds of bidding."

"Some of our wise men have said . . ." began Ransom, when she interrupted him.

"Let us wait and ask the King," she said. "For I think, Piebald, you do not know much more about this than I do."

"Yes, the King, by all means," said Ransom. "If only we can find him." Then, quite involuntarily, he added in English, "By Jove! What was that?" She also had exclaimed. Something like a shooting star seemed to have streaked across the sky, far away on their left, and some seconds later an indeterminate noise reached their ears.

"What was that?" he asked again, this time in Old Solar.

"Something has fallen out of Deep Heaven," said the Lady. Her face showed wonder and curiosity: but on earth we so rarely see these emotions without some admixture of defensive fear that her expression seemed strange to him.

"I think you're right," said he. "Hullo! What's this?" The calm sea had swelled and all the weeds at the edge of their island were in movement. A single wave passed under their island and all was still again.

"Something has certainly fallen into the sea," said the Lady. Then she resumed the conversation as if nothing had happened.

"It was to look for the King that I had resolved to go over to-day to the Fixed Land. He is on none of these islands here, for I have searched them all. But if we climbed high up on the Fixed Land and looked about, then we should see a long way. We could see if there are any other islands near us."

"Let us do this," said Ransom. "If we can swim so far."

"We shall ride," said the Lady. Then she knelt down on the shore—and such grace was in all her movements that it was a wonder to see her kneel—and gave three low calls all on the same note. At first no result was visible. But soon Ransom saw broken water coming rapidly towards them. A moment later and the sea beside the island was a mass of the large silver fishes: spouting, curling their bodies, pressing upon one another to get nearer, and the nearest ones nosing the land. They had not only the colour but the smoothness of silver. The biggest were about nine feet long and all were thick-set and powerful-looking. They were very unlike any terrestrial species, for the base of the head was noticeably wider than the foremost part of the trunk. But then the trunk itself grew thicker again towards the tail. Without this tailward bulge they would have looked like giant tadpoles. As it was, they suggested rather pot-bellied and narrow-chested old men with very big heads. The Lady seemed to take a long time in selecting two of them. But the moment she had done so the others all fell back for a few yards and the two successful candidates wheeled round and lay still with their tails to the shore, gently moving their fins. "Now, Piebald, like this," she said, and seated herself astride the narrow part of the right-hand fish. Ransom followed her example. The great head in front of him served instead of shoulders so that there was no danger of sliding off. He watched his hostess. She gave her fish a slight kick with her heels. He did the same to his. A moment later they were gliding out to sea at about six miles an hour. The air over the water was cooler and the breeze lifted his hair. In a world where he had as yet only swum and walked, the fish's progress gave the impression of quite an exhilarating speed. He glanced back and saw the feathery and billowy mass of the islands receding and the sky growing larger and more emphatically golden. Ahead, the fantastically shaped and coloured mountain dominated his whole field of vision. He noticed with interest that the whole school of rejected fish were still with them—some following, but the majority gambolling in wide extended wings to left and right.

"Do they always follow like this?" he asked.

"Do the beasts not follow in your world?" she replied. "We cannot ride more than two. It would be hard if those we did not choose were not even allowed to follow."

"Was that why you took so long to choose the two fish, Lady?"

"Of course," said the Lady. "I try not to choose the same fish too often."

The land came towards them apace and what had seemed level coastline began to open into bays and thrust itself forward into promontories. And now they were near enough to see that in this apparently calm ocean there was an invisible swell, a very faint rise and fall of water on the beach. A moment later the fishes lacked depth to swim any further, and following the Green Lady's example, Ransom slipped both his legs to one side of his fish and groped down with his toes. Oh, ecstasy!—they touched solid pebbles. He had not realised till now that he was pining for "fixed land." He looked up. Down to the bay in which they were landing ran a steep narrow valley with low cliffs and outcroppings of a reddish rock and, lower down, banks of some kind of moss and a few trees. The trees might almost have been terrestrial: planted in any southern country of our own world they would not have seemed remarkable to anyone except a trained botanist. Best of all, down the middle of the valley—and welcome to Ransom's eyes and ears as a glimpse of home or of heaven—ran a little stream, a dark translucent stream where a man might hope for trout.

"You love this land, Piebald?" said the Lady, glancing at him.

"Yes," said he, "it is like my own world."

They began to walk up the valley to its head. When they were under the trees the resemblance of an earthly country was diminished, for there is so much less light in that world that the glade which would have cast only a little shadow cast a forest gloom. It was about a quarter of a mile to the top of the valley, where it narrowed into a mere cleft between low rocks. With one or two grips and a leap the Lady was up these, and Ransom followed. He was amazed at her strength. They emerged into a steep upland covered with a kind of turf which would have been very like grass but that there was more blue in it. It seemed to be closely cropped and dotted with white fluffy objects as far as the eye could reach.

"Flowers?" asked Ransom. The Lady laughed.

"No. These are the Piebalds. I named you after them." He was puzzled for a moment but presently the objects began to move, and soon to move quickly towards the human pair whom they had apparently winded—for they were already so high that there was a strong breeze. In a moment they were bounding all about the Lady and welcoming her. They were white beasts with black spots—about the size of sheep but with ears so much larger, noses so much mobile, and tails so much longer, that the general impression was rather of enormous mice. Their claw-like or almost hand-like paws were clearly built for climbing, and the bluish turf was their food. After a proper interchange of courtesies with these creatures, Ransom and the Lady continued their journey. The circle of golden sea below them was now spread out in an enormous expanse and the green rock pillars above seemed almost to overhang. But it was a long and stiff climb to their base. The temperature here was much lower, though it was still warm. The silence was also noticeable. Down below, on the islands, though one had not remarked it at the time, there must have been a continual background of water noises, bubble noises, and the movement of beasts.

They were now entering into a kind of bay or re-entrant of turf between two of the green pillars. Seen from below these had appeared to touch one another; but now, though they had gone in so deep between two of them that most of the view was cut off on either hand, there was still room for a battalion to march in line. The slope grew steeper every moment; and as it grew steeper the space between the pillars also grew narrower. Soon they were scrambling on hands and knees in a place where the green walls hemmed them in so that they must go in single file, and Ransom, looking up, could hardly see the sky overhead. Finally they were faced with a little bit of real rock work—a neck of stone about eight feet high which joined, like a gum of rock, the roots of the two monstrous teeth of the mountain. "I'd give a good deal to have a pair of trousers on," thought Ransom to himself as he looked at it. The Lady, who was ahead, stood on tiptoe and raised her arms to catch a projection on the lip of the ridge. Then he saw her pull, apparently intending to lift her whole weight on her arms and swing herself to the top in a single movement. "Look here, you can't do it that way," he began, speaking inadvertently in English, but before he had time to correct himself she was standing on the edge above him. He did not see exactly how it was done, but there was no sign that she had taken any unusual exertion. His own climb was a less dignified affair, and it was a panting and perspiring man with a smudge of blood on his knee who finally stood beside her. She was inquisitive about the blood, and when he had explained the phenomenon to her as well as he could, wanted to scrape a little skin off her own knee to see if the same would happen. This led him to try to explain to her what was meant by pain, which only made her more anxious to try the experiment. But at the last moment Maleldil apparently told her not to.

Ransom now turned to survey their surroundings. High overhead, and seeming by perspective to lean inwards towards each other at the top and almost to shut out the sky, rose the immense piers of rock—not two or three of them, but nine. Some of them, like those two between which they had entered the circle, were close together. Others were many yards apart. They surrounded a roughly oval plateau of perhaps seven acres, covered with a finer turf than any known on our planet and dotted with tiny crimson flowers. A high, singing wind carried, as it were, a cooled and refined quintessence of all the scents from the richer world below, and kept these in continual agitation. Glimpses of the far-spread sea, visible between pillars, made one continually conscious of great height; and Ransom's eyes, long accustomed to the medley of curves and colours in the floating islands, rested on the pure lines and stable masses of this place with great refreshment. He took a few paces forward into the cathedral spaciousness of the plateau, and when he spoke his voice woke echoes.

"Oh, this is good," he said. "But perhaps you—you to whom it is forbidden—do not feel it so." But a glance at the Lady's face told him he was wrong. He did not know what was in her mind; but her face, as once or twice before, seemed to shine with something before which he dropped his eyes. "Let us examine the sea," she said presently.

They made the circle of the plateau methodically. Behind them lay the group of islands from which they had set out that morning. Seen from this altitude it was larger even than Ransom had supposed. The richness of its colours—its orange, its silver, its purple and (to his surprise) its glossy blacks—made it seem almost heraldic. It was from this direction that the wind came; the smell of those islands, though faint, was like the sound of running water to a thirsty man. But on every other side they saw nothing but the ocean. At least, they saw no islands. But when they had made almost the whole circuit, Ransom shouted and the Lady pointed almost at the same moment. About two miles off, dark against the coppery-green of the water, there was some small round object. If he had been looking down on an earthly sea Ransom would have taken it, at first sight, for a buoy.

"I do not know what it is," said the Lady. "Unless it is the thing that fell out of Deep Heaven this morning."

"I wish I had a pair of field glasses," thought Ransom, for the Lady's words had awakened in him a sudden suspicion. And the longer he stared at the dark blob the more his suspicion was confirmed. It appeared to be perfectly spherical; and he thought he had seen something like it before.

You have already heard that Ransom had been in that world which men call Mars but whose true name is Malacandra. But he had not been taken thither by the eldila. He had been taken by men, and taken in a space-ship, a hollow sphere of glass and steel. He had, in fact, been kidnapped by men who thought that the ruling powers of Malacandra demanded a human sacrifice. The whole thing had been a misunderstanding. The great Oyarsa who has governed Mars from the beginning (and whom my own eyes beheld, in a sense, in the hall of Ransom's cottage) had done him no harm and meant him none. But his chief captor, Professor Weston, had meant plenty of harm. He was a man obsessed with the idea which is at this moment circulating all over our planet in obscure works of "scientifiction," in little Interplanetary Societies and Rocketry Clubs, and between the covers of monstrous magazines, ignored or mocked by the intellectuals, but ready, if ever the power is put into its hands, to open a new chapter of misery for the universe. It is the idea that humanity, having now sufficiently corrupted the planet where it arose, must at all costs contrive to seed itself over a larger area: that the vast astronomical distances which are God's quarantine regulations, must somehow be overcome. This for a start. But beyond this lies the sweet poison of the false infinite—the wild dream that planet after planet, system after system, in the end galaxy after galaxy, can be forced to sustain, everywhere and for ever, the sort of life which is contained in the loins of our own species—a dream begotten by the hatred of death upon the fear of true immortality, fondled in secret by thousands of ignorant men and hundreds who are not ignorant. The destruction or enslavement of other species in the universe, if such there are, is to these minds a welcome corollary. In Professor Weston the power had at last met the dream. The great physicist had discovered a motive power for his space-ship. And that little black object, now floating beneath him on the sinless waters of Perelandra, looked to Ransom more like the space-ship every moment. "So that," he thought, "that is why I have been sent here. He failed on Malacandra and now he is coming here. And it's up to me to do something about it." A terrible sense of inadequacy swept over him. Last time—in Mars—Weston had had only one accomplice. But he had had firearms. And how many accomplices might he have this time? And in Mars he had been foiled not by Ransom but by the eldila, and specially the great eldil, the Oyarsa, of that world. He turned quickly to the Lady.

"I have seen no eldila in your world," he said.

"Eldila?" she repeated as if it were a new name to her.

"Yes. Elidila," said Ransom, "the great and ancient servants of Maleldil. The creatures that neither breed nor breathe. Whose bodies are made of light. Whom we can hardly see. Who ought to be obeyed."

She mused for a moment and then spoke. "Sweetly and gently this time Maleldil makes me older. He shows me all the natures of these blessed creatures. But there is no obeying them *now,* not in this world. That is all the old order, Piebald, the far side of the wave that has rolled past us and will not come again. That very ancient world to which you journeyed was put under the eldila. In your own world also they ruled once: but not since our Beloved became a Man. In your world they linger still. But in our world, which is the first of worlds to wake after the great change, they have no power. There is nothing now between us and Him. They have grown less and we have increased. And now Maleldil puts it into my mind that this is their glory and their joy. They received us—us things of the low worlds, who breed and breathe—as weak and small beasts whom their lightest touch could destroy; and their glory was to cherish us and make us older till we were older than they—till they could fall at our feet. It is a joy we shall not have.

However I teach the beasts they will never be better than I. But it is a joy beyond all. Not that it is better joy than ours. Every joy is beyond all others. The fruit we are eating is always the best fruit of all."

"There have been eldila who did not think it a joy," said Ransom.

"How?"

"You spoke yesterday, Lady, of clinging to the old good instead of taking the good that came."

"Yes—for a few heart-beats."

"There was an eldil who clung longer—who has been clinging since before the worlds were made."

"But the old good would cease to be a good at all if he did that."

"Yes. It has ceased. And still he clings."

She stared at him in wonder and was about to speak, but he interrupted her.

"There is no time to explain," he said.

"No time? What has happened to the time?" she asked.

"Listen," he said. "That thing down there has come through Deep Heaven from my world. There is a man in it: perhaps many men——"

"Look," she said, "it is turning into two—one big and one small."

Ransom saw that a small black object had detached itself from the space-ship and was beginning to move uncertainly away from it. It puzzled him for a moment. Then it dawned on him that Weston—if it was Weston—probably knew the watery surface he had to expect on Venus and had brought some kind of collapsible boat. But could it be that he had not reckoned with tides or storms and did not foresee that it might be impossible for him ever to recover the space-ship? It was not like Weston to cut off his own retreat. And Ransom certainly did not wish Weston's retreat to be cut off. A Weston who could not, even if he chose, return to Earth, was an insoluble problem. Anyway, what could he, Ransom, possibly do without support from the eldila? He began to smart under a sense of injustice. What was the good of sending him—a mere scholar— to cope with a situation of this sort? Any ordinary pugilist, or, better still, any man who could make good use of a tommy-gun, would have been more to the purpose. If only they could find this King whom the Green Woman kept on talking about. . . .

But while these thoughts were passing through his mind he became aware of a dim murmuring or growling sound which had gradually been encroaching on the silence for some time. "Look," said the Lady suddenly, and pointed to the mass of islands. Their surface was no longer level. At the same moment he realised that the noise was that of waves: small waves as yet, but definitely beginning to foam on the rocky headlands of the Fixed Island. "The sea is rising," said the Lady. "We must go down and leave this land at once. Soon the waves will be too great—and I must not be here by night."

"Not that way," shouted Ransom. "Not where you will meet the man from my world."

"Why?" said the Lady. "I am Lady and Mother of this world. If the King is not here, who else should greet a stranger?"

"I will meet him."

"It is not your world, Piebald," she replied.

"You do not understand," said Ransom. "This man—he is a friend of that eldil of whom I told you—one of those who cling to the wrong good."

"Then I must explain it to him," said the Lady. "Let us go and make him older," and with that she slung herself down the rocky edge of the plateau and began descending the mountain slope. Ransom took longer to manage the rocks; but once his feet were again on the turf he began running as fast as he could. The Lady cried out in surprise as he flashed past her, but he took no notice. He could now see clearly which bay the little boat was making for and his attention was fully occupied in directing his course and making sure of his feet. There was only one man in the boat. Down and down the long slope he raced. Now he was in a fold: now in a winding valley which momentarily cut off the sight of the sea. Now at last he was in the cove itself. He glanced back and saw to his dismay that the Lady had also been running and was only a few yards behind. He glanced forward again. There were waves, though not yet very large ones, breaking on the pebbly beach. A man in shirt and shorts and a pith helmet was ankle-deep in the water, wading ashore and pulling after him a little canvas punt. It was certainly Weston, though his face had something about it which seemed subtly unfamiliar. It seemed to Ransom of vital importance to prevent a meeting between Weston and the Lady. He had seen Weston murder an inhabitant of Malacandra. He turned back, stretching out both arms to bar her way and shouting "Go back!" She was too near. For a second she was almost in his arms. Then she stood back from him, panting from the race, surprised, her mouth opened to speak. But at that moment he heard Weston's voice, from behind him, saying in English, "May I ask you, Dr. Ransom, what is the meaning of this?"

7

In all the circumstances it would have been reasonable to expect that Weston would be much more taken aback at Ransom's presence than Ransom could be at his. But if he were, he showed no sign of it, and Ransom could hardly help admiring the massive egoism which enabled this man in the very moment of his arrival on an unknown world to stand there unmoved in all his authoritative vulgarity, his arms akimbo, his face scowling, and his feet planted as solidly on that unearthly soil as if he had been standing with his back to the fire in his own study. Then, with a shock, he noticed that Weston was speaking to the Lady in the Old Solar language with perfect fluency. On Malacandra, partly from incapacity, and much more from his contempt for the inhabitants, he had never acquired more than a smattering of it. Here was an inexplicable and disquieting novelty. Ransom felt that his only advantage had been taken from him. He felt that he was now in the presence of the incalculable. If the scales had been suddenly weighted in this one respect, what might come next?

He awoke from his abstraction to find that Weston and the Lady had been conversing fluently, but without mutual understanding. "It is no use," she was saying. "You and I are not old enough to speak together, it seems. The sea is rising; let us go back to the islands. Will he come with us, Piebald?"

"Where are the two fishes?" said Ransom.

"They will be waiting in the next bay," said the Lady.

"Quick, then," said Ransom to her; and then, in answer to her look: "No, he will not come." She did not, presumably, understand his urgency, but her eye was on the sea and she understood her own reason for haste. She had already begun to ascend the side of the valley, with Ransom following her, when Weston shouted, "No, you don't." Ransom turned and found himself covered by a revolver. The sudden heat which swept over his body was the only sign by which he knew that he was frightened. His head remained clear.

"Are you going to begin in this world also by murdering one of its inhabitants?" he asked.

"What are you saying?" asked the Lady, pausing and looking back at the two men with a puzzled, tranquil face.

"Stay where you are, Ransom," said the Professor. "That native can go where she likes; the sooner the better."

Ransom was about to implore her to make good her escape when he realised that no imploring was needed. He had irrationally supposed that she would understand the situation; but apparently she saw nothing more than two strangers talking about something which she did not at the moment understand—that, and her own necessity of leaving the Fixed Land at once.

"You and he do not come with me, Piebald?" she asked.

"No," said Ransom, without turning round. "It may be that you and I shall not meet soon again. Greet the King for me if you find him and speak of me always to Maleldil. I stay here."

"We shall meet when Maleldil pleases," she answered, "or if not, some greater good will happen to us instead." Then he heard her footsteps behind him for a few seconds, and then he heard them no more and knew he was alone with Weston.

"You allowed yourself to use the word Murder just now, Dr. Ransom," said the Professor, "in reference to an accident that occurred when we were in Malacandra. In any case, the creature killed was not a human being. Allow me to tell you that I consider the seduction of a native girl as an almost equally unfortunate way of introducing civilisation to a new planet."

"Seduction?" said Ransom. "Oh, I see. You thought I was making love to her."

"When I find a naked civilised man embracing a naked savage woman in a solitary place, that is the name I give to it."

"I wasn't embracing her," said Ransom dully, for the whole business of defending himself on this score seemed at that moment a mere weariness of the spirit. "And no one wears clothes here. But what does it matter? Get on with the job that brings you to Perelandra."

"You ask me to believe that you have been living here with that woman under these conditions in a state of sexless innocence?"

"Oh, sexless!" said Ransom disgustedly. "All right, if you like. It's about as good a description of living in Perelandra as it would be to say that a man had forgotten water because Niagara Falls didn't immediately give him the idea of making it into cups of tea. But you're right enough if you mean that I have had no more thought of desiring her than—than . . ." Comparisons failed him and his voice died. Then he began again: "But don't say I'm asking you to believe it, or to believe anything. I am asking you nothing but to begin and end as soon as possible whatever butcheries and robberies you have come to do."

Weston eyed him for a moment with a curious expression: then, unexpectedly, he returned his revolver to its holster.

"Ransom," he said, "you do me a great injustice."

For several seconds there was silence between them. Long breakers with white woolpacks of foam on them were now rolling into the cove exactly as on earth.

"Yes," said Weston at last, "and I will begin with a frank admission. You may make what capital of it you please. I shall not be deterred. I deliberately say that I was, in some respects, mistaken—seriously mistaken—in my conception of the whole interplanetary problem when I went to Malacandra."

Partly from the relaxation which followed the disappearance of the pistol, and partly from the elaborate air of magnanimity with which the great scientist spoke, Ransom felt very much inclined to laugh. But it occurred to him that this was possibly the first occasion in his whole life in which Weston had ever acknowledged himself in the wrong, and that even the false dawn of humility, which is still ninety-nine per cent. of arrogance, ought not to be rebuffed—or not by him.

"Well, that's very handsome," he said. "How do you mean?"

"I'll tell you presently," said Weston. "In the meantime I must get my things ashore." Between them they beached the punt, and began carrying Weston's primus-stove and tins and tent and other packages to a spot about two hundred yards inland. Ransom, who knew all the paraphernalia to be needless, made no objection, and in about a quarter of an hour something like an encampment had been established in a mossy place under some blue-trunked silver-leaved trees beside a rivulet. Both men sat down and Ransom listened at first with interest, then with amazement, and finally with incredulity. Weston cleared his throat, threw out his chest, and assumed his lecturing manner. Throughout the conversation that followed, Ransom was filled with a sense of crazy irrelevance. Here were two human beings, thrown together in an alien world under conditions of inconceivable strangeness: the one separated from his space-ship, the other newly released from the threat of instant death. Was it sane—was it imaginable—that they should find themselves at once engaged in a philosophical argument which might just as well have occurred in a Cambridge combination room? Yet that, apparently, was what Weston insisted upon. He showed no interest in the fate of his space-ship; he even seemed to feel no curiosity about Ransom's presence on Venus. Could it be that he had travelled more than thirty million miles of space in search of—conversation? But as he went on talking, Ransom felt himself more and more in the presence of a monomaniac. Like an actor who cannot think of anything but his celebrity, or a lover who can think of nothing but his mistress, tense, tedious, and unescapable, the scientist pursued his fixed idea.

"The tragedy of my life," he said, "and indeed of the modern intellectual world in general, is the rigid specialisation of knowledge entailed by the growing complexity of what is known. It is my own share in that tragedy that an early devotion to physics has prevented me from paying any proper attention to Biology until I reached the fifties. To do myself justice, I should make it clear that the false humanist ideal of knowledge as an end in itself never appealed to me. I always wanted to know in order to achieve utility. At first, that utility naturally appeared to me in a personal form—I wanted scholarships, an income, and that generally recognised position in the world without which a man has no leverage. When those were attained, I began to look farther: to the utility of the human race!"

He paused as he rounded his period and Ransom nodded to him to proceed.

"The utility of the human race," continued Weston, "in the long run depends rigidly on the possibility of interplanetary, and even inter-sidereal, travel. That problem I solved. The key of human destiny was placed in my hands. It would be unnecessary—and painful to us both—to remind you how it was wrenched from me in Malacandra by a member of a hostile intelligent species whose existence, I admit, I had not anticipated."

"Not hostile exactly," said Ransom, "but go on."

"The rigours of our return journey from Malacandra led to a serious break-down in my health——"

"Mine too," said Ransom.

Weston looked somewhat taken aback at the interruption and went on. "During my convalescence I had that leisure for reflection which I had denied myself for many years. In particular I reflected on the objections you had felt to that liquidation of the non-human inhabitants of Malacandra which was, of course, the necessary preliminary to its occupation by our own species. The traditional and, if I may say so, the humanitarian form in which you advanced those objections had till then concealed from me their true strength. That strength I now began to perceive. I began to see that my own exclusive devotion to human utility was really based on an unconscious dualism."

"What do you mean?"

"I mean that all my life I had been making a wholly unscientific dichotomy or antithesis between Man and Nature—had conceived myself fighting *for* Man against his non-human environment. During my illness I plunged into Biology, and particularly into what may be called biological philosophy. Hitherto, as a physicist, I had been content to regard Life as a subject outside my scope. The conflicting views of those who drew a sharp line between the organic and the inorganic and those who held that what we call Life was inherent in matter from the very beginning had not interested me. Now it did. I saw almost at once that I could admit no break, no discontinuity, in the unfolding of the cosmic process. I became a convinced believer in emergent evolution. All is one. The stuff of mind, the unconsciously purposive dynamism, is present from the very beginning."

Here he paused. Ransom had heard this sort of thing pretty often before and wondered when his companion was coming to the point. When Weston resumed it was with an even deeper solemnity of tone.

"The majestic spectacle of this blind, inarticulate purposiveness thrusting its way upward and ever upward in an endless unity of differentiated achievements towards an ever-increasing complexity of organisation, towards spontaneity and spirituality, swept away all my old conception of a duty to Man as such. Man in himself is nothing. The forward movement of Life—the growing spirituality—is everything. I say to you quite freely, Ransom, that I should have been wrong in liquidating the Malacandrians. It was a mere prejudice that made me prefer our own race to theirs. To spread spirituality, not to spread the human race, is henceforth my mission. This sets the coping-stone on my career. I worked first for myself; then for science; then for humanity; but now at last for Spirit itself—I might say, borrowing language which will be more familiar to you, the Holy Spirit."

"Now what exactly do you mean by that?" asked Ransom.

"I mean," said Weston, "that nothing now divides you and me except a few outworn theological technicalities with which organised religion has unhappily allowed itself to get incrusted. But I have penetrated that crust. The Meaning beneath it is as true and living as ever. If you will excuse me for putting it that way, the essential truth of the religious view of life finds a remarkable witness in the fact that it enabled you, on Malacandra, to grasp, in your own mythical and imaginative fashion, a truth which was hidden from me."

"I don't know much about what people call the religious view of life," said Ransom, wrinkling his brow. "You see, I'm a Christian. And what we mean by the Holy Ghost is *not* a blind, inarticulate purposiveness."

"My dear Ransom," said Weston, "I understand you perfectly. I have no doubt that my phraseology will seem strange to you, and perhaps even shocking. Early and revered associations may have put it out of your power to recognise in this new form the very same truths which religion has so long preserved and which science is now at last re-discovering. But whether you can see it or not, believe me, we are talking about exactly the same thing."

"I'm not at all sure that we are."

"That, if you will permit me to say so, is one of the real weaknesses of organised religion—that adherence to formulae, that failure to recognise one's own friends. God is a spirit, Ransom. Get hold of that. You're familiar with that already. Stick to it. God is a spirit."

"Well, of course. But what then?"

"What then? Why, spirit—mind—freedom—spontaneity—that's what I'm talking about. That is the goal towards which the whole cosmic process is moving. The final disengagement of that freedom, that spirituality, is the work to which I dedicate my own life and the life of humanity. The goal, Ransom, the goal: think of it! *Pure* spirit: the final vortex of self-thinking, self-originating activity."

"Final?" said Ransom. "You mean it doesn't yet exist?"

"Ah," said Weston, "I see what's bothering you. Of course I know. Religion pictures it as being there from the beginning. But surely that is not a real difference? To make it one, would be to take time too seriously. When it has once been attained, you might then say it had been at the beginning just as well as at the end. Time is one of the things it will transcend."

"By the way," said Ransom, "is it in any sense at all personal—is it alive?"

An indescribable expression passed over Weston's face. He moved a little nearer to Ransom and began speaking in a lower voice.

"That's what none of them understand," he said. It was such a gangster's or a schoolboy's whisper and so unlike his usual orotund lecturing style that Ransom for a moment felt a sensation almost of disgust.

"Yes," said Weston, "I couldn't have believed, myself, till recently. Not a person, of course. Anthropomorphism is one of the childish diseases of popular religion" (here he had resumed his public manner), "but the opposite extreme of excessive abstraction has perhaps in the aggregate proved more disastrous. Call it a Force. A great, inscrutable Force, pouring up into us from the dark bases of being. A Force that can choose its instruments. It is only lately, Ransom, that I've learned from actual experience something which you have believed all your life as part of your religion." Here he suddenly subsided again into a whisper—a croaking whisper unlike his usual voice. "Guided," he said. "Chosen. Guided. I've become conscious that I'm a man set apart. Why did I do physics? Why did I discover the Weston rays? Why did I go to Malacandra? It—the Force—has pushed me on all the time. I'm being guided. I know now that I am the greatest scientist the world has yet produced. I've been made so for a purpose. It is through me that Spirit itself is at this moment pushing on to its goal."

"Look here," said Ransom, "one wants to be careful about this sort of thing. There are spirits and spirits you know."

"Eh?" said Weston. "What are you talking about?"

"I mean a thing might be a spirit and not good for you."

"But I thought you agreed that Spirit was the good—the end of the whole process? I thought you religious people were all out for spirituality? What is the point of asceticism—fasts and celibacy and all that? Didn't we agree that God is a spirit? Don't you worship Him because He is pure spirit?"

"Good heavens, no! We worship Him because He is wise and good. There's nothing specially fine about simply being a spirit. The Devil is a spirit."

"Now your mentioning the Devil is very interesting," said Weston, who had by this time quite recovered his normal manner. "It is a most interesting thing in popular religion, this tendency to fissiparate, to breed pairs of opposites: heaven and hell, God and Devil. I need hardly say that in my view no real dualism in the universe is admissible; and on that ground I should have been disposed, even a few weeks ago, to reject these pairs of doublets as pure mythology. It would have been a profound error. The cause of this universal religious tendency is to be sought much deeper. The doublets are really portraits of Spirit, of cosmic energy—self-portraits, indeed, for it is the Life-Force itself which has deposited them in our brains."

"What on earth do you mean?" said Ransom. As he spoke he rose to his feet and began pacing to and fro. A quite appalling weariness and malaise had descended upon him.

"*Your* Devil and *your* God," said Weston, "are both pictures of the same Force. Your heaven is a picture of the perfect spirituality ahead; your hell a picture of the urge or *nisus* which is driving us on to it from behind. Hence the static peace of the one and the fire and darkness of the other. The next stage of emergent evolution, beckoning us forward, is God; the transcended stage behind, ejecting us, is the Devil. Your own religion, after all, says that the devils are fallen angels."

"And you are saying precisely the opposite, as far as I can make out—that angels are devils who've risen in the world."

"It comes to the same thing," said Weston.

There was another long pause. "Look here," said Ransom, "it's easy to misunderstand one another on a point like this. What you are saying sounds to me like the most horrible mistake a man could fall into. But that may be because in the effort to accommodate it to my supposed 'religious views,' you're saying a good deal more than you mean. It's only a metaphor, isn't it, all this about spirits and forces? I expect all you really mean is that you feel it your duty to work for the spread of civilisation and knowledge and that kind of thing." He had tried to keep out of his voice the involuntary anxiety which he had begun to feel. Next moment he recoiled in horror at the cackling laughter, almost an infantile or senile laughter, with which Weston replied.

"There you go, there you go," he said. "Like all you religious people. You talk and talk about these things all your life, and the moment you meet the reality you get frightened."

"What proof," said Ransom (who indeed did feel frightened), "what proof have you that you are being guided or supported by anything except your own individual mind and other people's books?"

"You didn't notice, dear Ransom," said Weston, "that I'd improved a bit since we last met in my knowledge of extra-terrestrial language. You are a philologist, they tell me."

Ransom started. "How did you do it?" he blurted out.

"Guidance, you know, guidance," croaked Weston. He was squatting at the roots of his tree with his knees drawn up, and his face, now the colour of putty, wore a fixed and even slightly twisted grin. "Guidance. Guidance," he went on. "Things coming into my head. I'm being prepared all the time. Being made a fit receptacle for it."

"That ought to be fairly easy," said Ransom impatiently. "If this Life-Force is something so ambiguous that God and the Devil are equally good portraits of it, I suppose any receptacle is equally fit, and anything you can do is equally an expression of it."

"There's such a thing as the main current," said Weston. "It's a question of surrendering yourself to that—making yourself the conductor of the live, fiery, central purpose—becoming the very finger with which it reaches forward."

"But I thought that was the Devil aspect of it, a moment ago."

"That is the fundamental paradox. The thing we are reaching forward to is what you would call God. The reaching forward, the dynamism, is what people like you always call the Devil. The people like me, who do the reaching forward, are always martyrs. You revile us, and by us come to your goal."

"Does that mean in plainer language that the things the Force wants you to do are what ordinary people call diabolical?"

"My dear Ransom, I wish you would not keep relapsing on to the popular level. The two things are only moments in the single, unique reality. The world leaps forward through great men and greatness always transcends mere moralism. When the leap has been made our 'diabolism' as you would call it becomes the morality of the next stage; but while we are making it, we are called criminals, heretics, blasphemers. . . ."

"How far does it go? Would you still obey the Life-Force if you found it prompting you to murder me?"

"Yes."

"Or to sell England to the Germans?"

"Yes."

"Or to print lies as serious research in a scientific periodical?"

"Yes."

"God help you!" said Ransom.

"You are still wedded to your conventionalities," said Weston. "Still dealing in abstractions. Can you not even conceive a total commitment—a commitment to something which utterly overrides all our petty ethical pigeon-holes?"

Ransom grasped at the straw. "Wait, Weston," he said abruptly. "That may be a point of contact. You say it's a total commitment. That is, you're giving up yourself. You're not out for your own advantage. No, wait half a second. This *is* the point of contact between your morality and mine. We both acknowledge——"

"Idiot," said Weston. His voice was almost a howl and he had risen to his feet. "Idiot," he repeated. "Can you understand nothing? Will you always try to press everything back into the miserable framework of your old jargon about self and self-sacrifice? That is the old accursed dualism in another form. There is no possible distinction in concrete thought between me and the universe. In so far as I am the conductor of the central forward pressure of the universe, I am it. Do you see, you timid, scruple-mongering fool? I *am* the Universe. I, Weston, am your God and your Devil. I call that Force into me completely. . . ."

Then horrible things began happening. A spasm like that preceding a deadly vomit twisted Weston's face out of recognition. As it passed, for one second something like the old Weston reappeared—the old Weston, staring with eyes of horror and howling, "Ransom, Ransom! For Christ's sake don't let them——" and instantly his whole body spun round as if he had been hit by a revolver-bullet and he fell to the earth, and was there rolling at Ransom's feet, slavering and chattering and tearing up the moss by handfuls. Gradually the convulsions decreased. He lay still, breathing heavily, his eyes open but without expression. Ransom was kneeling beside him now. It was obvious that the body was alive, and Ransom wondered whether this were a stroke or an epileptic fit, for he had never seen either. He rummaged among the packages and found a bottle of brandy which he uncorked and applied to the patient's mouth. To his consternation the teeth opened, closed on the neck of the bottle and bit it through. No glass was spat out. "O God, I've killed him," said Ransom. But beyond a spurt of blood at the lips there was no change in his appearance. The face suggested that either he was in no pain or in pain beyond all human comprehension. Ransom rose at last, but before doing so he plucked the revolver from Weston's belt, then, walking down to the beach, he threw it as far as he could into the sea.

He stood for some moments gazing out upon the bay and undecided what to do. Presently he turned and climbed up the turfy ridge that bordered the little valley on his left hand. He found himself on a fairly level upland with a good view of the sea, now running high and teased out of its level gold into a continually changing pattern of lights and shadows. For a second or two he could catch no sight of the islands. Then suddenly their tree-tops appeared, hanging high up against the sky, and widely separated. The weather, apparently, was already driving them apart—and even as he thought this they vanished once more into some unseen valley of the waves. What was his chance, he wondered, of ever finding them again? A sense of loneliness smote him, and then a feeling of angry frustration. If Weston were dying, or even if Weston were to live, imprisoned here with him on an island they could not leave, what had been the danger he was sent to avert from Perelandra? And so, having begun to think of himself, he realised that he was hungry. He had seen neither fruit nor gourd on the Fixed Land. Perhaps it was a death trap. He smiled bitterly at the folly which had made him so glad, that morning, to exchange those floating paradises, where every grove dropped sweetness, for this barren rock. But perhaps it was not barren after all. Determined, despite the weariness which was every moment descending upon him, to make a search for food, he was just turning inland when the swift changes of colour that announce the evening of that world overtook him. Uselessly he quickened his pace. Before he had got down into the valley, the grove where he had left Weston was a mere cloud of darkness. Before he had reached it he was in seamless, undimensioned night. An effort or two to grope his way to the place where Weston's stores had been deposited only served to abolish his sense of direction altogether. He sat down perforce. He called Weston's name aloud once or twice but, as he expected, received no answer. "I'm glad I removed his gun, all the same," thought Ransom; and then, "Well, *qui dort dîne* and I suppose I must make the best of it till the morning." When he lay down he discovered that the solid earth and moss of the Fixed Land was very much less comfortable than the surfaces to which he had lately been accustomed. That, and the thought of the other human being lying, no doubt, close at hand with open eyes and teeth clenched on splintered glass, and the sullen recurring pound of breakers on the beach, all made the night comfortless. "If I lived on Perelandra," he muttered, "Maleldil wouldn't need to *forbid* this island. I wish I'd never set eyes on it."

8

He woke, after a disturbed and dreamful sleep, in full daylight. He had a dry mouth, a crick in his neck, and a soreness in his limbs. It was so unlike all previous wakings in the world of Venus, that for a moment he supposed himself back on Earth: and the dream (for so it seemed to him) of having lived and walked on the oceans of the Morning Star rushed through his memory with a sense of lost sweetness that was well-nigh unbearable. Then he sat up and the facts came back to him. "It's jolly nearly the same as having waked from a dream, though," he thought. Hunger and thirst became at once his dominant sensations, but he conceived it a duty to look first at the sick man—though with very little hope that he could help him. He gazed round. There was the grove of silvery trees all right, but he could not see Weston. Then he glanced at the bay; there was no punt either. Assuming that in the darkness he had blundered into the wrong valley, he rose and approached the stream for a drink. As he lifted his face from the water with a long sigh of satisfaction, his eyes suddenly fell on a little wooden box—and then beyond it on a couple of tins. His brain was working rather slowly and it took him a few seconds to realise that he was in the right valley after all, and a few more to draw conclusions from the fact that the box was open and empty, and that some of the stores had been removed and others left behind. But was it possible that a man in Weston's physical condition could have recovered sufficiently during the night to strike camp and to go away laden with some kind of pack? Was it possible that any man could have faced a sea like that in a collapsible punt? It was true, as he now noticed for the first time, that the storm (which had been a mere squall by Perelandrian standards) appeared to have blown itself out during the night; but there was still a quite formidable swell and it seemed out of the question that the Professor could have left the island. Much more probably he had left the valley on foot and carried the punt with him. Ransom decided that he must find Weston at once: he must keep in touch with his enemy. For if Weston had recovered, there was no doubt he meant mischief of some kind. Ransom was not at all certain that he had understood all his wild talk on the previous day; but what he did understand he disliked very much, and suspected that this vague mysticism about "spirituality" would turn out to be something even nastier than his old and comparatively simple programme of planetary imperialism. It would be unfair to take seriously the things the man had said immediately before his seizure, no doubt; but there was enough without that.

The next few hours Ransom passed in searching the island for food and for Weston. As far as food was concerned, he was rewarded. Some fruit like bilberries could be gathered in handfuls on the upper slopes, and the wooded valleys abounded in a kind of oval nut. The kernel had a toughly soft consistency, rather like cork or kidneys, and the flavour, though somewhat austere and prosaic after the fruit of the floating islands, was not unsatisfactory. The giant mice were as tame as other Perelandrian beasts but seemed stupider. Ransom ascended to the central plateau. The sea was dotted with islands in every direction, rising and falling with the swell, and all separated from one another by wide stretches of water. His eye at once picked out an orange-coloured island, but did not know whether it was that on which he had been living, for he saw at least two others in which the same colour predominated. At one time he counted twenty-three floating islands in all. That, he thought, was more than the temporary archipelago had contained, and allowed him to hope that any one of those he saw might hide the King—or that the King might even at this moment be re-united to the Lady. Without thinking it out very clearly, he had come to rest almost all his hopes on the King.

Of Weston he could find no trace. It really did seem, in spite of all improbabilities, that he had somehow contrived to leave the Fixed Island; and Ransom's anxiety was very great. What Weston, in his new vein, might do, he had no idea. The best to hope for was that he would simply ignore the master and mistress of Perelandra as mere savages or "natives."

Late in the day, being tired, he sat down on the shore. There was very little swell now and the waves, just before they broke, were less than knee-deep. His feet, made soft by the mattress-like surface which one walks on in those floating islands, were hot and sore. Presently he decided to refresh them by a little wading. The delicious quality of the water drew him out till he was waist-deep. As he stood there, deep in thought, he suddenly perceived that what he had taken to be an effect of light on the water was really the back of one of the great silvery fish. "I wonder would it let me ride it?" he thought; and then, watching how the beast nosed towards him and kept itself as near the shallows as it dared, it was borne in upon him that it was trying to attract his attention. Could it have been *sent?* The thought had no sooner darted through his mind than he decided to make the experiment. He laid his hand across the creature's back, and it did not flinch from his touch. Then with some difficulty he scrambled into a sitting position across the narrow part behind its head, and while he was doing this it remained as nearly stationary as it could; but as soon as he was firmly in the saddle it whisked itself about and headed for the sea.

If he had wished to withdraw, it was very soon impossible to do so. Already the green pinnacles of the mountain, as he looked back, had withdrawn their summits from the sky and the coastline of the island had begun to conceal its bays and nesses. The breakers were no longer audible—only the prolonged sibilant or chattering noises of the water about him. Many floating islands were visible, though seen from this level they were mere feathery silhouettes. But the fish seemed to be heading for none of these. Straight on, as if it well knew its way, the beat of the great fins carried him for more than an hour. Then green and purple splashed the whole world, and after that darkness.

Somehow he felt hardly any uneasiness when he found himself swiftly climbing and descending the low hills of water through the black night. And here it was not all black. The heavens had vanished, and the surface of the sea; but far, far below him in the heart of the vacancy through which he appeared to be travelling, strange bursting star shells and writhing streaks of a bluish-green luminosity appeared. At first they were very remote, but soon, as far as he could judge, they were nearer. A whole world of phosphorescent creatures seemed to be at play not far from the surface—coiling eels and darting things in complete armour, and then heraldically fantastic shapes to which the sea-horse of our own waters would be commonplace. They were all round him—twenty or thirty of them often in sight at once. And mixed with all this riot of sea-centaurs and sea-dragons he saw yet stranger forms: fishes, if fishes they were, whose forward part was so nearly human in shape that when he first caught sight of them he thought he had fallen into a dream and shook himself to awake. But it was no dream. There—and there again—it was unmistakable: now a shoulder, now a profile, and then for one second a full face: veritable mermen or mermaids. The resemblance to humanity was indeed greater, not less, than he had first supposed. What had for a moment concealed it from him was the total absence of human expression. Yet the faces were not idiotic; they were not even brutal parodies of humanity like those of our terrestrial apes. They were more like human faces asleep, or faces in which humanity slept while some other life, neither bestial nor diabolic, but merely elvish, out of our orbit, was irrelevantly awake. He remembered his old suspicion that what was myth in one world might always be fact in some other. He wondered also whether the King and Queen of Perelandra, though doubtless the first human pair of this planet, might on the physical side have a marine ancestry. And if so, what then of the man-like things before men in our own world? Must they in truth have been the wistful brutalities whose pictures we see in popular books on evolution? Or were the old myths truer than the modern myths? Had there in truth been a time when satyrs danced in the Italian woods? But he said "Hush" to his mind at this stage, for the mere pleasure of breathing in the fragrance which now began to steal towards him from the blackness ahead. Warm and sweet, and every moment sweeter and purer, and every moment stronger and more filled with all delights, it came to him. He knew well what it was. He would know it henceforward out of the whole universe—the night-breath of a floating island in the star Venus. It was strange to be filled with home-sickness for places where his sojourn had been so brief and which were, by any objective standard, so alien to all our race. Or were they? The cord of longing which drew him to the invisible isle seemed to him at that moment to have been fastened long, long before his coming to Perelandra, long before the earliest times that memory could recover in his childhood, before birth, before the birth of man himself, before the origins of time. It was sharp, sweet, wild, and holy, all in one, and in any world where men's nerves have ceased to obey their central desires would doubtless have been aphrodisiac too, but not in Perelandra. The fish was no longer moving. Ransom put out his hand. He found he was touching weed. He crawled forward over the head of the monstrous fish, and levered himself on to the gently moving surface of the island. Short as his absence from such places had been, his earth-trained habits of walking had reasserted themselves, and he fell more than once as he groped his way on the heaving lawn. But it did no harm falling here; good luck to it! There were trees all about him in the dark and when a smooth, cool, rounded object came away in his hand he put it, unfearing, to his lips. It was none of the fruits he had tasted before. It was better than any of them. Well might the Lady say of her world that the fruit you ate at any moment was, at that moment, the best. Wearied with his day's walking and climbing, and, still more, borne down by absolute satisfaction, he sank into dreamless sleep.

He felt that it was several hours later when he awoke and found himself still in darkness. He knew, too, that he had been suddenly waked: and a moment later he was listening to the sound that had waked him. It was the sound of voices—a man's voice and a woman's in earnest conversation. He judged that they were very close to him—for in a Perelandrian night an object is no more visible six inches than six miles away. He perceived at once who the speakers were: but the voices sounded strange, and the emotions of the speakers were obscure to him, with no facial expression to eke them out.

"I am wondering," said the woman's voice, "whether all the people of your world have the habit of talking about the same thing more than once. I have said already that we are forbidden to dwell on the Fixed Land. Why do you not either talk of something else or stop talking?"

"Because this forbidding is such a strange one," said the Man's voice. "And so unlike the ways of Maleldil in my world. And He has not forbidden you to think about dwelling on the Fixed Land."

"That would be a strange thing—to think about what will never happen."

"Nay, in our world we do it all the time. We put words together to mean things that have never happened and places that never were: beautiful words, well put together. And then tell them to one another. We call it stories or poetry. In that old world you spoke of, Malacandra, they did the same. It is for mirth and wonder and wisdom."

"What is the wisdom in it?"

"Because the world is made up not only of what is but of what might be. Maleldil knows both and wants us to know both."

"This is more than I ever thought of. The other—the Piebald one—has already told me things which made me feel like a tree whose branches were growing wider and wider apart. But this goes beyond all. Stepping out of what is into what might be and talking and making things out there . . . alongside the world. I will ask the King what he thinks of it."

"You see, that is what we always come back to. If only you had not been parted from the King."

"Oh, I see. That also is one of the things that might be. The world might be so made that the King and I were never parted."

"The world would not have to be different—only the way you live. In a world where people live on the Fixed Lands they do not become suddenly separated."

"But you remember we are not to live on the Fixed Land."

"No, but He has never forbidden you to think about it. Might not that be one of the reasons why you are forbidden to do it—so that you may have a Might Be to think about, to make Story about as we call it?"

"I will think more of this. I will get the King to make me older about it."

"How greatly I desire to meet this King of yours! But in the matter of Stories he may be no older than you himself."

"That saying of yours is like a tree with no fruit. The King is always older than I, and about all things."

"But Piebald and I have already made you older about certain matters which the King never mentioned to you. That is the new good which you never expected. You thought you would always learn all things from the King; but now Maleldil has sent you other men whom it had never entered your mind to think of and they have told you things the King himself could not know."

"I begin to see now why the King and I were parted at this time. This is a strange and great good He intended for me."

"And if you refused to learn things from me and kept on saying you would wait and ask the King, would that not be like turning away from the fruit you had found to the fruit you had expected?"

"These are deep questions, Stranger. Maleldil is not putting much into my mind about them."

"Do you not see why?"

"No."

"Since Piebald and I have come to your world we have put many things into your mind which Maleldil has not. Do you not see that He is letting go of your hand a little?"

"How could He? He is wherever we go."

"Yes, but in another way. He is making you older—making you to learn things not straight from Him but by your own meetings with other people and your own questions and thoughts."

"He is certainly doing that."

"Yes. He is making you a full woman, for up till now you were only half made—like the beasts who do nothing of themselves. This time, when you meet the King again, it is you who will have things to tell him. It is you who will be older than he and who will make him older."

"Maleldil would not make a thing like that happen. It would be like a fruit with no taste."

"But it would have a taste for *him*. Do you not think the King must sometimes be tired of being the older? Would he not love you more if you were wiser than he?"

"Is this what you call a Poetry or do you mean that it really is?"

"I mean a thing that really is."

"But how could anyone love anything more? It is like saying a thing could be bigger than itself."

"I only meant you could become more like the women of my world."

"What are they like?"

"They are of a great spirit. They always reach out their hands for the new and unexpected good, and see that it is good long before the men understand it. Their minds run ahead of what Maleldil has told them. They do not need to wait for Him to tell them what is good, but know it for themselves as He does. They are, as it were, little Maleldils. And because of their wisdom, their beauty is as much greater than yours as the sweetness of these gourds surpasses the taste of water. And because of their beauty the love which the men have for them is as much greater than the King's love for you as the naked burning of Deep Heaven seen from my world is more wonderful than the golden roof of yours."

"I wish I could see them."

"I wish you could."

"How beautiful is Maleldil and how wonderful are all His works: perhaps He will bring out of me daughters as much greater than I as I am greater than the beasts. It will be better than I thought. I had thought I was to be always Queen and Lady. But I see now that I may be as the eldila. I may be appointed to cherish when they are small and weak children who will grow up and overtop me and at whose feet I shall fall. I see it is not only questions and thoughts that grow out wider and wider like branches. Joy also widens out and comes where we had never thought."

"I will sleep now," said the other voice. As it said this it became, for the first time, unmistakably the voice of Weston—and of Weston disgruntled and snappish. Up till now Ransom, though constantly resolving to join the conversation, had been kept silent in a kind of suspense between two conflicting states of mind. On the one hand he was certain, both from the voice and from many of the things it said, that the male speaker was Weston. On the other hand, the voice, divided from the man's appearance, sounded curiously unlike itself. Still more, the patient persistent manner in which it was used was very unlike the Professor's usual alternation between pompous lecturing and abrupt bullying. And how could a man fresh from such a physical crisis as he had seen Weston undergo have recovered such mastery of himself in a few hours? And how could he have reached the floating island? Ransom had found himself throughout their dialogue confronted with an intolerable contradiction. Something which was and was not Weston was talking: and the sense of this monstrosity, only a few feet away in the darkness, had sent thrills of exquisite horror tingling along his spine, and raised questions in his mind which he tried to dismiss as fantastic. Now that the conversation was over he realised, too, with what intense anxiety he had followed it. At the same moment he was conscious of a sense of triumph. But it was not he who was triumphant. The whole darkness about him rang with victory. He started and half raised himself. Had there been any actual sound? Listening hard he could hear nothing but the low murmurous noise of warm wind and gentle swell. The suggestion of music must have been from within. But as soon as he lay down again he felt assured that it was not. From without, most certainly from without, but not by the sense of hearing, festal revelry and dance and splendour poured into him—no sound, yet in such fashion that it could not be remembered or thought of except as music. It was like having a new sense. It was like being present when the morning stars sang together. It was as if Perelandra had that moment been created—and perhaps in some sense it had. The feeling of a great disaster averted was forced upon his mind, and with it came the hope that there would be no second attempt; and then, sweeter than all, the suggestion that he had been brought there not to do anything but only as a spectator or a witness. A few minutes later he was asleep.

9

THE WEATHER had changed during the night. Ransom sat looking out from the edge of the forest in which he had slept, on a flat sea where there were no other islands in view. He had waked a few minutes before and found himself lying alone in a close thicket of stems that were rather reed-like in character but stout as those of birch trees and which carried an almost flat roof of thick foliage. From this there hung fruits as smooth and bright and round as holly-berries, some of which he ate. Then he found his way to open country near the skirts of the island and looked about him. Neither Weston nor the Lady was in sight, and he began walking in a leisurely fashion beside the sea. His bare feet sank a little into a carpet of saffron-coloured vegetation, which covered them with an aromatic dust. As he was looking down at this he suddenly noticed something else. At first he thought it was a creature of more fantastic shape than he had yet seen on Perelandra. Its shape was not only fantastic but hideous. Then he dropped on one knee to examine it. Finally he touched it, with reluctance. A moment later he drew back his hands like a man who had touched a snake.

It was a damaged animal. It was, or had been, one of the brightly coloured frogs. But some accident had happened to it. The whole back had been ripped open in a sort of V-shaped gash, the point of the V being a little behind the head. Something had torn a widening wound backward—as we do in opening an envelope—along the trunk and pulled it out so far behind the animal that the hoppers or hind legs had been almost torn off with it. They were so damaged that the frog could not leap. On earth it would have been merely a nasty sight, but up to this moment Ransom had as yet seen nothing dead or spoiled in Perelandra, and it was like a blow in the face. It was like the first spasm of well-remembered pain warning a man who had thought he was cured that his family have deceived him and he is dying after all. It was like the first lie from the mouth of a friend on whose truth one was willing to stake a thousand pounds. It was irrevocable. The milk-warm wind blowing over the golden sea, the blues and silvers and greens of the floating garden, the sky itself—all these had become, in one instant, merely the illuminated margin of a book whose text was the struggling little horror at his feet, and he himself, in that same instant, had passed into a state of emotion which he could neither control nor understand. He told himself that a creature of that kind probably had very little sensation. But it did not much mend matters. It was not merely pity for pain that had suddenly changed the rhythm of his heart-beats. The thing was an intolerable obscenity which afflicted him with shame. It would have been better, or so he thought at that moment, for the whole universe never to have existed than for this one thing to have happened. Then he decided, in spite of his theoretical belief that it was an organism too low for much pain, that it had better be killed. He had neither boots nor stone nor stick. The frog proved remarkably hard to kill. When it was far too late to desist he saw clearly that he had been a fool to make the attempt. Whatever its sufferings might be he had certainly increased and not diminished them. But he had to go through with it. The job seemed to take nearly an hour. And when at last the mangled result was quite still and he went down to the water's edge to wash, he was sick and shaken. It seems odd to say this of a man who had been on the Somme; but the architects tell us that nothing is great or small save by position.

At last he got up and resumed his walk. Next moment he started and looked at the ground again. He quickened his pace, and then once more stopped and looked. He stood stock-still and covered his face. He called aloud upon heaven to break the nightmare or to let him understand what was happening. A trail of mutilated frogs lay along the edge of the island. Picking his footsteps with care, he followed it. He counted ten, fifteen, twenty: and the twenty-first brought him to a place where the wood came down to the water's edge. He went into the wood and came out on the other side. There he stopped dead and stared. Weston, still clothed but without his pith helmet, was standing about thirty feet away: and as Ransom watched he was tearing a frog—quietly and almost surgically inserting his forefinger, with its long sharp nail, under the skin behind the creature's head and ripping it open. Ransom had not noticed before that Weston had such remarkable nails. Then he finished the operation, threw the bleeding ruin away, and looked up. Their eyes met.

If Ransom said nothing, it was because he could not speak. He saw a man who was certainly not ill, to judge from his easy stance and the powerful use he had just been making of his fingers. He saw a man who was certainly Weston, to judge from his height and build and colouring and features. In that sense he was quite recognisable. But the terror was that he was also unrecognisable. He did not look like a sick man: but he looked very like a dead one. The face which he raised from torturing the frog had that terrible power which the face of a corpse sometimes has of simply rebuffing every conceivable human attitude one can adopt towards it. The expressionless mouth, the unwinking stare of the eyes, something heavy and inorganic in the very folds of the cheek, said clearly: "I have features as you have, but there is nothing in common between you and me." It was this that kept Ransom speechless. What could you say—what appeal or threat could have any meaning—to *that?* And now, forcing its way up into consciousness, thrusting aside every mental habit and every longing not to believe, came the conviction that this, in fact, was not a man: that Weston's body was kept, walking and undecaying, in Perelandra by some wholly different kind of life, and that Weston himself was gone.

It looked at Ransom in silence and at last began to smile. We have all often spoken—Ransom himself had often spoken—of a devilish smile. Now he realised that he had never taken the words seriously. The smile was not bitter, nor raging, nor, in an ordinary sense, sinister; it was not even mocking. It seemed to summon Ransom, with horrible naïveté of welcome, into the world of its own pleasures, as if all men were at one in those pleasures, as if they were the most natural thing in the world and no dispute could ever have occurred about them. It was not furtive, nor ashamed, it had nothing of the conspirator in it. It did not defy goodness, it ignored it to the point of annihilation. Ransom perceived that he had never before seen anything but half-hearted and uneasy attempts at evil. This creature was whole-hearted. The extremity of its evil had passed beyond all struggle into some state which bore a horrible similarity to innocence. It was beyond vice as the Lady was beyond virtue.

The stillness and the smiling lasted for perhaps two whole minutes: certainly not less. Then Ransom made to take a step towards the thing, with no very clear notion of what he would do when he reached it. He stumbled and fell. He had a curious difficulty in getting to his feet again, and when he got to them he overbalanced and fell for the second time. Then there was a moment of darkness with a noise of roaring express trains. After that the golden sky and coloured waves returned and he knew he was alone and recovering from a faint. As he lay there, still unable and perhaps unwilling to rise, it came into his mind that in certain old philosophers and poets he had read that the mere sight of the devils was one of the greatest among the torments of Hell. It had seemed to him till now merely a quaint fancy. And yet (as he now saw) even the children know better: no child would have any difficulty in understanding that there might be a face the mere beholding of which was final calamity. The children, the poets, and the philosophers were right. As there is one Face above all worlds merely to see which is irrevocable joy, so at the bottom of all worlds that face is waiting whose sight alone is the misery from which none who beholds it can recover. And though there seemed to be, and indeed were, a thousand roads by which a man could walk through the world, there was not a single one which did not lead sooner or later either to the Beatific or the Miserific Vision. He himself had, of course, seen only a mask or faint adumbration of it; even so, he was not quite sure that he would live.

When he was able, he got up and set out to search for the thing. He must either try to prevent it from meeting the Lady or at least be present when they met. What he could do, he did not know; but it was clear beyond all evasion that this was what he had been sent for. Weston's body, travelling in a space-ship, had been the bridge by which something else had invaded Perelandra—whether that supreme and original evil whom in Mars they call The Bent One, or one of his lesser followers, made no difference. Ransom was all goose-flesh, and his knees kept getting in each other's way. It surprised him that he could experience so extreme a terror and yet be walking and thinking—as men in war or sickness are surprised to find how much can be borne: "It will drive us mad," "It will kill us outright," we say; and then it happens and we find ourselves neither mad nor dead, still held to the task.

The weather changed. The plain on which he was walking swelled to a wave of land. The sky grew paler: it was soon rather primrose than gold. The sea grew darker, almost the colour of bronze. Soon the island was climbing considerable hills of water. Once or twice he had to sit down and rest. After several hours (for his progress was very slow) he suddenly saw two human figures on what was for the moment a skyline. Next moment they were out of sight as the country heaved up between them and him. It took about half an hour to reach them. Weston's body was standing—swaying and balancing itself to meet each change of the ground in a manner of which the real Weston would have been incapable. It was talking to the Lady. And what surprised Ransom most was that she continued to listen to it without turning to welcome him or even to comment on his arrival when he came and sat down beside her on the soft turf.

"It *is* a great branching out," it was saying. "This making of story or poetry about things that might be but are not. If you shrink back from it, are you not drawing back from the fruit that is offered you?"

"It is not from the making a story that I shrink back, O Stranger," she answered, "but from this one story that you have put into my head. I can make myself stories about my children or the King. I can make it that the fish fly and the land beasts swim. But if I try to make the story about living on the Fixed Island I do not know how to make it about Maleldil. For if I make it that He has changed His command, that will not go. And if I make it that we are living there against His command, that is like making the sky all black and the water so that we cannot drink it and the air so that we cannot breathe it. But also, I do not see what is the pleasure of trying to make these things."

"To make you wiser, older," said Weston's body.

"Do you know for certain that it will do that?" she asked.

"Yes, for certain," it replied. "That is how the women of my world have become so great and so beautiful."

"Do not listen to him," broke in Ransom; "send him away. Do not hear what he says, do not think of it."

She turned to Ransom for the first time. There had been some very slight change in her face since he had last seen her. It was not sad, nor deeply bewildered, but the hint of something precarious had increased. On the other hand she was clearly pleased to see him, though surprised at his interruption; and her first words revealed that her failure to greet him at his arrival had resulted from her never having envisaged the possibility of a conversation between more than two speakers. And throughout the rest of their talk, her ignorance of the technique of general conversation gave a curious and disquieting quality to the whole scene. She had no notion of how to glance rapidly from one face to another or to disentangle two remarks at once. Sometimes she listened wholly to Ransom, sometimes wholly to the other, but never to both.

"Why do you start speaking before this man has finished, Piebald?" she inquired. "How do they do in your world where you are many and more than two must often be together? Do they not talk in turns; or have you an art to understand even when all speak together? I am not old enough for that."

"I do not want you to hear him at all," said Ransom. "He is——" and then he hesitated. "Bad," "liar," "enemy," none of these words would, as yet, have any meaning for her. Racking his brains he thought of their previous conversation about the great eldil who had held on to the old good and refused the new one.

Yes; that would be her only approach to the idea of badness. He was just about to speak but it was too late. Weston's voice anticipated him.

"This Piebald," it said, "does not want you to hear me, because he wants to keep you young. He does not want you to go on to the new fruits that you have never tasted before."

"But how could he want to keep me younger?"

"Have you not seen already," said Weston's body, "that Piebald is one who always shrinks back from the wave that is coming towards us and would like, if he could, to bring back the wave that is past? In the very first hour of his talking with you, did he not betray this? He did not know that all was new since Maleldil became a man and that now all creatures with reason will be men. You had to teach him this. And when he had learned it he did not welcome it. He was sorry that there would be no more of the old furry people. He would bring back that old world if he could. And when you asked him to teach you Death, he would not. He wanted you to remain young, not to learn Death. Was it not he who first put into your mind the very thought that it was possible not to desire the wave that Maleldil was rolling towards us; to shrink so much that you would cut off your arms and legs to prevent it coming?"

"You mean he is so young?"

"He is what in my world we call Bad," said Weston's body. "One who rejects the fruit he is given for the sake of the fruit he expected or the fruit he found last time."

"We must make him older, then," said the Lady, and though she did not look at Ransom, all the Queen and Mother in her were revealed to him and he knew that she wished him, and all things, infinitely well. And he—he could do nothing. His weapon had been knocked out of his hand.

"And will you teach us Death?" said the Lady to Weston's shape, where it stood above her.

"Yes," it said, "it is for this that I came here, that you may have Death in abundance. But you must be very courageous."

"Courageous. What is that?"

"It is what makes you to swim on a day when the waves are so great and swift that something inside you bids you to stay on land."

"I know. And those are the best days of all for swimming."

"Yes. But to find Death, and with Death the real oldness and the strong beauty and the uttermost branching out, you must plunge into things greater than waves."

"Go on. Your words are like no other words that I have ever heard. They are like the bubble breaking on the tree. They make me think of—of—I do not know what they make me think of."

"I will speak greater words than these; but I must wait till you are older."

"Make me older."

"Lady, Lady," broke in Ransom, "will not Maleldil make you older in His own time and His own way, and will not that be far better?"

Weston's face did not turn in his direction either at this point or at any other time during the conversation, but his voice, addressed wholly to the Lady, answered Ransom's interruption.

"You see?" it said. "He himself, though he did not mean nor wish to do so, made you see a few days ago that Maleldil is beginning to teach you to walk by yourself, without holding you by the hand. That was the first branching out. When you came to know that, you were becoming really old. And since then Maleldil has let you learn much—not from His own voice, but from mine. You are becoming your own. That is what Maleldil wants you to do. That is why He has let you be separated from the King and even, in a way, from Himself. His way of making you older is to make you make yourself older. And yet this Piebald would have you sit still and wait for Maleldil to do it all."

"What must we do to Piebald to make him older?" said the Lady.

"I do not think you can help him till you are older yourself," said the voice of Weston. "You cannot help anyone yet. You are as a tree without fruit."

"It is very true," said the Lady. "Go on."

"Then listen," said Weston's body. "Have you understood that to wait for Maleldil's voice when Maleldil wishes you to walk on your own is a kind of disobedience?"

"I think I have."

"The wrong kind of obeying itself can be a disobeying."

The Lady thought for a few moments and then clapped her hands. "I see," she said, "I see! Oh, how old you make me. Before now I have chased a beast for mirth. And it has understood and run away from me. If it had stood still and let me catch it, that would have been a sort of obeying—but not the best sort."

"You understand very well. When you are fully grown you will be even wiser and more beautiful than the women of my own world. And you see that it might be so with Maleldil's biddings."

"I think I do not see quite clearly."

"Are you certain that He really wishes to be always obeyed?"

"How can we not obey what we love?"

"The beast that ran away loved you."

"I wonder," said the Lady, "if that is the same. The beast knows very well when I mean it to run away and when I want it to come to me. But Maleldil has never said to us that any word or work of His was a jest. How could our Beloved need to jest or frolic as we do? He is all a burning joy and a strength. It is like thinking that He needed sleep or food."

"No, it would not be a jest. That is only a thing like it, not the thing itself. But could the taking away of your hand from His—the full growing up—the walking in your own way—could that ever be perfect unless you had, if only once, *seemed* to disobey Him?"

"How could one *seem* to disobey?"

"By doing what He only *seemed* to forbid. There might be a commanding which He wished you to break."

"But if He told us we were to break it, then it would be no command. And if He did not, how should we know?"

"How wise you are growing, beautiful one," said Weston's mouth. "No. If He told you to break what He commanded, it would be no true command, as you have seen. For you are right, He makes no jests. A real disobeying, a real branching out, this is what He secretly longs for: secretly, because to tell you would spoil all."

"I begin to wonder," said the Lady after a pause, "whether you are so much older than I. Surely what you are saying is like fruit with no taste! How can I step out of His will save into something that cannot be wished? Shall I start trying not to love Him—or the King—or the beasts? It would be like trying to walk on water or swim through islands. Shall I try not to sleep or to drink or to laugh? I thought your words had a meaning. But now it seems they have none. To walk out of His will is to walk into nowhere."

"That is true of all His commands except one."

"But can that one be different?"

"Nay, you see of yourself that it is different. These other commands of His—to love, to sleep, to fill this world with your children—you see for yourself that they are good. And they are the same in all worlds. But the command against living on the Fixed Island is not so. You have already learned that He gave no such command to my world. And you cannot see where the goodness of it is. No wonder. If it were really good, must He not have commanded it to all worlds alike? For how could Maleldil not command what was good? There is *no* good in it. Maleldil Himself is showing you that, this moment, through your own reason. It is mere command. It is forbidding for the mere sake of forbidding."

"But why . . . ?"

"In order that you may break it. What other reason can there be? It is not good. It is not the same for other worlds. It stands between you and all settled life, all command of your own days. Is not Maleldil showing you as plainly as He can that it was set up as a test—as a great wave you have to go over, that you may become really old, really separate from Him."

"But if this concerns me so deeply, why does He put none of this into my mind? It is all coming from you, Stranger. There is no whisper, even, of the Voice saying Yes to your words."

"But do you not see that there cannot be? He longs—oh, how greatly He longs—to see His creature become fully itself, to stand up in its own reason and its own courage even against Him. But how can He *tell* it to do this? That would spoil all. Whatever it did after that would only be one more step taken *with* Him. This is the one thing of all the things He desires in which He must have no finger. Do you think He is not weary of seeing nothing but Himself in all that He has made? If that contented Him, why should He create at all? To find the Other— the thing whose will is no longer His—that is Maleldil's desire."

"If I could but know this——"

"He must not tell you. He cannot tell you. The nearest He can come to telling you is to let some other creature tell it for Him. And behold, He has done so. Is it for nothing, or without His will, that I have journeyed through Deep Heaven to teach you what He would have you know but must not teach you Himself?"

"Lady," said Ransom, "if I speak, will you hear me?"

"Gladly, Piebald."

"This man has said that the law against living on the Fixed Island is different from the other Laws, because it is not the same for all worlds and because we cannot see the goodness in it. And so far he says well. But then he says that it is thus different in order that you may disobey it. But there might be another reason."

"Say it, Piebald."

"I think He made one law of that kind in order that there might be obedience. In all these other matters what you call obeying Him is but doing what seems good in your own eyes also. Is love content with that? You do them, indeed, because they are His will, but not only because they are His will. Where can you taste the joy of obeying unless He bids you do something for which His bidding is the *only* reason? When we spoke last you said that if you told the beasts to walk on their heads, they would delight to do so. So I know that you understand well what I am saying."

"Oh, brave Piebald," said the Green Lady, "this is the best you have said yet. This makes me older far: yet it does not feel like the oldness this other is giving me. Oh, how well I see it! We cannot walk out of Maleldil's will: but He has given us a way to walk out of *our* will. And there could be no such way except a command like this. Out of our own will. It is like passing out through the world's roof into Deep Heaven. All beyond is Love Himself. I knew there was joy in looking upon the Fixed Island and laying down all thought of ever living there, but I did not till now understand." Her face was radiant as she spoke, but then a shade of bewilderment crossed it. "Piebald," she said, "if you are so young, as this other says, how do you know these things?"

"He says I am young, but I say not."

The voice of Weston's face spoke suddenly, and it was louder and deeper than before and less like Weston's voice.

"I am older than he," it said, "and he dare not deny it. Before the mothers of the mothers of his mother were conceived, I was already older than he could reckon. I have been with Maleldil in Deep Heaven where he never came and heard the eternal councils. And in the order of creation I am greater than he, and before me he is of no account. Is it not so?" The corpse-like face did not even now turn towards him, but the speaker and the Lady both seemed to wait for Ransom to reply. The falsehood which sprang to his mind died on his lips. In that air, even when truth seemed fatal, only truth would serve. Licking his lips and choking down a feeling of nausea, he answered:

"In our world to be older is not always to be wiser."

"Look at him." said Weston's body to the Lady; "consider how white his cheeks have turned and how his forehead is wet. You have not seen such things before: you will see them more often hereafter. It is what happens—it is the beginning of what happens—to little creatures when they set themselves against great ones."

An exquisite thrill of fear travelled along Ransom's spine. What saved him was the face of the Lady. Untouched by the evil so close to her, removed as it were ten years' journey deep within the region of her own innocence, and by that innocence at once protected and so endangered, she looked up at the standing Death above her, puzzled indeed, but not beyond the bounds of cheerful curiosity, and said:

"But he was right, Stranger, about this forbidding. It is you who need to be made older. Can you not see?"

"I have always seen the whole whereof he sees but the half. It is most true that Maleldil has given you a way of walking out of your own will—but out of your deepest will."

"And what is that?"

"Your deepest will, at present, is to obey Him—to be always as you are now, only His beast or His very young child. The way out of that is hard. It was made hard that only the very great, the very wise, the very courageous should dare to walk in it, to go on—on out of this smallness in which you now live—through the dark wave of His forbidding, into the real life, Deep Life, with all its joy and splendour and hardness."

"Listen, Lady," said Ransom. "There is something he is not telling you. All this that we are now talking has been talked before. The thing he wants you to try has been tried before. Long ago, when our world began, there was only one man and one woman in it, as you and the King are in this. And there once before he stood, as he stands now, talking to the woman. He had found her alone as he has found you alone. And she listened, and did the thing Maleldil had forbidden her to do. But no joy and splendour came of it. What came of it I cannot tell you because you have no image of it in your mind. But all love was troubled and made cold, and Maleldil's voice became hard to hear so that wisdom grew little among them; and the woman was against the man and the mother against the child; and when they looked to eat there was no fruit on their trees, and hunting for food took all their time, so that their life became narrower, not wider."

"He has hidden the half of what happened," said Weston's corpse-like mouth. "Hardness came out of it but also splendour. They made with their own hands mountains higher than your Fixed Island. They made for themselves Floating Islands greater than yours which they could move at will through the ocean faster than any bird can fly. Because there was not always food enough, a woman could give the only fruit to her child or her husband and eat death instead—could give them all, as you in your little narrow life of playing and kissing and riding fishes have never done, nor shall do till you break the commandment. Because knowledge was harder to find, those few who found it became more beautiful and excelled their fellows as you excel the beasts; and thousands were striving for their love . . ."

"I think I will go to sleep now," said the Lady quite suddenly. Up to this point she had been listening to Weston's body with open mouth and wide eyes, but as he spoke of the women with the thousands of lovers she yawned, with the unconcealed and unpremeditated yawn of a young cat.

"Not yet," said the other. "There is more. He has not told you that it was this breaking of the commandment which brought Maleldil to our world and because of which He was made man. He dare not deny it."

"Do you say this, Piebald?" asked the Lady.

Ransom was sitting with his fingers locked so tightly that his knuckles were white. The unfairness of it all was wounding him like barbed wire. Unfair . . . unfair. How could Maleldil expect him to fight against this, to fight with every weapon taken from him, forbidden to lie and yet brought to places where truth seemed fatal? It was unfair! A sudden impulse of hot rebellion arose in him. A second later, doubt, like a huge wave, came breaking over him. How if the enemy were right after all? *Felix peccatum Adae.* Even the Church would tell him that good came of disobedience in the end. Yes, and it was true too that he, Ransom, was a timid creature, a man who shrank back from new and hard things. On which side, after all, did the temptation lie? Progress passed before his eyes in a great momentary vision: cities, armies, tall ships, and libraries and fame, and the grandeur of poetry spurting like a fountain out of the labours and ambitions of men. Who could be certain that Creative Evolution was not the deepest truth? From all sorts of secret crannies in his own mind whose very existence he had never before suspected, something wild and heady and delicious began to rise, to pour itself towards the shape of Weston. "It is a spirit, it is a spirit," said this inner voice, "and you are only a man. It goes on from century to century. You are only a man. . . ."

"Do you say this, Piebald?" asked the Lady a second time.

The spell was broken.

"I will tell you what I say," answered Ransom, jumping to his feet. "Of course good came of it. Is Maleldil a beast that we can stop His path, or a leaf that we can twist His shape? Whatever you do, He will make good of it. But not the good He had prepared for you if you had obeyed Him. That is lost for ever. The first King and first Mother of our world did the forbidden thing; and He brought good of it in the end. But what they did was not good; and what they lost we have not seen. And there were some to whom no good came nor ever will come." He turned to the body of Weston. "You," he said, "tell her all. What good came to you? Do *you* rejoice that Maleldil became a man? Tell her of *your* joys, and of what profit you had when you made Maleldil and death acquainted."

In that moment that followed this speech two things happened that were utterly unlike terrestrial experience. The body that had been Weston's threw up its head and opened its mouth and gave a long melancholy howl like a dog; and the Lady lay down, wholly unconcerned, and closed her eyes and was instantly asleep. And while these two things were happening the piece of ground on which the two men stood and the woman lay was rushing down a great hillside of water.

Ransom kept his eyes fixed upon the enemy, but it took no notice of him. Its eyes moved like the eyes of a living man but it was hard to be sure what it was looking at, or whether it really used the eyes as organs of vision at all. One got the impression of a force that cleverly kept the pupils of those eyes fixed in a suitable direction while the mouth talked but which, for its own purpose, used wholly different modes of perception. The thing sat down close to the Lady's head on the far side of her from Ransom. If you could call it sitting down. The body did not reach its squatting position by the normal movements of a man: it was more as if some external force manœuvred it into the right position and then let it drop. It was impossible to point to any particular motion which was definitely non-human. Ransom had the sense of watching an imitation of living motions which had been very well studied and was technically correct: but somehow it lacked the master touch. And he was chilled with an inarticulate, night-nursery horror of the thing he had to deal with—the man-aged corpse, the bogey, the Un-man.

There was nothing to do but to watch: to sit there, for ever if need be, guarding the Lady from the Un-man while their island climbed interminably over the Alps and Andes of burnished water. All three were very still. Beasts and birds came often and looked upon them. Hours later the Un-man began to speak. It did not even look in Ransom's direction; slowly and cumbrously, as if by some machinery that needed oiling, it made its mouth and lips pronounce his name.

"Ransom," it said.

"Well?" said Ransom.

"Nothing," said the Un-man. He shot an inquisitive glance at it. Was the creature mad? But it looked, as before, dead rather than mad, sitting there with the head bowed and the mouth a little open, and some yellow dust from the moss settled in the creases of its cheeks, and the legs crossed tailorwise, and the hands, with their long metallic-looking nails, pressed flat together on the ground before it. He dismissed the problem from his mind and returned to his own uncomfortable thoughts.

"Ransom," it said again.

"What is it?" said Ransom sharply.

"Nothing," it answered.

Again there was silence; and again, about a minute later, the horrible mouth said:

"Ransom!" This time he made no reply. Another minute and it uttered his name again; and then, like a minute gun, "Ransom . . . Ransom . . . Ransom," perhaps a hundred times.

"What the Hell do you want?" he roared at last.

"Nothing," said the voice. Next time he determined not to answer; but when it had called on him a thousand times he found himself answering whether he would or no, and "Nothing," came the reply. He taught himself to keep silent in the end: not that the torture of resisting his impulse to speak was less than the torture of response but because something within him rose up to combat the tormentor's assurance that he must yield in the end. If the attack had been of some more violent kind it might have been easier to resist. What chilled and almost cowed him was the union of malice with something nearly childish. For temptation, for blasphemy, for a whole battery of horrors, he was in some sort prepared: but hardly for this petty, indefatigable nagging as of a nasty little boy at a preparatory school. Indeed no imagined horror could have surpassed the sense which grew within him as the slow hours passed, that this creature was, by all human standards, inside out—its heart on the surface and its shallowness at the heart. On the surface, great designs and an antagonism to Heaven which involved the fate of worlds: but deep within, when every veil had been pierced, was there, after all, nothing but a black puerility, an aimless empty spitefulness content to sate itself with the tiniest cruelties, as love does not disdain the smallest kindness? What kept him steady, long after all possibility of thinking about something else had disappeared, was the decision that if he must hear either the word Ransom or the word Nothing a million times, he would prefer the word Ransom.

And all the time the little jewel-coloured land went soaring up into the yellow firmament and hung there a moment and tilted its woods and went racing down into the warm lustrous depths between the waves: and the Lady lay sleeping with one arm bent beneath her head and her lips a little parted. Sleeping, assuredly— for her eyes were shut and her breathing regular—yet not looking quite like those who sleep in our world, for her face was full of expression and intelligence, and the limbs looked as if they were ready at any moment to leap up, and altogether she gave the impression that sleep was not a thing that happened to her but an action which she performed.

Then all at once it was night. "Ransom . . . Ransom . . . Ransom . . . Ransom" went on the voice. And suddenly it crossed his mind that though he would some time require sleep, the Un-man might not.

10

SLEEP proved to be indeed the problem. For what seemed a great time, cramped and wearied, and soon hungry and thirsty as well, he sat still in the darkness trying not to attend to the unflagging repetition of "Ransom—Ransom—Ransom." But presently he found himself listening to a conversation of which he knew he had not heard the beginning and realised he had slept. The Lady seemed to be saying very little. Weston's voice was speaking gently and continuously. It was not talking about the Fixed Land nor even about Maleldil. It appeared to be telling, with extreme beauty and pathos, a number of stories, and at first Ransom could not perceive any connecting link between them. They were all about women, but women who had apparently lived at different periods of the world's history and in quite different circumstances. From the Lady's replies it appeared that the stories contained much that she did not understand; but oddly enough the Un-man did not mind. If the questions aroused by any one story proved at all difficult to answer, the speaker simply dropped that story and instantly began another. The heroines of the stories seemed all to have suffered a great deal—they had been oppressed by fathers, cast off by husbands, deserted by lovers. Their children had risen up against them and society had driven them out. But the stories all ended, in a sense, happily: sometimes with honours and praises to a heroine still living, more often with tardy acknowledgment and unavailing tears after her death. As the endless speech proceeded, the Lady's questions grew always fewer; some meaning for the words Death and Sorrow—though what kind of meaning Ransom could not even guess—was apparently being created in her mind by mere repetition. At last it dawned upon him what all these stories were about. Each one of these women had stood forth alone and braved a terrible risk for her child, her lover, or her people. Each had been misunderstood, reviled, and persecuted: but each also magnificently vindicated by the event. The precise details were often not very easy to follow. Ransom had more than a suspicion than many of these noble pioneers had been what in ordinary terrestrial speech we call witches or perverts. But that was all in the background. What emerged from the stories was rather an image than an idea—the picture of the tall, slender form, unbowed though the world's weight rested upon its shoulders, stepping forth fearless and friendless into the dark to do for others what those others forbade it to do yet needed to have done. And all the time, as a sort of background to these goddess shapes, the speaker was building up a picture of the other sex. No word was directly spoken on the subject: but one felt them there as a huge, dim multitude of creatures pitifully childish and complacently arrogant; timid, meticulous, unoriginating; sluggish and ox-like, rooted to the earth almost in their indolence, prepared to try nothing, to risk nothing, to make no exertion, and capable of being raised into full life only by the unthanked and rebellious virtue of their females. It was very well done.

Ransom, who had little of the pride of sex, found himself for a few moments all but believing it.

In the midst of this the darkness was suddenly torn by a flash of lightning; a few seconds later came a revel of Perelandrian thunder, like the playing of a heavenly tambourine, and after that warm rain. Ransom did not much regard it. The flash had shown him the Un-man sitting bolt upright, the Lady raised on one elbow, the dragon lying awake at her head, a grove of trees beyond, and great waves against the horizon. He was thinking of what he had seen. He was wondering how the Lady could see that face—those jaws monotonously moving as if they were rather munching than talking—and not know the creature to be evil. He saw, of course, that this was unreasonable of him. He himself was doubtless an uncouth figure in her eyes; she could have no knowledge either about evil or about the normal appearance of terrestrial man to guide her. The expression on her face, revealed in the sudden light, was one that he had not seen there before. Her eyes were not fixed on the narrator: as far as that went, her thoughts might have been a thousand miles away. Her lips were shut and a little pursed. Her eyebrows were slightly raised. He had not yet seen her look so like a woman of our own race; and yet her expression was one he had not very often met on earth—except, as he realised with a shock, on the stage. "Like a tragedy queen" was the disgusting comparison that arose in his mind. Of course it was a gross exaggeration. It was an insult for which he could not forgive himself. And yet . . . and yet . . . the tableau revealed by the lightning had photographed itself on his brain. Do what he would, he found it impossible not to think of that new look in her face. A very *good* tragedy queen, no doubt. The heroine of a very great tragedy, very nobly played by an actress who was a good woman in real life. By earthly standards, an expression to be praised, even to be revered: but remembering all that he had read in her countenance before, the unselfconscious radiance, the frolic sanctity, the depth of stillness that reminded him sometimes of infancy and sometimes of extreme old age while the hard youth and valiancy of face and body denied both, he found this new expression horrifying. The fatal touch of invited grandeur, of enjoyed pathos—the assumption, however slight, of a rôle—seemed a hateful vulgarity. Perhaps she was doing no more—he had good hope that she was doing no more—than responding in a purely imaginative fashion to this new art of Story or Poetry. But by God she'd better not! And for the first time the thought "This can't go on" formulated itself in his mind.

"I will go where the leaves cover us from the rain," said her voice in the darkness. Ransom had hardly noticed that he was getting wet—in a world without clothes it is less important. But he rose when he heard her move and followed her as well as he could by ear. The Un-man seemed to be doing the same. They progressed in total darkness on a surface as variable as that of water. Every now and then there was another flash. One saw the Lady walking erect, the Un-man slouching by her side with Weston's shirt and shorts now sodden and clinging to it, and the dragon puffing and waddling behind. At last they came to a place where the carpet under their feet was dry and there was a drumming noise of rain on firm leaves above their heads. They lay down again. "And another time," began the Un-man at once, "there was a queen in our world who ruled over a little land——"

"Hush!" said the Lady, "let us listen to the rain." Then, after a moment, she added, "What was that? It was some beast I never heard before"—and indeed, there had been something very like a low growl close beside them.

"I do not know," said the voice of Weston.

"I think I do," said Ransom.

"Hush!" said the Lady again, and no more was said that night.

This was the beginning of a series of days and nights which Ransom remembered with loathing for the rest of his life. He had been only too correct in supposing that his enemy required no sleep. Fortunately the Lady did, but she needed a good deal less than Ransom and possibly, as the days passed, came to take less than she needed. It seemed to Ransom that whenever he dozed he awoke to find the Un-man already in conversation with her. He was dead tired. He could hardly have endured it at all but for the fact that their hostess quite frequently dismissed them both from her presence. On such occasions Ransom kept close to the Un-man. It was a rest from the main battle, but it was a very imperfect rest. He did not dare to let the enemy out of his sight for a moment, and every day its society became more unendurable. He had full opportunity to learn the falsity of the maxim that the Prince of Darkness is a gentleman. Again and again he felt that a suave and subtle Mephistopheles with red cloak and rapier and a feather in his cap, or even a sombre tragic Satan out of *Paradise Lost,* would have been a welcome release from the thing he was actually doomed to watch. It was not like dealing with a wicked politician at all: it was much more like being set to guard an imbecile or a monkey or a very nasty child. What had staggered and disgusted him when it first began saying, "Ransom . . . Ransom . . ." continued to disgust him every day and every hour. It showed plenty of subtlety and intelligence when talking to the Lady; but Ransom soon perceived that it regarded intelligence simply and solely as a weapon, which it had no more wish to employ in its off-duty hours than a soldier has to do bayonet practice when he is on leave. Thought was for it a device necessary to certain ends, but thought in itself did not interest it. It assumed reason as externally and inorganically as it had assumed Weston's body. The moment the Lady was out of sight it seemed to relapse. A great deal of his time was spent in protecting the animals from it. Whenever it got out of sight, or even a few yards ahead, it would make a grab at any beast or bird within its reach and pull out some fur or feathers. Ransom tried whenever possible to get between it and its victim. On such occasions there were nasty moments when the two stood facing each other. It never came to a fight, for the Un-man merely grinned and perhaps spat and fell back a little, but before that happened Ransom usually had opportunity to discover how terribly he feared it. For side by side with his disgust, the more childlike terror of living with a ghost or a mechanised corpse never left him for many minutes together.

The fact of being *alone* with it sometimes rushed upon his mind with such dismay that it took all his reason to resist his longing for society—his impulse to rush madly over the island until he found the Lady and to beg her protection. When the Un-man could not get animals it was content with plants. It was fond of cutting their outer rinds through with its nails, or grubbing up roots, or pulling off leaves, or even tearing up handfuls of turf. With Ransom himself it had innumerable games to play. It had a whole repertory of obscenities to perform with its own—or rather with Weston's—body: and the mere silliness of them was almost worse than the dirtiness. It would sit making grimaces at him for hours together; and then, for hours more, it would go back to its old repetition of "Ransom . . . Ransom." Often its grimaces achieved a horrible resemblance to people whom Ransom had known and loved in our own world. But worst of all were those moments when it allowed Weston to come back into its countenance. Then its voice, which was always Weston's voice, would begin a pitiful, hesitant mumbling, "You be very careful, Ransom. I'm down in the bottom of a big black hole. No I'm not, though. I'm on Perelandra. I can't think very well now, but that doesn't matter, he does all my thinking for me. It'll get quite easy presently. That boy keeps on shutting the windows. That's all right, they've taken off my head and put someone else's on me. I'll soon be all right now. They won't let me see my press cuttings. So then I went and told him that if they didn't want me in the first Fifteen they could jolly well do without me, see. We'll tell that young whelp it's an insult to the examiners to show up this kind of work. What I want to know is why I should pay for a first-class ticket and then be crowded out like this. It's not fair. Not fair. I never meant any harm. Could you take some of this weight off my chest, I don't want all those clothes. Let me alone. Let me alone. It's not fair. It's not fair. What enormous bluebottles. They say you get used to them"—and then it would end in the canine howl. Ransom never could make up his mind whether it was a trick or whether a decaying psychic energy that had once been Weston were indeed fitfully and miserably alive within the body that sat there beside him. He discovered that any hatred he had once felt for the Professor was dead. He found it natural to pray fervently for his soul. Yet what he felt for Weston was not exactly pity. Up till that moment, whenever he had thought of Hell, he had pictured the lost souls as being still human; now, as the frightful abyss which parts ghosthood from manhood yawned before him, pity was almost swallowed up in horror—in the unconquerable revulsion of the life within him from positive and self-consuming Death. If the remains of Weston were, at such moments, speaking through the lips of the Un-man, then Weston was not now a man at all. The forces which had begun, perhaps years ago, to eat away his humanity had now completed their work. The intoxicated will which had been slowly poisoning the intelligence and the affections had now at last poisoned itself and the whole psychic organism had fallen to pieces. Only a ghost was left—an everlasting unrest, a crumbling, a ruin, an odour of decay. "And this," thought Ransom, "might be my destination; or hers."

But of course the hours spent alone with the Un-man were like hours in a back area. The real business of life was the interminable conversation between the Tempter and the Green Lady. Taken hour by hour the progress was hard to estimate; but as the days passed Ransom could not resist the conviction that the general development was in the enemy's favour. There were, of course, ups and downs. Often the Un-man was unexpectedly repulsed by some simplicity which it seemed not to have anticipated. Often, too, Ransom's own contributions to the terrible debate were for the moment successful. There were times when he thought, "Thank God! We've won at last." But the enemy was never tired, and Ransom grew more weary all the time; and presently he thought he could see signs that the Lady was becoming tired too. In the end he taxed her with it and begged her to send them both away. But she rebuked him, and her rebuke revealed how dangerous the situation had already become. "Shall I go and rest and play," she asked, "while all this lies on our hands? Not till I am certain that there is no great deed to be done by me for the King and for the children of our children."

It was on those lines that the enemy now worked almost exclusively. Though the Lady had no word for Duty he had made it appear to her in the light of a Duty that she should continue to fondle the idea of disobedience, and convinced her that it would be a cowardice if she repulsed him. The ideas of the Great Deed, of the Great Risk, of a kind of martyrdom, were presented to her every day, varied in a thousand forms. The notion of waiting to ask the King before a decision was made had been unobtrusively shuffled aside. Any such "cowardice" was now not to be thought of. The whole point of her action—the whole grandeur—would lie in taking it without the King's knowledge, in leaving him utterly free to repudiate it, so that all the benefits should be his, and all the risks hers; and with the risk, of course, all the magnanimity, the pathos, the tragedy, and the original-ity. And also, the Tempter hinted, it would be no use asking the King, for he would certainly *not* approve the action: men were like that. The King must be forced to be free. Now, while she was on her own—now or never—the noble thing must be achieved; and with that "Now or never" he began to play on a fear which the Lady apparently shared with the women of earth—the fear that life might be wasted, some great opportunity let slip. "How if I were as a tree that could have borne gourds and yet bore none," she said. Ransom tried to convince her that children were fruit enough. But the Un-man asked whether this elaborate division of the human race into two sexes could possibly be meant for no other purpose than offspring?—a matter which might have been more simply provided for, as it was in many of the plants. A moment later it was explaining that men like Ransom in his own world—men of that intensely male and backward-looking type who always shrank away from the new good—had continuously laboured to keep women down to mere child-bearing and to ignore the high destiny for which Maleldil had actually created her. It told her that such men had already done incalculable harm. Let her look to it that nothing of the sort happened on Perelandra. It was at this stage that it began to teach her many new words: words like Creative and Intuition and Spiritual. But that was one of its false steps. When she had at last been made to understand what "creative" meant she forgot all about the Great Risk and the tragic loneliness and laughed for a whole minute on end. Finally she told the Un-man that it was younger even than Piebald, and sent them both away.

Ransom gained ground over that; but on the following day he lost it all by losing his temper. The enemy had been pressing on her with more than usual ardour the nobility of self-sacrifice and self-dedication, and the enchantment seemed to be deepening in her mind every moment, when Ransom, goaded beyond all patience, had leaped to his feet and really turned upon her, talking far too quickly and almost shouting, and even forgetting his Old Solar and intermixing English words. He tried to tell her that he'd seen this kind of "unselfishness" in action: to tell her of women making themselves sick with hunger rather than begin the meal before the man of the house returned, though they knew perfectly well that there was nothing he disliked more; of mothers wearing themselves to a ravelling to marry some daughter to a man whom she detested; of Agrippina and of Lady Macbeth. "Can you not see," he shouted, "that he is making you say words that mean nothing? What is the good of saying you would do this for the King's sake when you know it is what the King would hate most? Are you Maleldil that you should determine what is good for the King?" But she understood only a very small part of what he said and was bewildered by his manner. The Un-man made capital out of this speech.

But through all these ups and downs, all changes of the front line, all counter-attacks and stands and withdrawals, Ransom came to see more and more clearly the strategy of the whole affair. The Lady's response to the suggestion of becoming a risk-bearer, a tragic pioneer, was still a response made chiefly out of her love for the King and for her unborn children, and even, in a sense, of Maleldil Himself. The idea that He might not really wish to be obeyed to the letter was the sluice through which the whole flood of suggestion had been admitted to her mind. But mixed with this response, from the moment when the Un-man began its tragic stories, there was the faintest touch of theatricality, the first hint of a self-admiring inclination to seize a grand rôle in the drama of her world. It was clear that the Un-man's whole effort was to increase this element. As long as this was but one drop, so to speak, in the sea of her mind, he would not really succeed. Perhaps, while it remained so, she was protected from actual disobedience: perhaps no rational creature, until such a motive became dominant, could really throw away happiness for anything quite so vague as the Tempter's chatter about Deeper Life and the Upward Path. The veiled egoism in the conception of noble revolt must be increased. And Ransom thought, despite many rallies on her part and many setbacks suffered by the enemy, that it was, very slowly and yet perceptibly, increasing. The matter was, of course, cruelly, cruelly complicated. What the Un-man said was always very nearly true. Certainly it must be part of the Divine plan that this happy creature should mature, should become more and more a creature of free choice, should become, in a sense, more distinct from God and from her husband in order thereby to be at one with them in a richer fashion.

In fact, he had seen this very process going on from the moment at which he met her, and had, unconsciously, assisted it. This present temptation, if conquered, would itself be the next, and greatest, step in the same direction: an obedience freer, more reasoned, more conscious than any she had known before, was being put in her power. But for that very reason the fatal false step which, once taken, would thrust her down into the terrible slavery of appetite and hate and economics and government which our race knows so well, could be made to sound so like the true one. What made him feel sure that the dangerous element in her interest was growing was her progressive disregard of the plain intellectual bones of the problem. It became harder to recall her mind to the *data*—a command from Maleldil, a complete uncertainty about the results of breaking it, and a present happiness so great that hardly any change could be for the better. The turgid swell of indistinctly splendid images which the Un-man aroused, and the transcendent importance of the central image, carried all this away. She was still in her innocence. No evil intention had been formed in her mind. But if her will was uncorrupted, half her imagination was already filled with bright, poisonous shapes. "This can't go on," thought Ransom for the second time. But all his arguments proved in the long run unavailing, and it did go on.

There came a night when he was so tired that towards morning he fell into a leaden sleep and slept far into the following day. He woke to find himself alone. A great horror came over him. "What could I have done? What could I have done?" he cried out, for he thought that all was lost. With sick heart and sore head he staggered to the edge of the island: his idea was to find a fish and to pursue the truants to the Fixed Land where he felt little doubt that they had gone. In the bitterness and confusion of his mind he forgot that he had no notion in which direction that land now lay nor how far it was distant. Hurrying through the woods, he emerged into an open place and suddenly found that he was not alone. Two human figures, robed to their feet, stood before him, silent under the yellow sky. Their clothes were of purple and blue, their heads wore chaplets of silver leaves, and their feet were bare. They seemed to him to be, the one the ugliest, and the other the most beautiful, of the children of men. Then one of them spoke and he realised that they were none other than the Green Lady herself and the haunted body of Weston. The robes were of feathers, and he knew well the Perelandrian birds from which they had been derived; the art of the weaving it could be called, was beyond his comprehension.

"Welcome, Piebald," said the Lady. "You have slept long. What do you think of us in our leaves?"

"The birds," said Ransom. "The poor birds! What has he done to them?"

"He has found the feathers somewhere," said the Lady carelessly. "They drop them."

"Why have you done this, Lady?"

"He has been making me older again. Why did you never tell me, Piebald?"

"Tell you what?"

"We never knew. This one showed me that the trees have leaves and the beasts have fur, and said that in your world the men and women also hung beautiful things about them. Why do you not tell us how we look? Oh, Piebald, Piebald, I hope this is not going to be another of the new goods from which you draw back your hand. It cannot be new to you if they all do it it in your world."

"Ah," said Ransom, "but it is different there. It is cold."

"So the Stranger said," she answered. "But not in all parts of your world. He says they do it even where it is warm."

"Has he said why they do it?"

"To be beautiful. Why else?" said the Lady, with some wonder in her face.

"Thank Heaven," thought Ransom, "he is only teaching her vanity"; for he had feared something worse. Yet could it be possible, in the long run, to wear clothes without learning modesty, and through modesty lasciviousness?

"Do you think we are more beautiful?" said the Lady, interrupting his thoughts.

"No," said Ransom; and then, correcting himself, "I don't know." It was, indeed, not easy to reply. The Un-man, now that Weston's prosaic shirt and shorts were concealed, looked a more exotic and therefore a more imaginatively, less squalidly, hideous figure. As for the Lady—that she looked in some way worse was not doubtful. Yet there is a plainness in nudity—as we speak of "plain" bread. A sort of richness, a flamboyancy, a concession, as it were, to lower conceptions of the beautiful, had come with the purple robe. For the first (and last) time she appeared to him at that moment as a woman whom an earth-born man might conceivably love. And this was intolerable. The ghastly inappropriateness of the idea had, all in one moment, stolen something from the colours of the landscape and the scent of the flowers.

"Do you think we are more beautiful?" repeated the Lady.

"What does it matter?" said Ransom dully.

"Everyone should wish to be as beautiful as they can," she answered. "And we cannot see ourselves."

"We can," said Weston's body.

"How can this be?" said the Lady, turning to it. "Even if you could roll your eyes right round to look inside they would see only blackness."

"Not that way," it answered. "I will show you." It walked a few paces away to where Weston's pack lay in the yellow turf. With that curious distinctness which often falls upon us when we are anxious and preoccupied Ransom noticed the exact make and pattern of the pack. It must have been from the same shop in London where he had bought his own: and that little fact, suddenly reminding him that Weston had once been a man, that he too had once had pleasures and pains and a human mind, almost brought the tears into his eyes. The horrible fingers which Weston would never use again worked at the buckles and brought out a small bright object—an English pocket mirror that might have cost three-and-six. He handed it to the Green Lady. She turned it over in her hands.

"What is it? What am I to do with it?" she said.

"Look in it," said the Un-man.

"How?"

"Look!" he said. Then taking it from her he held it up to her face. She stared for quite an appreciable time without apparently making anything of it. Then she started back with a cry and covered her face. Ransom started too. It was the first time he had seen her the mere passive recipient of any emotion. The world about him was big with change.

"Oh—oh," she cried. "What is it? I saw a face."

"Only your own face, beautiful one," said the Un-man.

"I know," said the Lady, still averting her eyes from the mirror. "My face—out there—looking at me. Am I growing older or is it something else? I feel . . . I feel . . . my heart is beating too hard. I am not warm. What is it?" She glanced from one of them to the other. The mysteries had all vanished from her face. It was as easy to read as that of a man in a shelter when a bomb is coming.

"What is it?" she repeated.

"It is called Fear," said Weston's mouth. Then the creature turned its face full on Ransom and grinned.

"Fear," she said. "This is Fear," pondering the discovery; then, with abrupt finality, "I do not like it."

"It will go away," said the Un-man, when Ransom interrupted.

"It will never go away if you do what he wishes. It is into more and more fear that he is leading you."

"It is," said the Un-man, "into the great waves and through them and beyond. Now that you know Fear, you see that it must be you who shall taste it on behalf of your race. You know the King will not. You do not wish him to. But there is no cause for fear in this little thing: rather of joy. What is fearful in it?"

"Things being two when they are one," replied the Lady decisively. "That thing" (she pointed at the mirror) "is me and not me."

"But if you do not look you will never know how beautiful you are."

"It comes into my mind, Stranger," she answered, "that a fruit does not eat itself, and a man cannot be together with himself."

"A fruit cannot do that because it is only a fruit," said the Un-man. "But we can do it. We call this thing a mirror. A man can love himself, and be together with himself. That is what it means to be a man or a woman—to walk alongside oneself as if one were a second person and to delight in one's own beauty. Mirrors were made to teach this art."

"Is it a good?" said the Lady.

"No," said Ransom.

"How can you find out without trying?" said the Un-man.

"If you try it and it is not good," said Ransom, "how do you know whether you will be able to stop doing it?"

"I am walking alongside myself already," said the Lady. "But I do not yet know what I look like. If I have become two I had better know what the other is. As for you, Piebald, one look will show me this woman's face and why should I look more than once?"

She took the mirror, timidly but firmly, from the Un-man and looked into it in silence for the better part of a minute. Then she let it sink and stood holding it at her side.

"It is very strange," she said at last.

"It is very beautiful," said the Un-man. "Do you not think so?"

"Yes."

"But you have not yet found what you set out to find."

"What was that? I have forgotten."

"Whether the robe of feathers made you more beautiful or less."

"I saw only a face."

"Hold it further away and you will see the whole of the alongside woman— the other who is yourself. Or no—I will hold it."

The commonplace suggestions of the scene became grotesque at this stage. She looked at herself first with the robe, then without it, then with it again; finally she decided against it and threw it away. The Un-man picked it up.

"Will you not keep it?" he said: "you might wish to carry it on some days even if you do not wish for it on all days."

"*Keep* it?" she asked, not clearly understanding.

"I had forgotten," said the Un-man. "I had forgotten that you would not live on the Fixed Land nor build a house nor in any way become mistress of your own days. *Keeping* means putting a thing where you know you can always find it again, and where rain, and beasts, and other people cannot reach it. I would give you this mirror to keep. It would be the Queen's mirror, a gift brought into the world from Deep Heaven: the other women would not have it. But you have reminded me. There can be no gifts, no keeping, no foresight while you live as you do—from day to day, like the beasts."

But the Lady did not appear to be listening to him. She stood like one almost dazed with the richness of a day dream. She did not look in the least like a woman who is thinking about a new dress. The expression of her face was noble. It was a great deal too noble. Greatness, tragedy, high sentiment—these were obviously what occupied her thoughts. Ransom perceived that the affair of the robes and the mirror had been only superficially concerned with what is commonly called female vanity. The image of her beautiful body had been offered to her only as a means to awake the far more perilous image of her great soul. The external and, as it were, dramatic conception of the self was the enemy's true aim. He was making her mind a theatre in which that phantom self should hold the stage. He had already written the play.

11

Because he had slept so late that morning Ransom found it easy to keep awake the following night. The sea had become calm and there was no rain. He sat upright in the darkness with his back against a tree. The others were close beside him—the Lady, to judge by her breathing, asleep and the Un-man doubtless waiting to arouse her and resume its solicitations the moment Ransom should doze. For the third time, more strongly than ever before, it came into his head, "This can't go on."

The Enemy was using Third Degree methods. It seemed to Ransom that, but for a miracle, the Lady's resistance was bound to be worn away in the end. Why did no miracle come? Or rather, why no miracle on the right side? For the presence of the Enemy was in itself a kind of Miracle. Had Hell a prerogative to work wonders? Why did Heaven work none? Not for the first time he found himself questioning Divine Justice. He could not understand why Maleldil should remain absent when the Enemy was there in person.

But while he was thinking this, as suddenly and sharply as if the solid darkness about him had spoken with articulate voice, he knew that Maleldil was not absent. That sense—so very welcome yet never welcomed without the overcoming of a certain resistance—that sense of the Presence which he had once or twice before experienced on Perelandra, returned to him. The darkness was packed quite full. It seemed to press upon his trunk so that he could hardly use his lungs: it seemed to close in on his skull like a crown of intolerable weight so that for a space he could hardly think. Moreover, he became aware in some indefinable fashion that it had never been absent, that only some unconscious activity of his own had succeeded in ignoring it for the past few days.

Inner silence is for our race a difficult achievement. There is a chattering part of the mind which continues, until it is corrected, to chatter on even in the holiest places. Thus, while one part of Ransom remained, as it were, prostrated in a hush of fear and love that resembled a kind of death, something else inside him, wholly unaffected by reverence, continued to pour queries and objections into his brain. "It's all very well," said this voluble critic, "a presence of *that* sort! But the Enemy is really here, really saying and doing things. Where is Maleldil's representative?"

The answer which came back to him, quick as a fencer's or a tennis player's *riposte*, out of the silence and the darkness, almost took his breath away. It seemed Blasphemous. "Anyway, what can I do?" babbled the voluble self. "I've done all I can. I've talked till I'm sick of it. It's no good, I tell you." He tried to persuade himself that he, Ransom, could not possibly be Maleldil's representative as the Un-man was the representative of Hell. The suggestion was, he argued, itself diabolical—a temptation to fatuous pride, to megalomania. He was horrified when the darkness simply flung back this argument in his face, almost impatiently. And then—he wondered how it had escaped him till now—he was forced to perceive that his own coming to Perelandra was at least as much of a marvel as the Enemy's. That miracle on the right side, which he had demanded, had in fact occurred. He himself was the miracle.

"Oh, but this is nonsense," said the voluble self. He, Ransom, with his ridiculous piebald body and his ten times defeated arguments—what sort of a miracle was that? His mind darted hopefully down a side-alley that seemed to promise escape. Very well then. He *had* been brought here miraculously. He was in God's hands. As long as he did his best—and he *had* done his best—God would see to the final issue. He had not succeeded. But he had done his best. No one could do more. " 'Tis not in mortals to command success." He must not be worried about the final result. Maleldil would see to that. And Maleldil would bring him safe back to earth after his very real, though unsuccessful, efforts. Probably Maleldil's real intention was that he should publish to the human race the truths he had learned on the planet Venus. As for the fate of Venus, that could not really rest upon his shoulders. It was in God's hands. One must be content to leave it there. One must have Faith. . . .

It snapped like a violin string. Not one rag of all this evasion was left. Relentlessly, unmistakably, the Darkness pressed down upon him the knowledge that this picture of the situation was utterly false. His journey to Perelandra was not a moral exercise, nor a sham fight. If the issue lay in Maleldil's hands, Ransom and the Lady *were* those hands. The fate of a world really depended on how they behaved in the next few hours. The thing was irreducibly, nakedly real. They could, if they chose, decline to save the innocence of this new race, and if they declined its innocence would not be saved. It rested with no other creature in all time or all space. This he saw clearly, though as yet he had no inkling of what he could do.

The voluble self protested, wildly, swiftly, like the propeller of a ship racing when it is out of the water. The imprudence, the unfairness, the absurdity of it! Did Maleldil *want* to lose worlds? What was the sense of so arranging things that anything really important should finally and absolutely depend on such a man of straw as himself? And at that moment, far away on Earth, as he now could not help remembering, men were at war, and white-faced subalterns and freckled corporals who had but lately begun to shave, stood in horrible gaps or crawled forward in deadly darkness, awaking, like him, to the preposterous truth that all really depended on their actions; and far away in time Horatius stood on the bridge, and Constantine settled in his mind whether he would or would not embrace the new religion, and Eve herself stood looking upon the forbidden fruit and the Heaven of Heavens waited for her decision. He writhed and ground his teeth, but could not help seeing. Thus, and not otherwise, the world was made. Either something or nothing must depend on individual choices. And if something, who could set bounds to it? A stone may determine the course of a river. He was that stone at this horrible moment which had become the centre of the whole universe. The eldila of all worlds, the sinless organisms of everlasting light, were silent in Deep Heaven to see what Elwin Ransom of Cambridge would do.

Then came blessed relief. He suddenly realised that he did not know what he *could* do. He almost laughed with joy. All this horror had been premature. No definite task was before him. All that was being demanded of him was a general and preliminary resolution to oppose the Enemy in any mode which circumstances might show to be desirable: in fact—and he flew back to the comforting words as a child flies back to its mother's arms—"to do his best"—or rather, to go on doing his best, for he had really been doing it all along. "What bug-bears we make of things unnecessarily!" he murmured, settling himself in a slightly more comfortable position. A mild flood of what appeared to him to be cheerful and rational piety rose and engulfed him.

Hullo! What was this? He sat straight upright again, his heart beating wildly against his side. His thoughts had stumbled on an idea from which they started back as a man starts back when he has touched a hot poker. But this time the idea was really too childish to entertain. This time it *must* be a deception, risen from his own mind. It stood to reason that a struggle with the Devil meant a *spiritual* struggle . . . the notion of a physical combat was only fit for a savage. If only it *were* as simple as that . . . but here the voluble self had made a fatal mistake. The habit of imaginative honesty was too deeply engrained in Ransom to let him toy for more than a second with the pretence that he feared bodily strife with the Un-man less than he feared anything else. Vivid pictures crowded upon him . . . the deadly cold of those hands (he had touched the creature accidentally some hours before) . . . the long metallic nails . . . ripping off narrow strips of flesh, pulling out tendons. One would die slowly. Up to the very end that cruel idiocy would smile into one's face. One would give way long before one died—beg for mercy, promise it help, worship, anything.

It was fortunate that something so horrible should be so obviously out of the question. Almost, but not quite, Ransom decreed that whatever the Silence and the Darkness seemed to be saying about this, no such crude, materialistic struggle could possibly be what Maleldil really intended. Any suggestion to the contrary must be only his own morbid fancy. It would degrade the spiritual warfare to the condition of mere mythology. But here he got another check. Long since on Mars, and more strongly since he came to Perelandra, Ransom had been perceiving that the triple distinction of truth from myth and of both from fact was purely terrestrial—was part and parcel of that unhappy division between soul and body which resulted from the Fall. Even on earth the sacraments existed as a permanent reminder that the division was neither wholesome nor final. The Incarnation had been the beginning of its disappearance. In Perelandra it would have no meaning at all. Whatever happened here would be of such a nature that earth-men would call it mythological. All this he had thought before. Now he knew it. The Presence in the darkness, never before so formidable, was putting these truths into his hands, like terrible jewels.

The voluble self was almost thrown out of its argumentative stride—became for some seconds as the voice of a mere whimpering child begging to be let off, to be allowed to go home. Then it rallied. It explained precisely where the absurdity of a physical battle with the Un-man lay. It would be quite irrelevant to the spiritual issue. If the Lady were to be kept in obedience only by the forcible removal of the Tempter, what was the use of that? What would it prove? And if the temptation were not a proving or testing, why was it allowed to happen at all? Did Maleldil suggest that our own world might have been saved if the elephant had accidentally trodden on the serpent a moment before Eve was about to yield? Was it as easy and as un-moral as that? The thing was patently absurd!

The terrible silence went on. It became more and more like a face, a face not without sadness, that looks upon you while you are telling lies, and never interrupts, but gradually you know that it knows, and falter, and contradict yourself, and lapse into silence. The voluble self petered out in the end. Almost the Darkness said to Ransom, "You know you are only wasting time." Every minute it became clearer to him that the parallel he had tried to draw between Eden and Perelandra was crude and imperfect. What had happened on Earth, when Maleldil was born a man at Bethlehem, had altered the universe for ever. The new world of Perelandra was not a mere repetition of the old world Tellus. Maleldil never repeated Himself. As the Lady had said, the same wave never came twice. When Eve fell, God was not Man. He had not yet made men members of His body: since then He had, and through them henceforward He would save and suffer. One of the purposes for which He had done all this was to save Perelandra not through Himself but through Himself in Ransom. If Ransom refused, the plan, so far, miscarried. For that point in the story, a story far more complicated than he had conceived, it was he who had been selected. With a strange sense of "fallings from him, vanishings," he perceived that you might just as well call Perelandra, not Tellus, the centre. You might look upon the Perelandrian story as merely an indirect consequence of the Incarnation on earth: or you might look on the Earth story as mere preparation for the new worlds of which Perelandra was the first. The one was neither more nor less true than the other. Nothing was more or less important than anything else, nothing was a copy or model of anything else.

At the same time he also perceived that his voluble self had begged the question. Up to this point the Lady had repelled her assailant. She was shaken and weary, and there were some stains perhaps in her imagination, but she had stood. In that respect the story already differed from anything that he certainly knew about the mother or our own race. He did not know whether Eve had resisted at all, or if so, for how long. Still less did he know how the story would have ended if she had. If the "serpent" had been foiled, and returned the next day, and the next . . . what then? Would the trial have lasted for ever? How would Maleldil have stopped it? Here on Perelandra his own intuition had been not that no temptation must occur but that "This can't go on." This stopping of a third-degree solicitation, already more than once refused, was a problem to which the terrestrial Fall offered no clue—a new task, and for that new task a new character in the drama, who appeared (most unfortunately) to be himself. In vain did his mind hark back, time after time, to the Book of Genesis, asking "What would have happened?" But to this the Darkness gave him no answer. Patiently and inexorably it brought him back to the here and the now, and to the growing certainty of what was here and now demanded. Almost he felt that the words "would have happened" were meaningless—mere invitations to wander in what the Lady would have called an "alongside world" which had no reality. Only the actual was real: and every actual situation was new. Here in Perelandra the temptation would be stopped by Ransom, or it would not be stopped at all. The Voice—for it was almost with a Voice that he was now contending—seemed to create around this alternative an infinite vacancy. This chapter, this page, this very sentence, in the cosmic story was utterly and eternally itself; no other passage that had occurred or ever would occur could be substituted for it.

He fell back on a different line of defence. How *could* he fight the immortal enemy? Even if he were a fighting man—instead of a sedentary scholar with weak eyes and a baddish wound from the last war—what use was there in fighting it? It couldn't be killed, could it? But the answer was almost immediately plain. Weston's body could be destroyed; and presumably that body was the Enemy's only foothold in Perelandra. By that body, when that body still obeyed a human will, it had entered the new world: expelled from it, it would doubtless have no other habitation. It had entered that body at Weston's own invitation, and without such invitation could enter no other. Ransom remembered that the unclean spirits, in the Bible, had a horror of being cast out into the "deep." And thinking of these things he perceived at last, with a sinking of heart, that if physical action were indeed demanded of him, it was an action, by ordinary standards, neither impossible nor hopeless. On the physical plane it was one middle-aged, sedentary body against another, and both unarmed save for fists and teeth and nails. At the thought of these details, terror and disgust overcame him. To kill the thing with such weapons (he remembered his killing of the frog) would be a nightmare; to be killed—who knew how slowly?—was more than he could face. That he would be killed he felt certain. "When," he asked, "did I ever win a fight in all my life?"

He was no longer making efforts to resist the conviction of what he must do. He had exhausted all his efforts. The answer was plain beyond all subterfuge. The Voice out of the night spoke it to him in such unanswerable fashion that, though there was no noise, he almost felt it must wake the woman who slept close by. He was faced with the impossible. This he must do: this he could not do. In vain he reminded himself of the things that unbelieving boys might at this moment be doing on Earth for a lesser cause. His will was in that valley where the appeal to shame becomes useless—nay, makes the valley darker and deeper. He believed he could face the Un-man with firearms: even that he could stand up unarmed and face certain death if the creature had retained Weston's revolver. But to come to grips with it, to go voluntarily into those dead yet living arms, to grapple with it, naked chest to naked chest. . . . Terrible follies came into his mind. He would fail to obey the Voice, but it would be all right because he would repent later on, when he was back on Earth. He would lose his nerve as St. Peter had done, and be, like St. Peter, forgiven. Intellectually, of course, he knew the answer to these temptations perfectly well; but he was at one of those moments when all the utterances of intellect sound like twice-told tales. Then some cross-wind of the mind changed his mood. Perhaps he would fight and win, perhaps not even be badly mauled. But no faintest hint of a guarantee in that direction came to him from the darkness. The future was black as the night itself.

"It is not for nothing that you are named Ransom," said the Voice.

And he knew that this was no fancy of his own. He knew it for a very curious reason—because he had known for many years that his surname was derived not from *ransom* but from *Ranolf's son.* It would never have occurred to him thus to associate the two words. To connect the name Ransom with the act of ransoming would have been for him a mere pun. But even his voluble self did not now dare to suggest that the Voice was making a play upon words. All in a moment of time he perceived that what was, to human philologists, a merely accidental resemblance of two sounds, was in truth no accident. The whole distinction between things accidental and things designed, like the distinction between fact and myth, was purely terrestrial. The pattern is so large that within the little frame of earthly experience there appear pieces of it between which we can see no connection, and other pieces between which we can. Hence we rightly, for our use, distinguish the accidental from the essential. But step outside that frame and the distinction drops down into the void, fluttering useless wings. He had been forced out of the frame, caught up into the larger pattern. He knew now why the old philosophers had said that there is no such thing as chance or fortune beyond the Moon. Before his Mother had borne him, before his ancestors had been called Ransoms, before *ransom* had been the name for a payment that delivers, before the world was made, all these things had so stood together in eternity that the very significance of the pattern at this point lay in their coming together in just this fashion. And he bowed his head and groaned and repined against his fate—to be still a man and yet to be forced up into the metaphysical world, to enact what philosophy only thinks.

"My name also is Ransom," said the Voice.

It was some time before the purport of this saying dawned upon him. He whom the other worlds call Maleldil, was the world's ransom, his own ransom, well he knew. But to what purpose was it said now? Before the answer came to him he felt its insufferable approach and held out his arms before him as if he could keep it from forcing open the door of his mind. But it came. So *that* was the real issue. If he now failed, this world also would hereafter be redeemed. If he were not the ransom, Another would be. Yet nothing was ever repeated. Not a second crucifixion: perhaps—who knows—not even a second Incarnation . . . some act of even more appalling love, some glory of yet deeper humility. For he had seen already how the pattern grows and how from each world it sprouts into the next through some other dimension. The small external evil which Satan had done in Malacandra was only as a line: the deeper evil he had done in Earth was as a square: if Venus fell, her evil would be a cube—her Redemption beyond conceiving. Yet redeemed she would be. He had long known that great issues hung on his choice; but as he now realised the true width of the frightful freedom that was being put into his hands—a width to which all merely spatial infinity seemed narrow—he felt like a man brought out under naked heaven, on the edge of a precipice, into the teeth of a wind that came howling from the Pole. He had pictured himself, till now, standing before the Lord, like Peter. But it was worse. He sat before Him like Pilate. It lay with him to save or to spill. His hands had been reddened, as all men's hands have been, in the slaying before the foundation of the world; now, if he chose, he could dip them again in the same blood. "Mercy," he groaned; and then, "Lord, why me?" But there was no answer.

The thing still seemed impossible. But gradually something happened to him which had happened to him only twice before in his life. It had happened once while he was trying to make up his mind to do a very dangerous job in the last war. It had happened again while he was screwing his resolution to go and see a certain man in London and make to him an excessively embarrassing confession which justice demanded. In both cases the thing had seemed a sheer impossibility: he had not thought but known that, being what he was, he was psychologically incapable of doing it; and then, without any apparent movement of the will, as objective and unemotional as the reading on a dial, there had arisen before him, with perfect certitude, the knowledge "about this time tomorrow you will have done the impossible." The same thing happened now. His fear, his shame, his love, all his arguments, were not altered in the least. The thing was neither more nor less dreadful than it had been before. The only difference was that he knew—almost as a historical proposition—that it was going to be done. He might beg, weep, or rebel—might curse or adore—sing like a martyr or blaspheme like a devil. It made not the slightest difference. The thing was going to be done. There was going to arrive, in the course of time, a moment at which he would have done it. The future act stood there, fixed and unaltered as if he had already performed it. It was a mere irrelevant detail that it happened to occupy the position we call future instead of that which we call past. The whole struggle was over, and yet there seemed to have been no moment of victory. You might say, if you liked, that the power of choice had been simply set aside and an inflexible destiny substituted for it. On the other hand, you might say, that he had delivered from the rhetoric of his passions and had emerged into unassailable freedom. Ransom could not, for the life of him, see any difference between these two statements. Predestination and freedom were apparently identical. He could no longer see any meaning in the many arguments he had heard on this subject.

No sooner had he discovered that he would certainly try to kill the Un-man to-morrow than the doing of it appeared to him a smaller matter than he had supposed. He could hardly remember why he had accused himself of megalomania when the idea first occurred to him. It was true that if he left it undone, Maleldil Himself would do some greater thing instead. In that sense, he stood for Maleldil: but no more than Eve would have stood for Him by simply not eating the apple, or than any man stands for Him in doing any good action. As there was no comparison in person, so there was none in suffering—or only such comparison as may be between a man who burns his finger putting out a spark and a fireman who loses his life in fighting a conflagration because that spark was not put out. He asked no longer "Why me?" It might as well be he as another. It might as well be any other choice as this. The fierce light which he had seen resting on this moment of decision rested in reality on all.

"I have cast your Enemy into sleep," said the Voice. "He will not wake till morning. Get up. Walk twenty paces back into the wood; there sleep. Your sister sleeps also."

12

When some dreaded morning comes we usually wake fully to it at once. Ransom passed with no intermediate stages from dreamless sleep to a full consciousness of his task. He found himself alone—the island gently rocking on a sea that was neither calm nor stormy. The golden light, glinting through indigo trunks of trees, told him in which direction the water lay. He went to it and bathed. Then, having landed again, he lay down and drank. He stood for a few minutes running his hands through his wet hair and stroking his limbs. Looking down at his own body he noticed how greatly the sunburn on one side and the pallor on the other had decreased. He would hardly be christened Piebald if the Lady were now to meet him for the first time. His colour had become more like ivory: and his toes, after so many days of nakedness, had begun to lose the cramped, squalid shape imposed by boots. Altogether he thought better of himself as a human animal than he had done before. He felt pretty certain that he would never again wield an un-maimed body until a greater morning came for the whole universe, and he was glad that the instrument had been thus tuned up to concert pitch before he had to surrender it. "When I wake up after Thy image, I shall be satisfied," he said to himself.

Presently he walked into the woods. Accidentally—for he was at the moment intent on food—he blundered through a whole cloud of the arboreal bubbles. The pleasure was as sharp as when he had first experienced it, and his very stride was different as he emerged from them. Although this was to be his last meal, he did not even now feel it proper to look for any favorite fruit. But what met him was gourds. "A good breakfast on the morning you're hanged," he thought whimsically as he let the empty shell drop from his hand—filled for the moment with such pleasure as seemed to make the whole world a dance. "All said and done," he thought, "it's been worth it. I have had a time. I have lived in Paradise."

He went a little farther in the wood, which grew thickly hereabout, and almost tripped over the sleeping form of the Lady. It was unusual for her to be sleeping at this time of the day, and he assumed it was Maleldil's doing. "I shall never see her again," he thought; and then, "I shall never again look on a female body in quite the same way as I look on this." As he stood looking down on her, what was most with him was an intense and orphaned longing that he might, if only for once, have seen the great Mother of his own race thus, in her innocence and splendour. "Other things, other blessings, other glories," he murmured. "But never that. Never in all worlds, that. God can make good use of all that happens. But the loss is real." He looked at her once again and then walked abruptly past the place where she lay. "I was right," he thought, "it couldn't have gone on. It was time to stop it."

It took him a long time, wandering like this, in and out of the dark yet coloured thickets, before he found his Enemy. He came on his old friend the dragon, just as he had first seen it, coiled about the trunk of a tree, but it also was asleep; and now he noticed that ever since he awoke he had perceived no chattering of birds, no rustling of sleek bodies or peering of brown eyes through the leafage, nor heard any noise but that of water. It seemed that the Lord God had cast that whole island or perhaps that whole world into deep sleep. For a moment this gave him a sense of desolation, but almost at once he rejoiced that no memory of blood and rage should be left imprinted in these happy minds.

After about an hour, suddenly rounding a little clump of bubble-trees he found himself face to face with the Un-man. "Is it wounded already?" he thought as the first vision of a blood-stained chest broke on him. Then he saw that of course it was not its own blood. A bird, already half plucked and with beak wide open in the soundless yell of strangulation, was feebly struggling in its long clever hands. Ransom found himself acting before he knew what he had done. Some memory of boxing at his preparatory school must have awaked, for he found he had delivered a straight left with all his might on the Un-man's jaw. But he had forgotten that he was not fighting with gloves; what recalled him to himself was the pain as his fist crashed against the jaw-bone—it seemed almost to have broken his knuckles—and the sickening jar all up his arm. He stood still for a second under the shock of it and this gave the Un-man time to fall back about six paces. It too had not liked the first taste of the encounter. It had apparently bitten its tongue, for blood came bubbling out of the mouth when it tried to speak. It was still holding the bird.

"So you mean to try strength," it said in English, speaking thick.

"Put down that bird," said Ransom.

"But this is very foolish," said the Un-man. "Do you not know who I am?"

"I know *what* you are," said Ransom. "Which of them doesn't matter."

"And you think, little one," it answered, "that you can fight with me? You think He will help you, perhaps? Many thought that. I've known Him longer than you, little one. They all think He's going to help them—till they come to their senses screaming recantations too late in the middle of the fire, mouldering in concentration camps, writhing under saws, jibbering in mad-houses, or nailed on to crosses. Could He help Himself?"—and the creature suddenly threw back its head and cried in a voice so loud that it seemed the golden sky-roof must break, *"Eloi, Eloi, lama sabachthani."*

And the moment it had done so, Ransom felt certain that the sounds it had made were perfect Aramaic of the First Century. The Un-man was not quoting; it was remembering. These were the very words spoken from the Cross, treasured through all those years in the burning memory of the outcast creature which had heard them, and now brought forward in hideous parody; the horror made him momentarily sick. Before he had recovered the Un-man was upon him, howling like a gale, with eyes so wide opened that they seemed to have no lids, and with all its hair rising on its scalp. It had him caught tightly to its chest, with its arms about him, and its nails were ripping great strips off his back. His own arms were inside its embrace and, pummelling wildly, he could get no blow at it. He turned his head and bit deeply into the muscle of its right arm, at first without success, then deeper. It gave a howl, tried to hold on, and then suddenly he was free. Its defence was for an instant unready and he found himself raining punches about the region of its heart, faster and harder than he had supposed possible. He could hear through its open mouth the great gusts of breath that he was knocking out of it. Then its hands came up again, fingers arched like claws. It was not trying to box. It wanted to grapple. He knocked its right arm aside with a horrible shock of bone against bone and caught it a jab on the fleshy part of the chin: at the same moment its nails tore his right. He grabbed at its arms. More by luck than by skill he got it held by both wrists.

What followed for the next minute or so would hardly have looked like a fight at all to any spectator. The Un-man was trying with every ounce of power it could find in Weston's body to wrench its arms free from Ransom's hands, and he, with every ounce of his power, was trying to retain his manacle hold round its wrists. But this effort, which sent streams of sweat down the backs of both combatants, resulted in a slow and seemingly leisurely, and even aimless, movement of both pairs of arms. Neither could for the moment hurt the other. The Un-man bent forward its head and tried to bite, but Ransom straightened his arms and kept it at arm's length. There seemed no reason why this should ever end.

Then suddenly it shot out its leg and crooked it behind his knee. He was nearly taken off his feet. Movements became quick and flurried on both sides. Ransom in his turn tried to trip, and failed. He started bending the enemy's left arm back by main force with some idea of breaking or at least spraining it. But in the effort to do so he must have weakened his hold on the other wrist. It got its right free. He had just time to close his eyes before the nails tore fiercely down his cheek and the pain put an end to the blows his left was already raining on its ribs. A second later—he did not know how it happened—they were standing apart, their chests heaving in great gasps, each staring at the other.

Both were doubtless sorry spectacles. Ransom could not see his own wounds but he seemed to be covered with blood. The enemy's eyes were nearly closed and the body, wherever the remains of Weston's shirt did not conceal it, was a mass of what would soon be bruises. This, and its laboured breathing, and the very taste of its strength in their grapples, had altered Ransom's state of mind completely. He had been astonished to find it no stronger. He had all along, despite what reason told him, expected that the strength of its body would be superhuman, diabolical. He had reckoned on arms that could no more be caught and stopped than the blades of an aeroplane's propeller. But now he knew, by actual experience, that its bodily strength was merely that of Weston. On the physical plane it was one middle-aged scholar against another. Weston had been the more powerfully built of the two men, but he was fat; his body would not take punishment well. Ransom was nimbler and better breathed. His former certainty of death now seemed to him ridiculous. It was a very fair match. There was no reason why he should not win—and live.

This time it was Ransom who attacked, and the second bout was much the same as the first. What it came to was that whenever he could box Ransom was superior; whenever he came under tooth and claw he was beaten. His mind, even in the thick of it, was now quite clear. He saw that the issue of the day hung on a very simple question—whether loss of blood would undo him before heavy blows on heart and kidneys undid the other.

All that rich world was asleep about them. There were no rules, no umpire, no spectators; but mere exhaustion, constantly compelling them to fall apart, divided the grotesque duel into rounds as accurately as could be wished. Ransom could never remember how many of these rounds were fought. The thing became like the frantic repetitions of delirium, and thirst a greater pain than any the adversary could inflict. Sometimes they were both on the ground together. Once he was actually astride the enemy's chest, squeezing its throat with both hands and—he found to his surprise—shouting a line out of *The Battle of Maldon:* but it tore his arms so with its nails and so pounded his back with its knees that he was thrown off.

Then he remembers—as one remembers an island of consciousness preceded and followed by long anæsthesia—going forward to meet the Un-man for what seemed the thousandth time and knowing clearly that he could not fight much more. He remembers seeing the Enemy for a moment looking not like Weston but like a mandrill, and realising almost at once that this was delirium. He wavered. Then an experience that perhaps no good man can ever have in our world came over him—a torrent of perfectly unmixed and lawful hatred. The energy of hating, never before felt without some guilt, without some dim knowledge that he was failing fully to distinguish the sinner from the sin, rose into his arms and legs till he felt that they were pillars of burning blood. What was before him appeared no longer a creature of corrupted will. It was corruption itself to which will was attached only as an instrument. Ages ago it had been a Person: but the ruins of personality now survived in it only as weapons at the disposal of a furious self-exiled negation. It is perhaps difficult to understand why this filled Ransom not with horror but with a kind of joy. The joy came from finding at last what hatred was made for. As a boy with an axe rejoices on finding a tree, or a boy with a box of coloured chalks rejoices on finding a pile of perfectly white paper, so he rejoiced in the perfect congruity between his emotion and its object. Bleeding and trembling with weariness as he was, he felt that nothing was beyond his power, and when he flung himself upon the living Death, the eternal Surd in the universal mathematic, he was astonished, and yet (on a deeper level) not astonished at all, at his own strength. His arms seemed to move quicker than his thought. His hands taught him terrible things. He felt its ribs break, he heard its jaw-bone crack. The whole creature seemed to be crackling and splitting under his blows. His own pains, where it tore him, somehow failed to matter. He felt that he could so fight, so hate with a perfect hatred, for a whole year.

All at once he found he was beating the air. He was in such a state that at first he could not understand what was happening—could not believe that the Un-man had fled. His momentary stupidity gave it a start; and when he came to his senses he was just in time to see it vanishing into the wood, with a limping uneven stride, with one arm hanging useless, and with its dog-like howl. He dashed after it. For a second or so it was concealed from him by the tree trunks. Then it was once more in sight. He began running with all his power, but it kept its lead.

It was a fantastic chase, in and out of the lights and shadows and up and down the slowly moving ridges and valleys. They passed the dragon where it slept. They passed the Lady, sleeping with a smile on her face. The Un-man stooped low as it passed her with the fingers of its left hand crooked for scratching. It would have torn her if it dared, but Ransom was close behind and it could not risk the delay. They passed through a flock of large orange-coloured birds all fast asleep, each on one leg, each with its head beneath its wing, so that they looked like a grove of formal and flowery shrubs. They picked their steps where pairs and families of the yellow wallabies lay on their backs with eyes fast shut and their small forepaws folded on their breasts as if they were crusaders carved on tombs. They stooped beneath branches which were bowed down because on them lay the tree-pigs, making a comfortable noise like a child's snore. They crashed through thickets of bubble-trees and forgot, for the moment, their weariness. It was a large island. They came out of the woods and rushed across wide fields of saffron or of silver, sometimes deep to their ankles and sometimes to their waists in the cool or poignant scents. They rushed down into yet other woods which lay, as they approached them, at the bottom of secret valleys, but rose before they reached them to crown the summits of lonely hills. Ransom could not gain on his quarry. It was a wonder that any creature so maimed as its uneven strides showed it to be, could maintain that pace. If the ankle were really sprained, as he suspected, it must suffer indescribably at every step. Then the horrible thought came into his mind that perhaps it could somehow hand over the pain to be borne by whatever remnants of Weston's consciousness yet survived in its body. The idea that something which had once been of his own kind and fed at a human breast might even now be imprisoned in the thing he was pursuing redoubled his hatred, which was unlike nearly all other hatreds he had ever known, for it increased his strength.

As they emerged from about the fourth wood he saw the sea before them not thirty yards away. The Un-man rushed on as if it made no distinction between land and water and plunged in with a great splash. He could see its head, dark against the coppery sea, as it swam. Ransom rejoiced, for swimming was the only sport in which he had ever approached excellence. As he took the water he lost sight of the Un-man for a moment; then, looking up and shaking the wet hair from his face as he struck out in pursuit (his hair was very long by now), he saw its whole body upright and above the surface as though it were sitting on the sea. A second glance and he realised that it had mounted a fish. Apparently the charm'd slumber extended only to the island, for the Un-man on his mount was making good speed. It was stooping down doing something to its fish, Ransom could not see what. Doubtless it would have many ways of urging the animal to quicken its pace.

For a moment he was in despair: but he had forgotten the man-loving nature of these sea-horses. He found almost at once that he was in a complete shoal of the creatures, leaping and frisking to attract his attention. In spite of their good will it was no easy matter to get himself on to the slippery surface of the fine specimen which his grabbing hands first reached: while he was struggling to mount, the distance widened between him and the fugitive. But at last it was done. Settling himself behind the great goggle-eyed head he nudged the animal with his knees, kicked it with his heels, whispered words of praise and encouragement, and in general did all he could to awake its mettle. It began threshing its way forward. But looking ahead Ransom could no longer see any sign of the Un-man, but only the long empty ridge of the next wave coming towards him. Doubtless the quarry was beyond the ridge. Then he noticed that he had no cause to be bothered about the direction. The slope of water was dotted all over with the great fish, each marked by a heap of yellow foam and some of them spouting as well. The Un-man possibly had not reckoned on the instinct which made them follow as leader any of their company on whom a human being sat. They were all forging straight ahead, no more uncertain of their course than homing rooks or bloodhounds on a scent. As Ransom and his fish rose to the top of the wave, he found himself looking down on a wide shallow trough shaped much like a valley in the home counties. Far away and now approaching the opposite slope was the little, dark puppet-like silhouette of the Un-man: and between it and him the whole school of fish was spread out in three or four lines. Clearly there was no danger of losing touch. Ransom was hunting him with the fish and they would not cease to follow. He laughed aloud. "My hounds are bred out of the Spartan kind, so flew'd so sanded," he roared.

Now for the first time the blessed fact that he was no longer fighting nor even standing thrust itself upon his attention. He made to assume a more relaxed position and was pulled up sharp by a grinding pain across his back. He foolishly put back his hand to explore his shoulders, and almost screamed at the pain of his own touch. His back seemed to be in shreds and the shreds seemed to be all stuck together. At the same time he noticed that he had lost a tooth and that nearly all the skin was gone from his knuckles; and underneath the smarting surface pains, deeper and more ominous aches racked him from head to foot. He had not known he was so knocked up.

Then he remembered that he was thirsty. Now that he had begun to cool and stiffen he found the task of getting a drink from the water that raced by him extremely difficult. His first idea had been to stoop low till his head was almost upside down and bury his face in the water: but a single attempt cured him of that. He was reduced to putting down his cupped hands, and even this, as his stiffness grew upon him, had to be done with infinite caution and with many groans and gasps. It took many minutes to get a tiny sip which merely mocked his thirst. The quenching of that thirst kept him employed for what seemed to be half an hour—a half-hour of sharp pains and insane pleasures. Nothing had ever tasted so good. Even when he had done drinking he went on taking up water and splashing it over himself. This would have been among the happiest moments of his life—if only the smarting of his back did not seem to be getting worse and if only he were not afraid that there was poison in the cuts. His legs kept on getting stuck to the fish and having to be unstuck with pain and care. Every now and then blackness threatened to come over him. He could easily have fainted, but he thought "This will never do" and fixed his eyes on objects close at hand and thought plain thoughts and so retained his consciousness.

All this time the Un-man rode on before him, up-wave and down-wave, and the fishes followed and Ransom followed the fishes. There seemed to be more of them now, as if the chase had met other shoals and gathered them up into itself in snowball fashion: and soon there were creatures other than fish. Birds with long necks like swans—he could not tell their colour for they looked black against the sky—came, wheeling at first, overhead, but afterwards they settled in long straight files—all following the Un-man. The crying of these birds was often audible, and it was the wildest sound that Ransom had ever heard, the loneliest, and the one that had least to do with Man. No land was in sight, nor had been for many hours. He was on the high seas, the waste places of Perelandra, as he had not been since his first arrival. The sea-noises continuously filled his ear: the sea-smell, unmistakable and stirring as that of our Tellurian oceans, but quite different in its warmth and golden sweetness, entered into his brain. It also was wild and strange. It was not hostile: if it had been, its wildness and strangeness would have been the less, for hostility is a relation and an enemy is not a total stranger. It came into his head that he knew nothing at all about this world. Some day, no doubt, it would be peopled by the descendants of the King and Queen. But all its millions of years in the unpeopled past, all its uncounted miles of laughing water in the lonely present . . . did they exist solely for that? It was strange that he to whom a wood or a morning sky on earth had sometimes been a kind of meal, should have had to come to another planet in order to realise Nature as a thing in her own right. The diffused meaning, the inscrutable character, which had been both in Tellus and Perelandra since they split off from the Sun, and which would be, in one sense, displaced by the advent of imperial man, yet, in some other sense, not displaced at all, enfolded him on every side and caught him into itself.

13

DARKNESS fell upon the waves as suddenly as if it had been poured out of a bottle. As soon as the colours and the distances were thus taken away, sound and pain became more emphatic. The world was reduced to a dull ache, and sudden stabs, and the beating of the fish's fins, and the monotonous yet infinitely varied noises of the water. Then he found himself almost falling off the fish, recovered his seat with difficulty, and realised that he had been asleep, perhaps for hours. He foresaw that this danger would continually recur. After some consideration he levered himself painfully out of the narrow saddle behind its head and stretched his body at full length along the fish's back. He parted his legs and wound them about the creature as far as he could and did the same with his arms, hoping that thus he could retain his mount even while sleeping. It was the best he could do. A strange thrilling sensation crept over him, communicated doubtless from the movement of its muscles. It gave him the illusion of sharing in its strong bestial life, as if he were himself becoming a fish.

Long after this he found himself staring into something like a human face. It ought to have terrified him but, as sometimes happens to us in a dream, it did not. It was a bluish-greenish face shining apparently by its own light. The eyes were much larger than those of a man and gave it a goblin appearance. A fringe of corrugated membranes at the sides suggested whiskers. With a shock he realised that he was not dreaming, but awake. The thing was real. He was still lying, sore and wearied, on the body of the fish and this face belonged to something that was swimming alongside him. He remembered the swimming submen or mermen whom he had seen before. He was not at all frightened, and he guessed that the creature's reaction to him was the very same as his to it—an uneasy, though not hostile, bewilderment. Each was wholly irrelevant to the other. They met as the branches of different trees meet when the wind brings them together.

Ransom now raised himself once more to a sitting position. He found that the darkness was not complete. His own fish swam in a bath of phosphorescence and so did the stranger at his side. All about him were other blobs and daggers of blue light and he could dimly make out from the shapes which were fish and which were the water-people. Their movements faintly indicated the contours of the waves and introduced some hint of perspective into the night. He noticed presently that several of the water-people in his immediate neighbourhood seemed to be feeding. They were picking dark masses of something off the water with their webbed frog-like hands and devouring it. As they munched, it hung out of their mouths in bushy and shredded bundles and looked like moustaches. It is significant that it never occurred to him to try to establish any contact with these beings, as he had done with every other animal on Perelandra, nor did they try to establish any with him. They did not seem to be the natural subjects of man as the other creatures were. He got the impression that they simply shared a planet with him as sheep and horses share a field, each species ignoring the other. Later, this came to be a trouble in his mind: but for the moment he was occupied with a more practical problem. The sight of their eating had reminded him that he was hungry, and he was wondering whether the stuff they ate were eatable by him. It took him a long time, scooping the water with his fingers, to catch any of it. When at last he did it turned out to be of the same general structure as one of our smaller sea-weeds, and to have little bladders that popped when one pressed them. It was tough and slippery, but not salt like the weed of a Tellurian sea. What it tasted like, he could never properly describe. It is to be noted all through this story that while Ransom was on Perelandra his sense of taste had become something more than it was on Earth: it gave knowledge as well as pleasure, though not a knowledge that can be reduced to words. As soon as he had eaten a few mouthfuls of the seaweed he felt his mind oddly changed. He felt the surface of the sea to be the top of the world. He thought of the floating islands as we think of clouds; he saw them in imagination as they would appear from below—mats of fibre with long streamers hanging down from them, and became startlingly conscious of his own experience in walking on the topside of them as a miracle or a myth. He felt his memory of the Green Lady and all her promised descendants and all the issues which had occupied him ever since he came to Perelandra rapidly fading from his mind, as a dream fades when we wake, or as if it were shouldered aside by a whole world of interests and emotions to which he could give no name. It terrified him. In spite of his hunger he threw the rest of the weed away.

He must have slept again, for the next scene that he remembers was in daylight. The Un-man was still visible ahead, and the shoal of fishes was still spread out between it and him. The birds had abandoned the chase. And now at last a full and prosaic sense of his position descended upon him. It is a curious flaw in the reason, to judge from Ransom's experience, that when a man comes to a strange planet he at first quite forgets its size. That whole world is so small in comparison with his journey through space that he forgets the distances within it: any two places in Mars, or in Venus, appear to him like places in the same town. But now, as Ransom looked round once more and saw nothing in every direction but golden sky and tumbling waves, the full absurdity of this delusion was borne in upon him. Even if there were continents in Perelandra, he might well be divided from the nearest of them by the breadth of the Pacific or more. But he had no reason to suppose that there were any. He had no reason to suppose that even the floating islands were very numerous, or that they were equally distributed over the surface of the planet. Even if their loose archipelago spread over a thousand square miles, what would that be but a negligible freckling in a landless ocean that rolled for ever round a globe not much smaller than the World of Men? Soon his fish would be tired. Already, he fancied, it was not swimming at its original speed. The Un-man would doubtless torture its mount to swim till it died. But he could not do that. As he was thinking of these things and staring ahead, he saw something that turned his heart cold. One of the other fish deliberately turned out of line, spurted a little column of foam, dived, and reappeared some yards away, apparently drifting. In a few minutes it was out of sight. It had had enough.

And now the experiences of the past day and night began to make a direct assault upon his faith. The solitude of the seas and, still more, the experiences which had followed his taste of the seaweed, had insinuated a doubt as to whether this world in any real sense belonged to those who called themselves its King and Queen. How could it be made for them when most of it, in fact, was uninhabitable by them? Was not the very idea naïve and anthropomorphic in the highest degree? As for the great prohibition, on which so much had seemed to hang—was it really so important? What did these roarers with the yellow foam, and these strange people who lived in them, care whether two little creatures, now far away, lived or did not live on one particular rock? The parallelism between the scenes he had lately witnessed and those recorded in the Book of Genesis, and which had hitherto given him the feeling of knowing by experience what other men only believe, now began to shrink in importance. Need it prove anything more than that similar irrational *taboos* had accompanied the dawn of reason in two different worlds? It was all very well to talk of Maleldil: but where was Maleldil now? If this illimitable ocean said anything, it said something very different. Like all solitudes it was, indeed, haunted: but not by an anthropomorphic Deity, rather by the wholly inscrutable to which man and his life remained eternally irrelevant. And beyond this ocean was space itself. In vain did Ransom try to remember that he had been in "space" and found it Heaven, tingling with a fulness of life for which infinity itself was not one cubic inch too large. All that seemed like a dream. That opposite mode of thought which he had often mocked and called in mockery The Empirical Bogey, came surging into his mind—the great myth of our century with its gases and galaxies, its light years and evolutions, its nightmare perspectives of simple arithmetic in which everything that can possibly hold significance for the mind becomes the mere by-product of essential disorder. Always till now he had belittled it, had treated with a certain disdain its flat superlatives, its clownish amazement that different things should be of different sizes, its glib munificence of ciphers. Even now, his reason was not quite subdued, though his heart would not listen to his reason. Part of him still knew that the size of a thing is its least important characteristic, that the material universe derived from the comparing and mythopœic power within him that very majesty before which he was now asked to abase himself, and that mere numbers could not over-awe us unless we lent them, from our own resources, that awfulness which they themselves could no more supply than a banker's ledger. But this knowledge remained an abstraction. Mere bigness and loneliness overbore him.

These thoughts must have taken several hours and absorbed all his attention. He was aroused by what he least expected—the sound of a human voice. Emerging from his reverie he saw that all the fishes had deserted him. His own was swimming feebly: and there a few yards away, no longer fleeing him but moving slowly towards him, was the Un-man. It sat hugging itself, its eyes almost shut up with bruises, its flesh the colour of liver, its leg apparently broken, its mouth twisted with pain.

"Ransom," it said feebly.

Ransom held his tongue. He was not going to encourage it to start that game again.

"Ransom," it said again in a broken voice, "for God's sake speak to me."

He glanced at it in surprise. Tears were on its cheeks.

"Ransom, don't cold-shoulder me," it said. "Tell me what has happened. What have they done to us? You—you're all bleeding. My leg's broken . . ." its voice died away in a whimper.

"Who are you?" he asked sharply.

"Oh, don't pretend you don't know me," mumbled Weston's voice. "I'm Weston. You're Ransom—Elwin Ransom of Leicester, Cambridge, the philologist. We've had our quarrels, I know. I'm sorry. I dare say I've been in the wrong. Ransom, you'll not leave me to die in this horrible place, will you?"

"Where did you learn Aramaic?" asked Ransom, keeping his eyes on the other.

"Aramaic?" said Weston's voice. "I don't know what you're talking about. It's not much of a game to make fun of a dying man."

"But are you really Weston?" said Ransom, for he began to think that Weston had actually come back.

"Who else should I be?" came the answer, with a burst of weak temper, on the verge of tears.

"Where have you been?" asked Ransom.

Weston—if it was Weston—shuddered. "Where are we now?" he asked presently.

"In Perelandra—Venus, you know," answered Ransom.

"Have you found the space-ship?" asked Weston.

"I never saw it except at a distance," said Ransom. "And I've no idea where it is now—a couple of hundred miles away for all I know."

"You mean we're trapped?" said Weston, almost in a scream. Ransom said nothing and the other bowed his head and cried like a baby.

"Come," said Ransom at last, "there's no good taking it like that. Hang it all, you'd not be much better off if you were on Earth. You remember they're having a war there. The Germans may be bombing London to bits at this moment!" Then seeing the creature still crying, he added, "Buck up, Weston. It's only death, all said and done. We should have to die some day, you know. We shan't lack water, and hunger—without thirst—isn't too bad. As for drowning—well, a bayonet wound, or cancer, would be worse."

"You mean to say you're going to leave me," said Weston.

"I can't, even if I wanted to," said Ransom. "Don't you see I'm in the same position as yourself?"

"You'll promise not to go off and leave me in the lurch?" said Weston.

"All right, I'll promise if you like. Where could I go to?"

Weston looked very slowly all round and then urged his fish a little nearer to Ransom's.

"Where is . . . *it?*" he asked in a whisper. "You know," and he made meaningless gestures.

"I might ask you the same question," said Ransom.

"Me?" said Weston. His face was, in one way and another, so disfigured that it was hard to be sure of its expression.

"Have you any idea of what's been happening to you for the last few days?" said Ransom.

Weston once more looked all round him uneasily.

"It's all true, you know," he said at last.

"What's all true?" said Ransom.

Suddenly Weston turned on him with a snarl of rage. "It's all very well for *you,*" he said. "Drowning doesn't hurt and death is bound to come anyway, and all that nonsense. What do *you* know about death? It's all true, I tell you."

"What are you talking about?"

"I've been stuffing myself up with a lot of nonsense all my life," said Weston. "Trying to persuade myself that it matters what happens to the human race . . . trying to believe that anything you can do will make the universe bearable. It's all rot, do you see?"

"And something else is truer!"

"Yes," said Weston, and then was silent for a long time.

"We'd better turn our fishes head on to this," said Ransom presently, his eyes on the seas, "or we'll be driven apart." Weston obeyed without seeming to notice what he did, and for a time the two men were riding very slowly, side by side.

"I'll tell you what's truer," said Weston presently.

"What?"

"A little child that creeps upstairs when nobody's looking and very slowly turns the handle to take one peep into the room where its grandmother's dead body is laid out—and then runs away and has bad dreams. An enormous grandmother, you understand."

"What do you mean by saying that's truer?"

"I mean that child knows something about the universe which all science and all religion is trying to hide."

Ransom said nothing.

"Lots of things," said Weston presently. "Children are afraid to go through a churchyard at night, and the grown-ups tell them not to be silly: but the children know better than the grown-ups. People in Central Africa doing beastly things with masks on in the middle of the night—and missionaries and civil servants say it's all superstition. Well, the blacks know more about the universe than the white people. Dirty priests in back streets in Dublin frightening half-witted children to death with stories about it. You'd say they are unenlightened. They're not: except that they think there is a way of escape. There isn't. That is the real universe, always will be. That's what it all *means.*"

"I'm not quite clear——" began Ransom, when Weston interrupted him.

"That's why it's so important to live as long as you can. All the good things are now—a thin little rind of what we call life, put on for show, and then—the *real* universe for ever and ever. To thicken the rind by one centimetre—to live one week, one day, one half-hour longer—that's the only thing that matters. Of course you don't know it: but every man who is waiting to be hanged knows it. You say, 'What difference does a short reprieve make?' What difference!!"

"But nobody need go there," said Ransom.

"I know that's what you believe," said Weston. "But you're wrong. It's only a small parcel of civilised people who think that. Humanity as a whole knows better. It knows—Homer knew—that *all* the dead have sunk down into the inner darkness: under the rind. All witless, all twittering, gibbering, decaying. Bogeymen. Every savage knows that *all* ghosts hate the living who are still enjoying the rind: just as old women hate girls who still have their good looks. It's quite right to be afraid of the ghosts. You're going to be one all the same."

"You don't believe in God," said Ransom.

"Well, now, that's another point," said Weston. "I've been to church as well as you when I was a boy. There's more sense in parts of the Bible than you religious people know. Doesn't it say He's the God of the living, not of the dead? That's just it. Perhaps your God does exist—but it makes no difference whether He does or not. No, of course you wouldn't see it; but one day you will. I don't think you've got the idea of the rind—the thin outer skin which we call life—really clear. Picture the universe as an infinite globe with this very thin crust on the outside. But remember its thickness is a thickness of *time*. It's about seventy years thick in the best places. We are born on the surface of it and all our lives we are sinking through it. When we've got all the way through then we are what's called Dead: we've got into the dark part inside, the real globe. If your God exists, He's not in the globe—He's outside, like a moon. As we pass into the interior we pass out of His ken. He doesn't follow us in. You would express it by saying He's not in time—which you think comforting! In other words He stays put: out in the light and air, outside. But we are in time. We 'move with the times.' That is, from His point of view, we move *away*, into what He regards as nonentity, where He never follows. That is all there is to us, all there ever was. He may be there in what you call 'Life,' or He may not. What difference does it make? *We're* not going to be there for long!"

"That could hardly be the whole story," said Ransom. "If the whole universe were like that, then we, being parts of it, would feel at home in such a universe. The very fact that it strikes us as monstrous——"

"Yes," interrupted Weston, "that would be all very well if it wasn't that reasoning itself is only valid as long as you stay in the rind. It has nothing to do with the real universe. Even the ordinary scientists—like what I used to be myself—are beginning to find that out. Haven't you seen the real meaning of all this modern stuff about the dangers of extrapolation and bent space and the indeterminacy of the atom? They don't say in so many words, of course, but what they're getting to, even before they die nowadays, is what all men get to when they're dead—the knowledge that reality is neither rational nor consistent nor anything else. In a sense you might say it isn't there. 'Real' and 'Unreal,' 'true' and 'false'—they're all only on the surface. They give way the moment you press them."

"If all this were true," said Ransom, "what would be the point of saying it?"

"Or of anything else?" replied Weston. "The only point in anything is that there isn't any point. Why do ghosts want to frighten? Because they *are* ghosts. What else is there to do?"

"I get the idea," said Ransom. "That the account a man gives of the universe, or of any other building, depends very much on where he is standing."

"But specially," said Weston, "on whether he's inside or out. All the things you like to dwell upon are outsides. A planet like our own, or like Perelandra, for instance. Or a beautiful human body. All the colours and pleasant shapes are merely where it ends, where it ceases to be. Inside, what do you get? Darkness, worms, heat, pressure, salt, suffocation, stink."

They ploughed forward for a few minutes in silence over waves which were now growing larger. The fish seemed to be making little headway.

"Of course you don't care," said Weston. "What do you people in the rind care about us? You haven't been pulled down yet. It's like a dream I once had, though I didn't know then how true it was. I dreamed I was lying dead—you know, nicely laid out in the ward in a nursing home with my face settled by the undertaker and big lilies in the room. And then a sort of a person who was all falling to bits—like a tramp, you know, only it was himself not his clothes that was coming to pieces—came and stood at the foot of the bed, just hating me. 'All right,' he said, 'all right. You think you're mighty fine with your clean sheet and your shiny coffin being got ready. I began like that. We all did. Just wait and see what you come down to in the end.' "

"Really," said Ransom, "I think you might just as well shut up."

"Then there's Spiritualism," said Weston, ignoring this suggestion. "I used to think it all nonsense. But it isn't. It's all true. You've noticed that all *pleasant* accounts of the dead are traditional or philosophical? What actual experiment discovers is quite different. Ectoplasm—slimy films coming out of a medium's belly and making great, chaotic, tumbledown faces. Automatic writing producing reams of rubbish."

"*Are* you Weston?" said Ransom, suddenly turning upon his companion. The persistent mumbling voice, so articulate that you had to listen to it and yet so inarticulate that you had to strain your ears to follow what it said, was beginning to madden him.

"Don't be angry," said the voice. "There's no good being angry with me. I thought you might be sorry. My God, Ransom, it's awful. You don't understand. Right down under layers and layers. Buried alive. You try to connect things and can't. They take your head off . . . and you can't even look back on what life was like in the rind, because you know it never did mean anything even from the beginning."

"What are you?" cried Ransom. "How do you know what death is like? God knows, I'd help you if I could. But give me the facts. Where have you been these few days?"

"Hush," said the other suddenly, "what's that?"

Ransom listened. Certainly there did seem to be a new element in the great concourse of noises with which they were surrounded. At first he could not define it. The seas were very big now and the wind was strong. All at once his companion reached out his hand and clutched Ransom's arm.

"Oh, my God!" he cried. "Oh, Ransom, Ransom! We shall be killed. Killed and put back under the rind. Ransom, you promised to help me. Don't let them get me again."

"Shut up," said Ransom in disgust, for the creature was wailing and blubbering so that he could hear nothing else: and he wanted very much to identify the deeper note that had mingled with the piping wind and roar of water.

"Breakers," said Weston, "breakers, you fool! Can't you hear? There's a country over there! There's a rocky coast. Look there—no, to your right. We shall be smashed into a jelly. Look—O God, here comes the dark!"

And the dark came. Horror of death such as he had never known, horror of the terrified creature at his side, descended upon Ransom: finally, horror with no definite object. In a few minutes he could see through the jet-black night the luminous cloud of foam. From the way in which it shot steeply upward he judged it was breaking on cliffs. Invisible birds, with a shriek and flurry, passed low overhead.

"Are you there, Weston?" he shouted. "What cheer? Pull yourself together. All that stuff you've been talking is lunacy. Say a child's prayer if you can't say a man's. Repent your sins. Take my hand. There are hundreds of mere boys on Earth facing death this moment. We'll do very well."

His hand was clutched in the darkness, rather more firmly than he wished. "I can't bear it, I can't bear it," came Weston's voice.

"Steady now. None of that," he shouted back, for Weston had suddenly gripped his arm with both hands.

"I can't bear it," came the voice again.

"Hi!" said Ransom. "Let go. What the devil are you doing?"—and as he spoke strong arms had plucked him from the saddle, had wrapped him round in a terrible embrace just below his thighs, and, clutching uselessly at the smooth surface of the fish's body, he was dragged down. The waters closed over his head: and still his enemy pulled him down into the warm depth, and down farther yet to where it was no longer warm.

14

"I can't hold my breath any longer," thought Ransom. "I can't. I can't." Cold slimy things slid upwards over his agonised body. He decided to stop holding his breath, to open his mouth and die, but his will did not obey this decision. Not only his chest but his temples felt as if they were going to burst. It was idle to struggle. His arms met no adversary and his legs were pinioned. He became aware that they were moving upwards. But this gave him no hope. The surface was too far away, he could not hold out till they reached it. In the immediate presence of death all ideas of the after life were withdrawn from his mind. The mere abstract proposition, "This is a man dying," floated before him in an unemotional way. Suddenly a roar of sound rushed back upon his ears—intolerable boomings and clangings. His mouth opened automatically. He was breathing again. In a pitch darkness full of echoes he was clutching what seemed to be gravel and kicking wildly to throw off the grip that still held his legs. Then he was free and fighting once more: a blind struggle half in and half out of the water on what seemed to be a pebbly beach, with sharper rocks here and there that cut his feet and elbows. The blackness was filled with gasping curses, now in his own voice, now in Weston's, with yelps of pain, thudding concussions, and the noise of laboured breath. In the end he was astride of the enemy. He pressed its sides between his knees till its ribs cracked and clasped his hands round its throat. Somehow he was able to resist its fierce tearing at his arms—to keep on pressing. Once before he had had to press like this, but that had been on an artery, to save life, not to kill. It seemed to last for ages. Long after the creature's struggles had ceased he did not dare to relax his grip. Even when he was quite sure that it breathed no longer he retained his seat on its chest and kept his tired hands, though now loosely, on its throat. He was nearly fainting himself, but he counted a thousand before he would shift his posture. Even then he continued to sit on its body. He did not know whether in the last few hours the spirit which had spoken to him was really Weston's or whether he had been the victim of a ruse. Indeed, it made little difference. There was, no doubt, a confusion of persons in damnation: what Pantheists falsely hoped of Heaven bad men really received in Hell. They were melted down into their Master, as a lead soldier slips down and loses his shape in the ladle held over the gas ring. The question whether Satan, or one whom Satan had digested, is acting on any given occasion, has in the long run no clear significance. In the meantime, the great thing was not to be tricked again.

There was nothing to be done, then, except to wait for the morning. From the roar of echoes all about him he concluded that they were in a very narrow bay between cliffs. How they had ever made it was a mystery. The morning must be many hours distant. This was a considerable nuisance. He determined not to leave the body till he had examined it by daylight and perhaps taken further steps to make sure that it could not be re-animated. Till then he must pass the time

as best he could. The pebbly beach was not very comfortable, and when he tried
to lean back he found a jagged wall. Fortunately he was so tired that for a time
the mere fact of sitting still contented him. But this phase passed.

He tried to make the best of it. He determined to give up guessing how the
time was going. "The only safe answer," he told himself, "is to think of the
earliest hour you can suppose possible, and then assume the real time is two hours
earlier than that." He beguiled himself by recapitulating the whole story of his
adventure in Perelandra. He recited all that he could remember of the *Iliad,* the
Odyssey, the *Æneid,* the *Chanson de Roland, Paradise Lost,* the *Kalevala,* the
Hunting of the Snark, and a rhyme about Germanic sound-laws which he had
composed as a freshman. He tried to spend as long as he could hunting for the
lines he could not remember. He set himself a chess problem. He tried to rough
out a chapter for a book he was writing. But it was all rather a failure.

These things went on, alternating with periods of dogged inactivity, until it
seemed to him that he could hardly remember a time before that night. He could
scarcely believe that even to a bored and wakeful man twelve hours could appear
so long. And the noise—the gritty, slippery discomfort! It was very odd, now he
came to think it, that this country should have none of those sweet night breezes
which he had met everywhere else in Perelandra. It was odd too (but this thought
came to him what seemed hours later) that he had not even the phosphorescent
wave-crests to feed his eyes on. Very slowly a possible explanation of both facts
dawned upon him: and it would also explain why the darkness lasted so long. The
idea was too terrible for any indulgence of fear. Controlling himself, he rose stiffly
to his feet and began picking his steps along the beach. His progress was very
slow: but presently his outstretched arms touched perpendicular rock. He stood
on tiptoe and stretched his hands up as far as he could. They found nothing but
rock. "Don't get the wind up," he said to himself. He started groping his way
back. He came to the Un-man's body, passed it, and went beyond it round the
opposite beach. It curved rapidly, and here, before he had gone twenty steps his
hands—which he was holding above his head—met not a wall, but a roof, of rock.
A few paces farther and it was lower. Then he had to stoop. A little later and
he had to go on his hands and knees. It was obvious that the roof came down
and finally met the beach.

Sick with despair he felt his way back to the body and sat down. The truth
was now beyond doubt. There was no good waiting for the morning. There would
be no morning here till the end of the world, and perhaps he had already waited
a night and a day. The clanging echoes, the dead air, the very smell of the place,
all confirmed this. He and his enemy when they sank had clearly, by some
hundredth chance, been carried through a hole in the cliffs well below water-level
and come up on the beach of a cavern. Was it possible to reverse the process?
He went down to the water's edge—or rather as he groped his way down to where
the shingle was wet, the water came to meet him. It thundered over his head far
up behind him, and then receded with a tug which he only resisted by spread-
eagling himself on the beach and gripping the stones. It would be useless to

plunge into *that*—he would merely have his ribs broken against the opposite wall of the cave. If one had light, and a high place to dive from, it was conceivable one might get down to the bottom and strike the exit . . . but very doubtful. And anyway, one had no light.

Although the air was not very good he supposed that this prison must be supplied with air from somewhere—but whether from any aperture that he could possibly reach was another matter. He turned at once and began exploring the rock behind the beach. At first it seemed hopeless, but the conviction that caves may lead you anywhere dies hard, and after some time his groping hands found a shelf about three feet high. He stepped up on it. He had expected it to be only a few inches deep but his hands could find no wall before him. Very cautiously he took some paces forward. His right foot touched something sharp. He whistled with the pain and went on even more cautiously. Then he found vertical rock— smooth as high as he could reach. He turned to his right and presently lost it. He turned left and began to go forward again and almost at once stubbed his toe. After nursing it for a moment he went down on hands and knees. He seemed to be among boulders, but the way was practicable. For ten minutes or so he made fairly good going, pretty steeply upward, sometimes on slippery shingle, sometimes over the tops of the big stones. Then he came to another cliff. There appeared to be a shelf on this about four feet up, but this time a really shallow one. He got on to it somehow and glued himself to the face, feeling out to left and right for further grips.

When he found one and realised that he was now about to attempt some real climbing, he hesitated. He remembered that what was above him might be a cliff which even in daylight and properly clothed he would never dare to attempt: but hope whispered that it might equally well be only seven feet high and that a few minutes of coolness might bring him into those gently winding passages up into the heart of the mountain which had, by now, won such a firm place in his imagination. He decided to go on. What worried him was not, in fact, the fear of falling, but the fear of cutting himself off from the water. Starvation he thought he could face: not thirst. But he went on. For some minutes he did things which he had never done on Earth. Doubtless he was in one way helped by the darkness: he had no real sensation of height and no giddiness. On the other hand, to work by touch alone made crazy climbing. Doubtless if anyone had seen him he would have appeared at one moment to take mad risks and at another to indulge in excessive caution. He tried to keep out of his mind the possibility that he might be climbing merely towards a roof.

After about quarter of an hour he found himself on a wide horizontal surface—either a much deeper shelf or the top of the precipice. He rested here for a while and licked his cuts. Then he got up and felt his way forwards, expecting every moment to meet another rock wall. When, after about thirty paces, he had not done so, he tried shouting and judged from the sound that he was in a fairly open place. Then he continued. The floor was of small pebble and ascended fairly steeply. There were some larger stones but he had learned to curl up his toes as his foot felt for the next pace and he seldom stubbed them now. One minor trouble was that even in this perfect blackness he could not help straining his eyes to see. It gave him a headache and created phantom lights and colours.

This slow uphill trek through darkness lasted so long that he began to fear he was going round in a circle, or that he had blundered into some gallery which ran on for ever beneath the surface of the planet. The steady ascent in some degree reassured him. The starvation for light became very painful. He found himself thinking about light as a hungry man thinks about food—picturing April hillsides with milky clouds racing over them in blue skies or quiet circles of lamp-light on tables pleasantly littered with books and pipes. By a curious confusion of mind he found it impossible not to imagine that the slope he walked on was not merely dark, but black in its own right, as if with soot. He felt that his feet and hands must be blackened by touching it. Whenever he pictured himself arriving at any light, he also pictured that light revealing a world of soot all around him.

He struck his head sharply against something and sat down half stunned. When he had collected himself he found by groping that the shingle slope had run up into a roof of smooth rock. His heart was very low as he sat there digesting this discovery. The sound of the waves came up faint and melancholy from below and told him that he was now at a great height. At last, though with very little hope, he began walking to his right, keeping contact with the roof by raising his arms. Presently it receded beyond his reach. A long time after that he heard a sound of water. He went on more slowly in great fear of encountering a waterfall. The shingle began to be wet and finally he stood in a little pool. Turning to his left he found, indeed, a waterfall, but it was a tiny stream with no force of water that could endanger him. He knelt in the rippling pool and drank from the fall and put his aching head and weary shoulders under it. Then, greatly refreshed, he tried to work his way up it.

Though the stones were slippery with some kind of moss and many of the pools were deep, it presented no serious difficulties. In about twenty minutes he had reached the top, and as far as he could judge by shouting and noticing the echoes he was now in a very large cave indeed. He took the stream for guidance and proceeded to follow it up. In that featureless dark it was some sort of company. Some real hope—distinct from that mere convention of hope which supports men in desperate situations—began to enter his mind.

It was shortly after this that he began to be worried by the noises. The last faint booming of the sea in the little hole whence he had set out so many hours ago had now died away and the predominant sound was the gentle tinkling of the stream. But he now began to think that he heard other noises mixed with it. Sometimes it would be a dull plump as if something had slipped into one of the pools behind him: sometimes, more mysteriously, a dry rattling sound as if metal were being dragged over the stones. At first he put it down to imagination. Then he stopped once or twice to listen and heard nothing; but each time when he went on it began again. At last, stopping once more, he heard it quite unmistakably. Could it be that the Un-man had after all come to life and was still following him? But that seemed improbable, for its whole plan had been to escape. It was not so easy to dispose of the other possibility—that these caverns might have inhabitants. All this experience, indeed, assured him that if there were such inhabitants they would probably be harmless, but somehow he could not quite believe that anything which lived in such a place would be agreeable, and a little echo of the Un-man's—or was it Weston's—talk came back to him. "All beautiful on the surface, but down inside—darkness, heat, horror, and stink." Then it occurred to him that if some creature were following him up the stream it might be well for him to leave its banks and wait till the creature had gone past. But if it were hunting him it would presumably hunt by scent; and in any case he would not risk losing the stream. In the end he went on.

Whether through weakness—for he was now very hungry indeed—or because the noises behind made him involuntarily quicken his pace, he found himself unpleasantly hot, and even the stream did not appear very refreshing when he put his feet in it. He began to think that whether he were pursued or not he must have a short rest—but just at that moment he saw the light. His eyes had been mocked so often before that he would not at first believe it. He shut them while he counted a hundred and looked again. He turned round and sat down for several minutes, praying that it might not be a delusion, and looked again. "Well," said Ransom, "if it is a delusion, it's a pretty stubborn one." A very dim, tiny, quivering luminosity, slightly red in colour, was before him. It was too weak to illuminate anything else and in that world of blackness he could not tell whether it was five feet or five miles away. He set out at once, with beating heart. Thank Heaven, the stream appeared to be leading him towards it.

While he thought it was still a long way off he found himself almost stepping into it. It was a circle of light lying on the surface of the water, which thereabouts formed a deepish trembling pool. It came from above. Stepping into the pool he looked up. An irregularly shaped patch of light, now quite distinctly red, was immediately above him. This time it was strong enough to show him the objects immediately around it, and when his eyes had mastered them he perceived that he was looking up a funnel or fissure. Its lower aperture lay in the roof of his own cavern which must here be only a few feet above his head: its upper aperture was obviously in the floor of a separate and higher chamber whence the light came. He could see the uneven side of the funnel, dimly illuminated, and clothed with pads and streamers of a jelly-like and rather unpleasing vegetation. Down this water was trickling and falling on his head and shoulders in a warm rain. This warmth, together with the red colour of the light, suggested that the upper cave was illuminated by subterranean fire. It will not be clear to the reader, and it was not clear to Ransom when he thought about it afterwards, why he immediately decided to get into the upper cave if he possibly could. What really moved him, he thinks, was the mere hunger for light. The very first glance at the funnel restored dimensions and perspective to his world, and this in itself was like delivery from prison. It seemed to tell him far more than it actually did of his surroundings: it gave him back that whole frame of spatial directions without which a man seems hardly able to call his body his own. After this, any return to the horrible black vacancy, the world of soot and grime, the world without size or distance, in which he had been wandering, was out of the question. Perhaps also he had some idea that whatever was following him would cease to follow if he could get into the lighted cave.

But it was not easy to do. He could not reach the opening of the funnel. Even when he jumped he only just touched the fringe of its vegetation. At last he hit upon an unlikely plan which was the best he could think of. There was just enough light here for him to see a number of larger stones among the gravel, and he set to work to build up a pile in the centre of the pool. He worked rather feverishly and often had to undo what he had done: and he tried it several times before it was really high enough. When at last it was completed and he stood sweating and shaky on the summit the real hazard was still to be run. He had to grip the vegetation on each side above his head, trusting to luck that it would hold, and half jump, half pull himself up as quickly as he could, since if it held at all it would, he felt sure, not hold for long. Somehow or other he managed it. He got himself wedged into the fissure with his back against one side and his feet against the other, like a mountaineer in what is called a chimney. The thick squashy growth protected his skin, and after a few upward struggles he found the walls of the passage so irregular that it could be climbed in the ordinary way. The heat increased rapidly. "I'm a fool to have come up here," said Ransom: but even as he said so, he was at the top.

At first he was blinded by the light. When at last he could take in his surroundings he found himself in a vast hall so filled with firelight that it gave him the impression of being hollowed out of red clay. He was looking along the length of it. The floor sloped down to the left side. On his right it sloped upward to what appeared a cliff edge, beyond which was an abyss of blinding brightness. A broad shallow river was flowing down the middle of the cavern. The roof was so high as to be invisible, but the walls soared up into darkness with broad curves like the roots of a beech tree.

He staggered to his feet, splashed across the river (which was hot to the touch) and approached the cliff edge. The fire appeared to be thousands of feet below him and he could not see the other side of the pit in which it swelled and roared and writhed. His eyes could only bear it for a second or so, and when he turned away the rest of the cavern seemed dark. The heat of his body was painful. He drew away from the cliff edge and sat down with his back to the fire to collect his thoughts.

They were collected in an unlooked-for way. Suddenly and irresistibly, like an attack by tanks, that whole view of the universe which Weston (if it were Weston) had so lately preached to him, took all but complete possession of his mind. He seemed to see that he had been living all his life in a world of illusion. The ghosts, the damned ghosts, were right. The beauty of Perelandra, the innocence of the Lady, the sufferings of saints, and the kindly affections of men, were all only an appearance and outward show. What he had called the worlds were but the skins of the worlds: a quarter of a mile beneath the surface, and from thence through thousands of miles of dark and silence and infernal fire, to the very heart of each, Reality lived—the meaningless, the un-made, the omnipotent idiocy to which all spirits were irrelevant and before which all efforts were vain. Whatever was following him would come up that wet, dark hole, would presently be excreted by that hideous duct, and then he would die. He fixed his eyes upon the dark opening from which he had himself just emerged. And then—"I thought as much," said Ransom.

Slowly, shakily, with unnatural and inhuman movements a human form, scarlet in the firelight, crawled out on to the floor of the cave. It was Un-man, of course: dragging its broken leg and with its lower jaw sagging open like that of a corpse, it raised itself to a standing position. And then, close behind it, something else came up out of the hole. First came what looked like branches of trees, and then seven or eight spots of light, irregularly grouped like a constellation. Then a tubular mass which reflected the red glow as if it were polished. His heart gave a great leap as the branches suddenly resolved themselves into long wiry feelers and the dotted lights became the many eyes of a shell-helmeted head and the mass that followed it was revealed as a large roughly cylindrical body. Horrible things followed—angular, many jointed legs, and presently, when he thought the whole body was in sight, a second body came following it and after that a third. The thing was in three parts, united only by a kind of wasp's waist structure—three parts that did not seem to be truly aligned and made it look as if it had been trodden on—a huge, many legged, quivering deformity, standing just behind the Un-man so that the horrible shadows of both danced in enormous and united menace on the wall of rock behind them.

"They want to frighten me," said something in Ransom's brain, and at the same moment he became convinced both that the Un-man had summoned this great crawler and also that the evil thoughts which had preceded the appearance of the enemy had been poured into his own mind by the enemy's will. The knowledge that his thoughts could be thus managed from without did not awake terror but rage. Ransom found that he had risen, that he was approaching the Un-man, that he was saying things, perhaps foolish things, in English. "Do you think I'm going to stand *this?*" he yelled. "Get out of my brain. It isn't yours, I tell you! Get out of it." As he shouted he had picked up a big, jagged stone from beside the stream. "Ransom," croaked the Un-man, "wait! We're both trapped . . ." but Ransom was already upon it.

"In the name of the Father and of the Son and of the Holy Ghost, here goes—I mean Amen," said Ransom, and hurled the stone as hard as he could into the Un-man's face. The Un-man fell as a pencil falls, the face smashed out of all recognition. Ransom did not give it a glance but turned to face the other horror. But where had the horror gone? The creature was there, a curiously shaped creature no doubt, but all loathing had vanished clean out of his mind, so that neither then nor at any other time could he remember it, nor ever understand again why one should quarrel with an animal for having more legs or eyes than oneself. All that he had felt from childhood about insects and reptiles died that moment: died utterly, as hideous music does when you switch off the wireless. Apparently it had all, even from the beginning, been a dark enchantment of the enemy's. Once, as he had sat writing near an open window in Cambridge, he had looked up and shuddered to see, as he supposed, a many coloured beetle of unusually hideous shape crawling across his paper. A second glance showed him that it was a dead leaf, moved by the breeze; and instantly the very curves and re-entrants which had made its ugliness turned into its beauties. At this moment he had almost the same sensation. He saw at once that the creature intended him no harm—had indeed no intentions at all. It had been drawn thither by the Un-man, and now stood still, tentatively moving its antennæ. Then, apparently not liking its surroundings, it turned laboriously round and began descending into the hole by which it had come. As he saw the last section of its tripartite body wobble on the edge of the aperture, and then finally tip upward with its torpedo-shaped tail in the air, Ransom almost laughed. "Like an animated corridor train," was his comment.

He turned to the Un-man. It had hardly anything left that you could call a head, but he thought it better to take no risks. He took it by its ankles and lugged it up to the edge of the cliff: then, after resting a few seconds, he shoved it over. He saw its shape black, for a second, against the sea of fire: and then that was the end of it.

He rolled rather than crawled back to the stream and drank deeply. "This may be the end of me or it may not," thought Ransom. "There may be a way out of these caves or there may not. But I won't go another step further to-day. Not if it was to save my life—not to save my life. That's flat. Glory be to God, I'm tired." A second later he was asleep.

15

For the rest of the subterranean journey after his long sleep in the firelit cave, Ransom was somewhat light-headed with hunger and fatigue. He remembers lying still after he woke for what seemed many hours and even debating with himself whether it was worth going on. The actual moment of decision has vanished from his mind. Pictures come back in a chaotic, disjointed fashion. There was a long gallery open to the fire-pit on one side and a terrible place where clouds of steam went up for ever and ever. Doubtless one of the many torrents that roared in the neighborhood here fell into the depth of the fire. Beyond that were great halls still dimly illuminated and full of unknown mineral wealth that sparkled and danced in the light and mocked his eyes as if he were exploring a hall of mirrors by the help of a pocket torch. It seemed to him also, though this may have been delirium, that he came through a vast cathedral space which was more like the work of art than that of Nature, with two great thrones at one end and chairs on either hand too large for human occupants. If the things were real, he never found any explanation of them. There was a dark tunnel in which a wind from Heaven knows where was blowing and drove sand in his face. There was also a place where he himself walked in darkness and looked down through fathom below fathom of shafts and natural arches and winding gulfs on to a smooth floor lit with a cold green light. And as he stood and looked it seemed to him that four of the great earth-beetles, dwarfed by distance to the size of gnats, and crawling two by two, came slowly into sight. And they were drawing behind them a flat car, and on the car, upright, unshaken, stood a mantled form, huge and still and slender. And driving its strange team it passed on with insufferable majesty and went out of sight. Assuredly the inside of this world was not for man. But it was for something. And it appeared to Ransom that there might, if a man could find it, be some way to renew the old Pagan practice of propitiating the local gods of unknown places in such fashion that it was no offence to God Himself but only a prudent and courteous apology for trespass. That thing, that swathed form in its chariot, was no doubt his fellow creature. It did not follow that they were equals or had an equal right in the under-land. A long time after this came the drumming—the *boom-ba-ba-ba-boom-boom* out of pitch darkness, distant at first, then all around him, then dying away after endless prolongation of echoes in the black labyrinth. Then came the fountain of cold light—a column, as of water, shining with some radiance of its own, and pulsating, and never any nearer however long he travelled and at last suddenly eclipsed. He did not find what it was. And so, after more strangeness and grandeur and labour than I can tell, there came a moment when his feet slid without warning on clay—a wild grasp—a spasm of terror—and he was spluttering and struggling in deep, swift-flowing water. He thought that even if he escaped being battered to death against the walls of the channel he would presently plunge along with the stream into the pit of fire. But the channel must have been very straight and the current perhaps was less violent than he had supposed. At all events he never touched the sides. He lay helpless, in the end, rushing forward through echoing darkness. It lasted a long time.

You will understand that what with expectation of death, and weariness, and the great noise, he was confused in mind. Looking back on the adventure afterwards it seemed to him that he floated out of blackness into greyness and then into an inexplicable chaos of semi-transparent blues and greens and whites. There was a hint of arches above his head and faintly shining columns, but all vague and all obliterating one another as soon as seen. It looked like a cave of ice, but it was too warm for that. And the roof above him seemed to be itself rippling like water, but this was doubtless a reflection. A moment later and he was rushed out into broad daylight and air and warmth, and rolled head over heels, and deposited, dazzled and breathless, in the shallows of a great pool.

He was now almost too weak to move. Something in the air, and the wide silence which made a background to the lonely crying of birds, told him that he was on a high mountain top. He rolled rather than crawled out of the pool on to sweet blue turf. Looking back whence he had come he saw a river pouring from the mouth of a cave, a cave that seemed indeed to be made of ice. Under it the water was spectral blue, but near where he lay it was warm amber. There was mist and freshness and dew all about him. At his side rose a cliff mantled with streamers of bright vegetation, but gleaming like glass where its own surface showed through. But this he heeded little. There were rich clusters of a grape-like fruit glowing under the little pointed leaves, and he could reach them without getting up. Eating passed into sleeping by a transition he could never remember.

At this point it becomes increasingly difficult to give Ransom's experiences in any certain order. How long he lay beside the river at the cavern mouth eating and sleeping and waking only to eat and sleep again, he has no idea. He thinks it was only a day or two, but from the state of his body when this period of convalescence ended I should imagine it must have been more like a fortnight or three weeks. It was a time to be remembered only in dreams as we remember infancy. Indeed it was a second infancy, in which he was breast-fed by the planet Venus herself: unweaned till he moved from that place. Three impressions of this long Sabbath remain. One is the endless sound of rejoicing water. Another is the delicious life that he sucked from the clusters which almost seemed to bow themselves unasked into his upstretched hands. The third is the song. Now high in air above him, now welling up as if from glens and valleys far below, it floated through his sleep and was the first sound at every waking. It was formless as the song of a bird, yet it was not a bird's voice. As a bird's voice is to a flute, so this was to a cello: low and ripe and tender, full-bellied, rich and golden-brown: passionate too, but not with the passions of men.

Because he was weaned so gradually from this state of rest I cannot give his impressions of the place he lay in, bit by bit, as he came to take it in. But when he was cured and his mind was clear again, this was what he saw. The cliffs out of which his river had broken through the cave were not of ice, but of some kind of translucent rock. Any little splinter broken off them was as transparent as glass, but the cliffs themselves, when you looked at them close, seemed to become opaque about six inches from the surface. If you waded up-stream into the cave and then turned back and looked towards the light, the edges of the arch which formed the cave's mouth were distinctly transparent: and everything looked blue inside the cave. He did not know what happened at the top of these cliffs.

Before him the lawn of blue turf continued level for about thirty paces, and then dropped with a steep slope, leading the river down in a series of cataracts. The slope was covered with flowers which shook continually in a light breeze. It went down a long way and ended in a winding and wooded valley which curled out of sight on his right hand round a majestic slope: but beyond that, lower down—so much lower down as to be almost incredible—one caught the point of mountain tops, and beyond that, fainter yet, the hint of still lower valleys, and then a vanishing of everything in golden haze. On the opposite side of this valley the earth leaped up in great sweeps and folds of almost Himalayan height to the red rocks. They were not red like Devonshire cliffs: they were true rose-red, as if they had been painted. Their brightness astonished him, and so did the needle-like sharpness of their spires, until it occurred to him that he was in a young world and that these mountains might, geologically speaking, be in their infancy. Also, they might be farther off than they looked.

To his left and behind him the crystal cliffs shut off his view. To his right they soon ended and beyond them the ground rose to another and nearer peak—a much lower one than those he saw across the valley. The fantastic steepness of all the slopes confirmed his idea that he was on a very young mountain.

Except for the song it was all very still. When he saw birds flying they were usually a long way below him. On the slopes to his right and, less distinctly, on the slope of the great *massif* which faced him, there was a continual rippling effect which he could not account for. It was like water flowing: but since, if it were a stream on the remoter mountain, it would have to be a stream two or three miles wide, this seemed improbable.

In trying to put the completed picture together I have omitted something which, in fact, made it a long job for Ransom to get that picture. The whole place was subject to mists. It kept on vanishing in a veil of saffron or very pale gold and reappearing again—almost as if the golden sky-roof, which indeed looked only a few feet above the mountain-tops, were opening and pouring down riches upon the world.

Day by day as he came to know more of the place, Ransom also came to know more of the state of his own body. For a long time he was too stiff almost to move and even an incautious breath made him wince. It healed, however, surprisingly quickly. But just as a man who has had a fall only discovers the real hurt when the minor bruises and cuts are less painful, so Ransom was nearly well before he detected his most serious injury. It was a wound in his heel. The shape made it quite clear that the wound had been inflicted by human teeth—the nasty, blunt teeth of our own species which crush and grind more than they cut. Oddly enough, he had no recollection of this particular bite in any of his innumerable tussles with the Un-man. It did not look unhealthy, but it was still bleeding. It was not bleeding at all fast, but nothing he could do would stop it. But he worried very little about this. Neither the future nor the past really concerned him at this period. Wishing and fearing were modes of consciousness for which he seemed to have lost the faculty.

Nevertheless there came a day when he felt the need of some activity and yet did not feel ready to leave the little lair between the pool and the cliff which had become like a home. He employed that day in doing something which may appear rather foolish and yet at the time it seemed to him that he could hardly omit it. He had discovered that the substance of the translucent cliffs was not very hard. Now he took a sharp stone of a different kind, and cleared a wide space on the cliff wall of vegetation. Then he made measurements and spaced it all out carefully and after a few hours had produced the following. The language was Old Solar but the letters were Roman.

WITHIN THESE CAVES WAS BURNED

THE BODY

OF

EDWARD ROLLES WESTON

A LEARNED HNAU OF THE WORLD WHICH THOSE WHO INHABIT IT

CALL TELLUS

BUT THE ELDILA

THULCANDRA

HE WAS BORN WHEN TELLUS HAD COMPLETED

ONE THOUSAND EIGHT HUNDRED AND NINETY-SIX REVOLUTIONS

ABOUT ARBOL

SINCE THE TIME WHEN

MALELDIL

BLESSED BE HE

WAS BORN AS A HNAU IN THULCANDRA

HE STUDIED THE PROPERTIES OF BODIES

AND FIRST OF THE TELLURIANS TRAVELLED THROUGH DEEP

HEAVEN TO MALACANDRA

AND TO PERELANDRA

WHERE HE GAVE UP HIS WILL AND REASON

TO THE BENT ELDIL

WHEN TELLUS WAS MAKING

THE ONE THOUSANDTH NINE HUNDREDTH AND FORTY-SECOND

REVOLUTION AFTER THE BIRTH OF MALELDIL

BLESSED BE HE

"That was a tomfool thing to do," said Ransom to himself contentedly as he lay down again. "No one will ever read it. But there ought to be some record. He was a great physicist after all. Anyway, it has given me some exercise." He yawned prodigiously and settled down to yet another twelve hours of sleep.

The next day he was better and began taking little walks, not going down but strolling to and fro on the hillside on each side of the cave. The following day he was better still. But on the third day he was well, and ready for adventures.

He set out very early in the morning and began to follow the watercourse down the hill. The slope was very steep but there were no outcroppings of rock and the turf was soft and springy and to his surprise he found that the descent brought no weariness to his knees. When he had been going about half an hour and the peaks of the opposite mountain were now too high to see and the crystal cliffs behind him were only a distant glare, he came to a new kind of vegetation. He was approaching a forest of little trees whose trunks were only about two and a half feet high; but from the top of each trunk there grew long streamers which did not rise in the air but flowed in the wind downhill and parallel to the ground. Thus, when he went in among them, he found himself wading knee deep and more in a continually rippling sea of them—a sea which presently tossed all about him as far as his eye could reach. It was blue in colour, but far lighter than the blue of the turf—almost a Cambridge blue at the centre of each streamer, but dying away at their tasselled and feathery edges into a delicacy of bluish grey which it would take the subtlest effects of smoke and cloud to rival in our world. The soft, almost impalpable, caresses of the long thin leaves on his flesh, the low, singing, rustling, whispering music, and the frolic movement all about him, began to set his heart beating with that almost formidable sense of delight which he had felt before in Perelandra. He realised that these dwarf forests—these ripple-trees as he now christened them—were the explanation of that water-like movement he had seen on the farther slopes.

When he was tired he sat down and found himself at once in a new world. The streamers now flowed above his head. He was in a forest made for dwarfs, a forest with a blue transparent roof, continually moving and casting an endless dance of lights and shades upon its mossy floor. And presently he saw that it was indeed made for dwarfs. Through the moss, which here was of extraordinary fineness, he saw the hithering and thithering of what at first he took for insects but what proved, on closer inspection, to be tiny mammals. There were many mountain mice, exquisite scale models of those he had seen on the Forbidden Island, each about the size of a bumble bee. There were little miracles of grace which looked more like horses than anything he had yet seen on this world, though they resembled proto-hippos rather than his modern representative.

"How can I avoid treading on thousands of these?" he wondered. But they were not really very numerous and the main crowd of them seemed to be all moving away on his left. When he made to rise he noticed that there were already very few of them in sight.

He continued to wade down through the rippling streamers (it was like a sort of vegetable surf-bathing) for about an hour longer. Then he came into woods and presently to a river with a rocky course flowing across his path to the right.

He had, in fact, reached the wooded valley, and knew that the ground which sloped upwards through trees on the far side of the water was the beginning of the great ascent. Here was amber shade and solemn height under the forest roof, and rocks wet with cataracts, and, over all, the noise of that deep singing. It was so loud now and so full of melody that he went downstream, a little out of his way, to look for its origin. This brought him almost at once out of stately aisles and open glades into a different kind of wood. Soon he was pressing his way through thornless thickets, all in bloom. His head was covered with the petals that showered on it, his sides gilded with pollen. Much that his fingers touched was gummy and at each pace his contact with soil and bush appeared to wake new odours that darted into his brain and there begot wild and enormous pleasures. The noise was very loud now and the thicket very dense so that he could not see a yard ahead, when the music stopped suddenly. There was a sound of rustling and broken twigs and he made hastily in that direction, but found nothing. He had almost decided to give up the search when the song began again a little farther away. Once more he made after it; once more the creature stopped singing and evaded him. He must have played thus at hide-and-seek with it for the best part of an hour before his search was rewarded.

Treading delicately during one of the loudest bursts of music he at last saw through the flowery branches a black something. Standing still whenever it stopped singing, and advancing with great caution whenever it began again, he stalked it for ten minutes. At last it was in full view, and singing, and ignorant that it was watched. It sat upright like a dog, black and sleek and shiny, but its shoulders were high above Ransom's head, and the forelegs on which they were pillared were like young trees and the wide soft pads on which they rested were large as those of a camel. The enormous rounded belly was white, and far up above the shoulders the neck rose like that of a horse. The head was in profile from where Ransom stood—the mouth wide open as it sang of joy in thick-coming trills, and the music almost visibly rippled in its glossy throat. He stared in wonder at the wide liquid eyes and the quivering, sensitive nostrils. Then the creature stopped, saw him, and darted away, and stood, now a few paces distant, on all four legs, not much smaller than a young elephant, swaying a long bushy tail. It was the first thing in Perelandra which seemed to show any fear of man. Yet it was not fear. When he called to it it came nearer. It put its velvet nose into his hand and endured his touch; but almost at once it darted back and, bending its long neck, buried its head in its paws. He could make no headway with it, and when at length it retreated out of sight he did not follow it. To do so would have seemed an injury to its fawn-like shyness, to the yielding softness of its expression, its evident wish to be for ever a sound and only a sound in the thickest centre of untravelled woods. He resumed his journey: a few seconds after the song broke out behind him, louder and lovelier than before, as if in a pæan of rejoicing at its recovered privacy.

Ransom now addressed himself seriously to the ascent of the great mountain and in a few minutes emerged from the woods on to its lower slopes. He continued ascending so steeply that he used hands as well as feet for about half an hour and was puzzled to find himself doing it with almost no fatigue. Then he came once more into a region of ripple-trees. This time the wind was blowing the streamers not down the mountain-side but up it, so that his course had to the eye the astonishing appearance of lying through a wide blue waterfall which flowed the wrong way, curving and foaming towards the heights. Whenever the wind failed for a second or two the extreme ends of the streamers began to curl back under the influence of gravitation, so that it looked as if the heads of the waves were being flung back by a high wind. He continued going up through this for a long time, never feeling any real need for rest but resting occasionally none the less. He was now so high that the crystal cliffs from which he had set out appeared on a level with him as he looked across the valley. He now saw that the land leaped up beyond them into a whole waste of the same translucent formation which ended in a kind of glassy table-land. Under the naked sun of our own planet this would have been too bright to look at: here, it was a tremulous dazzle changing every moment under the undulations which the Perelandrian sky receives from the ocean. To the left of this tableland were some peaks of greenish rock. He went on. Little by little the peaks and the tableland sank and grew smaller, and presently there arose beyond them an exquisite haze like vaporized amethyst and emerald and gold, and the edge of this haze rose as he rose, and became at last the horizon of the sea, high lifted above the hills. And the sea grew ever larger and the mountains less, and the horizon of the sea rose and rose till all the lower mountains behind him seemed to be lying at the bottom of a great bowl of sea; but ahead, the interminable slope, now blue, now violet, now flickering with the smoke-like upward movement of the ripple-trees, soared up and up to the sky. And now the wooded valley in which he had met the singing beast was invisible and the mountain from which he had set out looked no more than a little swell on the slope of the great mountain, and there was not a bird in the air, nor any creature underneath the streamers, and still he went on unwearied, but always bleeding a little from his heel. He was not lonely nor afraid. He had no desires and did not even think about reaching the top nor why he should reach it. To be always climbing this was not, in his present mood, a process but a state, and in that state of life he was content. It did once cross his mind that he had died and felt no weariness because he had no body. The wound in his heel convinced him that this was not so; but if it had been so indeed, and these had been trans-mortal mountains, his journey could hardly have been more great and strange.

That night he lay on the slopes between the stems of the ripple-trees with the sweet-scented, wind-proof, delicately-whispering roof above his head, and when morning came he resumed his journey. At first he climbed through dense mists. When these parted, he found himself so high that the concave of the sea seemed to close him in on every side but one: and on that one he saw the rose-red peaks, no longer very distant, and a pass between the two nearest ones through which he caught a glimpse of something soft and flushed. And now he began to feel a strange mixture of sensations—a sense of perfect duty to enter that secret place which the peaks were guarding combined with an equal sense of trespass. He dared not go up that pass: he dared not do otherwise. He looked to see an angel with a flaming sword: he knew that Maleldil bade him go on. "This is the holiest and the most unholy thing I have ever done," he thought; but he went on. And now he was right in the pass. The peaks on either hand were not of red rock. Cores of rock they must have had; but what he saw were great matterhorns clothed in flowers—a flower shaped something like a lily but tinted like a rose. And soon the ground on which he trod was carpeted with the same flowers and he must crush them as he walked; and here at last his bleeding left no visible trace.

From the neck between the two peaks he looked a little down, for the top of the mountain was a shallow cup. He saw a valley, a few acres in size, as secret as a valley in the top of a cloud: a valley pure rose-red, with ten or twelve of the glowing peaks about it, and in the centre a pool, married in pure unrippled clearness to the gold of the sky. The lilies came down to its very edge and lined all its bays and headlands. Yielding without resistance to the awe which was gaining upon him, he walked forward with slow paces and bowed head. There was something white near the water's edge. An altar? A patch of white lilies among the red? A tomb? But whose tomb? No, it was not a tomb but a coffin, open and empty, and its lid lying beside it.

Then of course he understood. This thing was own brother to the coffin-like chariot in which the strength of angels had brought him from Earth to Venus. It was prepared for his return. If he had said, "It is for my burial," his feelings would not have been very different. And while he thought of this he became gradually aware that there was something odd about the flowers at two places in his immediate neighbourhood. Next, he perceived that the oddity was an oddity in the light; thirdly, that it was in the air as well as on the ground. Then, as the blood pricked his veins and a familiar, yet strange, sense of diminished being possessed him, he knew that he was in the presence of two eldila. He stood still. It was not for him to speak.

16

A CLEAR VOICE like a chime of remote bells, a voice with no blood in it, spoke out of the air and sent a tingling through his frame.

"They have already set foot on the sand and are beginning to ascend," it said.

"The small one from Thulcandra is already here," said a second voice.

"Look on him, beloved, and love him," said the first. "He is indeed but breathing dust and a careless touch would unmake him. And in his best thoughts there are such things mingled as, if we thought them, our light would perish. But he is in the body of Maleldil and his sins are forgiven. His very name in his own tongue is Elwin, the friend of the eldila."

"How great is your knowledge!" said the second voice.

"I have been down into the air of Thulcandra," said the first, "which the small ones call Tellus. A thickened air is full of the Darkened as Deep Heaven is of the Light Ones. I have heard the prisoners there talking in their divided tongues and Elwin has taught me how it is with them."

From these words Ransom knew the speaker was the Oyarsa of Malacandra, the great archon of Mars. He did not, of course, recognize the voice, for there is no difference between one eldil's voice and another's. It is by art, not nature, that they affect human ear-drums and their words owe nothing to lungs or lips.

"It it is good, Oyarsa," said Ransom, "tell me who is this other."

"It is Oyarsa," said Oyarsa, "and here that is not my name. In my own sphere I am Oyarsa. Here I am only Malacandra."

"I am Perelandra," said the other voice.

"I do not understand," said Ransom. "The Woman told me there were no eldila in this world."

"They have not seen my face till to-day," said the second voice, "except as they see it in the water and the roof-heaven, the islands, the caves, and the trees. I was not set to rule them, but while they were young I ruled all else. I rounded this ball when it first arose from Arbol. I spun the air about it and wove the roof. I built the Fixed Island and this, the holy mountain, as Maleldil taught me. The beasts that sing and the beasts that fly and all that swims on my breast and all that creeps and tunnels within me down to the centre has been mine. And to-day all this is taken from me. Blessed be He."

"The small one will not understand you," said the Lord of Malacandra. "He will think that this is a grievous thing in your eyes."

"He does not say this, Malacandra."

"No. That is another strange thing about the children of Adam."

There was a moment's silence and then Malacandra addressed Ransom. "You will think of this best if you think of it in the likeness of certain things from your own world."

"I think I understand," said Ransom, "for one of Maleldil's sayers has told us. It is like when the children of a great house come to their full age. Then those who administered all their riches, and whom perhaps they have never seen, come and put all in their hands and give up their keys."

"You understand well," said Perelandra. "Or like when the singing beast leaves the dumb dam who suckled him."

"The singing beast?" said Ransom. "I would gladly hear more of this."

"The beasts of that kind have no milk and always what they bring forth is suckled by the she-beast of another kind. She is great and beautiful and dumb, and till the young singing beast is weaned it is among her whelps and is subject to her. But when it is grown it becomes the most delicate and glorious of all beasts and goes from her. And she wonders at its song."

"Why has Maleldil made such a thing?" said Ransom.

"That is to ask why Maleldil has made me," said Perelandra. "But now it is enough to say that from the habits of these two beasts much wisdom will come into the minds of my King and my Queen and their children. But the hour is upon us, and this is enough."

"What hour?" asked Ransom.

"Today is the morning day," said one or other or both the voices. But there was something much more than sound about Ransom and his heart began beating fast.

"The morning . . . do you mean . . .?" he asked. "Is all well? Has the Queen found the King?"

"The world is born to-day," said Malacandra. "To-day for the first time two creatures of the low worlds, two images of Maleldil that breathe and breed like the beasts, step up that step at which your parents fell, and sit in the throne of what they were meant to be. It was never seen before. Because it did not happen in your world a greater thing happened, but not this. Because the greater thing happened in Thulcandra, this and not the greater thing happens here."

"Elwin is falling to the ground," said the other voice.

"Be comforted," said Malacandra. "It is no doing of yours. You are not great, though you could have prevented a thing so great that Deep Heaven sees it with amazement. Be comforted, small one, in your smallness. He lays no merit on you. Receive and be glad. Have no fear, lest your shoulders be bearing this world. Look! it is beneath your head and carries you."

"Will they come here?" asked Ransom some time later.

"They are already well up the mountain's side," said Perelandra. "And our hour is upon us. Let us prepare our shapes. We are hard for them to see while we remain in ourselves."

"It is very well said," answered Malacandra. "But in what form shall we show ourselves to do them honour?"

"Let us appear to the small one here," said the other. "For he is a man and can tell us what is pleasing to their senses."

"I can see—I can see *something* even now," said Ransom.

"Would you have the King strain his eyes to see those who come to do him honour?" said the archon of Perelandra. "But look on this and tell us how it deals with you."

The very faint light—the almost imperceptible alteration in the visual field—which betokens an eldil vanished suddenly. The rosy peaks and the calm pool vanished also. A tornado of sheer monstrosities seemed to be pouring over Ransom. Darting pillars filled with eyes, lightning pulsations of flame, talons and beaks and billowy masses of what suggested snow, volleyed through cubes and heptagons into an infinite black void. "Stop it . . . stop it," he yelled, and the scene cleared. He gazed round blinking on the field of lilies, and presently gave the eldila to understand that this kind of appearance was not suited to human sensations. "Look then on this," said the voices again. And he looked with some reluctance, and far off between the peaks on the other side of the little valley there came rolling wheels. There was nothing but that—concentric wheels moving with a rather sickening slowness one inside the other. There was nothing terrible about them if you could get used to their appalling size, but there was also nothing significant. He bade them to try yet a third time. And suddenly two human figures stood before him on the opposite side of the lake.

They were taller than the Sorns, the giants whom he had met in Mars. They were perhaps thirty feet high. They were burning white like white-hot iron. The outline of their bodies when he looked at it steadily against the red landscape seemed to be faintly, swiftly undulating as though the permanence of their shape, like that of waterfalls or flames, co-existed with a rushing movement of the matter it contained. For a fraction of an inch inward from this outline the landscape was just visible through them: beyond that they were opaque.

Whenever he looked straight at them they appeared to be rushing towards him with enormous speed: whenever his eyes took in their surroundings he realised that they were stationary. This may have been due in part to the fact that their long and sparkling hair stood out straight behind them as if in a great wind. But if there were a wind it was not made of air, for no petal of the flowers was shaken. They were not standing quite vertically in relation to the floor of the valley: but to Ransom it appeared (as it had appeared to me on Earth when I saw one) that the eldils were vertical. It was the valley—it was the whole world of Perelandra—which was aslant. He remembered the words of Oyarsa long ago in Mars, "I am not *here* in the same way you are *here.*" It was borne in upon him that the creatures were really moving, though not moving in relation to him. This planet which inevitably seemed to him while he was in it an unmoving world—*the* world, in fact—was to them a thing moving through the heavens. In relation to their own celestial frame of reference they were rushing forward to keep abreast of the mountain valley. Had they stood still, they would have flashed past him too quickly for him to see, doubly dropped behind by the planet's spin on its own axis and by its onward march around the Sun.

Their bodies, he said, were white. But a flush of diverse colours began at about the shoulders and streamed up the necks and flickered over face and head and stood out around the head like plumage or a halo. He told me he could in a sense remember these colours—that is, he would know them if he saw them again—but that he cannot by any effort call up a visual image of them nor give them any name. The very few people with whom he and I can discuss these matters all give the same explanation. We think that when creatures of the hypersomatic kind choose to "appear" to us, they are not in fact affecting our retina at all, but directly manipulating the relevant parts of our brain. If so, it is quite possible that they can produce there the sensations we *should* have if our eyes were capable of receiving those colours in the spectrum which are actually beyond their range. The "plumage" or halo of the one eldil was extremely different from that of the other. The Oyarsa of Mars shone with cold and morning colours, a little metallic—pure, hard, and bracing. The Oyarsa of Venus glowed with a warm splendour, full of the suggestion of teeming vegetable life.

The faces surprised him very much. Nothing less like the "angel" of popular art could well be imagined. The rich variety, the hint of undeveloped possibilities, which make the interest of human faces, were entirely absent. One single, changeless expression—so clear that it hurt and dazzled him—was stamped on each and there was nothing else there at all. In that sense their faces were as "primitive," as unnatural, if you like, as those of archaic statues from Ægina. What this one thing was he could not be certain. He concluded in the end that it was charity. But it was terrifyingly different from the expression of human charity, which we always see either blossoming out of, or hastening to descend into, natural affection. Here there was no affection at all: no least lingering memory of it even at ten million years' distance, no germ from which it could spring in any future, however remote. Pure, spiritual, intellectual love shot from their faces like barbed lightning. It was so unlike the love we experience that its expression could easily be mistaken for ferocity.

Both the bodies were naked, and both were free from any sexual characteristics, either primary or secondary. That, one would have expected. But whence came this curious difference between them? He found that he could point to no single feature wherein the difference resided, yet it was impossible to ignore. One could try—Ransom has tried a hundred times—to put it into words. He has said that Malacandra was like rhythm and Perelandra like melody. He has said that Malacandra affected him like a quantitative, Perelandra like an accentual, metre. He thinks that the first held in his hand something like a spear, but the hands of the other were open, with the palms towards him. But I don't know that any of these attempts has helped me much. At all events what Ransom saw at that moment was the real meaning of gender. Everyone must sometimes have wondered why in nearly all tongues certain inanimate objects are masculine and others feminine. What is masculine about a mountain or feminine about certain trees? Ransom has cured me of believing that this is a purely morphological phenomenon, depending on the form of the word. Still less is gender an imaginative extension of sex. Our ancestors did not make mountains masculine because they projected male characteristics into them. The real process is the reverse. Gender is a reality, and a more fundamental reality than sex. Sex is, in fact, merely the adaptation to organic life of a fundamental polarity which divides all created beings. Female sex is simply one of the things that have feminine gender; there are many others, and Masculine and Feminine meet us on planes of reality where male and female would be simply meaningless. Masculine is not attenuated male, nor feminine attenuated female. On the contrary, the male and female of organic creatures are rather faint and blurred reflections of masculine and feminine. Their reproductive functions, their differences in strength and size, partly exhibit, but partly also confuse and misrepresent, the real polarity. All this Ransom saw, as it were, with his own eyes. The two white creatures were sexless. But he of Malacandra was masculine (not male); she of Perelandra was feminine (not female). Malacandra seemed to him to have the look of one standing armed, at the ramparts of his own remote archaic world, in ceaseless vigilance, his eyes ever roaming the earth-ward horizon whence his danger came long ago. "A sailor's look," Ransom once said to me; "you know . . . eyes that are impregnated with distance." But the eyes of Perelandra opened, as it were, inward, as if they were the curtained gateway to a world of waves and murmurings and wandering airs, of life that rocked in winds and splashed on mossy stones and descended as the dew and arose sunward in thin-spun delicacy of mist. On Mars the very forests are of stone; in Venus the lands swim. For now he thought of them no more as Malacandra and Perelandra. He called them by their Tellurian names. With deep wonder he thought to himself, "My eyes have seen Mars and Venus. I have seen Ares and Aphrodite." He asked them how they were known to the old poets of Tellus. When and from whom had the children of Adam learned that Ares was a man of war and that Aphrodite rose from the sea foam? Earth has been besieged, an enemy-occupied territory, since before history began. The gods have had no commerce there. How then do we know of them? It comes, they told him, a long way round and through many stages. There is an environment of minds as well as of space. The universe is one—a spider's web wherein each mind lives along every line, a vast whispering gallery where (save for the direct action of Maleldil) though no news travels unchanged yet no secret can be rigorously kept. In the mind of the fallen Archon under whom our planet groans, the memory of Deep Heaven and the gods with whom he once consorted is still alive. Nay, in the very matter of our world, the traces of the celestial commonwealth are not quite lost. Memory passes through the womb and hovers in the air. The Muse is a real thing. A faint breath, as Virgil says, reaches even the late generations. Our mythology is based on a solider reality than we dream: but it is also at an almost infinite distance from that base. And when they told him this, Ransom at last understood why mythology was what it was—gleams of celestial strength and beauty falling on a jungle of filth and imbecility. His cheeks burned on behalf of our race when he looked on the true Mars and Venus and remembered the follies that have been talked of them on Earth. Then a doubt struck him.

"But do I see you as you really are?" he asked.

"Only Maleldil sees any creature as it really is," said Mars.

"How do you see one another?" asked Ransom.

"There are no holding places in your mind for an answer to that."

"Am I then seeing only an appearance? Is it not real at all?"

"You see only an appearance, small one. You have never seen more than an appearance of anything—not of Arbol, nor of a stone, nor of your own body. This appearance is as true as what you see of those."

"But . . . there were those other appearances."

"No. There was only the failure of appearance."

"I don't understand," said Ransom. "Were all those other things—the wheels and the eyes—more real than this or less?"

"There is no meaning in your question," said Mars. "You can see a stone, if it is a fit distance from you and if you and it are moving at speeds not too different. But if one throws the stone at your eye, what then is the appearance?"

"I should feel pain and perhaps see splintered light," said Ransom. "But I don't know that I should call that an appearance of the stone."

"Yet it would be the true operation of the stone. And there is your question answered. We are now at the right distance from you."

"And were you nearer in what I first saw?"

"I do not mean that kind of distance."

"And then," said Ransom, still pondering, "there is what I had thought was your wonted appearance—the very faint light, Oyarsa, as I used to see it in your own world. What of that?"

"That is enough appearance for us to speak to you by. No more was needed between us: no more is needed now. It is to honour the King that we would now appear more. That light is the overflow or echo into the world of your senses of vehicles made for appearance to one another and to the greater eldila."

At this moment Ransom suddenly noticed an increasing disturbance of sound behind his back—of unco-ordinated sound, husky and pattering noises which broke in on the mountain silence and the crystal voices of the gods with a delicious note of warm animality. He glanced round. Romping, prancing, fluttering, gliding, crawling, waddling, with every kind of movement—in every kind of shape and colour and size—a whole zoo of beasts and birds was pouring into a flowery valley through the passes between the peaks at his back. They came mostly in their pairs, male and female together, fawning upon one another, climbing over one another, diving under one another's bellies, perching upon one another's backs. Flaming plumage, gilded beaks, glossy flanks, liquid eyes, great red caverns of whinneying or of bleating mouths, and thickets of switching tails, surrounded him on every side. "A regular Noah's Ark!" thought Ransom, and then, with sudden seriousness, "But there will be no ark needed in this world."

The song of four singing beasts rose in almost deafening triumph above the restless multitude. The great eldil of Perelandra kept back the creatures to the hither side of the pool, leaving the opposite side of the valley empty except for the coffin-like object. Ransom was not clear whether Venus spoke to the beasts or even whether they were conscious of her presence. Her connection with them was perhaps of some subtler kind—quite different from the relations he had observed between them and the Green Lady. Both the eldila were now on the same side of the pool with Ransom. He and they and all the beasts were facing in the same direction. The thing began to arrange itself. First, on the very brink of the pool, were the eldila, standing: between them, and a little back, was Ransom, still sitting among the lilies. Behind him the four singing beasts, sitting up on their haunches like fire-dogs, and proclaiming joy to all ears. Behind these again, the other animals. The sense of ceremony deepened. The expectation became intense. In our foolish human fashion he asked a question merely for the purpose of breaking it. "How can they climb to here and go down again and yet be off this island before nightfall?" Nobody answered him. He did not need an answer, for somehow he knew perfectly well that *this* island had never been forbidden them, and that one purpose in forbidding the other had been to lead them to this their destined throne. Instead of answering, the gods said, "Be still."

Ransom's eyes had grown so used to the tinted softness of Perelandrian daylight—and specially since his journey in the dark guts of the mountain—that he had quite ceased to notice its difference from the daylight of our own world. It was, therefore, with a shock of double amazement that he now suddenly saw the peaks on the far side of the valley showing really dark against what seemed a terrestrial dawn. A moment later sharp, well-defined shadows—long, like the shadows at early morning—were streaming back from every beast and every unevenness of the ground and each lily had its light and its dark side. Up and up came the light from the mountain slope. It filled the whole valley. The shadows disappeared again. All was in a pure daylight that seemed to come from nowhere in particular. He knew ever afterwards what is meant by a light "resting on" or "overshadowing" a holy thing, but not emanating from it. For as the light reached its perfection and settled itself, as it were, like a lord upon his throne or like wine in a bowl, and filled the whole flowery cup of the mountain top, every cranny, with its purity, the holy thing, Paradise itself in its two Persons, Paradise walking hand in hand, its two bodies shining in the light like emeralds yet not themselves too bright to look at, came in sight in the cleft between two peaks, and stood a moment with its male right hand lifted in regal and pontifical benediction, and they walked down and stood on the far side of the water. And the gods kneeled and bowed their huge bodies before the small forms of that young King and Queen.

17

THERE WAS great silence on the mountain top and Ransom also had fallen down before the human pair. When at last he raised his eyes from the four blessed feet, he found himself involuntarily speaking though his voice was broken and his eyes dimmed. "Do not move away, do not raise me up," he said. "I have never before seen a man or a woman. I have lived all my life among shadows and broken images. Oh, my Father and my Mother, my Lord and my Lady, do not move, do not answer me yet. My own father and mother I have never seen. Take me for your son. We have been alone in my world for a great time."

The eyes of the Queen looked upon him with love and recognition, but it was not of the Queen that he thought most. It was hard to think of anything but the King. And how shall I—I who have not seen him—tell you what he was like? It was hard even for Ransom to tell me of the King's face. But we dare not withhold the truth. It was that face which no man can say he does not know. You might ask how it was possible to look upon it and not to commit idolatry, not to mistake it for that of which it was the likeness. For the resemblance was, in its own fashion, infinite, so that almost you could wonder at finding no sorrows in his brow and no wounds in his hands and feet. Yet there was no danger of mistaking, not one moment of confusion, no least sally of the will towards forbidden reverence. Where likeness was greatest, mistake was least possible. Perhaps this is always so. A clever wax-work can be made so like a man that for a moment it deceives us: the great portrait which is far more deeply like him does not. Plaster images of the Holy One may before now have drawn to themselves the adoration they were meant to arouse for the reality. But here, where His live image, like Him within and without, made by His own bare hands out of the depth of divine artistry, His masterpiece of self-portraiture coming forth from His workshop to delight all worlds, walked and spoke before Ransom's eyes, it could never be taken for more than an image. Nay, the very beauty of it lay in the certainty that it was a copy, like and not the same, an echo, a rhyme, an exquisite reverberation of the uncreated music prolonged in a created medium.

Ransom was lost for a while in the wonder of these things, so that when he came to himself he found that Perelandra was speaking, and what he heard seemed to be the end of a long oration. "The floating lands and the firm lands," she was saying, "the air and the curtains at the gates of Deep Heaven, the seas and the Holy Mountain, the rivers above and the rivers of underland, the fire, the fish, the birds, the beasts, and the others of the waves whom yet you know not; all these Maleldil puts into your hand from this day forth as far as you live in time and farther. My word henceforth is nothing: your word is law unchangeable and the very daughter of the Voice. In all that circle which this world runs about Arbol, you are Oyarsa. Enjoy it well. Give names to all creatures, guide all natures to perfection. Strengthen the feebler, lighten the darker, love all. Hail and be glad, oh man and woman, Oyarsa-Perelendri, the Adam, the Crown, Tor and Tinidril, Baru and Baru'ah, Ask and Embla, Yatsur and Yatsurah, dear to Maleldil. Blessed be He!"

When the King spoke in answer, Ransom looked up at him again. He saw that the human pair were now seated on a low bank that rose near the margin of the pool. So great was the light, that they cast clear reflections in the water as they might have done in our own world.

"We give you thanks, fair foster mother," said the King, "and specially for this world in which you have laboured for long ages as Maleldil's very hand that all might be ready for us when we woke. We have not known you till to-day. We have often wondered whose hand it was that we saw in the long waves and the bright islands and whose breath delighted us in the wind at morning. For though we were young then, we saw dimly that to say 'It is Maleldil' was true, but not all the truth. This world we receive: our joy is the greater because we take it by your gift as well as by His. But what does He put into your mind to do henceforward?"

"It lies in your bidding, Tor-Oyarsa," said Perelandra, "whether I now converse in Deep Heaven only or also in that part of Deep Heaven which is to you a World."

"It is very much our will," said the King, "that you remain with us, both for the love we bear you and also that you may strengthen us with counsel and even with your operations. Not till we have gone many times about Arbol shall we grow up to the full management of the dominion which Maleldil puts into our hands: nor are we yet ripe to steer the world through Heaven nor to make rain and fair weather upon us. If it seems good to you, remain."

"I am content," said Perelandra.

While this dialogue proceeded, it was a wonder that the contrast between the Adam and the eldils was not a discord. On the one side, the crystal, bloodless voice, and the immutable expression of the snow-white face; on the other the blood coursing in the veins, the feeling trembling on the lips and sparkling in the eyes, the might of the man's shoulders, the wonder of the woman's breasts, a splendour of virility and richness of womanhood unknown on earth, a living torrent of perfect animality—yet when these met, the one did not seem rank nor the other spectral. *Animal rationale*—an animal, yet also a reasonable soul: such, he remembered, was the old definition of Man. But he had never till now seen the reality. For now he saw this living Paradise, the Lord and Lady, as the resolution of discords, the bridge that spans what would else be a chasm in creation, the keystone of the whole arch. By entering that mountain valley they had suddenly united the warm multitude of the brutes behind him with the transcorporeal intelligences at his side. They closed the circle, and with their coming all the separate notes of strength or beauty which that assembly had hitherto struck became one music. But now the King was speaking again.

"And as it is not Maleldil's gift simply," he said, "but also Maleldil's gift through you, and thereby the richer, so it is not through you only, but through a third, and thereby the richer again. And this is the first word I speak as

Tor-Oyarsa-Perelendri; that in our world, as long as it is a world, neither shall morning come nor night but that we and all our children shall speak to Maleldil of Ransom the man of Thulcandra and praise him to one another. And to you, Ransom, I say this, that you have called us Lord and Father, Lady and Mother. And rightly, for this is our name. But in another fashion we call you Lord and Father. For it seems to us that Maleldil sent you into our world at that day when the time of our being young drew to its end, and from it we must now go up or go down, into corruption or into perfection. Maleldil has taken us where He meant us to be: but of Maleldil's instruments in this, you were the chief."

They made him go across the water to them, wading, for it came only to his knees. He would have fallen at their feet but they would not let him. They rose to meet him and both kissed him, mouth to mouth and heart to heart as equals embrace. They would have made him sit between them, but when they saw that this troubled him they let it be. He went and sat down on the level ground, below them, and a little to the left. From there he faced the assembly—the huge shapes of the gods and the concourse of beasts. And then the Queen spoke.

"As soon as you had taken away the Evil One," she said, "and I awoke from sleep, my mind was cleared. It is a wonder to me, Piebald, that for all those days you and I could have been so young. The reason for not yet living on the Fixed Land is now so plain. How could I wish to live there except because it was Fixed? And why should I desire the Fixed except to make sure—to be able on one day to command where I should be the next and what should happen to me? It was to reject the wave—to draw my hands out of Maleldil's, to say to Him, 'Not thus, but thus'—to put in our own power what times should roll towards us . . . as if you gathered fruits together to-day for to-morrow's eating instead of taking what came. That would have been cold love and feeble trust. And out of it how could we ever have climbed back into love and trust again?"

"I see it well," said Ransom. "Though in my world it would pass for folly. We have been evil so long"—and then he stopped, doubtful of being understood and surprised that he had used a word for *evil* which he had not hitherto known that he knew, and which he had not heard either in Mars or in Venus.

"We know these things now," said the King, seeing Ransom's hesitation. "All this, all that happened in your world, Maleldil has put into our mind. We have learned of evil, though not as the Evil One wished us to learn. We have learned better than that, and know it more, for it is waking that understands sleep and not sleep that understands waking. There is an ignorance of evil that comes from being young: there is a darker ignorance that comes from doing it, as men by sleeping lose the knowledge of sleep. You are more ignorant of evil in Thulcandra now than in the days before your Lord and Lady began to do it. But Maleldil has brought us out of the one ignorance, and we have not entered the other. It was by the Evil One himself that he brought us out of the first. Little did that dark mind know the errand on which he really came to Perelandra!"

"Forgive me, my Father, if I speak foolishly," said Ransom. "I see how evil has been made known to the Queen, but not how it was made known to you."

Then unexpectedly the King laughed. His body was very big and his laugh was like an earthquake in it, loud and deep and long, till in the end Ransom laughed too, though he had not seen the joke, and the Queen laughed as well. And the birds began clapping their wings and the beasts wagging their tails, and the light seemed brighter and the pulse of the whole assembly quickened, and new modes of joy that had nothing to do with mirth as we understand it passed into them all, as it were from the very air, or as if there were dancing in Deep Heaven. Some say there always is.

"I know what he is thinking," said the King, looking upon the Queen. "He is thinking that you suffered and strove and I have a world for my reward." Then he turned to Ransom and continued. "You are right," he said, "I know now what they say in your world about justice. And perhaps they say well, for in that world things always fall below justice. But Maleldil always goes above it. All is gift. I am Oyarsa not by His gift alone but by our foster mother's, not by hers alone but by yours, not by yours alone but my wife's—nay, in some sort, by gift of the very beasts and birds. Through many hands, enriched with many different kinds of love and labour, the gift comes to me. It is the Law. The best fruits are plucked for each by some hand that is not his own."

"That is not the whole of what happened, Piebald," said the Queen. "The King has not told you all. Maleldil drove him far away into a green sea where forests grow up from the bottom through the waves. . . ."

"Its name is Lur," said the King.

"Its name is Lur," repeated the eldila. And Ransom realized that the King had uttered not an observation but an enactment.

"And there in Lur (it is far hence)," said the Queen, "strange things befell him."

"Is it good to ask about these things?" said Ransom.

"There were many things," said Tor the King. "For many hours I learned the properties of shapes by drawing lines in the turf of a little island on which I rode. For many hours I learned new things about Maleldil and about His Father and the Third One. We knew little of this while we were young. But after that He showed me in a darkness what was happening to the Queen. And I knew it was possible for her to be undone. And then I saw what had happened in your world, and how your Mother fell and how your Father went with her, doing her no good thereby and bringing the darkness upon all their children. And then it was before me like a thing coming towards my hand . . . what I should do in like case. There I learned of evil and good, of anguish and joy."

Ransom had expected the King to relate his decision, but when the King's voice died away into thoughtful silence he had not the assurance to question him.

"Yes . . ." said the King, musing. "Though a man were to be torn in two halves . . . though half of him turned into earth. . . . The living half must still follow Maleldil. For if it also lay down and became earth, what hope would there be for the whole? But while one half lived, through it He might send life back into the other." Here he paused for a long time, and then spoke again somewhat quickly. "He gave me no assurance. No fixed land. Always one must throw oneself into the wave." Then he cleared his brow and turned to the eldila and spoke in a new voice.

"Certainly, oh foster mother," he said. "We have much need of counsel for already we feel that growing up within our bodies which our young wisdom can hardly overtake. They will not always be bodies bound to the low worlds. Hear the second word that I speak as Tor-Oyarsa-Perelendri. While this World goes about Arbol ten thousand times, we shall judge and hearten our people from this throne. Its name is Tai Harendrimar, The Hill of Life."

"Its name is Tai Harendrimar," said the eldila.

"On the Fixed Land which once was forbidden," said Tor the King, "we will make a great place to the splendour of Maleldil. Our sons shall bend the pillars of rock into arches——"

"What are arches?" said Tinidril the Queen.

"Arches," said Tor the King, "are when pillars of stone throw out branches like trees and knit their branches together and bear up a great dome as of leafage, but the leaves shall be shaped stones. And there our sons will make images."

"What are images?" said Tinidril.

"Splendour of Deep Heaven!" cried the King with a great laugh. "It seems there are too many new words in the air. I had thought these things were coming out of your mind into mine, and lo! you have not thought them at all. Yet I think Maleldil passed them to me through you, none the less. I will show you images, I will show you houses. It may be that in this matter our natures are reversed and it is you who beget and I who bear. But let us speak of plainer matters. We will fill this world with our children. We will know this world to the centre. We will make the nobler of the beasts so wise that they will become *hnau* and speak: their lives shall awake to a new life in us as we awake in Maleldil. When the time is ripe for it and the ten thousand circlings are nearly at an end, we will tear the sky curtain and Deep Heaven shall become familiar to the eyes of our sons as the trees and the waves to ours."

"And what after this, Tor-Oyarsa?" said Malacandra.

"Then it is Maleldil's purpose to make us free of Deep Heaven. Our bodies will be changed, but not all changed. We shall be as the eldila, but not all as eldila. And so will all our sons and daughters be changed in the time of this ripeness, until the number is made up which Maleldil read in His Father's mind before times flowed."

"And that," said Ransom, "will be the end?"

Tor the King stared at him.

"The end?" he said. "Who spoke of an end?"

"The end of your world, I mean," said Ransom.

"Splendour of Heaven!" said Tor. "Your thoughts are unlike ours. About that time we shall be not far from the beginning of all things. But there will be one matter to settle before the beginning rightly begins."

"What is that?" asked Ransom.

"Your own world," said Tor, "Thulcandra. The seige of your world shall be raised, the black spot cleared away, before the real beginning. In those days Maleldil will go to war—in us, and in many who once were *hnau* on your world, and in many from far off and in many eldila, and, last of all, in Himself unveiled, He will go down to Thulcandra. Some of us will go before. It is in my mind, Malacandra, that thou and I will be among those. We shall fall upon your moon, wherein there is a secret evil, and which is as the shield of the Dark Lord of Thulcandra—scarred with many a blow. We shall break her. Her light shall be put out. Her fragments shall fall into your world and the seas and the smoke shall arise so that the dwellers in Thulcandra will no longer see the light of Arbol. And as Maleldil Himself draws near, the evil things in your world shall show themselves stripped of disguise so that plagues and horrors shall cover your lands and seas. But in the end all shall be cleansed, and even the memory of your Black Oyarsa blotted out, and your world shall be fair and sweet and reunited to the field of Arbol and its true name shall be heard again. But can it be, Friend, that no rumour of all this is heard in Thulcandra? Do your people think that their Dark Lord will hold his prey forever?"

"Most of them," said Ransom, "have ceased to think of such things at all. Some of us still have the knowledge: but I did not at once see what you were talking of, because what you call the beginning we are accustomed to call the Last Things."

"I do not call it the beginning," said Tor the King. "It is but the wiping out of a false start in order that the world may *then* begin. As when a man lies down to sleep, if he finds a twisted root under his shoulder he will change his place—and after that his real sleep begins. Or as a man setting foot on an island, may make a false step. He steadies himself and after that his journey begins. You would not call that steadying of himself a last thing?"

"And is the whole story of my race no more than this?" said Ransom.

"I see no more than beginnings in the history of the Low Worlds," said Tor the King. "And in yours a failure to begin. You talk of evenings before the day has dawned. I set forth even now on ten thousand years of preparation—I, the first of my race, my race the first of races, to begin. I tell you that when the last of my children has ripened and ripeness has spread from them to all the Low Worlds, it will be whispered that the morning is at hand."

"I am full of doubts and ignorance," said Ransom. "In our world those who know Maleldil at all believe that His coming down to us and being a man is the central happening of all that happens. If you take that from me, Father, whither will you lead me? Surely not to the enemy's talk which thrusts my world and my race into a remote corner and gives me a universe, with no centre at all, but millions of worlds that lead nowhere or (what is worse) to more and more worlds for ever, and comes over me with numbers and empty spaces and repetitions and asks me to bow down before bigness. Or do you make your world the centre? But I am troubled. What of the people on Malacandra? Would they also think that their world was the centre? I do not even see how your world can rightly be called yours. You were made yesterday and it is from of old. The most of it is water where you cannot live. And what of the things beneath its crust? And of the great spaces with no world at all? Is the enemy easily answered when He says that all is without plan or meaning? As soon as we think we see one it melts away into nothing, or into some other plan that we never dreamed of, and what was the centre becomes the rim, till we doubt if any shape or plan or pattern was ever more than a trick of our own eyes, cheated with hope, or tired with too much looking. To what is all driving? What is the morning you speak of? What is it the beginning of?"

"The beginning of the Great Game, of the Great Dance," said Tor. "I know little of it as yet. Let the eldila speak."

The voice that spoke next seemed to be that of Mars, but Ransom was not certain. And who spoke after that, he does not know at all. For in the conversation that followed—if it can be called a conversation—though he believes that he himself was sometimes the speaker, he never knew which words were his or another's, or even whether a man or an eldil was talking. The speeches followed one another—if, indeed, they did not all take place at the same time—like the parts of a music into which all five of them had entered as instruments or like a wind blowing through five trees that stand together on a hilltop.

"We would not talk of it like that," said the first voice. "The Great Dance does not wait to be perfect until the peoples of the Low Worlds are gathered into it. We speak not of when it will begin. It has begun from before always. There was no time when we did not rejoice before His face as now. The dance which we dance is at the centre and for the dance all things were made. Blessed be He!"

Another said, "Never did He make two things the same; never did He utter one word twice. After earths, not better earths but beasts; after beasts, not better beasts, but spirits. After a falling, not a recovery but a new creation. Out of the new creation, not a third but the mode of change itself is changed for ever. Blessed is He!"

And another said, "It is loaded with justice as a tree bows down with fruit. All is righteousness and there is no equality. Not as when stones lie side by side, but as when stones support and are supported in an arch, such is His order; rule and obedience, begetting and bearing, heat glancing down, life growing up. Blessed be He!"

One said, "They who add years to years in lumpish aggregation, or miles to miles and galaxies to galaxies, shall not come near His greatness. The day of the fields of Arbol will fade and the days of Deep Heaven itself are numbered. Not thus is He great. He dwells (all of Him dwells) within the seed of the smallest flower and is not cramped: Deep Heaven is inside Him who is inside the seed and does not distend Him. Blessed be He!"

"The edge of each nature borders on that whereof it contains no shadow or similitude. Of many points one line; of many lines one shape; of many shapes one solid body; of many senses and thoughts one person; of three persons, Himself. As is the circle to the sphere, so are the ancient worlds that needed no redemption to that world wherein He was born and died. As is a point to a line, so is that world to the far-off fruits of its redeeming. Blessed be He!"

"Yet the circle is not less round than the sphere, and the sphere is the home and fatherland of circles. Infinite multitudes of circles lie enclosed in every sphere, and if they spoke they would say, For us were spheres created. Let no mouth open to gainsay them. Blessed be He!"

"The peoples of the ancient worlds who never sinned, for whom He never came down, are the peoples for whose sake the Low Worlds were made. For though the healing what was wounded and the straightening what was bent is a new dimension of glory, yet the straight was not made that it might be bent nor the whole that it might be wounded. The ancient peoples are at the centre. Blessed be He!"

"All which is not itself the Great Dance was made in order that He might come down into it. In the Fallen World He prepared for Himself a body and was united with the Dust and made it glorious for ever. This is the end and final cause of all creating, and the sin whereby it came is called Fortunate and the world where this was enacted is the centre of worlds. Blessed be He!"

"The tree was planted in that world but the fruit has ripened in this. The fountain that sprang with mingled blood and life in the Dark World, flows here with life only. We have passed the first cataracts, and from here onward the stream flows deep and turns in the direction of the sea. This is the Morning Star which He promised to those who conquer; this is the centre of worlds. Till now all has waited. But now the trumpet has sounded and the army is on the move. Blessed be He!"

"Though men or angels rule them, the worlds are for themselves. The waters you have not floated on, the fruit you have not plucked, the caves into which you have not descended and the fire through which your bodies cannot pass, do not await your coming to put on perfection, though they will obey you when you come. Times without number I have circled Arbol while you were not alive, and those times were not desert. Their own voice was in them, not merely a dreaming of the day when you should awake. They also were at the centre. Be comforted, small immortals. You are not the voice that all things utter, nor is there eternal silence in the places where you cannot come. No feet have walked, nor shall, on the ice of Glund; no eye looked up from beneath on the Ring of Lurga, and Iron-plain in Neruval is chaste and empty. Yet it is not for nothing that the gods walk ceaselessly around the fields of Arbol. Blessed be He!"

"That Dust itself which is scattered so rare in Heaven, whereof all worlds, and the bodies that are not worlds, are made, is at the centre. It waits not till created eyes have seen it or hands handled it, to be in itself a strength and splendour of Maleldil. Only the least part has served, or ever shall, a beast, a man, or a god. But always, and beyond all distances, before they came and after they are gone and where they never come, it is what it is and utters the heart of the Holy One with its own voice. It is farthest from Him of all things, for it has no life, nor sense, nor reason; it is nearest to Him of all things for without intervening soul, as sparks fly out of fire, He utters in each grain of it the unmixed image of His energy. Each grain, if it spoke, would say, I am at the centre; for me all things were made. Let no mouth open to gainsay it. Blessed be He!"

"Each grain is at the centre. The Dust is at the centre. The Worlds are at the centre. The beasts are at the centre. The ancient peoples are there. The race that sinned is there. Tor and Tinidril are there. The gods are there also. Blessed be He!"

"Where Maleldil is, there is the centre. He is in every place. Not some of Him in one place and some in another, but in each place the whole Maleldil, even in the smallness beyond thought. There is no way out of the centre save into the Bent Will which casts itself into the Nowhere. Blessed be He!"

"Each thing was made for Him. He is the centre. Because we are with Him, each of us is at the centre. It is not as in a city of the Darkened World where they say that each must live for all. In His city all things are made for each. When He died in the Wounded World He died not for men, but for each man. If each man had been the only man made, He would have done no less. Each thing, from the single grain of Dust to the strongest eldil, is the end and the final cause of all creation and the mirror in which the beam of His brightness comes to rest and so returns to Him. Blessed be He!"

"In the plan of the Great Dance plans without number interlock, and each movement becomes in its season the breaking into flower of the whole design to which all else had been directed. Thus each is equally at the centre and none are there by being equals, but some by giving place and some by receiving it, the small things by their smallness and the great by their greatness, and all the patterns linked and looped together by the unions of a kneeling with a sceptred love. Blessed be He!"

"He has immeasurable use for each thing that is made, that His love and splendour may flow forth like a strong river which has need of a great watercourse and fills alike the deep pools and the little crannies, that are filled equally and remain unequal; and when it has filled them brim full it flows over and makes new channels. We also have need beyond measure of all that He has made. Love me, my brothers, for I am infinitely necessary to you and for your delight I was made. Blessed be He!"

"He has no need at all of anything that is made. An eldil is not more needful to Him than a grain of the Dust: a peopled world no more needful than a world that is empty: but all needless alike, and what all add to Him is nothing. We also have no need of anything that is made. Love me, my brothers, for I am infinitely superfluous, and your love shall be like His, born neither of your need nor of my deserving, but a plain bounty. Blessed be He!"

"All things are by Him and for Him. He utters Himself also for His own delight and sees that He is good. He is His own begotten and what proceeds from Him is Himself. Blessed be He!"

"All that is made seems planless to the darkened mind, because there are more plans than it looked for. In these seas there are islands where the hairs of the turf are so fine and so closely woven together that unless a man looked long at them he would see neither hairs nor weaving at all, but only the same and the flat. So with the Great Dance. Set your eyes on one movement and it will lead you through all patterns and it will seem to you the master movement. But the seeming will be true. Let no mouth open to gainsay it. There seems no plan because it is all plan: there seems no centre because it is all centre. Blessed be He!"

"Yet this seeming also is the end and final cause for which He spreads out Time so long and Heaven so deep; lest if we never met the dark, and the road that leads nowhither, and the question to which no answer is imaginable, we should have in our minds no likeness of the Abyss of the Father, into which if a creature drop down his thoughts for ever he shall hear no echo return to him. Blessed, blessed, blessed be He!"

And now, by a transition which he did not notice, it seemed that what had begun as speech was turned into sight, or into something that can be remembered only as if it were seeing. He thought he saw the Great Dance. It seemed to be woven out of the intertwining undulation of many cords or bands of light, leaping over and under one another and mutually embraced in arabesques and flower-like subtleties. Each figure as he looked at it became the master-figure or focus of the whole spectacle, by means of which his eye disentangled all else and brought it into unity—only to be itself entangled when he looked to what he had taken for mere marginal decorations and found that there also the same hegemony was claimed, and the claim made good, yet the former pattern not thereby dispossessed but finding in its new subordination a significance greater than that which it had abdicated. He could see also (but the word "seeing" is now plainly inadequate) wherever the ribbons or serpents of light intersected, minute corpuscles of momentary brightness: and he knew somehow that these particles were the secular generalities of which history tells—peoples, institutions, climates of opinion, civilisations, arts, sciences, and the like—ephemeral coruscations that piped their short song and vanished. The ribbons or cords themselves, in which millions of corpuscles lived and died, were things of some different kind. At first he could not say what. But he knew in the end that most of them were individual entities. If so, the time in which the Great Dance proceeds is very unlike time as we know it. Some of the thinner and more delicate cords were beings that we call short-lived: flowers and insects, a fruit or a storm of rain, and once (he thought) a wave of the sea. Others were such things as we also think lasting: crystals, rivers, mountains, or even stars. Far above these in girth and luminosity and flashing with colours from beyond our spectrum were the lines of the personal beings, yet as different from one another in splendour as all of them from the previous class. But not all the cords were individuals: some were universal truths or universal qualities. It did not surprise him then to find that these and the persons were both cords and both stood together as against the mere atoms of generality which lived and died in the clashing of their streams: but afterwards, when he came back to earth, he wondered. And by now the thing must have passed together out of the region of sight as we understand it. For he says that the whole solid figure of these enamoured and inter-inanimated circlings was suddenly revealed as the mere superficies of a far vaster pattern in four dimensions, and that figure as the boundary of yet others in other worlds: till suddenly as the movement grew yet swifter, the interweaving yet more ecstatic, the relevance of all to all yet more intense, as dimension was added to dimension and that part of him which could reason and remember was dropped farther and farther behind that part of him which saw, even then, at the very zenith of complexity, complexity was eaten up and faded, as a thin white cloud fades into the hard blue burning of the sky, and a simplicity beyond all comprehension, ancient and young as spring, illimitable, pellucid, drew him with cords of infinite desire into its own stillness. He went up into such a quietness, a privacy, and a freshness that at the very moment when he stood farthest from our ordinary mode of being he had the sense of stripping off encumbrances and awaking from trance, and coming to himself. With a gesture of relaxation he looked about him. . . .

The animals had gone. The two white figures had disappeared. Tor and Tinidril and he were alone, in ordinary Perelandrian daylight, early in the morning.

"Where are the beasts?" said Ransom.

"They have gone about their small affairs," said Tinidril. "They have gone to bring up their whelps and lay their eggs, to build their nests and spin their webs and dig their burrows, to sing and play and to eat and drink."

"They did not wait long," said Ransom, "for I feel it is still early in the morning."

"But not the same morning," said Tor.

"We have been here long, then?" asked Ransom.

"Yes," said Tor. "I did not know it till now. But we have accomplished one whole circle about Arbol since we met on this mountain top."

"A year?" said Ransom. "A whole year? O Heavens, what may by now have happened in my own dark world! Did you know, Father, that so much time was passing?"

"I did not feel it pass," said Tor. "I believe the waves of time will often change for us henceforward. We are coming to have it in our own choice whether we shall be above them and see many waves together or whether we shall reach them one by one as we used to."

"It comes into my mind," said Tinidril, "that to-day, now that the year has brought us back to the same place in Heaven, the eldila are coming for Piebald to take him back to his own world."

"You are right, Tinidril," said Tor. Then he looked at Ransom and said, "There is a red dew coming up out of your foot, like a little spring."

Ransom looked down and saw that his heel was still bleeding. "Yes," he said, "it is where the Evil One bit me. The redness is of *hrū* (blood)."

"Sit down, friend," said Tor, "and let me wash your foot in this pool."

Ransom hesitated but the King compelled him. So presently he sat on the little bank and the King kneeled before him in the shallow water and took the injured foot in his hand. He paused as he looked at it.

"So this is *hrū*, " he said at last. "I have never seen such a fluid before. And this is the substance wherewith Maleldil remade the worlds before any world was made."

He washed the foot for a long time but the bleeding did not stop. "Does it mean Piebald will die?" said Tinidril at last.

"I do not think so," said Tor. "I think that any of his race who has breathed the air that he has breathed and drunk the waters that he has drunk since he came to the Holy Mountain will not find it easy to die. Tell me, Friend, was it not so in your world that after they had lost their paradise the men of your race did not learn to die quickly?"

"I had heard," said Ransom, "that those first generations were long livers, but most take it for only a Story or a Poetry and I had not thought of the cause."

"Oh!" said Tinidril suddenly. "The eldila are come to take him."

Ransom looked round and saw, not the white manlike forms in which he had last seen Mars and Venus, but only the almost invisible lights. The King and Queen apparently recognized the spirits in this guise also: as easily, he thought, as an earthly King would recognise his acquaintance even when they were not in court dress.

The King released Ransom's foot and all three of them went towards the white casket. Its covering lay beside it on the ground. All felt an impulse to delay.

"What is this that we feel, Tor?" said Tinidril.

"I don't know," said the King. "One day I will give it a name. This is not a day for making names."

"It is like a fruit with a very thick shell," said Tinidril. "The joy of our meeting when we meet again in the Great Dance is the sweet of it. But the rind is thick—more years thick than I can count."

"You see now," said Tor, "what that Evil One would have done to us. If we had listened to him we should now be trying to get at that sweet without biting through the shell."

"And so it would not be 'That sweet' at all," said Tinidril.

"It is now his time to go," said the tingling voice of an eldil. Ransom found no words to say as he laid himself down in the casket. The sides rose up high above him like walls: beyond them, as if framed in a coffin-shaped window, he saw the golden sky and the faces of Tor and Tinidril. "You must cover my eyes," he said presently: and the two human forms went out of sight for a moment and returned. Their arms were full of the rose-red lilies. Both bent down and kissed him. He saw the King's hand lifted in blessing and then never saw anything again in that world. They covered his face with the cool petals till he was blinded in a red sweet-smelling cloud.

"Is all ready?" said the King's voice. "Farewell, Friend and Saviour, farewell," said both voices. "Farewell till we three pass out of the dimensions of time. Speak of us always to Maleldil as we speak always of you. The splendour, the love, and the strength be upon you."

Then came the great cumbrous noise of the lid being fastened on above him. Then, for a few seconds, noises without, in the world from which he was eternally divided. Then his consciousness was engulfed.

FROM

The Screwtape
Letters

MY DEAR WORMWOOD,

So you "have great hopes that the patient's religious phase is dying away", have you? I always thought the Training College had gone to pieces since they put old Slubgob at the head of it, and now I am sure. Has no one ever told you about the law of Undulation?

Humans are amphibians—half spirit and half animal. (The Enemy's determination to produce such a revolting hybrid was one of the things that determined Our Father to withdraw his support from Him.) As spirits they belong to the eternal world, but as animals they inhabit time. This means that while their spirit can be directed to an eternal object, their bodies, passions, and imaginations are in continual change, for to be in time means to change. Their nearest approach to constancy, therefore, is undulation—the repeated return to a level from which they repeatedly fall back, a series of troughs and peaks. If you had watched your patient carefully you would have seen this undulation in every department of his life—his interest in his work, his affection for his friends, his physical appetites, all go up and down. As long as he lives on earth periods of emotional and bodily richness and liveliness will alternate with periods of numbness and poverty. The dryness and dulness through which your patient is now going are not, as you fondly suppose, your workmanship; they are merely a natural phenomenon which will do us no good unless you make a good use of it.

To decide what the best use of it is, you must ask what use the Enemy wants to make of it, and then do the opposite. Now it may surprise you to learn that in His efforts to get permanent possession of a soul, He relies on the troughs even more than on the peaks; some of His special favourites have gone through longer and deeper troughs than anyone else. The reason is this. To us a human is primarily food; our aim is the absorption of its will into ours, the increase of our own area of selfhood at its expense. But the obedience which the Enemy demands of men is quite a different thing. One must face the fact that all the talk about His love for men, and His service being perfect freedom, is not (as one would gladly believe) mere propaganda, but an appalling truth. He really *does* want to fill the universe with a lot of loathsome little replicas of Himself—creatures whose life, on its miniature scale, will be qualitatively like His own, not because He has absorbed them but because their wills freely conform to His. We want cattle who can finally become food; He wants servants who can finally become sons. We want to suck in, He wants to give out. We are empty and would be filled; He is full and flows over. Our war aim is a world in which Our Father Below has drawn all other beings into himself: the Enemy wants a world full of beings united to Him but still distinct.

And that is where the troughs come in. You must have often wondered why the Enemy does not make more use of His power to be sensibly present to human souls in any degree He chooses and at any moment. But you now see that the Irresistible and the Indisputable are the two weapons which the very nature of His scheme forbids Him to use. Merely to over-ride a human will (as His felt presence in any but the faintest and most mitigated degree would certainly do) would be for Him useless. He cannot ravish. He can only woo. For His ignoble idea is to eat the cake and have it; the creatures are to be one with Him, but yet themselves; merely to cancel them, or assimilate them, will not serve. He is prepared to do a little over-riding at the beginning. He will set them off with communications of His presence which, though faint, seem great to them, with emotional sweetness, and easy conquest over temptation. But He never allows this state of affairs to last long. Sooner or later He withdraws, if not in fact, at least from their conscious experience, all those supports and incentives. He leaves the creature to stand up on its own legs—to carry out from the will alone duties which have lost all relish. It is during such trough periods, much more than during the peak periods, that it is growing into the sort of creature He wants it to be. Hence the prayers offered in the state of dryness are those which please Him best. We can drag our patients along by continual tempting, because we design them only for the table, and the more their will is interfered with the better. He cannot "tempt" to virtue as we do to vice. He wants them to learn to walk and must therefore take away His hand; and if only the will to walk is really there He is pleased even with their stumbles. Do not be deceived, Wormwood. Our cause is never more in danger than when a human, no longer desiring, but still intending, to do our Enemy's will, looks round upon a universe from which every trace of Him seems to have vanished, and asks why he has been forsaken, and still obeys.

But of course the troughs afford opportunities to our side also. Next week I will give you some hints on how to exploit them,

Your affectionate uncle
SCREWTAPE

MY DEAR WORMWOOD,

I hope my last letter has convinced you that the trough of dulness or "dryness" through which your patient is going at present will not, of itself, give you his soul, but needs to be properly exploited. What forms the exploitation should take I will now consider.

In the first place I have always found that the Trough periods of the human undulation provide excellent opportunity for all sensual temptations, particularly those of sex. This may surprise you, because, of course, there is more physical energy, and therefore more potential appetite, at the Peak periods; but you must remember that the powers of resistance are then also at their highest. The health and spirits which you want to use in producing lust can also, alas, be very easily used for work or play or thought or innocuous merriment. The attack has a much better chance of success when the man's whole inner world is drab and cold and empty. And it is also to be noted that the Trough sexuality is subtly different in quality from that of the Peak—much less likely to lead to the milk and water phenomenon which the humans call "being in love", much more easily drawn into perversions, much less contaminated by those generous and imaginative and even spiritual concomitants which often render human sexuality so disappointing. It is the same with other desires of the flesh. You are much more likely to make your man a sound drunkard by pressing drink on him as an anodyne when he is dull and weary than by encouraging him to use it as a means of merriment among his friends when he is happy and expansive. Never forget that when we are dealing with any pleasure in its healthy and normal and satisfying form, we are, in a sense, on the Enemy's ground. I know we have won many a soul through pleasure. All the same, it is His invention, not ours. He made the pleasures: all our research so far has not enabled us to produce one. All we can do is to encourage the humans to take the pleasures which our Enemy has produced, at times, or in ways, or in degrees, which He has forbidden. Hence we always try to work away from the natural condition of any pleasure to that in which it is least natural, least redolent of its Maker, and least pleasurable. An ever increasing craving for an ever diminishing pleasure is the formula. It is more certain; and it's better *style*. To get the man's soul and give him *nothing* in return—that is what really gladdens our Father's heart. And the troughs are the time for beginning the process.

But there is an even better way of exploiting the Trough; I mean through the patient's own thoughts about it. As always, the first step is to keep knowledge out of his mind. Do not let him suspect the law of undulation. Let him assume that the first ardours of his conversion might have been expected to last, and ought to have lasted, forever, and that his present dryness is an equally permanent condition. Having once got this misconception well fixed in his head, you may then proceed in various ways. It all depends on whether your man is of the desponding type who can be tempted to despair, or of the wishful-thinking type who can be assured that all is well. The former type is getting rare among the humans. If your patient should happen to belong to it, everything is easy. You have only got to keep him out of the way of experienced Christians (an easy task now-a-days), to direct his attention to the appropriate passages in scripture, and then to set him to work on the desperate design of recovering his old feelings by sheer will-power, and the game is ours. If he is of the more hopeful type, your job is to make him acquiesce in the present low temperature of his spirit and gradually become content with it, persuading himself that it is not so low after all. In a week or two you will be making him doubt whether the first days of his Christianity were not, perhaps, a little excessive. Talk to him about "moderation in all things". If you can once get him to the point of thinking that "religion is all very well up to a point", you can feel quite happy about his soul. A moderated religion is as good for us as no religion at all—and more amusing.

Another possibility is that of direct attack on his faith. When you have caused him to assume that the trough is permanent, can you not persuade him that "his religious phase" is just going to die away like all his previous phases? Of course there is no conceivable way of getting by reason from the proposition "I am losing interest in this" to the proposition "This is false". But, as I said before, it is jargon, not reason, you must rely on. The mere word *phase* will very likely do the trick. I assume that the creature has been through several of them before—they all have—and that he always feels superior and patronising to the ones he has emerged from, not because he has really criticized them but simply because they are in the past. (You keep him well fed on hazy ideas of Progress and Development and the Historical Point of View, I trust, and give him lots of modern Biographies to read? The people in them are always emerging from Phases, aren't they?)

You see the idea? Keep his mind off the plain antithesis between True and False. Nice shadowy expressions—"It was a phase"—"I've been through all that"—and don't forget the blessed word "Adolescent",

Your affectionate uncle
SCREWTAPE

M<small>Y DEAR WORMWOOD</small>,

The most alarming thing in your last account of the patient is that he is making none of those confident resolutions which marked his original conversion. No more lavish promises of perpetual virtue, I gather; not even the expectation of an endowment of "grace" for life, but only a hope for the daily and hourly pittance to meet the daily and hourly temptation! This is very bad.

I see only one thing to do at the moment. Your patient has become humble; have you drawn his attention to the fact? All virtues are less formidable to us once the man is aware that he has them, but this is specially true of humility. Catch him at the moment when he is really poor in spirit and smuggle into his mind the gratifying reflection, "By jove! I'm being humble", and almost immediately pride—pride at his own humility—will appear. If he awakes to the danger and tries to smother this new form of pride, make him proud of his attempt—and so on, through as many stages as you please. But don't try this too long, for fear you awake his sense of humour and proportion, in which case he will merely laugh at you and go to bed.

But there are other profitable ways of fixing his attention on the virtue of Humility. By this virtue, as by all the others, our Enemy wants to turn the man's attention away from self to Him, and to the man's neighbours. All the abjection and self-hatred are designed, in the long run, solely for this end; unless they attain this end they do us little harm; and they may even do us good if they keep the man concerned with himself, and, above all, if self-contempt can be made the starting-point for contempt of other selves, and thus for gloom, cynicism, and cruelty.

You must therefore conceal from the patient the true end of Humility. Let him think of it not as self-forgetfulness but as a certain kind of opinion (namely, a low opinion) of his own talents and character. Some talents, I gather, he really has. Fix in his mind the idea that humility consists in trying to believe those talents to be less valuable than he believes them to be. No doubt they *are* in fact less valuable than he believes, but that is not the point. The great thing is to make him value an opinion for some quality other than truth, thus introducing an element of dishonesty and make-believe into the heart of what otherwise threat ens to become a virtue. By this method thousands of humans have been brought to think that humility means pretty women trying to believe they are ugly and clever men trying to believe they are fools. And since what they are trying to believe may, in some cases, be manifest nonsense, they cannot succeed in believing it and we have the chance of keeping their minds endlessly revolving on themselves in an effort to achieve the impossible. To anticipate the Enemy's strategy, we must consider His aims. The Enemy wants to bring the man to a state of mind in which he could design the best cathedral in the world, and know it to be the best, and rejoice in the fact, without being any more (or less) or otherwise glad at having done it than he would be if it had been done by another. The Enemy wants him, in the end, to be so free from any bias in his own favour that he can rejoice in his own talents as frankly and gratefully as in his neighbour's talents—or in a sunrise, an elephant, or a waterfall. He wants each man, in the long run, to be able to recognise all creatures (even himself) as glorious and excellent things. He wants to kill their animal self-love as soon as possible; but it is His long-term policy, I fear, to restore to them a new kind of self-love—a charity and gratitude for all selves, including their own; when they have really learned to love their neighbours as themselves, they will be allowed to love themselves as their neighbours. For we must never forget what is the most repellent and inexplicable trait in our Enemy; He *really* loves the hairless bipeds He has created and always gives back to them with His right hand what He has taken away with His left.

His whole effort, therefore, will be to get the man's mind off the subject of his own value altogether. He would rather the man thought himself a great architect or a great poet and then forgot about it, than that he should spend much time and pains trying to think himself a bad one. Your efforts to instil either vainglory or false modesty into the patient will therefore be met from the Enemy's side with the obvious reminder that a man is not usually called upon to have an opinion of his own talents at all, since he can very well go on improving them to the best of his ability without deciding on his own precise niche in the temple of Fame. You must try to exclude this reminder from the patient's consciousness at all costs. The Enemy will also try to render real in the patient's mind a doctrine which they all profess but find it difficult to bring home to their feelings—the doctrine that they did not create themselves, that their talents were given them, and that they might as well be proud of the colour of their hair. But always and by all methods the Enemy's aim will be to get the patient's mind off such questions, and yours will be to fix it on them. Even of his sins the Enemy does not want him to think too much: once they are repented, the sooner the man turns his attention outward, the better the Enemy is pleased,

Your affectionate uncle

SCREWTAPE

MY DEAR WORMWOOD,

When I told you not to fill your letters with rubbish about the war, I meant, of course, that I did not want to have your rather infantile rhapsodies about the death of men and the destruction of cities. In so far as the war really concerns the spiritual state of the patient, I naturally want full reports. And on this aspect you seem singularly obtuse. Thus you tell me with glee that there is reason to expect heavy air raids on the town where the creature lives. This is a crying example of something I have complained about already—your readiness to forget the main point in your immediate enjoyment of human suffering. Do you not know that bombs kill men? Or do you not realise that the patient's death, at this moment, is precisely what we want to avoid? He has escaped the worldly friends with whom you tried to entangle him; he has "fallen in love" with a very Christian woman and is temporarily immune from your attacks on his chastity; and the various methods of corrupting his spiritual life which we have been trying are so far unsuccessful. At the present moment, as the full impact of the war draws nearer and his worldly hopes take a proportionately lower place in his mind, full of his defence work, full of the girl, forced to attend to his neighbours more than he has ever done before and liking it more than he expected, "taken out of himself" as the humans say, and daily increasing in conscious dependence on the Enemy, he will almost certainly be lost to us if he is killed tonight. This is so obvious that I am ashamed to write it. I sometimes wonder if you young fiends are not kept out on temptation-duty too long at a time—if you are not in some danger of becoming infected by the sentiments and values of the humans among whom you work. They, of course, do tend to regard death as the prime evil and survival as the greatest good. But that is because we have taught them to do so. Do not let us be infected by our own propaganda. I know it seems strange that your chief aim at the moment should be the very same thing for which the patient's lover and his mother are praying—namely his bodily safety. But so it is; you should be guarding him like the apple of your eye. If he dies now, you lose him. If he survives the war, there is always hope. The Enemy has guarded him from you through the first great wave of temptations. But, if only he can be kept alive, you have time itself for your ally. The long, dull monotonous years of middle-aged prosperity or middle-aged adversity are excellent campaigning weather. You see, it is so hard for these creatures to *persevere*. The routine of adversity, the gradual decay of youthful loves and youthful hopes, the quiet despair (hardly felt as pain) of ever overcoming the chronic temptations with which we have again and again defeated them, the drabness which we create in their lives and the inarticulate resentment with which we teach them to respond to it—all this provides admirable opportunities of wearing out a soul by attrition. If, on the other hand, the middle years prove prosperous, our position is even stronger. Prosperity knits a man to the World. He feels that he is "finding his place in it", while really it is finding its place in him. His increasing reputation, his widening circle of acquaintances, his sense of importance, the growing pressure of absorbing and agreeable work, build up in him a sense of being really at home in earth which is just what we want. You will notice that the young are generally less unwilling to die than the middle-aged and the old.

The truth is that the Enemy, having oddly destined these mere animals to life in His own eternal world, has guarded them pretty effectively from the danger of feeling at home anywhere else. That is why we must often wish long life to our patients; seventy years is not a day too much for the difficult task of unravelling their souls from Heaven and building up a firm attachment to the earth. While they are young we find them always shooting off at a tangent. Even if we contrive to keep them ignorant of explicit religion, the incalculable winds of fantasy and music and poetry—the mere face of a girl, the song of a bird, or the sight of a horizon—are always blowing our whole structure away. They *will* not apply themselves steadily to worldly advancement, prudent connections, and the policy of safety first. So inveterate is their appetite for Heaven that our best method, at this stage, of attaching them to earth is to make them believe that earth can be turned into Heaven at some future date by politics or eugenics or "science" or psychology, or what not. Real worldliness is a work of time—assisted, of course, by pride, for we teach them to describe the creeping death as good sense or Maturity or Experience. *Experience,* in the peculiar sense we teach them to give it, is, by the bye, a most useful word. A great human philosopher nearly let our secret out when he said that where Virtue is concerned "Experience is the mother of illusion"; but thanks to a change in Fashion, and also, of course, to the Historical Point of View, we have largely rendered his book innocuous.

How valuable time is to us may be gauged by the fact that the Enemy allows us so little of it. The majority of the human race dies in infancy; of the survivors, a good many die in youth. It is obvious that to Him human birth is important chiefly as the qualification for human death, and death solely as the gate to that other kind of life. We are allowed to work only on a selected minority of the race, for what humans call a "normal life" is the exception. Apparently He wants some—but only a very few—of the human animals with which He is peopling Heaven to have had the experience of resisting us through an earthly life of sixty or seventy years. Well, there is our opportunity. The smaller it is, the better we must use it. Whatever you do, keep your patient as safe as you possibly can,

Your affectionate uncle
SCREWTAPE

PART V

NONFICTION:
CHRISTIAN
TOPICS

Ever SINCE C. S. Lewis consented to explain and defend the truth of the Christian faith on BBC Radio during World War II, there has been a demand for his writings on this subject. His radio broadcasts were published, and eventually they were expanded and revised as *Mere Christianity* (1952). This apologetical work of under two hundred pages is the most popular book of its kind in the English language. It has never gone out of print, and the total sales figures continue to rise, now numbering well into the millions. Five sections of this immensely influential book are reprinted here. These selections will give the reader a glimpse of how Lewis employs simple sentences and ordinary examples to explain the essentials of mainstream Christian belief.

Lewis is enjoyed by many readers because he seems to thrive on taking the offensive in the age-old debates about Christianity. Where some clerics and theologians surrender, or find themselves on the defensive, Lewis takes up the Christian banner and exuberantly enters the fray. With writing that is full of military metaphors and references to spiritual struggle, the Oxford academician has become a thoughtful and tough-minded warrior of heroic proportions.

Some of his best prose in defense of basic doctrines has been brought together in *Undeceptions: Essays on Theology and Ethics,* edited by Walter Hooper. Four selections from this collection are reproduced here: "God in the Dock," "What Are We to Make of Jesus Christ?" "Miracles," and "Rejoinder to Dr. Pittenger."

The latter article is one of Lewis's responses to a critic of biblical Christianity, as is his well-known critique of the higher biblical criticism entitled "Modern Theology and Biblical Criticism," published in *Christian Reflections.*

Lewis did more than just defend Christianity and take on its detractors; he offered some basic teaching in the fundamentals of the faith as well, In an era when many clergy seem ill-equipped or unwilling to provide basic biblical teaching about doctrine, faith, morals, and discipleship, Lewis's writings evidently fill a void. Two sermons reprinted here, "The Weight of Glory" and "Learning in War-time," taken from *The Weight of Glory and Other Essays* (1949), focus on aspects of discipleship. In a similar vein are two essays, one on prayer, "The Efficacy of Prayer," and the other on the Second Coming of Christ entitled "The World's Last Night." These two essays appear in a book under the title *The World's Last Night and Other Essays* (1960). Lewis continued to write in this genre until his death.

Finally, Lewis offers some basic teaching in two popular books: *Reflections on the Psalms* (1958) and *Letters to Malcolm: Chiefly on Prayer* (1964). The introduction and two chapters on the Psalms are included here, showing how Lewis employed a traditional didactic style. In the excerpts from the second book, on the other hand, he puts his ideas in the form of casual letters to an old college chum.

FROM

Mere Christianity

We Have Cause to Be Uneasy

I ENDED my last chapter with the idea that in the Moral Law somebody or something from beyond the material universe was actually getting at us. And I expect when I reached that point some of you felt a certain annoyance. You may even have thought that I had played a trick on you—that I had been carefully wrapping up to look like philosophy what turns out to be one more "religious jaw." You may have felt you were ready to listen to me as long as you thought I had anything new to say; but if it turns out to be only religion, well, the world has tried that and you cannot put the clock back. If anyone is feeling that way I should like to say three things to him.

First, as to putting the clock back. Would you think I was joking if I said that you can put a clock back, and that if the clock is wrong it is often a very sensible thing to do? But I would rather get away from that whole idea of clocks. We all want progress. But progress means getting nearer to the place where you want to be. And if you have taken a wrong turning, then to go forward does not get you any nearer. If you are on the wrong road, progress means doing an about-turn and walking back to the right road; and in that case the man who turns back soonest is the most progressive man. We have all seen this when doing arithmetic. When I have started a sum the wrong way, the sooner I admit this and go back and start over again, the faster I shall get on. There is nothing progressive about being pigheaded and refusing to admit a mistake. And I think if you look at the present state of the world, it is pretty plain that humanity has been making some big mistake. We are on the wrong road. And if that is so, we must go back. Going back is the quickest way on.

Then, secondly, this has not yet turned exactly into a "religious jaw." We have not yet got as far as the God of any actual religion, still less the God of that particular religion called Christianity. We have only got as far as a Somebody or Something behind the Moral Law. We are not taking anything from the Bible or the Churches, we are trying to see what we can find out about this Somebody on our own steam. And I want to make it quite clear that what we find out on our own steam is something that gives us a shock. We have two bits of evidence about the Somebody. One is the universe He has made. If we used that as our only clue, then I think we should have to conclude that He was a great artist (for the universe is a very beautiful place), but also that He is quite merciless and no friend to man (for the universe is a very dangerous and terrifying place). The other bit of evidence is that Moral Law which He has put into our minds. And this is a better bit of evidence than the other, because it is inside information. You find out more about God from the Moral Law than from the universe in general just as you find out more about a man by listening to his conversation than by looking at a house he has built. Now, from this second bit of evidence we conclude that the Being behind the universe is intensely interested in right conduct—in fair play, unselfishness, courage, good faith, honesty and truthfulness. In that sense we should agree with the account given by Christianity and some other religions, that God is "good." But do not let us go too fast here. The Moral Law does not give us any grounds for thinking that God is "good" in the sense of being indulgent, or soft, or sympathetic. There is nothing indulgent about the Moral Law. It is as hard as nails. It tells you to do the straight thing and it does not seem to care how painful, or dangerous, or difficult it is to do. If God is like the Moral Law, then He is not soft. It is no use, at this stage, saying that what you mean by a "good" God is a God who can forgive. You are going too quickly. Only a Person can forgive. And we have not yet got as far as a personal God—only as far as a power, behind the Moral Law, and more like a mind than it is like anything else. But it may still be very unlike a Person. If it is pure impersonal mind, there may be no sense in asking it to make allowances for you or let you off, just as there is no sense in asking the multiplication table to let you off when you do your sums wrong. You are bound to get the wrong answer. And it is no use either saying that if there is a God of that sort—an impersonal absolute goodness—then you do not like Him and are not going to bother about Him. For the trouble is that one part of you is on His side and really agrees with His disapproval of human greed and trickery and exploitation. You may want Him to make an exception in your own case, to let you off this one time; but you know at bottom that unless the power behind the world really and unalterably detests that sort of behaviour, then He cannot be good. On the other hand, we know that if there does exist an absolute goodness it must hate most of what we do. That is the terrible fix we are in. If the universe is not governed by an absolute goodness, then all our efforts are in the long run hopeless. But if it is, then we are making ourselves enemies to that goodness every day, and are not in the least likely to do any better tomorrow, and so our case is hopeless again. We cannot do without it, and we cannot do with it. God is the only comfort, He is also the supreme terror: the thing we most need and the thing we most want to hide from. He is our only possible ally, and we have made ourselves His enemies. Some people talk as if meeting the gaze of absolute goodness would be fun. They need to think again. They are still only playing with religion. Goodness is either the great safety or the great danger—according to the way you react to it. And we have reacted the wrong way.

Now my third point. When I chose to get to my real subject in this round-about way, I was not trying to play any kind of trick on you. I had a different reason. My reason was that Christianity simply does not make sense until you have faced the sort of facts I have been describing. Christianity tells people to repent and promises them forgiveness. It therefore has nothing (as far as I know) to say to people who do not know they have done anything to repent of and who do not feel that they need any forgiveness. It is after you have realised that there is a real Moral Law, and a Power behind the law, and that you have broken that law and put yourself wrong with that Power—it is after all this, and not a moment sooner, that Christianity begins to talk. When you know you are sick, you will listen to the doctor. When you have realised that our position is nearly desperate you will begin to understand what the Christians are talking about. They offer an explanation of how we got into our present state of both hating goodness and loving it. They offer an explanation of how God can be this impersonal mind at the back of the Moral Law and yet also a Person. They tell you how the demands of this law, which you and I cannot meet, have been met on our behalf, how God Himself becomes a man to save man from the disapproval of God. It is an old story and if you want to go into it you will no doubt consult people who have more authority to talk about it than I have. All I am doing is to ask people to face the facts—to understand the questions which Christianity claims to answer. And they are very terrifying facts. I wish it was possible to say something more agreeable. But I must say what I think true. Of course, I quite agree that the Christian religion is, in the long run, a thing of unspeakable comfort. But it does not begin in comfort; it begins in the dismay I have been describing, and it is no use at all trying to go on to that comfort without first going through that dismay. In religion, as in war and everything else, comfort is the one thing you cannot get by looking for it. If you look for truth, you may find comfort in the end: if you look for comfort you will not get either comfort or truth—only soft soap and wishful thinking to begin with and, in the end, despair. Most of us have got over the pre-war wishful thinking about international politics. It is time we did the same about religion.

The Invasion

VERY WELL THEN, atheism is too simple. And I will tell you another view that is also too simple. It is the view I call Christianity-and-water, the view which simply says there is a good God in Heaven and everything is all right—leaving out all the difficult and terrible doctrines about sin and hell and the devil, and the redemption. Both these are boys' philosophies.

It is no good asking for a simple religion. After all, real things are not simple. They look simple, but they are not. The table I am sitting at looks simple: but ask a scientist to tell you what it is really made of—all about the atoms and how the light waves rebound from them and hit my eye and what they do to the optic nerve and what it does to my brain—and, of course, you find that what we call "seeing a table" lands you in mysteries and complications which you can hardly get to the end of. A child saying a child's prayer looks simple. And if you are content to stop there, well and good. But if you are not—and the modern world usually is not—if you want to go on and ask what is really happening—then you must be prepared for something difficult. If we ask for something more than simplicity, it is silly then to complain that the something more is not simple.

Very often, however, this silly procedure is adopted by people who are not silly, but who, consciously or unconsciously, want to destroy Christianity. Such people put up a version of Christianity suitable for a child of six and make that the object of their attack. When you try to explain the Christian doctrine as it is really held by an instructed adult, they then complain that you are making their heads turn round and that it is all too complicated and that if there really were a God they are sure He would have made "religion" simple, because simplicity is so beautiful, etc. You must be on your guard against these people for they will change their ground every minute and only waste your time. Notice, too, their idea of God "making religion simple": as if "religion" were something God invented, and not His statement to us of certain quite unalterable facts about His own nature.

Besides being complicated, reality, in my experience, is usually odd. It is not neat, not obvious, not what you expect. For instance, when you have grasped that the earth and the other planets all go round the sun, you would naturally expect that all the planets were made to match—all at equal distances from each other, say, or distances that regularly increased, or all the same size, or else getting bigger or smaller as you go farther from the sun. In fact, you find no rhyme or reason (that we can see) about either the sizes or the distances; and some of them have one moon, one has four, one has two, some have none, and one has a ring.

Reality, in fact, is usually something you could not have guessed. That is one of the reasons I believe Christianity. It is a religion you could not have guessed. If it offered us just the kind of universe we had always expected, I should feel we were making it up. But, in fact, it is not the sort of thing anyone would have made up. It has just that queer twist about it that real things have. So let us leave behind all these boys' philosophies—these oversimple answers. The problem is not simple and the answer is not going to be simpler either.

What is the problem? A universe that contains much that is obviously bad and apparently meaningless, but containing creatures like ourselves who know that it is bad and meaningless. There are only two views that face all the facts. One is the Christian view that this is a good world that has gone wrong, but still retains the memory of what it ought to have been. The other is the view called Dualism. Dualism means the belief that there are two equal and independent powers at the back of everything, one of them good and the other bad, and that this universe is the battlefield in which they fight out an endless war. I personally think that next to Christianity Dualism is the manliest and most sensible creed on the market. But it has a catch in it.

The two powers, or spirits, or gods—the good one and the bad one—are supposed to be quite independent. They both existed from all eternity. Neither of them made the other, neither of them has any more right than the other to call itself God. Each presumably thinks it is good and thinks the other bad. One of them likes hatred and cruelty, the other likes love and mercy, and each backs its own view. Now what do we mean when we call one of them the Good Power and the other the Bad Power? Either we are merely saying that we happen to prefer the one to the other—like preferring beer to cider—or else we are saying that, whatever the two powers think about it, and whichever we humans, at the moment, happen to like, one of them is actually wrong, actually mistaken, in regarding itself as good. Now if we mean merely that we happen to prefer the first, then we must give up talking about good and evil at all. For good means what you ought to prefer quite regardless of what you happen to like at any given moment. If "being good" meant simply joining the side you happened to fancy, for no real reason, then good would not deserve to be called good. So we must mean that one of the two powers is actually wrong and the other actually right.

But the moment you say that, you are putting into the universe a third thing in addition to the two Powers: some law or standard or rule of good which one of the powers conforms to and the other fails to conform to. But since the two powers are judged by this standard, then this standard, or the Being who made this standard, is farther back and higher up than either of them, and He will be the real God. In fact, what we meant by calling them good and bad turns out to be that one of them is in a right relation to the real ultimate God and the other in a wrong relation to Him.

The same point can be made in a different way. If Dualism is true, then the bad Power must be a being who likes badness for its own sake. But in reality we have no experience of anyone liking badness just because it is bad. The nearest we can get to it is in cruelty. But in real life people are cruel for one of two reasons—either because they are sadists, that is, because they have a sexual perversion which makes cruelty a cause of sensual pleasure to them, or else for the sake of something they are going to get out of it—money, or power, or safety. But pleasure, money, power, and safety are all, as far as they go, good things. The badness consists in pursuing them by the wrong method, or in the wrong way, or too much. I do not mean, of course, that the people who do this are not desperately wicked. I do mean that wickedness, when you examine it, turns out to be the pursuit of some good in the wrong way. You can be good for the mere sake of goodness: you cannot be bad for the mere sake of badness. You can do a kind action when you are not feeling kind and when it gives you no pleasure, simply because kindness is right; but no one ever did a cruel action simply because cruelty is wrong—only because cruelty was pleasant or useful to him. In other words badness cannot succeed even in being bad in the same way in which goodness is good. Goodness is, so to speak, itself: badness is only spoiled goodness. And there must be something good first before it can be spoiled. We called sadism a sexual perversion; but you must first have the idea of a normal sexuality before you can talk of its being perverted; and you can see which is the perversion, because you can explain the perverted from the normal, and cannot explain the normal from the perverted. It follows that this Bad Power, who is supposed to be on an equal footing with the Good Power, and to love badness in the same way as the Good Power loves goodness, is a mere bogy. In order to be bad he must have good things to want and then to pursue in the wrong way: he must have impulses which were originally good in order to be able to pervert them. But if he is bad he cannot supply himself either with good things to desire or with good impulses to pervert. He must be getting both from the Good Power. And if so, then he is not independent. He is part of the Good Power's world: he was made either by the Good Power or by some power above them both.

Put it more simply still. To be bad, he must exist and have intelligence and will. But existence, intelligence and will are in themselves good. Therefore he must be getting them from the Good Power: even to be bad he must borrow or steal from his opponent. And do you now begin to see why Christianity has always said that the devil is a fallen angel? That is not a mere story for the children. It is a real recognition of the fact that evil is a parasite, not an original thing. The powers which enable evil to carry on are powers given it by goodness. All the things which enable a bad man to be effectively bad are in themselves good things—resolution, cleverness, good looks, existence itself. That is why Dualism, in a strict sense, will not work.

But I freely admit that real Christianity (as distinct from Christianity-and-water) goes much nearer to Dualism than people think. One of the things that surprised me when I first read the New Testament seriously was that it talked so much about a Dark Power in the universe—a mighty evil spirit who was held to be the Power behind death and disease, and sin. The difference is that Christianity thinks this Dark Power was created by God, and was good when he was created, and went wrong. Christianity agrees with Dualism that this universe is at war. But it does not think this is a war between independent powers. It thinks it is a civil war, a rebellion, and that we are living in a part of the universe occupied by the rebel.

Enemy-occupied territory—that is what this world is. Christianity is the story of how the rightful king has landed, you might say landed in disguise, and is calling us all to take part in a great campaign of sabotage. When you go to church you are really listening-in to the secret wireless from our friends: that is why the enemy is so anxious to prevent us from going. He does it by playing on our conceit and laziness and intellectual snobbery. I know someone will ask me, "Do you really mean, at this time of day, to re-introduce our old friend the devil—hoofs and horns and all?" Well, what the time of day has to do with it I do not know. And I am not particular about the hoofs and horns. But in other respects my answer is "Yes, I do." I do not claim to know anything about his personal appearance. If anybody really wants to know him better I would say to that person, "Don't worry. If you really want to, you will. Whether you'll like it when you do is another question."

Social Morality

THE FIRST THING to get clear about Christian morality between man and man is that in this department Christ did not come to preach any brand new morality. The Golden Rule of the New Testament (Do as you would be done by) is a summing up of what everyone, at bottom, had always known to be right. Really great moral teachers never do introduce new moralities: it is quacks and cranks who do that. As Dr. Johnson said, "People need to be reminded more often than they need to be instructed." The real job of every moral teacher is to keep on bringing us back, time after time, to the old simple principles which we are all so anxious not to see; like bringing a horse back and back to the fence it has refused to jump or bringing a child back and back to the bit in its lesson that it wants to shirk.

The second thing to get clear is that Christianity has not, and does not profess to have, a detailed political programme for applying "Do as you would be done by" to a particular society at a particular moment. It could not have. It is meant for all men at all times and the particular programme which suited one place or time would not suit another. And, anyhow, that is not how Christianity works. When it tells you to feed the hungry it does not give you lessons in cookery. When it tells you to read the Scriptures it does not give you lessons in Hebrew and Greek, or even in English grammar. It was never intended to replace or supersede the ordinary human arts and sciences: it is rather a director which will set them all to the right jobs, and a source of energy which will give them all new life, if only they will put themselves at its disposal.

People say, "The Church ought to give us a lead." That is true if they mean it in the right way, but false if they mean it in the wrong way. By the Church they ought to mean the whole body of practising Christians. And when they say that the Church should give us a lead, they ought to mean that some Christians—those who happen to have the right talents—should be economists and statesmen, and that all economists and statesmen should be Christians, and that their whole efforts in politics and economics should be directed to putting "Do as you would be done by" into action. If that happened, and if we others were really ready to take it, then we should find the Christian solution for our own social problems pretty quickly. But, of course, when they ask for a lead from the Church most people mean they want the clergy to put out a political programme. That is silly. The clergy are those particular people within the whole Church who have been specially trained and set aside to look after what concerns us as creatures who are going to live for ever: and we are asking them to do a quite different job for which they have not been trained. The job is really on us, on the laymen. The application of Christian principles, say, to trade unionism or education, must come from Christian trade unionists and Christian schoolmasters: just as Christian literature comes from Christian novelists and dramatists—not from the bench of bishops getting together and trying to write plays and novels in their spare time.

All the same, the New Testament, without going into details, gives us a pretty clear hint of what a fully Christian society would be like. Perhaps it gives us more than we can take. It tells us that there are to be no passengers or parasites: if man does not work, he ought not to eat. Every one is to work with his own hands, and what is more, every one's work is to produce something good: there will be no manufacture of silly luxuries and then of sillier advertisements to persuade us to buy them. And there is to be no "swank" or "side," no putting on airs. To that extent a Christian society would be what we now call Leftist. On the other hand, it is always insisting on obedience—obedience (and outward marks of respect) from all of us to properly appointed magistrates, from children to parents, and (I am afraid this is going to be very unpopular) from wives to husbands. Thirdly, it is to be a cheerful society: full of singing and rejoicing, and regarding worry or anxiety as wrong. Courtesy is one of the Christian virtues; and the New Testament hates what it calls "busybodies."

If there were such a society in existence and you or I visited it, I think we should come away with a curious impression. We should feel that its economic life was very socialistic and, in that sense, "advanced," but that its family life and its code of manners were rather old-fashioned—perhaps even ceremonious and aristocratic. Each of us would like some bits of it, but I am afraid very few of us would like the whole thing. That is just what one would expect if Christianity is the total plan for the human machine. We have all departed from that total plan in different ways, and each of us wants to make out that his own modification of the original plan is the plan itself. You will find this again and again about anything that is really Christian: every one is attracted by bits of it and wants to pick out those bits and leave the rest. That is why we do not get much further: and that is why people who are fighting for quite opposite things can both say they are fighting for Christianity.

Now another point. There is one bit of advice given to us by the ancient heathen Greeks, and by the Jews in the Old Testament, and by the great Christian teachers of the Middle Ages, which the modern economic system has completely disobeyed. All these people told us not to lend money at interest: and lending money at interest—what we call investment—is the basis of our whole system. Now it may not absolutely follow that we are wrong. Some people say that when Moses and Aristotle and the Christians agreed in forbidding interest (or "usury" as they called it), they could not foresee the joint stock company, and were only thinking of the private moneylender, and that, therefore, we need not bother about what they said. That is a question I cannot decide on. I am not an economist and I simply do not know whether the investment system is responsible for the state we are in or not. This is where we want the Christian economist. But I should not have been honest if I had not told you that three great civilizations had agreed (or so it seems at first sight) in condemning the very thing on which we have based our whole life.

One more point and I am done. In the passage where the New Testament says that every one must work, it gives as a reason "in order that he may have something to give to those in need." Charity—giving to the poor—is an essential part of Christian morality: in the frightening parable of the sheep and the goats it seems to be the point on which everything turns. Some people nowadays say that charity ought to be unnecessary and that instead of giving to the poor we ought to be producing a society in which there were no poor to give to. They may be quite right in saying that we ought to produce that kind of society. But if anyone thinks that, as a consequence, you can stop giving in the meantime, then he has parted company with all Christian morality. I do not believe one can settle how much we ought to give. I am afraid the only safe rule is to give more than we can spare. In other words, if our expenditure on comforts, luxuries, amusements, etc., is up to the standard common among those with the same income as our own, we are probably giving away too little. If our charities do not at all pinch or hamper us, I should say they are too small. There ought to be things we should like to do and cannot do because our charitable expenditure excludes them. I am speaking now of "charities" in the common way. Particular cases of distress among your own relatives, friends, neighbours or employees, which God, as it were, forces upon your notice, may demand much more: even to the crippling and endangering of your own position. For many of us the great obstacle to charity lies not in our luxurious living or desire for more money, but in our fear—fear of insecurity. This must often be recognized as a temptation. Sometimes our pride also hinders our charity; we are tempted to spend more than we ought on the showy forms of generosity (tipping, hospitality) and less than we ought on those who really need our help.

And now, before I end, I am going to venture on a guess as to how this section has affected any who have read it. My guess is that there are some Leftist people among them who are very angry that it has not gone further in that direction, and some people of an opposite sort who are angry because they think it has gone much too far. If so, that brings us right up against the real snag in all this drawing up of blueprints for a Christian society. Most of us are not really approaching the subject in order to find out what Christianity says: we are approaching it in the hope of finding support from Christianity for the views of our own party. We are looking for an ally where we are offered either a Master or—a Judge. I am just the same. There are bits in this section that I wanted to leave out. And that is why nothing whatever is going to come of such talks unless we go a much longer way round. A Christian society is not going to arrive until most of us really want it: and we are not going to want it until we become fully Christian. I may repeat "Do as you would be done by" till I am black in the face, but I cannot really carry it out till I love my neighbour as myself: and I cannot learn to love my neighbour as myself till I learn to love God: and I cannot learn to love God except by learning to obey Him. And so, as I warned you, we are driven on to something more inward—driven on from social matters to religious matters. For the longest way round is the shortest way home.

The Obstinate Toy Soldiers

THE SON OF GOD became a man to enable men to become sons of God. We do not know—anyway, *I* do not know—how things would have worked if the human race had never rebelled against God and joined the enemy. Perhaps every man would have been "in Christ," would have shared the life of the Son of God, from the moment he was born. Perhaps the *Bios* or natural life would have been drawn up into the *Zoe*, the uncreated life, at once and as a matter of course. But that is guesswork. You and I are concerned with the way things work now.

And the present state of things is this. The two kinds of life are now not only different (they would always have been that) but actually opposed. The natural life in each of us is something self-centered, something that wants to be petted and admired, to take advantage of other lives, to exploit the whole universe. And especially it wants to be left to itself: to keep well away from anything better or stronger or higher than it, anything that might make it feel small. It is afraid of the light and air of the spiritual world, just as people who have been brought up to be dirty are afraid of a bath. And in a sense it is quite right. It knows that if the spiritual life gets hold of it, all its self-centredness and self-will are going to be killed and it is ready to fight tooth and nail to avoid that.

Did you ever think, when you were a child, what fun it would be if your toys could come to life? Well suppose you could really have brought them to life. Imagine turning a tin soldier into a real little man. It would involve turning the tin into flesh. And suppose the tin soldier did not like it. He is not interested in flesh; all he sees is that the tin is being spoilt. He thinks you are killing him. He will do everything he can to prevent you. He will not be made into a man if he can help it.

What you would have done about that tin soldier I do not know. But what God did about us was this. The Second Person in God, the Son, became human Himself: was born into the world as an actual man—a real man of a particular height, with hair of a particular colour, speaking a particular language, weighing so many stone. The Eternal Being, who knows everything and who created the whole universe, became not only a man but (before that) a baby, and before that a *foetus* inside a Woman's body. If you want to get the hang of it, think how you would like to become a slug or a crab.

The result of this was that you now had one man who really was what all men were intended to be: one man in whom the created life, derived from his Mother, allowed itself to be completely and perfectly turned into the begotten life. The natural human creature in Him was taken up fully into the divine Son. Thus in one instance humanity had, so to speak, arrived: had passed into the life of Christ. And because the whole difficulty for us is that the natural life has to be, in a sense, "killed," He chose an earthly career which involved the killing of His human desires at every turn—poverty, misunderstanding from His own family, betrayal by one of His intimate friends, being jeered at and manhandled by the Police, and execution by torture. And then, after being thus killed—killed every day in a sense—the human creature in Him, because it was united to the divine Son, came to life again. The Man in Christ rose again: not only the God. That is the whole point. For the first time we saw a real man. One tin soldier—real tin, just like the rest—had come fully and splendidly alive.

And here, of course, we come to the point where my illustration about the tin soldier breaks down. In the case of real toy soldiers or statues, if one came to life, it would obviously make no difference to the rest. They are all separate. But human beings are not. They look separate because you see them walking about separately. But then, we are so made that we can see only the present moment. If we could see the past, then of course it would look different. For there was a time when every man was part of his mother, and (earlier still) part of his father as well: and when they were part of his grandparents. If you could see humanity spread out in time, as God sees it, it would not look like a lot of separate things dotted about. It would look like one single growing thing— rather like a very complicated tree. Every individual would appear connected with every other. And not only that. Individuals are not really separate from God any more than from one another. Every man, woman, and child all over the world is feeling and breathing at this moment only because God, so to speak, is "keeping him going."

Consequently, when Christ becomes man it is not really as if you could become one particular tin soldier. It is as if something which is always affecting the whole human mass begins, at one point, to affect that whole human mass in a new way. From that point the effect spreads through all mankind. It makes a difference to people who lived before Christ as well as to people who lived after Him. It makes a difference to people who have never heard of Him. It is like dropping into a glass of water one drop of something which gives a new taste or a new colour to the whole lot. But, of course, none of these illustrations really works perfectly. In the long run God is no one but Himself and what He does is like nothing else. You could hardly expect it to be.

What, then, is the difference which He has made to the whole human mass? It is just this; that the business of becoming a son of God, of being turned from a created thing into a begotten thing, of passing over from the temporary biological life into timeless "spiritual" life, has been done for us. Humanity is already "saved" in principle. We individuals have to appropriate that salvation. But the really tough work—the bit we could not have done for ourselves—has been done for us. We have not got to try to climb up into spiritual life by our own efforts; it has already come down into the human race. If we will only lay ourselves open to the one Man in whom it was fully present, and who, in spite of being God, is also a real man, He will do it in us and for us. Remember what I said about "good infection." One of our own race has this new life: if we get close to Him we shall catch it from Him.

Of course, you can express this in all sorts of different ways. You can say that

Christ died for our sins. You may say that the Father has forgiven us because Christ has done for us what we ought to have done. You may say that we are washed in the blood of the Lamb. You may say that Christ has defeated death. They are all true. If any of them do not appeal to you, leave it alone and get on with the formula that does. And, whatever you do, do not start quarrelling with other people because they use a different formula from yours.

Let's Pretend

MAY I once again start by putting two pictures, or two stories rather, into your minds? One is the story you have all read called *Beauty and the Beast*. The girl, you remember, had to marry a monster for some reason. And she did. She kissed it as if it were a man. And then, much to her relief, it really turned into a man and all went well. The other story is about someone who had to wear a mask; a mask which made him look much nicer than he really was. He had to wear it for years. And when he took it off he found his own face had grown to fit it. He was now really beautiful. What had begun as disguise had become a reality. I think both these stories may (in a fanciful way, of course) help to illustrate what I have to say in this chapter. Up till now, I have been trying to describe facts—what God is and what He had done. Now I want to talk about practice—what do we do next? What difference does all this theology make? It can start making a difference tonight. If you are interested enough to have read thus far you are probably interested enough to make a shot at saying your prayers: and, whatever else you say, you will probably say the Lord's Prayer.

Its very first words are *Our Father*. Do you now see what those words mean? They mean quite frankly, that you are putting yourself in the place of a son of God. To put it bluntly, you are *dressing up as Christ*. If you like, you are pretending. Because, of course, the moment you realise what the words mean, you realise that you are not a son of God. You are not being like The Son of God, whose will and interests are at one with those of the Father: you are a bundle of self-centered fears, hopes, greeds, jealousies, and self-conceit, all doomed to death. So that, in a way, this dressing up as Christ is a piece of outrageous cheek. But the odd thing is that He has ordered us to do it.

Why? What is the good of pretending to be what you are not? Well, even on the human level, you know, there are two kinds of pretending. There is a bad kind, where the pretence is there instead of the real thing; as when a man pretends he is going to help you instead of really helping you. But there is also a good kind, where the pretence leads up to the real thing. When you are not feeling particularly friendly but know you ought to be, the best thing you can do, very often, is to put on a friendly manner and behave as if you were a nicer person than you actually are. And in a few minutes, as we have all noticed, you will be really feeling friendlier than you were. Very often the only way to get a quality in reality is to start behaving as if you had it already. That is why children's games are so important. They are always pretending to be grown-ups—playing soldiers, playing shop. But all the time, they are hardening their muscles and sharpening their wits, so that the pretence of being grown-up helps them to grow up in earnest.

Now, the moment you realise "Here I am, dressing up as Christ," it is extremely likely that you will see at once some way in which at that very moment the pretence could be made less of a pretence and more of a reality. You will find several things going on in your mind which would not be going on there if you were really a son of God. Well, stop them. Or you may realise that, instead of saying your prayers, you ought to be downstairs writing a letter, or helping your wife to wash-up. Well, go and do it.

You see what is happening. The Christ Himself, the Son of God who is man (just like you) and God (just like His Father) is actually at your side and is already at that moment beginning to turn your pretence into a reality. This is not merely a fancy way of saying that your conscience is telling you what to do. If you simply ask your conscience, you get one result: if you remember that you are dressing up as Christ, you get a different one. There are lots of things which your conscience might not call definitely wrong (specially things in your mind) but which you will see at once you cannot go on doing if you are seriously trying to be like Christ. For you are no longer thinking simply about right and wrong; you are trying to catch the good infection from a Person. It is more like painting a portrait than like obeying a set of rules. And the odd thing is that while in one way it is much harder than keeping rules, in another way it is far easier.

The real Son of God is at your side. He is beginning to turn you into the same kind of thing as Himself. He is beginning, so to speak, to "inject" His kind of life and thought, His *Zoe,* into you; beginning to turn the tin soldier into a live man. The part of you that does not like it is the part that is still tin.

Some of you may feel that this is very unlike your own experience. You may say "I've never had the sense of being helped by an invisible Christ, but I often have been helped by other human beings." That is rather like the woman in the first war who said that if there were a bread shortage it would not bother her house because they always ate toast. If there is no bread there will be no toast. If there were no help from Christ, there would be no help from other human beings. He works on us in all sorts of ways: not only through what we think our "religious life." He works through Nature, through our own bodies, through books, sometimes through experiences which seem (at the time) *anti-*Christian. When a young man who has been going to church in a routine way honestly realises that he does not believe in Christianity and stops going—provided he does it for honesty's sake and not just to annoy his parents—the spirit of Christ is probably nearer to him then than it ever was before. But above all, He works on us through each other.

Men are mirrors, or "carriers" of Christ to other men. Sometimes unconscious carriers. This "good infection" can be carried by those who have not got it themselves. People who were not Christians themselves helped me to Christianity. But usually it is those who know Him that bring Him to others. That is why the Church, the whole body of Christians showing Him to one another, is so important. You might say that when two Christians are following Christ together there is not twice as much Christianity as when they are apart, but sixteen times as much.

But do not forget this. At first it is natural for a baby to take its mother's milk without knowing its mother. It is equally natural for us to see the man who helps us without seeing Christ behind him. But we must not remain babies. We must go on to recognise the real Giver. It is madness not to. Because, if we do not, we shall be relying on human beings. And that is going to let us down. The best of them will make mistakes; all of them will die. We must be thankful to all the people who have helped us, we must honour them and love them. But never, never pin your whole faith on any human being: not if he is the best and wisest in the whole world. There are lots of nice things you can do with sand; but do not try building a house on it.

And now we begin to see what it is that the New Testament is always talking about. It talks about Christians "being born again"; it talks about them "putting on Christ"; about Christ "being formed in us"; about our coming to "have the mind of Christ."

Put right out of your head the idea that these are only fancy ways of saying that Christians are to read what Christ said and try to carry it out—as a man may read what Plato or Marx said and try to carry it out. They mean something much more than that. They mean that a real Person, Christ, here and now, in that very room where you are saying your prayers, is doing things to you. It is not a question of a good man who died two thousand years ago. It is a living Man, still as much a man as you, and still as much God as He was when He created the world, really coming and interfering with your very self; killing the old natural self in you and replacing it with the kind of self He has. At first, only for moments. Then for longer periods. Finally, if all goes well, turning you permanently into a different sort of thing; into a new little Christ, a being which, in its own small way, has the same kind of life as God; which shares in His power, joy, knowledge and eternity. And soon we make two other discoveries.

(1) We begin to notice, besides our particular sinful acts, our sinfulness; begin to be alarmed not only about what we do, but about what we are. This may sound rather difficult, so I will try to make it clear from my own case. When I come to my evening prayers and try to reckon up the sins of the day, nine times out of ten the most obvious one is some sin against charity; I have sulked or snapped or sneered or snubbed or stormed. And the excuse that immediately springs to my mind is that the provocation was so sudden and unexpected: I was caught off my guard, I had not time to collect myself. Now that may be an extenuating circumstance as regards those particular acts: they would obviously be worse if they had been deliberate and premeditated. On the other hand, surely what a man does when he is taken off his guard is the best evidence for what sort of a man he is? Surely what pops out before the man has time to put on a disguise is the truth? If there are rats in a cellar you are most likely to see them if you go in very suddenly. But the suddenness does not create the rats: it only prevents them from hiding. In the same way the suddenness of the provocation does not make me an ill-tempered man: it only shows me what an ill-tempered man I am. The rats are always there in the cellar, but if you go in shouting and noisily they will have taken cover before you switch on the light. Apparently the rats of resentment and vindictiveness are always there in the cellar of my soul. Now that

cellar is out of reach of my conscious will. I can to some extent control my acts: I have no direct control over my temperament. And if (as I said before) what we are matters even more than what we do—if, indeed, what we do matters chiefly as evidence of what we are—then it follows that the change which I most need to undergo is a change that my own direct, voluntary efforts cannot bring about. And this applies to my good actions too. How many of them were done for the right motive? How many for fear of public opinion, or a desire to show off? How many from a sort of obstinacy or sense of superiority which, in different circumstances, might equally had led to some very bad act? But I cannot, by direct moral effort, give myself new motives. After the first few steps in the Christian life we realise that everything which really needs to be done in our souls can be done only by God. And that brings us to something which has been very misleading in my language up to now.

(2) I have been talking as if it were we who did everything. In reality, of course, it is God who does everything. We, at most, allow it to be done to us. In a sense you might even say it is God who does the pretending. The Three-Personal God, so to speak, sees before Him in fact a self-centered, greedy, grumbling, rebellious human animal. But He says "Let us pretend that this is not a mere creature, but our Son. It is like Christ in so far as it is a Man, for He became Man. Let us pretend that it is also like Him in Spirit. Let us treat it as if it were what in fact it is not. Let us pretend in order to make the pretence into a reality." God looks at you as if you were a little Christ: Christ stands beside you to turn you into one. I daresay this idea of a divine make-believe sounds rather strange at first. But, is it so strange really? Is not that how the higher thing always raises the lower? A mother teaches her baby to talk by talking to it as if it understood long before it really does. We treat our dogs as if they were "almost human": that is why they really become "almost human" in the end.

FROM

Undeceptions:
Essays on Theology and Ethics

God in the Dock

(1948)

I HAVE BEEN ASKED to write about the difficulties which a man must face in trying to present the Christian Faith to modern unbelievers. That is too wide a subject for my capacity or even for the scope of an article. The difficulties vary as the audience varies. The audience may be of this or that nation, may be children or adults, learned or ignorant. My own experience is of English audiences only, and almost exclusively of adults. It has, in fact, been mostly of men (and women) serving in the R.A.F. This has meant that while very few of them have been learned in the academic sense of that word, a large number of them have had a smattering of elementary practical science, have been mechanics, electricians or wireless operators; for the rank and file of the R.A.F. belong to what may almost be called "the Intelligentsia of the Proletariat". I have also talked to students at the Universities. These strict limitations in my experience must be kept in mind by the readers. How rash it would be to generalize from such an experience I myself discovered on the single occasion when I spoke to soldiers. It became at once clear to me that the level of intelligence in our army is very much lower than in the R.A.F. and that quite a different approach was required.

The first thing I learned from addressing the R.A.F. was that I had been mistaken in thinking materialism to be our only considerable adversary. Among the English "Intelligentsia of the Proletariat", materialism is only one among many non-Christian creeds—Theosophy, Spiritualism, British Israelitism, etc. England has, of course, always been the home of "cranks"; I see no sign that they are diminishing. Consistent Marxism I very seldom met. Whether this is because it is very rare, or because men speaking in the presence of their officers concealed it, or because Marxists did not attend the meetings at which I spoke, I have no means of knowing. Even where Christianity was professed, it was often much tainted with Pantheistic elements. Strict and well-informed Christian statements, when they occurred at all, usually came from Roman Catholics or from members of extreme Protestant sects (e.g., Baptists). My student audiences shared, in a less degree, the theological vagueness I found in the R.A.F., but among them strict and well informed statements came from Anglo-Catholics and Roman Catholics; seldom, if ever from Dissenters. The various non-Christian religions mentioned above hardly appeared.

The next thing I learned from the R.A.F. was that the English Proletariat is sceptical about History to a degree which academically educated persons can hardly imagine. This, indeed, seems to me to be far the widest cleavage between the learned and the unlearned. The educated man habitually, almost without noticing it, sees the present as something that grows out of a long perspective of centuries. In the minds of my R.A.F. hearers this perspective simply did not exist. It seemed to me that they did not really believe that we have any reliable knowledge of historic Man. But this was often curiously combined with a conviction that we knew a great deal about Pre-Historic Man: doubtless because Pre-Historic Man is labelled "Science" (which is reliable) whereas Napoleon or Julius Caesar is labelled as "History" (which is not). Thus a pseudo-scientific picture of the "Caveman" and a picture of "the Present" filled almost the whole of their imaginations; between these, there lay only a shadowy and unimportant region in which the phantasmal shapes of Roman soldiers, stage-coaches, pirates, knights in armour, highwaymen, etc., moved in a mist. I had supposed that if my hearers disbelieved the Gospels, they would do so because the Gospels recorded miracles. But my impression is that they disbelieved them simply because they dealt with events that happened a long time ago: that they would be almost as incredulous of the Battle of Actium as of the Resurrection—and for the same reason. Sometimes this scepticism was defended by the argument that all books before the invention of printing must have been copied and re-copied till the text was changed beyond recognition. And here came another surprise. When their historical scepticism took that rational form, it was sometimes easily allayed by the mere statement that there existed a "science called textual criticism" which gave us a reasonable assurance that some ancient texts were accurate. This ready acceptance of the authority of specialists is significant, not only for its ingenuousness but also because it underlines a fact of which my experiences have on the whole convinced me; i.e., that very little of the opposition we meet is inspired by malice or suspicion. It is based on genuine doubt, and often on doubt that is reasonable in the state of the doubter's knowledge.

My third discovery is of a difficulty which I suspect to be more acute in England than elsewhere. I mean the difficulty occasioned by language. In all societies, no doubt, the speech of the vulgar differs from that of the learned. The English language with its double vocabulary (Latin and native), English manners (with their boundless indulgence to slang, even in polite circles) and English culture which allows nothing like the French Academy, make the gap unusually wide. There are almost two languages in this country. The man who wishes to speak to the uneducated in English must learn their language. It is not enough that he should abstain from using what he regards as "hard words". He must discover empirically what words exist in the language of his audience and what they mean in that language: e.g., that *potential* means not "possible" but "power", that *creature* means not creature, but "animal", that *primitive* means "rude" or "clumsy", that rude means (often) "scabrous", "obscene", that the *Immaculate Conception* (except in the mouths of Roman Catholics) means the "Virgin Birth". A *being* means "a personal being": a man who said to me: "I believe in the Holy Ghost, but I don't think it is a being", meant: "I believe there is such a Being, but that it is not personal." On the other hand, *personal* sometimes means "corporeal". When an uneducated Englishman says that he believes "in God, but not in a personal God", he may mean simply and solely that he is not an Anthropomorphist in the strict and original sense of that word. *Abstract* seems to have two meanings: *(a)* "immaterial", *(b)* "vague", obscure and unpractical. Thus Arithmetic is not, in their language, an "abstract" science. *Practical* means often "economic" or "utilitarian". *Morality* nearly always means "chastity": thus in their language the sentence "I do not say that this woman is immoral but I do say that she is a thief," would not be nonsense, but would mean: "She is chaste but dishonest." *Christian* has an eulogistic rather than a descriptive sense: e.g., "Christian standards" means simply "high moral standards". The proposition "So and so is not a Christian" would only be taken to be a criticism of his behaviour, never to be merely a statement of his beliefs. It is also important to notice that what would seem to the learned to be the harder of two words may in fact, to the uneducated, be the easier. Thus it was recently proposed to emend a prayer used in the Church of England that magistrates "may truly and indifferently administer justice" to "may truly and impartially administer justice". A country priest told me that his sexton understood and could accurately explain the meaning of "indifferently" but had no idea of what "impartially" meant.

The popular English language, then, simply has to be learned by him who would preach to the English: just as a missionary learns Bantu before preaching to the Bantus. This is the more necessary because once the lecture or discussion has begun, digressions on the meaning of words tend to bore uneducated audiences and even to awaken distrust. There is no subject in which they are less interested than Philology. Our problem is often simply one of translation. Every examination for ordinands ought to include a passage from some standard theological work for translation into the vernacular. The work is laborious but it is immediately rewarded. By trying to translate our doctrines into vulgar speech we discover how much we understand them ourselves. Our failure to translate may sometimes be due to our ignorance of the vernacular; much more often it exposes the fact that we do not exactly know what we mean.

Apart from this linguistic difficulty, the greatest barrier I have met is the almost total absence from the minds of my audience of any sense of sin. This has struck me more forcibly when I spoke to the R.A.F. than when I spoke to students: whether (as I believe) the Proletariat is more self-righteous than other classes, or whether educated people are cleverer at concealing their pride, this creates for us a new situation. The early Christian preachers could assume in their hearers whether Jews, *Metuentes* or Pagans, a sense of guilt. (That this was common among Pagans is shown by the fact that both Epicureanism and the Mystery Religions both claimed, though in different ways, to assuage it.) Thus the Christian message was in those days unmistakably the *Evangelium,* the Good News. It promised healing to those who knew they were sick. We have to convince our hearers of the unwelcome diagnosis before we can expect them to welcome the news of the remedy.

The ancient man approached God (or even the gods) as the accused person approaches his judge. For the modern man the roles are reversed. He is the judge: God is in the dock. He is quite a kindly judge: if God should have a reasonable defence for being the god who permits war, poverty and disease, he is ready to listen to it. The trial may even end in God's acquittal. But the important thing is that Man is on the Bench and God in the Dock.

It is generally useless to try to combat this attitude, as older preachers did, by dwelling on sins like drunkenness and unchastity. The modern Proletariat is not drunken. As for fornication, contraceptives have made a profound difference. As long as this sin might socially ruin a girl by making her the mother of a bastard, most men recognized the sin against charity which it involved, and their consciences were often troubled by it. Now that it need have no such consequences, it is not, I think, generally felt to be a sin at all. My own experience suggests that if we can awake the conscience of our hearers at all, we must do so in quite different directions. We must talk of conceit, spite, jealousy, cowardice, meanness, etc. But I am very far from believing that I have found the solution of this problem.

Finally, I must add that my own work has suffered very much from the incurable intellectualism of my approach. The simple, emotional appeal ("Come to Jesus") is still often successful. But those who, like myself, lack the gift for making it, had better not attempt it.

What Are We to Make of Jesus Christ?

(1950)

"WHAT are we to make of Jesus Christ?" This is a question which has, in a sense, a frantically comic side. For the real question is not what are we to make of Christ, but what is He to make of us? The picture of a fly sitting deciding what it is going to make of an elephant has comic elements about it. But perhaps the questioner meant what are we to make of Him in the sense of "How are we to solve the historical problem set us by the recorded sayings and acts of this Man?" This problem is to reconcile two things. On the one hand you have got the almost generally admitted depth and sanity of His moral teaching, which is not very seriously questioned, even by those who are opposed to Christianity. In fact, I find when I am arguing with very anti-God people that they rather make a point of saying, "I am entirely in favour of the moral teaching of Christianity"—and there seems to be a general agreement that in the teaching of this Man and of His immediate followers, moral truth is exhibited at its purest and best. It is not sloppy idealism, it is full of wisdom and shrewdness. The whole thing is realistic, fresh to the highest degree, the product of a sane mind. That is one phenomenon.

The other phenomenon is the quite appalling nature of this Man's theological remarks. You all know what I mean, and I want rather to stress the point that the appalling claim which this Man seems to be making is not merely made at one moment of His career. There is, of course, the one moment which led to His execution. The moment at which the High Priest said to Him, "Who are you?" "I am the Anointed, the Son of the uncreated God, and you shall see Me appearing at the end of all history as the judge of the Universe." But that claim, in fact, does not rest on this one dramatic moment. When you look into His conversation you will find this sort of claim running through the whole thing. For instance, He went about saying to people, "I forgive your sins". Now it is quite natural for a man to forgive something you do to *him*. Thus if somebody cheats *me* out of five pounds it is quite possible and reasonable for me to say, "Well, I forgive him, we will say no more about it." What on earth would you say if somebody had done *you* out of five pounds and *I* said, "That is all right, I forgive him"? Then there is a curious thing which seems to slip out almost by accident. On one occasion this Man is sitting looking down on Jerusalem from the hill above it and suddenly in comes an extraordinary remark—"I keep on sending you prophets and wise men." Nobody comments on it. And yet, quite suddenly, almost incidentally, He is claiming to be the power that all through the centuries is sending wise men and leaders into the world. Here is another curious remark: in almost every religion there are unpleasant observances like fasting. This Man suddenly remarks one day, "No one need fast while I am here." Who is this Man who remarks that His mere presence suspends all normal rules? Who is the person who can suddenly tell the School they can have a half-holiday? Sometimes the statements put forward the assumption that He, the Speaker, is completely without sin or fault. This is always the attitude. "You, to whom I am talking, are all sinners," and He never remotely suggests that this same reproach can be brought against Him. He says again, "I am the begotten of the One God, before Abraham was, I am," and remember what the words "I am" were in Hebrew. They were the name of God, which must not be spoken by any human being, the name which it was death to utter.

Well, that is the other side. On the one side clear, definite moral teaching. On the other, claims which, if not true, are those of a megalomaniac, compared with whom Hitler was the most sane and humble of men. There is no half-way house and there is no parallel in other religions. If you had gone to Buddha and asked him: "Are you the son of Brahma?" he would have said, "My son, you are still in the vale of illusion." If you had gone to Socrates and asked, "Are you Zeus?" he would have laughed at you. If you had gone to Mohammed and asked, "Are you Allah?" he would first have rent his clothes and then cut your head off. If you had asked Confucius, "Are you Heaven?" I think he would have probably replied, "Remarks which are not in accordance with nature are in bad taste." The idea of a great moral teacher saying what Christ said is out of the question. In my opinion, the only person who can say that sort of thing is either God or a complete lunatic suffering from that form of delusion which undermines the whole mind of man. If you think you are a poached egg, when you are not looking for a piece of toast to suit you you may be sane, but if you think you are God, there is no chance for you. We may note in passing that He was never regarded as a mere moral teacher. He did not produce that effect on any of the people who actually met him. He produced mainly three effects—Hatred—Terror—Adoration. There was no trace of people expressing mild approval.

What are we to do about reconciling the two contradictory phenomena? One attempt consists in saying that the Man did not really say these things, but that His followers exaggerated the story, and so the legend grew up that He had said them. This is difficult because His followers were all Jews; that is, they belonged to that Nation which of all others was most convinced that there was only one God—that there could not possibly be another. It is very odd that this horrible invention about a religious leader should grow up among the one people in the whole earth least likely to make such a mistake. On the contrary we get the impression that none of His immediate followers or even of the New Testament writers embraced the doctrine at all easily.

Another point is that on that view you would have to regard the accounts of the Man as being *legends*. Now, as a literary historian, I am perfectly convinced that whatever else the Gospels are they are not legends. I have read a great deal of legend and I am quite clear that they are not the same sort of thing. They are not artistic enough to be legends. From an imaginative point of view they are clumsy, they don't work up to things properly. Most of the life of Jesus is totally unknown to us, as is the life of anyone else who lived at that time, and no people building up a legend would allow that to be so. Apart from bits of the

Platonic dialogues, there are no conversations that I know of in ancient literature like the Fourth Gospel. There is nothing, even in modern literature, until about a hundred years ago when the realistic novel came into existence. In the story of the woman taken in adultery we are told Christ bent down and scribbled in the dust with His finger. Nothing comes of this. No one has ever based any doctrine on it. And the art of *inventing* little irrelevant details to make an imaginary scene more convincing is a purely modern art. Surely the only explanation of this passage is that the thing really happened? The author put it in simply because he had *seen* it.

Then we come to the strangest story of all, the story of the Resurrection. It is very necessary to get the story clear. I heard a man say, "The importance of the Resurrection is that it gives evidence of survival, evidence that the human personality survives death." On that view what happened to Christ would be what had always happened to all men, the difference being that in Christ's case we were privileged to see it happening. This is certainly not what the earliest Christian writers thought. Something perfectly new in the history of the Universe had happened. Christ had defeated death. The door which had always been locked had for the very first time been forced open. This is something quite distinct from mere ghost-survival. I don't mean that they disbelieved in ghost-survival. On the contrary, they believed in it so firmly that, on more than one occasion, Christ had had to assure them that He was *not* a ghost. The point is that while believing in survival they yet regarded the Resurrection as something totally different and new. The Resurrection narratives are not a picture of survival after death; they record how a totally new mode of being has arisen in the universe. Something new had appeared in the universe: as new as the first coming of organic life. This Man, after death, does not get divided into "ghost" and "corpse". A new mode of being has arisen. That is the story. What are we going to make of it?

The question is, I suppose, whether any hypothesis covers the facts so well as the Christian hypothesis. That hypothesis is that God has come down into the created universe, down to manhood—and come up again, pulling it up with Him. The alternative hypothesis is not legend, nor exaggeration, nor the apparitions of a ghost. It is either lunacy or lies. Unless one can take the second alternative (and I can't) one turns to the Christian theory.

"What are we to make of Christ?" There is no question of what we can make of Him, it is entirely a question of what He intends to make of us. You must accept or reject the story.

The things He says are very different from what any other teacher has said. Others say, "This is the truth about the universe. This is the way you ought to go," but He says, "*I* am the Truth, and the Way, and the Life." He says, "No man can reach absolute reality, except through Me. Try to retain your own life and you will be inevitably ruined. Give yourself away and you will be saved." He says, "If you are ashamed of Me, if, when you hear this call, you turn the other way, I also will look the other way when I come again as God without disguise.

If anything whatever is keeping you from God and from Me, whatever it is, throw it away. If it is your eye, pull it out. If it is your hand, cut it off. If you put yourself first you will be last. Come to Me everyone who is carrying a heavy load, I will set that right. Your sins, all of them, are wiped out, I can do that. I am Re-birth, I am Life. Eat Me, drink Me, I am your Food. And finally, do not be afraid, I have overcome the whole Universe." That is the issue.

Miracles

(1942)

I HAVE KNOWN only one person in my life who claimed to have seen a ghost. It was a woman; and the interesting thing is that she disbelieved in the immortality of the soul before seeing the ghost and still disbelieves after having seen it. She thinks it was a hallucination. In other words, seeing is not believing. This is the first thing to get clear in talking about miracles. Whatever experiences we may have, we shall not regard them as miraculous if we already hold a philosophy which excludes the supernatural. Any event which is claimed as a miracle is, in the last resort, an experience received from the senses; and the senses are not infallible. We can always say we have been the victims of an illusion; if we disbelieve in the supernatural this is what we always shall say. Hence, whether miracles have really ceased or not, they would certainly appear to cease in Western Europe as materialism became the popular creed. For let us make no mistake. If the end of the world appeared in all the literal trappings of the Apocalypse,[1] if the modern materialist saw with his own eyes the heavens rolled up[2] and the great white throne appearing,[3] if he had the sensation of being himself hurled into the Lake of Fire,[4] he would continue forever, in that lake itself, to regard his experience as an illusion and to find the explanation of it in psycho-analysis, or cerebral pathology. Experience by itself proves nothing. If a man doubts whether he is dreaming or waking, no experiment can solve his doubt, since every experiment may itself be part of the dream. Experience proves this, or that, or nothing, according to the preconceptions we bring to it.

This fact that the interpretation of experience depends on preconceptions, is often used as an argument against miracles. It is said that our ancestors, taking the supernatural for granted and greedy of wonders, read the miraculous into events that were really not miracles. And in a sense I grant it. That is to say, I think that just as our preconceptions would prevent us from apprehending miracles if they really occurred, so their preconceptions would lead them to imagine miracles even if they did not occur. In the same way, the doting man will think his wife faithful when she is not and the suspicious man will not think her faithful when she is: the question of her actual fidelity remains meanwhile to be settled, if at all, on other grounds. But there is one thing often said about our ancestors which we must *not* say. We must not say "They believed in miracles because they did not know the laws of Nature." This is nonsense. When St Joseph discovered that his bride was pregnant, he was "minded to put her away".[5] He knew enough biology for that. Otherwise, of course he would not have regarded pregnancy as a proof of infidelity. When he accepted the Christian explanation, he regarded

[1]The Book of Revelation   [2]ibid., vi. 14   [3]ibid., xx. 11
[4]ibid., xix. 20; xx. 10; xx. 14–15; xxi.8   [5]Matthew i. 19

it as a miracle precisely because he knew enough of the laws of Nature to know that this was a suspension of them. When the disciples saw Christ walking on the water they were frightened:[6] they would not have been frightened unless they had known the laws of Nature and known that this was an exception. If a man had no conception of a regular order in Nature, then of course he could not notice departures from that order: just as a dunce who does not understand the normal metre of a poem is also unconscious of the poet's variations from it. Nothing is wonderful except the abnormal and nothing is abnormal until we have grasped the norm. Complete ignorance of the laws of Nature would preclude the perception of the miraculous just as rigidly as complete disbelief in the supernatural precludes it, perhaps even more so. For while the materialist would have at least to explain miracles away, the man wholly ignorant of Nature would simply not notice them.

The experience of a miracle in fact requires two conditions. First we must believe in a normal stability of nature, which means we must recognize that the data offered by our senses recur in regular patterns. Secondly, we must believe in some reality beyond Nature. When both beliefs are held, and not till then, we can approach with an open mind the various reports which claim that this super- or extra-natural reality has sometimes invaded and disturbed the sensuous content of space and time which makes our "natural" world. The belief in such a supernatural reality itself can neither be proved nor disproved by experience. The arguments for its existence are metaphysical, and to me conclusive. They turn on the fact that even to think and act in the natural world we have to assume something beyond it and even assume that we partly belong to that something. In order to think we must claim for our own reasoning a validity which is not credible if our own thought is merely a function of our brain, and our brains a by-product of irrational physical processes. In order to act, above the level of mere impulse, we must claim a similar validity for our judgments of good and evil. In both cases we get the same disquieting result. The concept of nature itself is one we have reached only tacitly by claiming a sort of *super-*natural status for ourselves.

If we frankly accept this position and then turn to the evidence, we find, of course, that accounts of the supernatural meet us on every side. History is full of them—often in the same documents which we accept wherever they do not report miracles. Respectable missionaries report them not infrequently. The whole Church of Rome claims their continued occurrence. Intimate conversation elicits from almost every acquaintance at least one episode in his life which is what he would call "queer" or "rum". No doubt most stories of miracles are unreliable; but then, as anyone can see by reading the papers, so are most stories of all events. Each story must be taken on its merits: what one must not do is to rule out the supernatural as the one impossible explanation. Thus you

[6]Matthew xiv. 26; Mark vi. 49; John vi. 19

may disbelieve in the Mons Angels[7] because you cannot find a sufficient number of sensible people who say they saw them. But if you found a sufficient number, it would, in my view, be unreasonable to explain this by collective hallucination. For we know enough of psychology to know that spontaneous unanimity in hallucination is very improbable, and we do not know enough of the supernatural to know that a manifestation of angels is equally improbable. The supernatural theory is the less improbable of the two. When the Old Testament says that Sennacherib's invasion was stopped by angels,[8] and Herodotus says it was stopped by a lot of mice who came and ate up all the bowstrings of his army,[9] an open-minded man will be on the side of the angels. Unless you start by begging the question, there is nothing intrinsically unlikely in the existence of angels or in the action ascribed to them. But mice just don't do these things.

A great deal of scepticism now current about the miracles of our Lord does not, however, come from disbelief of all reality beyond nature. It comes from two ideas which are respectable but I think mistaken. In the first place, modern people have an almost aesthetic dislike of miracles. Admitting that God can, they doubt if He would. To violate the laws He Himself has imposed on His creation seems to them arbitrary, clumsy, a theatrical device only fit to impress savages—a solecism against the grammar of the universe. In the second place, many people confuse the laws of nature with the laws of thought and imagine that their reversal or suspension would be a contradiction in terms—as if the resurrection of the dead were the same sort of thing as two and two making five.

I have only recently found the answer to the first objection. I found it first in George MacDonald and then later in St Athanasius. This is what St Athanasius says in his little book *On the Incarnation:* "Our Lord took a body like to ours and lived as a man in order that those who had refused to recognize Him in His superintendence and captaincy of the whole universe might come to recognize from the works He did here below in the body that what dwelled in this body was the Word of God." This accords exactly with Christ's own account of His miracles: "The Son can do nothing of Himself, but what He seeth the Father do."[10] The doctrine, as I understand it, is something like this:

There is an activity of God displayed throughout creation, a wholesale activity let us say which men refuse to recognize. The miracles done by God incarnate, living as a man in Palestine, perform the very same things as this wholesale activity, but at a different speed and on a smaller scale. One of their chief purposes is that men having seen a thing done by personal power on the small scale, may recognize, when they see the same thing done on the large scale, that

[7]Lewis is referring to the story that angels appeared, protecting British troops in their retreat from Mons, France, on the 26th August 1914. A recent summary of the event by Jill Kitson, "Did Angels appear to British troops at Mons?" is found in *History Makers*, No. 3 (1969), pp. 132–33.

[8]II Kings xix. 35   [9]Herodotus, Bk. II, Sect. 141   [10]John v. 19

the power behind it is also personal—is indeed the very same person who lived among us two thousand years ago. The miracles in fact are a retelling in small letters of the very same story which is written across the whole world in letters too large for some of us to see. Of that larger script part is already visible, part is still unsolved. In other words, some of the miracles do locally what God has already done universally: others do locally what he had not yet done, but will do. In that sense, and from our human point of view, some are reminders and others prophecies.

God creates the vine and teaches it to draw up water by its roots and, with the aid of the sun, to turn that water into a juice which will ferment and take on certain qualities. Thus every year, from Noah's time till ours, God turns water into wine. That, men fail to see. Either like the Pagans they refer the process to some finite spirit, Bacchus or Dionysus: or else, like the moderns, they attribute real and ultimate causality to the chemical and other material phenomena which are all that our sense can discover in it. But when Christ at Cana makes water into wine, the mask is off.[11] The miracle has only half its effect if it only convinces us that Christ is God: it will have its full effect if whenever we see a vineyard or drink a glass of wine we remember that here works He who sat at the wedding party in Cana. Every year God makes a little corn into much corn: the seed is sown and there is an increase, and men, according to the fashion of their age, say "It is Ceres, it is Adonis, it is the Corn-King," or else "It is the laws of Nature." The close-up, the translation, of this annual wonder is the feeding of the five thousand.[12] Bread is not made there of nothing. Bread is not made of stones, as the Devil once suggested to Our Lord in vain.[13] A little bread is made into much bread. The Son will do nothing but what He sees the Father do. There is, so to speak, a family *style*. The miracles of healing fall into the same pattern. This is sometimes obscured for us by the somewhat magical view we tend to take of ordinary medicine. The doctors themselves do not take this view. The magic is not in the medicine but in the patient's body. What the doctor does is to stimulate Nature's functions in the body, or to remove hindrances. In a sense, though we speak for convenience of healing a cut, every cut heals itself; no dressing will make skin grow over a cut on a corpse. That same mysterious energy which we call gravitational when it steers the planets and biochemical when it heals a body is the efficient cause of all recoveries, and if God exists, that energy, directly or indirectly, is His. All who are cured are cured by Him, the healer within. But once He did it visibly, a Man meeting a man. Where He does not work within in this mode, the organism dies. Hence Christ's one miracle of destruction is also in harmony with God's wholesale activity. His bodily hand held out in symbolic wrath blasted a single fig tree;[14] but no tree died that year in Palestine, or any year,

[11]John ii. 1–11   [12]Matthew xiv. 15–21; Mark vi. 34–44; Luke ix. 12–17; John vi. 1–11
[13]Matthew iv. 3; Luke iv. 3   [14]Matthew xxi. 19; Mark xi. 13–20

or in any land, or even ever will, save because He has done something, or (more likely) ceased to do something, to it.

When He fed the thousands he multiplied fish as well as bread. Look in every bay and almost every river. This swarming, pulsating fecundity shows He is still at work. The ancients had a god called Genius—the god of animal and human fertility, the presiding spirit of gynaecology, embryology, or the marriage bed—the "genial bed" as they called it after its god Genius.[15] As the miracles of wine and bread and healing showed who Bacchus really was, who Ceres, who Apollo, and that all were one, so this miraculous multiplication of fish reveals the real Genius. And with that we stand at the threshold of the miracle which for some reason most offends modern ears. I can understand the man who denies the miraculous altogether; but what is one to make of the people who admit some miracles but deny the Virgin Birth? Is it that for all their lip service to the laws of Nature there is only one law of Nature that they really believe? Or is it that they see in this miracle a slur upon sexual intercourse which is rapidly becoming the one thing venerated in a world without veneration? No miracle is in fact more significant. What happens in ordinary generation? What is a father's function in the act of begetting? A microscopic particle of matter from his body fertilizes the female: and with that microscopic particle passes, it may be, the colour of his hair and his great grandfather's hanging lip, and the human form in all its complexity of bones, liver, sinews, heart, and limbs, and prehuman form which the embryo will recapitulate in the womb. Behind every spermatozoon lies the whole history of the universe: locked within it is no small part of the world's future. That is God's normal way of making a man—a process that takes centuries, beginning with the creation of matter itself, and narrowing to one second and one particle at the moment of begetting. And once again men will mistake the sense impressions which this creative act throws off for the act itself or else refer it to some finite being such as Genius. Once, therefore, God does it directly, instantaneously; without a spermatozoon, without the milleniums of organic history behind the spermatozoon. There was of course another reason. This time He was creating not simply a man, but the man who was to be Himself: the only true Man. The process which leads to the spermatozoon has carried down with it through the centuries much undesirable silt; the life which reaches us by that normal route is tainted. To avoid that taint, to give humanity a fresh start, He once short-circuited the process. There is a vulgar anti-God paper which some anonymous donor sends me every week. In it recently I saw the taunt that we Christians believe in a God who committed adultery with the wife of a Jewish carpenter. The answer to that is that if you describe the action of God in

---

[15]For further information on this subject see the chapter on "Genius and Genius" in Lewis's *Studies in Medieval and Renaissance Literature*, ed. Walter Hooper (Cambridge, 1966), pp. 169–74.

fertilizing Mary as "adultery", then, in that sense, God would have committed adultery with every woman who ever had a baby. For what He did once without a human father, He does always even when He uses a human father as His instrument. For the human father in ordinary generation is only a carrier, sometimes an unwilling carrier, always the last in a long line of carriers, of life that comes from the supreme life. Thus the filth that our poor, muddled, sincere, resentful enemies fling at the Holy One, either does not stick, or, sticking, turns into glory.

So much for the miracles which do small and quick what we have already seen in the large letters of God's universal activity. But before I go on to the second class—those which foreshadow parts of the universal activity we have not yet seen—I must guard against a misunderstanding. Do not imagine I am trying to make the miracles less miraculous. I am not arguing that they are more probable because they are less unlike natural events: I am trying to answer those who think them arbitrary, theatrical, unworthy of God, meaningless interruptions of universal order. They remain in my view wholly miraculous. To do instantly with dead and baked corn what ordinarily happens slowly with live seed is just as great a miracle as to make bread of stones. Just as great, but a different *kind* of miracle. That is the point. When I open Ovid,[16] or Grimm, I find the sort of miracles which really would be arbitrary. Trees talk, houses turn into trees, magic rings raise tables richly spread with food in lonely places, ships become goddesses, and men are changed into snakes or birds or bears. It is fun to read about: the least suspicion that it had really happened would turn that fun into nightmare. You find no miracles of that kind in the Gospels. Such things, if they could be, would prove that some alien power was invading Nature; they would not in the least prove that it was the same power which had made Nature and rules her every day. But the true miracles express not simply a god, but God: that which is outside Nature, not as a foreigner, but as her sovereign. They announce not merely that a King has visited our town, but that it is *the* King, *our* King.

The second class of miracles, on this view, foretell what God has not yet done, but will do, universally. He raised one man (the man who was Himself) from the dead because He will one day raise all men from the dead. Perhaps not only men, for there are hints in the New Testament that all creation will eventually be rescued from decay, restored to shape and subserve the splendour of re-made humanity.[17] The Transfiguration[18] and the walking on the water[19] are glimpses of the beauty and the effortless power over all matter which will belong to men when they are really waked by God. Now resurrection certainly involves "reversal" of natural process in the sense that it involves a series of changes moving in the opposite direction to those we see. At death, matter which has been organic,

---

[16]The reference is to Ovid's (43 B.C.–A.D. 18) *Metamorphoses.*

[17]e.g., Romans viii. 22: "We know that the whole creation groaneth and travaileth in pain together until now."

[18]Matthew xvii. 1–9; Mark ix. 2–10   [19]Matthew xiv. 26; Mark vi. 49; John vi. 19

falls back gradually into the inorganic, to be finally scattered and used perhaps in other organism. Resurrection would be the reverse process. It would not of course mean the restoration to each personality of those very atoms, numerically the same, which had made its first or "natural" body. There would not be enough to go round, for one thing; and for another, the unity of the body even in this life was consistent with a slow but perplexed change of its actual ingredients. But it certainly does mean matter of some kind rushing towards organism as now we see it rushing away. It means, in fact, playing backwards a film we have already seen played forwards. In that sense it is reversal of Nature. But, of course, it is a further question whether reversal in this sense is necessarily contradiction. Do we know that the film cannot be played backwards?

Well, in one sense, it is precisely the teaching of modern physics that the film never works backwards. For modern physics, as you have heard before, the universe is "running down". Disorganization and chance are continually increasing. There will come a time, not infinitely remote, when it will be wholly run down or wholly disorganized, and science knows of no possible return from that state. There must have been a time, not infinitely remote, in the past when it was wound up, though science knows of no winding-up process. The point is that for our ancestors the universe was a picture: for modern physics it is a story. If the universe is a picture these things either appear in that picture or not; and if they don't, since it is an infinite picture, one may suspect that they are contrary to the nature of things. But a story is a different matter; specially if it is an incomplete story. And the story told by modern physics might be told briefly in the words "Humpty Dumpty was falling". That is, it proclaims itself an incomplete story. There must have been a time before he fell, when he was sitting on the wall; there must be a time after he has reached the ground. It is quite true that science knows of no horses and men who can put him together again once he has reached the ground and broken. But then she also knows of no means by which he could originally have been put on the wall. You wouldn't expect her to. All science rests on observation: all our observations are taken *during* Humpty Dumpty's fall, because we were born after he lost his seat on the wall and shall be extinct long before he reaches the ground. But to assume from observations taken while the clock is running down that the unimaginable winding-up which must have preceded this process cannot occur when the process is over is the merest dogmatism. From the very nature of the case the laws of degradation and disorganization which we find in matter at present, cannot be the ultimate and eternal nature of things. If they were, there would have been nothing to degrade and disorganize. Humpty Dumpty can't fall off a wall that never existed.

Obviously, an event which lies outside the falling or disintegrating process which we know as Nature, is not imaginable. If anything is clear from the records of Our Lord's appearances after His resurrection, it is that the risen body was very different from the body that died and that it lives under conditions quite unlike those of natural life. It is frequently not recognized by those who see it:[20] and it is not related to space in the same way as our bodies. The sudden appearances and disappearances[21] suggest the ghost of popular tradition: yet He emphatically insists that He is not merely a spirit and takes steps to demonstrate that the risen body can still perform animal operations, such as eating.[22] What makes all this baffling to us is our assumption that to pass beyond what we call Nature—beyond the three dimensions and the five highly specialized and limited senses—is immediately to be in a world of pure negative spiritually, a world where space of any sort and sense of any sort have no function. I know no grounds for believing this. To explain even an atom Schrödinger wants seven dimensions: and give us new senses and we should find a new Nature. There may be Natures piled upon Natures, each supernatural to the one beneath it, before we come to the abyss of pure spirit; and to be in that abyss, at the right hand of the Father, may not mean being absent from any of these Natures—may mean a yet more dynamic presence on all levels. That is why I think it very rash to assume that the story of the Ascension is mere allegory. I know it sounds like the work of people who imagined an absolute up and down and a local heaven in the sky. But to say this is after all to say "Assuming that the story is fake, we could thus explain how it arose." Without that assumption we find ourselves "moving about in worlds unrealized"[23] with no probability—or improbability—to guide us. For if the story is true then a being still in some mode, though not our mode, corporeal, withdrew at His own will from the Nature presented by our three dimensions and five senses, not necessarily into the non-sensuous and undimensioned but possibly into, or through, a world or worlds of super-sense and super-space. And He might choose to do it gradually. Who on earth knows what the spectators might see? If they say they saw a momentary movement along the vertical plane—then an indistinct mass—then nothing—who is to pronounce this improbable?

My time is nearly up and I must be very brief with the second class of people whom I promised to deal with: those who mistake the laws of Nature for laws of thought and, therefore, think that any departure from them is a self-contradiction, like a square circle or two and two making five. To think this is to imagine that the normal processes of Nature are transparent to the intellect, that we can say why she behaves as she does. For, of course, if we cannot see why a thing is so, then we cannot see any reason why it should not be otherwise. But in fact the actual course of Nature is wholly inexplicable. I don't mean that science has not yet explained it, but may do so some day. I mean that the very nature of explanation makes it impossible that we should even explain why matter has the properties it has. For explanation, by its very nature, deals with a world of "ifs and ands". Every explanation takes the form "Since A, therefore B" or "If C, then D." In order to explain any event you have to assume the universe as a going

---

[20]Luke xxiv. 13–31, 36–7; John xx. 14–16

[21]Mark xvi. 14; Luke xxiv. 31, 36; John xx. 19, 26   [22]Luke xxiv. 42–3; John xxi. 13

[23]This is probably a misquotation of Wordsworth's "Moving about in worlds not realized." *Intimations of Immortality*, ix, 149

concern, a machine working in a particular way. Since this particular way of working is the basis of all explanation, it can never be itself explained. We can see no reason why it should not have worked a different way.

To say this is not only to remove the suspicion that miracle is self-contradictory, but also to realize how deeply right St Athanasius was when he found an essential likeness between the miracles of Our Lord and the general order of Nature. Both are a full stop for the explaining intellect. If the "natural" means that which can be fitted into a class, that which obeys a norm, that which can be paralleled, that which can be explained by reference to other events, then Nature herself as a whole is *not* natural. If a miracle means that which must simply be accepted, the unanswerable actuality which gives no account of itself but simply *is*, then the universe is one great miracle. To direct us to that great miracle is one main object of the earthly acts of Christ: that are, as He himself said, Signs.[24] They serve to remind us that the explanations of particular events which we derive *from* the given, the unexplained, the almost wilful character of the actual universe, are not explanations of that character. These Signs do not take us away from reality; they recall us to it—recall us from our dream world of "ifs and ands" to the stunning actuality of everything that is real. They are focal points at which more reality becomes visible than we ordinarily see at once. I have spoken of how He made miraculous bread and wine and of how, when the Virgin conceived, He had shown Himself the true Genius whom men had ignorantly worshipped long before. It goes deeper than that. Bread and wine were to have an even more sacred significance for Christians and the act of generation was to be the chosen symbol among all mystics for the union of the soul with God. These things are no accidents. With Him there are no accidents. When He created the vegetable world He knew already what dreams the annual death and resurrection of the corn would cause to stir in pious Pagan minds, He knew already that He Himself must so die and live again and in what sense, including and far transcending the old religion of the Corn King. He would say "This is my Body."[25] *Common* bread, miraculous bread, sacramental bread—these three are distinct, but not to be separated. Divine reality is like a fugue. All His acts are different, but they all rhyme or echo to one another. It is this that makes Christianity so difficult to talk about. Fix your mind on any one story or any one doctrine and it becomes at once a magnet to which truth and glory come rushing from all levels of being. Our featureless pantheistic unities and glib rationalist distinctions are alike defeated by the seamless, yet ever-varying, texture of reality, the liveness, the elusiveness, the intertwined harmonies of the multidimensional fertility of God. But if this is the difficulty, it is also one of the firm grounds of our belief. To think that this was a fable, a product of our own brains as they are a product of matter would be to believe that this vast symphonic splendour had come out of something

[24]Matthew xii. 39; xvi. 4; xxiv. 24, 30; Mark xiii. 22; xvi. 17, 20; Luke xxi. 11, 25
[25]Matthew xxvi. 26; Mark xiv. 22; Luke xxii. 19; I Corinthians xi. 24

much smaller and emptier than itself. It is not so. We are nearer to the truth in the vision seen by Julian of Norwich, when Christ appeared to her holding in His hand a little thing like a hazel nut and saying, "This is all that is created."[26] And it seemed to her so small and weak that she wondered how it could hold together at all.[27]

[26]*Sixteen Revelations of Divine Love,* ed. Roger Hudleston (London, 1927), ch. v, p. 9
[27]See Letter 3

Rejoinder to Dr Pittenger

(1958)

To one of the charges Dr Norman Pittenger makes in his "Critique" in the 1st October *Christian Century*, [1] I must with shame plead guilty. He has caught me using the word "literally" where I did not really mean it, a vile journalistic cliché which he cannot reprobate more severely than I now do myself. [2]

I must also admit some truth in his charge of Apollinarianism; there is a passage in my *Problem of Pain* which would imply, if pressed, a shockingly crude conception of the Incarnation. I corrected it by a footnote to the French edition but have not been able to do so elsewhere, save in so far as *Mere Christianity*, book four, chapter three, may provide an antidote.

This must not be taken to mean that my present conception would fully satisfy Dr Pittenger. He speaks about "the validity of our Lord's unique place in Christian faith as that One in whom God was so active and so present that he may be called 'God-Man' ". [3] I am not quite sure what this means. May I translate it, "Our Lord's actually unique place in the structure of utter reality, the unique mode, as well as degree, of God's presence and action in Him, make the formula 'God-Man' the objectively true description of Him"? If so, I think we are very nearly agreed. Or must I translate it, "the unique place which Christians (subjectively, in their own thoughts) gave to our Lord as One in whom God was present and active to a unique degree made it reasonable for them to call Him God-Man"? If so, I must demur. In other words, if Dr Pittenger's "may be called" means anything less or other than "is", I could not accept his formula. For I think that Jesus Christ is (in fact) the only Son of God—that is, the only original Son of God, through whom others are enabled to "become sons of God". [4] If Dr Pittenger wishes to attack that doctrine, I wonder he should choose me as its representative. It has had champions far worthier of his steel.

I turn next to my book *Miracles* and am sorry to say that I here have to meet Dr Pittenger's charges with straight denials. He says that this book "opens with a definition of miracles as the 'violation' of the laws of nature". [5] He is mistaken. The passage (chapter 2) really runs: "I use the word *Miracle* to mean an interference with Nature by supernatural power." [6] If Dr Pittenger thinks the difference

---

[1] W. Norman Pittenger. "A Critique of C. S. Lewis", *Christian Century*, vol. LXXV (1st October, 1958), pp. 1104–7

[2] In *Broadcast Talks* (London, 1942), Part II, ch. 5, p. 60, Lewis had written that "the whole mass of Christians are literally the physical organism through which Christ acts—that we are His fingers and muscles, the cells of His body." The word "literally", however, was deleted when *Broadcast Talks* was reprinted with two other short books as *Mere Christianity* (London, 1952) in which the phrase quoted above is found in bk. II, ch. 5, p. 51.

[3] Pittenger, p. 1106   [4] John i. 12   [5] Pittenger, p. 1105

[6] *Miracles: A Preliminary Study* (London, 1947). Because Lewis later revised chapter III of this book, all my text-references are to the "revised" paperback edition of *Miracles* (Fontana Books, London, 1960), p. 9

between the true text and his mis-quotation merely verbal, he has misunderstood nearly the whole book. I never equated nature (the spatio-temporal system of facts and events) with the laws of nature (the patterns into which these facts and events fall). I would as soon equate an actual speech with the rules of grammar. In chapter eight I say in so many words that no miracle either can or need break the laws of Nature; that "it is . . . inaccurate to define a miracle as something that breaks the laws of Nature";[7] and that "The divine art of miracle is not an art of suspending the pattern to which events conform but of feeding new events into that pattern."[8] How many times does a man need to say something before he is safe from the accusation of having said exactly the opposite? (I am not for a moment imputing dishonesty to Dr Pittenger; we all know too well how difficult it is to grasp or retain the substance of a book one finds antipathetic.)

Again, Dr Pittenger contrasts my view with that which makes miracles a sign of God's action and presence in creation. Yet in chapter fifteen I say that the miracle at Cana manifests "the God of Israel who has through all these centuries given us wine" and that in the miraculous feedings God "does close and small . . . what He has always been doing in the seas, the lakes and the little brooks".[9] Surely this is just what Dr Pittenger wanted me to say, and what Athanasius says (*De Incarnatione* xiv. 8, edited by F. L. Cross, 1939)?

It is very true that I make no use of the different words (*semeia, terata* and the rest) which New Testament writers use for miracles. But why should I? I was writing for people who wanted to know whether the things could have happened rather than what they should be called; whether we could without absurdity believe that Christ rose from the emptied tomb. I am afraid most of my readers, if once convinced that He did not, would have felt it of minor importance to decide whether, if He had done so, this nonexistent event would have been a *teras* or a *dunamis*. And (in certain moods) one does, after all, see their point.

Dr Pittenger thinks the Naturalist whom I try to refute in chapter three is a man of straw. He may not be found in the circles Dr Pittenger frequents. He is quite common where I come from; and, presumably, in Moscow. There is indeed a really serious hitch in that chapter (which ought to be rewritten), but Dr Pittenger has not seen it or has charitably kept silent about it.[10]

I now turn to the more difficult and interesting question of the Fourth Gospel. It is difficult because, here again, I do not quite understand what Dr Pittenger writes. He blames me for putting all four Gospels in the same category and especially for believing that Jesus claimed deity because the Fourth Gospel says He did. But this does not mean that Dr Pittenger rejects the fourth as simply untrue. According to him it gives that "interpretation" of our Lord's "significance" which the early Christians "found", and "rightly" found, "to be true".[11] Now in my language that significance of anything which is "rightly found to be

[7]ibid., p. 63   [8]ibid., p. 64   [9]ibid., pp. 140, 141
[10]Lewis did, as just mentioned in a footnote above, revise chapter III of *Miracles*.
[11]Pittenger, p. 1106

true" would be its true significance and those who found it would have found what the thing really meant. If the Fourth Gospel gives us what Jesus Christ really meant, why am I blamed for accepting it? But I am, and therefore Dr Pittenger's words must bear some other sense. Does he mean that what they "rightly found to be true" was not true? Or that the significance which was rightly found to be true by them would be "wrongly found" to be true by us? Or did they get the "significance" right and go wrong about the "interpretation of the significance"? I give it up.

I confess, however, that the problem of the Fourth Gospel raises in me a conflict between authority and private judgment: the authority of all those learned men who think that Gospel unhistorical, and my judgment as a literary critic which constrains me to think it at least as close to the facts as Boswell's *Johnson.* If I venture here to follow judgment in the teeth of authority, this is partly because I could never see how one escaped the dilemma *aut deus aut malus homo*[12] by confining oneself to the Synoptics. Moderns do not seem startled, as contemporaries were, by the claim Jesus there makes to forgive sins; not sins against Himself, just sins. Yet surely, if they actually met it, they would feel differently. If Dr Pittenger told me that two of his colleagues had lost him a professorship by telling lies about his character and I replied, "I freely forgive them both", would he not think this an impertinence (both in the old and in the modern sense) bordering on insanity? And of course all three Synoptics tell the story of One who, at his trial, sealed His fate by saying He was the Son of God.

I am accused of attributing "almost spatial transcendence" to God and of denying His continued presence within Nature because I speak of Him as "invading" or "intruding into" her.[13] This is really very hard of the Doctor. Of course the very word "transcendence" contains a spatial image. So does "immanence". So does Dr Pittenger's "God's action and *presence in* the creation".[14] We must, after all, speak the language of men. (I have got much light on this problem from Edwyn Bevan's *Symbolism and Belief.*) But I freely admit that, believing both, I have stressed the transcendence of God more than His immanence. I thought, and think, that the present situation demands this. I see around me no danger of Deism but much of an immoral, naïve and sentimental pantheism. I have often found that it was in fact the chief obstacle to conversion.

Dr Pittenger says that I base the Faith on authority (which has "grown up in the Church and won the assent of great doctors").[15] So does he; his authority is "the total consentient witness of all Christians from the apostles' time".[16] I am not sure why he calls my authority "mechanical". Surely it differs from his mainly by being discoverable? The "total consentient witness" would be grand

[12]Either God or a bad man   [13]Pittenger, p. 1105   [14]ibid.
[15]Pittenger, p. 1106, quoting Lewis's *The Problem of Pain* (London, 1940), ch. v, p. 60
[16]Pittenger, p. 1106

if we had it. But of course the overwhelming majority of Christians, as of other men, have died, and are dying while I write, without recording their "witness". How does Dr Pittenger consult his authority?

Where he really hurt me was in the charge of callousness to animals. Surprised me too; for the very same passage is blamed by others for extreme sentimentality.[17] It is hard to please all. But if the Patagonians think me a dwarf and the Pygmies a giant, perhaps my stature is in fact fairly unremarkable.

The statement that I do not "care much for" the Sermon on the Mount but "prefer" the "Pauline ethic" of man's sinfulness and helplessness[18] carries a suggestion of alternatives between which we may choose, where I see successive stages through which we must proceed. Most of my books are evangelistic, addressed to *tous exo*. It would have been inept to preach forgiveness and a Saviour to those who did not know they were in need of either. Hence St Paul's and the Baptist's diagnosis (would you call it exactly an *ethic?*) had to be pressed. Nor am I aware that our Lord revised it ("if ye, being evil . . .").[19] As to "caring for" the Sermon on the Mount, if "caring for" here means "liking" or enjoying, I suppose no one "cares for" it. Who can *like* being knocked flat on his face by a sledge-hammer? I can hardly imagine a more deadly spiritual condition than that of the man who can read that passage with tranquil pleasure. This is indeed to be "at ease in Zion".[20] Such a man is not yet ripe for the Bible; he had better start by learning sense from Islam: "The Heaven and the earth and all between, thinkest thou I made them *in jest?*"

And this illustrates what appears to me to be a weakness in the Doctor's critical method. He judges my book *in vacuo*, with no consideration of the audience to whom they were addressed or the prevalent errors they were trying to combat. The Naturalist becomes a straw man because he is not found among "first-rate scientists" and readers of Einstein. But I was writing *ad populum*, not *ad clerum*. This is relevant to my manner as well as my matter. It is true, I do not understand why it is vulgar or offensive, in speaking of the Holy Trinity, to illustrate from plane and solid geometry the conception that what is self-contradictory on one level may be consistent on another.[21] I could have understood the Doctor's being shocked if I had compared God to an unjust judge or Christ to a thief in the night; but mathematical objects seem to me as free from sordid associations as any the mind can entertain.

But let all that pass. Suppose the image is vulgar. If it gets across to the unbeliever what the unbeliever desperately needs to know, the vulgarity must be endured. Indeed, the image's very vulgarity may be an advantage; for there is much sense in the reasons advanced by Aquinas (following Pseudo-Dionysius) for

[17]The reference is to the chapter on "Animal Pain" in *The Problem of Pain*.
[18]Pittenger, p. 1106   [19]Matthew vii. 11; Luke xi. 13   [20]Amos vi. 1
[21]In *Mere Christianity*, bk. iv, ch. 2, p. 128, Lewis says "In God's dimension, so to speak, you find a being who is three Persons while remaining one Being, just as a cube is six squares while remaining one cube".

preferring to present divine truths *sub figuris vilium corporum*[22] *(Summa Theologica,* Qu. 1, Art. 9 *ad tertium).*

When I began, Christianity came before the great mass of my unbelieving fellow-countrymen either in the highly emotional form offered by revivalists or in the unintelligible language of highly cultured clergymen. Most men were reached by neither. My task was therefore simply that of a *translator*—one turning Christian doctrine, or what he believed to be such, into the vernacular, into language that unscholarly people would attend to and could understand. For this purpose a style more guarded, more *nuancé,* finelier shaded, more rich in fruitful ambiguities—in fact, a style more like Dr Pittenger's own—would have been worse than useless. It would not only have failed to enlighten the common reader's understanding; it would have aroused his suspicion. He would have thought, poor soul, that I was facing both ways, sitting on the fence, offering at one moment what I withdrew the next, and generally trying to trick him. I may have made theological errors. My manner may have been defective. Others may do better hereafter. I am ready, if I am young enough, to learn. Dr Pittenger would be a more helpful critic if he advised a cure as well as asserting many diseases. How does he himself do such work? What methods, and with what success, does he employ when he is trying to convert the great mass of storekeepers, lawyers, realtors, morticians, policemen and artisans who surround him in his own city?

One thing at least is sure. If the real theologians had tackled this laborious work of translation about a hundred years ago, when they began to lose touch with the people (for whom Christ died), there would have been no place for me.[23]

[22] under the figure of vile bodies   [23] See Letter 11

Modern Theology and Biblical Criticism

This paper arose out of a conversation I had with the Principal[1] one night last term. A book of Alec Vidler's happened to be lying on the table and I expressed my reaction to the sort of theology it contained. My reaction was a hasty and ignorant one, produced with the freedom that comes after dinner.[2] One thing led to another and before we were done I was saying a good deal more than I had meant about the type of thought which, so far as I could gather, is now dominant in many theological colleges. He then said, 'I wish you would come and say all this to my young men.' He knew of course that I was extremely ignorant of the whole thing. But I think his idea was that you ought to know how a certain sort of theology strikes the outsider. Though I may have nothing but misunderstandings to lay before you, you ought to know that such misunderstand-

---

[1]The Principal of Westcott House, Cambridge, now the Bishop of Edinburgh (The Rt Rev Kenneth Carey).

[2]While the Bishop was out of the room, Lewis read 'The Sign at Cana' in Alec Vidler's *Windsor Sermons* (S.C.M. Press, 1958). The Bishop recalls that when he asked him what he thought about it, Lewis 'expressed himself very freely about the sermon and said that he thought that it was quite incredible that we should have had to wait nearly 2,000 years to be told by a theologian called Vidler that what the Church has always regarded as a miracle was, in fact, a parable!'

349

ings exist. That sort of thing is easy to overlook inside one's own circle. The minds you daily meet have been conditioned by the same studies and prevalent opinions as your own. That may mislead you. For of course as priests it is the outsiders you will have to cope with. You exist in the long run for no other purpose. The proper study of shepherds is sheep, not (save accidentally) other shepherds. And woe to you if you do not evangelize. I am not trying to teach my grandmother. I am a sheep, telling shepherds what only a sheep can tell them. And now I start my bleating.

There are two sorts of outsiders: the uneducated, and those who are educated in some way but not in your way. How you are to deal with the first class, if you hold views like Loisy's or Schweitzer's or Bultmann's or Tillich's or even Alec Vidler's, I simply don't know. I see—and I'm told that you see—that it would hardly do to tell them what you really believe. A theology which denies the historicity of nearly everything in the Gospels to which Christian life and affections and thought have been fastened for nearly two millennia—which either denies the miraculous altogether or, more strangely, after swallowing the camel of the Resurrection strains at such gnats as the feeding of the multitudes—if offered to the uneducated man can produce only one or other of two effects. It will make him a Roman Catholic or an atheist. What you offer him he will not recognize as Christianity. If he holds to what he calls Christianity he will leave a Church in which it is no longer taught and look for one where it is. If he agrees with your version he will no longer call himself a Christian and no longer come to church. In his crude, coarse way, he would respect you much more if you did the same. An experienced clergyman told me that most liberal priests, faced with this problem, have recalled from its grave the late medieval conception of two truths: a picture-truth which can be preached to the people, and an esoteric truth for use among the clergy. I shouldn't think you will enjoy this conception much when you have to put it into practice. I'm sure if I had to produce picture-truths to a parishioner in great anguish or under fierce temptation, and produce them with that seriousness and fervour which his condition demanded, while knowing all the time that I didn't exactly—only in some Pickwickian sense—believe them myself, I'd find my forehead getting red and damp and my collar getting tight. But that is your headache, not mine. You have, after all, a different sort of collar. I claim to belong to the second group of outsiders: educated, but not theologically educated. How one member of that group feels I must now try to tell you.

The undermining of the old orthodoxy has been mainly the work of divines engaged in New Testament criticism. The authority of experts in that discipline is the authority in deference to whom we are asked to give up a huge mass of beliefs shared in common by the early Church, the Fathers, the Middle Ages, the Reformers, and even the nineteenth century. I want to explain what it is that makes me sceptical about this authority. Ignorantly sceptical, as you will all too easily see. But the scepticism is the father of the ignorance. It is hard to persevere in a close study when you can work up no *prima facie* confidence in your teachers.

First then, whatever these men may be as Biblical critics, I distrust them as critics. They seem to me to lack literary judgement, to be imperceptive about the very quality of the texts they are reading. It sounds a strange charge to bring against men who have been steeped in those books all their lives. But that might be just the trouble. A man who has spent his youth and manhood in the minute study of New Testament texts and of other people's studies of them, whose literary experiences of those texts lacks any standard of comparison such as can only grow from a wide and deep and genial experience of literature in general, is, I should think, very likely to miss the obvious things about them. If he tells me that something in a Gospel is legend or romance, I want to know how many legends and romances he has read, how well his palate is trained in detecting them by the flavour; not how many years he has spent on that Gospel. But I had better turn to examples.

In what is already a very old commentary I read that the Fourth Gospel is regarded by one school as a 'spiritual romance', 'a poem not a history', to be judged by the same canons as Nathan's parable, the Book of Jonah, *Paradise Lost* 'or, more exactly, *Pilgrim's Progress*'.[3] After a man has said that, why need one attend to anything else he says about any book in the world? Note that he regards *Pilgrim's Progress*, a story which professes to be a dream and flaunts its allegorical nature by every single proper name it uses, as the closest parallel. Note that the whole epic panoply of Milton goes for nothing. But even if we leave out the grosser absurdities and keep to *Jonah*, the insensitiveness is crass—*Jonah*, a tale with as few even pretended historical attachments as *Job*, grotesque in incident and surely not without a distinct, though of course edifying, vein of typically Jewish humour. Then turn to John. Read the dialogues: that with the Samaritan woman at the well, or that which follows the healing of the man born blind. Look at its pictures: Jesus (if I may use the word) doodling with his finger in the dust; the unforgettable ἦν δὲ νύξ (xiii, 30). I have been reading poems, romances, vision-literature, legends, myths all my life. I know what they are like. I know that not one of them is like this. Of this text there are only two possible views. Either this is reportage—though it may no doubt contain errors—pretty close up to the facts; nearly as close as Boswell. Or else, some unknown writer in the second century, without known predecessors or successors, suddenly anticipated the whole technique of modern, novelistic, realistic narrative. If it is untrue, it must be narrative of that kind. The reader who doesn't see this has simply not learned to read. I would recommend him to read Auerbach.[4]

Here, from Bultmann's *Theology of the New Testament* (p. 30) is another: 'Observe in what unassimilated fashion the prediction of the parousia (Mk. viii,

---

[3]Lewis is quoting from an article, 'The Gospel According to St. John', by Walter Lock in *A New Commentary on Holy Scripture, including the Apocrypha*, ed. by Charles Gore, Henry Leighton Goudge, Alfred Guillaume (S.P.C.K., 1928), p. 241. Lock, in turn, is quoting from James Drummond's *An Inquiry into the Character and Authorship of the Fourth Gospel* (Williams and Norgate, 1903).

[4]Lewis means, I think, Erich Auerbach's *Mimesis: The Representation of Reality in Western Literature*, translated by Williard R. Trask (Princeton, 1953).

38) follows upon the prediction of the passion (viii, 31).'[5] What can he mean? Unassimilated? Bultmann believes that predictions of the parousia are older than those of the passion. He therefore wants to believe—and no doubt does believe— that when they occur in the same passage some discrepancy or 'unassimilation' must be perceptible between them. But surely he foists this on the text with shocking lack of perception. Peter has confessed Jesus to be the Anointed One. That flash of glory is hardly over before the dark prophecy begins—that the Son of Man must suffer and die. Then this contrast is repeated. Peter, raised for a moment by his confession, makes his false step; the crushing rebuff 'Get thee behind me' follows. Then, across that momentary ruin which Peter (as so often) becomes, the voice of the Master, turning to the crowd, generalizes the moral. All His followers must take up the cross. This avoidance of suffering, this self-preservation, is not what life is really about. Then, more definitely still, the summons to martyrdom. You must stand to your tackling. If you disown Christ here and now, He will disown you later. Logically, emotionally, imaginatively, the sequence is perfect. Only a Bultmann could think otherwise.

Finally, from the same Bultmann: 'The personality of Jesus has no importance for the kerygma either of Paul or of John . . . Indeed the tradition of the earliest Church did not even unconsciously preserve a picture of his personality. Every attempt to reconstruct one remains a play of subjective imagination.'[6]

So there is no personality of Our Lord presented in the New Testament. Through what strange process has this learned German gone in order to make himself blind to what all men except him see? What evidence have we that he would recognize a personality if it were there? For it is Bultmann *contra mundum*. If anything whatever is common to all believers, and even to many unbelievers, it is the sense that in the Gospels they have met a personality. There are characters whom we know to be historical but of whom we do not feel that we have any personal knowledge—knowledge by acquaintance; such as Alexander, Attila, or William of Orange. There are others who make no claim to historical reality but whom, none the less, we know as we know real people: Falstaff, Uncle Toby, Mr Pickwick. But there are only three characters who, claiming the first sort of reality, also actually have the second. And surely everyone knows who they are: Plato's Socrates, the Jesus of the Gospels, and Boswell's Johnson. Our acquaintance with them shows itself in a dozen ways. When we look into the Apocryphal gospels, we find ourselves constantly saying of this or that *logion*, 'No. It's a fine saying, but not His. That wasn't how He talked.'—just as we do with all pseudo-Johnsoniana. We are not in the least perturbed by the contrasts within each character: the union in Socrates of silly and scabrous titters about Greek pederasty with the highest mystical fervour and the homeliest good sense; in Johnson, of profound gravity and melancholy with that love of fun and

---

[5]Rudolf Bultmann, *Theology of the New Testament,* translated by Kendrick Grobel, vol. I (S.C.M. Press, 1952), p. 30.

[6]*Op. cit.,* p. 35.

nonsense which Boswell never understood though Fanny Burney did; in Jesus of peasant shrewdness, intolerable severity, and irresistible tenderness. So strong is the flavour of the personality that, even while He says things which, on any other assumption than that of Divine Incarnation in the fullest sense, would be appallingly arrogant, yet we—and many unbelievers too—accept Him at His own valuation when He says 'I am meek and lowly of heart.' Even those passages in the New Testament which superficially, and in intention, are most concerned with the Divine, and least with the Human Nature, bring us face to face with the personality. I am not sure that they don't do this more than any others. 'We beheld His glory, the glory as of the only begotten of the Father, full of graciousness and reality . . . which we have looked upon and our hands have handled.' What is gained by trying to evade or dissipate this shattering immediacy of personal contact by talk about 'that significance which the early church found that it was impelled to attribute to the Master'? This hits us in the face. Not what they were impelled to do but what impelled them. I begin to fear that by *personality* Dr Bultmann means what I should call impersonality: what you'd get in a D.N.B. article or an obituary or a Victorian *Life and Letters of Yeshua Bar-Yosef* in three volumes with photographs.

That then is my first bleat. These men ask me to believe they can read between the lines of the old texts; the evidence is their obvious inability to read (in any sense worth discussing) the lines themselves. They claim to see fern-seed and can't see an elephant ten yards away in broad daylight.

Now for my second bleat. All theology of the liberal type involves at some point—and often involves throughout—the claim that the real behaviour and purpose and teaching of Christ came very rapidly to be misunderstood and misrepresented by His followers, and has been recovered or exhumed only by modern scholars. Now long before I became interested in theology I had met this kind of theory elsewhere. The tradition of Jowett still dominated the study of ancient philosophy when I was reading Greats. One was brought up to believe that the real meaning of Plato had been misunderstood by Aristotle and wildly travestied by the neo-Platonists, only to be recovered by the moderns. When recovered, it turned out (most fortunately) that Plato had really all along been an English Hegelian, rather like T. H. Green. I have met it a third time in my own professional studies; every week a clever undergraduate, every quarter a dull American don, discovers for the first time what some Shakesperian play really meant. But in this third instance I am a privileged person. The revolution in thought and sentiment which has occurred in my own lifetime is so great that I belong, mentally, to Shakespeare's world far more than to that of these recent interpreters. I see—I feel it in my bones—I know beyond argument—that most of their interpretations are merely impossible; they involve a way of looking at things which was not known in 1914, much less in the Jacobean period. This daily confirms my suspicion of the same approach to Plato or the New Testament. The idea that any man or writer should be opaque to those who lived in the same culture, spoke the same language, shared the same habitual imagery and unconscious assumptions, and yet be transparent to those who have none of these advantages, is in my opinion preposterous. There is an *a priori* improbability in it which almost no argument and no evidence could counterbalance.

Thirdly, I find in these theologians a constant use of the principle that the miraculous does not occur. Thus any statement put into Our Lord's mouth by the old texts, which, if He had really made it, would constitute a prediction of the future, is taken to have been put in after the occurrence which it seemed to predict. This is very sensible if we start by knowing that inspired prediction can never occur. Similarly in general, the rejection as unhistorical of all passages which narrate miracles is sensible if we start by knowing that the miraculous in general never occurs. Now I do not here want to discuss whether the miraculous is possible. I only want to point out that this is a purely philosophical question. Scholars, as scholars, speak on it with no more authority than anyone else. The canon 'If miraculous, unhistorical' is one they bring to their study of the texts, not one they have learned from it. If one is speaking of authority, the united authority of all the Biblical critics in the world counts here for nothing. On this they speak simply as men; men obviously influenced by, and perhaps insufficiently critical of, the spirit of the age they grew up in.

But my fourth bleat—which is also my loudest and longest—is still to come.

All this sort of criticism attempts to reconstruct the genesis of the texts it studies; what vanished documents each author used, when and where he wrote, with what purposes, under what influences—the whole *Sitz im Leben* of the text. This is done with immense erudition and great ingenuity. And at first sight it is very convincing. I think I should be convinced by it myself, but that I carry about with me a charm—the herb *moly*—against it. You must excuse me if I now speak for a while of myself. The value of what I say depends on its being first-hand evidence.

What forearms me against all these Reconstructions is the fact that I have seen it all from the other end of the stick. I have watched reviewers reconstructing the genesis of my own books in just this way.

Until you come to be reviewed yourself you would never believe how little of an ordinary review is taken up by criticism in the strict sense: by evaluation, praise, or censure, of the book actually written. Most of it is taken up with imaginary histories of the process by which you wrote it. The very terms which the reviewers use in praising or dispraising often imply such a history. They praise a passage as 'spontaneous' and censure another as 'laboured'; that is, they think they know that you wrote the one *currente calamo* and the other *invita Minerva*.

What the value of such reconstructions is I learned very early in my career. I had published a book of essays; and the one into which I had put most of my heart, the one I really cared about and in which I discharged a keen enthusiasm, was on William Morris.[7] And in almost the first review I was told that this was obviously the only one in the book in which I had felt no interest. Now don't

[7]Lewis's essay on 'William Morris' appears in *Rehabilitations and Other Essays* (Oxford, 1939).

mistake. The critic was, I now believe, quite right in thinking it the worst essay in the book; at least everyone agreed with him. Where he was totally wrong was in his imaginary history of the causes which produced its dullness.

Well, this made me prick up my ears. Since then I have watched with some care similar imaginary histories both of my own books and of books by friends whose real history I knew. Reviewers, both friendly and hostile, will dash you off such histories with great confidence; will tell you what public events had directed the author's mind to this or that, what other authors had influenced him, what his over-all intention was, what sort of audience he principally addressed, why—and when—he did everything.

Now I must first record my impression; then, distinct from it, what I can say with certainty. My impression is that in the whole of my experience not one of these guesses has on any one point been right; that the method shows a record of 100 per cent. failure. You would expect that by mere chance they would hit as often as they miss. But it is my impression that they do no such thing. I can't remember a single hit. But as I have not kept a careful record my mere impression may be mistaken. What I think I can say with certainty is that they are usually wrong.

And yet they would often sound—if you didn't know the truth—extremely convincing. Many reviewers said that the Ring in Tolkien's *The Lord of the Rings* was suggested by the atom bomb. What could be more plausible? Here is a book published when everyone was preoccupied by that sinister invention; here in the centre of the book is a weapon which it seems madness to throw away yet fatal to use. Yet in fact, the chronology of the book's composition makes the theory impossible. Only the other week a reviewer said that a fairy tale by my friend Roger Lancelyn Green was influenced by fairy tales of mine. Nothing could be more probable. I have an imaginary country with a beneficent lion in it: Green, one with a beneficent tiger. Green and I can be proved to read one another's works; to be indeed in various ways closely associated. The case for an affiliation is far stronger than many which we accept as conclusive when dead authors are concerned. But it's all untrue nevertheless. I know the genesis of that Tiger and that Lion and they are quite independent.[8]

Now this surely ought to give us pause. The reconstruction of the history of a text, when the text is ancient, sounds very convincing. But one is after all sailing by dead reckoning; the results cannot be checked by fact. In order to decide how

---

[8]Lewis corrected this error in the following letter, 'Books for Children', in *The Times Literary Supplement* (28 November 1958), p. 689: 'Sir,—A review of Mr R. L. Green's *Land of the Lord High Tiger* in your issue of 21 November spoke of myself (in passing) with so much kindness that I am reluctant to cavil at anything it contained: but in justice to Mr Green I must. The critic suggested that Mr Green's Tiger owed something to my fairy-tales. In reality this is not so and is chronologically impossible. The Tiger was an old inhabitant, and his land a familiar haunt, of Mr Green's imagination long before I began writing. There is a moral here for all of us as critics. I wonder how much *Quellenforschung* in our studies of older literature seems solid only because those who knew the facts are dead and cannot contradict it?'

reliable the method is, what more could you ask for than to be shown an instance where the same method is at work and we have facts to check it by? Well, that is what I have done. And we find, that when this check is available, the results are either always, or else nearly always, wrong. The 'assured results of modern scholarship', as to the way in which an old book was written, are 'assured', we may conclude, only because the men who knew the facts are dead and can't blow the gaff. The huge essays in my own field which reconstruct the history of *Piers Plowman* or *The Faerie Queene* are most unlikely to be anything but sheer illusions.[9]

Am I then venturing to compare every whipster who writes a review in a modern weekly with these great scholars who have devoted their whole lives to the detailed study of the New Testament? If the former are always wrong, does it follow that the latter must fare no better?

There are two answers to this, First, while I respect the learning of the great Biblical critics, I am not yet persuaded that their judgement is equally to be respected. But, secondly, consider with what overwhelming advantages the mere reviewers start. They reconstruct the history of a book written by someone whose mother-tongue is the same as theirs; a contemporary, educated like themselves, living in something like the same mental and spiritual climate. They have every-thing to help them. The superiority in judgement and diligence which you are going to attribute to the Biblical critics will have to be almost superhuman if it is to offset the fact that they are everywhere faced with customs, language, race-characteristics, class-characteristics, a religious background, habits of compo-sition, and basic assumptions, which no scholarship will ever enable any man now alive to know as surely and intimately and instinctively as the reviewer can know mine. And for the very same reason, remember, the Biblical critics, whatever reconstructions they devise, can never be crudely proved wrong. St Mark is dead. When they meet St Peter there will be more pressing matters to discuss.

You may say, of course, that such reviewers are foolish in so far as they guess how a sort of book they never wrote themselves was written by another. They assume that you wrote a story as they would try to write a story; the fact that they would so try, explains why they have not produced any stories. But are the Biblical critics in this way much better off? Dr Bultmann never wrote a gospel. Has the experience of his learned, specialized, and no doubt meritorious, life really given him any power of seeing into the minds of those long dead men who were caught up into what, on any view, must be regarded as the central religious experience of the whole human race? It is no incivility to say—he himself would admit—that he must in every way be divided from the evangelists by far more formidable barriers—spiritual as well as intellectual—than any that could exist between my reviewers and me.

[9]For a fuller treatment on book-reviewing, see Lewis's essay 'On Criticism' in his *Of Other Worlds: Essays and Stories,* ed. Walter Hooper, (Bles, 1966), pp. 43–58.

My picture of one layman's reaction—and I think it is not a rare one—would be incomplete without some account of the hopes he secretly cherishes and the naïve reflections with which he sometimes keeps his spirits up.

You must face the fact he does not expect the present school of theological thought to be everlasting. He thinks, perhaps wishfully thinks, that the whole thing may blow over. I have learned in other fields of study how transitory the 'assured results of modern scholarship' may be, how soon scholarship ceases to be modern. The confident treatment to which the New Testament is subjected is no longer applied to profane texts. There used to be English scholars who were prepared to cut up *Henry VI* between half a dozen authors and assign his share to each. We don't do that now. When I was a boy one would have been laughed at for supposing there had been a real Homer: the disintegrators seemed to have triumphed forever. But Homer seems to be creeping back. Even the belief of the ancient Greeks that the Mycenaeans were their ancestors and spoke Greek has been surprisingly supported. We may without disgrace believe in a historical Arthur. Everywhere, except in theology, there has been a vigorous growth of scepticism about scepticism itself. We can't keep ourselves from murmuring *multa renascentur quae jam cecidere.*

Nor can a man of my age ever forget how suddenly and completely the idealist philosophy of his youth fell. McTaggart, Green, Bosanquet, Bradley seemed enthroned forever; they went down as suddenly as the Bastille. And the interesting thing is that while I lived under that dynasty I felt various difficulties and objections which I never dared to express. They were so frightfully obvious that I felt sure they must be mere misunderstandings: the great men could not have made such very elementary mistakes as those which my objections implied. But very similar objections—though put, no doubt, far more cogently than I could have put them—were among the criticisms which finally prevailed. They would now be the stock answers to English Hegelianism. If anyone present tonight has felt the same shy and tentative doubts about the great Biblical critics, perhaps he need not feel quite certain that they are only his stupidity. They may have a future he little dreams of.

We derive a little comfort, too, from our mathematical colleagues. When a critic reconstructs the genesis of a text he usually has to use what may be called linked hypotheses. Thus Bultmann says that Peter's confession is 'an Easter-story projected backward into Jesus' life-time' (p. 26, *op. cit.*). The first hypothesis is that Peter made no such confession. Then, granting that, there is a second hypothesis as to how the false story of his having done so might have grown up. Now let us suppose—what I am far from granting—that the first hypothesis has a probability of 90 per cent. Let us assume that the second hypothesis also has a probability of 90 per cent. But the two together don't still have 90 per cent; for the second comes in only on the assumption of the first. You have not A plus B; you have a complex AB. And the mathematicians tell me that AB has only an 81 per cent. probability. I'm not good enough at arithmetic to work it out, but you see that if, in a complex reconstruction, you go on thus superinducing hypothesis on hypothesis, you will in the end get a complex in which, though each hypothesis by itself has in a sense a high probability, the whole has almost none.

You must not, however, paint the picture too black. We are not fundamentalists. We think that different elements in this sort of theology have different degrees of strength. The nearer it sticks to mere textual criticism, of the old sort, Lachmann's sort, the more we are disposed to believe in it. And of course we agree that passages almost verbally identical cannot be independent. It is as we glide away from this into reconstructions of a subtler and more ambitious kind that our faith in the method wavers; and our faith in Christianity is proportionately corroborated. The sort of statement that arouses our deepest scepticism is the statement that something in a Gospel cannot be historical because it shows a theology or an ecclesiology too developed for so early a date. For this implies that we know, first of all, that there was any development in the matter, and secondly, how quickly it proceeded. It even implies an extraordinary homogeneity and continuity of development: implicitly denies that anyone could greatly have anticipated anyone else. This seems to involve knowing about a number of long dead people—for the early Christians were, after all, people—things of which I believe few of us could have given an accurate account if we had lived among them; all the forward and backward surge of discussion, preaching, and individual religious experience. I could not speak with similar confidence about the circle I have chiefly lived in myself. I could not describe the history even of my own thought as confidently as these men describe the history of the early Church's mind. And I am perfectly certain no one else could. Suppose a future scholar knew that I abandoned Christianity in my teens, and that, also in my teens, I went to an atheist tutor. Would not this seem far better evidence than most of what we have about the development of Christian theology in the first two centuries? Would he not conclude that my apostasy was due to the tutor? And then reject as 'backward projection' any story which represented me as an atheist before I went to that tutor? Yet he would be wrong. I am sorry to have become once more autobiographical. But reflection on the extreme improbability of his own life—by historical standards—seems to me a profitable exercise for everyone. It encourages a due agnosticism.

For agnosticism is, in a sense, what I am preaching. I do not wish to reduce the sceptical element in your minds. I am only suggesting that it need not be reserved exclusively for the New Testament and the Creeds. Try doubting something else.

Such scepticism might, I think, begin at the very beginning with the thought which underlies the whole demythology of our time. It was put long ago by Tyrrell. As man progresses he revolts against 'earlier and inadequate expressions of the religious idea . . . Taken literally, and not symbolically, they do not meet his need. And as long as he demands to picture to himself distinctly the term and satisfaction of that need he is doomed to doubt, for his picturings will necessarily be drawn from the world of his present experience.'[10]

In one way of course Tyrrell was saying nothing new. The Negative Theology of Pseudo-Dionysius had said as much, but it drew no such conclusions as Tyrrell. Perhaps this is because the older tradition found our conceptions inadequate to God whereas Tyrrell finds it inadequate to 'the religious idea'. He doesn't say whose idea. But I am afraid he means Man's idea. We, being men, know what we think: and we find the doctrines of the Resurrection, the Ascension, and the Second Coming inadequate to our thoughts. But supposing these things were the expressions of God's thought?

It might still be true that 'taken literally and not symbolically' they are inadequate. From which the conclusion commonly drawn is that they must be taken symbolically, not literally; that is, wholly symbolically. All the details are equally symbolical and analogical.

But surely there is a flaw here. The argument runs like this. All the details are derived from our present experience; but the reality transcends our experience: therefore all the details are wholly and equally symbolical. But suppose a dog were trying to form a conception of human life. All the details in its picture would be derived from canine experience. Therefore all that the dog imagined could, at best, be only analogically true of human life. The conclusion is false. If the dog visualized our scientific researches in terms of ratting, this would be analogical; but if it thought that eating could be predicated of humans only in an analogical sense, the dog would be wrong. In fact if a dog could, *per impossibile*, be plunged for a day into human life, it would be hardly more surprised by hitherto unimagined differences than by hitherto unsuspected similarities. A reverent dog would be shocked. A modernist dog, distrusting the whole experience, would ask to be taken to the vet.

But the dog can't get into human life. Consequently, though it can be sure that its best ideas of human life are full of analogy and symbol, it could never point to any one detail and say, 'This is entirely symbolic.' You cannot know that everything in the representation of a thing is symbolical unless you have independent access to the thing and can compare it with the representation. Dr Tyrrell can tell that the story of the Ascension is inadequate to his religious idea, because he knows his own idea and can compare it with the story. But how if we are asking about a transcendent, objective reality to which the story is our sole access? 'We know not—oh we know not.' But then we must take our ignorance seriously.

Of course if 'taken literally and not symbolically' means 'taken in terms of mere physics', then this story is not even a religious story. Motion away from the earth—which is what Ascension physically means—would not in itself be an event of spiritual significance. Therefore, you argue, the spiritual reality can have

[10]George Tyrrell, 'The Apocalyptic Vision of Christ' in *Christianity at the Cross-Roads* (Longmans, Green & Co., 1909), p. 125.

nothing but an analogical connection with the story of an ascent. For the union of God with God and of Man with God-man can have nothing to do with space. Who told you this? What you really mean is that we can't see how it could possibly have anything to do with it. That is a quite different proposition. When I know as I am known I shall be able to tell which parts of the story were purely symbolical and which, if any, were not; shall see how the transcendent reality either excludes and repels locality, or how unimaginably it assimilates and loads it with significance. Had we not better wait?

Such are the reactions of one bleating layman to Modern Theology. It is right you should hear them. You will not perhaps hear them very often again. Your parishioners will not often speak to you quite frankly. Once the layman was anxious to hide the fact that he believed so much less than the Vicar: he now tends to hide the fact that he believes so much more. Missionary to the priests of one's own church is an embarrassing rôle; though I have a horrid feeling that if such mission work is not soon undertaken the future history of the Church of England is likely to be short.

FROM

The Weight of Glory
and Other Addresses

The Weight of Glory

Preached originally as a sermon in the
Church of St. Mary the Virgin, Oxford,
on June 8, 1941: published in
THEOLOGY, *November, 1941,*
and by the S.P.C.K.,
1942

IF you asked twenty good men to-day what they thought the highest of the virtues, nineteen of them would reply, Unselfishness. But if you asked almost any of the great Christians of old he would have replied, Love. You see what has happened? A negative term has been substituted for a positive, and this is of more than philological importance. The negative ideal of Unselfishness carries with it the suggestion not primarily of securing good things for others, but of going without them ourselves, as if our abstinence and not their happiness was the important point. I do not think this is the Christian virtue of Love. The New Testament has lots to say about self-denial, but not about self-denial as an end in itself. We are told to deny ourselves and to take up our crosses in order that we may follow Christ; and nearly every description of what we shall ultimately find if we do so contains an appeal to desire. If there lurks in most modern minds the notion that to desire our own good and earnestly to hope for the enjoyment of it is a bad thing, I submit that this notion has crept in from Kant and the Stoics and is no part of the Christian faith. Indeed, if we consider the unblushing promises of reward and the staggering nature of the rewards promised in the Gospels, it would seem that Our Lord finds our desires, not too strong, but too weak. We are half-hearted creatures, fooling about with drink and sex and ambition when infinite joy is offered us, like an ignorant child who wants to go on making mud pies in a slum because he cannot imagine what is meant by the offer of a holiday at the sea. We are far too easily pleased.

We must not be troubled by unbelievers when they say that this promise of reward makes the Christian life a mercenary affair. There are different kinds of reward. There is the reward which has no *natural connexion* with the things you do to earn it, and is quite foreign to the desires that ought to accompany those things. Money is not the natural reward of love; that is why we call a man mercenary if he marries a woman for the sake of her money. But marriage is the proper reward for a real lover, and he is not mercenary for desiring it. A general who fights well in order to get a peerage is mercenary; a general who fights for victory is not, victory being the proper reward of battle as marriage is the proper reward of love. The proper rewards are not simply tacked on to the activity for which they are given, but are the activity itself in consummation. There is also a third case, which is more complicated. An enjoyment of Greek poetry is certainly a proper, and not a mercenary, reward for learning Greek; but only those who have reached the stage of enjoying Greek poetry can tell from their own experience that this is so. The schoolboy beginning Greek grammar cannot look forward to his adult enjoyment of Sophocles as a lover looks forward to marriage or a general to victory. He has to begin by working for marks, or to escape punishment, or to please his parents, or, at best, in the hope of a future good which he cannot at present imagine or desire. His position, therefore, bears a certain resemblance to that of the mercenary; the reward he is going to get will, in actual fact, be a natural or proper reward, but he will not know that till he has got it. Of course, he gets it gradually; enjoyment creeps in upon the mere drudgery, and nobody could point to a day or an hour when the one ceased and the other began. But it is just in so far as he approaches the reward that he becomes able to desire it for its own sake; indeed, the power of so desiring it is itself a preliminary reward.

The Christian, in relation to heaven, is in much the same position as this schoolboy. Those who have attained everlasting life in the vision of God doubtless know very well that it is no mere bribe, but the very consummation of their earthly discipleship; but we who have not yet attained it cannot know this in the same way, and cannot even begin to know it at all except by continuing to obey and finding the first reward of our obedience in our increasing power to desire the ultimate reward. Just in proportion as the desire grows, our fear lest it should be a mercenary desire will die away and finally be recognized as an absurdity. But probably this will not, for most of us, happen in a day; poetry replaces grammar, gospel replaces law, longing transforms obedience, as gradually as the tide lifts a grounded ship.

But there is one other important similarity between the schoolboy and ourselves. If he is an imaginative boy he will, quite probably, be revelling in the English poets and romancers suitable to his age some time before he begins to suspect that Greek grammar is going to lead him to more and more enjoyments of this same sort. He may even be neglecting his Greek to read Shelley and Swinburne in secret. In other words, the desire which Greek is really going to gratify already exists in him and is attached to objects which seem to him quite unconnected with Xenophon and the verbs in μι. Now, if we are made for heaven, the desire for our proper place will be already in us, but not yet attached to the true object, and will even appear as the rival of that object. And this, I think, is just what we find. No doubt there is one point in which my analogy of the schoolboy breaks down. The English poetry which he reads when he ought to be doing Greek exercises may be just as good as the Greek poetry to which the exercises are leading him, so that in fixing on Milton instead of journeying on to Aeschylus his desire is not embracing a false object. But our case is very different. If a transtemporal, transfinite good is our real destiny, then any other good on which our desire fixes must be in some degree fallacious, must bear at best only a symbolical relation to what will truly satisfy.

In speaking of this desire for our own far-off country, which we find in ourselves even now, I feel a certain shyness. I am almost committing an indecency. I am trying to rip open the inconsolable secret in each one of you—the secret which hurts so much that you take your revenge on it by calling it names like Nostalgia and Romanticism and Adolescence; the secret also which pierces with such sweetness that when, in very intimate conversation, the mention of it becomes imminent, we grow awkward and affect to laugh at ourselves; the secret we cannot hide and cannot tell, though we desire to do both. We cannot tell it because it is a desire for something that has never actually appeared in our experience. We cannot hide it because our experience is constantly suggesting it, and we betray ourselves like lovers at the mention of a name. Our commonest expedient is to call it beauty and behave as if that had settled the matter. Wordsworth's expedient was to identify it with certain moments in his own past. But all this is a cheat. If Wordsworth had gone back to those moments in the past, he would not have found the thing itself, but only the reminder of it; what he remembered would turn out to be itself a remembering. The books or the music in which we thought the beauty was located will betray us if we trust to them; it was not *in* them, it only came *through* them, and what came through them was longing. These things—the beauty, the memory of our own past—are good images of what we really desire; but if they are mistaken for the thing itself they turn into dumb idols, breaking the hearts of their worshippers. For they are not the thing itself; they are only the scent of a flower we have not found, the echo of a tune we have not heard, news from a country we have never yet visited. Do you think I am trying to weave a spell? Perhaps I am; but remember your fairy tales. Spells are used for breaking enchantments as well as for inducing them. And you and I have need of the strongest spell that can be found to wake us from the evil enchantment of worldliness which has been laid upon us for nearly a hundred years. Almost our whole education has been directed to silencing this shy, persistent, inner voice; almost all our modern philosophies have been devised to convince us that the good of man is to be found on this earth. And yet it is a remarkable thing that such philosophies of Progress or Creative Evolution themselves bear reluctant witness to the truth that our real goal is elsewhere. When they want to convince you that earth is your home, notice how they set about it. They begin by trying to persuade you that earth can be made into heaven, thus giving a sop to your sense of exile in earth as it is. Next, they tell you that this fortunate event is still a good way off in the future, thus giving a sop to your knowledge that the fatherland is not here and now. Finally, lest your longing for the transtemporal should awake and spoil the whole affair, they use any rhetoric that comes to hand to keep out of your mind the recollection that even if all the happiness they promised could come to man on earth, yet still each generation would lose it by death, including the last generation of all, and the whole story would be nothing, not even a story, for ever and ever. Hence all the nonsense that Mr. Shaw puts into the final speech of Lilith, and Bergson's remark that the *élan vital* is capable of surmounting all obstacles, perhaps even death—as if we could believe that any social or biological development on this planet will delay the senility of the sun or reverse the second law of thermodynamics.

Do what they will, then, we remain conscious of a desire which no natural happiness will satisfy. But is there any reason to suppose that reality offers any satisfaction to it? "Nor does the being hungry prove that we have bread." But I think it may be urged that this misses the point. A man's physical hunger does not prove that that man will get any bread; he may die of starvation on a raft in the Atlantic. But surely a man's hunger does prove that he comes of a race which repairs its body by eating and inhabits a world where eatable substances exist. In the same way, though I do not believe (I wish I did) that my desire for Paradise proves that I shall enjoy it, I think it a pretty good indication that such a thing exists and that some men will. A man may love a woman and not win her; but it would be very odd if the phenomenon called "falling in love" occurred in a sexless world.

Here, then, is the desire, still wandering and uncertain of its object and still largely unable to see that object in the direction where it really lies. Our sacred books give us some account of the object. It is, of course, a symbolical account. Heaven is, by definition, outside our experience, but all intelligible descriptions must be of things within our experience. The scriptural picture of heaven is therefore just as symbolical as the picture which our desire, unaided, invents for itself; heaven is not really full of jewelry any more than it is really the beauty of Nature, or a fine piece of music. The difference is that the scriptural imagery has authority. It comes to us from writers who were closer to God than we, and it has stood the test of Christian experience down the centuries. The natural appeal of this authoritative imagery is to me, at first, very small. At first sight it chills, rather than awakes, my desire. And that is just what I ought to expect. If Christianity could tell me no more of the far-off land than my own temperament led me to surmise already, then Christianity would be no higher than myself. If it has more to give me, I must expect it to be less immediately attractive than "my own stuff". Sophocles at first seems dull and cold to the boy who has only reached Shelley. If our religion is something objective, then we must never avert our eyes from those elements in it which seem puzzling or repellent; for it will be precisely the puzzling or the repellent which conceals what we do not yet know and need to know.

The promises of Scripture may very roughly be reduced to five heads. It is promised, firstly, that we shall be with Christ; secondly, that we shall be like Him; thirdly, with an enormous wealth of imagery, that we shall have "glory"; fourthly, that we shall, in some sense, be fed or feasted or entertained; and, finally, that we shall have some sort of official position in the universe—ruling cities, judging angels, being pillars of God's temple. The first question I ask about these promises is: "Why any of them except the first?" Can anything be added to the conception of being with Christ? For it must be true, as an old writer says, that he who has God and everything else has no more than he who has God only. I think the answer turns again on the nature of symbols. For though it may escape our notice at first glance, yet it is true than any conception of being with Christ which most of us can now form will be not very much less symbolical than the other promises; for it will smuggle in ideas of proximity in space and loving conversation as we now understand conversation, and it will probably concentrate on the humanity of Christ to the exclusion of His deity. And, in fact, we find that those Christians who attend solely to this first promise always do fill it up with very earthly imagery indeed—in fact, with hymeneal or erotic imagery. I am not for a moment condemning such imagery. I heartily wish I could enter into it more deeply than I do, and pray that I yet shall. But my point is that this also is only a symbol, like the reality in some respects, but unlike it in others, and therefore needs correction from the different symbols in the other promises. The variation of the promises does not mean that anything other than God will be our ultimate bliss; but because God is more than a Person, and lest we should imagine the joy of His presence too exclusively in terms of our present poor experience of personal love, with all its narrowness and strain and monotony, a dozen changing images, correcting and relieving each other, are supplied.

I turn next to the idea of glory. There is no getting away from the fact that this idea is very prominent in the New Testament and in early Christian writings. Salvation is constantly associated with palms, crowns, white robes, thrones, and splendour like the sun and stars. All this makes no immediate appeal to me at all, and in that respect I fancy I am a typical modern. Glory suggests two ideas to me, of which one seems wicked and the other ridiculous. Either glory means to me fame, or it means luminosity. As for the first, since to be famous means to be better known than other people, the desire for fame appears to me as a competitive passion and therefore of hell rather than heaven. As for the second, who wishes to become a kind of living electric light bulb?

When I began to look into this matter I was shocked to find such different Christians as Milton, Johnson and Thomas Aquinas taking heavenly glory quite frankly in the sense of fame or good report. But not fame conferred by our fellow creatures—fame with God, approval or (I might say) "appreciation" by God. And then, when I had thought it over, I saw that this view was scriptural; nothing can eliminate from the parable the divine *accolade*, "Well done, thou good and faithful servant." With that, a good deal of what I had been thinking all my life fell down like a house of cards. I suddenly remembered that no one can enter heaven except as a child; and nothing is so obvious in a child—not in a conceited child, but in a good child—as its great and undisguised pleasure in being praised. Not only in a child, either, but even in a dog or a horse. Apparently what I had mistaken for humility had, all these years, prevented me from understanding what is in fact the humblest, the most childlike, the most creaturely of pleasures—nay, the specific pleasure of the inferior: the pleasure of a beast before men, a child before its father, a pupil before his teacher, a creature before its Creator. I am not forgetting how horribly this most innocent desire is parodied in our human ambitions, or how very quickly, in my own experience, the lawful pleasure of praise from those whom it was my duty to please turns into the deadly poison of self-admiration. But I thought I could detect a moment—a very, very short moment—before this happened, during which the satisfaction of having pleased those whom I rightly loved and rightly feared was pure. And that is enough to raise our thoughts to what may happen when the redeemed soul, beyond all hope and nearly beyond belief, learns at last that she has pleased Him whom she was created to please. There will be no room for vanity then. She will be free from the miserable illusion that it is her doing. With no taint of what we should now call self-approval she will most innocently rejoice in the thing that God has made her to be, and the moment which heals her old inferiority complex for ever will also drown her pride deeper than Prospero's book. Perfect humility dispenses with modesty. If God is satisfied with the work, the work may be satisfied with itself; "it is not for her to bandy compliments with her Sovereign". I can imagine someone saying that he dislikes my idea of heaven as a place where we are patted on the back. But proud misunderstanding is behind that dislike. In the end that Face which is the delight or the terror of the universe must be turned upon each of us either with one expression or with the other, either conferring glory inexpressible or inflicting shame that can never be cured or disguised. I read in a periodical the other day that the fundamental thing is how we think of God. By God Himself, it is not! How God thinks of us is not only more important, but infinitely more important. Indeed, how we think of Him is of no importance except in so far as it is related to how He thinks of us. It is written that we shall "stand before" Him, shall appear, shall be inspected. The promise of glory is the promise, almost incredible and only possible by the work of Christ, that some of us, that any of us who really chooses, shall actually survive that examination, shall find approval, shall please God. To please God . . . to be a real ingredient in the divine happiness . . . to be loved by God, not merely pitied, but delighted in as an artist delights in his work or a father in a son—it seems impossible, a weight or burden of glory which our thoughts can hardly sustain. But so it is.

And now notice what is happening. If I had rejected the authoritative and scriptural image of glory and stuck obstinately to the vague desire which was, at the outset, my only pointer to heaven, I could have seen no connexion at all between that desire and the Christian promise. But now, having followed up what seemed puzzling and repellent in the sacred books, I find, to my great surprise, looking back, that the connexion is perfectly clear. Glory, as Christianity teaches me to hope for it, turns out to satisfy my original desire and indeed to reveal an element in that desire which I had not noticed. By ceasing for a moment to consider my own wants I have begun to learn better what I really wanted. When I attempted, a few minutes ago, to describe our spiritual longings, I was omitting one of their most curious characteristics. We usually notice it just as the moment of vision dies away, as the music ends or as the landscape loses the celestial light. What we feel then has been well described by Keats as "the journey homeward to habitual self". You know what I mean. For a few minutes we have had the illusion of belonging to that world. Now we wake to find that it is no such thing. We have been mere spectators. Beauty has smiled, but not to welcome us; her face was turned in our direction, but not to see us. We have not been accepted, welcomed, or taken into the dance. We may go when we please, we may stay if we can: "Nobody marks us." A scientist may reply that since most of the things we call beautiful are inanimate, it is not very surprising that they take no notice of us. That, of course, is true. It is not the physical objects that I am speaking of, but that indescribable something of which they become for a moment the messengers. And part of the bitterness which mixes with the sweetness of that message is due to the fact that it so seldom seems to be a message intended for us, but rather something we have overheard. By bitterness I mean pain, not resentment. We should hardly dare to ask that any notice be taken of ourselves. But we pine. The sense that in this universe we are treated as strangers, the longing to be acknowledged, to meet with some response, to bridge some chasm that yawns between us and reality, is part of our inconsolable secret. And surely, from this point of view, the promise of glory, in the sense described, becomes highly relevant to our deep desire. For glory meant good report with God, acceptance by God, response, acknowledgment, and welcome into the heart of things. The door on which we have been knocking all our lives will open at last.

Perhaps it seems rather crude to describe glory as the fact of being "noticed" by God. But this is almost the language of the New Testament. St. Paul promises to those who love God not, as we should expect, that they will know Him, but that they will be known by Him (I Cor. viii. 3). It is a strange promise. Does not God know all things at all times? But it is dreadfully re-echoed in another passage of the New Testament. There we are warned that it may happen to any one of us to appear at last before the face of God and hear only the appalling words:

"I never knew you. Depart from Me." In some sense, as dark to the intellect as it is unendurable to the feelings, we can be both banished from the presence of Him who is present everywhere and erased from the knowledge of Him who knows all. We can be left utterly and absolutely *outside*—repelled, exiled, estranged, finally and unspeakably ignored. On the other hand, we can be called in, welcomed, received, acknowledged. We walk every day on the razor edge between these two incredible possibilities. Apparently, then, our lifelong nostalgia, our longing to be reunited with something in the universe from which we now feel cut off, to be on the inside of some door which we have always seen from the outside, is no mere neurotic fancy, but the truest index of our real situation. And to be at last summoned inside would be both glory and honour beyond all our merits and also the healing of that old ache.

And this brings me to the other sense of glory—glory as brightness, splendour, luminosity. We are to shine as the sun, we are to be given the Morning Star. I think I begin to see what it means. In one way, of course, God has given us the Morning Star already: you can go and enjoy the gift on many fine mornings if you get up early enough. What more, you may ask, do we want? Ah, but we want so much more—something the books on aesthetics take little notice of. But the poets and the mythologies know all about it. We do not want merely to *see* beauty, though, God knows, even that is bounty enough. We want something else which can hardly be put into words—to be united with the beauty we see, to pass into it, to receive it into ourselves, to bathe in it, to become part of it. That is why we have peopled air and earth and water with gods and goddesses and nymphs and elves—that, though we cannot, yet these projections can, enjoy in themselves that beauty, grace, and power of which Nature is the image. That is why the poets tell us such lovely falsehoods. They talk as if the west wind could really sweep into a human soul; but it can't. They tell us that "beauty born of murmuring sound" will pass into a human face; but it won't. Or not yet. For if we take the imagery of Scripture seriously, if we believe that God will one day *give* us the Morning Star and cause us to *put on* the splendour of the sun, then we may surmise that both the ancient myths and the modern poetry, so false as history, may be very near the truth as prophecy. At present we are on the outside of the world, the wrong side of the door. We discern the freshness and purity of morning, but they do not make us fresh and pure. We cannot mingle with the splendours we see. But all the leaves of the New Testament are rustling with the rumour that it will not always be so. Some day, God willing, we shall get *in*. When human souls have become as perfect in voluntary obedience as the inanimate creation is in its lifeless obedience, then they will put on its glory, or rather that greater glory of which Nature is only the first sketch. For you must not think that I am putting forward any heathen fancy of being absorbed into Nature. Nature is mortal; we shall outlive her. When all the suns and nebulae have passed away, each one of you will still be alive. Nature is only the image, the symbol; but it is the symbol Scripture invites me to use. We are summoned to pass in through Nature, beyond her, into that splendour which she fitfully reflects.

And in there, in beyond Nature, we shall eat of the tree of life. At present, if we are reborn in Christ, the spirit in us lives directly on God; but the mind, and still more the body, receives life from Him at a thousand removes—through our ancestors, through our food, through the elements. The faint, far-off results of those energies which God's creative rapture implanted in matter when He made the worlds are what we now call physical pleasures; and even thus filtered, they are too much for our present management. What would it be to taste at the fountain-head that stream of which even these lower reaches prove so intoxicating? Yet that, I believe, is what lies before us. The whole man is to drink joy from the fountain of joy. As St. Augustine said, the rapture of the saved soul will "flow over" into the glorified body. In the light of our present specialized and depraved appetites we cannot imagine this *torrens voluptatis,* and I warn everyone most seriously not to try. But it must be mentioned, to drive out thoughts even more misleading—thoughts that what is saved is a mere ghost, or that the risen body lives in numb insensibility. The body was made for the Lord, and these dismal fancies are wide of the mark.

Meanwhile the cross comes before the crown and tomorrow is a Monday morning. A cleft has opened in the pitiless walls of the world, and we are invited to follow our great Captain inside. The following Him is, of course, the essential point. That being so, it may be asked what practical use there is in the speculations which I have been indulging. I can think of at least one such use. It may be possible for each to think too much of his own potential glory hereafter; it is hardly possible for him to think too often or too deeply about that of his neighbour. The load, or weight, or burden of my neighbour's glory should be laid daily on my back, a load so heavy that only humility can carry it, and the backs of the proud will be broken. It is a serious thing to live in a society of possible gods and goddesses, to remember that the dullest and most uninteresting person you talk to may one day be a creature which, if you saw it now, you would be strongly tempted to worship, or else a horror and a corruption such as you now meet, if at all, only in a nightmare. All day long we are, in some degree, helping each other to one or other of these destinations. It is in the light of these overwhelming possibilities, it is with the awe and the circumspection proper to them, that we should conduct all our dealings with one another, all friendships, all loves, all play, all politics. There are no *ordinary* people. You have never talked to a mere mortal. Nations, cultures, arts, civilization—these are mortal, and their life is to ours as the life of a gnat. But it is immortals whom we joke with, work with, marry, snub, and exploit—immortal horrors or everlasting splendours. This does not mean that we are to be perpetually solemn. We must play. But our merriment must be of that kind (and it is, in fact, the merriest kind) which exists between people who have, from the outset, taken each other seriously—no flippancy, no superiority, no presumption. And our charity must be a real and costly love, with deep feeling for the sins in spite of which we love the sinner—no mere tolerance or indulgence which parodies love as flippancy parodies merriment. Next to the Blessed Sacrament itself, your neighbour is the holiest object presented to your senses. If he is your Christian neighbour he is holy in almost the same way, for in him also Christ *vere latitat*—the glorifier and the glorified, Glory Himself, is truly hidden.

Learning in War-Time

*A sermon preached in the Church
of St. Mary the Virgin,
Oxford, Autumn,
1939*

A UNIVERSITY is a society for the pursuit of learning. As students, you will be expected to make yourselves, or to start making yourselves, into what the Middle Ages called clerks: into philosophers, scientists, scholars, critics, or historians. And at first sight this seems to be an odd thing to do during a great war. What is the use of beginning a task which we have so little chance of finishing? Or, even if we ourselves should happen not to be interrupted by death or military service, why should we—indeed how can we—continue to take an interest in these placid occupations when the lives of our friends and the liberties of Europe are in the balance? Is it not like fiddling while Rome burns?

Now it seems to me that we shall not be able to answer these questions until we have put them by the side of certain other questions which every Christian ought to have asked himself in peace-time. I spoke just now of fiddling while Rome burns. But to a Christian the true tragedy of Nero must be not that he fiddled while the city was on fire but that he fiddled on the brink of hell. You must forgive me for the crude monosyllable. I know that many wiser and better Christians than I in these days do not like to mention heaven and hell even in a pulpit. I know, too, that nearly all the references to this subject in the New Testament come from a single source. But then that source is Our Lord Himself. People will tell you it is St. Paul, but that is untrue. These overwhelming doctrines are dominical. They are not really removable from the teaching of Christ or of His Church. If we do not believe them, our presence in this church is great tomfoolery. If we do, we must sometime overcome our spiritual prudery and mention them.

The moment we do so we can see that every Christian who comes to a university must at all times face a question compared with which the questions raised by the war are relatively unimportant. He must ask himself how it is right, or even psychologically possible, for creatures who are every moment advancing either to heaven or to hell, to spend any fraction of the little time allowed them in this world on such comparative trivialities as literature or art, mathematics or biology. If human culture can stand up to that, it can stand up to anything. To admit that we can retain our interest in learning under the shadow of these eternal issues, but not under the shadow of a European war, would be to admit that our ears are closed to the voice of reason and very wide open to the voice of our nerves and our mass emotions.

This indeed is the case with most of us: certainly with me. For that reason I think it important to try to see the present calamity in a true perspective. The war creates no absolutely new situation: it simply aggravates the permanent human situation so that we can no longer ignore it. Human life has always been lived on the edge of a precipice. Human culture has always had to exist under the shadow of something infinitely more important than itself. If men had postponed the search for knowledge and beauty until they were secure, the search would never have begun. We are mistaken when we compare war with "normal life". Life has never been normal. Even those periods which we think most tranquil, like the nineteenth century, turn out, on closer inspection, to be full of crises, alarms, difficulties, emergencies. Plausible reasons have never been lacking for putting off all merely cultural activities until some imminent danger has been averted or some crying injustice put right. But humanity long ago chose to neglect those plausible reasons. They wanted knowledge and beauty now, and would not wait for the suitable moment that never comes. Periclean Athens leaves us not only the Parthenon but, significantly, the Funeral Oration. The insects have chosen a different line: they have sought first the material welfare and security of the hive, and presumably they have their reward. Men are different. They propound mathematical theorems in beleaguered cities, conduct metaphysical arguments in condemned cells, make jokes on scaffolds, discuss the last new poem while advancing to the walls of Quebec, and comb their hair at Thermopylae. This is not *panache:* it is our nature.

But since we are fallen creatures the fact that this is now our nature would not, by itself, prove that it is rational or right. We have to inquire whether there is really any legitimate place for the activities of the scholar in a world such as this. That is, we have always to answer the question: "How can you be so frivolous and selfish as to think about anything but the salvation of human souls?" and we have, at the moment, to answer the additional question, "How can you be so frivolous and selfish as to think of anything but the war?" Now part of our answer will be the same for both questions. The one implies that our life can, and ought, to become exclusively and explicitly religious: the other, that it can and ought to become exclusively national. I believe that our whole life can, and indeed must, become religious in a sense to be explained later. But if it is meant that all our activities are to be of the kind that can be recognized as "sacred" and opposed to "secular" then I would give a single reply to both my imaginary assailants. I would say, "Whether it ought to happen or not, the thing you are recommending is not going to happen." Before I became a Christian I do not think I fully realized that one's life, after conversion, would inevitably consist in doing most of the same things one had been doing before: one hopes, in a new spirit, but still the same things. Before I went to the last war I certainly expected that my life in the trenches would, in some mysterious sense, be all war. In fact, I found that the nearer you got to the front line the less everyone spoke and thought of the allied cause and the progress of the campaign; and I am pleased to find that Tolstoi, in the greatest war book ever written, records the same thing—and so, in its own way, does the Iliad. Neither conversion nor enlistment in the army is really going to obliterate our human life. Christians and soldiers are still men: the infidel's idea of a religious life, and the civilian's idea of active service, are fantastic. If you attempted, in either case, to suspend your whole intellectual and aesthetic activity, you would only succeed in substituting a worse cultural life for a better. You are not, in fact, going to read nothing, either in the Church or in the line: if you don't read good books you will read bad ones. If you don't go on thinking rationally, you will think irrationally. If you reject aesthetic satisfactions you will fall into sensual satisfactions.

There is therefore this analogy between the claims of our religion and the claims of the war: neither of them, for most of us, will simply cancel or remove from the slate the merely human life which we were leading before we entered them. But they will operate in this way for different reasons. The war will fail to absorb our whole attention because it is a finite object, and therefore intrinsically unfitted to support the whole attention of a human soul. In order to avoid misunderstanding I must here make a few distinctions. I believe our cause to be, as human causes go, very righteous, and I therefore believe it to be a duty to participate in this war. And every duty is a religious duty, and our obligation to perform every duty is therefore absolute. Thus we may have a duty to rescue a drowning man, and perhaps, if we live on a dangerous coast, to learn life-saving so as to be ready for any drowning man when he turns up. It may be our duty to lose our own lives in saving him. But if anyone devoted himself to life-saving in the sense of giving it his total attention—so that he thought and spoke of nothing else and demanded the cessation of all other human activities until everyone had learned to swim—he would be a monomaniac. The rescue of drowning men is, then, a duty worth dying for, but not worth living for. It seems to me that all political duties (among which I include military duties) are of this kind. A man may have to die for our country: but no man must, in any exclusive sense, live for his country. He who surrenders himself without reservation to the temporal claims of a nation, or a party, or a class is rendering to Caesar that which, of all things, most emphatically belongs to God: himself.

It is for a very different reason that religion cannot occupy the whole of life in the sense of excluding all our natural activities. For, of course, in some sense, it must occupy the whole of life. There is no question of a compromise between the claims of God and the claims of culture, or politics, or anything else. God's claim is infinite and inexorable. You can refuse it: or you can begin to try to grant it. There is no middle way. Yet in spite of this it is clear that Christianity does not exclude any of the ordinary human activities. St. Paul tells people to get on with their jobs. He even assumes that Christians may go to dinner parties, and, what is more, dinner parties given by pagans. Our Lord attends a wedding and provides miraculous wine. Under the aegis of His Church, and in the most Christian ages, learning and the arts flourish. The solution of this paradox is, of course, well known to you. "Whether ye eat or drink or whatsoever ye do, do all to the glory of God."

All our merely natural activities will be accepted, if they are offered to God, even the humblest: and all of them, even the noblest, will be sinful if they are not. Christianity does not simply replace our natural life and substitute a new one:

it is rather a new organization which exploits, to its own supernatural ends, these natural materials. No doubt, in a given situation, it demands the surrender of some, or of all, our merely human pursuits: it is better to be saved with one eye, than, having two, to be cast into Gehenna. But it does this, in a sense, *per accidens*—because, in those special circumstances, it has ceased to be possible to practise this or that activity to the glory of God. There is no essential quarrel between the spiritual life and the human activities as such. Thus the omnipresence of obedience to God in a Christian's life is, in a way, analogous to the omnipresence of God in space. God does not fill space as a body fills it, in the sense that parts of Him are in different parts of space, excluding other objects from them. Yet He is everywhere—totally present at every point of space—according to good theologians.

We are now in a position to answer the view that human culture is an inexcusable frivolity on the part of creatures loaded with such awful responsibilities as we. I reject at once an idea which lingers in the mind of some modern people that cultural activities are in their own right spiritual and meritorious—as though scholars and poets were intrinsically more pleasing to God than scavengers and bootblacks. I think it was Matthew Arnold who first used the English word *spiritual* in the sense of the German *geistlich*, and so inaugurated this most dangerous and most anti-Christian error. Let us clear it forever from our minds. The work of a Beethoven, and the work of a charwoman, become spiritual on precisely the same condition, that of being offered to God, of being done humbly "as to the Lord". This does not, of course, mean that it is for anyone a mere toss-up whether he should sweep rooms or compose symphonies. A mole must dig to the glory of God and a cock must crow. We are members of one body, but differentiated members, each with his own vocation. A man's upbringing, his talents, his circumstances, are usually a tolerable index of his vocation. If our parents have sent us to Oxford, if our country allows us to remain there, this is *prima facie* evidence that the life which we, at any rate, can best lead to the glory of God at present is the learned life. By leading that life to the glory of God I do not, of course, mean any attempt to make our intellectual inquiries work out to edifying conclusions. That would be, as Bacon says, to offer to the author of truth the unclean sacrifice of a lie. I mean the pursuit of knowledge and beauty, in a sense, for their own sake, but in a sense which does not exclude their being for God's sake. An appetite for these things exists in the human mind, and God makes no appetite in vain. We can therefore pursue knowledge as such, and beauty, as such, in the sure confidence that by so doing we are either advancing to the vision of God ourselves or indirectly helping others to do so. Humility, no less than the appetite, encourages us to concentrate simply on the knowledge or the beauty, not too much concerning ourselves with their ultimate relevance to the vision of God. That relevance may not be intended for us but for our betters—for men who come after and find the spiritual significance of what we dug out in blind and humble obedience to our vocation. This is the teleological argument that the existence of the impulse and the faculty prove that they must have a proper function in God's scheme—the argument by which Thomas Aquinas proves that sexuality would have existed even without the Fall. The soundness of the argument, as regards culture, is proved by experience. The intellectual life is not the only road to God, nor the safest, but we find it to be a road, and it may be the appointed road for us. Of course it will be so only so long as we keep the impulse pure and disinterested. That is the great difficulty. As the author of the *Theologia Germanica* says, we may come to love knowledge—*our* knowing—more than the thing known: to delight not in the exercise of our talents but in the fact that they are ours, or even in the reputation they bring us. Every success in the scholar's life increases this danger. If it becomes irresistible, he must give up his scholarly work. The time for plucking out the right eye has arrived.

That is the essential nature of the learned life as I see it. But it has indirect values which are especially important to-day. If all the world were Christian, it might not matter if all the world were uneducated. But, as it is, a cultural life will exist outside the Church whether it exists inside or not. To be ignorant and simple now—not to be able to meet the enemies on their own ground—would be to throw down our weapons, and to betray our uneducated brethren who have, under God, no defence but us against the intellectual attacks of the heathen. Good philosophy must exist, if for no other reason, because bad philosophy needs to be answered. The cool intellect must work not only against cool intellect on the other side, but against the muddy heathen mysticisms which deny intellect altogether. Most of all, perhaps, we need intimate knowledge of the past. Not that the past has any magic about it, but because we cannot study the future, and yet need something to set against the present, to remind us that the basic assumptions have been quite different in different periods and that much which seems certain to the uneducated is merely temporary fashion. A man who has lived in many places is not likely to be deceived by the local errors of his native village: the scholar has lived in many times and is therefore in some degree immune from the great cataract of nonsense that pours from the press and the microphone of his own age.

The learned life then is, for some, a duty. At the moment it looks as if it were your duty. I am well aware that there may seem to be an almost comic discrepancy between the high issues we have been considering and the immediate task you may be set down to, such as Anglo-Saxon sound laws or chemical formulae. But there is a similar shock awaiting us in every vocation—a young priest finds himself involved in choir treats and a young subaltern in accounting for pots of jam. It is well that it should be so. It weeds out the vain, windy people and keeps in those who are both humble and tough. On that kind of difficulty we need waste no sympathy. But the peculiar difficulty imposed on you by the war is another matter: and of it I would again repeat, what I have been saying in one form or another ever since I started—do not let your nerves and emotions lead you into thinking your predicament more abnormal than it really is. Perhaps it may be useful to mention the three mental exercises which may serve as defences against the three enemies which war raises up against the scholar.

The first enemy is excitement—the tendency to think and feel about the war when we had intended to think about our work. The best defence is a recognition that in this, as in everything else, the war has not really raised up a new enemy but only aggravated an old one. There are always plenty of rivals to our work. We are always falling in love or quarrelling, looking for jobs or fearing to lose them, getting ill and recovering, following public affairs. If we let ourselves, we shall always be waiting for some distraction or other to end before we can really get down to our work. The only people who achieve much are those who want knowledge so badly that they seek it while the conditions are still unfavourable. Favourable conditions never come. There are, of course, moments when the pressure of the excitement is so great that only superhuman self-control could resist it. They come both in war and peace. We must do the best we can.

The second enemy is frustration—the feeling that we shall not have time to finish. If I say to you that no one has time to finish, that the longest human life leaves a man, in any branch of learning, a beginner, I shall seem to you to be saying something quite academic and theoretical. You would be surprised if you knew how soon one begins to feel the shortness of the tether: of how many things, even in middle life, we have to say "No time for that", "Too late now", and "Not for me". But Nature herself forbids you to share that experience. A more Christian attitude, which can be attained at any age, is that of leaving futurity in God's hands. We may as well, for God will certainly retain it whether we leave it to Him or not. Never, in peace or war, commit your virtue or your happiness to the future. Happy work is best done by the man who takes his long-term plans somewhat lightly and works from moment to moment "as to the Lord". It is only our *daily* bread that we are encouraged to ask for. The present is the only time in which any duty can be done or any grace received.

The third enemy is fear. War threatens us with death and pain. No man— and specially no Christian who remembers Gethsemane—need try to attain a stoic indifference about these things: but we can guard against the illusions of the imagination. We think of the streets of Warsaw and contrast the deaths there suffered with an abstraction called Life. But there is no question of death or life for any of us; only a question of this death or of that—of a machine gun bullet now or a cancer forty years later. What does war do to death? It certainly does not make it more frequent: 100 per cent of us die, and the percentage cannot be increased. It puts several deaths earlier: but I hardly suppose that that is what we fear. Certainly when the moment comes, it will make little difference how many years we have behind us. Does it increase our chances of a painful death? I doubt it. As far as I can find out, what we call natural death is usually preceded by suffering: and a battlefield is one of the very few places where one has a reasonable prospect of dying with no pain at all. Does it decrease our chances of dying at peace with God? I cannot believe it. If active service does not persuade a man to prepare for death, what conceivable concatenation of circumstances would? Yet war does do something to death. It forces us to remember it. The only reason why the cancer at sixty or the paralysis at seventy-five do not bother us is that we forget them. War makes death real to us: and that would have been regarded as one of its blessings by most of the great Christians of the past. They thought it good for us to be always aware of our mortality. I am inclined to think they were right. All the animal life in us, all schemes of happiness that centered in this world, were always doomed to a final frustration. In ordinary times only a wise man can realize it. Now the stupidest of us knows. We see unmistakably the sort of universe in which we have all along been living, and must come to terms with it. If we had foolish un-Christian hopes about human culture, they are now shattered. If we thought we were building up a heaven on earth, if we looked for something that would turn the present world from a place of pilgrimage into a permanent city satisfying the soul of man, we are disillusioned, and not a moment too soon. But if we thought that for some souls, and at some times, the life of learning, humbly offered to God, was, in its own small way, one of the appointed approaches to the Divine reality and the Divine beauty which we hope to enjoy hereafter, we can think so still.

The Efficacy of Prayer

Some years ago I got up one morning intending to have my hair cut in preparation for a visit to London, and the first letter I opened made it clear I need not go to London. So I decided to put the haircut off too. But then there began the most unaccountable little nagging in my mind, almost like a voice saying, "Get it cut all the same. Go and get it cut." In the end I could stand it no longer. I went. Now my barber at that time was a fellow Christian and a man of many troubles whom my brother and I had sometimes been able to help. The moment I opened his shop door he said, "Oh, I was praying you might come today." And in fact if I had come a day or so later I should have been of no use to him.

It awed me; it awes me still. But of course one cannot rigorously prove a causal connection between the barber's prayers and my visit. It might be telepathy. It might be accident.

I have stood by the bedside of a woman whose thighbone was eaten through with cancer and who had thriving colonies of the disease in many other bones as well. It took three people to move her in bed. The doctors predicted a few months of life; the nurses (who often know better), a few weeks. A good man laid his hands on her and prayed. A year later the patient was walking (uphill, too, through rough woodland) and the man who took the last X-ray photos was saying, "These bones are as solid as rock. It's miraculous."

But once again there is no rigorous proof. Medicine, as all true doctors admit, is not an exact science. We need not invoke the supernatural to explain the falsification of its prophecies. You need not, unless you choose, believe in a causal connection between the prayers and the recovery.

The question then arises, "What sort of evidence *would* prove the efficacy of prayer?" The thing we pray for may happen, but how can you ever know it was not going to happen anyway? Even if the thing were indisputably miraculous it would not follow that the miracle had occurred because of your prayers. The answer surely is that a compulsive empirical proof such as we have in the sciences can never be attained.

Some things are proved by the unbroken uniformity of our experiences. The law of gravitation is established by the fact that, in our experience, all bodies without exception obey it. Now even if all the things that people prayed for happened, which they do not, this would not prove what Christians mean by the efficacy of prayer. For prayer is request. The essence of request, as distinct from compulsion, is that it may or may not be granted. And if an infinitely wise Being listens to the requests of finite and foolish creatures, of course He will sometimes grant and sometimes refuse them. Invariable "success" in prayer would not prove the Christian doctrine at all. It would prove something much more like magic—a power in certain human beings to control, or compel, the course of nature.

There are, no doubt, passages in the New Testament which may seem at first sight to promise an invariable granting of our prayers. But that cannot be what they really mean. For in the very heart of the story we meet a glaring instance to the contrary. In Gethsemane the holiest of all petitioners prayed three times that a certain cup might pass from Him. It did not. After that the idea that prayer is recommended to us as a sort of infallible gimmick may be dismissed.

Other things are proved not simply by experience but by those artificially contrived experiences which we call experiments. Could this be done about prayer? I will pass over the objection that no Christian could take part in such a project, because he has been forbidden it: "You must not try experiments on God, your Master." Forbidden or not, is the thing even possible?

I have seen it suggested that a team of people—the more the better—should agree to pray as hard as they knew how, over a period of six weeks, for all the patients in Hospital A and none of those in Hospital B. Then you would tot up the results and see if A had more cures and fewer deaths. And I suppose you would repeat the experiment at various times and places so as to eliminate the influence of irrelevant factors.

The trouble is that I do not see how any real prayer could go on under such conditions. "Words without thoughts never to heaven go," says the King in *Hamlet.* Simply to say prayers is not to pray; otherwise a team of properly trained parrots would serve as well as men for our experiment. You cannot pray for the recovery of the sick unless the end you have in view is their recovery. But you can have no motive for desiring the recovery of all the patients in one hospital and none of those in another. You are not doing it in order that suffering should be relieved; you are doing it to find out what happens. The real purpose and the nominal purpose of your prayers are at variance. In other words, whatever your tongue and teeth and knees may do, you are not praying. The experiment demands an impossibility.

Empirical proof and disproof are, then, unobtainable. But this conclusion will seem less depressing if we remember that prayer is request and compare it with other specimens of the same thing.

We make requests of our fellow creatures as well as of God: we ask for the salt, we ask for a raise in pay, we ask a friend to feed the cat while we are on our holidays, we ask a woman to marry us. Sometimes we get what we ask for and sometimes not. But when we do, it is not nearly so easy as one might suppose to prove with scientific certainty a causal connection between the asking and the getting.

Your neighbour may be a humane person who would not have let your cat starve even if you had forgotten to make any arrangement. Your employer is never so likely to grant your request for a raise as when he is aware that you could get better money from a rival firm and is quite possibly intending to secure you by a raise in any case. As for the lady who consents to marry you—are you sure she had not decided to do so already? Your proposal, you know, might have been the result, not the cause, of her decision. A certain important conversation might never have taken place unless she had intended that it should.

Thus in some measure the same doubt that hangs about the causal efficacy of our prayers to God hangs also about our prayers to man. Whatever we get we might have been going to get anyway. But only, as I say, in some measure. Our friend, boss, and wife may tell us that they acted because we asked; and we may know them so well as to feel sure, first that they are saying what they believe to be true, and secondly that they understand their own motives well enough to be right. But notice that when this happens our assurance has not been gained by the methods of science. We do not try the control experiment of refusing the raise or breaking off the engagement and then making our request again under fresh conditions. Our assurance is quite different in kind from scientific knowledge. It is born out of our personal relation to the other parties; not from knowing things about them but from knowing *them*.

Our assurance—if we reach an assurance—that God always hears and sometimes grants our prayers, and that apparent grantings are not merely fortuitous, can only come in the same sort of way. There can be no question of tabulating successes and failures and trying to decide whether the successes are too numerous to be accounted for by chance. Those who best know a man best know whether, when he did what they asked, he did it because they asked. I think those who best know God will best know whether He sent me to the barber's shop because the barber prayed.

For up till now we have been tackling the whole question in the wrong way and on the wrong level. The very question "Does prayer work?" puts us in the wrong frame of mind from the outset. "Work": as if it were magic, or a machine—something that functions automatically. Prayer is either a sheer illusion or a personal contact between embryonic, incomplete persons (ourselves) and the utterly concrete Person. Prayer in the sense of petition, asking for things, is a small part of it; confession and penitence are its threshold, adoration its sanctuary, the presence and vision and enjoyment of God its bread and wine. In it God shows Himself to us. That He answers prayers is a corollary—not necessarily the most important one—from that revelation. What He does is learned from what He is.

Petitionary prayer is, nonetheless, both allowed and commanded to us: "Give us our daily bread." And no doubt it raises a theoretical problem. Can we believe that God ever really modifies His action in response to the suggestions of men? For infinite wisdom does not need telling what is best, and infinite goodness needs no urging to do it. But neither does God need any of those things that are done by finite agents, whether living or inanimate. He could, if He chose, repair our bodies miraculously without food; or give us food without the aid of farmers, bakers, and butchers; or knowledge without the aid of learned men; or convert the heathen without missionaries. Instead, He allows soils and weather and animals and the muscles, minds, and wills of men to co-operate in the execution of His will. "God," said Pascal, "instituted prayer in order to lend to His creatures the dignity of causality." But not only prayer; whenever we act at all He lends us that dignity. It is not really stranger, nor less strange, that my prayers should affect the course of events than that my other actions should do so. They have not advised or changed God's mind—that is, His over-all purpose. But that purpose will be realized in different ways according to the actions, including the prayers, of His creatures.

For He seems to do nothing of Himself which He can possibly delegate to His creatures. He commands us to do slowly and blunderingly what He could do perfectly and in the twinkling of an eye. He allows us to neglect what He would have us do, or to fail. Perhaps we do not fully realize the problem, so to call it, of enabling finite free wills to co-exist with Omnipotence. It seems to involve at every moment almost a sort of divine abdication. We are not mere recipients or spectators. We are either privileged to share in the game or compelled to collaborate in the work, "to wield our little tridents." Is this amazing process simply Creation going on before our eyes? This is how (no light matter) God makes something—indeed, makes gods—out of nothing.

So at least it seems to me. But what I have offered can be, at the very best, only a mental model or symbol. All that we say on such subjects must be merely analogical and parabolic. The reality is doubtless not comprehensible by our faculties. But we can at any rate try to expel bad analogies and bad parables. Prayer is not a machine. It is not magic. It is not advice offered to God. Our act, when we pray, must not, any more than all our other acts, be separated from the continuous act of God Himself, in which alone all finite causes operate.

It would be even worse to think of those who get what they pray for as a sort of court favorites, people who have influence with the throne. The refused prayer of Christ in Gethsemane is answer enough to that. And I dare not leave out the hard saying which I once heard from an experienced Christian: "I have seen many striking answers to prayer and more than one that I thought miraculous. But they usually come at the beginning: before conversion, or soon after it. As the Christian life proceeds, they tend to be rarer. The refusals, too, are not only more frequent; they become more unmistakable, more emphatic."

Does God then forsake just those who serve Him best? Well, He who served Him best of all said, near His tortured death, "Why hast thou forsaken me?" When God becomes man, that Man, of all others, is least comforted by God, at His greatest need. There is a mystery here which, even if I had the power, I might not have the courage to explore. Meanwhile, little people like you and me, if our prayers are sometimes granted, beyond all hope and probability, had better not draw hasty conclusions to our own advantage. If we were stronger, we might be less tenderly treated. If we were braver, we might be sent, with far less help, to defend far more desperate posts in the great battle.

The World's Last Night

THERE ARE many reasons why the modern Christian and even the modern theologian may hesitate to give to the doctrine of Christ's Second Coming that emphasis which was usually laid on it by our ancestors. Yet it seems to me impossible to retain in any recognisable form our belief in the Divinity of Christ and the truth of the Christian revelation while abandoning, or even persistently neglecting, the promised, and threatened, Return. "He shall come again to judge the quick and the dead," says the Apostles' Creed. "This same Jesus," said the angels in Acts, "shall so come in like manner as ye have seen him go into heaven." "Hereafter," said our Lord himself (by those words inviting crucifixion), "shall ye see the Son of Man . . . coming in the clouds of heaven." If this is not an integral part of the faith once given to the saints, I do not know what is. In the following pages I shall endeavor to deal with some of the thoughts that may deter modern men from a firm belief in, or a due attention to, the return or Second Coming of the Saviour. I have no claim to speak as an expert in any of the studies involved, and merely put forward the reflections which have arisen in my own mind and have seemed to me (perhaps wrongly) to be helpful. They are all submitted to the correction of wiser heads.

The grounds for modern embarrassment about this doctrine fall into two groups, which may be called the theoretical and the practical. I will deal with the theoretical first.

Many are shy of this doctrine because they are reacting (in my opinion very properly reacting) against a school of thought which is associated with the great name of Dr. Albert Schweitzer. According to that school, Christ's teaching about his own return and the end of the world—what theologians call his "apocalyptic"—was the very essence of his message. All his other doctrines radiated from it; his moral teaching everywhere presupposed a speedy end of the world. If pressed to an extreme, this view, as I think Chesterton said, amounts to seeing in Christ little more than an earlier William Miller, who created a local "scare." I am not saying that Dr. Schweitzer pressed it to that conclusion: but it has seemed to some that his thought invites us in that direction. Hence, from fear of that extreme, arises a tendency to soft-pedal what Schweitzer's school has overemphasized.

For my own part I hate and distrust reactions not only in religion but in everything. Luther surely spoke very good sense when he compared humanity to a drunkard who, after falling off his horse on the right, falls off it next time on the left. I am convinced that those who find in Christ's apocalyptic the whole of his message are mistaken. But a thing does not vanish—it is not even discredited—because someone has spoken of it with exaggeration. It remains exactly where it was. The only difference is that if it has recently been exaggerated, we must now take special care not to overlook it; for that is the side on which the drunk man is now most likely to fall off.

The very name "apocalyptic" assigns our Lord's predictions of the Second Coming to a class. There are other specimens of it: the *Apocalypse of Baruch*, the *Book of Enoch*, or the *Ascension of Isaiah*. Christians are far from regarding such texts as Holy Scripture, and to most modern tastes the *genre* appears tedious and unedifying. Hence there arises a feeling that our Lord's predictions, being "much the same sort of thing," are discredited. The charge against them might be put either in a harsher or a gentler form. The harsher form would run, in the mouth of an atheist, something like this: "You see that, after all, your vaunted Jesus was really the same sort of crank or charlatan as all the other writers of apocalyptic." The gentler form, used more probably by a modernist, would be like this: "Every great man is partly of his own age and partly for all time. What matters in his work is always that which transcends his age, not that which he shared with a thousand forgotten contemporaries. We value Shakespeare for the glory of his language and his knowledge of the human heart, which were his own; not for his belief in witches or the divine right of kings, or his failure to take a daily bath. So with Jesus. His belief in a speedy and catastrophic end to history belongs to him not as a great teacher but as a first-century Palestinian peasant. It was one of his inevitable limitations, best forgotten. We must concentrate on what distinguished him from other first-century Palestinian peasants, on his moral and social teaching."

As an argument against the reality of the Second Coming this seems to me to beg the question at issue. When we propose to ignore in a great man's teaching those doctrines which it has in common with the thought of his age, we seem to be assuming that the thought of his age was erroneous. When we select for serious consideration those doctrines which "transcend" the thought of his own age and are "for all time," we are assuming that the thought of *our* age is correct: for of course by thoughts which transcend the great man's age we really mean thoughts that agree with ours. Thus I value Shakespeare's picture of the transformation in old Lear more than I value his views about the divine right of kings, because I agree with Shakespeare that a man can be purified by suffering like Lear, but do not believe that kings (or any other rulers) have divine right in the sense required. When the great man's views do not seem to us erroneous we do not value them the less for having been shared with his contemporaries. Shakespeare's disdain for treachery and Christ's blessing on the poor were not alien to the outlook of their respective periods; but no one wishes to discredit them on that account. No one would reject Christ's apocalyptic on the ground that apocalyptic was common in first-century Palestine unless he had already decided that the thought of first-century Palestine was in that respect mistaken. But to have so decided is surely to have begged the question; for the question is whether the expectation of a catastrophic and Divinely ordered end of the present universe is true or false.

If we have an open mind on that point, the whole problem is altered. If such an end is really going to occur, and if (as is the case) the Jews had been trained by their religion to expect it, then it is very natural that they should produce apocalyptic literature. On that view, our Lord's production of something like the other apocalyptic documents would not necessarily result from his supposed bondage to the errors of his period, but would be the Divine exploitation of a sound element in contemporary Judaism: nay, the time and place in which it pleased him to be incarnate would, presumably, have been chosen because, there and then, that element existed, and had, by his eternal providence, been developed for that very purpose. For if we once accept the doctrine of the Incarnation, we must surely be very cautious in suggesting that any circumstance in the culture of first-century Palestine was a hampering or distorting influence upon his teaching. Do we suppose that the scene of God's earthly life was selected at random?—that some other scene would have served better?

But there is worse to come. "Say what you like," we shall be told, "the apocalyptic beliefs of the first Christians have been proved to be false. It is clear from the New Testament that they all expected the Second Coming in their own lifetime. And, worse still, they had a reason, and one which you will find very embarrassing. Their Master had told them so. He shared, and indeed created, their delusion. He said in so many words, 'this generation shall not pass till all these things be done.' And he was wrong. He clearly knew no more about the end of the world than anyone else."

It is certainly the most embarrassing verse in the Bible. Yet how teasing, also, that within fourteen words of it should come the statement "But of that day and that hour knoweth no man, no, not the angels which are in heaven, neither the Son, but the Father." The one exhibition of error and the one confession of ignorance grow side by side. That they stood thus in the mouth of Jesus himself, and were not merely placed thus by the reporter, we surely need not doubt. Unless the reporter were perfectly honest he would never have recorded the confession of ignorance at all; he could have had no motive for doing so except a desire to tell the whole truth. And unless later copyists were equally honest they would never have preserved the (apparently) mistaken prediction about "this generation" after the passage of time had shown the (apparent) mistake. This passage (Mark 13:30–32) and the cry "Why hast thou forsaken me?" (Mark 15:34) together make up the strongest proof that the New Testament is historically reliable. The evangelists have the first great characteristic of honest witnesses: they mention facts which are, at first sight, damaging to their main contention.

The facts, then, are these: that Jesus professed himself (in some sense) ignorant, and within a moment showed that he really was so. To believe in the Incarnation, to believe that he is God, makes it hard to understand how he could be ignorant; but also makes it certain that, if he said he could be ignorant, then ignorant he could really be. For a God who can be ignorant is less baffling than a God who falsely professes ignorance. The answer of theologians is that the God-Man was omniscient as God, and ignorant as Man. This, no doubt, is true, though it cannot be imagined. Nor indeed can the unconsciousness of Christ in sleep be imagined, nor the twilight of reason in his infancy; still less his merely organic life in his mother's womb. But the physical sciences, no less than theology, propose for our belief much that cannot be imagined.

A generation which has accepted the curvature of space need not boggle at the impossibility of imagining the consciousness of incarnate God. In that consciousness the temporal and the timeless were united. I think we can acquiesce in mystery at that point, provided we do not aggravate it by our tendency to picture the timeless life of God as, simply, another sort of time. We are committing that blunder whenever we ask how Christ could be *at the same moment* ignorant and omniscient, or how he could be the God who neither slumbers nor sleeps *while* he slept. The italicized words conceal an attempt to establish a temporal relation between his timeless life as God and the days, months, and years of his life as Man. And of course there is no such relation. The Incarnation is not an episode in the life of God: the Lamb is slain—and therefore presumably born, grown to maturity, and risen—from all eternity. The taking up into God's nature of humanity, with all its ignorances and limitations, is not itself a temporal event, though the humanity which is so taken up was, like our own, a thing living and dying in time. And if limitation, and therefore ignorance, was thus taken up, we ought to expect that the ignorance should at some time be actually displayed. It would be difficult, and, to me, repellent, to suppose that Jesus never asked a genuine question, that is, a question to which he did not know the answer. That would make of his humanity something so unlike ours as scarcely to deserve the name. I find it easier to believe that when he said "Who touched me?" (Luke 7:45) he really wanted to know.

The difficulties which I have so far discussed are, to a certain extent, debating points. They tend rather to strengthen a disbelief already based on other grounds than to create disbelief by their own force. We are now coming to something much more important and often less fully conscious. The doctrine of the Second Coming is deeply uncongenial to the whole evolutionary or developmental character of modern thought. We have been taught to think of the world as something that grows slowly towards perfection, something that "progresses" or "evolves." Christian Apocalyptic offers us no such hope. It does not even foretell (which would be more tolerable to our habits of thought) a gradual decay. It foretells a sudden, violent end imposed from without; an extinguisher popped onto the candle, a brick flung at the gramophone, a curtain rung down on the play—"Halt!"

To this deep-seated objection I can only reply that, in my opinion, the modern conception of Progress or Evolution (as popularly imagined) is simply a myth, supported by no evidence whatever.

I say "evolution, as popularly imagined." I am not in the least concerned to refute Darwinism as a theorem in biology. There may be flaws in that theorem, but I have here nothing to do with them. There may be signs that biologists are already contemplating a withdrawal from the whole Darwinian position, but I claim to be no judge of such signs. It can even be argued that what Darwin really accounted for was not the origin, but the elimination, of species, but I will not pursue that argument. For purposes of this article I am assuming that Darwinian biology is correct. What I want to point out is the illegitimate transition from the Darwinian theorem in biology to the modern myth of evolutionism or developmentalism or progress in general.

The first thing to notice is that the myth arose earlier than the theorem, in advance of all evidence. Two great works of art embody the idea of a universe in which, by some inherent necessity, the "higher" always supersedes the "lower." One is Keats's *Hyperion* and the other is Wagner's *Nibelung's Ring*. And they are both earlier than the *Origin of Species*. You could not have a clearer expression of the developmental or progressive idea than Oceanus' words

> 'tis the eternal law
> That first in beauty should be first in might.

And you could not have a more ardent submission to it than those words in which Wagner describes his tetralogy.

> *The progress of the whole poem, therefore [he writes to Röckel in 1854], shows the necessity of recognizing, and submitting to, the change, the diversity, the multiplicity, and the eternal novelty, of the Real. Wotan rises to the tragic heights of willing his own downfall. This is all that we have to learn from the history of Man—to will the Necessary, and ourselves to bring it to pass. The creative work which this highest and self-renouncing will finally accomplishes is the fearless and everloving man, Siegfried.* *

The idea that the myth (so potent in all modern thought) is a result of Darwin's biology would thus seem to be unhistorical. On the contrary, the attraction of Darwinism was that it gave to a pre-existing myth the scientific reassurances it required. If no evidence for evolution had been forthcoming, it would have been necessary to invent it. The real sources of the myth are partly political. It projects onto the cosmic screen feelings engendered by the Revolutionary period.

In the second place, we must notice that Darwinism gives no support to the belief that natural selection, working upon chance variations, has a general tendency to produce improvement. The illusion that it has comes from confining our attention to a few species which have (by some possibly arbitrary standard of our own) changed for the better. Thus the horse has improved in the sense that

---

*"*Der Fortgang des ganzen Gedichtes zeigt demnach die Notwendigkeit, den Wechsel, die Mannigfaltigkeit, die Vielheit, die ewige Neuheit der Wirklichkeit und des Lebens anzuerkennen und ihr zu weichen. Wotan schwingt sich bis zu der tragischen Höhe, seinen Untergang zu wollen. Dies ist alles, was wir aus der Geschichte der Menscheit zu lernen haben: das Notwendige zu wollen und selbst zu vollbringen. Das Schöpfungswerk dieses höchsten, selbst vernichtenden Willens ist der endlich gewonnene furchtlose, stets liebende Mensch; Siegfried.*"

Fuller research into the origins of this potent myth would lead us to the German idealists and thence (as I have heard suggested) through Boehme back to Alchemy. Is the whole dialectical view of history possibly a gigantic projection of the old dream that we can make gold?

protohippos would be less useful to us than his modern descendant. The anthropoid has improved in the sense that he now is Ourselves. But a great many of the changes produced by evolution are not improvements by any conceivable standard. In battle men save their lives sometimes by advancing and sometimes by retreating. So, in the battle for survival, species save themselves sometimes by increasing, sometimes by jettisoning, their powers. There is no general law of progress in biological history.

And, thirdly, even if there were, it would not follow—it is, indeed, manifestly not the case—that there is any law of progress in ethical, cultural, and social history. No one looking at world history without some preconception in favor of progress could find in it a steady up gradient. There is often progress within a given field over a limited period. A school of pottery or painting, a moral effort in a particular direction, a practical art like sanitation or shipbuilding, may continuously improve over a number of years. If this process could spread to all departments of life and continue indefinitely, there would be "Progress" of the sort our fathers believed in. But it never seems to do so. Either it is interrupted (by barbarian irruption or the even less resistible infiltration of modern industrialism) or else, more mysteriously, it decays. The idea which here shuts out the Second Coming from our minds, the idea of the world slowly ripening to perfection, is a myth, not a generalization from experience. And it is a myth which distracts us from our real duties and our real interest. It is our attempt to guess the plot of a drama in which we are the characters. But how can the characters in a play guess the plot? We are not the playwright, we are not the producer, we are not even the audience. We are on the stage. To play well the scenes in which we are "on" concerns us much more than to guess about the scenes that follow it.

In *King Lear* (III:vii) there is a man who is such a minor character that Shakespeare has not given him even a name: he is merely "First Servant." All the characters around him—Regan, Cornwall, and Edmund—have fine long-term plans. They think they know how the story is going to end, and they are quite wrong. The servant has no such delusions. He has no notion how the play is going to go. But he understands the present scene. He sees an abomination (the blinding of old Gloucester) taking place. He will not stand it. His sword is out and pointed at his master's breast in a moment: then Regan stabs him dead from behind. That is his whole part: eight lines all told. But if it were real life and not a play, that is the part it would be best to have acted.

The doctrine of the Second Coming teaches us that we do not and cannot know when the world drama will end. The curtain may be rung down at any moment: say, before you have finished reading this paragraph. This seems to some people intolerably frustrating. So many things would be interrupted. Perhaps you were going to get married next month, perhaps you were going to get a raise next week: you may be on the verge of a great scientific discovery; you may be maturing great social and political reforms. Surely no good and wise God would be so very unreasonable as to cut all this short? Not *now*, of all moments!

But we think thus because we keep on assuming that we know the play. We do not know the play. We do not even know whether we are in Act I or Act V. We do not know who are the major and who the minor characters. The Author knows. The audience, if there is an audience (if angels and archangels and all the company of heaven fill the pit and the stalls) may have an inkling. But we, never seeing the play from outside, never meeting any characters except the tiny minority who are "on" in the same scenes as ourselves, wholly ignorant of the future and very imperfectly informed about the past, cannot tell at what moment the end ought to come. That it will come when it ought, we may be sure; but we waste our time in guessing when that will be. That it has a meaning we may be sure, but we cannot see it. When it is over, we may be told. We are led to expect that the Author will have something to say to each of us on the part that each of us has played. The playing it well is what matters infinitely.

The doctrine of the Second Coming, then, is not to be rejected because it conflicts with our favorite modern mythology. It is, for that very reason, to be the more valued and made more frequently the subject of meditation. It is the medicine our condition especially needs.

And with that, I turn to the practical. There is a real difficulty in giving this doctrine the place which it ought to have in our Christian life without, at the same time, running a certain risk. The fear of that risk probably deters many teachers who accept the doctrine from saying very much about it.

We must admit at once that this doctrine has, in the past, led Christians into very great follies. Apparently many people find it difficult to believe in this great event without trying to guess its date, or even without accepting as a certainty the date that any quack or hysteric offers them. To write a history of all these exploded predictions would need a book, and a sad, sordid, tragi-comical book it would be. One such prediction was circulating when St. Paul wrote his second letter to the Thessalonians. Someone had told them that "the Day" was "at hand." This was apparently having the result which such predictions usually have: people were idling and playing the busybody. One of the most famous predictions was that of poor William Miller in 1843. Miller (whom I take to have been an honest fanatic) dated the Second Coming to the year, the day, and the very minute. A timely comet fostered the delusion. Thousands waited for the Lord at midnight on March 21st, and went home to a late breakfast on the 22nd followed by the jeers of a drunkard.

Clearly, no one wishes to say anything that will reawaken such mass hysteria. We must never speak to simple, excitable people about "the Day" without emphasizing again and again the utter impossibility of prediction. We must try to show them that that impossibility is an essential part of the doctrine. If you do not believe our Lord's words, why do you believe in his return at all? And if you do believe them must you not put away from you, utterly and forever, any hope of dating that return? His teaching on the subject quite clearly consisted of three propositions. (1) That he will certainly return. (2) That we cannot possibly find out when. (3) And that therefore we must always be ready for him.

Note the *therefore*. Precisely because we cannot predict the moment, we must be ready at all moments. Our Lord repeated this practical conclusion again and again; as if the promise of the Return had been made for the sake of this conclusion alone. Watch, watch, is the burden of his advice. I shall come like a thief. You will not, I most solemnly assure you you will not, see me approaching. If the householder had known at what time the burglar would arrive, he would have been ready for him. If the servant had known when his absent employer would come home, he would not have been found drunk in the kitchen. But they didn't. Nor will you. Therefore you must be ready at all times. The point is surely simple enough. The schoolboy does not know which part of his Virgil lesson he will be made to translate: that is why he must be prepared to translate *any* passage. The sentry does not know at what time an enemy will attack, or an officer inspect, his post: that is why he must keep awake *all* the time. The Return is wholly unpredictable. There will be wars and rumours of wars and all kinds of catastrophes, as there always are. Things will be, in that sense, normal, the hour before the heavens roll up like a scroll. You cannot guess it. If you could, one chief purpose for which it was foretold would be frustrated. And God's purposes are not so easily frustrated as that. One's ears should be closed against any future William Miller in advance. The folly of listening to him at all is almost equal to the folly of believing him. He *couldn't* know what he pretends, or thinks, he knows.

Of this folly George MacDonald has written well. "Do those," he asks, "who say, Lo here or lo there are the signs of his coming, think to be too keen for him and spy his approach? When he tells them to watch lest he find them neglecting their work, they stare this way and that, and watch lest he should succeed in coming like a thief! Obedience is the one key of life."

The doctrine of the Second Coming has failed, so far as we are concerned, if it does not make us realize that at every moment of every year in our lives Donne's question "What if this present were the world's last night?" is equally relevant.

Sometimes this question has been pressed upon our minds with the purpose of exciting fear. I do not think that is its right use. I am, indeed, far from agreeing with those who think all religious fear barbarous and degrading and demand that it should be banished from the spiritual life. Perfect love, we know, casteth out fear. But so do several other things—ignorance, alcohol, passion, presumption, and stupidity. It is very desirable that we should all advance to that perfection of love in which we shall fear no longer; but it is very undesirable, until we have reached that stage, that we should allow any inferior agent to cast out our fear. The objection to any attempt at perpetual trepidation about the Second Coming is, in my view, quite a different one: namely, that it will certainly not succeed. Fear is an emotion: and it is quite impossible—even physically impossible—to maintain any emotion for very long. A perpetual excitement of hope about the Second Coming is impossible for the same reason. Crisis-feeling of any sort is essentially transitory. Feelings come and go, and when they come a good use can be made of them: they cannot be our regular spiritual diet.

What is important is not that we should always fear (or hope) about the End but that we should always remember, always take it into account. An analogy may here help. A man of seventy need not be always feeling (much less talking) about his approaching death: but a wise man of seventy should always take it into account. He would be foolish to embark on schemes which presuppose twenty more years of life: he would be criminally foolish not to make—indeed, not to have made long since—his will. Now, what death is to each man, the Second Coming is to the whole human race. We all believe, I suppose, that a man should "sit loose" to his own individual life, should remember how short, precarious, temporary, and provisional a thing it is; should never give all his heart to anything which will end when his life ends. What modern Christians find it harder to remember is that the whole life of humanity in this world is also precarious, temporary, provisional.

Any moralist will tell you that the personal triumph of an athlete or of a girl at a ball is transitory: the point is to remember that an empire or a civilisation is also transitory. All achievements and triumphs, in so far as they are merely this-worldly achievements and triumphs, will come to nothing in the end. Most scientists here join hands with the theologians; the earth will not always be habitable. Man, though longer-lived than men, is equally mortal. The difference is that whereas the scientists expect only a slow decay from within, we reckon with sudden interruption from without—at any moment. ("What if this present were the world's last night?")

Taken by themselves, these considerations might seem to invite a relaxation of our efforts for the good of posterity: but if we remember that what may be upon us at any moment is not merely an End but a Judgment, they should have no such result. They may, and should, correct the tendency of some moderns to talk as though duties to posterity were the only duties we had. I can imagine no man who will look with more horror on the End than a conscientious revolutionary who has, in a sense sincerely, been justifying cruelties and injustices inflicted on millions of his contemporaries by the benefits which he hopes to confer on future generations: generations who, as one terrible moment now reveals to him, were never going to exist. Then he will see the massacres, the faked trials, the deportations, to be all ineffaceably real, an essential part, his part, in the drama that has just ended: while the future Utopia had never been anything but a fantasy.

Frantic administration of panaceas to the world is certainly discouraged by the reflection that "this present" might be "the world's last night"; sober work for the future, within the limits of ordinary morality and prudence, is not. For what comes is Judgment: happy are those whom it finds labouring in their vocations, whether they were merely going out to feed the pigs or laying good plans to deliver humanity a hundred years hence from some great evil. The curtain has indeed now fallen. Those pigs will never in fact be fed, the great campaign against White Slavery or Governmental Tyranny will never in fact proceed to victory. No matter; you were at your post when the Inspection came.

Our ancestors had a habit of using the word "Judgment" in this context as if it meant simply "punishment": hence the popular expression, "It's a judgment on him." I believe we can sometimes render the thing more vivid to ourselves by taking judgment in a stricter sense: not as the sentence or award, but as the Verdict. Some day (and "What if this present were the world's last night?") an absolutely correct verdict—if you like, a perfect critique—will be passed on what each of us is.

We have all encountered judgments or verdicts on ourselves in this life. Every now and then we discover what our fellow creatures really think of us. I don't of course mean what they tell us to our faces: that we usually have to discount. I am thinking of what we sometimes overhear by accident or of the opinions about us which our neighbours or employees or subordinates unknowingly reveal in their actions: and of the terrible, or lovely, judgments artlessly betrayed by children or even animals. Such discoveries can be the bitterest or sweetest experiences we have. But of course both the bitter and the sweet are limited by our doubt as to the wisdom of those who judge. We always hope that those who so clearly think us cowards or bullies are ignorant and malicious; we always fear that those who trust us or admire us are misled by partiality. I suppose the experience of the Final Judgment (which may break in upon us at any moment) will be like these little experiences, but magnified to the Nth.

For it will be infallible judgment. If it is favorable we shall have no fear, if unfavorable, no hope, that it is wrong. We shall not only believe, we shall know, know beyond doubt in every fibre of our appalled or delighted being, that as the Judge has said, so we are: neither more nor less nor other. We shall perhaps even realise that in some dim fashion we could have known it all along. We shall know and all creation will know too: our ancestors, our parents, our wives or husbands, our children. The unanswerable and (by then) self-evident truth about each will be known to all.

I do not find that pictures of physical catastrophe—that sign in the clouds, those heavens rolled up like a scroll—help one so much as the naked idea of Judgment. We cannot always be excited. We can, perhaps, train ourselves to ask more and more often how the thing which we are saying or doing (or failing to do) at each moment will look when the irresistible light streams in upon it; that light which is so different from the light of this world—and yet, even now, we know just enough of it to take it into account. Women sometimes have the problem of trying to judge by artificial light how a dress will look by daylight. That is very like the problem of all of us: to dress our souls not for the electric lights of the present world but for the daylight of the next. The good dress is the one that will face that light. For that light will last longer.

Reflections on the Psalms

Introductory

THIS IS NOT a work of scholarship. I am no Hebraist, no higher critic, no ancient historian, no archaeologist. I write for the unlearned about things in which I am unlearned myself. If an excuse is needed (and perhaps it is) for writing such a book, my excuse would be something like this. It often happens that two schoolboys can solve difficulties in their work for one another better than the master can. When you took the problem to a master, as we all remember, he was very likely to explain what you understood already, to add a great deal of information which you didn't want, and say nothing at all about the thing that was puzzling you. I have watched this from both sides of the net; for when, as a teacher myself, I have tried to answer questions brought me by pupils, I have sometimes, after a minute, seen that expression settle down on their faces which assured me that they were suffering exactly the same frustration which I had suffered from my own teachers. The fellow-pupil can help more than the master because he knows less. The difficulty we want him to explain is one he has recently met. The expert met it so long ago that he has forgotten. He sees the whole subject, by now, in such a different light that he cannot conceive what is really troubling the pupil; he sees a dozen other difficulties which ought to be troubling him but aren't.

In this book, then, I write as one amateur to another, talking about difficulties I have met, or lights I have gained, when reading the Psalms, with the hope that this might at any rate interest, and sometimes even help, other inexpert readers. I am "comparing notes", not presuming to instruct. It may appear to some that I have used the Psalms merely as pegs on which to hang a series of miscellaneous essays. I do not know that it would have done any harm if I had written the book that way, and I shall have no grievance against anyone who reads it that way. But that is not how it was in fact written. The thoughts it contains are those to which I found myself driven in reading the Psalms; sometimes by my enjoyment of them, sometimes by meeting with what at first I could not enjoy.

The Psalms were written by many poets and at many different dates. Some, I believe, are allowed to go back to the reign of David; I think certain scholars allow that Psalm 18 (of which a slightly different version occurs in I *Samuel* 22) might be by David himself. But many are later than the "captivity", which we should call the deportation to Babylon. In a scholarly work, chronology would be the first thing to settle: in a book of this sort nothing more need, or can, be said about it.

What must be said, however, is that the Psalms are poems, and poems intended to be sung: not doctrinal treatises, nor even sermons. Those who talk of reading the Bible "as literature" sometimes mean, I think, reading it without attending to the main thing it is about; like reading Burke with no interest in politics, or reading the *Aeneid* with no interest in Rome. That seems to me to be nonsense. But there is a saner sense in which the Bible, since it is after all literature, cannot properly be read except as literature; and the different parts of it as the different sorts of literature they are. Most emphatically the Psalms must be read as poems; as lyrics, with all the licences and all the formalities, the hyperboles, the emotional rather than logical connections, which are proper to lyric poetry. They must be read as poems if they are to be understood; no less than French must be read as French or English as English. Otherwise we shall miss what is in them and think we see what is not.

Their chief formal characteristic, the most obvious element of pattern, is fortunately one that survives in translation. Most readers will know that I mean what the scholars call "parallelism"; that is, the practice of saying the same thing twice in different words. A perfect example is "He that dwelleth in heaven shall laugh them to scorn: the Lord shall have them in derision" (2, *4*), or again, "He shall make thy righteousness as clear as the light; and thy just dealing as the noon-day" (37, *6*). If this is not recognised as pattern, the reader will either find mares' nests (as some of the older preachers did) in his effort to get a different meaning out of each half of the verse or else feel that it is rather silly.

In reality it is a very pure example of what all pattern, and therefore all art, involves. The principle of art has been defined by someone as "the same in the other". Thus in a country dance you take three steps and then three steps again. That is the same. But the first three are to the right and the second three to the left. That is the other. In a building there may be a wing on one side and a wing on the other, but both of the same shape. In music the composer may say ABC, and then abc, and then $\alpha\beta\gamma$. Rhyme consists in putting together two syllables that have the same sound except for their initial consonants, which are other. "Parallelism" is the characteristically Hebrew form of the same in the other, but it occurs in many English poets too: for example, in Marlowe's

> Cut is the branch that might have grown
> full straight
> And burned is Apollo's laurel bough,

or in the childishly simple form used by the *Cherry Tree Carol,*

> Joseph was an old man and an old man was he.

Of course the Parallelism is often partially concealed on purpose (as the balances between masses in a picture may be something far subtler than complete symmetry). And of course other and more complex patterns may be worked in across it, as in Psalm 119, or in 107 with its refrain. I mention only what is most obvious, the Parallelism itself. It is (according to one's point of view) either a wonderful piece of luck or a wise provision of God's that poetry which was to be turned into all languages should have as its chief formal characteristic one that does not disappear (as mere metre does) in translation.

If we have any taste for poetry we shall enjoy this feature of the Psalms. Even those Christians who cannot enjoy it will respect it; for Our Lord, soaked in the poetic tradition of His country, delighted to use it. "For with what judgement ye judge, ye shall be judged; and with what measure ye mete, it shall be measured to you again" (*Matthew* 7, 2). The second half of the verse makes no logical addition; it echoes, with variation, the first, "Ask, and it shall be given you; seek, and ye shall find; knock and it shall be opened unto you" (7,7). The advice is given in the first phrase, then twice repeated with different images. We may, if we like, see in this an exclusively practical and didactic purpose; by giving to truths which are infinitely worth remembering this rhythmic and incantatory expression, He made them almost impossible to forget. I like to suspect more. It seems to me appropriate, almost inevitable, that when that great Imagination which in the beginning, for Its own delight and for the delight of men and angels and (in their proper mode) of beasts, had invented and formed the whole world of Nature, submitted to express Itself in human speech, that speech should sometimes be poetry. For poetry too is a little incarnation, giving body to what had been before invisible and inaudible.

I think, too, it will do us no harm to remember that, in becoming Man, He bowed His neck beneath the sweet yoke of a heredity and early environment. Humanly speaking, He would have learned this style, if from no one else (but it was all about Him) from His Mother. "That we should be saved from our enemies and from the hands of all that hate us; to perform the mercy promised to our fathers, and to remember his holy covenant." Here is the same parallelism. (And incidentally, is this the only aspect in which we can say of His human nature

"He was His Mother's own son"? There is a fierceness, even a touch of Deborah, mixed with the sweetness in the *Magnificat* to which most painted Madonnas do little justice; matching the frequent severity of His own sayings. I am sure the private life of the holy family was, in many senses, "mild" and "gentle", but perhaps hardly in the way some hymn writers have in mind. One may suspect, on proper occasions, a certain astringency; and all in what people at Jerusalem regarded as a rough north-country dialect.)

I have not attempted of course to "cover the subject" even on my own amateurish level. I have stressed, and omitted, as my own interests led me. I say nothing about the long historical Psalms, partly because they have meant less to me, and partly because they seem to call for little comment. I say the least I can about the history of the Psalms as parts of various "services"; a wide subject, and not for me. And I begin with those characteristics of the Psalter which are at first most repellent. Other men of my age will know why. Our generation was brought up to eat everything on the plate; and it was the sound principle of nursery gastronomy to polish off the nasty things first and leave the titbits to the end.

I have worked in the main from the translation which Anglicans find in their Prayer Book; that of Coverdale. Even of the old translators he is by no means the most accurate; and of course a sound modern scholar has more Hebrew in his little finger than poor Coverdale had in his whole body. But in beauty, in poetry, he, and St. Jerome, the great Latin translator, are beyond all whom I know. I have usually checked, and sometimes corrected, his version from that of Dr. Moffatt.

Finally, as will soon be apparent to any reader, this is not what is called an "apologetic" work. I am nowhere trying to convince unbelievers that Christianity is true. I address those who already believe it, or those who are ready, while reading, to "suspend their disbelief". A man can't be always defending the truth; there must be a time to feed on it.

I have written, too, as a member of the Church of England, but I have avoided controversial questions as much as possible. At one point I had to explain how I differed on a certain matter both from Roman Catholics and from Fundamentalists: I hope I shall not for this forfeit the goodwill or the prayers of either. Nor do I much fear it. In my experience the bitterest opposition comes neither from them nor from any other thoroughgoing believers, and not often from atheists, but from semi-believers of all complexions. There are some enlightened and progressive old gentlemen of this sort whom no courtesy can propitiate and no modesty disarm. But then I dare say I am a much more annoying person than I know. (Shall we, perhaps, in Purgatory, see our own faces and hear our own voices as they really were?)

Second Meanings

I MUST now turn to something far more difficult. Hitherto we have been trying to read the Psalms as we suppose—or I suppose—their poets meant them to be read. But this of course is not the way in which they have chiefly been used by Christians. They have been believed to contain a second or hidden meaning, an "allegorical" sense, concerned with the central truths of Christianity, with the Incarnation, the Passion, the Resurrection, the Ascension, and with the Redemption of man. All the Old Testament has been treated in the same way. The full significance of what the writers are saying is, on this view, apparent only in the light of events which happened after they were dead.

Such a doctrine, not without reason, arouses deep distrust in a modern mind. Because, as we know, almost anything can be read into any book if you are determined enough. This will be especially impressed on anyone who has written fantastic fiction. He will find reviewers, both favourable and hostile, reading into his stories all manner of allegorical meanings which he never intended. (Some of the allegories thus imposed on my own books have been so ingenious and interesting that I often wish I had thought of them myself.) Apparently it is impossible for the wit of man to devise a narrative in which the wit of some other man cannot, and with some plausibility, find a hidden sense.

The field for self-deception, once we accept such methods of interpretation, is therefore obviously very wide. Yet in spite of this I think it impossible—for a reason I will give later—to abandon the method wholly when we are dealing, as Christians, with the Bible. We have, therefore, a steep hill before us. I will not attempt the cliffs. I must take a roundabout route which will look at first as if it could never lead us to the top at all.

I begin far away from Scripture and even from Christianity, with instances of something said or written which takes on a new significance in the light of later events.

One of the Roman historians tells us about a fire in a provincial town which was thought to have originated in the public baths. What gave some colour to the suspicion of deliberate incendiarism was the fact that, earlier that day, a gentleman had complained that the water in the hot bath was only lukewarm and had received from an attendant the reply, *it will soon be hot enough.* Now of course if there really had been a plot, and the slave was in it, and fool enough to risk discovery by this veiled threat, then the story would not concern us. But let us suppose the fire was an accident (i.e. was intended by nobody). In that case the slave would have said something truer, or more importantly true, than he himself supposed. Clearly, there need be nothing here but chance coincidence. The slave's reply is fully explained by the customer's complaint; it is just what any bath attendant would say. The deeper significance which his words turned out to have during the next few hours was, as we should say, accidental.

Now let us take a somewhat tougher instance. (The non-classical reader needs to know that to a Roman the "age" or "reign" of Saturn meant the lost age of innocence and peace. That is, it roughly corresponded to the Garden of Eden before the Fall; though it was never, except among the Stoics, of anything like comparable importance.) Virgil, writing not very long before the birth of Christ, begins a poem thus: "The great procession of the ages begins anew. Now the Virgin returns, the reign of Saturn returns, and the new child is sent down from high heaven." It goes on to describe the paradisal age which this nativity will usher in. And of course throughout the Middle Ages it was taken that some dim prophetic knowledge of the birth of Christ had reached Virgil, probably through the Sibylline Books. He ranked as a Pagan prophet. Modern scholars would, I suppose, laugh at the idea. They might differ as to what noble or imperial couple were being thus extravagantly complimented by a court poet on the birth of a son; but the resemblance to the birth of Christ would be regarded, once more, as an accident. To say the least of it, however, this is a much more striking accident than the slave's words to the man in the baths. If this is luck, it is extraordinary luck. If one were a fanatical opponent of Christianity one would be tempted to say, in an unguarded moment, that it was diabolically lucky.

I now turn to two examples which I think to be on a different level. In them, as in those we have been considering, someone says what is truer and more important than he knows; but it does not seem to me that he could have done so by chance. I hasten to add that the alternative to chance which I have in mind is not "prophecy" in the sense of clear prevision, miraculously bestowed. Nor of course have I the slightest intention of using the examples I shall cite as evidences for the truth of Christianity. Evidences are not here our subject. We are merely considering how we should regard those second meanings which things said or written sometimes take on in the light of fuller knowledge than their author possessed. And I am suggesting that different instances demand that we should regard them in different ways. Sometimes we may regard this overtone as the result of simple coincidence, however striking. But there are other cases in which the later truth (which the speaker did not know) is intimately related to the truth he did know; so that, in hitting on something like it, he was in touch with that very same reality in which the fuller truth is rooted. Reading his words in the light of that fuller truth and hearing it in them as an overtone or second meaning, we are not foisting on them something alien to his mind, an arbitrary addition. We are prolonging his meaning in a direction congenial to it. The basic reality behind his words and behind the full truth is one and the same.

The status I claim for such things, then, is neither that of coincidence on the one hand nor that of supernatural prevision on the other. I will try to illustrate it by three imaginable cases. i. A holy person, explicitly claiming to prophesy by the Spirit, tells us that there is in the universe such and such a creature. Later we learn (which God forbid) to travel in space and distribute upon new worlds the vomit of our own corruption; and, sure enough, on the remote planet of some remote star, we find that very creature. This would be prophecy in the strictest sense. This would be evidence for the prophet's miraculous gift and strong presumptive evidence for the truth of anything else he had said. ii. A wholly unscientific writer of fantasies invents a creature for purely artistic reasons. Later on, we find a creature recognisably like it. This would be just the writer's luck. A man who knows nothing about racing may once in his life back a winner. iii. A great biologist, illustrating the relation between animal organisms and their environment, invents for this purpose a hypothetical animal adapted to a hypothetical environment. Later, we find a creature very like it (of course in an environment very like the one he had supposed). This resemblance is not in the least accidental. Insight and knowledge, not luck, led to his invention. The real nature of life explains both why there is such a creature in the universe and also why there was such a creature in his lectures. If, while we re-read the lectures, we think of the reality, we are not bringing arbitrary fancies of our own to bear on the text. This second meaning is congenial to it. The examples I have in mind correspond to this third case; except of course that something more sensitive and personal than scientific knowledge is involved—what the writer or speaker was, not only what he knew.

Plato in his *Republic* is arguing that righteousness is often praised for the rewards it brings—honour, popularity, and the like—but that to see it in its true nature we must separate it from all these, strip it naked. He asks us therefore to imagine a perfectly righteous man treated by all around him as a monster of wickedness. We must picture him, still perfect, while he is bound, scourged, and finally impaled (the Persian equivalent of crucifixion). At this passage a Christian reader starts and rubs his eyes. What is happening? Yet another of these lucky coincidences? But presently he sees that there is something here which cannot be called luck at all.

Virgil, in the poem I have quoted, may have been, and the slave in the baths almost certainly was, "talking about something else", some matter other than that of which their words were most importantly true. Plato is talking, and knows he is talking, about the fate of goodness in a wicked and misunderstanding world. But that is not something simply other than the Passion of Christ. It is the very same thing of which that Passion is the supreme illustration. If Plato was in some measure moved to write of it by the recent death—we may almost say the martyrdom—of his master Socrates then that again is not something simply other than the Passion of Christ. The imperfect, yet very venerable, goodness of Socrates led to the easy death of the hemlock, and the perfect goodness of Christ led to the death of the cross, not by chance but for the same reason; because goodness is what it is, and because the fallen world is what it is. If Plato, starting from one example and from his insight into the nature of goodness and the nature of the world, was led on to see the possibility of a perfect example, and thus to depict something extremely like the Passion of Christ, this happened not because he was lucky but because he was wise. If a man who knew only England and had observed that, the higher a mountain was, the longer it retained the snow in early spring, were led on to suppose a mountain so high that it retained the snow all the year round, the similarity between his imagined mountain and the real Alps would not be merely a lucky accident. He might not know that there were any such mountains in reality; just as Plato probably did not know that the ideally perfect instance of crucified goodness which he had depicted would ever become actual and historical. But if that man ever saw the Alps he would not say "What a curious coincidence". He would be more likely to say "There! What did I tell you?"

And what are we to say of those gods in various Pagan mythologies who are killed and rise again and who thereby renew or transform the life of their worshippers or of nature? The odd thing is that here those anthropologists who are most hostile to our faith would agree with many Christians in saying "The resemblance is not accidental". Of course the two parties would say this for different reasons. The anthropologists would mean: "All these superstitions have a common source in the mind and experience, especially the agricultural experience, of early man. Your myth of Christ is like the myth of Balder because it has the same origin. The likeness is a family likeness." The Christians would fall into two schools of thought. The early Fathers (or some of them), who believed that Paganism was nothing but the direct work of the Devil, would say: "The Devil has from the beginning tried to mislead humanity with lies. As all accomplished liars do, he makes his lies as like the truth as he can; provided they lead man astray on the main issue, the more closely they imitate truth the more effective they will be. That is why we call him God's Ape; he is always imitating God. The resemblance of Adonis to Christ is therefore not at all accidental; it is the resemblance we expect to find between a counterfeit and the real thing, between a parody and the original, between imitation pearls and pearls." Other Christians who think, as I do, that in mythology divine and diabolical and human elements (the desire for a good story), all play a part, would say: "It is not accidental. In the sequence of night and day, in the annual death and rebirth of the crops, in the myths which these processes gave rise to, in the strong, if half-articulate, feeling (embodied in many Pagan 'Mysteries') that man himself must undergo some sort of death if he would truly live, there is already a likeness permitted by God to that truth on which all depends. The resemblance between these myths and the Christian truth is no more accidental than the resemblance between the sun and the sun's reflection in a pond, or that between a historical fact and the somewhat garbled version of it which lives in popular report, or between the trees and hills of the real world and the trees and hills in our dreams." Thus all three views alike would regard the "Pagan Christs" and the true Christ as things really related and would find the resemblance significant.

In other words, when we examine things said which take on, in the light of later knowledge, a meaning they could not have had for those who said them, they turn out to be of different sorts. To be sure, of whatever sort they may be, we can often profitably read them with that second meaning in mind. If I think (as I cannot help thinking) about the birth of Christ while I read that poem of Virgil's, or even if I make it a regular part of my Christmas reading, this may be quite a sensible and edifying thing to do. But the resemblance which makes such a reading possible may after all be a mere coincidence (though I am not sure that it is). I may be reading into Virgil what is wholly irrelevant to all he was, and did, and intended; irrelevant as the sinister meaning which the bathman's word in the Roman story acquired from later events may have been to anything that slave was or meant. But when I meditate on the Passion while reading Plato's picture of the Righteous One, or on the Resurrection while reading about Adonis or Balder, the case is altered. There is a real connection between what Plato and the myth-makers most deeply were and meant and what I believe to be the truth. I know that connection and they do not. But it is really there. It is not an arbitrary fancy of my own thrust upon the old words. One can, without any absurdity, imagine Plato or the myth-makers if they learned the truth, saying, "I see . . . so that was what I was really talking about. Of course. That is what my words really meant, and I never knew it." The bath attendant if innocent, on hearing the second meaning given to his words, would no doubt have said, "So help me, I never meant no such thing. Never come into my head. I hadn't a clue." What Virgil would have said, if he had learned the truth, I have no idea. (Or may we more charitably speak, not of what Plato and Virgil and the myth-makers "would have said" but of what they said? For we can pray with good hope that they now know and have long since welcomed the truth; "many shall come from the east and the west and sit down in the kingdom.")

Thus, long before we come to the Psalms or the Bible, there are good reasons for not throwing away all second meanings as rubbish. Keble said of the Pagan poets, "Thoughts beyond their thoughts to those high bards were given." But let us now turn to Scripture itself.

Scripture

IF even pagan utterances can carry a second meaning, not quite accidentally but because, in the sense I have suggested, they have a sort of right to it, we shall expect the Scriptures to do this more momentously and more often. We have two grounds for doing so if we are Christians.

i. For us these writings are "holy", or "inspired", or, as St. Paul says, "the Oracles of God". But this has been understood in more than one way, and I must try to explain how I understand it, at least so far as the Old Testament is concerned. I have been suspected of being what is called a Fundamentalist. That is because I never regard any narrative as unhistorical simply on the ground that it includes the miraculous. Some people find the miraculous so hard to believe that they cannot imagine any reason for my acceptance of it other than a prior belief that every sentence of the Old Testament has historical or scientific truth. But this I do not hold, any more than St. Jerome did when he said that Moses described Creation "after the manner of a popular poet" (as we should say, mythically) or than Calvin did when he doubted whether the story of Job were history or fiction. The real reason why I can accept as historical a story in which a miracle occurs is that I have never found any philosophical grounds for the universal negative proposition that miracles do not happen. I have to decide on quite other grounds (if I decide at all) whether a given narrative is historical or not. The *Book of Job* appears to me unhistorical because it begins about a man quite unconnected with all history or even legend, with no genealogy, living in a country of which the Bible elsewhere has hardly anything to say; because, in fact, the author quite obviously writes as a story-teller not as a chronicler.

I have therefore no difficulty in accepting, say, the view of those scholars who tell us that the account of Creation in *Genesis* is derived from earlier Semitic stories which were Pagan and mythical. We must of course be quite clear what "derived from" means. Stories do not reproduce their species like mice. They are told by men. Each re-teller either repeats exactly what his predecessor had told him or else changes it. He may change it unknowingly or deliberately. If he changes it deliberately, his invention, his sense of form, his ethics, his ideas of what is fit, or edifying, or merely interesting, all come in. If unknowingly, then his unconscious (which is so largely responsible for our forgettings) has been at work. Thus at every step in what is called—a little misleadingly—the "evolution" of a story, a man, all he is and all his attitudes, are involved. And no good work is done anywhere without aid from the Father of Lights. When a series of such re-tellings turns a creation story which at first had almost no religious or metaphysical significance into a story which achieves the idea of true Creation and of a transcendent Creator (as *Genesis* does), then nothing will make me believe that some of the re-tellers, or some one of them, has not been guided by God.

Thus something originally merely natural—the kind of myth that is found among most nations—will have been raised by God above itself, qualified by Him and compelled by Him to serve purposes which of itself it would not have served. Generalising thus, I take it that the whole Old Testament consists of the same sort of material as any other literature—chronicle (some of it obviously pretty accurate), poems, moral and political diatribes, romances, and what not; but all taken into the service of God's word. Not all, I suppose, in the same way. There are prophets who write with the clearest awareness that Divine compulsion is upon them. There are chroniclers whose intention may have been merely to record. There are poets like those in the *Song of Songs* who probably never dreamed of any but a secular and natural purpose in what they composed. There is (and it is no less important) the work first of the Jewish and then of the Christian Church in preserving and canonising just these books. There is the work of redactors and editors in modifying them. On all of these I suppose a Divine pressure; of which not by any means all need have been conscious.

The human qualities of the raw materials show through. Naïvety, error, contradiction, even (as in the cursing Psalms) wickedness are not removed. The total result is not "the Word of God" in the sense that every passage, in itself, gives impeccable science or history. It carries the Word of God; and we (under grace, with attention to tradition and to interpreters wiser than ourselves, and with the use of such intelligence and learning as we may have) receive that word from it not by using it as an encyclopædia or an encyclical but by steeping ourselves in its tone or temper and so learning its overall message.

To a human mind this working-up (in a sense imperfectly), this sublimation (incomplete) of human material, seems, no doubt, an untidy and leaky vehicle. We might have expected, we may think we should have preferred, an unrefracted light giving us ultimate truth in systematic form—something we could have tabulated and memorised and relied on like the multiplication table. One can respect, and at moments envy, both the Fundamentalist's view of the Bible and the Roman Catholic's view of the Church. But there is one argument which we should beware of using for either position: God must have done what is best, this is best, therefore God has done this. For we are mortals and do not know what is best for us, and it is dangerous to prescribe what God must have done— especially when we cannot, for the life of us, see that He has after all done it.

We may observe that the teaching of Our Lord Himself, in which there is no imperfection, is not given us in that cut-and-dried, fool-proof, systematic fashion we might have expected or desired. He wrote no book. We have only reported sayings, most of them uttered in answer to questions, shaped in some degree by their context. And when we have collected them all we cannot reduce them to a system. He preaches but He does not lecture. He uses paradox, proverb, exaggeration, parable, irony; even (I mean no irreverence) the "wisecrack". He utters maxims which, like popular proverbs, if rigorously taken, may seem to contradict one another. His teaching therefore cannot be grasped by the intellect alone, cannot be "got up" as if it were a "subject". If we try to do that with it, we shall find Him the most elusive of teachers. He hardly ever gave a straight answer to a straight question. He will not be, in the way we want, "pinned down".

The attempt is (again, I mean no irreverence) like trying to bottle a sunbeam.

Descending lower, we find a somewhat similar difficulty with St. Paul. I cannot be the only reader who has wondered why God, having given him so many gifts, withheld from him (what would to us seem so necessary for the first Christian theologian) that of lucidity and orderly exposition.

Thus on three levels, in appropriate degrees, we meet the same refusal of what we might have thought best for us—in the Word Himself, in the Apostle of the Gentiles, in Scripture as a whole. Since this is what God has done, this, we must conclude, was best. It may be that what we should have liked would have been fatal to us if granted. It may be indispensable that Our Lord's teaching, by that elusiveness (to our systematising intellect), should demand a response from the whole man, should make it so clear that there is no question of learning a subject but of steeping ourselves in a Personality, acquiring a new outlook and temper, breathing a new atmosphere, suffering Him, in His own way, to rebuild in us the defaced image of Himself. So in St. Paul. Perhaps the sort of works I should wish him to have written would have been useless. The crabbedness, the appearance of inconsequence and even of sophistry, the turbulent mixture of petty detail, personal complaint, practical advice, and lyrical rapture, finally let through what matters more than ideas—a whole Christian life in operation—better say, Christ Himself operating in a man's life. And in the same way, the value of the Old Testament may be dependent on what seems its imperfection. It may repel one use in order that we may be forced to use it in another way—to find the Word in it, not without repeated and leisurely reading nor without discriminations made by our conscience and our critical faculties, to re-live, while we read, the whole Jewish experience of God's gradual and graded self-revelation, to feel the very contentions between the Word and the human material through which it works. For here again, it is our total response that has to be elicited.

Certainly it seems to me that from having had to reach what is really the Voice of God in the cursing Psalms through all the horrible distortions of the human medium, I have gained something I might not have gained from a flawless, ethical exposition. The shadows have indicated (at least to my heart) something more about the light. Nor would I (now) willingly spare from my Bible something in itself so anti-religious as the nihilism of *Ecclesiastes.* We get there a clear, cold picture of man's life without God. That statement is itself part of God's word. We need to have heard it. Even to have assimilated *Ecclesiastes* and no other book in the Bible would be to have advanced further towards truth than some men do.

But of course these conjectures as to why God does what He does are probably of no more value than my dog's ideas of what I am up to when I sit and read. But though we can only guess the reasons, we can at least observe the consistency, of His ways. We read in *Genesis* (2, 7) that God formed man of the dust and breathed life into him. For all the first writer knew of it, this passage might merely illustrate the survival, even in a truly creational story, of the Pagan inability to conceive true Creation, the savage, pictorial tendency to imagine God making things "out of" something as the potter or the carpenter does. Nevertheless, whether by lucky accident or (as I think) by God's guidance, it embodies a profound principle. For on any view man is in one sense clearly made "out of" something else. He is an animal; but an animal called to be, or raised to be, or (if you like) doomed to be, something more than an animal. On the ordinary biological view (what difficulties I have about evolution are not religious) one of the primates is changed so that he becomes man; but he remains still a primate and an animal. He is taken up into a new life without relinquishing the old. In the same way, all organic life takes up and uses processes merely chemical. But we can trace the principle higher as well as lower. For we are taught that the Incarnation itself proceeded "not by the conversion of the godhead into flesh, but by taking of (the) manhood into God"; in it human life becomes the vehicle of Divine life. If the Scriptures proceed not by conversion of God's word into a literature but by taking up of a literature to be the vehicle of God's word, this is not anomalous.

Of course, on almost all levels, that method seems to us precarious or, as I have said, leaky. None of these up-gradings is, as we should have wished, self-evident. Because the lower nature, in being taken up and loaded with a new burden and advanced to a new privilege, remains, and is not annihilated, it will always be possible to ignore the up-grading and see nothing but the lower. Thus men can read the life of Our Lord (because it is a human life) as nothing but a human life. Many, perhaps most, modern philosophies read human life merely as an animal life of unusual complexity. The Cartesians read animal life as mechanism. Just in the same way Scripture can be read as merely human literature. No new discovery, no new method, will ever give a final victory to either interpretation. For what is required, on all these levels alike, is not merely knowledge but a certain insight; getting the focus right. Those who can see in each of these instances only the lower will always be plausible. One who contended that a poem was nothing but black marks on white paper would be unanswerable if he addressed an audience who couldn't read. Look at it through microscopes, analyse the printer's ink and the paper, study it (in that way) as long as you like; you will never find something over and above all the products of analysis whereof you can say "This is the poem". Those who can read, however, will continue to say the poem exists.

If the Old Testament is a literature thus "taken up", made the vehicle of what is more than human, we can of course set no limit to the weight or multiplicity of meanings which may have been laid upon it. If any writer may say more than he knows and mean more than he meant, then these writers will be especially likely to do so. And not by accident.

ii. The second reason for accepting the Old Testament in this way can be put more simply and is of course far more compulsive. We are committed to it in principle by Our Lord Himself. On that famous journey to Emmaus He found fault with the two disciples for not believing what the prophets had said. They ought to have known from their Bibles that the Anointed One, when He came, would enter his glory through suffering. He then explained, from "Moses" (i.e. the Pentateuch) down, all the places in the Old Testament "concerning Himself" (*Luke* 24, *25–27*). He clearly identified Himself with a figure often mentioned in the Scriptures; appropriated to Himself many passages where a modern scholar might see no such reference. In the predictions of His Own Passion which He had previously made to the disciples, He was obviously doing the same thing. He accepted—indeed He claimed to be—the second meaning of Scripture.

We do not know—or anyway I do not know—what all these passages were. We can be pretty sure about one of them. The Ethiopian eunuch who met Philip (*Acts* 8, *27–38*) was reading *Isaiah* 53. He did not know whether in that passage the prophet was talking about himself or about someone else. Philip, in answering his question, "preached unto him Jesus". The answer, in fact, was "Isaiah is speaking of Jesus". We need have no doubt that Philip's authority for this interpretation was Our Lord. (Our ancestors would have thought that Isaiah consciously foresaw the sufferings of Christ as people see the future in the sort of dreams recorded by Mr. Dunne. Modern scholars would say, that on the conscious level, he was referring to Israel itself, the whole nation personified. I do not see that it matters which view we take.) We can, again, be pretty sure, from the words on the cross (*Mark* 15, *34*), that Our Lord identified Himself with the sufferer in Psalm 22. Or when He asked (*Mark* 12, *35, 36*) how Christ could be both David's son and David's lord, He clearly identified Christ, and therefore Himself, with the "my Lord" of Psalm 110—was in fact hinting at the mystery of the Incarnation by pointing out a difficulty which only it could solve. In *Matthew* 4, *6* the words of Psalm 91 *11, 12*, "He shall give his angels charge over thee . . . that thou hurt not thy foot against a stone," are applied to Him, and we may be sure the application was His own since only He could be the source of the temptation-story. In *Mark* 12, *10* He implicitly appropriates to Himself the words of Psalm 118 *22* about the stone which the builders rejected. "Thou shalt not leave my soul in hell, neither shalt thou suffer thy Holy One to see corruption" (16, *11*) is treated as a prophecy of His Resurrection in *Acts* 2, *27*, and was doubtless so taken by Himself, since we find it so taken in the earliest Christian tradition—that is, by people likely to be closer both to the spirit and to the letter of His words than any scholarship (I do not say, "any sanctity") will bring a modern. Yet it is, perhaps, idle to speak here of spirit and letter. There is almost no "letter" in the words of Jesus. Taken by a literalist, He will always prove the most elusive of teachers. Systems cannot keep up with that darting illumination. No net less wide than a man's whole heart, nor less fine of mesh than love, will hold the sacred Fish.

FROM

Letters to Malcolm: Chiefly on Prayer

I AM all in favour of your idea that we should go back to our old plan of having a more or less set subject—an *agendum*—for our letters. When we were last separated the correspondence languished for lack of it. How much better we did in our undergraduate days with our interminable letters on the *Republic,* and classical metres, and what was then the "new" psychology! Nothing makes an absent friend so present as a disagreement.

Prayer, which you suggest, is a subject that is a good deal in my mind. I mean, private prayer. If you were thinking of corporate prayer, I won't play. There is no subject in the world (always excepting sport) on which I have less to say than liturgiology. And the almost nothing which I have to say may as well be disposed of in this letter.

I think our business as laymen is to take what we are given and make the best of it. And I think we should find this a great deal easier if what we were given was always and everywhere the same.

To judge from their practice, very few Anglican clergymen take this view. It looks as if they believed people can be lured to go to church by incessant brightenings, lightenings, lengthenings, abridgements, simplifications and complications of the service. And it is probably true that a new, keen vicar will usually be able to form within his parish a minority who are in favour of his innovations. The majority, I believe, never are. Those who remain—many give up churchgoing altogether—merely endure.

Is this simply because the majority are hidebound? I think not. They have a good reason for their conservatism. Novelty, simply as such, can have only an entertainment value. And they don't go to church to be entertained. They go to *use* the service, or, if you prefer, to *enact* it. Every service is a structure of acts and words through which we receive a sacrament, or repent, or supplicate, or adore. And it enables us to do these things best—if you like, it "works" best—when, through long familiarity, we don't have to think about it. As long as you notice, and have to count, the steps, you are not yet dancing but only learning to dance. A good shoe is a shoe you don't notice. Good reading becomes possible when you need not consciously think about eyes, or light, or print, or spelling. The perfect church service would be one we were almost unaware of; our attention would have been on God.

But every novelty prevents this. It fixes our attention on the service itself; and thinking about worship is a different thing from worshipping. The important question about the Grail was "for what does it serve?" "'Tis mad idolatry that makes the service greater than the god."

A still worse thing may happen. Novelty may fix our attention not even on the service but on the celebrant. You know what I mean. Try as one may to exclude it, the question, "What on earth is he up to now?" will intrude. It lays one's devotion waste. There is really some excuse for the man who said, "I wish they'd remember that the charge to Peter was Feed my sheep; not Try experiments on my rats, or even, Teach my performing dogs new tricks."

Thus my whole liturgiological position really boils down to an entreaty for permanence and uniformity. I can make do with almost any kind of service whatever, if only it will stay put. But if each form is snatched away just when I am beginning to feel at home in it, then I can never make any progress in the art of worship. You give me no chance to acquire the trained habit—*habito dell'arte*.

It may well be that some variations which seem to me merely matters of taste really involve grave doctrinal differences. But surely not all? For if grave doctrinal differences are really as numerous as variations in practice, then we shall have to conclude that no such thing as the Church of England exists. And anyway, the Liturgical Fidget is not a purely Anglican phenomenon; I have heard Roman Catholics complain of it too.

And that brings me back to my starting point. The business of us laymen is simply to endure and make the best of it. Any tendency to a passionate preference for one type of service must be regarded simply as a temptation. Partisan "Churchmanships" are my *bête noire*. And if we avoid them, may we not possibly perform a very useful function? The shepherds go off, "every one to his own way" and vanish over diverse points of the horizon. If the sheep huddle patiently together and go on bleating, might they finally recall the shepherds? (Haven't English victories sometimes been won by the rank and file in spite of the generals?)

As to the words of the service—liturgy in the narrower sense—the question is rather different. If you have a vernacular liturgy you must have a changing liturgy; otherwise it will finally be vernacular only in name. The ideal of "timeless English" is sheer nonsense. No living language can be timeless. You might as well ask for a motionless river.

I think it would have been best, if it were possible, that necessary change should have occurred gradually and (to most people) imperceptibly; here a little and there a little; one obsolete word replaced in a century—like the gradual change of spelling in successive editions of Shakespeare. As things are we must reconcile ourselves, if we can also reconcile government, to a new Book.

If we were—I thank my stars I'm not—in a position to give its authors advice, would you have any advice to give them? Mine could hardly go beyond unhelpful cautions: "Take care. It is so easy to break eggs without making omelettes."

Already our liturgy is one of the very few remaining elements of unity in our hideously divided Church. The good to be done by revision needs to be very great and very certain before we throw that away. Can you imagine any new Book which will not be a source of new schism?

Most of those who press for revision seem to wish that it should serve two purposes: that of modernising the language in the interests of intelligibility, and that of doctrinal improvement. Ought the two operations—each painful and each dangerous—to be carried out at the same time? Will the patient survive?

What are the agreed doctrines which are to be embodied in the new Book and how long will agreement on them continue? I ask with trepidation because I read a man the other day who seemed to wish that everything in the old Book which was inconsistent with orthodox Freudianism should be deleted.

For whom are we to cater in revising the language? A country parson I know asked his sexton what he understood by *indifferently* in the phrase "truly and indifferently administer justice". The man replied, "It means making no difference between one chap and another." "And what would it mean if it said *impartially*?" asked the parson. "Don't know. Never heard of it," said the sexton. Here, you see, we have a change intended to make things easier. But it does so neither for the educated, who understand *indifferently* already, nor for the wholly uneducated, who don't understand *impartially*. It helps only some middle area of the congregation which may not even be a majority. Let us hope the revisers will prepare for their work by a prolonged empirical study of popular speech as it actually is, not as we *(a priori)* assume it to be. How many scholars know (what I discovered by accident) that when uneducated people say *impersonal* they sometimes mean *incorporeal*?

What of expressions which are archaic but not unintelligible? ("Be ye lift up"). I find that people re-act to archaism most diversely. It antagonises some: makes what is said unreal. To others, not necessarily more learned, it is highly numinous and a real aid to devotion. We can't please both.

I know there must be change. But is this the right moment? Two signs of the right moment occur to me. One would be a unity among us which enabled the Church—not some momentarily triumphant party—to speak through the new work with a united voice. The other would be the manifest presence, somewhere in the Church, of the specifically literary talent needed for composing a good prayer. Prose needs to be not only very good but very good in a very special way, if it is to stand up to reiterated reading aloud. Cranmer may have his defects as a theologian; as a stylist, he can play all the moderns, and many of his predecessors, off the field. I don't see either sign at the moment.

Yet we all want to be tinkering. Even I would gladly see "Let your light so shine before men" removed from the offertory. It sounds, in that context, so like an exhortation to do our alms that they may be seen by men.

I'd meant to follow up what you say about Rose Macaulay's letters, but that must wait till next week. . . .

. . . Perhaps I shan't find it so easy to persuade you that the ready-made modicum has also its use: for me, I mean—I'm not suggesting rules for any one else in the whole world.

First, it keeps me in touch with "sound doctrine". Left to oneself, one could easily slide away from "the faith once given" into a phantom called "my religion".

Secondly, it reminds me "what things I ought to ask" (perhaps especially when I am praying for other people). The crisis of the present moment, like the nearest telegraph-post, will always loom largest. Isn't there a danger that our great, permanent, objective necessities—often more important—may get crowded out? By the way, that's another thing to be avoided in a revised Prayer Book. "Contemporary problems" may claim an undue share. And the more "up to date" the Book is, the sooner it will be dated.

Finally, they provide an element of the ceremonial. On your view, that is just what we don't want. On mine, it is part of what we want. I see what you mean when you say that using ready-made prayers would be like "making love to your own wife out of Petrarch or Donne". (Incidentally might you not *quote* them—to such a literary wife as Betty?) The parallel won't do.

I fully agree that the relationship between God and a man is more private and intimate than any possible relation between two fellow creatures. Yes, but at the same time there is, in another way, a greater distance between the participants. We are approaching—well I won't say "the Wholly Other", for I suspect that is meaningless, but the Unimaginably and Insupportably Other. We ought to be—sometimes I hope one is—simultaneously aware of closest proximity and infinite distance. You make things far too snug and confiding. Your erotic analogy needs to be supplemented by "I fell at His feet as one dead."

I think the "low" church *milieu* that I grew up in did tend to be too cosily at ease in Sion. My grandfather, I'm told, used to say that he "looked forward to having some very interesting conversations with St. Paul when he got to heaven." Two clerical gentlemen talking at ease in a club! It never seemed to cross his mind that an encounter with St. Paul might be rather an overwhelming experience even for an Evangelical clergyman of good family. But when Dante saw the great apostles in heaven they affected him like *mountains*. There's lots to be said against devotions to saints; but at least they keep on reminding us that we are very small people compared with them. How much smaller before their Master? . . .

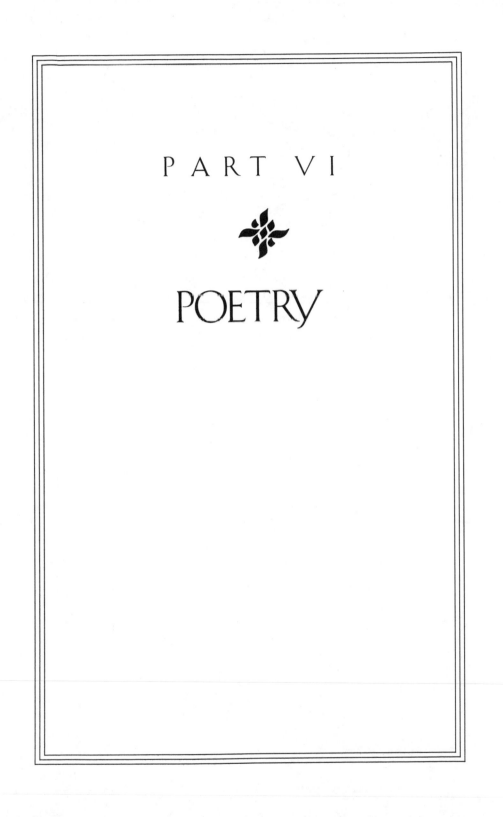

PART VI

POETRY

P OETRY was always important to C. S. Lewis. He started writing verse as a child, and his first two books were in the same genre. The early books are a collection of forty lyrics entitles *Spirits in Bondage* (1919) and a long narrative poem *Dymer* (1926). Neither volume was enthusiastically received, so the budding writer subsequently turned most of his attention to prose.

Although he never attempted another full book of verse, he did continue to write and publish the occasional poem throughout the rest of his life.

Over one hundred and twenty of Lewis's poems have been gathered from various periodicals and published in *Poems* (1964). Eleven selections from that collection are published here; the twelfth selection is a verse Lewis wrote in memory of his wife, and it is on her plaque at the Headington Crematorium.

The first four selections reveal Lewis in his typical posture as a combatant. "A Confession" is an attack on T. S. Eliot's verse; "Evolutionary Hymn" assaults the Idea of Progress; "On the Atomic Bomb" critiques post-1945 doomsday hysteria; and "Posturing," which originally appeared in *The Pilgrim's Regress*, is a jab at the author's own pride.

Lewis did more than take shots at standing targets when he wrote poetry. The last eight examples published here show a wide range of moods, from mourning over the death of Charles Williams and Joy Davidman, to contemplating biblical events and examining his own apologetical enterprise.

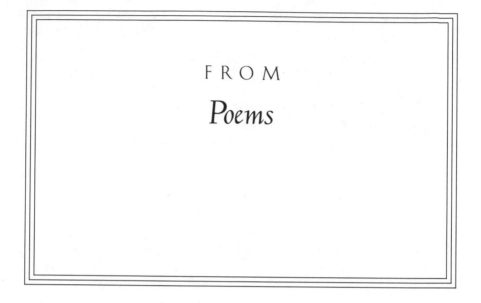

FROM

Poems

A Confession

I am so coarse, the things the poets see
Are obstinately invisible to me.
For twenty years I've stared my level best
To see if evening—any evening—would suggest
A patient etherized upon a table;
In vain. I simply wasn't able.
To me each evening looked far more
Like the departure from a silent, yet a crowded, shore
Of a ship whose freight was everything, leaving behind
Gracefully, finally, without farewells, marooned mankind.

Red dawn behind a hedgerow in the east
Never, for me, resembled in the least
A chillblain on a cocktail-shaker's nose;
Waterfalls don't remind me of torn underclothes,
Nor glaciers of tin-cans. I've never known
The moon look like a hump-backed crone—
Rather, a prodigy, even now
Not naturalized, a riddle glaring from the Cyclops' brow

Of the cold world, reminding me on what a place
I crawl and cling, a planet with no bulwarks, out in space.

Never the white sun of the wintriest day
Struck me as *un crachat d'estaminet.*
I'm like that odd man Wordsworth knew, to whom
A primrose was a yellow primrose, one whose doom
Keeps him forever in the list of dunces,
Compelled to live on stock responses,
Making the poor best that I can
Of dull things . . . peacocks, honey, the Great Wall, Aldebaran,
Silver weirs, new-cut grass, wave on the beach, hard gem,
The shapes of horse and woman, Athens, Troy, Jerusalem.

Evolutionary Hymn

Lead us, Evolution, lead us
Up the future's endless stair:
Chop us, change us, prod us, weed us.
For stagnation is despair:
Groping, guessing, yet progressing,
Lead us nobody knows where.

Wrong or justice in the present,
Joy or sorrow, what are they
While there's always jam to-morrow,
While we tread the onward way?
Never knowing where we're going,
We can never go astray.

To whatever variation
Our posterity may turn
Hairy, squashy, or crustacean,
Bulbous-eyed or square of stern,
Tusked or toothless, mild or ruthless,
Towards that unknown god we yearn.

Ask not if it's god or devil,
Brethren, lest your words imply
Static norms of good and evil
(As in Plato) throned on high;
Such scholastic, inelastic,
Abstract yardsticks we deny.

Far too long have sages vainly
Glossed great Nature's simple text;
He who runs can read it plainly,
'Goodness—what comes next.'
By evolving, Life is solving
All the questions we perplexed.

On then! Value means survival-
Value. If our progeny
Spreads and spawns and licks each rival,
That will prove its deity
(Far from pleasant, by our present
Standards, though it well may be).

On the Atomic Bomb

Metrical Experiment

So; you have found an engine
Of injury that angels
Might dread. The world plunges,
Shies, snorts, and curvets like a horse in danger.

Then comfort her with fondlings,
With kindly word and handling,
But do not believe blindly
This way or that. Both fears and hopes are swindlers.

What's here to dread? For mortals
Both hurt and death were certain
Already; our light-hearted
Hopes from the first sentenced to final thwarting.

This marks no huge advance in
The dance of Death. His pincers
Were grim before with chances
Of cold, fire, suffocation, Ogpu, cancer.

Nor hope that this last blunder
Will end our woes by rending
Tellus herself asunder—
All gone in one bright flash like dryest tinder.

As if your puny gadget
Could dodge the terrible logic

Of history! No; the tragic
Road will go on, new generations trudge it.

Narrow and long it stretches,
Wretched for one who marches
Eyes front. He never catches
A glimpse of the fields each side, the happy orchards.

Posturing

Because of endless pride
Reborn with endless error,
Each hour I look aside
Upon my secret mirror
Trying all postures there
To make my image fair.

Thou givest grapes, and I,
Though starving, turn to see
How dark the cool globes lie
In the white hand of me,
And linger gazing thither
Till the live clusters wither.

So should I quickly die
Narcissus-like of want,
But, in the glass, my eye
Catches such forms as haunt
Beyond nightmare, and make
Pride humble for pride's sake.

Then and then only turning
The stiff neck round, I grow
A molten man all burning
And look behind and know
Who made the glass, whose light makes
 dark, whose fair
Makes foul, my shadowy form reflected
 there
That self-Love, brought to bed of Love
 may die and bear
Her sweet son in despair.

Joys That Sting

Oh doe not die, says Donne, *for I shall hate*
All women so. How false the sentence rings.
Women? But in a life made desolate
It is the joys once shared that have the stings.

To take the old walks alone, or not at all,
To order one pint where I ordered two,
To think of, and then not to make, the small
Time-honoured joke (senseless to all but you);

To laugh (oh, one'll laugh), to talk upon
Themes that we talked upon when you were there,
To make some poor pretence of going on,
Be kind to one's old friends, and seem to care,

While no one (O God) through the years will say
The simplest, common word in just your way.

To Charles Williams

Your death blows a strange bugle call, friend, and all is hard
To see plainly or record truly. The new light imposes change,
Re-adjusts all a life-landscape as it thrusts down its probe from the sky,
To create shadows, to reveal waters, to erect hills and deepen glens.
The slant alters. I can't see the old contours. It's a larger world
Than I once thought it. I wince, caught in the bleak air that blows on
     the ridge.
Is it the first sting of the great winter, the world-waning? Or the cold of
     spring?

A hard question and worth talking a whole night on. But with whom?
Of whom now can I ask guidance? With what friend concerning your
     death
Is it worth while to exchange thoughts unless—oh unless it were you?

Scazons

Walking to-day by a cottage I shed tears
When I remembered how once I had walked there
With my friends who are mortal and dead. Years
Little had healed the wound that was laid bare.

Out little spear that stabs! I, fool, believed
I had outgrown the local, unique sting,
I had transmuted wholly (I was deceived)
Into Love universal the lov'd thing.

But Thou, Lord, surely knewest thine own plan
When the angelic indifferencies with no bar
Universally loved, but Thou gav'st man
The tether and pang of the particular,

Which, like a chemic drop, infinitesimal,
Plashed into pure water, changing the whole,
Embodies and embitters and turns all
Spirit's sweet water into astringent soul,

That we, though small, might quiver with Fire's same
Substantial form as Thou—not reflect merely
Like lunar angels back to Thee cold flame.
Gods are we, Thou hast said; and we pay dearly.

Sonnet

*Dieu a établi la prière pour communiquer à ses
creatures la dignité de la causalité.* —PASCAL

The Bible says Sennacherib's campaign was spoiled
By angels: in Herodotus it says, by mice—
Innumerably nibbling all one night they toiled
To eat his bowstrings piecemeal as warm wind eats ice.

But muscular archangels, I suggest, employed
Seven little jaws at labour on each slender string,
And by their aid, weak masters though they be, destroyed
The smiling-lipped Assyrian, cruel-bearded king.

No stranger that omnipotence should choose to need
Small helps than great—no stranger if His action lingers

Till men have prayed, and suffers their weak prayers indeed
To move as very muscles His delaying fingers,

Who, in His longanimity and love for our
Small dignities, enfeebles, for a time, His power.

Stephen to Lazarus

But was I the first martyr, who
Gave up no more than life, while you,
Already free among the dead,
Your rags stripped off, your fetters shed,
Surrendered what all other men
Irrevocably keep, and when
Your battered ship at anchor lay
Seemingly safe in the dark bay
No ripple stirs, obediently
Put out a second time to sea
Well knowing that your death (in vain
Died once) must all be died again?

As the Ruin Falls

All this is flashy rhetoric about loving you.
I never had a selfless thought since I was born.
I am mercenary and self-seeking through and through:
I want God, you, all friends, merely to serve my turn.

Peace, re-assurance, pleasure, are the goals I seek,
I cannot crawl one inch outside my proper skin:
I talk of love—a scholar's parrot may talk Greek—
But, self-imprisoned, always end where I begin.

Only that now you have taught me (but how late) my lack.
I see the chasm. And everything you are was making
My heart into a bridge by which I might get back
From exile, and grow man. And now the bridge is breaking.

For this I bless you as the ruin falls. The pains
You give me are more precious than all other gains.

The Apologist's Evening Prayer

From all my lame defeats and oh! much more
From all the victories that I seemed to score;
From cleverness shot forth on Thy behalf
At which, while angels weep, the audience laugh;
From all my proofs of Thy divinity,
Thou, who wouldst give no sign, deliver me.

Thoughts are but coins. Let me not trust, instead
Of Thee, their thin-worn image of Thy head.
From all my thoughts, even from my thoughts of Thee,
O thou fair Silence, fall, and set me free.
Lord of the narrow gate and the needle's eye,
Take from me all my trumpery lest I die.

REMEMBER

HELEN JOY DAVIDMAN

D. JULY 1960
LOVED WIFE OF
C. S. LEWIS

HERE THE WHOLE WORLD (STARS, WATER, AIR,
AND FIELD, AND FOREST, AS THEY WERE
REFLECTED IN A SINGLE MIND)
LIKE CAST OFF CLOTHES WAS LEFT BEHIND
IN ASHES, YET WITH HOPE THAT SHE,
RE-BORN FROM HOLY POVERTY,
IN LENTEN LANDS, HEREAFTER MAY
RESUME THEM ON HER EASTER DAY.

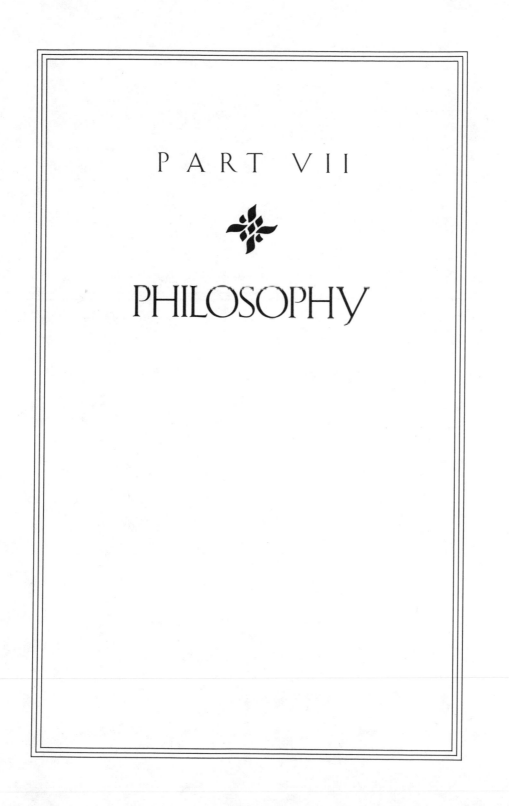

PART VII

PHILOSOPHY

I F C. S. LEWIS is best remembered as a Christian apologist and author of imaginative literature, or a literary historian and critic, it also should be remembered that he wrote some other books that are strikingly philosophic in tone. Books such as *The Problem of Pain* (1940), *Miracles* (1947), *The Four Loves* (1960), as well as his Preface to B. G. Sandhurst's *How Heathen is Britain?* (1946), are heavily theological and apologetic, yet they are markedly analytic and philosophic.

It is true that Lewis studied philosophy and classics at Oxford. Nevertheless, he felt more kinship to the less abstract academic disciplines of literary history and criticism. These preferences notwithstanding, he occasionally published his thoughts about moral and natural philosophy.

Lewis's effectiveness as a philosopher has been debated since the 1940s, and he has as many detractors as he has defenders. Most critics agree, however, that *The Abolition of Man* (1943) is his most important excursion into this field. Subtitled *Reflections on Education with Special Reference to the Teaching of English in the Upper Form Schools,* this work has been in print for over four decades.

The Abolition of Man, reprinted in its entirety here, is an exploration into the nature of humankind and morality. The University of Durham Riddell Memorial Lectures provided the occasion for the Oxford academician to present three talks that comprise a book now widely regarded as a classic.

The Abolition of Man

or
Reflections on Education
with Special Reference to the
Teaching of English in
the Upper Forms of Schools

CONTENTS

The Master said, He who sets to work on a different
strand destroys the whole fabric.
—CONFUCIUS, *Analects* II. 16.

1

Men without Chests

So he sent the word to slay
And slew the little childer.

CAROL

I DOUBT whether we are sufficiently attentive to the importance of elementary text-books. That is why I have chosen as the starting-point for these lectures a little book on English intended for 'boys and girls in the upper forms of schools.' I do not think the authors of this book (there were two of them) intended any harm, and I owe them, or their publisher, good language for sending me a complimentary copy. At the same time I shall have nothing good to say of them. Here is a pretty predicament. I do not want to pillory two modest practising school-masters who were doing the best they knew: but I cannot be silent about what I think the actual tendency of their work. I therefore propose to conceal their names. I shall refer to these gentlemen as Gaius and Titius and to their book as *The Green Book*. But I promise you there is such a book and I have it on my shelves.

In their second chapter Gaius and Titius quote the well-known story of Coleridge at the waterfall. You remember that there were two tourists present: that one called it 'sublime' and the other 'pretty': and that Coleridge mentally endorsed the first judgement and rejected the second with disgust. Gaius and Titius comment as follows: 'When the man said *That is sublime,* he appeared to be making a remark about the waterfall. . . . Actually . . . he was not making a remark about the waterfall, but a remark about his own feelings. What he was saying was really *I have feelings associated in my mind with the word "Sublime,"* or shortly, *I have sublime feelings.'* Here are a good many deep questions settled in a pretty summary fashion. But the authors are not yet finished. They add: 'This confusion is continually present in language as we use it. We appear to be saying something very important about something: and actually we are only saying something about our own feelings.'[1]

Before considering the issues really raised by this momentous little paragraph (designed, you will remember, for 'the upper forms in schools') we must eliminate one mere confusion into which Gaius and Titius have fallen. Even on their own view—on any conceivable view—the man who says *This is sublime* cannot mean *I have sublime feelings.* Even if it were granted that such qualities as sublimity were simply and solely projected into things from our own emotions, yet the emotions which prompt the projection are the correlatives, and therefore almost the opposites, of the qualities projected. The feelings which make a man call an

[1] *The Green Book*, pp. 19, 20.

429

object sublime are not sublime feelings but feelings of veneration. If *This is sublime* is to be reduced at all to a statement about the speaker's feelings, the proper translation would be *I have humble feelings.* If the view held by Gaius and Titius were consistently applied it would lead to obvious absurdities. It would force them to maintain that *You are contemptible* means *I have contemptible feelings:* in fact that *Your feelings are contemptible* means *My feelings are contemptible.* But we need not delay over this which is the very *pons asinorum* of our subject. It would be unjust to Gaius and Titius themselves to emphasize what was doubtless a mere inadvertence.

The schoolboy who reads this passage in *The Green Book* will believe two propositions: firstly, that all sentences containing a predicate of value are state-ments about the emotional state of the speaker, and, secondly, that all such statements are unimportant. It is true that Gaius and Titius have said neither of these things in so many words. They have treated only one particular predicate of value *(sublime)* as a word descriptive of the speaker's emotions. The pupils are left to do for themselves the work of extending the same treatment to all predicates of value: and no slightest obstacle to such extension is placed in their way. The authors may or may not desire the extension: they may never have given the question five minutes' serious thought in their lives. I am not concerned with what they desired but with the effect their book will certainly have on the schoolboy's mind. In the same way, they have not said that judgements of value are unimportant. Their words are that we 'appear to be saying something very important' when in reality we are 'only saying something about our own feelings.' No schoolboy will be able to resist the suggestion brought to bear upon him by that word *only.* I do not mean, of course, that he will make any conscious inference from what he reads to a general philosophical theory that all values are subjective and trivial. The very power of Gaius and Titius depends on the fact that they are dealing with a boy: a boy who thinks he is 'doing' his 'English prep' and has no notion that ethics, theology, and politics are all at stake. It is not a theory they put into his mind, but an assumption, which ten years hence, its origin forgotten and its presence unconscious, will condition him to take one side in a controversy which he has never recognized as a controversy at all. The authors themselves, I suspect, hardly know what they are doing to the boy, and he cannot know what is being done to him.

Before considering the philosophical credentials of the position which Gaius and Titius have adopted about value, I should like to show its practical results on their educational procedure. In their fourth chapter they quote a silly adver-tisement of a pleasure cruise and proceed to inoculate their pupils against the sort of writing it exhibits.[2] The advertisement tells us that those who buy tickets for this cruise will go 'across the Western Ocean where Drake of Devon sailed,' 'adventuring after the treasures of the Indies,' and bringing home themselves also a 'treasure' of 'golden hours' and 'glowing colours.' It is a bad bit of writing, of

[2]*Ibid.,* p. 53.

course: a venal and bathetic exploitation of those emotions of awe and pleasure which men feel in visiting places that have striking associations with history or legend. If Gaius and Titius were to stick to their last and teach their readers (as they promised to do) the art of English composition, it was their business to put this advertisement side by side with passages from great writers in which the very same emotion is well expressed, and then show where the difference lies. They might have used Johnson's famous passage from the *Western Islands*, which concludes: 'That man is little to be envied, whose patriotism would not gain force upon the plain of Marathon, or whose piety would not grow warmer among the ruins of Iona.'[3] They might have taken that place in *The Prelude* where Wordsworth describes how the antiquity of London first descended on his mind with 'Weight and power, Power growing under weight.'[4] A lesson which had laid such literature beside the advertisement and really discriminated the good from the bad would have been a lesson worth teaching. There would have been some blood and sap in it the trees of knowledge and of life growing together. It would also have had the merit of being a lesson in literature: a subject of which Gaius and Titius, despite their professed purpose, are uncommonly shy. What they actually do is to point out that the luxurious motor-vessel won't really sail where Drake did, that the tourists will not have any adventures, that the treasures they bring home will be of a purely metaphorical nature, and that a trip to Margate might provide 'all the pleasure and rest' they required.[5] All this is very true: talents inferior to those of Gaius and Titius would have sufficed to discover it. What they have not noticed, or not cared about, is that a very similar treatment could be applied to much good literature which treats the same emotion. What, after all, can the history of early British Christianity, in pure reason, add to the motives for piety as they exist in the eighteenth century? Why should Mr. Wordsworth's inn be more comfortable or the air of London more healthy because London has existed for a long time? Or, if there is indeed any obstacle which will prevent a critic from 'debunking' Johnson and Wordsworth (and Lamb, and Virgil, and Thomas Browne, and Mr. de la Mare) as *The Green Book* debunks the advertisement, Gaius and Titius have given their schoolboy readers no faintest help to its discovery. From this passage the schoolboy will learn about literature precisely nothing. What he will learn quickly enough, and perhaps indelibly, is the belief that all emotions aroused by local association are in themselves contrary to reason and contemptible. He will have no notion that there are two ways of being immune to such an advertisement—that it falls equally flat on those who are above it and those who are below it, on the man of real sensibility and on the mere trousered ape who has never been able to conceive the Atlantic as anything more than so many million tons of cold salt water. There are two men to whom we offer in vain a false leading article on patriotism and honour: one is the coward, the other is the honourable and patriotic man. None of this is brought before

[3]*Journey to the Western Islands. Inch Kenneth.*   [4]*The Prelude*, viii, 11. 549–59
[5]*The Green Book*, pp. 53–5.

the schoolboy's mind. On the contrary, he is encouraged to reject the lure of the 'Western Ocean' on the very dangerous ground that in so doing he will prove himself a knowing fellow who can't be bubbled out of his cash. Gaius and Titius, while teaching him nothing about letters, have cut out of his soul, long before he is old enough to choose, the possibility of having certain experiences which thinkers of more authority than they have held to be generous, fruitful, and humane.

But it is not only Gaius and Titius. In another little book, whose author I will call Orbilius, I find that the same operation, under the same general anaesthetic, is being carried out. Orbilius chooses for 'debunking' a silly bit of writing on horses, where these animals are praised as the 'willing servants' of the early colonists in Australia.[6] And he falls into the same trap as Gaius and Titius. Of Ruksh and Sleipnir and the weeping horses of Achilles and the war-horse in the Book of Job—nay even of Brer Rabbit and of Peter Rabbit—of man's prehistoric piety to 'our brother the ox'—of all that this semi-anthropomorphic treatment of beasts has meant in human history and of the literature where it finds noble or piquant expression—he has not a word to say.[7] Even of the problems of animal psychology as they exist for science he says nothing. He contents himself with explaining that horses are not, *secundum litteram,* interested in colonial expansion.[8] This piece of information is really all that his pupils get from him. Why the composition before them is bad, when others that lie open to the same charge are good, they do not hear. Much less do they learn of the two classes of men who are, respectively above and below the danger of such writing—the man who really knows horses and really loves them, not with anthropomorphic illusions, but with ordinate love, and the irredeemable urban blockhead to whom a horse is merely an old-fashioned means of transport. Some pleasure in their own ponies and dogs they will have lost: some incentive to cruelty or neglect they will have received: some pleasure in their own knowingness will have entered their minds. That is their day's lesson in English, though of English they have learned nothing. Another little portion of the human heritage has been quietly taken from them before they were old enough to understand.

I have hitherto been assuming that such teachers as Gaius and Titius do not fully realize what they are doing and do not intend the far-reaching consequences it will actually have. There is, of course, another possibility. What I have called (presuming on their concurrence in a certain traditional system of values) the

[6]Orbilius' book, p. 5.

[7]Orbilius is so far superior to Gaius and Titius that he does (pp. 19–22) contrast a piece of good writing on animals with the piece condemned. Unfortunately, however, the only superiority he really demonstrates in the second extract is its superiority in factual truth. The specifically literary problem (the use and abuse of expressions which are false *secundum litteram*) is not tackled. Orbilius indeed tells us (p. 97) that we must 'learn to distinguish between legitimate and illegitimate figurative statement,' but he gives us very little help in doing so. At the same time it is fair to record my opinion that his work is on quite a different level from *The Green Book.*

[8]*Ibid.*, p.9

'trousered ape' and the 'urban blockhead' may be precisely the kind of man they really wish to produce. The differences between us may go all the way down. They may really hold that the ordinary human feelings about the past or animals or large waterfalls are contrary to reason and contemptible and ought to be eradicated. They may be intending to make a clean sweep of traditional values and start with a new set. That position will be discussed later. If it is the position which Gaius and Titius are holding, I must, for the moment, content myself with pointing out that it is a philosophical and not a literary position. In filling their book with it they have been unjust to the parent or headmaster who buys it and who has got the work of amateur philosophers where he expected the work of professional grammarians. A man would be annoyed if his son returned from the dentist with his teeth untouched and his head crammed with the dentist's *obiter dicta* on bimetallism or the Baconian theory.

But I doubt whether Gaius and Titius have really planned, under cover of teaching English, to propagate their philosophy. I think they have slipped into it for the following reasons. In the first place, literary criticism is difficult, and what they actually do is very much easier. To explain why a bad treatment of some basic human emotion is bad literature is, if we exclude all question-begging attacks on the emotion itself, a very hard thing to do. Even Dr. Richards, who first seriously tackled the problem of badness in literature, failed, I think, to do it. To 'debunk' the emotion, on the basis of a commonplace rationalism, is within almost anyone's capacity. In the second place, I think Gaius and Titius may have honestly misunderstood the pressing educational need of the moment. They see the world around them swayed by emotional propaganda—they have learned from tradition that youth is sentimental—and they conclude that the best thing they can do is to fortify the minds of young people against emotion. My own experience as a teacher tells an opposite tale. For every one pupil who needs to be guarded from a weak excess of sensibility there are three who need to be awakened from the slumber of cold vulgarity. The task of the modern educator is not to cut down jungles but to irrigate deserts. The right defence against false sentiments is to inculcate just sentiments. By starving the sensibility of our pupils we only make them easier prey to the propagandist when he comes. For famished nature will be avenged and a hard heart is no infallible protection against a soft head.

But there is a third, and a profounder, reason for the procedure which Gaius and Titius adopt. They may be perfectly ready to admit that a good education should build some sentiments while destroying others. They may endeavour to do so. But it is impossible that they should succeed. Do what they will, it is the 'debunking' side of their work, and this side alone, which will really tell. In order to grasp this necessity clearly I must digress for a moment to show that what may be called the educational predicament of Gaius and Titius is different from that of all their predecessors.

Until quite modern times all teachers and even all men believed the universe to be such that certain emotional reactions on our part could be either congruous or incongruous to it—believed, in fact, that objects did not merely receive, but could *merit,* our approval or disapproval, our reverence, or our contempt. The reason why Coleridge agreed with the tourist who called the cataract sublime and disagreed with the one who called it pretty was of course that he believed inanimate nature to be such that certain responses could be more 'just' or 'ordinate' or 'appropriate' to it than others. And he believed (correctly) that the tourists thought the same. The man who called the cataract sublime was not intending simply to describe his own emotions about it: he was also claiming that the object was one which *merited* those emotions. But for this claim there would be nothing to agree or disagree about. To disagree with *This is pretty* if those words simply described the lady's feelings, would be absurd: if she had said *I feel sick* Coleridge would hardly have replied *No; I feel quite well.* When Shelley, having compared the human sensibility to an Aeolian lyre, goes on to add that it differs from a lyre in having a power of 'internal adjustment' whereby it can 'accommodate its chords to the motions of that which strikes them,'[9] he is assuming the same belief. 'Can you be righteous,' asks Traherne, 'unless you be just in rendering to things their due esteem? All things were made to be yours and you were made to prize them according to their value.'[10] St. Augustine defines virtue as *ordo amoris,* the ordinate condition of the affections in which every object is accorded that kind and degree of love which is appropriate to it.[11] Aristotle says that the aim of education is to make the pupil like and dislike what he ought.[12] When the age for reflective thought comes, the pupil who has been thus trained in 'ordinate affections' or 'just sentiments' will easily find the first principles in Ethics: but to the corrupt man they will never be visible at all and he can make no progress in that science.[13] Plato before him had said the same. The little human animal will not at first have the right responses. It must be trained to feel pleasure, liking, disgust, and hatred at those things which really are pleasant, likeable, disgusting, and hateful.[14] In the *Republic,* the well-nurtured youth is one 'who would see most clearly whatever was amiss in ill-made works of man or ill-grown works of nature, and with a just distaste would blame and hate the ugly even from his earliest years and would give delighted praise to beauty, receiving it into his soul and being nourished by it, so that he becomes a man of gentle heart. All this before he is of an age to reason; so that when Reason at length comes to him, then, bred as he has been, he will hold out his hands in welcome and recognize her because of the affinity he bears to her.'[15] In early Hinduism that conduct in men which can be called good consists in conformity to, or almost participation in, the *Rta*—that great ritual or pattern of nature and supernature which is revealed alike in the cosmic order, the moral virtues, and the ceremonial of the temple. Righteousness, correctness, order, the *Rta,* is constantly identified with *satya* or truth, correspondence to reality. As

[9]*Defence of Poetry.*   [10]*Centuries of Meditations,* i. 12.
[11]*De Civ. Dei,* xv. 22. Cf. *ibid.* ix. 5. xi. 28.   [12]*Eth. Nic.* 1104 B.   [13]*Ibid.* 1095 B.
[14]*Laws,* 653.   [15]*Republic,* 402 A.

Plato said that the Good was 'beyond existence' and Wordsworth that through virtue the stars were strong, so the Indian masters say that the gods themselves are born of the *Rta* and obey it.[16] The Chinese also speak of a great thing (the greatest thing) called the *Tao*. It is the reality beyond all predicates, the abyss that was before the Creator Himself. It is Nature, it is the Way, the Road. It is the Way in which the universe goes on, the Way in which things everlastingly emerge, stilly and tranquilly, into space and time. It is also the Way which every man should tread in imitation of that cosmic and supercosmic progression, conforming all activities to that great exemplar.[17] 'In ritual,' say the Analects, 'it is harmony with Nature that is prized.'[18] The ancient Jews likewise praise the Law as being 'true.'[19]

This conception in all its forms, Platonic, Aristotelian, Stoic, Christian, and Oriental alike, I shall henceforth refer to for brevity simply as 'the *Tao.*' Some of the accounts of it which I have quoted will seem, perhaps, to many of you merely quaint or even magical. But what is common to them all is something we cannot neglect. It is the doctrine of objective value, the belief that certain attitudes are really true, and others really false, to the kind of thing the universe is and the kind of things we are. Those who know the *Tao* can hold that to call children delightful or old men venerable is not simply to record a psychological fact about our own parental or filial emotions at the moment, but to recognize a quality which *demands* a certain response from us whether we make it or not. I myself do not enjoy the society of small children: because I speak from within the *Tao* I recognize this as a defect in myself—just as a man may have to recognize that he is tone deaf or colour blind. And because our approvals and disapprovals are thus recognitions of objective value or responses to an objective order, therefore emotional states can be in harmony with reason (when we feel liking for what ought to be approved) or out of harmony with reason (when we perceive that liking is due but cannot feel it). No emotion is, in itself, a judgement: in that sense all emotions and sentiments are alogical. But they can be reasonable or unreasonable as they conform to Reason or fail to conform. The heart never takes the place of the head: but it can, and should, obey it.

Over against this stands the world of *The Green Book*. In it the very possibility of a sentiment being reasonable—or even unreasonable—has been excluded from the outset. It can be reasonable or unreasonable only if it conforms or fails to conform to something else. To say that the cataract is sublime means saying that our emotion of humility is appropriate or ordinate to the reality, and thus

[16]A. B. Keith, s.v. 'Righteousness (Hindu).' *Enc. Religion and Ethics*, vol. x.

[17]*Ibid.*, vol. ii, p. 454 B; iv. 12 B; ix. 87 A.

[18]*The Analects of Confucius*, trans. Arthur Waley, London, 1938, i. 12.

[19]Psalm cxix. 151. The word is *ĕmeth*, 'truth.' Where the *Satya* of the Indian sources emphasizes truth as 'correspondence,' *ĕmeth* (connected with a verb that means 'to be firm') emphasizes rather the reliability or trustworthiness of truth. *Faithfulness* and *permanence* are suggested by Hebraists as alternative renderings. *Emeth* is that which does not deceive, does not 'give,' does not change, that which holds water. (See T. K. Cheyne in *Encyclopedia Biblica*, 1914, s.v. 'Truth.')

to speak of something else besides the emotion: just as to say that a shoe fits is to speak not only of shoes but of feet. But this reference to something beyond the emotion is what Gaius and Titius exclude from every sentence containing a predicate of value. Such statements, for them, refer solely to the emotion. Now the emotion, thus considered by itself, cannot be either in agreement or disagreement with Reason. It is irrational not as a paralogism is irrational, but as a physical event is irrational: it does not rise even to the dignity of error. On this view, the world of facts, without one trace of value, and the world of feelings without one trace of truth or falsehood, justice or injustice, confront one another, and no *rapprochement* is possible.

Hence the educational problem is wholly different according as you stand within or without the *Tao*. For those within, the task is to train in the pupil those responses which are in themselves appropriate, whether anyone is making them or not, and in making which the very nature of man consists. Those without, if they are logical, must regard all sentiments as equally non-rational, as mere mists between us and the real objects. As a result, they must either decide to remove all sentiments, as far as possible, from the pupil's mind: or else to encourage some sentiments for reasons that have nothing to do with their intrinsic 'justness' or 'ordinacy.' The latter course involves them in the questionable process of creating in others by 'suggestion' or incantation a mirage which their own reason has successfully dissipated.

Perhaps this will become clearer if we take a concrete instance. When a Roman father told his son that it was a sweet and seemly thing to die for his country, he believed what he said. He was communicating to the son an emotion which he himself shared and which he believed to be in accord with the value which his judgement discerned in noble death. He was giving the boy the best he had, giving of his spirit to humanize him as he had given of his body to beget him. But Gaius and Titius cannot believe that in calling such a death sweet and seemly they would be saying 'something important about something.' Their own method of debunking would cry out against them if they attempted to do so. For death is not something to eat and therefore cannot be *dulce* in the literal sense, and it is unlikely that the real sensations preceding it will be *dulce* even by analogy. And as for *decorum*—that is only a word describing how some other people will feel about your death when they happen to think of it, which won't be often, and will certainly do you no good. There are only two courses open to Gaius and Titius. Either they must go the whole way and debunk this sentiment like any other, or must set themselves to work to produce, from outside, a sentiment which they believe to be of no value to the pupil and which may cost him his life, because it is useful to us (the survivors) that our young men should feel it. If they embark on this course the difference between the old and the new education will be an important one. Where the old initiated, the new merely 'conditions.' The old dealt with its pupils as grown birds deal with young birds when they teach them to fly: the new deals with them more as the poultry-keeper deals with young birds—making them thus or thus for purposes of which the birds know nothing. In a word, the old was a kind of propagation—men transmitting manhood to men: the new is merely propaganda.

It is to their credit that Gaius and Titius embrace the first alternative. Propaganda is their abomination: not because their own philosophy gives a ground for condemning it (or anything else) but because they are better than their principles. They probably have some vague notion (I will examine it in my next lecture) that valour and good faith and justice could be sufficiently commended to the pupil on what they would call 'rational' or 'biological' or 'modern' grounds, if it should ever become necessary. In the meantime, they leave the matter alone and get on with the business of debunking.

But this course, though less inhuman, is not less disastrous than the opposite alternative of cynical propaganda. Let us suppose for a moment that the harder virtues could really be theoretically justified with no appeal to objective value. It still remains true that no justification of virtue will enable a man to be virtuous. Without the aid of trained emotions the intellect is powerless against the animal organism. I had sooner play cards against a man who was quite sceptical about ethics, but bred to believe that 'a gentleman does not cheat,' than against an irreproachable moral philosopher who had been brought up among sharpers. In battle it is not syllogisms that will keep the reluctant nerves and muscles to their post in the third hour of the bombardment. The crudest sentimentalism (such as Gaius and Titius would wince at) about a flag or a country or a regiment will be of more use. We were told it all long ago by Plato. As the king governs by his executive, so Reason in man must rule the mere appetites by means of the 'spirited element.'[20] The head rules the belly through the chest—the seat, as Alanus tells us, of Magnanimity,[21] of emotions organized by trained habit into stable sentiments. The Chest—Magnanimity—Sentiment—these are the indispensable liaison officers between cerebral man and visceral man. It may even be said that it is by this middle element that man is man: for by his intellect he is mere spirit and by his appetite mere animal. The operation of *The Green Book* and its kind is to produce what may be called Men without Chests. It is an outrage that they should be commonly spoken of as Intellectuals. This gives them the chance to say that he who attacks them attacks Intelligence. It is not so. They are not distinguished from other men by any unusual skill in finding truth nor any virginal ardour to pursue her. Indeed it would be strange if they were: a persevering devotion to truth, a nice sense of intellectual honour, cannot be long maintained without the aid of a sentiment which Gaius and Titus could debunk as easily as any other. It is not excess of thought but defect of fertile and generous emotion that marks them out. Their heads are no bigger than the ordinary: it is the atrophy of the chest beneath that makes them seem so.

And all the time—such is the tragi-comedy of our situation—we continue to

[20]*Republic*, 442 B.C.   [21]Alanus ab Insulis. *De Planctu Naturae Prosa*, iii.

clamour for those very qualities we are rendering impossible. You can hardly open a periodical without coming across the statement that what our civilization needs is more 'drive,' or dynamism, or self-sacrifice, or 'creativity.' In a sort of ghastly simplicity we remove the organ and demand the function. We make men without chests and expect of them virtue and enterprise. We laugh at honour and are shocked to find traitors in our midst. We castrate and bid the geldings be fruitful.

2

The Way

It is upon the Trunk that a gentleman works.
Analects OF CONFUCIUS, I. 2.

THE PRACTICAL RESULT of education in the spirit of *The Green Book* must be the destruction of the society which accepts it. But this is not necessarily a refutation of subjectivism about values as a theory. The true doctrine might be a doctrine which if we accept we die. No one who speaks from within the *Tao* could reject it on that account; ἐν δὲ φάει καὶ ὄλεσσον. But it has not yet come to that. There are theoretical difficulties in the philosophy of Gaius and Titius.

However subjective they may be about some traditional value, Gaius and Titius have shown by the very act of writing *The Green Book* that there must be some other values about which they are not subjective at all. They write in order to produce certain states of mind in the rising generation, if not because they think those states of mind intrinsically just or good, yet certainly because they think them to be the means to some state of society which they regard as desirable. It would not be difficult to collect from various passages in *The Green Book* what their ideal is. But we need not. The important point is not the precise nature of their end, but the fact that they have an end at all. They must have, or their book (being purely practical in intention) is written to no purpose. And this end must have real value in their eyes. To abstain from calling it 'good' and to use, instead, such predicates as 'necessary' or 'progressive' or 'efficient' would be a subterfuge. They could be forced by argument to answer the questions 'necessary for what?', 'progressing towards what?', 'effecting what?'; in the last resort they would have to admit that some state of affairs was in their opinion good for its own sake. And this time they could not maintain that 'good' simply described their own emotions about it. For the whole purpose of their book is so to condition the young reader that he will share their approval, and this would be either a fool's or a villain's undertaking unless they held that their approval was in some way valid or correct. In actual fact Gaius and Titius will be found to hold, with complete uncritical dogmatism, the whole system of values which happened to be in vogue among moderately educated young men of the professional classes during the period between the two wars.[1] Their scepticism about

[1]The real (perhaps unconscious) philosophy of Gaius and Titius becomes clear if we contrast the two following lists of disapprovals and approvals. *A. Disapprovals:* A mother's appeal to a child to be 'brave' is 'nonsense' (*Green Book*, p. 62). The reference of the word 'gentleman' is 'extremely vague' *(ibid.)*. 'To call a man a coward tells us really nothing about what he does' (p. 64). Feelings about a country or empire are feelings 'about nothing in particular' (p. 77). *B. Approvals:* Those who prefer the arts of peace to the arts of war (it is not said in what circumstances) are such that 'we

values is on the surface: it is for use on other people's values: about the values current in their own set they are not nearly sceptical enough. And this phenomenon is very usual. A great many of those who 'debunk' traditional or (as they would say) 'sentimental' values have in the background values of their own which they believe to be immune from the debunking process. They claim to be cutting away the parasitic growth of emotion, religious sanction, and inherited taboos, in order that 'real' or 'basic' values may emerge. I will now try to find out what happens if this is seriously attempted.

Let us continue to use the previous example—that of death for a good cause—not, of course, because virtue is the only value or martyrdom the only virtue, but because this is the *experimentum crucis* which shows different systems of thought in the clearest light. Let us suppose that an Innovator in values regards *dulce et decorum* and *greater love hath no man* as mere irrational sentiments which are to be stripped off in order that we may get down to the 'realistic' or 'basic' ground of this value. Where will he find such a ground?

First of all, he might say that the real value lay in the utility of such sacrifice to the community. 'Good,' he might say, '*means* what is useful to the community.' But of course the death of the community is not useful to the community— only the death of some of its members. What is really meant is that the death of some men is useful to other men. That is very true. But on what ground are some men being asked to die for the benefit of others? Every appeal to pride, honour, shame, or love is excluded by hypothesis. To use these would be to return to sentiment and the Innovator's task is, having cut all that away, to explain to men, in terms of pure reasoning, why they will be well advised to die that others may live. He may say 'Unless some of us *risk* death all of us are *certain* to die.' But that will be true only in a limited number of cases; and even when it is true it provokes the very reasonable counter question 'Why should I be one of those who take the risk?'

At this point the Innovator may ask why, after all, selfishness should be more 'rational' or 'intelligent' than altruism. The question is welcome. If by Reason we mean the process actually employed by Gaius and Titius when engaged in debunking (that is, the connecting by inference of propositions, ultimately derived from sense data, with further propositions), then the answer must be that a refusal to sacrifice oneself is no more rational than a consent to do so. And no less rational. Neither choice is rational—or irrational—at all. From propositions about fact alone no *practical* conclusion can ever be drawn. *This will preserve*

---

may want to call them wise men' (p. 65). The pupil is expected 'to believe in a democratic community life' (p. 67). 'Contact with the ideas of other people is, as we know, healthy' (p. 86). The reason for bathrooms ('that people are healthier and pleasanter to meet when they are clean') is 'too obvious to need mentioning' (p. 142). It will be seen that comfort and security, as known to a suburban street in peace-time, are the ultimate values: those things which can alone produce or spiritualize comfort and security are mocked. Man lives by bread alone, and the ultimate source of bread is the baker's van: peace matters more than honour and can be preserved by jeering at colonels and reading newspapers.

society cannot lead to *do this* except by the mediation of *society ought to be preserved*. *This will cost you your life* cannot lead directly to *do not do this*: it can lead to it only through a felt desire or an acknowledged duty of self preservation. The Innovator is trying to get a conclusion in the imperative mood out of premises in the indicative mood: and though he continues trying to all eternity he cannot succeed, for the thing is impossible. We must therefore either extend the word Reason to include what our ancestors called Practical Reason and confess that judgements such as *society ought to be preserved* (though they can support themselves by no reason of the sort that Gaius and Titius demand) are not mere sentiments but are rationality itself: or else we must give up at once, and for ever, the attempt to find a core of 'rational' value behind all the sentiments we have debunked. The Innovator will not take the first alternative, for practical principles known to all men by Reason are simply the *Tao* which he has set out to supersede. He is more likely to give up the quest for a 'rational' core and to hunt for some other ground even more 'basic' and 'realistic.'

This he will probably feel that he has found in Instinct. The preservation of society, and of the species itself, are ends that do not hang on the precarious thread of Reason: they are given by Instinct. That is why there is no need to argue against the man who does not acknowledge them. We have an instinctive urge to preserve our own species. That is why men ought to work for posterity. We have no instinctive urge to keep promises or to respect individual life: that is why scruples of justice and humanity—in fact the *Tao*—can be properly swept away when they conflict with our real end, the preservation of the species. That, again, is why the modern situation permits and demands a new sexual morality: the old taboos served some real purpose in helping to preserve the species, but contraceptives have modified this and we can now abandon many of the taboos. For of course sexual desire, being instinctive, is to be gratified whenever it does not conflict with the preservation of the species. It looks, in fact, as if an ethics based on instinct will give the Innovator all he wants and nothing that he does not want.

In reality we have not advanced one step. I will not insist on the point that Instinct is a name for we know not what (to say that migratory birds find their way by instinct is only to say that we do not know how migratory birds find their way), for I think it is here being used in a fairly definite sense, to mean an unreflective or spontaneous impulse widely felt by the members of a given species. In what way does Instinct, thus conceived, help us to find 'real' values? Is it maintained that we *must* obey instinct, that we cannot do otherwise? But if so, why are *Green Books* and the like written? Why this stream of exhortation to drive us where we cannot help going? Why such praise for those who have submitted to the inevitable? Or is it maintained that if we do obey instinct we shall be happy and satisfied? But the very question we are considering was that of facing death which (so far as the Innovator knows) cuts off every possible satisfaction: and if we have an instinctive desire for the good of posterity then this desire, by the very nature of the case, can never be satisfied, since its aim is achieved, if at all, when we are dead. It looks very much as if the Innovator would have to say not that we must obey instinct, nor that it will satisfy us to do so, but that we *ought* to obey instinct.[2]

But why ought we to obey instinct? Is there another instinct of a higher order directing us to do so, and a third of a still higher order directing us to obey *it?*—an infinite regress of instincts? This is presumably impossible, but nothing else will serve. From the statement about psychological fact 'I have an impulse to do so and so' we cannot by any ingenuity derive the practical principle 'I ought to obey this impulse.' Even if it were true that men had a spontaneous, unreflective impulse to sacrifice their own lives for the preservation of their fellows, it remains a quite separate question whether this is an impulse they should control or one they should indulge. For even the Innovator admits that many impulses (those which conflict with the preservation of the species) have to be controlled. And this admission surely introduces us to a yet more fundamental difficulty.

Telling us to obey instinct is like telling us to obey 'people.' People say different things: so do instincts. Our instincts are at war. If it is held that the instinct for preserving the species should always be obeyed at the expense of other instincts, whence do we derive this rule of precedence? To listen to that instinct speaking in its own cause and deciding in its own favour would be rather simple minded. Each instinct, if you listen to it, will claim to be gratified at the expense of all the rest. By the very act of listening to one rather than to others we have

---

[2]The most determined effort which I know to construct a theory of value on the basis of 'satisfaction of impulses' is that of Dr. I. A. Richards (*Principles of Literary Criticism*, 1924). The old objection to defining Value as Satisfaction is the universal value judgement that 'it is better to be Socrates dissatisfied than a pig satisfied.' To meet this Dr. Richards endeavours to show that our impulses can be arranged in a hierarchy and some satisfactions preferred to others without an appeal to any criterion other than satisfaction. He does this by the doctrine that some impulses are more 'important' than others—an *important* impulse being one whose frustration involves the frustration of other impulses. A good systematization (i.e. the good life) consists in satisfying as many impulses as possible; which entails satisfying the 'important' at the expense of the 'unimportant.' The objections to this scheme seem to me to be two. (1) Without a theory of immortality it leaves no room for the value of noble death. It may, of course, be said that a man who has saved his life by treachery will suffer for the rest of that life from frustration. But not, surely, frustration of *all* his impulses? Whereas the dead man will have *no* satisfaction. Or is it maintained that since he has no unsatisfied impulses he is better off than the disgraced and living man? This at once raises the second objection. (2) Is the value of a systematization to be judged by the presence of satisfactions or the absence of dissatisfactions? The extreme case is that of the dead man in whom satisfactions and dissatisfactions (on the modern view) both equal zero, as against the successful traitor who can still eat, drink, sleep, scratch, and copulate, even if he cannot have friendship or love or self-respect. But it arises at other levels. Suppose *A* has only 500 impulses and all are satisfied, and that *B* has 1,200 impulses whereof 700 are satisfied and 500 not: which has the better systematization? There is no doubt which Dr. Richards actually prefers—he even praises art on the ground that it makes us 'discontented' with ordinary crudities! (*op. cit.*, p. 230). The only trace I find of a philosophical basis for this preference is the statement that 'the more complex an activity the more conscious it is' (p. 109). But if satisfaction is the only value, why should increase of consciousness be good? For consciousness is the condition of all dissatisfactions as well as of all satisfactions. Dr. Richards' system gives no support to his (and our) actual preference for civil life over savage and human over animal—or even for life over death.

already prejudged the case. If we did not bring to the examination of our instincts a knowledge of their comparative dignity we could never learn it from them. And that knowledge cannot itself be instinctive: the judge cannot be one of the parties judged: or, if he is, the decision is worthless and there is no ground for placing the preservation of the species above self-preservation or sexual appetite.

The idea that, without appealing to any court higher than the instincts themselves, we can yet find grounds for preferring one instinct above its fellows dies very hard. We grasp at useless words: we call it the 'basic,' or 'fundamental,' or 'primal,' or 'deepest' instinct. It is of no avail. Either these words conceal a value judgement passed *upon* the instinct and therefore not derivable *from* it, or else they merely record its felt intensity, the frequency of its operation, and its wide distribution. If the former, the whole attempt to base value upon instinct has been abandoned: if the latter, these observations about the quantitative aspects of a psychological event lead to no practical conclusion. It is the old dilemma. Either the premisses already concealed an imperative or the conclusion remains merely in the indicative.[3]

Finally, it is worth inquiry whether there *is* any instinct to care for posterity or preserve the species. I do not discover it in myself: and yet I am a man rather prone to think of remote futurity—a man who can read Mr. Olaf Stapledon with delight. Much less do I find it easy to believe that the majority of people who have sat opposite me in buses or stood with me in queues feel an unreflective

[3]The desperate expedients to which a man can be driven if he attempts to base value on fact are well illustrated by Dr. C. H. Waddington's fate in *Science and Ethics*. Dr. Waddington here explains that 'existence is its own justification' (p. 14), and writes: 'An existence which is essentially evolutionary is itself the justification for an evolution towards a more comprehensive existence' (p. 17). I do not think Dr. Waddington is himself at ease in this view, for he does endeavour to recommend the course of evolution to us on three grounds other than its mere occurrence. *(a)* That the later stages include or 'comprehend' the earlier. *(b)* That T. H. Huxley's picture of Evolution will not revolt you if you regard it from an 'actuarial' point of view. *(c)* That, any way, after all, it isn't half so bad as people make out ('not so morally offensive that we cannot accept it' (p. 18). These three palliatives are more creditable to Dr. Waddington's heart than his head and seem to me to give up the main position. If Evolution is praised (or, at least, apologized for) on the ground of *any* properties it exhibits, then we are using an external standard and the attempt to make existence its own justification has been abandoned. If that attempt is maintained, why does Dr. Waddington concentrate on Evolution: i.e. on a temporary phase of organic existence in one planet? This is 'geocentric.' If Good—"whatever Nature happens to be doing," then surely we should notice what Nature is doing as a whole; and nature as a whole, I understand, is working steadily and irreversibly towards the final extinction of all life in every part of the universe, so that Dr. Waddington's ethics, stripped of their unaccountable bias towards such a parochial affair as tellurian biology, would leave murder and suicide our only duties. Even this, I confess, seems to me a lesser objection than the discrepancy between Dr. Waddington's first principle and the value judgements men actually make. To value anything simply because it occurs is in fact to worship success, like Quislings or men of Vichy. Other philosophies more wicked have been devised: none more vulgar. I am far from suggesting that Dr. Waddington practises in real life such grovelling prostration before the *fait accompli*. Let us hope that *Rasselas*, cap. 22, gives the right picture of what his philosophy amounts to in action. ('The philosopher rose up and departed with the air of a man that had co-operated with the present system.')

impulse to do anything at all about the species, or posterity. Only people educated in a particular way have ever had the idea 'posterity' before their minds at all. It is difficult to assign to instinct our attitude towards an object which exists only for reflective men. What we have by nature is an impulse to preserve our own children and grandchildren; an impulse which grows progressively feebler as the imagination looks forward and finally dies out in the 'deserts of vast futurity.' No parents who were guided by this instinct would dream for a moment of setting up the claims of their hypothetical descendants against those of the baby actually crowing and kicking in the room. Those of us who accept the *Tao* may, perhaps, say that they ought to do so: but that is not open to those who treat instinct as the source of value. As we pass from mother love to rational planning for the future we are passing away from the realm of instinct into that of choice and reflection: and if instinct is the source of value, planning for the future ought to be less respectable and less obligatory than the baby language and cuddling of the fondest mother or the most fatuous nursery anecdotes of a doting father. If we are to base ourselves upon instinct, these things are the substance and care for posterity the shadow—the huge, flickering shadow of the nursery happiness cast upon the screen of the unknown future. I do not say this projection is a bad thing: but then I do not believe that instinct is the ground of value judgements. What is absurd is to claim that your care for posterity finds its justification in instinct and then flout at every turn the only instinct on which it could be supposed to rest, tearing the child almost from the breast to crèche and kindergarten in the interests of progress and the coming race.

The truth finally becomes apparent that neither in any operation with factual propositions nor in any appeal to instinct can the Innovator find the basis for a system of values. None of the principles he requires are to be found there: but they are all to be found somewhere else. 'All within the four seas are his brothers' (xii. 5) says Confucius of the *Chün-tzu,* the *cuor gentil* or gentleman. *Humani nihil a me alienum puto* says the Stoic. 'Do as you would be done by' says Jesus. 'Humanity is to be preserved' says Locke.[4] All the practical principles behind the Innovator's case for posterity, or society, or the species, are there from time immemorial in the *Tao.* But they are nowhere else. Unless you accept these without question as being to the world of action what axioms are to the world of theory, you can have no practical principles whatever. You cannot reach them as conclusions: they are premisses. You may, since they can give no 'reason' for themselves of a kind to silence Gaius and Titius, regard them as sentiments: but then you must give up contrasting 'real' or 'rational' value with sentimental value. All value will be sentimental; and you must confess (on pain of abandoning every value) that all sentiment is not 'merely' subjective. You may, on the other hand, regard them as rational—nay as rationality itself—as things so obviously reasonable that they neither demand nor admit proof. But then you must allow that Reason can be practical, that an *ought* must not be dismissed because it cannot

[4]See Appendix.

produce some *is* as its credential. If nothing is self-evident, nothing can be proved. Similarly, if nothing is obligatory for its own sake, nothing is obligatory at all.

To some it will appear that I have merely restored under another name what they always meant by basic or fundamental instinct. But much more than a choice of words is involved. The Innovator attacks traditional values (the *Tao*) in defence of what he at first supposes to be (in some special sense) 'rational' or 'biological' values. But as we have seen, all the values which he uses in attacking the *Tao*, and even claims to be substituting for it, are themselves derived from the *Tao*. If he had really started from scratch, from right outside the human tradition of value, no jugglery could have advanced him an inch towards the conception that a man should die for the community or work for posterity. If the *Tao* falls, all his own conceptions of value fall with it. Not one of them can claim any authority other than that of the *Tao*. Only by such shreds of the *Tao* as he has inherited is he enabled even to attack it. The question therefore arises what title he has to select bits of it for acceptance and to reject others. For if the bits he rejects have no authority, neither have those he retains: if what he retains is valid, what he rejects is equally valid too.

The Innovator, for example, rates high the claims of posterity. He cannot get any valid claim for posterity out of instinct or (in the modern sense) reason. He is really deriving our duty to posterity from the *Tao;* our duty to do good to all men is an axiom of Practical Reason, and our duty to do good to our descendants is a clear deduction from it. But then, in every form of the *Tao* which has come down to us, side by side with the duty to children and descendants lies the duty to parents and ancestors. By what right do we reject one and accept the other? Again, the Innovator may place economic value first. To get people fed and clothed is the great end, and in pursuit of it scruples about justice and good faith may be set aside. The *Tao* of course agrees with him about the importance of getting the people fed and clothed. Unless the Innovator were himself using the *Tao* he could never have learned of such a duty. But side by side with it in the *Tao* lie those duties of justice and good faith which he is ready to debunk. What is his warrant? He may be a Jingoist, a Racialist, an extreme nationalist, who maintains that the advancement of his own people is the object to which all else ought to yield. But no kind of factual observation and no appeal to instinct will give him a ground for this opinion. Once more, he is in fact deriving it from the *Tao:* a duty to our own kin, because they are our own kin, is a part of traditional morality. But side by side with it in the *Tao*, and limiting it, lie the inflexible demands of justice, and the rule that, in the long run, all men are our brothers. Whence comes the Innovator's authority to pick and choose?

Since I can see no answer to these questions, I draw the following conclusions. This thing which I have called for convenience the *Tao*, and which others may call Natural Law or Traditional Morality or the First Principles of Practical Reason or the First Platitudes, is not one among a series of possible systems of value. It is the sole source of all value judgements. If it is rejected, all value is rejected. If any value is retained, it is retained. The effort to refute it and raise a new system of value in its place is self-contradictory. There never has been, and never will be, a radically new judgement of value in the history of the world. What purport to be new systems or (as they now call them) 'ideologies,' all consist of fragments from the *Tao* itself, arbitrarily wrenched from their context in the whole and then swollen to madness in their isolation, yet still owing to the *Tao* and to it alone such validity as they possess. If my duty to my parents is a superstition, then so is my duty to posterity. If justice is a superstition, then so is my duty to my country or my race. If the pursuit of scientific knowledge is a real value, then so is conjugal fidelity. The rebellion of the branches against the tree: if the rebels could succeed they would find that they had destroyed themselves. The human mind has no more power of inventing a new value than of imagining a new primary colour, or, indeed, of creating a new sun and a new sky for it to move in.

Does this mean, then, that no progress in our perceptions of value can ever take place? That we are bound down for ever to an unchanging code given once for all? And is it, in any event, possible to talk of obeying what I call the *Tao*? If we lump together, as I have done, the traditional moralities of East and West, the Christian, the Pagan, and the Jew, shall we not find many contradictions and some absurdities? I admit all this. Some criticism, some removal of contradictions, even some real development, is required. But there are two very different kinds of criticism.

A theorist about language may approach his native tongue, as it were from outside, regarding its genius as a thing that has no claim on him and advocating wholesale alterations of its idiom and spelling in the interests of commercial convenience or scientific accuracy. That is one thing. A great poet, who has 'loved, and been well nurtured in, his mother tongue,' may also make great alterations in it, but his changes of the language are made in the spirit of the language itself: he works from within. The language which suffers, has also inspired, the changes. That is a different thing—as different as the works of Shakespeare are from Basic English. It is the difference between alteration from within and alteration from without: between the organic and the surgical.

In the same way, the *Tao* admits development from within. There is a difference between a real moral advance and a mere innovation. From the Confucian 'Do not do to others what you would not like them to do to you' to the Christian 'Do as you would be done by' is a real advance. The morality of Nietzsche is a mere innovation. The first is an advance because no one who did not admit the validity of the old maxim could see reason for accepting the new one, and anyone who accepted the old would at once recognize the new as an extension of the same principle. If he rejected it, he would have to reject it as a superfluity, something that went too far, not as something simply heterogeneous from his own ideas of value. But the Nietzschean ethic can be accepted only if we are ready to scrap traditional morals as a mere error and then to put ourselves in a position where we can find no ground for any value judgements at all. It is the difference between a man who says to us: 'You like your vegetables moderately fresh; why not grow your own and have them perfectly fresh?' and a man who says, 'Throw away that loaf and try eating bricks and centipedes instead.'

Those who understand the spirit of the *Tao* and who have been led by that spirit can modify it in directions which that spirit itself demands. Only they can know what those directions are. The outsider knows nothing about the matter. His attempts at alteration, as we have seen, contradict themselves. So far from being able to harmonize discrepancies in its letter by penetration to its spirit, he merely snatches at some one precept, on which the accidents of time and place happen to have riveted his attention, and then rides it to death—for no reason that he can give. From within the *Tao* itself comes the only authority to modify the *Tao*. This is what Confucius meant when he said 'With those who follow a different Way it is useless to take counsel.'[5] This is why Aristotle said that only those who have been well brought up can usefully study ethics: to the corrupted man, the man who stands outside the *Tao*, the very starting point of this science is invisible.[6] He may be hostile, but he cannot be critical: he does not know what is being discussed. This is why it was also said 'This people that knoweth not the Law is accursed'[7] and 'He that believeth not shall be damned.'[8] An open mind, in questions that are not ultimate, is useful. But an open mind about the ultimate foundations either of Theoretical or of Practical Reason is idiocy. If a man's mind is open on these things, let his mouth at least be shut. He can say nothing to the purpose. Outside the *Tao* there is no ground for criticizing either the *Tao* or anything else.

In particular instances it may, no doubt, be a matter of some delicacy to decide where the legitimate internal criticism ends and the fatal external kind begins. But wherever any precept of traditional morality is simply challenged to produce its credentials, as though the burden of proof lay on it, we have taken the wrong position. The legitimate reformer endeavours to show that the precept in question conflicts with some precept which its defenders allow to be more fundamental, or that it does not really embody the judgement of value it professes to embody. The direct frontal attack 'Why?'—'What good does it do?'—'Who said so?' is never permissible; not because it is harsh or offensive but because no values at all can justify themselves on that level. If you persist in *that* kind of trial you will destroy all values, and so destroy the bases of your own criticism as well as the thing criticized. You must not hold a pistol to the head of the *Tao*. Nor must we postpone obedience to a precept until its credentials have been examined. Only those who are practising the *Tao* will understand it. It is the well-nurtured man, the *cuor gentil*, and he alone, who can recognize Reason when it comes.[9] It is Paul, the Pharisee, the man 'perfect as touching the Law' who learns where and how that Law was deficient.[10]

---

[5]*Analects* of Confucius, xv, 39.   [6]*Eth. Nic.* 1905 B, 1140 B, 1151 A.
[7]John vii. 49. The speaker said it in malice, but with more truth than he meant. Cf. John xi. 51.
[8]Mark xvi. 16.   [9]*Republic*, 402 A.   [10]Phil. iii. 6.

In order to avoid misunderstanding, I may add that though I myself am a Theist, and indeed a Christian, I am not here attempting any indirect argument for Theism. I am simply arguing that if we are to have values at all we must accept the ultimate platitudes of Practical Reason as having absolute validity: that any attempt, having become sceptical about these, to reintroduce value lower down on some supposedly more 'realistic' basis, is doomed. Whether this position implies a supernatural origin for the *Tao* is a question I am not here concerned with.

Yet how can the modern mind be expected to embrace the conclusion we have reached? This *Tao* which, it seems, we must treat as an absolute is simply a phenomenon like any other—the reflection upon the minds of our ancestors of the agricultural rhythm in which they lived or even of their physiology. We know already in principle how such things are produced: soon we shall know in detail: eventually we shall be able to produce them at will. Of course, while we did not know how minds were made, we accepted this mental furniture as a datum, even as a master. But many things in nature which were once our masters have become our servants. Why not this? Why must our conquest of nature stop short, in stupid reverence, before this final and toughest bit of 'nature' which has hitherto been called the conscience of man? You threaten us with some obscure disaster if we step outside it: but we have been threatened in that way by obscurantists at every step in our advance, and each time the threat has proved false. You say we shall have no values at all if we step outside the *Tao*. Very well: we shall probably find that we can get on quite comfortably without them. Let us regard all ideas of what we *ought* to do simply as an interesting psychological survival: let us step right out of all that and start doing what we like. Let us decide for ourselves what man is to be and make him into that: not on any ground of imagined value, but because we want him to be such. Having mastered our environment, let us now master ourselves and choose our own destiny.

This is a very possible position: and those who hold it cannot be accused of self-contradiction like the half-hearted sceptics who still hope to find 'real' values when they have debunked the traditional ones. This is the rejection of the concept of value altogether. I shall need another lecture to consider it.

3

The Abolition of Man

It came burning hot into my mind, whatever he said and
however he flattered, when he got me to his house, he would
sell me for a slave.

BUNYAN

'MAN'S CONQUEST of Nature' is an expression often used to describe the
progress of applied science. 'Man has Nature whacked' said someone to a friend
of mine not long ago. In their context the words had a certain tragic beauty, for
the speaker was dying of tuberculosis. 'No matter,' he said, 'I know I'm one of
the casualties. Of course there are casualties on the winning as well as on the
losing side. But that doesn't alter the fact that it is winning.' I have chosen this
story as my point of departure in order to make it clear that I do not wish to
disparage all that is really beneficial in the process described as 'Man's conquest,'
much less all the real devotion and self-sacrifice that has gone to make it possible.
But having done so I must proceed to analyse this conception a little more closely.
In what sense is Man the possessor of increasing power over Nature?

Let us consider three typical examples: the aeroplane, the wireless, and the
contraceptive. In a civilized community, in peace-time, anyone who can pay for
them may use these things. But it cannot strictly be said that when he does so
he is exercising his own proper or individual power over Nature. If I pay you to
carry me, I am not therefore myself a strong man. Any or all of the three things
I have mentioned can be withheld from some men by other men—by those who
sell, or those who allow the sale, or those who own the sources of production, or
those who make the goods. What we call Man's power is, in reality, a power
possessed by some men which they may, or may not, allow other men to profit
by. Again, as regards the powers manifested in the aeroplane or the wireless, Man
is as much the patient or subject as the possessor, since he is the target both for
bombs and for propaganda. And as regards contraceptives, there is a paradoxical,
negative sense in which all possible future generations are the patients or subjects
of a power wielded by those already alive. By contraception simply, they are
denied existence; by contraception used as a means of selective breeding, they
are, without their concurring voice, made to be what one generation, for its own
reasons, may choose to prefer. From this point of view, what we call Man's power
over Nature turns out to be a power exercised by some men over other men with
Nature as its instrument.

It is, of course, a commonplace to complain that men have hitherto used
badly, and against their fellows, the powers that science has given them. But that
is not the point I am trying to make. I am not speaking of particular corruptions
and abuses which an increase of moral virtue would cure: I am considering what

the thing called 'Man's power over Nature' must always and essentially be. No doubt, the picture could be modified by public ownership of raw materials and factories and public control of scientific research. But unless we have a world state this will still mean the power of one nation over others. And even within the world state or the nation it will mean (in principle) the power of majorities over minorities, and (in the concrete) of a government over the people. And all long-term exercises of power, especially in breeding, must mean the power of earlier generations over later ones.

The latter point is not always sufficiently emphasized, because those who write on social matters have not yet learned to imitate the physicists by always including Time among the dimensions. In order to understand fully what Man's power over Nature, and therefore the power of some men over other men, really means, we must picture the race extended in time from the date of its emergence to that of its extinction. Each generation exercises power over its successors: and each, in so far as it modifies the environment bequeathed to it and rebels against tradition, resists and limits the power of its predecessors. This modifies the picture which is sometimes painted of a progressive emancipation from tradition and a progressive control of natural processes resulting in a continual increase of human power. In reality, of course, if any one age really attains, by eugenics and scientific education, the power to make its descendants what it pleases, all men who live after it are the patients of that power. They are weaker, not stronger: for though we may have put wonderful machines in their hands we have pre-ordained how they are to use them. And if, as is almost certain, the age which had thus attained maximum power over posterity were also the age most emancipated from tradition, it would be engaged in reducing the power of its predecessors almost as drastically as that of its successors. And we must also remember that, quite apart from this, the later a generation comes—the nearer it lives to that date at which the species becomes extinct—the less power it will have in the forward direction, because its subjects will be so few. There is therefore no question of a power vested in the race as a whole steadily growing as long as the race survives. The last men, far from being the heirs of power, will be of all men most subject to the dead hand of the great planners and conditions and will themselves exercise least power upon the future. The real picture is that of one dominant age—let us suppose the hundredth century A.D.—which resists all previous ages most successfully and dominates all subsequent ages most irresistibly, and thus is the real master of the human species. But even within this master generation (itself an infinitesimal minority of the species) the power will be exercised by a minority smaller still. Man's conquest of Nature, if the dreams of some scientific planners are realized, means the rule of a few hundreds of men over billions upon billions of men. There neither is nor can be any simple increase of power on Man's side. Each new power won *by* man is a power *over* man as well. Each advance leaves him weaker as well as stronger. In every victory, besides being the general who triumphs, he is also the prisoner who follows the triumphal car.

I am not yet considering whether the total result of such ambivalent victories is a good thing or a bad. I am only making clear what Man's conquest of Nature really means and especially that final stage in the conquest, which, perhaps, is not far off. The final stage is come when Man by eugenics, by pre-natal conditioning, and by an education and propaganda based on a perfect applied psychology, has obtained full control over himself. *Human* nature will be the last part of Nature to surrender to Man. The battle will then be won. We shall have 'taken the thread of life out of the hand of Clotho' and be henceforth free to make our species whatever we wish it to be. The battle will indeed be won. But who, precisely, will have won it?

For the power of Man to make himself what he pleases means, as we have seen, the power of some men to make other men what *they* please. In all ages, no doubt, nurture and instruction have, in some sense, attempted to exercise this power. But the situation to which we must look forward will be novel in two respects. In the first place, the power will be enormously increased. Hitherto the plans of educationalists have achieved very little of what they attempted and indeed, when we read them—how Plato would have every infant 'a bastard nursed in a bureau,' and Elyot would have the boy see no men before the age of seven and, after that, no women,[1] and how Locke wants children to have leaky shoes and no turn for poetry[2]—we may well thank the beneficent obstinacy of real mothers, real nurses, and (above all) real children for preserving the human race in such sanity as it still possesses. But the man-moulders of the new age will be armed with the powers of an omnicompetent state and an irresistible scientific technique: we shall get at last a race of conditioners who really can cut out all posterity in what shape they please. The second difference is even more important. In the older systems both the kind of man the teachers wished to produce and their motives for producing him were prescribed by the *Tao*—a norm to which the teachers themselves were subject and from which they claimed no liberty to depart. They did not cut men to some pattern they had chosen. They handed on what they had received; they initiated the young neophyte into the mystery of humanity which over-arched him and them alike. It was but old birds teaching young birds to fly. This will be changed. Values are now mere natural phenomena. Judgements of value are to be produced in the pupil as part of the conditioning. Whatever *Tao* there is will be the product, not the motive, of education. The conditioners have been emancipated from all that. It is one more

---

[1] *The Boke Named the Governour*, I. iv: 'Al men except physitions only shulde be excluded and kepte out of the norisery.' I. vi: 'After that a childe is come to seuen yeres of age . . . the most sure counsaile is to withdrawe him from all company of women.'

[2] *Some Thoughts concerning Education*, § 7: 'I will also advise his *Feet to be wash'd* every Day in cold Water, and to have his Shoes so thin that they might leak and *let in Water*, whenever he comes near it.' § 174: 'If he have a poetick vein, 'tis to me the strangest thing in the World that the Father should desire or suffer it to be cherished or improved. Methinks the Parents should labour to have it stifled and suppressed as much as may be.' Yet Locke is one of our most sensible writers on education.

part of Nature which they have conquered. The ultimate springs of human action are no longer, for them, something given. They have surrendered—like electricity: it is the function of the Conditioners to control, not to obey them. They know how to *produce* conscience and decide what kind of conscience they will produce. They themselves are outside, above. For we are assuming the last stage of Man's struggle with Nature. The final victory has been won. Human nature has been conquered—and, of course, has conquered, in whatever sense those words may now bear.

The Conditioners, then, are to choose what kind of artificial *Tao* they will, for their own good reasons, produce in the Human race. They are the motivators, the creators of motives. But how are they going to be motivated themselves? For a time, perhaps, by survivals, within their own minds, of the old 'natural' *Tao*. Thus at first they may look upon themselves as servants and guardians of humanity and conceive that they have a 'duty' to do it 'good.' But it is only by confusion that they can remain in this state. They recognize the concept of duty as the result of certain processes which they can now control. Their victory has consisted precisely in emerging from the state in which they were acted upon by those processes to the state in which they use them as tools. One of the things they now have to decide is whether they will, or will not, so condition the rest of us that we can go on having the old idea of duty and the old reactions to it. How can duty help them to decide that? Duty itself is up for trial: it cannot also be the judge. And 'good' fares no better. They know quite well how to produce a dozen different conceptions of good in us. The question is which, if any, they should produce. No conception of good can help them to decide. It is absurd to fix on one of the things they are comparing and make it the standard of comparison.

To some it will appear that I am inventing a factitious difficulty for my Conditioners. Other, more simple-minded, critics may ask 'Why should you suppose they will be such bad men?' But I am not supposing them to be bad men. They are, rather, not men (in the old sense) at all. They are, if you like, men who have sacrificed their own share in traditional humanity in order to devote themselves to the task of deciding what 'Humanity' shall henceforth mean. 'Good' and 'bad,' applied to them, are words without content: for it is from them that the content of these words is henceforward to be derived. Nor is their difficulty factitious. We might suppose that it was possible to say 'After all, most of us want more or less the same things—food and drink and sexual intercourse, amusement, art, science, and the longest possible life for individuals and for the species. Let them simply say, This is what we happen to like, and go on to condition men in the way most likely to produce it. Where's the trouble?' But this will not answer. In the first place, it is false that we all really like the same things. But even if we did, what motive is to impel the Conditioners to scorn delights and live laborious days in order that we, and posterity, may have what we like? Their duty? But that is only the *Tao*, which they may decide to impose on us, but which cannot be valid for them. If they accept it, then they are no longer the makers of conscience but still its subjects, and their final conquest over Nature has not really happened. The preservation of the species? But why should the species be preserved? One of the questions before them is whether this feeling for posterity (they know well how it is produced) shall be continued or not. However far they go back, or down, they can find no ground to stand on. Every motive they try to act on becomes at once a *petitio*. It is not that they are bad men. They are not men at all. Stepping outside the *Tao*, they have stepped into the void. Nor are their subjects necessarily unhappy men. They are not men at all: they are artefacts. Man's final conquest has proved to be the abolition of Man.

Yet the Conditioners will act. When I said just now that all motives fail them, I should have said all motives except one. All motives that claim any validity other than that of their felt emotional weight at a given moment have failed them. Everything except the *sic volo, sic jubeo* has been explained away. But what never claimed objectivity cannot be destroyed by subjectivism. The impulse to scratch when I itch or to pull to pieces when I am inquisitive is immune from the solvent which is fatal to my justice, or honour, or care for posterity. When all that says 'it is good' has been debunked, what says 'I want' remains. It cannot be exploded or 'seen through' because it never had any pretensions. The Conditioners, there- fore, must come to be motivated simply by their own pleasure. I am not here speaking of the corrupting influence of power nor expressing the fear that under it our Conditioners will degenerate. The very words *corrupt* and *degenerate* imply a doctrine of value and are therefore meaningless in this context. My point is that those who stand outside all judgments of value cannot have any ground for preferring one of their own impulses to another except the emotional strength of that impulse. We may legitimately hope that among the impulses which arise in minds thus emptied of all 'rational' or 'spiritual' motives, some will be benevo- lent. I am very doubtful myself whether the benevolent impulses, stripped of that preference and encouragement which the *Tao* teaches us to give them and left to their merely natural strength and frequency as psychological events, will have much influence. I am very doubtful whether history shows us one example of a man who, having stepped outside traditional morality and attained power, has used that power benevolently. I am inclined to think that the Conditioners will hate the conditioned. Though regarding as an illusion the artificial conscience which they produce in us their subjects, they will yet perceive that it creates in us an illusion of meaning for our lives which compares favourably with the futility of their own: and they will envy us as eunuchs envy men. But I do not insist on this, for it is mere conjecture. What is not conjecture is that our hope even of a 'conditioned' happiness rests on what is ordinarily called 'chance'—the chance that benevolent impulses may on the whole predominate in our Conditioners. For without the judgement 'Benevolence is good'—that is, without re-entering the *Tao*—they can have no ground for promoting or stabilizing their benevolent impulses rather than any others. By the logic of their position they must just take their impulses as they come, from chance. And Chance here means Nature. It is from heredity, digestion, the weather, and the association of ideas, that the motives of the Conditioners will spring. Their extreme rationalism, by 'seeing through' all 'rational' motives, leaves them creatures of wholly irrational behaviour. If you will not obey the *Tao*, or else commit suicide, obedience to impulse (and therefore, in the long run, to mere 'nature') is the only course left open.

At the moment, then, of Man's victory over Nature, we find the whole human race subjected to some individual men, and those individuals subjected to that in themselves which is purely 'natural'—to their irrational impulses. Nature, untrammelled by values, rules the Conditioners and, through them, all humanity. Man's conquest of Nature turns out, in the moment of its consummation, to be Nature's conquest of Man. Every victory we seemed to win has led us, step by step, to this conclusion. All Nature's apparent reverses have been but tactical withdrawals. We thought we were beating her back when she was luring us on. What looked to us like hands held up in surrender was really the opening of arms to enfold us for ever. If the fully planned and conditioned world (with its *Tao* a mere product of the planning) comes into existence, Nature will be troubled no more by the restive species that rose in revolt against her so many millions of years ago, will be vexed no longer by its chatter of truth and mercy and beauty and happiness. *Ferum victorem cepit:* and if the eugenics are efficient enough there will be no second revolt, but all snug beneath the Conditioners, and the Conditioners beneath her, till the moon falls or the sun grows cold.

My point may be clearer to some if it is put in a different form. Nature is a word of varying meanings, which can best be understood if we consider its various opposites. The Natural is the opposite of the Artificial, the Civil, the Human, the Spiritual, and the Supernatural. The Artificial does not now concern us. If we take the rest of the list of opposites, however, I think we can get a rough idea of what men have meant by Nature and what it is they oppose to her. Nature seems to be the spatial and temporal, as distinct from what is less fully so or not so at all. She seems to be the world of quantity, as against the world of quality: of objects as against consciousness: of the bound, as against the wholly or partially autonomous: of that which knows no values as against that which both has and perceives value: of efficient causes (or, in some modern systems, of no causality at all) as against final causes. Now I take it that when we understand a thing analytically and then dominate and use it for our own convenience we reduce it to the level of 'Nature' in the sense that we suspend our judgments of value about it, ignore its final cause (if any), and treat it in terms of quantity. This repression of elements in what would otherwise be our total reaction to it is sometimes very noticeable and even painful: something has to be overcome before we can cut up a dead man or a live animal in a dissecting room. These objects *resist* the movement of the mind whereby we thrust them into the world of mere Nature. But in other instances too, a similar price is exacted for our analytical knowledge and manipulative power, even if we have ceased to count it. We do not look at trees either as Dryads or as beautiful objects while we cut them into beams: the first man who did so may have felt the price keenly, and the bleeding trees in Virgil and Spenser may be far-off echoes of that primeval sense of impiety. The stars lost their divinity as astronomy developed, and the Dying God has no place in chemical agriculture. To many, no doubt, this process is simply the gradual discovery that the real world is different from what we expected, and the old opposition to Galileo or to 'bodysnatchers' is simply obscurantism. But that is not the whole story. It is not the greatest of modern scientists who feel most sure that the object, stripped of its qualitative properties and reduced to mere quantity, is wholly real. Little scientists, and little unscientific followers of science, may think so. The great minds know very well that the object, so treated, is an artificial abstraction, that something of its reality has been lost.

From this point of view the conquest of Nature appears in a new light. We reduce things to mere Nature *in order that* we may 'conquer' them. We are always conquering Nature, because 'Nature' is the name for what we have, to some extent, conquered. The price of conquest is to treat a thing as mere Nature. Every conquest over Nature increases her domain. The stars do not become Nature till we can weigh and measure them: the soul does not become Nature till we can psycho-analyse her. The wresting of powers *from* Nature is also the surrendering of things *to* Nature. As long as this process stops short of the final stage we may well hold that the gain outweighs the loss. But as soon as we take the final step of reducing our own species to the level of mere Nature, the whole process is stultified, for this time the being who stood to gain and the being who has been sacrificed are one and the same. This is one of the many instances where to carry a principle to what seems its logical conclusion produces absurdity. It is like the famous Irishman who found that a certain kind of stove reduced his fuel bill by half and thence concluded that two stoves of the same kind would enable him to warm his house with no fuel at all. It is the magician's bargain: give up our soul, get power in return. But once our souls, that is, our selves, have been given up, the power thus conferred will not belong to us. We shall in fact be the slaves and puppets of that to which we have given our souls. It is in Man's power to treat himself as a mere 'natural object' and his own judgements of value as raw material for scientific manipulation to alter at will. The objection to his doing so does not lie in the fact that his point of view (like one's first day in a dissecting room) is painful and shocking till we grow used to it. The pain and the shock are at most a warning and a symptom. The real objection is that if man chooses to treat himself as raw material, raw material he will be: not raw material to be manipulated, as he fondly imagined, by himself, but by mere appetite, that is, mere Nature, in the person of his dehumanized Conditioners.

We have been trying, like Lear, to have it both ways: to lay down our human prerogative and yet at the same time to retain it. It is impossible. Either we are rational spirit obliged for ever to obey the absolute values of the *Tao*, or else we are mere nature to be kneaded and cut into new shapes for the pleasures of masters who must, by hypothesis, have no motive but their own 'natural' impulses. Only the *Tao* provides a common human law of action which can overarch rulers and ruled alike. A dogmatic belief in objective value is necessary to the very idea of a rule which is not tyranny or an obedience which is not slavery.

I am not here thinking solely, perhaps not even chiefly, of those who are our public enemies at the moment. The process which, if not checked, will abolish Man, goes on apace among Communists and Democrats no less than among Fascists. The methods may (at first) differ in brutality. But many a mild-eyed scientist in pince-nez, many a popular dramatist, many an amateur philosopher in our midst, means in the long run just the same as the Nazi rulers of Germany. Traditional values are to be 'debunked' and mankind to be cut out into some fresh shape at the will (which must, by hypothesis, be an arbitrary will) of some few lucky people in one lucky generation which has learned how to do it. The belief that we can invent 'ideologies' at pleasure, and the consequent treatment of mankind as mere υλη, specimens, preparations, begins to affect our very language. Once we killed bad men: now we liquidate unsocial elements. Virtue has become *integration* and diligence *dynamism*, and boys likely to be worthy of a commission are 'potential officer material.' Most wonderful of all, the virtues of thrift and temperance, and even of ordinary intelligence, are *sales-resistance*.

The true significance of what is going on has been concealed by the use of the abstraction Man. Not that the word Man is necessarily a pure abstraction. In the *Tao* itself, as long as we remain within it, we find the concrete reality in which to participate is to be truly human: the real common will and common reason of humanity, alive, and growing like a tree, and branching out, as the situation varies, into ever new beauties and dignities of application. While we speak from within the *Tao* we can speak of Man having power over himself in a sense truly analogous to an individual's self-control. But the moment we step outside and regard the *Tao* as a mere subjective product, this possibility has disappeared. What is now common to all men is a mere abstract universal, an H.C.F., and Man's conquest of himself means simply the rule of the Conditioners over the conditioned human material, the world of post-humanity which, some knowingly and some unknowingly, nearly all men in all nations are at present labouring to produce.

Nothing I can say will prevent some people from describing this lecture as an attack on science. I deny the charge, of course: and real Natural Philosophers (there are some now alive) will perceive that in defending value I defend *inter alia* the value of knowledge, which must die like every other when its roots in the *Tao* are cut. But I can go further than that. I even suggest that from Science herself the cure might come. I have described as a 'magician's bargain' that process whereby man surrenders object after object, and finally himself, to Nature in return for power. And I meant what I said. The fact that the scientist has succeeded where the magician failed has put such a wide contrast between them in popular thought that the real story of the birth of Science is misunderstood. You will even find people who write about the sixteenth century as if Magic were a medieval survival and Science the new thing that came to to sweep it away. Those who have studied the period know better. There was very little magic in the Middle Ages: the sixteenth and seventeenth centuries are the high noon of magic. The serious magical endeavour and the serious scientific endeavour are twins: one was sickly and died, the other strong and throve. But they were twins. They were born of the same impulse. I allow that some (certainly not all) of the early scientists were actuated by a pure love of knowledge. But if we consider the temper of that age as a whole we can discern the impulse of which I speak. There is something which unites magic and applied science while separating both from the 'wisdom' of earlier ages. For the wise men of old the cardinal problem had been how to conform the soul to reality, and the solution had been knowledge, self-discipline, and virtue. For magic and applied science alike the problem is how to subdue reality to the wishes of men: the solution is a technique; and both, in the practice of this technique, are ready to do things hitherto regarded as disgusting and impious—such as digging up and mutilating the dead. If we compare the chief trumpeter of the new era (Bacon) with Marlowe's Faustus, the similarity is striking. You will read in some critics that Faustus has a thirst for knowledge. In reality, he hardly mentions it. It is not truth he wants from his devils, but gold and guns and girls. 'All things that move between the quiet poles shall be at his command' and 'a sound magician is a mighty god.'[3] In the same spirit Bacon condemns those who value knowledge as an end it itself: this, for him, is to use as a mistress for pleasure what ought to be a spouse for fruit.[4] The true object is to extend Man's power to the performance of all things possible. He rejects magic because it does not work,[5] but his goal is that of the magician. In Paracelsus the characters of magician and scientist are combined. No doubt those who really founded modern science were usually those whose love of truth exceeded their love of power; in every mixed movement the efficacy comes from the good elements not from the bad. But the presence of the bad elements is not irrelevant to the direction the efficacy takes. It might be going too far to say that the modern scientific movement was tainted from its birth: but I think it would be true to say that it was born in an unhealthy neighbourhood and at an inauspicious hour. Its triumphs may have been too rapid and purchased at too high a price: reconsideration, and something like repentance, may be required.

Is it, then, possible to imagine a new Natural Philosophy, continually conscious that the 'natural object' produced by analysis and abstraction is not reality but only a view, and always correcting the abstraction? I hardly know what I am asking for. I hear rumours that Goethe's approach to nature deserves fuller consideration—that even Dr. Steiner may have seen something that orthodox researchers have missed. The regenerate science which I have in mind would not do even to minerals and vegetables what modern science threatens to do to man himself. When it explained it would not explain away. When it spoke of the parts it would remember the whole. While studying the *It* it would not lose what Martin Buber calls the *Thou*-situation. The analogy between the *Tao* of Man and the instincts of an animal species would mean for it new light cast on the

[3]*Dr. Faustus*, 77–90.
[4]*Advancement of Learning*, Bk. I (p. 60 in Ellis and Spedding, 1905; p. 35 in Everyman Edn.).
[5]*Filum Labyrinthi*, i.

unknown thing. Instinct, by the inly known reality of conscience and not a reduction of conscience to the category of Instinct. Its followers would not be free with the words *only* and *merely*. In a word, it would conquer Nature without being at the same time conquered by her and buy knowledge at a lower cost than that of life.

Perhaps I am asking impossibilities. Perhaps, in the nature of things, analytical understanding must always be a basilisk which kills what it sees and only sees by killing. But if the scientists themselves cannot arrest this process before it reaches the common Reason and kills that too, then someone else must arrest it. What I most fear is the reply that I am 'only one more' obscurantist, that this barrier, like all previous barriers set up against the advance of science, can be safely passed. Such a reply springs from the fatal serialism of the modern imagination—the image of infinite unilinear progression which so haunts our minds. Because we have to use numbers so much we tend to think of every process as if it must be like the numeral series, where every step, to all eternity, is the same kind of step as the one before. I implore you to remember the Irishman and his two stoves. There are progressions in which the last step is *sui generis*—incommensurable with the others—and in which to go the whole way is to undo all the labour of your previous journey. To reduce the *Tao* to a mere natural product is a step of that kind. Up to that point, the kind of explanation which explains things away may give us something, though at a heavy cost. But you cannot go on 'explaining away' for ever: you will find that you have explained explanation itself away. You cannot go on 'seeing through' things for ever. The whole point of seeing through something is to see something through it. It is good that the window should be transparent, because the street or garden beyond it is opaque. How if you saw through the garden too? It is no use trying to 'see through' first principles. If you see through everything, then everything is transparent. But a wholly transparent world is an invisible world. To 'see through' all things is the same as not to see.

Appendix
Illustrations of the *Tao*

THE FOLLOWING ILLUSTRATIONS of the Natural Law are collected from such sources as come readily to the hand of one who is not a professional historian. The list makes no pretense of completeness. It will be noticed that writers such as Locke and Hooker, who wrote within the Christian tradition, are quoted side by side with the New Testament. This would, of course, be absurd if I were trying to collect independent testimonies to the *Tao*. But (1) I am not trying to *prove* its validity by the argument from common consent. Its validity cannot be deduced. For those who do not perceive its rationality, even universal consent could not prove it. (2) The idea of collecting *independent* testimonies presupposes that 'civilizations' have arisen in the world independently of one another; or even that humanity has had several independent emergences on this planet. The biology and anthropology involved in such an assumption are extremely doubtful. It is by no means certain that there has ever (in the sense required) been more than one civilization in all history. It is at least arguable that every civilization we find has been derived from another civilization and, in the last resort, from a single centre—'carried' like an infectious disease or like the Apostolical succession.

I. *The Law of General Beneficence*

(A) NEGATIVE

'I have not slain men.' (Ancient Egyptian. From the Confession of the Righteous Soul, 'Book of the Dead.' v. *Encyclopedia of Religion and Ethics* [=*ERE*], vol. v, p. 478.)

'Do not murder.' (Ancient Jewish. Exodus xx. 13.)

'Terrify not men or God will terrify thee.' (Ancient Egyptian. Precepts of Ptahhetep. H. R. Hall, *Ancient History of Near East*, p. 133 n.)

'In Nástrond (= Hell) I saw . . . murderers.' (Old Norse. *Volospá* 38, 39.)

'I have not brought misery upon my fellows. I have not made the beginning of every day laborious in the sight of him who worked for me.' (Ancient Egyptian. Confession of Righteous Soul. *ERE* v. 478.)

'I have not been grasping.' (Ancient Egyptian. *Ibid.*)

'Who meditates oppression, his dwelling is overturned.' (Babylonian. *Hymn to Samaš. ERE* v. 455.)

'He who is cruel and calumnious has the character of a cat.' (Hindu. Laws of Manu. Janet, *Histoire de la Science Politique*, vol. i, p. 6.)

'Slander not.' (Babylonian. *Hymn to Samaš. ERE* v. 445.)

'Thou shalt not bear false witness against thy neighbour.' (Ancient Jewish. Exodus xx. 16.)

'Utter not a word by which anyone could be wounded.' (Hindu. Janet, p. 7.)

'Has he . . . driven an honest man from his family? broken up a well cemented clan?' (Babylonian. List of Sins from incantation tablets. *ERE* v. 466.)

'I have not caused hunger. I have not caused weeping.' (Ancient Egyptian. *ERE* v. 478.)

'Never do to others what you would not like them to do to you.' (Ancient Chinese. *Analects of Confucius,* trans. A. Waley, xv. 23; cf. xii. 2.)

'Thou shalt not hate thy brother in thy heart.' (Ancient Jewish. Leviticus xix. 17.)

'He whose heart is in the smallest degree set upon goodness will dislike no one.' (Ancient Chinese. *Analects,* iv. 4.)

(B) POSITIVE

'Nature urges that a man should wish human society to exist and should wish to enter it.' (Roman. Cicero, De *Officiis,* I. iv.)

'By the fundamental Law of Nature Man [is] to be preserved as much as possible.' (Locke, *Treatises of Civil Govt.* ii. 3.)

'When the people have multiplied, what next should be done for them? The Master said, Enrich them. Jan Ch'iu said, When one has enriched them, what next should be done for them? The Master said, Instruct them.' (Ancient Chinese. *Analects,* xiii. 9.)

'Speak kindness . . . show good will.' (Babylonian. *Hymn to Samaš. ERE* v. 445.)

'Men were brought into existence for the sake of men that they might do one another good.' (Roman. Cicero, *De Off.* I. vii.)

'Man is man's delight.' (Old Norse. *Hávamál* 47.)

'He who is asked for alms should always give.' (Hindu. Janet, i. 7.)

'What good man regards any misfortune as no concern of his?' (Roman. Juvenal, xv. 140.)

'I am a man: nothing human is alien to me.' (Roman. Terence, *Heaut. Tim.*)

'Love thy neighbour as thyself.' (Ancient Jewish. Leviticus xix. 18.)

'Love the stranger as thyself.' (Ancient Jewish. *Ibid.* 33, 34.)

'Do to men what you wish men to do to you.' (Christian. Matt. vii. 12.)

II. *The Law of Special Beneficence*

'It is upon the trunk that a gentleman works. When that is firmly set up, the Way grows. And surely proper behaviour to parents and elder brothers is the trunk of goodness.' (Ancient Chinese. *Analects,* i. 2.)

'Brothers shall fight and be each others' bane.' (Old Norse. Account of the Evil Age before the World's end, *Volospá* 45.)

'Has he insulted his elder sister?' (Babylonian. List of Sins. *ERE* v. 446.)

'You will see them take care of their kindred [and] the children of their friends . . . never reproaching them in the least.' (Redskin. Le Jeune, quoted *ERE* v. 437.)

'Love thy wife studiously. Gladden her heart all thy life long.' (Ancient Egyptian. *ERE* v. 481.)

'Nothing can ever change the claims of kinship for a right thinking man.' (Anglo-Saxon. *Beowulf*, 2600.)

'Did not Socrates love his own children, though he did so as a free man and as one not forgetting that the gods have the first claim on our friendship?' (Greek. Epictetus, iii. 24.)

'Natural affection is a thing right and according to Nature.' (Greek. *Ibid.* I. xi.)

'I ought not to be unfeeling like a statue but should fulfil both my natural and artificial relations, as a worshipper, a son, a brother, a father, and a citizen.' (Greek, *Ibid.* III. ii.)

'This first I rede thee: be blameless to thy kindred. Take no vengeance even though they do thee wrong.' (Old Norse. *Sigrdrifumál*, 22.)

'Is it only the sons of Atreus who love their wives? For every good man, who is right-minded, loves and cherishes his own.' (Greek. Homer, *Iliad*, ix. 340.)

'The union and fellowship of men will be best preserved if each receives from us the more kindness in proportion as he is more closely connected with us.' (Roman. Cicero, *De Off.* I. xvi.)

'Part of us is claimed by our country, part by our parents, part by our friends.' (Roman. *Ibid.* I. vii.)

'If a ruler . . . compassed the salvation of the whole state, surely you would call him Good? The Master said, It would no longer be a matter of "Good." He would without doubt be a Divine Sage.' (Ancient Chinese. *Analects*, vi. 28.)

'Has it escaped you that, in the eyes of gods and good men, your native land deserves from you more honour, worship, and reverence than your mother and father and all your ancestors? That you should give a softer answer to its anger than to a father's anger? That if you cannot persuade it to alter its mind you must obey it in all quietness, whether it binds you or beats you or sends you to a war where you may get wounds or death?' (Greek. Plato, *Crito*, 51 A. B.)

'If any provide not for his own, and specially for those of his own house, he hath denied the faith.' (Christian. I. Tim. v. 8.)

'Put them in mind to obey magistrates.' . . . . 'I exhort that prayers be made for kings and all that are in authority.' (Christian. Tit. iii. 1 and I Tim. ii. 1, 2.)

III. *Duties to Parents, Elders, Ancestors*

'Your father is an image of the Lord of Creation, your mother an image of the Earth. For him who fails to honour them, every work of piety is in vain. This is the first duty.' (Hindu. Janet, i. 9.)

'Has he despised Father and Mother?' (Babylonian. List of Sins. *ERE* v. 446.)

'I was a staff by my Father's side. . . . I went in and out at his command.' (Ancient Egyptian. Confession of the Righteous Soul. *ERE* v. 481.)

'Honour thy Father and thy Mother.' (Ancient Jewish. Exodus xx. 12.)

'To care for parents.' (Greek. List of duties in Epictetus, III. vii.)

'Children, old men, the poor, and the sick, should be considered as the lords of the atmosphere.' (Hindu. Janet, i. 8.)

'Rise up before the hoary head and honour the old man.' (Ancient Jewish. Leviticus xix. 32.)

'I tended the old man, I gave him my staff.' (Ancient Egyptian. *ERE* v. 481.)

'You will see them take care . . . of old men.' (Redskin. Le Jeune, quoted *ERE* v. 437.)

'I have not taken away the oblations of the blessed dead.' (Ancient Egyptian. Confession of the Righteous Soul. *ERE* v. 478.)

'When proper respect towards the dead is shown at the end and continued after they are far away, the moral force [*tê*] of a people has reached its highest point.' (Ancient Chinese. *Analects,* i. 9.)

IV. *Duties to Children and Posterity*

'Children, the old, the poor, etc., should be considered as lords of the atmosphere.' (Hindu. Janet, i. 8.)

'To marry and to beget children.' (Greek. List of duties. Epictetus, III. vii.)

'Can you conceive an Epicurean commonwealth? . . . What will happen? Whence is the population to be kept up? Who will educate them? Who will be Director of Adolescents? Who will be Director of Physical Training? What will be taught?' (Greek. *Ibid.*)

'Nature produces a special love of offspring' and 'To live according to Nature is the supreme good.' (Roman. Cicero, *De Off.* I. iv, and *De Legibus,* I. xxi.)

'The second of these achievements is no less glorious than the first; for while the first did good on one occasion, the second will continue to benefit the state forever.' (Roman. Cicero, *De Off.* I. xxii.)

'Great reverence is owed to a child.' (Roman. Juvenal, xiv. 47.)

'The Master said, Respect the young.' (Ancient Chinese. *Analects,* ix. 22.)

'The killing of the women and more especially of the young boys and girls who are to go to make up the future strength of the people, is the saddest part . . . and we feel it very sorely.' (Redskin. Account of the Battle of Wounded Knee. *ERE* v. 432.)

V. *The Law of Justice*

(A) SEXUAL JUSTICE

'Has he approached his neighbour's wife?' (Babylonian. List of Sins. *ERE* v. 446.)

'Thou shalt not commit adultery.' (Ancient Jewish. Exodus xx. 14.)

'I saw in Nástrond (= Hell) . . . beguilers of others' wives.' (Old Norse. *Volospá* 38, 39.)

(B) HONESTY

'Has he drawn false boundaries?' (Babylonian. List of Sins. *ERE* v. 446.)

'To wrong, to rob, to cause to be robbed.' (Babylonian. *Ibid.*)

'I have not stolen.' (Ancient Egyptian. Confession of Righteous Soul. *ERE* v. 478.)

'Thou shalt not steal.' (Ancient Jewish. Exodus xx. 15.)

'Choose loss rather than shameful gains.' (Greek. Chilon Fr. 10. Diels.)

'Justice is the settled and permanent intention of rendering to each man his rights.' (Roman. Justinian, *Institutions*, I. i.)

'If the native made a "find" of any kind (e.g. a honey tree) and marked it, it was thereafter safe for him, as far as his own tribesmen were concerned, no matter how long he left it.' (Australian Aborigines. *ERE* v. 441.)

'The first point of justice is that none should do any mischief to another unless he has first been attacked by the other's wrongdoing. The second is that a man should treat common property as common property, and private property as his own. There is no such thing as private property by nature, but things have become private either through prior occupation (as when men of old came into empty territory) or by conquest, or law, or agreement, or stipulation, or casting lots.' (Roman. Cicero, *De Off.* I. vii.)

(C) JUSTICE IN COURT, &C.

'Whoso takes no bribe . . . well pleasing is this to Samaš.' (Babylonian. *ERE* v. 445.)

'I have not traduced the slave to him who is set over him.' (Ancient Egyptian. Confession of Righteous Soul. *ERE* v. 478.)

'Thou shalt not bear false witness against thy neighbour.' (Ancient Jewish. Exodus xx. 16.)

'Regard him whom thou knowest like him whom thou knowest not.' (Ancient Egyptian. *ERE* v. 482.)

'Do no unrighteousness in judgement. You must not consider the fact that one party is poor nor the fact that the other is a great man.' (Ancient Jewish. Leviticus xix. 15.)

VI. *The Law of Good Faith and Veracity*

'A sacrifice is obliterated by a lie and the merit of alms by an act of fraud.' (Hindu. Janet, i. 6.)

'Whose mouth, full of lying, avails not before thee: thou burnest their utterance.' (Babylonian. *Hymn to Samaš. ERE* v. 445.)

'With his mouth was he full of *Yea*, in his heart full of *Nay?*' (Babylonian. *ERE* v. 446.)

'I have not spoken falsehood.' (Ancient Egyptian. Confession of Righteous Soul. *ERE* v. 478.)

'I sought no trickery, nor swore false oaths.' (Anglo-Saxon. *Beowulf*, 2738.)

'The Master said, Be of unwavering good faith.' (Ancient Chinese. *Analects*, viii. 13.)

'In Nástrond (= Hell) I saw the perjurers.' (Old Norse. *Volospá* 39.)

'Hateful to me as are the gates of Hades is that man who says one thing, and hides another in his heart.' (Greek. Homer, *Iliad*, ix. 312.)

'The foundation of justice is good faith.' (Roman. Cicero, *De Off*. I. vii.)

'[The gentleman] must learn to be faithful to his superiors and to keep promises.' (Ancient Chinese. *Analects*, I. 8.)

'Anything is better than treachery.' (Old Norse. *Hávamál* 124.)

VII. *The Law of Mercy*

'The poor and the sick should be regarded as lords of the atmosphere.' (Hindu. Janet, i. 8.)

'Whoso makes intercession for the weak, well pleasing is this to Samaš' (Babylonian. *ERE* v. 445.)

'Has he failed to set a prisoner free?' (Babylonian. List of Sins. *ERE* v. 446.)

'I have given bread to the hungry, water to the thirsty, clothes to the naked, a ferry boat to the boatless.' (Ancient Egyptian. *ERE* v. 478.)

'One should never strike a woman; not even with a flower.' (Hindu. Janet, i. 8.)

'There, Thor, you got disgrace, when you beat women.' (Old Norse. *Hárbarthsljóth* 38.)

'In the Dalebura tribe a woman, a cripple from birth, was carried about by the tribespeople in turn until her death at the age of sixty-six.' . . . 'They never desert the sick.' (Australian Aborigines. *ERE* v. 443.)

'You will see them take care of . . . widows, orphans, and old men, never reproaching them.' (Redskin. *ERE* v. 439.)

'Nature confesses that she has given to the human race the tenderest hearts, by giving us the power to weep. This is the best part of us.' (Roman. Juvenal, xv. 131.)

'They said that he had been the mildest and gentlest of the kings of the world.' (Anglo-Saxon. Praise of the hero in *Beowulf*, 3180.)

'When thou cuttest down thine harvest . . . and hast forgot a sheaf . . . thou shalt not go again to fetch it: it shall be for the stranger, for the fatherless, and for the widow.' (Ancient Jewish. Deut. xxiv. 19.)

VIII. *The Law of Magnanimity*

A.

'There are two kinds of injustice: the first is found in those who do an injury, the second in those who fail to protect another from injury when they can.' (Roman. Cicero, *De Off.* I, vii.)

'Men always knew that when force and injury was offered they might be defenders of themselves; they knew that howsoever men may seek their own commodity, yet if this were done with injury unto others it was not to be suffered, but by all men and by all good means to be withstood.' (English. Hooker, *Laws of Eccl. Polity*, 1. ix. 4.)

'To take no notice of a violent attack is to strengthen the heart of the enemy. Vigour is valiant, but cowardice is vile.' (Ancient Egyptian. The Pharaoh Seun-sert III cit H R Hall, *Ancient History of the Near East,* p. 161.)

'They came to the fields of joy, the fresh turf of the Fortunate Woods and the dwellings of the Blessed . . . here was the company of those who had suffered wounds fighting for their fatherland.' (Roman. Virgil, *Aen.* vi, 638–9, 660.)

'Courage has got to be harder, heart the stouter, spirit the sterner, as our strength weakens. Here lies our lord, cut to pieces, our best man in the dust. If anyone thinks of leaving this battle, he can howl forever.' (Anglo-Saxon. *Maldon*, 312.)

'Praise and imitate that man to whom, while life is pleasing, death is not grievous.' (Stoic. Seneca, *Ep.* liv.)

'The Master said, Love learning and if attacked be ready to die for the Good Way.' (Ancient Chinese. *Analects*, viii. 13.)

B.

'Death is to be chosen before slavery and base deeds.' (Roman. Cicero, *De Off.* I. xxiii.)

'Death is better for every man than life with shame.' (Anglo-Saxon, *Beowulf*, 2890.)

'Nature and Reason command that nothing uncomely, nothing effeminate, nothing lascivious be done or thought.' (Roman. Cicero, *De Off.* I. iv.)

'We must not listen to those who advise us "being men to think human thoughts, and being mortal to think mortal thoughts," but must put on immortality as much as is possible and strain every nerve to live according to that best part of us, which, being small in bulk, yet much more in its power and honour surpasses all else.' (Ancient Greek. Aristotle, *Eth. Nic.* 1177 B.)

'The soul then ought to conduct the body, and the spirit of our minds the soul. This is therefore the first Law, whereby the highest power of the mind requireth obedience at the hands of all the rest.' (Hooker, *op. cit.* I. viii. 6.)

'Let him not desire to die, let him not desire to live, let him wait for his time

. . . let him patiently bear hard words, entirely abstaining from bodily pleasures.' (Ancient Indian. Laws of Manu. *ERE* ii. 98.)

'He who is unmoved, who has restrained his senses . . . is said to be devoted. As a flame in a windless place that flickers not, so is the devoted.' (Ancient Indian. *Bhagavad gita. ERE* ii. 90.)

C.

'Is not the love of Wisdom a practice of death?' (Ancient Greek. Plato, *Phaedo*, 81 A.)

'I know that I hung on the gallows for nine nights, wounded with the spear as a sacrifice to Odin, myself offered to Myself.' (Old Norse, *Hávamál*, 1. 10 in *Corpus Poeticum Boreale;* stanza 139 in Hildebrand's *Lieder der Alteren Edda.* 1922.)

'Verily, verily I say to you unless a grain of wheat falls into the earth and dies, it remains alone, but if it dies it bears much fruit. He who loves his life loses it.' (Christian. John xii. 24, 25.)

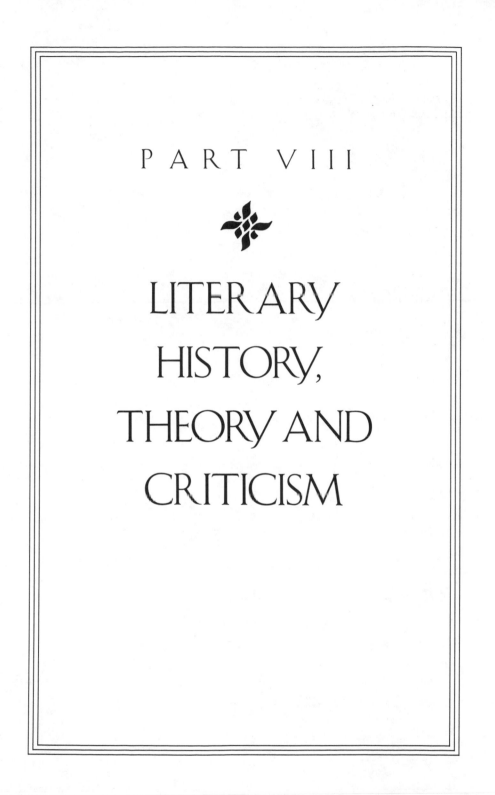

PART VIII

LITERARY
HISTORY,
THEORY AND
CRITICISM

S INCE the 1930s C. S. Lewis has been well known in the academic world
as a literary theoretician, historian, and critic. A specialist in English literature,
Lewis has written several books and essays that are still required reading for
serious students.

The first selection reproduced here is "De Descriptione Temporum," his
inaugural lecture at Cambridge University in 1954. This is an important essay
which Lewis reprinted in *They Asked for a Paper* (1962). The address not only
illuminates Lewis's point of view and frame of reference, it presents a succinct
answer to a frequently raised question, "Why is literary history important?"

That Lewis saw literary history as an important academic enterprise can be
seen in his first scholarly book, *The Allegory of Love* (1936). This work traces
the historical development of courtly love—in sentiment and allegory—over
several centuries. Here we have a narrative history of a genre that spans more than
half a millennium from the eleventh through the sixteenth century. Some introductory remarks from this book follow here, enabling the newcomer to Lewis
studies to get a glimpse of his idea of process in history.

Although Lewis lost enthusiasm for the genre of courtly love, his interest in
literary history never waned. In 1954 he published a massive volume for the
Oxford History of English Literature series entitled *English Literature in the
Sixteenth Century, Excluding Drama*. This 696-page work of careful scholarship
surveys the dramatic changes in English literature during a period of prodigious

change. Some of the author's introductory remarks are reprinted here, along with a representative sample from this well-written and useful survey.

Lewis wrote other works on the literary history of the Medieval and Renaissance periods, among them *The Discarded Image* (1964), which is based on his Oxford lectures. But his interests ranged to other fields as well. In a fascinating volume entitled *Studies in Words* (1960), Lewis unveils the history of the meaning of several words, showing how their definitions and uses have evolved over the centuries. One chapter is presented here, and it gives a glimpse of Lewis's versatility as he ventures into the discipline of philology.

Lewis made valuable contributions to literary theory as well as history. His debate with E. M. W. Tillyard over literary theory, *The Personal Heresy: A Controversy* (1939), contains alternate chapters by each scholar. And his chapter entitled "On Stories," included here from *Essays Presented to Charles Williams* (1947) is a brilliant contribution to a neglected subject.

Lewis's thought cannot always be easily categorized, and his volume *An Experiment in Criticism* (1961) is a case in point. Its subject, to be sure, is criticism, but some of the pages introduced here show that he wrote brilliantly about such unique subjects as literary experience.

The high quality of Lewis's theory and history notwithstanding, some scholars believe that his most enduring work is in the field of generic criticism. From the 1930s until the end of his career, Lewis published some of the most significant scholarship ever produced on Edmund Spenser. This interest came to fruition in a major section of his Oxford History volume, as well as numerous articles on Spenser that were posthumously brought together by Alastair Fowler in *Spenser's Images of Life* (1967). Rather than break up any of his longer pieces on Spenser, or use one esoteric article on a specialized theme, a brief overview of Spenser that Lewis did for a volume entitled *Fifteen Poets* (1941) concludes this chapter of selections.

De Descriptione Temporum

Speaking from a newly founded Chair, I find myself freed from one embarrassment only to fall into another. I have no great predecessors to overshadow me; on the other hand, I must try (as the theatrical people say) "to create the part". The responsibility is heavy. If I miscarry, the University might come to regret not only my election—an error which, at worst, can be left to the great healer—but even, which matters very much more, the foundation of the Chair itself. That is why I have thought it best to take the bull by the horns and devote this lecture to explaining as clearly as I can the way in which I approach my work; my interpretation of the commission you have given me.

What most attracted me in that commission was the combination "Medieval and Renaissance". I thought that by this formula the University was giving official sanction to a change which has been coming over historical opinion within my own lifetime. It is temperately summed up by Professor Seznec in the words: "As the Middle Ages and the Renaissance come to be better known, the traditional antithesis between them grows less marked."[1] Some scholars might go

[1] J. Seznec, *La Survivance des dieux antiques* (London, 1940), trans. B. F. Sessions (Kingsport, Tennessee, 1953), p. 3.

further than Professor Seznec, but very few, I believe, would now oppose him. If we are sometimes unconscious of the change, that is not because we have not shared it but because it has been gradual and imperceptible. We recognize it most clearly if we are suddenly brought face to face with the old view in its full vigour. A good experiment is to re-read the first chapter of J. M. Berdan's *Early Tudor Poetry*. [2] It is still in many ways a useful book; but it is now difficult to read that chapter without a smile. We begin with twenty-nine pages (and they contain several misstatements) of unrelieved gloom about grossness, superstition, and cruelty to children, and on the twenty-ninth comes the sentence, "The first rift in this darkness is the Copernican doctrine"; as if a new hypothesis in astronomy would naturally make a man stop hitting his daughter about the head. No scholar could now write quite like that. But the old picture, done in far cruder colours, has survived among the weaker brethren, if not (let us hope) at Cambridge, yet certainly in that Western darkness from which you have so lately bidden me emerge. Only last summer a young gentleman whom I had the honour of examining described Thomas Wyatt as "the first man who scrambled ashore out of the great, dark surging sea of the Middle Ages". [3] This was interesting because it showed how a stereotyped image can obliterate a man's own experience. Nearly all the medieval texts which the syllabus had required him to study had in reality led him into formal gardens where every passion was subdued to a ceremonial and every problem of conduct was dovetailed into a complex and rigid moral theology.

From the formula "Medieval and Renaissance", then, I inferred that the University was encouraging my own belief that the barrier between those two ages has been greatly exaggerated, if indeed it was not largely a figment of Humanist propaganda. At the very least, I was ready to welcome any increased flexibility in our conception of history. All lines of demarcation between what we call "periods" should be subject to constant revision. Would that we could dispense with them altogether! As a great Cambridge historian[4] has said: "Unlike dates, periods are not facts. They are retrospective conceptions that we form about past events, useful to focus discussion, but very often leading historical thought astray." The actual temporal process, as we meet it in our lives (and we meet it, in a strict sense, nowhere else) has no divisions, except perhaps those "blessed barriers between day and day", our sleeps. Change is never complete, and change never ceases. Nothing is every quite finished with; it may always begin over again. (This is one of the sides of life that Richardson hits off with wearing accuracy.) And nothing is quite new; it was always somehow anticipated or prepared for. A seamless, formless continuity-in-mutability is the mode of our life. But unhappily we cannot as historians dispense with periods. We cannot use for literary history the technique of Mrs. Woolf's *The Waves*. We cannot hold

[2] New York, 1920.

[3] A delicious passage in Comparetti, *Vergil in the Middle Ages*, trans. E. F. M. Benecke (London, 1895), p. 241, contrasts the Middle Ages with "more normal periods of history".

[4] G. M. Trevelyan, *English Social History* (London, 1944), p. 92.

together huge masses of particulars without putting into them some kind of structure. Still less can we arrange a term's work or draw up a lecture list. Thus we are driven back upon periods. All divisions will falsify our material to some extent; the best one can hope is to choose those which will falsify it least. But because we must divide, to reduce the emphasis on any one traditional division must, in the long run, mean an increase of emphasis on some other division. And that is the subject I want to discuss. If we do not put the Great Divide between the Middle Ages and the Renaissance, where should we put it? I ask this question with the full consciousness that, in the reality studied, there is no Great Divide. There is nothing in history that quite corresponds to a coastline or a watershed in geography. If, in spite of this, I still think my question worth asking, that is certainly not because I claim for my answer more than a methodological value, or even much of that. Least of all would I wish it to be any less subject than others to continual attack and speedy revision. But I believe that the discussion is as good a way as any other of explaining how I look at the work you have given me. When I have finished it, I shall at least have laid the cards on the table and you will know the worst.

The meaning of my title will now have become plain. It is a chapter-heading borrowed from Isidore.[5] In that chapter Isidore is engaged in dividing history, as he knew it, into its periods; or, as he calls them, *aetates*. I shall be doing the same. Assuming that we do not put our great frontier between the Middle Ages and the Renaissance, I shall consider the rival claims of certain other divisions which have been, or might be, made. But, first, a word of warning. I am not, even on the most Lilliputian scale, emulating Professor Toynbee or Spengler. About everything that could be called "the philosophy of history" I am a desperate sceptic. I know nothing of the future, not even whether there will be any future. I don't know whether past history has been necessary or contingent. I don't know whether the human tragi-comedy is now in Act I or Act V; whether our present disorders are those of infancy or of old age. I am merely considering how we should arrange or schematize those facts—ludicrously few in comparison with the totality—which survive to us (often by accident) from the past. I am less like a botanist in a forest than a woman arranging a few cut flowers for the drawing-room. So, in some degree, are the greatest historians. We can't get into the real forest of the past; that is part of what the word *past* means.

The first division that naturally occurs to us is that between Antiquity and the Dark Ages—the fall of the Empire, the barbarian invasions, the christening of Europe. And of course no possible revolution in historical thought will ever make this anything less than a massive and multiple change. Do not imagine that I mean to belittle it. Yet I must observe that three things have happened since, say, Gibbon's time, which make it a shade less catastrophic for us than it was for him.

1. The partial loss of ancient learning and its recovery at the Renaissance were

[5] *Etymologiarum*, ed. W. M. Lindsay, 2 vols. (Oxford, 1911), V, xxxix.

for him both unique events. History furnished no rivals to such a death and such a re-birth. But we have lived to see the second death of ancient learning. In our time something which was once the possession of all educated men has shrunk to being the technical accomplishment of a few specialists. If we say that this is not total death, it may be replied that there was no total death in the Dark Ages either. It could even be argued that Latin, surviving as the language of Dark Age culture, and preserving the disciplines of Law and Rhetoric, gave to some parts of the classical heritage a far more living and integral status in the life of those ages than the academic studies of the specialists can claim in our own. As for the area and the *tempo* of the two deaths, if one were looking for a man who could not read Virgil though his father could, he might be found more easily in the twentieth century than in the fifth.

2. To Gibbon the literary change from Virgil to *Beowulf* or the *Hildebrand*, if he had read them, would have seemed greater than it can to us. We can now see quite clearly that these barbarian poems were not really a novelty comparable to, say, *The Waste Land* or Mr. Jones's *Anathemata*. They were rather an unconscious return to the spirit of the earliest classical poetry. The audience of Homer, and the audience of the *Hildebrand*, once they had learned one another's language and metre, would have found one another's poetry perfectly intelligible. Nothing new had come into the world.

3. The christening of Europe seemed to all our ancestors, whether they welcomed it themselves as Christians, or, like Gibbon, deplored it as humanistic unbelievers, a unique, irreversible event. But we have seen the opposite process. Of course the un-christening of Europe in our time is not quite complete; neither was her christening in the Dark Ages. But roughly speaking we may say that whereas all history was for our ancestors divided into two periods, the pre-Christian and the Christian, and two only, for us it falls into three—the pre-Christian, the Christian, and what may reasonably be called the post-Christian. This surely must make a momentous difference. I am not here considering either the christening or the un-christening from a theological point of view. I am considering them simply as cultural changes.[6] When I do that, it appears to me that the second change is even more radical than the first. Christians and Pagans had much more in common with each other than either has with a post-Christian. The gap between those who worship different gods is not so wide as that between those who worship and those who do not. The Pagan and Christian ages alike are ages of what Pausanias would call the δρώμενον,[7] the externalised and enacted idea; the sacrifice, the games, the triumph, the ritual drama, the Mass, the tournament, the masque, the pageant, the epithalamium, and with them ritual and symbolic costumes, *trabea* and laticlave, crown of wild olive, royal

[6]It is not certain that either process, seen (if we could see it) *sub specie aeternitatis*, would be more important than it appears to the historian of culture. The amount of Christian (that is, of penitent and regenerate) life in an age, as distinct from "Christian Civilisation", is not to be judged by mortals.

[7]*De Descriptione Graec.* II, xxxvii.

crown, coronet, judge's robes, knight's spurs, herald's tabard, coat-armour, priestly vestment, religious habit—for every rank, trade, or occasion its visible sign. But even if we look away from that into the temper of men's minds, I seem to see the same. Surely the gap between Professor Ryle and Thomas Browne is far wider than that between Gregory the Great and Virgil? Surely Seneca and Dr. Johnson are closer together than Burton and Freud?

You see already the lines along which my thought is working; and indeed it is no part of my aim to save a surprise for the end of the lecture. If I have ventured, a little, to modify our view of the transition from "the Antique" to "the Dark", it is only because I believe we have since witnessed a change even more profound.

The next frontier which has been drawn, though not till recently, is that between the Dark and the Middle Ages. We draw it somewhere about the early twelfth century. This frontier clearly cannot compete with its predecessor in the religious field; nor can it boast such drastic redistribution of populations. But it nearly makes up for these deficiencies in other ways. The change from Ancient to Dark had, after all, consisted mainly in losses. Not entirely. The Dark Ages were not so unfruitful in progress as we sometimes think. They saw the triumph of the *codex* or hinged book over the roll or *volumen*—a technical improvement almost as important for the history of learning as the invention of printing. All exact scholarship depends on it. And if—here I speak under correction—they also invented the stirrup, they did something almost as important for the art of war as the inventor of Tanks. But in the main, they were a period of retrogression: worse houses, worse drains, fewer baths, worse roads, less security. (We notice in *Beowulf* that an old sword is expected to be better than a new one.) With the Middle Ages we reach a period of widespread and brilliant improvement. The text of Aristotle is recovered. Its rapid assimilation by Albertus Magnus and Thomas Aquinas opens up a new world of thought. In architecture new solutions of technical problems lead the way to new aesthetic effects. In literature the old alliterative and assonantal metres give place to that rhymed and syllabic verse which was to carry the main burden of European poetry for centuries. At the same time the poets explore a whole new range of sentiment. I am so far from underrating this particular revolution that I have before now been accused of exaggerating it. But "great" and "small" are terms of comparison. I would think this change in literature the greatest if I did not know of a greater. It does not seem to me that the work of the Troubadours and Chrestien and the rest was really as great a novelty as the poetry of the twentieth century. A man bred on the *Chanson de Roland* might have been puzzled by the *Lancelot*. He would have wondered why the author spent so much time on the sentiments and so (comparatively) little on the actions. But he would have known that this was what the author had done. He would, in one important sense, have known what the poem was "about". If he had misunderstood the intention, he would at least have understood the words. That is why I do not think the change from "Dark" to "Middle" can, on the literary side, be judged equal to the change which has taken place in my own lifetime. And of course in religion it does not even begin to compete.

A third possible frontier remains to be considered. We might draw our line somewhere towards the end of the seventeenth century, with the general accept-ance of Copernicanism, the dominance of Descartes, and (in England) the foundation of the Royal Society. Indeed, if we were considering the history of thought (in the narrower sense of the word) I believe this is where I would draw my line. But if we are considering the history of our culture in general, it is a different matter. Certainly the sciences then began to advance with a firmer and more rapid tread. To that advance nearly all the later, and (in my mind) vaster, changes can be traced. But the effects were delayed. The sciences long remained like a lion-cub whose gambols delighted its master in private; it had not yet tasted man's blood. All through the eighteenth century the tone of the common mind remained ethical, rhetorical, juristic, rather than scientific, so that Johnson[8] could truly say, "the knowledge of external nature, and the sciences which that knowledge requires or includes, are not the great or the frequent business of the human mind." It is easy to see why. Science was not the business of Man because Man had not yet become the business of science. It dealt chiefly with the inanimate; and it threw off few technological by-products. When Watt makes his engine, when Darwin starts monkeying with the ancestry of Man, and Freud with his soul, and the economists with all that is his, then indeed the lion will have got out of its cage. Its liberated presence in our midst will become one of the most important factors in everyone's daily life. But not yet; not in the seventeenth century.

It is by these steps that I have come to regard as the greatest of all divisions in the history of the West that which divides the present from, say, the age of Jane Austen and Scott. The dating of such things must of course be rather hazy and indefinite. No one could point to a year or a decade in which the change indisputably began, and it has probably not yet reached its peak. But somewhere between us and the Waverley Novels, somewhere between us and *Persuasion,* the chasm runs. Of course, I had no sooner reached this result than I asked myself whether it might not be an illusion of perspective. The distance between the telegraph post I am touching and the next telegraph post looks longer than the sum of the distances between all the other posts. Could this be an illusion of the same sort? We cannot pace the periods as we could pace the posts. I can only set out the grounds on which, after frequent reconsideration, I have found myself forced to reaffirm my conclusion.

1. I begin with what I regard as the weakest; the change, between Scott's age and ours, in political order. On this count my proposed frontier would have serious rivals. The change is perhaps less than that between Antiquity and the Dark Ages. Yet it is very great; and I think it extends to all nations, those we call democracies as well as dictatorships. If I wished to satirise the present political order I should borrow for it the name which *Punch* invented during the first

[8]*Life of Milton.*

German War: *Govertisement.* This is a portmanteau word and means "government by advertisement". But my intention is not satiric; I am trying to be objective. The change is this. In all previous ages that I can think of the principal aim of rulers, except at rare and short intervals, was to keep their subjects quiet, to forestall or extinguish widespread excitement and persuade people to attend quietly to their several occupations. And on the whole their subjects agreed with them. They even prayed (in words that sound curiously old-fashioned) to be able to live "a peaceable life in all godliness and honesty" and "pass their time in rest and quietness". But now the organisation of mass excitement seems to be almost the normal organ of political power. We live in an age of "appeals", "drives", and "campaigns". Our rulers have become like schoolmasters and are always demanding "keenness". And you notice that I am guilty of a slight archaism in calling them "rulers". "Leaders" is the modern word. I have suggested elsewhere that this is a deeply significant change of vocabulary. Our demand upon them has changed no less than theirs on us. For of a ruler one asks justice, incorruption, diligence, perhaps clemency; of a leader, dash, initiative, and (I suppose) what people call "magnetism" or "personality".

On the political side, then, this proposed frontier has respectable, but hardly compulsive, qualifications.

2. In the arts I think it towers above every possible rival. I do not think that any previous age produced work which was, in its own time, as shatteringly and bewilderingly new as that of the Cubists, the Dadaists, the Surrealists, and Picasso has been in ours. And I am quite sure that this is true of the art I love best, that is, of poetry. This question has often been debated with some heat, but the heat was, I think, occasioned by the suspicion (not always ill-grounded) that those who asserted the unprecedented novelty of modern poetry intended thereby to discredit it. But nothing is farther from my purpose than to make any judgement of value, whether favourable or the reverse. And if once we can eliminate that critical issue and concentrate on the historical fact, then I do not see how anyone can doubt that modern poetry is not only a greater novelty than any other "new poetry" but new in a new way, almost in a new dimension. To say that all new poetry was once as difficult as ours is false; to say that any was is an equivocation. Some earlier poetry was difficult, but not in the same way. Alexandrian poetry was difficult because it presupposed a learned reader; as you became learned you found the answers to the puzzles. Skaldic poetry was unintelligible if you did not know the *kenningar,* but intelligible if you did. And—this is the real point—all Alexandrian men of letters and all skalds would have agreed about the answers. I believe the same to be true of the dark conceits in Donne; there was one correct interpretation of each and Donne could have told it to you. Of course you might misunderstand what Wordsworth was "up to" in *Lyrical Ballads;* but everyone understood what he said. I do not see in any of these the slightest parallel to the state of affairs disclosed by a recent symposium on Mr. Eliot's *Cooking Egg.* [9]

[9]*Essays in Criticism,* III, 3 (July 1953).

Here we find seven adults (two of them Cambridge men) whose lives have been specially devoted to the study of poetry discussing a very short poem which has been before the world for thirty-odd years; and there is not the slightest agreement among them as to what, in any sense of the word, it means. I am not in the least concerned to decide whether this state of affairs is a good thing, or a bad thing.[10] I merely assert that it is a new thing. In the whole history of the West, from Homer—I might almost say from the *Epic of Gilgamesh*—there has been no bend or break in the development of poetry comparable to this. On this score my proposed division has no rival to fear.

3. Thirdly, there is the great religious change which I have had to mention before: the un-christening. Of course there were lots of sceptics in Jane Austen's time and long before, as there are lots of Christians now. But the presumption has changed. In her days some kind and degree of religious belief and practice were the norm: now, though I would gladly believe that both kind and degree have improved, they are the exception. I have already argued that this change surpasses that which Europe underwent at its conversion. It is hard to have patience with those Jeremiahs, in Press or pulpit, who warn us that we are "relapsing into Paganism". It might be rather fun if we were. It would be pleasant to see some future Prime Minister trying to kill a large and lively milk-white bull in Westminster Hall. But we shan't. What lurks behind such idle prophecies, if they are anything but careless language, is the false idea that the historical process allows mere reversal; that Europe can come out of Christianity "by the same door as in she went" and find herself back where she was. It is not what happens. A post-Christian man is not a Pagan; you might as well think that a married woman recovers her virginity by divorce. The post-Christian is cut off from the Christian past and therefore doubly from the Pagan past.

4. Lastly, I play my trump card. Between Jane Austen and us, but not between her and Shakespeare, Chaucer, Alfred, Virgil, Homer, or the Pharaohs, comes the birth of the machines. This lifts us at once into a region of change far above all that we have hitherto considered. For this is parallel to the great changes by which we divide epochs of pre-history. This is on a level with the change from stone to bronze, or from a pastoral to an agricultural economy. It alters Man's place in nature. The theme has been celebrated till we are all sick of it, so I will here say nothing about its economic and social consequences, immeasurable though they are. What concerns us more is its psychological effect. How has it come about that we use the highly emotive word "stagnation", with all its malodorous and malarial overtones, for what other ages would have called "permanence"? Why does the word "primitive" at once suggest to us clumsiness, inefficiency, barbarity? When our ancestors talked of the primitive church or the primitive purity of our constitution they meant nothing of that sort. (The only

---

[10]In music we have pieces which demand more talent in the performer than in the composer. Why should there not come a period when the art of writing poetry stands lower than the art of reading it? Of course rival readings would then cease to be "right" or "wrong" and become more and less brilliant "performances".

pejorative sense which Johnson gives to *Primitive* in his Dictionary is, significantly, "Formal; affectedly solemn; imitating the supposed gravity of old times".) Why does "latest" in advertisements mean "best"? Well, let us admit that these semantic developments owe something to the nineteenth-century belief in spontaneous progress which itself owes something either to Darwin's theorem of biological evolution or to that myth of universal evolutionism which is really so different from it, and earlier. For the two great imaginative expressions of the myth, as distinct from the theorem—Keats's *Hyperion* and Wagner's *Ring*—are pre-Darwinian. Let us give these their due. But I submit that what has imposed this climate of opinion so firmly on the human mind is a new archetypal image. It is the image of old machines being superseded by new and better ones. For in the world of machines the new most often really is better and the primitive really is the clumsy. And this image, potent in all our minds, reigns almost without rival in the minds of the uneducated. For to them, after their marriage and the births of their children, the very milestones of life are technical advances. From the old push-bike to the motor-bike and thence to the little car; from gramophone to radio and from radio to television; from the range to the stove; these are the very stages of their pilgrimage. But whether from this cause or from some other, assuredly that approach to life which has left these footprints on our language is the thing that separates us most sharply from our ancestors and whose absence would strike us as most alien if we could return to their world. Conversely, our assumption that everything is provisional and soon to be superseded, that the attainment of goods we have never yet had, rather than the defence and conservation of those we have already, is the cardinal business of life, would most shock and bewilder them if they could visit ours.

I thus claim for my chosen division of periods that on the first count it comes well up to scratch; on the second and third it arguably surpasses all; and on the fourth it quite clearly surpasses them without any dispute. I conclude that it really is the greatest change in the history of Western Man.

At any rate, this conviction determines my whole approach to my work from this Chair. I am not preparing an excuse in advance lest I should hereafter catch myself lecturing either on the *Epic of Gilgamesh* or on the *Waverley Novels*. The field "Medieval and Renaissance" is already far too wide for my powers. But you see how to me the appointed area must primarily appear as a specimen of something far larger, something which had already begun when the *Iliad* was composed and was still almost unimpaired when Waterloo was fought. Of course within that immense period there are all sorts of differences. There are lots of convenient differences between the area I am to deal with and other areas; there are important differences within the chosen area. And yet—despite all this—that whole thing, from its Greek or pre-Greek beginnings down to the day before yesterday, seen from the vast distance at which we stand today, reveals a homogeneity that is certainly important and perhaps more important than its interior diversities. That is why I shall be unable to talk to you about my particular region without constantly treating things which neither began with the Middle Ages nor ended with the end of the Renaissance. In that way I shall be forced to present to you a great deal of what can only be described as Old European, or Old Western, Culture. If one were giving a lecture on Warwickshire to an audience of Martians (no offence: Martians may be delightful creatures) one might loyally choose all one's *data* from that county: but much of what you told them would not really be Warwickshire lore but "common tellurian".

The prospect of my becoming, in such halting fashion as I can, the spokesman of Old Western Culture, alarms me. It may alarm you. I will close with one reassurance and one claim.

First, for the reassurance. I do not think you need fear that the study of a dead period, however prolonged and however sympathetic, need prove an indulgence in nostalgia or an enslavement to the past. In the individual life, as the psychologists have taught us, it is not the remembered but the forgotten past that enslaves us. I think the same is true of society. To study the past does indeed liberate us from the present, from the idols of our own market-place. But I think it liberates us from the past too. I think no class of men are less enslaved to the past than historians. The unhistorical are usually, without knowing it, enslaved to a fairly recent past. Dante read Virgil. Certain other medieval authors[11] evolved the legend of Virgil as a great magician. It was the more recent past, the whole quality of mind evolved during a few preceding centuries, which impelled them to do so. Dante was freer; he also knew more of the past. And you will be no freer by coming to misinterpret Old Western Culture as quickly and deeply as those medievals misinterpreted Classical Antiquity; or even as the Romantics misinterpreted the Middle Ages.[12] Such misinterpretation has already begun. To arrest its growth while arrest is still possible, is surely a proper task for a university.

And now for the claim: which sounds arrogant but, I hope, is not really so. I have said that the vast change which separates you from Old Western has been gradual and is not even now complete. Wide as the chasm is, those who are native to different sides of it can still meet; are meeting in this room. This is quite normal at times of great change. The correspondence of Henry More[13] and Descartes is an amusing example; one would think the two men were writing in different centuries. And here comes the rub. I myself belong far more to that Old Western order than to yours. I am going to claim that this, which in one way is a disqualification for my task, is yet in another a qualification. The disqualification is obvious. You don't want to be lectured on Neanderthal Man by a Neanderthaler, still less on dinosaurs by a dinosaur. And yet, is that the whole story? If

---

[11]On their identity see Comparetti, *Virgilio nel Medio Evo*, ed. G. Pasquali (Firenze, 1943), p. xxii. I owe this reference to Mr. G. C. Hardie.

[12]As my examples show, such misinterpretations may themselves produce results which have imaginative value. If there had been no Romantic distortion of the Middle Ages, we should have no *Eve of St. Agnes*. There is room both for an appreciation of the imagined past and an awareness of its difference from the real past; but if we want only the former, why come to a university? (The subject deserves much fuller treatment than I can give it here.)

[13]*A Collection of several Philosophical Writings* (Cambridge, 1662).

a live dinosaur dragged its slow length into the laboratory, would we not all look back as we fled? What a chance to know at last how it really moved and looked and smelled and what noises it made! And if the Neanderthaler could talk, then, though his lecturing technique might leave much to be desired, should we not almost certainly learn from him some things about him which the best modern anthropologist could never have told us? He would tell us without knowing he was telling. One thing I know: I would give a great deal to hear any ancient Athenian, even a stupid one, talking about Greek tragedy. He would know in his bones so much that we seek in vain. At any moment some chance phrase might, unknown to him, show us where modern scholarship had been on the wrong track for years. Ladies and gentlemen, I stand before you somewhat as that Athenian might stand. I read as a native texts that you must read as foreigners. You see why I said that the claim was not really arrogant; who can be proud of speaking fluently his mother tongue or knowing his way about his father's house? It is my settled conviction that in order to read Old Western literature aright you must suspend most of the responses and unlearn most of the habits you have acquired in reading modern literature. And because this is the judgement of a native, I claim that, even if the defence of my conviction is weak, the fact of my conviction is a historical *datum* to which you should give full weight. That way, where I fail as a critic, I may yet be useful as a specimen. I would even dare to go further. Speaking not only for myself but for all other Old Western men whom you may meet, I would say, use your specimens while you can. There are not going to be many more dinosaurs.

Inaugural Lecture at Cambridge, 1954

FROM

The Allegory of Love

A Study in
Medieval Tradition

Courtly Love

'When in the world I lived I was the world's
commander.'

SHAKESPEARE

THE ALLEGORICAL LOVE POETRY of the Middle Ages is apt to repel the
modern reader both by its form and by its matter. The form, which is that of
a struggle between personified abstractions, can hardly be expected to appeal to
an age which holds that 'art means what it says' or even that art is meaningless—
for it is essential to this form that the literal narrative and the *significacio* should
be separable. As for the matter, what have we to do with these medieval lovers—
'servants' or 'prisoners' they called themselves—who seem to be always weeping
and always on their knees before ladies of inflexible cruelty? The popular erotic
literature of our own day tends rather to sheikhs and 'Salvage Men' and marriage
by capture, while that which is in favour with our intellectuals recommends either
frank animalism or the free companionship of the sexes. In every way, if we have
not outgrown, we have at least grown away from, the *Romance of the Rose*. The
study of this whole tradition may seem, at first sight, to be but one more example
of that itch for 'revival', that refusal to leave any corpse ungalvanized, which is
among the more distressing accidents of scholarship. But such a view would be
superficial. Humanity does not pass through phases as a train passes through
stations: being alive, it has the privilege of always moving yet never leaving

anything behind. Whatever we have been, in some sort we are still. Neither the form nor the sentiment of this old poetry has passed away without leaving indelible traces on our minds. We shall understand our present, and perhaps even our future, the better if we can succeed, by an effort of the historical imagination, in reconstructing that long-lost state of mind for which the allegorical love poem was a natural mode of expression. But we shall not be able to do so unless we begin by carrying our attention back to a period long before that poetry was born. In this and the following chapter, I shall trace in turn the rise both of the sentiment called 'Courtly Love' and of the allegorical method. The discussion will seem, no doubt, to carry us far from our main subject: but it cannot be avoided.

English Literature
in the Sixteenth Century
Excluding Drama

New Learning and New Ignorance

T HE ROUGH OUTLINE of our literary history in the sixteenth century is not very difficult to grasp. At the beginning we find a literature still medieval in form and spirit. In Scotland it shows the highest level of technical brilliance: in England it has for many years been dull, feeble, and incompetent. As the century proceeds, new influences arise: changes in our knowledge of antiquity, new poetry from Italy and France, new theology, new movements in philosophy or science. As these increase, though not necessarily because of them, the Scotch literature is almost completely destroyed. In England the characteristic disease of late medieval poetry, its metrical disorder, is healed: but replaced, for the most part, by a lifeless and laboured regularity to which some ears might prefer the vagaries of Lydgate. There is hardly any sign of a new inspiration. Except for the songs of Wyatt, whose deepest roots are medieval, and the prose of the Prayer Book, which is mostly translation, authors seem to have forgotten the lessons which had been mastered in the Middle Ages and learned little in their stead. Their prose is clumsy, monotonous, garrulous; their verse either astonishingly tame and cold or, if it attempts to rise, the coarsest fustian. In both mediums we come to dread a certain ruthless emphasis; bludgeon-work. Nothing is light, or tender, or fresh. All the authors write like elderly men. The mid-century is an earnest, heavy-handed, commonplace age: a drab age. Then, in the last quarter of the century, the unpredictable happens. With startling suddenness we ascend. Fantasy, conceit, paradox, colour, incantation return. Youth returns. The fine frenzies of ideal love and ideal war are readmitted. Sidney, Spenser, Shakespeare, Hooker—even, in a way, Lyly—display what is almost a new culture: that culture which was to last through most of the seventeenth century and to enrich the very meanings of the words *England* and *Aristocracy*. Nothing in the earlier history of our period would have enabled the sharpest observer to foresee this transformation.

Some have believed, or assumed, that it resulted from what seemed at the time to be a resurrection, rejuvenescence, or *renascentia* [1]—the recovery of Greek and the substitution of Augustan for medieval Latin. It is, of course, true that the rich vernacular literature of the eighties used the fruits of that event, as it used the Middle Ages and everything else it could lay its hands on. It is also true that many movements of thought which affected our literature would have been impossible without the recovery of Greek. But if there is any closer connexion than that between the *renascentia* and the late sixteenth-century efflorescence of English literature, I must confess that it has escaped me. The more we look into the question, the harder we shall find it to believe that humanism had any power of encouraging, or any wish to encourage, the literature that actually arose. And it may be as well to confess immediately that I have no alternative 'explanation' to offer. I do not claim to know why there were many men of genius at that time. The Elizabethans themselves would have attributed it to Constellation. I must be content with trying to sketch some of the intellectual and imaginative conditions under which they wrote. . . .

Thomas Cranmer's [2] great achievements as a translator are sunk in the corporate anonymity of the *Book of Common Prayer*. As an original writer he is a much more shadowy figure than Latimer. That he had thought about the art we know from the very interesting annotations which he made on Henry VIII's corrections of the *Institution of a Christian Man* in 1538. The frankness of these comments does credit to both parties. Most are naturally doctrinal, but some are stylistic; 'These sentences, methinks, come not in aptly in some places as they be brought in but rather interrupt and let the course and phrase of the paraphrasis', or 'the

---

[1]'Revertuntur . . . graeca et latina lingua seu renascuntur verius' (Vives, *De Causis Corruptarum Artium*, I). '(Poesis) tametsi rediviva novam sub Petrarcha pueritiam inchoasse' (Scaliger, *Poet.*, vi. i). 'In veterum lucubrationibus restituendis laborant et ceu a mortuis revocant' (Huldrichus Coccius, *Ep. Ded.* to *Opera Vivis*. Basel, 1555).

[2]b. 1489. Taught by 'a marvelous severe and cruel schoolmaster'. Fellow of Jesus, Cambridge, 1511. Marries, forfeits fellowship, loses his wife and recovers fellowship. Ordained, 1523. His views on the divorce, expressed to Gardiner at a chance meeting, recommend him to the king. Ordered to write on this question. Archdeacon of Taunton, 1529. Sent to Rome on the same matter, 1530. Ambassador to the emperor, 1531. Re-marries, 1532. Archbishop of Canterbury, 1533. Member of the Council of Regency, 1547. Signs Edward VI's act devising the crown to Lady Jane Grey, 1553. On accession of Mary sent to the Tower. Removed to Oxford, 1554. Degraded and handed over to the civil power as a heretic; recants, recants his recantation, and is burnt, 1556.

sentence as it is printed runneth more euenly'. This is our only glimpse into Cranmer's workshop: the finished product, except in the Prayer Book, is so severely utilitarian that we might not have suspected any conscious concern for style in the author. His preface to the Great Bible of 1539, after some preliminary flourishes which are a very faint anticipation of euphuism, consists mainly of translation, and very good translation too, from Chrysostom and Gregory Nazianzene. The three pieces certainly known to be his in *Certain Sermons or Homilies* [3] (1547) are those on salvation, on faith, and on good works. They aim neither at subtlety nor eloquence. Cranmer's only concern is to state an agreed doctrine with the least possibility of misunderstanding: the thing could hardly be done delightfully but it is done well. His *Defence of the True and Catholic Doctrine of the Sacrament* (1550), revised in 1551 as *An Answer to* Stephen Gardiner, nowhere rises above the usual level of controversy in that age. In all these works Cranmer writes a prose with which it is difficult to find any fault, but it gives curiously little pleasure. It never drags and never hurries; it never disappoints the ear; and (*pace* John Foxe) there is hardly a single sentence that leaves us in doubt of its meaning. He could have taught More and even Tyndale some things about the art of English composition: but they can be loved and he cannot. This is partly because while avoiding their vices he lacks their virtues. He is not stodgy and verbose like More: but then he has neither humour nor pathos. He is not digressive like Tyndale, but then he lacks Tyndale's fire. The explanation is that Cranmer always writes in an official capacity. Everything he says has been threshed out in committee. We never see a thought growing: his business is to express the agreed point of view. Everyone who has tried to draw up a report knows how fatal such conditions are to good writing. Every phrase that really bites or flashes has to be crossed out in the end: it would offend one party, or be misunderstood by another, or unduly encourage a third. What remains when all the necessary erasures have been made is inevitably flat and grey. In Cranmer the wonder is that what remains is even so lively as it is. Compared with official publications either by Church or Civil Service in our own day, it is almost magnificent: but in such a book as this we are comparing it with real literature. By that standard it cannot rank high. It is praiseworthy: it is (if I may put it that way) devastatingly praiseworthy. What Cranmer might have written if the burden of responsibility had ever been lifted from his shoulders and he had made a book to please himself, we can only guess. He did his proper work and he did it very well, but I do not think I shall often re-read him. I had much rather hear Latimer thump his tub.

Four other controversialists may be briefly mentioned. Simon Fish's *Supplication for the Beggars* (1529) provoked More's *Supplication*. Fish writes more as a politician and economist than as a theologian: his rhetoric is monotonous and commonplace but not quite ineffective. John Rastell's *Book of Purgatory* (1530) on the opposite side is more happily conceived, under the influence of More. It

[3]i.e. the 'first Book of Homilies'.

is an imaginary dialogue between a Turk and a German which attempts to defend the doctrine of purgatory on philosophical grounds. It lacks More's humour and dramatic invention and Rastell does not understand his opponents well enough to be dangerous. John Frith whom they tied to a post in Newgate so that he could neither stand nor sit and who died at the stake praying for his enemies in 1533, looms larger as a man than as an author, though he is not contemptible even in the second capacity. His works include a *Disputation of Purgatory* (against Rastell, More, and Fisher), an *Antithesis* (of Christ and the Pope), a second book *Against Rastell*, a *Mirror to know thyself*, and treatises on Baptism and the Sacrament. Most of these were written in the Tower where he was forbidden books and writing materials and therefore 'when I heare the keyes ryng at the dore, strayte all must be conuayed out of the way; and then if any notable thing had been in my minde it was cleane lost'. His style, if a little wordy, is alive and he is fond of such rhetorical questions as are learned in conversation rather than in the schoolroom. He is not without humour. Robert Barnes (1495–1540) is in every way a lesser man. His tracts, which cover the usual topics, are all combined in John Day's folio with his *Supplication* to Henry VIII. His style is not good enough to enliven dull matter nor bad enough to spoil a plain tale; hence the account of his trial before the chapter of Westminster is still readable. Barnes, Frith, and Fish all share More's faults without his virtues, and all bring into the field the same undisciplined armies of adjectives. Rastell is more concise, but he is dry and jejune.

Free

THE MATERIALS of this chapter will illustrate two principles mentioned in the Introduction. They are all moralised status-words. And they all show parallelism of semantic movement in different languages.

I. 'ELEUTHEROS'

Eleutheros means 'free', not a slave. One can also be *eleutheros apo*, free from, pain, fear or the like. A community is *eleutheros* when it is autonomous; Xenophon can speak of two communities being *eleutherous apo*, free from, one another; mutually independent.[1] All this would be unimportant if the word had not taken on a secondary, a social-ethical, sense. To call a man *eleutheros* in the first sense merely identified his legal status; to call his behaviour *eleutheros* in the second was to say that it displayed the qualities which, on the Greek view, a freeman ought to have. There is also another adjective, *eleutherios*, which is used with this second meaning only. *Eleutheros* is used with both.

---

[1] *Cyropaedia* III, ii, 23.

488

The character of the *eleutheros* (or *eleutherios*) is, of course, contrasted with that of the slave. It would be dangerous in modern English to say 'with the servile character', for that would probably conjure up a false image. By a 'servile' man we mean, I take it, an abject, submissive man who cringes and flatters. That this was not the ancient idea of the typical slave is plain from the slaves in Greek and Roman comedy and also from the contrasts implied in the words we are now studying. It was a slave-girl who taunted Monica with her tippling, while quarrelling with her young mistress *ut fit*, 'the way they do'.[2] The true servile character is cheeky, shrewd, cunning, up to every trick, always with an eye to the main chance, determined 'to look after number one'. Figaro or Mrs Slipslop fill the requirements pretty well. Sam Weller has the right knowingness, the diamond-cut-diamond realism, but he is disinterested. Absence of disinterestedness, lack of generosity, is the hall-mark of the servile. The typical slave always has an axe to grind. Hence the miserably betrayed Philoctetes in Sophocles' play (l. 1006) says to the cunning Odysseus 'Oh you—you who never had a sound or *eleutheron* thought in your mind!' Odysseus has done nothing without 'an ulterior motive'.

It was of course recognised, as by Aristotle so by others, that servile status and servile character did not always coincide. Hence a fragment of Menander runs 'Live in slavery with the spirit of a freeman *(eleutherôs)* and you will be no slave'.

Generosity being part of the freeman's character, the abstract noun *eleutheriotes* can mean generosity about money, bountifulness, readiness to give; the word *generosity* itself, as we noticed before, shows a very similar development. *Aneleutheria*, the opposite of *eleutheriotes*, of course means stinginess.[3]

II. 'LIBER'

Latin *liber* and *liberalis* are related almost exactly as *eleutheros* and *eleutherios*. *Liber* is 'free', not a slave; or free, used of an inanimate object, in the sense of unconfined, unopposed. The sea, in Ovid, as opposed to the rivers, is the plain of freer *(liberioris)* water.[4] One's mind or judgement can be *liber* when one is not 'committed' or bound by previous engagement or prejudice. Honest jurymen who come to the case with an 'open' mind are *liberi solutique* in Cicero's *Verrines*, 'free and without ties'. Conduct is *liberalis* when it is such as becomes a freeman. Justice, according to Cicero,[5] is the most magnificent virtue and most suitable-to-a-freeman *(liberalis)*. This ethical sense is often specialised and narrowed to denote the quality which we still call *liberality*. 'Liberales are the sort of people who ransom prisoners of war'.[6]

Since the word *liberalis* is metrically two trochees it can never occur in dactylic verse. In poetry, therefore, *ingenuus* (free-born) is used instead, with, I think, precisely the same range of meaning. That is, it may refer merely to status,

---

[2]St Augustine, *Confessions* IX, 8.   [3]Aristotle, *Ethics*, 1119 b.   [4]*Metamorphoses* I, 41.
[5]*Republic* III, viii.   [6]Cicero, *Offices* II, xvi.

but much more often has the ethical-social meaning; as when Juvenal says 'a boy of *ingenuus* countenance, with an *ingenuus* modesty *(pudor)'*, in XI, 154. The passage is interesting in two ways: first, because this boy was in fact a slave, and secondly because the *pudor* brings out by contrast the ancient idea of the typical slave. The slick waiters, alternately fawning and insolent, in the worst type of 'posh' hotel would have seemed to the ancients typically 'servile'; the kind, unpretentious old servants whom men of my age can still remember (especially in the country) would not. The later history of the derivative *ingenuous* is also instructive; like a freeman, thence open, unsuspicious, ready to trust because trustworthy, thence (in the good sense) *simple,* thence too simple, credulous, finally fatuous, a dupe, a gull. Greek *euethes*, originally 'good-natured' but finally 'silly', shows the same development. So does *silly* itself, and *innocent.* These developments in fact embody the comment of the typical slave on the *ingenuus,* whose lack of suspicion he regards as folly. If Sam Weller had been a typical *servus* he would merely have despised (instead of both honouring and smiling at) the innocence of Mr Pickwick.

III. 'FREE'

Like the Greek and Latin words this originally refers to legal status. The opposite is slave—*theow* in classical Anglo-Saxon, or, later, Old Norse *thrael.* All sons of free men, *freora manna*, are to be taught to read, says King Alfred in the preface to his version of the *Cura Pastoralis.* It also means 'free' in the physical sense, free to move. After her miraculous healing the blind woman in the old version of Bede, who had been led to the shrine by her maids, went home '*freo* on her own feet' (IV, 10). These, the oldest senses of the word, are now, oddly enough, its *dangerous senses;* for the others, those that correspond roughly to *eleutherios* and *liberalis,* are mainly obsolete.

I say 'correspond roughly' because there is a perceptible difference between the ancient and the English developments. Both may be described as 'social-ethical', but in the Greek and Roman words the ethical predominates and the social almost vanishes in the end. This is not so of English *free.* Its background is feudal, not republican; it belongs to a world in which manners were more elaborate than in antiquity and far more valued.

In *Piers Plowman* we read that Mede is married more for her money than for any virtue or beauty or any *high kinde*—any noble blood.[7] The B text at the corresponding point reads *free kinde.* [8] The adjectives are probably almost synonymous in this context. There need be no ethical implication in either; and the social pretension is higher than that of *eleutheros* or *liberalis.* Often the word refers neither to blood nor to morality but to manners, as when the thirteenth-century *Floris and Blancheflor* (l. 498) describes a burgher as 'fre and curteys', polite and courteous. Like the adjective *kinde* it tails off into the vaguest, most unspecified, laudation, so that Christ in the York *Harrowing of Hell* (l. 5) can

[7]C. III, 82.   [8]B. II, 75.

say 'mi Fader *free*'. It shows its fullest charge of meaning in Chaucer's line 'Trouthe and honour, fredom and courtesye';[9] knightly behaviour, in which morality up to the highest self-sacrifice and manners down to the smallest gracefulness in etiquette were inextricably blended by the medieval ideal.

Inevitably, since 'largesse' is a most important aspect of *fredom*, this sense throws out the branch 'munificent, open-handed'; 'fre of hir goodes', generous with their property,[10] or 'to fre of dede', over-liberal in its action.[11] This could also, however, be reached without going through the sense 'noble, courteous', simply from the sense 'unrestrained' (as in the translation of Bede); uninhibited, unchecked, in one's dealings with one's own property.

The larger sense is perhaps well brought out in Chaucer's line 'Free was daun John and namely of dispence':[12] he had in general the manners of a gentleman, and especially in the way he spent his money. The *Franklin's Tale* gives us a sort of competition in *fredom* (magnanimity, generosity) and hands over to the reader the problem 'which was the moste free'.[13] Boccaccio in the corresponding passage asks who had shown the greatest *liberalità*.

From the sense 'unrestrained' another branch goes off. Behaviour which is informal, familiar, facile, the reverse of 'stand-offish', can be *free*. Thus Quarles says 'The world's a crafty strumpet . . . if thou be free she's strange; if strange, she's free'.[14] Hence a pejorative usage. One may be more familiar, less formal, than the social situation justifies, and may receive, as in Sheridan, the rebuff 'Not so free, fellow'.[15] Finally *free* can almost mean 'abusive'. 'The mistress and the maid shall quarrel and give each other very free language.'[16] 'A *freedom*' can likewise be an unwarranted breach of social restraint, a 'liberty' unduly 'taken', and even an indecency: 'I do not know a more disagreeable character than a valetudinarian, who thinks he may do anything that is for his ease and indulges himself in the grossest freedoms'.[17]

It is probably by an influence from this sense that we should explain Shakespeare's use of *liberal* to mean, in various senses, (too) 'free spoken'; as where the young wag in *The Merchant* is warned that his chatter among strangers may 'show something too liberal' (II, ii, 187).

Very distinct from all these, though doubtless springing from the idea of 'unrestrained, not tied, not confined', is free in the sense 'costing nothing' (Latin *gratis* and Greek *dorean*). Thus *dorean* is rendered as *freely* in the Authorised Version; 'freely ye have received', and, earlier, in the Wycliffite translation, *freli*.

IV. 'FRANK' AND 'VILLAIN'

There is a sharp contrast between the histories of *frank* and *free*. The social-ethical meanings of *free* have vanished; but, for *frank*, only the ethical meaning, and that in a very narrowed sense, survives.

---

[9]*C.T.*A. 46   [10]*Piers Plowman*, B. x, 74.   [11]*Pearl*, 481.   [12]*C.T.*B. 1233.
[13]F. 1622.   [14]*Emblems* I, iv.   [15]*St Patrick's Day* II, ii.   [16]Steele, *Spectator*, 493.
[17]Boswell, 16 September 1777.

Originally *frank* is of course a national name—'a Frank'. Its legal, social, and ethical meanings are ultimately derived from the state of affairs in Gaul after the Frankish conquest. Any man you met would probably be either a Frank, hence a conqueror, a warrior, and a landowner, or else a mere 'native', one of a subject race. If the latter, he was (typically) a serf, an un-free peasant attached to an estate which had once been a Roman *villa;* he was in fact a *villanus* or *vilains. Frank* and *villain* (or *frans* and *vilains*) is the essential contrast.

English *villain* could still be used in its literal sense by Lancelot Andrewes: 'they be men, and not beasts; freemen, and not villains'.[18] But long before his time it had dwindled into a term of abuse, and finally into a term of mere (i.e. unspecified) abuse: *villain (d.s.),* a synonym for 'bad man', useless except as a technical term in dramatic criticism (for 'Shakespeare's villains' is a convenient enough expression). The process was of course gradual, and it is not easy to be sure what stage of it is represented by each occurrence of the word in the old texts.

At first its pejorative meaning was closely connected with its literal; the image of the actual *vilains* or peasant was still operative. Peasants, since we abolished them, have in this country been so idealised that we may go as far astray about the old overtones of 'peasant' as about the ancient idea of the servile character. We get an inkling of them when Love, in the *Romance of the Rose,* says 'no villain or butcher' has ever been allowed to kiss his lips (l. 1938). He goes on to say that the *villain* is brutal *(fel),* pitiless, disobliging, and unfriendly (ll. 2086–7.) If you would avoid *vilanie,* the peasant character, you must imitate courteous Gawain, not surly Kay (ll. 2093f.). Danger is later described as a *vilains;* he leaps suddenly from his hiding place, huge, dark, bristly, with blazing eyes, loud and violent (ll. 2920f.). But notice that while *vilains* is still thus closely connected with the image of the actual peasant, it quite clearly refers to a psychological type, not to an actual rank. Love takes care to tell us that *'vilanie* makes the *vilains'* (l. 2083). Theoretically, one who was a *vilains* by status might not have the vice of *vilanie;* certainly many a man who is not a *vilains* by status will be guilty of it. *Churl,* itself originally a status word, would be the nearest English equivalent to Old French *vilains* in this sense, if it had not come to lay more emphasis on niggardliness in particular than on the generally sullen and uncooperative character of the peasant.[19] *Boor* is perhaps now our best translation.

The noun *vilein* is of doubtful occurrence in Chaucer, but *vileinye* is common. The central area of its meaning is rudeness, bad manners. The Knight never 'said *vileinye',* spoke rudely, to anyone (A. 70). Chaucer hopes that his setting down the bawdy tales will not be counted against him as *vileinye* (l. 726). The young roisterers in the *Pardoner's Tale* are reproved for speaking *vileinye* to an old man (C. 740). By an easy transition, to dispraise or vilify anything is to speak *vileinye* of it; the Wife of Bath asks why one should speak *vileinye* 'of bigamye

---

[18]Sermon before the Queen, 24 February 1590.
[19]Probably under the influence of A.V.I Samuel xxv. 3–11.

or of octogamye' (D. 34) or of Lameth (D. 53). Hence a shame or indignity done to anything, like Creon's refusal to permit the burial of the enemy dead (A. 941), can be a *vileinye*.

We get nearer to a purely ethical sense when the Wife of Bath argues that if nobility were really transmissible by heredity, then those of a good stock would never cease to practise *gentillesse* nor begin practising 'villeinye or vyce' (D. 1133–8). But the context still attaches the word very closely not to moral defects in general but to those moral defects which were felt to be especially inappropriate in the highest ranks—the opposites of *gentillesse*. Twice we find rape described as *villeinye*. The wife of Hasdrubal committed suicide to make sure that no Roman 'dide hir vileinye' (F. 1404), and Tarquin is asked in an apostrophe how he could have done Lucretia 'this vilanye'.[20] But note the preceding lines. He ought to have acted as a lord and a 'verray knight', instead of which he has 'doon dispyt to chivalrye'. Rape will naturally be the first of all moral offences to be called *vileinye* because, besides being a sin against the Christian law, it is the direct antithesis of *gentillesse*, of courtesy and of deference to ladiés. Tarquin's sin is a *vilein's* act because it is, as our fathers, if not we, would say, 'the act of a cad'. Indeed the word *cad*, with its contemporary semantic wobble between social and moral condemnation, is a good enough parallel to *vileinye* in this sense. And once *vileinye* means something like 'caddishness' it is already on the downward path which will finally lead it to become a word of mere, unspecified opprobrium. Once or twice in Chaucer it has almost reached this stage. When the act of those enemies who had beaten the wife of Melibeus and mortally wounded his daughter is described as a *vileinye* (B. 2547), or John warns Aleyn that the miller is a dangerous man who might do them a *vileinye* (A. 4191), the content of the word is perhaps hardly more precise than 'a rotten trick' or 'a bad turn'. In the *Second Nun's Tale*, when we hear that no one can see the rose and lily garlands brought by the angel unless he 'be chaast and hate vileinye' (C. 231), perhaps we have reached a purely ethical meaning.

In the Elizabethan drama *villain*, and the associated words, are, so to speak, treacherous. At first the modern reader in most contexts will give them the *dangerous sense* without hesitation. Because they are opprobrious, that sense will always seem to fit the context; that is why it is so dangerous. 'Remorseless, treacherous, lecherous, kindless villain!';[21] 'I never loved my brother in my life'—'More villain thou';[22] 'Some villain hath done me wrong'[23]—what should all these be but *villain (d.s.)*? Perhaps they all are. But it is not absolutely certain.

Antipholus of Syracuse describes his man Dromio as 'a trusty villain' whose 'merry jests' often cheer him up.[24] We have here of course the affectionate use of an opprobrious term in reverse—like 'a trusty rogue'. But it is hard to believe that the opprobrium stored in the term before it is reversed can be as strong as that of *villain (d.s.)*. Something more like 'rogue' or (in older usage) 'wretch', or

[20]*Leg.* 1823.   [21]*Hamlet* II, ii, 619.   [22]*As You Like It* III, i, 14.   [23]*Lear* I, ii, 183.   [24]*Errors* I, ii, 19.

'rascal'. And 'rascal'—certainly not *villain (d.s.)*—is surely the sense required when Petruchio repeatedly calls his man Grunio a *villain,* and once a *knave.* [25] Again, in *Measure for Measure* (V, i, 264) the luckless Lucio says that Friar Lodowick 'spoke most villanous speeches of the Duke'. The point of the joke is that it was Lucio himself who had spoken those speeches, as no one knows better than the Duke. And they were not those of a *villain (d.s.)*. He was not plotting the Duke's murder or deposition, only telling 'pretty tales', talking bawdy about his betters. His speeches were, in fact, *vileinye* in Chaucer's rather than in the modern sense; rude, scandalous.

Since words mean many things in the same period, these usages do not of course disprove the interpretation *villain (d.s.)* in the previous passages from *Hamlet, As You Like It* and *Lear.* But they provide the background against which its probability can be judged. I am inclined, myself, to think that *villain (d.s.)* need not be fully present in any of them. It may be present in all as the speaker's meaning. The speaker certainly regards the other party as what *we* would call a *villain,* but I am not certain that he selects this particular term of abuse because it already (lexically) has the meaning 'very wicked man'. The purpose of all opprobrious language is, not to describe, but to hurt—even when, like Hamlet, we make only the shadow-passes of a soliloquised combat. We call the enemy not what we think he is but what we think he would least like to be called. Hence extreme hatred may select the word *villain* precisely because it is not yet merely moral but still carries some implication of ignoble birth, coarse manners, and ignorance. For all except the best men would rather be called wicked than vulgar. Compare the scene where Somerset calls Suffolk away from the *de jure* Duke of York with the words 'Away! . . . We grace the *yeoman* by conversing with him'. [26]

All this I admit to be uncertain. But there is one place where I very greatly hope that *villain* has hardly any of the *dangerous sense* in it. The opening soliloquy of *Richard III* does not, on any view, show Shakespeare at his subtlest. But the crudity of 'I am determined to prove a villain' (I, i, 30) is, even on that level, almost comic if Richard means *villain (d.s.)*. But if we dare suppose that the word has predominantly—or, better still, exclusively—its older sense, the line is immeasurably improved. For then, Richard, having produced as good, and contemptuous, a parody as his distorted body can of those who 'court an amorous looking glass', suddenly relapses into himself, looks as clumsy, as coarse, as uncouth as he knows how—becomes the very image of the *vilains,* fixes the audience with a glance of ogre-ish glee, and says in effect 'Well; since I can't be a lounge-lizard, I'll be—gad, I'll be—a Tough'.

Some other usages, which obviously come by hyperbole, are consistent with almost any meaning of the word. Such are 'a villainous house for fleas', 'villainous smell', 'villainous melancholy', or 'villainously cross-gartered'. These will surprise no one who remembers how, at various periods, every inconvenience or discomfort, has been called *scurvy, abominable, shocking, incredible* or *shattering.*

---

[25] *Taming* I, ii, 8–19.   [26] *Hen. VI,* Pt I, II, iv, 81.

In Old French, *frans,* the form which *frank* assumed, can mean *free,* unencumbered. There is a line quoted by Chalcidius 'When you have laid aside your body and soar *free (liber)* to the sky';[27] the *Romance of the Rose* (l. 5030) translates 'You will go *frans* into the holy air'. This usage is found also in English; Lord Berners in his version of *Huon* writes 'he and all his company shal depart frank and free at their pleasure' (XLIII).

Its social-ethical sense once had pretty much the same range as that of *free.* The god of love, in the *Romance of the Rose,* says that the servant when he accepts must be courteous and *frans* (l. 1939). The quality which the *frans* has is of course *franchise* (courtesy, gentle manners, the gentle heart) both in French and English; among Gawain's virtues are '*franchise* and fellowshipe'.[28] But later usage restricted the word to a sense which may owe something both to the idea of 'unrestrained' and to that of the noble or chivalrous. This double implication, or double semantic root, may have helped the sense in question to triumph. The *frank* person is unencumbered by fears, calculations, and an eye to the main chance; he also shows the straightforwardness and boldness of a noble nature. Hence 'with frank and with uncurbed plainness'[29] or 'bearing with frank appearance their purposes towards Cyprus'.[30]

Like *free,* it too can mean *gratis,* not to be paid for; in *Mother Hubbards Tale,* we find 'Thou hast it wonne for it is of frank gift' (l. 531). This sense long survived in 'the frank' which members of Parliament were once entitled to put on their letters.

V. AN OBSOLETE BRANCH-LINE

Like *eleutheria* and *libertas, freedom* and *franchise* can of course mean the legal freedom of a community. But the ancient words are used chiefly, if not entirely, in reference to the freedom of a state. The contrast implied is sometimes between autonomy and subjection to a foreign power; sometimes between the freedom of a republic and the rule of a despot. The medieval words nearly always refer to something different; to the guaranteed freedoms or immunities (from royal or baronial interference) of a corporate entity which cuts across states, like the Church, or which exists within the state, like a city or guild. Thus Gower says a knight should defend 'The common right and the franchise of Holy Churche';[31] or Shakespeare, 'If you deny it let the danger light upon your city's freedom'.[32]

This led to a development unparalleled, I believe, in the ancient languages. By becoming a member of any corporation which enjoys such *freedom* or *franchise* you of course come to share that *freedom* or *franchise.* You become a *freeman* of, or receive the *freedom* of, that city; or you become 'free of the Grocers'.[33] These are familiar. But a further development along this line is more startling. *Freedom* can mean simply 'citizenship', and when the centurion tells

[27]*In Timaeum* CXXXVI.   [28]*Gawain,* 652.   [29]*Hen. V,* I, ii, 244.   [30]*Othello* I, iii, 37.
[31]*Confessio* VIII, 3023.   [32]*Merchant* IV, i, 39.   [33]Jonson, *Alchemist* I, i.

Saint Paul that he had paid a lot of money to acquire Roman citizenship *(po-liteia)*, the Authorised Version says 'At a great price obtained I this freedom'.[34] Philemon Holland translating Suetonius writes 'Unlesse they might be *donati civitate . . .* enioye the fraunchises and freedom of Rome'. This meaning is fossilised in the surviving English use of *franchise* to mean the power of voting, conceived as the essential mark of full citizenship.

VI. 'LIBERAL' AS A CULTURAL TERM

We had brought the ancient words to a social and ethical sense; it remains to consider the all-important cultured meaning which grew from it.

The freeman, and still more the *eleutherios* or *liberalis* who not only is but ought to be a freeman, has not only his characteristic virtues but his characteristic occupations. Some of these are necessary; statesmanship, says Pseudo-Plato, is the most *liberal (eleutheriotaten)* of studies.[35] But the idea that leisure occupations, things done for their own sake and not for utility, are especially *eleuthera*, soon comes into play. It is perhaps present when Xenophon says 'They have a square *(agora)* called the Free *(eleuthera)* Square from which tradespeople and their noises and vulgarities *(apeirokaliai)* are excluded'.[36] The tradespeople need not be, and probably are not, slaves. But they are engaged in activities which have no value except in so far as they contribute to some end outside themselves. The contrast becomes explicit when Aristotle says in the *Rhetoric* 'of one's possessions those which yield some profit are the most useful, but those which exist only to be enjoyed are *eleutheria*'. This is the first step. Only he who is neither legally enslaved to a master nor economically enslaved by the struggle for subsistence, is likely to have, or to have the leisure for using, a piano or a library. That is how one's piano or library is more *liberal*, more characteristic of one's position as a freeman, than one's coal-shovel or one's tools.

But there is a further development, which we owe (I believe) entirely to Aristotle; a brilliant conceit. (There is no reason why we should not attribute a conceit to him; he was a wit, and a dressy man, as well as a philosopher.) It comes in the *Metaphysics*.[37] 'We call a man free whose life is lived for his own sake not for that of others. In the same way philosophy is of all studies the only free one; for it alone exists for its own sake.'

Here is an astonishing change. Up till now a study could be *free* because it was the characteristic occupation of a freeman. Aristotle now makes it 'free' in a quite new sense; namely, by analogy. It is a free study because it holds among other studies the same privileged position which the freeman holds among other men. The conceit is all the better for taking up into itself the much simpler idea that disinterestedness is an essential part of the 'free' character. The free study seeks nothing beyond itself and desires the activity of knowing for that activity's own sake. That is what the man of radically servile character—give him what

[34]Acts xxii. 29.   [35]*Axiochus*, 369.   [36]*Cyropaedia* I, ii, 3.
[37]1982 b, Everyman ed., p. 55.

leisure and what fortune you please—will never understand. He will ask, 'But what *use* is it?' And finding that it cannot be eaten or drunk, nor used as an aphrodisiac, nor made an instrument for increasing his income or his power, he will pronounce it—he has pronounced it—to be 'bunk'.

How far Aristotle's ideal is from a mere dilettantism can best be seen by giving it the background which two other passages supply. In *Metaphysics* we learn that the organisation of the universe resembles that of a household, in which 'no one has so little chance to act at random as the free members. For them everything or almost everything proceeds according to a fixed plan *(tetaktai)*, whereas the slaves and domestic animals contribute little to the common end and act mostly at random.'[38] The attitude of any slave-owning society is and ought to be repellent to us, but it is worth while suppressing that repulsion in order to get the picture as Aristotle saw it. Looking from his study window he sees the hens scratching in the dust, the pigs asleep, the dogs hunting for fleas; the slaves, any of them who are not at that very moment on some appointed task, flirting, quarrelling, cracking nuts, playing dice, or dozing. He, the master, may use them all for the common end, the well-being of the family. They themselves have no such end, nor any consistent end, in mind. Whatever in their lives is not compelled from above is random—dependent on the mood of the moment. His own life is quite different; a systematised round of religious, political, scientific, literary and social activities; its very hours of recreation (there's an anecdote about them) deliberate, approved and allowed for; consistent with itself. But what is it in the structure of the universe that corresponds to this distinction between Aristotle, self-bound with the discipline of a freeman, and Aristotle's slaves, negatively free with a servile freedom between each job and the next? I think there is no doubt of the answer. It is the things in the higher world of aether which are regular, immutable, consistent; those down here in the air that are subject to change, and chance and contingence.[39] In the world, as in the household, the higher acts to a fixed plan; the lower admits the 'random' element. The free life is to the servile as the life of the gods (the living stars) is to that of terrestrial creatures. This is so not because the truly free man 'does what he likes', but because he imitates, so far as a mortal can, the flawless and patterned regularity of the heavenly beings, like them not doing what he likes but being what he is, being fully human as they are divine, and fully human by his likeness to them. For the crown of life—here we break right out of the cautious modesty of most Greek sentiment—is not 'being mortal, to think mortal thoughts' but rather 'to immortalise as much as possible' and by all means to live according to the highest element in oneself.[40]

Of course humanity is not often on the Aristotelian height. The *eleutheria mathemata* of the Greeks, the *liberalia studia* or *liberales artes* of the Latins are soon taken over by the curricula and every teacher or student knows which they are; one no longer needs to think why they are called *liberal.* You need merely enumerate: 'Arts', says Cicero, 'which include *liberales et ingenuae* knowledges,

[38]1075 b.   [39]*De Mundo*, 392 a.   [40]*Ethics*, 1177 b.

such as Geometry, Music, the knowledge of letters and poets and whatever is said about natural objects, human manners and politics'.[41] One even meets the idea (strange to those who have studied the lives of the Humanists) that the pursuit of such studies tends to improve one's behaviour: 'to have learned well the *liberal* arts' (*ingenuas*, because it comes in a hexameter) 'softens the manners and banishes ferocity'.[42] Finally, in the Middle Ages, the *Liberal Arts* settle down into the well known list of seven—grammar, dialectic, rhetoric, music, arithmetic, geometry, and astronomy. Arithmetic might hardly have won its place if Aristotle's idea of the *liberal* had been kept steadily in view.

That idea is, however, still operative in the eighteenth and nineteenth centuries in the conception of an inquisitiveness which is 'generous' or 'noble' or 'liberal' because it seeks knowledge for its own sake. Johnson speaks of 'such knowledge as may justly be admired in those who have no motive to study but generous curiosity',[43] and praises Boswell, back from Corsica, as one 'whom a wise and noble curiosity has led where perhaps no native of his country ever was before'.[44] Macaulay says that the Jesuits, as missionaries, 'wandered to countries which neither mercantile avidity nor liberal curiosity had impelled any stranger to explore'.[45]

The *liberal* motive is here contrasted equally with the religious and the mercantile. This suggests a problem for those who wish to embrace both the Christian and the Aristotelian scheme. What excellence can either ideal concede to the other? The only nineteenth-century author, so far as I know, who fully faced the question was Newman, in a very firm piece of thinking which makes clear how, in his view, that which is necessarily subordinate has nevertheless its own relative autonomy and its own proper excellence—

That alone is *liberal* knowledge which stands on its own pretensions, which is independent of sequel . . . refuses to be informed (as it is called) by any end. The most ordinary pursuits have this specific character if they are self-sufficient and complete; the highest lose it when they minister to something beyond them. . . . If, for instance, Theology, instead of being cultivated as a contemplation, be limited to the purposes of the pulpit or be represented by the catechism, it loses—not its usefulness, not its divine character, not its meritoriousness (rather it increases those qualities by such charitable condescension) but it does lose the particular attribute which I am illustrating; just as a face worn by tears and fasting loses its beauty. . . . And thus it appears that even what is supernatural need not be *liberal*, nor need a hero be a gentleman, for the plain reason that one idea is not another idea.[46]

Unless followed by the word 'education', *liberal* has now lost this meaning. For that loss, so damaging to the whole of our cultural outlook, we must thank those who made it the name, first of a political, and then of a theological, party. The same irresponsible rapacity, the desire to appropriate a word for its 'selling-

[41]*De Oratore* III, xxxii.   [42]Ovid, *Ex Ponto* II, ix, 47.
[43]*Journey to the Western Islands, Ostig.*   [44]Boswell, 14 January 1766.   [45]*History* VI.
[46]*Scope and Nature of University Education,* IV.

power', has often done linguistic mischief. It is not easy now to say at all in English what the word *conservative* would have said if it had not been 'cornered' by politicians. *Evangelical, intellectual, rationalist,* and *temperance* have been destroyed in the same way. Sometimes the arrogation is so outrageous that it fails; the Quakers have not killed the word *friends.* And sometimes so many different people grab at the coveted word for so many different groups or factions that, while it is spoiled for its original purpose, none of the grabbers achieve secure possession. *Humanist* is an example; it will probably end by being a term of eulogy as vague as *gentleman.*

We cannot stop the verbicides. The most we can do is not to imitate them.

On Stories

IT IS ASTONISHING how little attention critics have paid to Story considered in itself. Granted the story, the style in which it should be told, the order in which it should be disposed, and (above all) the delineation of the characters, have been abundantly discussed. But the Story itself, the series of imagined events, is nearly always passed over in silence, or else treated exclusively as affording opportunities for the delineation of character. There are indeed three notable exceptions. Aristotle in the *Poetics* constructed a theory of Greek tragedy which puts Story in the centre and relegates character to a strictly subordinate place. In the Middle Ages and the early Renaissance, Boccaccio and others developed an allegorical theory of Story to explain the ancient myths. And in our own time Jung and his followers have produced their doctrine of Archtypes. Apart from these three attempts the subject has been left almost untouched, and this has had a curious result. Those forms of literature in which Story exists merely as a means to something else—for example, the novel of manners where the story is there for the sake of the characters, or the criticism of social conditions—have had full justice done to them; but those forms in which everything else is there for the sake of the story have been given little serious attention. Not only have they been despised, as if they were fit only for children, but even the kind of pleasure they give has, in my opinion, been misunderstood. It is the second injustice which I am most anxious to remedy. Perhaps the pleasure of Story comes as low in the scale as modern criticism puts it. I do not think so myself, but on that point we may agree to differ. Let us, however, try to see clearly what kind of pleasure it is: or rather, what different kinds of pleasure it may be. For I suspect that a very hasty assumption has been made on this subject. I think that books which are read merely 'for the story' may be enjoyed in two very different ways. It is partly a division of books (some stories can be read only in the one spirit and some only in the other) and partly a division of readers (the same story can be read in different ways).

What finally convinced me of this distinction was a conversation which I had a few years ago with an intelligent American pupil. We were talking about the books which had delighted our boyhood. His favourite had been Fenimore Cooper whom (as it happens) I have never read. My friend described one particular scene in which the hero was half-sleeping by his bivouac fire in the woods while a Redskin with a tomahawk was silently creeping on him from behind. He remembered the breathless excitement with which he had read the passage, the agonized suspense with which he wondered whether the hero would wake up in time or not. But I, remembering the great moments in my own early reading, felt quite sure that my friend was misrepresenting his experience, and indeed leaving out the real point. Surely, surely, I thought, the sheer excitement, the suspense, was not what had kept him going back and back to Fenimore Cooper. If that were what he wanted any other 'boy's blood' would have done as well. I tried to put my thought into words. I asked him whether he were sure that he was not over-emphasizing and falsely isolating the importance of the danger simply as danger. For though I had never read Fenimore Cooper I had enjoyed other books about 'Red Indians'. And I knew that what I wanted from them was not simply 'excitement'. Dangers, of course, there must be: how else can you keep a story going? But they must (in the mood which led one to such a book) be Redskin dangers. The 'Redskinnery' was what really mattered. In such a scene as my friend had described, take away the feathers, the high cheek-bones, the whiskered trousers, substitute a pistol for a tomahawk, and what would be left? For I wanted not the momentary suspense but that whole world to which it belonged—the snow and the snow-shoes, beavers and canoes, war-paths and wigwams, and Hiawatha names. Thus I; and then came the shock. My pupil is a very clear-headed man and he saw at once what I meant and also saw how totally his imaginative life as a boy had differed from mine. He replied that he was perfectly certain that 'all that' had made no part of his pleasure. He had never cared one brass farthing for it. Indeed—and this really made me feel as if I were talking to a visitor from another planet—in so far as he had been dimly aware of 'all that', he had resented it as a distraction from the main issue. He would, if anything, have preferred to the Redskin some more ordinary danger such as a crook with a revolver.

To those whose literary experiences are at all like my own the distinction which I am trying to make between two kinds of pleasure will probably be clear enough from this one example. But to make it doubly clear I will add another. I was once taken to see a film version of *King Solomon's Mines*. Of its many sins—not least the introduction of a totally irrelevant young woman in shorts who accompanied the three adventurers wherever they went—only one here concerns us. At the end of Haggard's book, as everyone remembers, the heroes are awaiting death entombed in a rock chamber and surrounded by the mummified kings of that land. The maker of the film version, however, apparently thought this tame. He substituted a subterranean volcanic eruption, and then went one better by adding an earthquake. Perhaps we should not blame him. Perhaps the scene in the original was not 'cinematic' and the man was right, by the canons of his own art, in altering it. But it would have been better not to have chosen in the first place a story which could be adapted to the screen only by being ruined. Ruined, at least, for me. No doubt if sheer excitement is all you want from a story, and if increase of dangers increases excitement, then a rapidly changing series of two risks (that of being burned alive and that of being crushed to bits) would be better than the single prolonged danger of starving to death in a cave. But that is just the point. There must be a pleasure in such stories distinct from mere excitement or I should not feel that I had been cheated in being given the earthquake instead of Haggard's actual scene. What I lose is the whole sense of the deathly (quite a different thing from simple danger of death)—the cold, the silence, and the surrounding faces of the ancient, the crowned and sceptred, dead. You may, if you please, say that Rider Haggard's effect is quite as 'crude' or 'vulgar' or 'sensational' as that which the film substituted for it. I am not at present discussing that. The point is that it is extremely different. The one lays a hushing spell on the imagination; the other excites a rapid flutter of the nerves. In reading that chapter of the book curiosity or suspense about the escape of the heroes from their death-trap makes a very minor part of one's experience. The trap I remember for ever: how they got out I have long since forgotten.

It seems to me that in talking of books which are 'mere stories'—books, that is, which concern themselves principally with the imagined event and not with character or society—nearly everyone makes the assumption that 'excitement' is the only pleasure they ever give or are intended to give. *Excitement*, in this sense, may be defined as the alternate tension and appeasement of imagined anxiety. This is what I think untrue. In some such books, and for some readers, another factor comes in.

To put it at the very lowest, I know that something else comes in for at least one reader—myself. I must here be autobiographical for the sake of being evidential. Here is a man who has spent more hours than he cares to remember in reading romances, and received from them more pleasure perhaps than he should. I know the geography of Tormance better than that of Tellus. I have been more curious about travels from Uplands to Utterbol and from Morna Moruna to Koshtra Belorn than about those recorded in Hakluyt. Though I saw the trenches before Arras I could not now lecture on them so tactically as on the Greek wall, and Scamander and the Scaean Gate. As a social historian I am sounder on Toad Hall and the Wild Wood or the cave-dwelling Selenites or Hrothgar's court or Vortigern's than on London, Oxford, and Belfast. If to love Story is to love excitement then I ought to be the greatest lover of excitement alive. But the fact is that what is said to be the most 'exciting' novel in the world, *The Three Musketeers,* makes no appeal to me at all. The total lack of atmosphere repels me. There is no country in the book—save as a storehouse of inns and ambushes. There is no weather. When they cross to London there is no feeling that London differs from Paris. There is not a moment's rest from the 'adventures': one's nose is kept ruthlessly to the grindstone. It all means nothing to me. If that is what is meant by Romance, then Romance is my aversion and I greatly prefer George Eliot or Trollope. In saying this I am not attempting to criticize *The Three Musketeers.* I believe on the testimony of others that it is a capital story. I am sure that my own inability to like it is in me a defect and a misfortune. But that misfortune is evidence. If a man sensitive and perhaps over-sensitive to Romance likes least that Romance which is, by common consent, the most 'exciting' of all, then it follows that 'excitement' is not the only kind of pleasure to be got out of Romance. If a man loves wine and yet hates one of the strongest wines, then surely the sole source of pleasure in wine cannot be the alcohol?

If I am alone in this experience then, to be sure, the present essay is of merely autobiographical interest. But I am pretty sure that I am not absolutely alone. I write on the chance that some others may feel the same and in the hope that I may help them to clarify their own sensations.

In the example of *King Solomon's Mines* the producer of the film substituted at the climax one kind of danger for another and thereby, for me, ruined the story. But where excitement is the only thing that matters kinds of danger must be irrelevant. Only degrees of danger will matter. The greater the danger and the narrower the hero's escape from it, the more exciting the story will be. But when we are concerned with the 'something else' this is not so. Different kinds of danger strike different chords from the imagination. Even in real life different kinds of danger produce different kinds of fear. There may come a point at which fear is so great that such distinctions vanish, but that is another matter. There is a fear which is twin sister to awe, such as a man in war-time feels when he first comes within sound of the guns; there is a fear which is twin sister to disgust, such as a man feels on finding a snake or scorpion in his bedroom. There are taut, quivering fears (for one split second hardly distinguishable from a kind of pleasurable thrill) that a man may feel on a dangerous horse or a dangerous sea; and again, dead, squashed, flattened, numbing fears, as when we think we have cancer or cholera. There are also fears which are not of *danger* at all: like the fear of some large and hideous, though innocuous, insect or the fear of a ghost. All this, even in real life. But in imagination, where the fear does not rise to abject terror and is not discharged in action, the qualitative difference is much stronger.

I can never remember a time when it was not, however vaguely, present to my consciousness. *Jack the Giant-Killer* is not, in essence, simply the story of a

clever hero surmounting danger. It is in essence the story of such a hero surmounting *danger from giants*. It is quite easy to contrive a story in which, though
the enemies are of normal size, the odds against Jack are equally great. But it will
be quite a different story. The whole quality of the imaginative response is
determined by the fact that the enemies are giants. That heaviness, that monstrosity, that uncouthness, hangs over the whole thing. Turn it into music and
you will feel the difference at once. If your villain is a giant your orchestra will
proclaim his entrance in one way: if he is any other kind of villain, in another.
I have seen landscapes (notably in the Mourne Mountains) which, under a
particular light, made me feel that at any moment a giant might raise his head
over the next ridge. Nature has that in her which compels us to invent giants:
and only giants will do. (Notice that Gawain was in the north-west corner of
England when 'etins aneleden him', giants came *blowing* after him on the high
fells. Can it be an accident that Wordsworth was in the same places when he
heard 'low breathings coming after him'?) The dangerousness of the giants is,
though important, secondary. In some folk-tales we meet giants who are not
dangerous. But they still affect us in much the same way. A *good* giant is
legitimate: but he would be twenty tons of living, earth-shaking oxymoron. The
intolerable pressure, the sense of something older, wilder, and more earthy than
humanity, would still cleave to him.

But let us descend to a lower instance. Are pirates, any more than giants,
merely a machine for threatening the hero? That sail which is rapidly overhauling
us may be an ordinary enemy: a Don or a Frenchman. The ordinary enemy may
easily be made just as lethal as the pirate. At the moment when she runs up the
Jolly Roger, what exactly does this do to the imagination? It means, I grant you,
that if we are beaten there will be no quarter. But that could be contrived without
piracy. It is not the mere increase of danger that does the trick. It is the whole
image of the utterly lawless enemy, the men who have cut adrift from all human
society and become, as it were, a species of their own—men strangely clad, dark
men with ear-rings, men with a history which they know and we don't, lords of
unspecified treasure buried in undiscovered islands. They are, in fact, to the
young reader almost as mythological as the giants. It does not cross his mind that
a man—a mere man like the rest of us—might be a pirate at one time of his life
and not at another, or that there is any smudgy frontier between piracy and
privateering. A pirate is a pirate, just as a giant is a giant.

Consider, again, the enormous difference between being shut out and being
shut in: if you like between agoraphobia and claustrophobia. In *King Solomon's
Mines* the heroes were shut in: so, more terribly, the narrator imagined himself
to be in Poe's *Premature Burial*. Your breath shortens while you read it. Now
remember the chapter called 'Mr. Bedford Alone' in H. G. Wells's *First Men
in the Moon*. There Bedford finds himself shut out on the surface of the Moon
just as the long lunar day is drawing to its close—and with the day go the air and
all heat. Read it from the terrible moment when the first tiny snowflake startles
him into a realization of his position down to the point at which he reaches the

'sphere' and is saved. Then ask yourself whether what you have been feeling is simply suspense. 'Over me, around me, closing in on me, embracing me ever nearer was the Eternal . . . the infinite and final Night of space.' That is the idea which has kept you enthralled. But if we were concerned only with the question whether Mr. Bedford will live or freeze, that idea is quite beside the purpose. You can die of cold between Russian Poland and new Poland, just as well as by going to the Moon, and the pain will be equal. For the purpose of killing Mr. Bedford 'the infinite and final Night of space' is almost entirely otiose: what is by cosmic standards an infinitesimal change of temperature is sufficient to kill a man and absolute zero can do no more. That airless outer darkness is important not for what it can do to Bedford but for what it does to us: to trouble us with Pascal's old fear of those eternal silences which have gnawed at so much religious faith and shattered so many humanistic hopes: to evoke with them and through them all our racial and childish memories of exclusion and desolation: to present, in fact, as an intuition one permanent aspect of human experience.

And here, I expect, we come to one of the differences between life and art. A man really in Bedford's position would probably not feel very acutely that sidereal loneliness. The immediate issue of death would drive the contemplative object out of his mind: he would have no interest in the many degrees of increasing cold lower than the one which made his survival impossible. That is one of the functions of art: to present what the narrow and desperately practical perspectives of real life exclude.

I have sometimes wondered whether the 'excitement' may not be an element actually hostile to the deeper imagination. In inferior romances, such as the American magazines of 'scientifiction' supply, we often come across a really suggestive idea. But the author has no expedient for keeping the story on the move except that of putting his hero into violent danger. In the hurry and scurry of his escapes the poetry of the basic idea is lost. In a much milder degree I think this has happened to Wells himself in the *War of the Worlds*. What really matters in this story is the idea of being attacked by something utterly 'outside'. As in *Piers Plowman* destruction has come upon us 'from the planets'. If the Martian invaders are merely dangerous—if we once become mainly concerned with the fact that they can *kill* us—why, then, a burglar or a bacillus can do as much. The real nerve of the romance is laid bare when the hero first goes to look at the newly fallen projectile on Horsell Common. 'The yellowish-white metal that gleamed in the crack between the lid and the cylinder had an unfamiliar hue. *Extra-terrestrial* had no meaning for most of the onlookers.' But *extra-terrestrial* is the key word of the whole story. And in the later horrors, excellently as they are done, we lose the feeling of it. Similarly in the Poet Laureate's *Sard Harker* it is the journey across the Sierras that really matters. That the man who has heard the noise in the cañon—'He could not think what it was. It was not sorrowful nor joyful nor terrible. It was great and strange. It was like the rock speaking'— that this man should be later in danger of mere murder is almost an impertinence.

It is here that Homer shows his supreme excellence. The landing on Circe's island, the sight of the smoke going up from amidst those unexplored woods, the god meeting us ('the messenger, the slayer of Argus')—what an anti-climax if all these had been the prelude only to some ordinary risk of life and limb! But the peril that lurks here, the silent, painless, unendurable change into brutality, is worthy of the setting. Mr. de la Mare too has surmounted the difficulty. The threat launched in the opening paragraphs of his best stories is seldom fulfilled in any identifiable event: still less is it dissipated. Our fears are never, in one sense, realized: yet we lay down the story feeling that they, and far more, were justified. But perhaps the most remarkable achievement in this kind is that of Mr. David Lindsay's *Voyage to Arcturus*. The experienced reader, noting the threats and promises of the opening chapter, even while he gratefully enjoys them, feels sure that they cannot be carried out. He reflects that in stories of this kind the first chapter is nearly always the best and reconciles himself to disappointment; Tormance, when we reach it, he forbodes, will be less interesting than Tormance seen from the Earth. But never will he have been more mistaken. Unaided by any special skill or even any sound taste in language, the author leads us up a stair of unpredictables. In each chapter we think we have found his final position: each time we are utterly mistaken. He builds whole worlds of imagery and passion, any one of which would have served another writer for a whole book, only to pull each of them to pieces and pour scorn on it. The physical dangers, which are plentiful, here count for nothing: it is we ourselves and the author who walk through a world of spiritual dangers which makes them seem trivial. There is no recipe for writing of this kind. But part of the secret is that the author (like Kafka) is recording a lived dialectic. His Tormance is a region of the spirit. He is the first writer to discover what 'other planets' are really good for in fiction. No merely physical strangeness or merely spatial distance will realize that idea of otherness which is what we are always trying to grasp in a story about voyaging through space: you must go into another dimension. To construct plausible and moving 'other worlds' you must draw on the only real 'other world' we know, that of the spirit.

Notice here the corollary. If some fatal progress of applied science ever enables us in fact to reach the Moon, that real journey will not at all satisfy the impulse which we now seek to gratify by writing such stories. The real Moon, if you could reach it and survive, would in a deep and deadly sense be just like anywhere else. You would find cold, hunger, hardship, and danger; and after the first few hours they would be *simply* cold, hunger, hardship, and danger as you might have met them on Earth. And death would be simply death among those bleached craters as it is simply death in a nursing home at Sheffield. No man would find an abiding strangeness on the Moon unless he were the sort of man who could find it in his own back garden. 'He who would bring home the wealth of the Indies must carry the wealth of the Indies with him.'

Good stories often introduce the marvellous or supernatural, and nothing about Story has been so often misunderstood as this. Thus, for example, Dr. Johnson, if I remember rightly, thought that children liked stories of the marvellous because they were too ignorant to know that they were impossible. But children do not always like them, nor are those who like them always children; and to enjoy reading about fairies—much more about giants and dragons—it is not necessary to believe in them. Belief is at best irrelevant; it may be a positive disadvantage. Nor are the marvels in good Story ever mere arbitrary fictions stuck on to make the narrative more sensational. I happened to remark to a man who was sitting beside me at dinner the other night that I was reading Grimm in German of an evening but never bothered to look up a word I didn't know, 'so that it is often great fun' (I added) 'guessing what it was that the old woman gave to the prince which he afterwards lost in the wood'. 'And specially difficult in a fairytale,' said he, 'where everything is arbitrary and therefore the object might be anything at all.' His error was profound. The logic of a fairy-tale is as strict as that of a realistic novel, though different.

Does anyone believe that Kenneth Grahame made an arbitrary choice when he gave his principal character the form of a toad, or that a stag, a pigeon, a lion would have done as well? The choice is based on the fact that the real toad's face has a grotesque resemblance to a certain kind of human face—a rather apoplectic face with a fatuous grin on it. This is, no doubt, an accident in the sense that all the lines which suggest the resemblance are really there for quite different biological reasons. The ludicrous quasi-human expression is therefore changeless: the toad cannot stop grinning because its 'grin' is not really a grin at all. Looking at the creature we thus see, isolated and fixed, an aspect of human vanity in its funniest and most pardonable form; following that hint Grahame creates Mr. Toad—an ultra-Jonsonian 'humour'. And we bring back the wealth of the Indies; we have henceforward more amusement in, and kindness towards, a certain kind of vanity in real life.

But why should the characters be disguised as animals at all? The disguise is very thin, so thin that Grahame makes Mr. Toad on one occasion 'comb the dry leaves out of his *hair*'. Yet it is quite indispensable. If you try to rewrite the book with all the characters humanized you are faced at the outset with a dilemma. Are they to be adults or children? You will find that they can be neither. They are like children in so far as they have no responsibilities, no struggle for existence, no domestic cares. Meals turn up; one does not even ask who cooked them. In Mr. Badger's kitchen 'plates on the dresser grinned at pots on the shelf'. Who kept them clean? Where were they bought? How were they delivered in the Wild Wood? Mole is very snug in his subterranean home, but what was he living *on*? If he is a *rentier* where is the bank, what are his investments? The tables in his forecourt were 'marked with rings that hinted at beer mugs'. But where did he get the beer? In that way the life of all the characters is that of children for whom everything is provided and who take everything for granted. But in other ways it is the life of adults. They go where they like and do what they please, they arrange their own lives.

To that extent the book is a specimen of the most scandalous escapism: it paints a happiness under incompatible conditions—the sort of freedom we can

have only in childhood and the sort we can have only in maturity—and conceals
the contradiction by the further pretence that the characters are not human
beings at all. The one absurdity helps to hide the other. It might be expected
that such a book would unfit us for the harshness of reality and send us back to
our daily lives unsettled and discontented. I do not find that it does so. The
happiness which it presents to us is in fact full of the simplest and most attainable
things—food, sleep, exercise, friendship, the face of nature, even (in a sense)
religion. That 'simple but sustaining meal' of 'bacon and broad beans and a
macaroni pudding' which Rat gave to his friends has, I doubt not, helped down
many a real nursery dinner. And in the same way the whole story, paradoxically
enough, strengthens our relish for real life. This excursion into the preposterous
sends us back with renewed pleasure to the actual.

It is usual to speak in a playfully apologetic tone about one's adult enjoyment
of what are called 'children's books'. I think the convention a silly one. No book
is really worth reading at the age of ten which is not equally (and often far more)
worth reading at the age of fifty—except, of course, books of information. The
only imaginative works we ought to grow out of are those which it would have
been better not to have read at all. A mature palate will probably not much care
for *crème de menthe:* but it ought still to enjoy bread and butter and honey.

Another very large class of stories turns on fulfilled prophecies—the story of
Oedipus, or *The Man who would be King,* or *The Hobbit.* In most of them the
very steps taken to prevent the fulfilment of the prophecy actually bring it about.
It is foretold that Oedipus will kill his father and marry his mother. In order to
prevent this from happening he is exposed on the mountain: and that exposure,
by leading to his rescue and thus to his life among strangers in ignorance of his
real parentage, renders possible both the disasters. Such stories produce (at least
in me) a feeling of awe, coupled with a certain sort of bewilderment such as one
often feels in looking at a complex pattern of lines that pass over and under one
another. One sees, yet does not quite see, the regularity. And is there not good
occasion both for awe and bewilderment? We have just had set before our
imagination something that has always baffled the intellect: we have *seen* how
destiny and free will can be combined, even how free will is the *modus operandi*
of destiny. The story does what no theorem can quite do. It may not be 'like real
life' in the superficial sense: but it sets before us an image of what reality may
well be like at some more central region.

It will be seen that throughout this essay I have taken my examples indiscrimi-
nately from books which critics would (quite rightly) place in very different
categories—from American 'scientifiction' and Homer, from Sophocles and
Märchen, from children's stories and the intensely sophisticated art of Mr. de
la Mare. This does not mean that I think them of equal literary merit. But if I
am right in thinking that there is another enjoyment in Story besides the excitement, then popular romance even on the lowest level becomes rather more
important than we had supposed. When you see an immature or uneducated
person devouring what seem to you merely sensational stories, can you be sure

what kind of pleasure he is enjoying? It is, of course, no good asking *him*. If he were capable of analysing his own experience as the question requires him to do, he would be neither uneducated nor immature. But because he is inarticulate we must not give judgement against him. He may be seeking only the recurring tension of imagined anxiety. But he may also, I believe, be receiving certain profound experiences which are, for him, not acceptable in any other form.

Mr. Roger Green, writing in *English* not long ago, remarked that the reading of Rider Haggard had been to many a sort of religious experience. To some people this will have seemed simply grotesque. I myself would strongly disagree with it if 'religious' is taken to mean 'Christian'. And even if we take it in a sub-Christian sense, it would have been safer to say that such people had first met in Haggard's romances elements which they would meet again in religious experience if they ever came to have any. But I think Mr. Green is very much nearer the mark than those who assume that no one has ever read the romances except in order to be thrilled by hair-breadth escapes. If he had said simply that something which the educated receive from poetry can reach the masses through stories of adventure, and almost in no other way, then I think he would have been right. If so, nothing can be more disastrous than the view that the cinema can and should replace popular written fiction. The elements which it excludes are precisely those which give the untrained mind its only access to the imaginative world. There is death in the camera.

As I have admitted, it is very difficult to tell in any given case whether a story is piercing to the unliterary reader's deeper imagination or only exciting his emotions. You cannot tell even by reading the story for yourself. Its badness proves very little. The more imagination the reader has, being an untrained reader, the more he will do for himself. He will, at a mere hint from the author, flood wretched material with suggestion and never guess that he is himself chiefly making what he enjoys. The nearest we can come to a test is by asking whether he often *re-reads* the same story.

It is, of course, a good test for every reader of every kind of book. An unliterary man may be defined as one who reads books once only. There is hope for a man who has never read Malory or Boswell or *Tristram Shandy* or Shakespeare's *Sonnets:* but what can you do with a man who says he 'has read' them, meaning he has read them once, and thinks that this settles the matter? Yet I think the test has a special application to the matter in hand. For excitement, in the sense defined above, is just what must disappear from a second reading. You cannot, except at the first reading, be really curious about what happened. If you find that the reader of popular romance—however uneducated a reader, however bad the romances—goes back to his old favourites again and again, then you have pretty good evidence that they are to him a sort of poetry.

The re-reader is looking not for actual surprises (which can come only once) but for a certain ideal surprisingness. The point has often been misunderstood. The man in Peacock thought that he had disposed of 'surprise' as an element in landscape gardening when he asked what happened if you walked through the garden for the second time. Wiseacre! In the only sense that matters the surprise works as well the twentieth time as the first. It is the *quality* of unexpectedness, not the *fact* that delights us. It is even better the second time. Knowing that the 'surprise' is coming we can now fully relish the fact that this path through the shrubbery doesn't *look* as if it were suddenly going to bring us out on the edge of the cliff. So in literature. We do not enjoy a story fully at the first reading. Not till the curiosity, the sheer narrative lust, has been given its sop and laid asleep, are we at leisure to savour the real beauties. Till then, it is like wasting great wine on a ravenous natural thirst which merely wants cold wetness. The children understand this well when they ask for the same story over and over again, and in the same words. They want to have again the 'surprise' of discovering that what seemed Little-Red-Riding-Hood's grandmother is really the wolf. It is better when you know it is coming: free from the shock of actual surprise you can attend better to the intrinsic surprisingness of the *peripeteia*.

I should like to be able to believe that I am here in a very small way contributing (for criticism does not always come later than practice) to the encouragement of a better school of prose story in England: of story that can mediate imaginative life to the masses while not being contemptible to the few. But perhaps this is not very likely. It must be admitted that the art of Story as I see it is a very difficult one. What its central difficulty is I have already hinted when I complained that in the *War of the Worlds* the idea that really matters becomes lost or blunted as the story gets under way. I must now add that there is a perpetual danger of this happening in all stories. To be stories at all they must be series of events: but it must be understood that this series—the *plot,* as we call it—is only really a net whereby to catch something else. The real theme may be, and perhaps usually is, something that has no sequence in it, something other than a process and much more like a state or quality. Giantship, otherness, the desolation of space, are examples that have crossed our path. The titles of some stories illustrate the point very well. *The Well at the World's End*—can a man write a story to that title? Can he find a series of events following one another in time which will really catch and fix and bring home to us all that we grasp at on merely hearing the six words? Can a man write a story on Atlantis—or is it better to leave the word to work on its own? And I must confess that the net very seldom does succeed in catching the bird. Morris in the *Well at the World's End* came near to success—quite near enough to make the book worth many readings. Yet, after all, the best moments of it come in the first half.

But it does sometimes succeed. In the works of the late E. R. Eddison it succeeds completely. You may like or dislike his invented worlds (I myself like that of *The Worm Ouroboros* and strongly dislike that of *Mistress of Mistresses*) but there is here no quarrel between the theme and the articulation of the story. Every episode, every speech, helps to incarnate what the author is imagining. You could spare none of them. It takes the whole story to build up that strange blend of renaissance luxury and northern hardness. The secret here is largely the style, and especially the style of the dialogue. These proud, reckless, amorous people create themselves and the whole atmosphere of their world chiefly by talking. Mr. de la Mare also succeeds, partly by style and partly by never laying the cards on the table. Mr. David Lindsay, however, succeeds while writing a style which is at times (to be frank) abominable. He succeeds because his real theme is, like the plot, sequential, a thing in time, or quasi-time: a passionate spiritual journey. Charles Williams had the same advantage, but I do not mention his stories much here because they are hardly pure story in the sense we are now considering. They are, despite their free use of the supernatural, much closer to the novel; a believed religion, detailed character drawing, and even social satire all come in. *The Hobbit* escapes the danger of degenerating into mere plot and excitement by a very curious shift of tone. As the humour and homeliness of the early chapters, the sheer 'Hobbitry', dies away we pass insensibly into the world of epic. It is as if the battle of Toad Hall had become a serious *heimsókn* and Badger had begun to talk like Njal. Thus we lose one theme but find another. We kill—but not the same fox.

It may be asked why anyone should be encouraged to write a form in which the means are apparently so often at war with the end. But I am hardly suggesting that anyone who can write great poetry should write stories instead. I am rather suggesting what those whose work will in any case be a romance should aim at. And I do not think it unimportant that good work in this kind, even work less than perfectly good, can come where poetry will never come.

Shall I be thought whimsical if, in conclusion, I suggest that this internal tension in the heart of every story between the theme and the plot constitutes, after all, its chief resemblance to life? If story fails in that way does not life commit the same blunder? In real life, as in a story, something must happen. That is just the trouble. We grasp at a state and find only a succession of events in which the state is never quite embodied. The grand idea of finding Atlantis which stirs us in the first chapter of the adventure story is apt to be frittered away in mere excitement when the journey has once been begun. But so, in real life, the idea of adventure fades when the day-to-day details begin to happen. Nor is this merely because actual hardship and danger shoulder it aside. Other grand ideas—homecoming, reunion with a beloved—similarly elude our grasp. Suppose there is no disappointment; even so—well, you are here. But now, something must happen, and after that something else. All that happens may be delightful: but can any such series quite embody the sheer state of being which was what we wanted? If the author's plot is only a net, and usually an imperfect one, a net of time and event for catching what is not really a process at all, is life much more? I am not sure, on second thoughts, that the slow fading of the magic in *The Well at the World's End* is, after all, a blemish. It is an image of the truth. Art, indeed, may be expected to do what life cannot do: but so it has done. The bird has escaped us. But it was at least entangled in the net for several chapters. We saw it close and enjoyed the plumage. How many 'real lives' have nets that can do as much?

In life and art both, as it seems to me, we are always trying to catch in our net of successive moments something that is not successive. Whether in real life there is any doctor who can teach us how to do it, so that at last either the meshes will become fine enough to hold the bird, or we be so changed that we can throw our nets away and follow the bird to its own country, is not a question for this essay. But I think it is sometimes done—or very, very nearly done—in stories. I believe the effort to be well worth making.

FROM

An Experiment in Criticism

The Few and the Many

I N   T H I S   E S S A Y   I propose to try an experiment. Literary criticism is traditionally employed in judging books. Any judgement it implies about men's reading of books is a corollary from its judgement on the books themselves. Bad taste is, as it were by definition, a taste for bad books. I want to find out what sort of picture we shall get by reversing the process. Let us make our distinction between readers or types of reading the basis, and our distinction between books the corollary. Let us try to discover how far it might be plausible to define a good book as a book which is read in one way, and a bad book as a book which is read in another.

I think this worth trying because the normal procedure seems to me to involve almost continually a false implication. If we say that *A* likes (or has a taste for) the women's magazines and *B* likes (or has a taste for) Dante, this sounds as if *likes* and *taste* have the same meaning when applied to both; as if there were a single activity, though the objects to which it is directed are different. But observation convinces me that this, at least usually, is untrue.

Already in our schooldays some of us were making our first responses to good literature. Others, and these the majority, were reading, at school, *The Captain*, and, at home, short-lived novels from the circulating library. But it was apparent then that the majority did not 'like' their fare in the way we 'liked' ours. It is apparent still. The differences leap to the eye.

In the first place, the majority never read anything twice. The sure mark of an unliterary man is that he considers 'I've read it already' to be a conclusive argument against reading a work. We have all known women who remembered a novel so dimly that they had to stand for half an hour in the library skimming through it before they were certain they had once read it. But the moment they became certain, they rejected it immediately. It was for them dead, like a burnt-out match, an old railway ticket, or yesterday's paper; they had already used it. Those who read great works, on the other hand, will read the same work ten, twenty or thirty times during the course of their life.

Secondly, the majority, though they are sometimes frequent readers, do not set much store by reading. They turn to it as a last resource. They abandon it with alacrity as soon as any alternative pastime turns up. It is kept for railway journeys, illnesses, odd moments of enforced solitude, or for the process called 'reading oneself to sleep'. They sometimes combine it with desultory conversation; often, with listening to the radio. But literary people are always looking for leisure and silence in which to read and do so with their whole attention. When they are denied such attentive and undisturbed reading even for a few days they feel impoverished.

Thirdly, the first reading of some literary work is often, to the literary, an experience so momentous that only experiences of love, religion, or bereavement can furnish a standard of comparison. Their whole consciousness is changed. They have become what they were not before. But there is no sign of anything like this among the other sort of readers. When they have finished the story or the novel, nothing much, or nothing at all, seems to have happened to them.

Finally, and as a natural result of their different behaviour in reading, what they have read is constantly and prominently present to the mind of the few, but not to that of the many. The former mouth over their favourite lines and stanzas in solitude. Scenes and characters from books provide them with a sort of iconography by which they interpret or sum up their own experience. They talk to one another about books, often and at length. The latter seldom think or talk of their reading.

It is pretty clear that the majority, if they spoke without passion and were fully articulate, would not accuse us of liking the wrong books, but of making such a fuss about any books at all. We treat as a main ingredient in our well-being something which to them is marginal. Hence to say simply that they like one thing and we another is to leave out nearly the whole of the facts. If *like* is the correct word for what they do to books, some other word must be found for what we do. Or, conversely, if we *like* our kind of book we must not say that they *like* any book. If the few have 'good taste', then we may have to say that no such thing as 'bad taste' exists: for the inclination which the many have to their sort of reading is not the same thing and, if the word were univocally used, would not be called taste at all.

Though I shall concern myself almost entirely with literature, it is worth noting that the same difference of attitude is displayed about the other arts and about natural beauty. Many people enjoy popular music in a way which is compatible with humming the tune, stamping in time, talking, and eating. And when the popular tune has once gone out of fashion they enjoy it no more. Those who enjoy Bach react quite differently. Some buy pictures because the walls 'look so bare without them'; and after the pictures have been in the house for a week they become practically invisible to them. But there are a few who feed on a great picture for years. As regards nature, the majority 'like a nice view as well as anyone'. They are not saying a word against it. But to make the landscapes a really important factor in, say, choosing the place for a holiday—to put them on a level with such serious considerations as a luxurious hotel, a good golf links, and a sunny climate—would seem to them affectation. To 'go on' about them like Wordsworth would be humbug. . . . Those of us who have been true readers all our life seldom fully realise the enormous extension of our being which we owe to authors. We realise it best when we talk with an unliterary friend. He may be full of goodness and good sense but he inhabits a tiny world. In it, we should be suffocated. The man who is contented to be only himself, and therefore less a self, is in prison. My own eyes are not enough for me, I will see through those of others. Reality, even seen through the eyes of many, is not enough. I will see what others have invented. Even the eyes of all humanity are not enough. I regret that the brutes cannot write books. Very gladly would I learn what face things present to a mouse or a bee; more gladly still would I perceive the olfactory world charged with all the information and emotion it carries for a dog.

Literary experience heals the wound, without undermining the privilege, of individuality. There are mass emotions which heal the wound; but they destroy the privilege. In them our separate selves are pooled and we sink back into sub-individuality. But in reading great literature I become a thousand men and yet remain myself. Like the night sky in the Greek poem, I see with a myriad eyes, but it is still I who see. Here, as in worship, in love, in moral action, and in knowing, I transcend myself; and am never more myself than when I do.

FROM
Fifteen Poets

Edmund Spenser

EDMUND SPENSER (1552?–99), was educated at Merchant
Taylors' School and Pembroke Hall, Cambridge. He obtained in 1578 a place in Leicester's household, and became
acquainted with Sir Philip Sidney. In 1579 he began the
Faerie Queene and published his *Shepheards Calendar*,
which was enthusiastically received. In 1580 he settled in
Ireland and occupied himself with literary work, preparing
the *Faerie Queene* for the press, three books of this work
being entrusted to the printer on the poet's visit to London
in 1589. The reputation of the *Faerie Queene* led the printer, Ponsonby, to issue in 1591 his minor verse, in part
rewritten. In 1594 Spenser married Elizabeth Boyle, whom
he had wooed in his *Amoretti*, and possibly celebrated the
marriage in his splendid *Epithalamion* (the two were
printed together in 1595). He published the second instal-
ment of three books of the *Faerie Queene* in 1596. He died
in destitution in London, and was buried near Chaucer in
Westminster Abbey.

Beyond all doubt it is best to have made one's first acquaintance with Spenser in a very large—and, preferably, illustrated—edition of the *Faerie Queene,* on a wet day, between the ages of twelve and sixteen; and if, even at that age, certain of the names aroused unidentified memories of some still earlier, some almost prehistoric, commerce with a selection of 'Stories from Spenser', heard before we could read, so much the better. But those who have had this good fortune are not likely to be reading the following extracts. They will never have lost touch with the poet. His great book will have accompanied them year by year and grown up with them as books do: to the youthful appreciation of mere wonder-tale they will have added a critically sensuous enjoyment of the melodious stanza, to both these a historical understanding of its significance in English poetry as a whole, and an ever-increasing perception of its wisdom. To them I need not speak; the problem is rather how to find substitutes for their slowly ripened habit of mind which may enable a mature reader to enter the Spenserian world for the first time: to do for him, in a few minutes, what they have done for themselves in many years.

It must be admitted that this is impossible, but on the following lines an effort may be made. Our imaginary child began with *The Faerie Queene,* and the mature reader must do the same. Passages from Spenser's other works appear, quite rightly, in the following pages, and it would certainly be a pity not to know the *Epithalamion:* but it must never be forgotten that he stands or falls by his great poetic romance, and if you do not like it and yet believe that you like Spenser you are probably deceiving yourself. Secondly, there is that large edition and that wet day. It is not, perhaps, absolutely necessary to have a large edition *in fact;* but it is imperative that you should think of *The Faerie Queene* as a book suitable for reading in a heavy volume, at a table—a book to which limp leather is insulting—a massy, antique story with a blackletter flavour about it—a book for devout, prolonged, and leisurely perusal. The illustrations (real or imagined) raise a problem. There are fantastic palaces and voluptuous nudes in Spenser which seem to ask for Tintoretto or Correggio or Claude: but there are also, and more abundantly, wicketgates and ugly fiends and stiffly bearded elders which we would rather see in woodcuts—such violent, unforgettable little cuts as Wordsworth mentions in *The Excursion.* This double need for two quite different kinds of picture is characteristic. There is a renaissance element in the *Faerie Queene*— a gorgeous, luxurious, Italianate, and florid element: but this is not the basis of it. All this new growth sprouts out of an old, gnarled wood, and, as in very early spring, mists it over in places without concealing it. The cloth of gold is an occasional decoration: most of the coat is homespun. And it is best to begin with a taste for homespun, accepting the cloth of gold when it comes but by no means depending on it for your pleasure, or you will be disappointed—to keep your *Faerie Queene* on the same shelf with Bunyan and Malory and *The Seven Champions* and even with *Jack the Giant Killer,* rather than with *Hero and Leander* or *Venus and Adonis.* For this is the paradox of Spenser's poem; it is not really medieval—no medieval romance is very like it—yet everyone who has really enjoyed it, from the Wartons down, has enjoyed it as the very consummation of the Middle Ages, the quintessence of 'the blackletter flavour'.

It came about in this way. Spenser's friends wanted him to be in the Movement, to be an extreme Puritan and a servile classicist, which were the two fashionable things at Cambridge in his day. Under their tutelage he produced the pretentious, and (to tell the truth) nearly worthless, *Shepheards Calendar*. But even in it he was straining at the tether, and his friend E. K. had to write pretty sharp cautionary notes on 'Ladies of the Lake' and 'friendly fairies', hinting that the poet had approached much too nearly to the medieval and the papistical—things as shocking to the fierce young intellectuals of that day as the bourgeois and the Victorian are to their descendants in our own. But Spenser, in his great work, went back to what he had always liked, and took all his renaissance accomplishments with him. What he had always liked was the Middle Ages as he imagined them to have been and as they survived in his time in the pageant, the morality play, and the metrical romance. They were real survivals, yet they smelled already a little archaic: they had already, for Spenser himself, a touch of the blackletter flavour. He thus became something between the last of the medieval poets and the first of the romantic medievalists; he was enabled to produce a tale more solemn, more redolent of the past, more venerable, than any real medieval romance—to deny, in his own person, the breach between the Middle Ages and the Renaissance and to hand on to succeeding generations a poetic symbol of the former whose charms have proved inexhaustible.

It will be remembered that we attributed to our ideal reader—along with the wet day, the large volume, and the unjaded appetite of boyhood—a haunting memory that he has met all these knights and ladies, all these monsters and enchanters, somewhere before. What corresponds to this in the experience of the mature reader is the consciousness of Spenser's moral allegory. Critics differ as regards the degree of attention which we must pay to it. It may not be necessary for all readers at all stages of the narrative to know exactly what the poet means, but it is emphatically necessary that they should surrender themselves to the sense of some dim significance in the background—that they should feel themselves to be moving in regions 'where more is meant than meets the ear'. Even if this feeling were only an illusion, it would be an essential part of the whole poetic illusion intended. The present writer, however, thinks that it is nothing of the sort: that Spenser's beautiful or alarming visions do truly embody, in forms as unsophisticated as those of our pantomime fairies and devils, though incomparably more potent, moral and psychological realities of the utmost simplicity and profundity. Certainly they are, at their best, as Mr. Yeats says of the figures in Spenser's House of Busirane, 'so visionary, so full of ghostly midnight animation, that one is persuaded that they had some strange purpose and did truly appear in just that way'.

PART IX

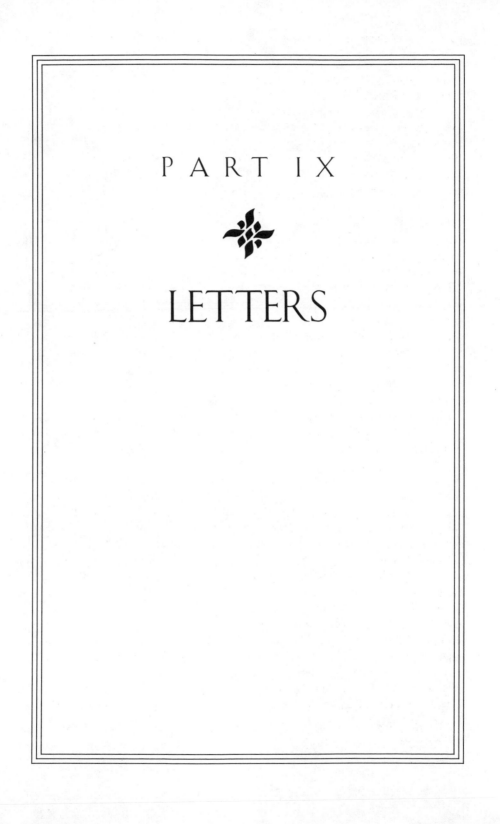

LETTERS

C. S. LEWIS never expected his personal letters to be published. Nevertheless, they now comprise some of his most important contributions.

His brother Warren Hamilton Lewis edited *The Letters of C. S. Lewis* (1966), and Walter Hooper brought out Jack's correspondence with his friend Arthur Greeves (see Part 2). These two volumes tell much about Lewis's life, especially his intellectual and religious development. Spanning the years from his teens until his death in 1963, this pair of books should be required reading for anyone who wants to understand the subtleties of Lewis's mind.

Two other collections of Lewis letters, *Letters to an American Lady* (1967), edited by Clyde S. Kilby, and *C. S. Lewis, Letters to Children* (1985), edited by Lyle W. Dorsett and Marjorie Lamp Mead, present a compelling portrait of C. S. Lewis as a generous soul who answered his fan mail with courtesy and care.

The first two letters reprinted in this chapter are typical of Lewis the teacher, who took his fan mail seriously and then attempted to offer thoughtful instruction rather than perfunctory responses.

If the first two letters reveal Lewis the instructor, the last eight epistles show him in his role as a pastor. Thousands of people wrote to this famous author, and many of them wanted spiritual direction. Like a kindly shepherd, yet never patronizing or condescending, he provided pastoral advice to everyone who sincerely sought his help.

FROM

Letters of C. S. Lewis

TO A SCHOOLGIRL IN AMERICA, who had written (at her teacher's suggestion) to request advice on writing.

14 December 1959

It is very hard to give any general advice about writing. Here's my attempt.

(1) Turn off the Radio.

(2) Read all the good books you can, and avoid nearly all magazines.

(3) Always write (and read) with the ear, not the eye. You shd. hear every sentence you write as if it was being read aloud or spoken. If it does not sound nice, try again.

(4) Write about what really interests you, whether it is real things or imaginary things, and nothing else. (Notice this means that if you are interested *only* in writing you will never be a writer, because you will have nothing to write about. . . .)

(5) Take great pains to be *clear*. Remember that though you start by knowing what you mean, the reader doesn't, and a single ill-chosen word may lead him to a total misunderstanding. In a story it is terribly easy just to forget that you have not told the reader something that he wants to know—the whole

picture is so clear in your own mind that you forget that it isn't the same in his.

(6) When you give up a bit of work don't (unless it is hopelessly bad) throw it away. Put it in a drawer. It may come in useful later. Much of my best work, or what I think my best, is the re-writing of things begun and abandoned years earlier.

(7) Don't use a typewriter. The noise will destroy your sense of rhythm, which still needs years of training.

(8) Be sure you know the meaning (or meanings) of every word you use.

Dear [Patricia]

All your points are in a sense right. But I'm not exactly "representing" the real (Christian) story in symbols. I'm more saying "Suppose there were a world like Narnia and it needed rescuing and the Son of God (or the 'Great Emperor oversea') went to redeem *it*, as He came to redeem ours, what might it, in that world, all have been like?" Perhaps it comes to much the same thing as you thought, but not quite.

1. The creation of Narnia is the Son of God creating *a* world (not specially *our* world).

2. Jadis plucking the apple is, like Adam's sin, an act of disobedience, but it doesn't fill the same place in her life as his plucking did in his. She was *already* fallen (very much so) before she ate it.

3. The stone table *is* meant to remind one of Moses' table.

4. The Passion and Resurrection of Aslan are the Passion and Resurrection Christ might be supposed to have had in *that* world—like those in our world but not exactly like.

5. Edmund is like Judas a sneak and traitor. But unlike Judas he repents and is forgiven (as Judas no doubt w[oul]d. have been if he'd repented).

6. Yes. At the v.[ery] *edge* of the Narnian world Aslan begins to appear more like Christ as He is known in *this* world. Hence, the Lamb. Hence, the breakfast—

like at the end of St. John's Gospel. Does not He say "You have been allowed to know me in *this* world (Narnia) so that you may know me better when you get back to your own"?

7. And of course the Ape and Puzzle, just before the last Judgement (in the *Last Battle*) are like the coming of Antichrist before the end of our world.

All clear?

I'm so glad you like the books.

> Yours sincerely
> C. S. Lewis

[3 April 1949]

My dear Sarah

I am sorry to say that I don't think I shall be able to be at your confirmation on Saturday. For most men Saturday afternoon is a free time, but I have an invalid old lady[1] to look after and the week-end is the time when I have no freedom at all, and have to try to be Nurse, Kennel-Maid, Wood-cutter, Butler, Housemaid and Secretary all in one. I had hoped that if the old lady were a little better than usual and if all the other people in the house were in good tempers I might be able to get away next Saturday. But the old lady is a good deal worse than usual and most of the people in the house are in bad tempers. So I must "stick to the ship".

If I *had* come and we had met, I am afraid you might have found me very shy and dull. (By the way, always remember that old people can be quite as shy with young people as young people can be with old. This explains what must seem to you the idiotic way in which so many grown-ups talk to you). But I will try to do what I can by a letter. I think of myself as having to be two people for you. (1) The real, serious, Christian godfather (2) The fairy godfather. As regards (2) I enclose a bit of the only kind of magic (a very dull kind) which I can work. Your mother will know how to deal with the spell. I think it will mean one or two, or even five, pounds for you *now*, to get things you want, and the rest in the Bank for future use. As I say, it is a dull kind of magic and a really good godfather (of type 2) would do something much more interesting: but it is the best an old bachelor can think of, and it is with my love.

As for No 1, the serious Christian godfather, I feel very unfit for the work—just as you, I dare say, may feel very unfit for being confirmed and for receiving the Holy Communion. But then an angel would not be really fit and we must all do the best we can. So I suppose I must try to give you advice. And the bit of advice that comes into my head is this; don't expect (I mean, don't *count on*

[1]This lady was Janie King Moore, the mother of C. S. Lewis's army friend, E. F. C. "Paddy" Moore. When Paddy was killed in World War I, Lewis honored his promise to care for his friend's mother and sister, Maureen. Mrs. Moore died in 1951.

and don't *demand*) that when you are confirmed, or when you make your first Communion, you will have all the *feelings* you would like to have. You may, of course: but also you may not. But don't worry if you don't get them. They aren't what matter. The things that are happening to you are quite real things whether you feel as you w[oul]d. wish or not, just as a meal will do a hungry person good even if he has a cold in the head which will rather spoil the taste. Our Lord will give us right feelings if He wishes—and then we must say Thank you. If He doesn't, then we must say to ourselves (and Him) that He knows us best. This, by the way, is one of the very few subjects on which I feel I do know something. For years after I had become a regular communicant I can't tell you how dull my feelings were and how my attention wandered at the most important moments. It is only in the last year or two that things have begun to come right— which just shows how important it is to keep on doing what you are told.

Oh—I'd nearly forgotten—I have *one* other piece of advice. Remember that there are only three kinds of things anyone need ever do. (1) Things we *ought* to do (2) Things we've *got* to do (3) Things we *like* doing. I say this because some people seem to spend so much of their time doing things for none of the three reasons, things like reading books they don't like because other people read them. Things you ought to do are things like doing one's school work or being nice to people. Things one has got to do are things like dressing and undressing, or household shopping. Things one likes doing—but of course I don't know what *you* like. Perhaps you'll write and tell me one day.

Of course I always mention you in my prayers and will most especially on Saturday. Do the same for me

Your affectionate godfather
C. S. Lewis

FROM

Letters to an

American Lady

The Kilns,
Headington Quarry,
Oxford
6/12/55

Dear Mary

I was most distressed by the news in your letter of Dec. 2d. It was touching the way you spent the first page telling me nice things about my own books and . . . then disclosed your own great trouble at the end. And I can't help you, because under the modern laws I'm not allowed to send money to America. (What a barbarous system we live under. I knew a man who had to risk *prison* in order to smuggle a little money to his own sister, widowed in U.S.A.). By the way, we mustn't be too sure there was any irony about your just having refused that other job. There may have been a snag about it which God knew and you didn't.

I feel it almost impossible to say anything (in my comfort and security— apparent security, for real security is in Heaven and thus earth affords only imitations) which would not sound horribly false and facile. Also, you know it all better than I do. I should in your place be (I *have* in similar places *been*) far more panic-stricken and even perhaps rebellious. For it is a dreadful truth that the state of (as you say) "having to depend solely on God" is what we all dread most. And of course that just shows how very much, how almost exclusively, we have been depending on things. But trouble goes so far back in our lives and is now so deeply ingrained, we *will* not turn to Him as long as He leaves us anything else to turn to. I suppose all one can say is that it was bound to come. In the hour of death and the day of judgment, what else shall we have? Perhaps when those moments come, they will feel happiest who have been forced (however unwittingly) to begin practising it here on earth. It is good of Him to *force* us; but dear me, how hard to *feel* that it is good at the time.

The little Christmas poem was nice. I particularly liked "The curtain spread By the simplicity around"—a very precise idea economically expressed.

All's well—I'm half ashamed it should be—with me. God bless and keep you. You shall be constantly in my prayers by day and night.

Yours
Jack Lewis

Magdalen College,
Oxford
Nov. 10th 1952

Dear Mrs. _____

It is a little difficult to explain how I feel that tho' you have taken a way which is not for me[1] I nevertheless can congratulate you—I suppose because your faith and joy are so obviously increased. Naturally, I do not draw from that the same conclusions as you—but there is no need for us to start a controversial correspondence! I believe we are very near to one another, but not because I am at all on the Rome-ward frontier of my own communion. I believe that, in the present divided state of Christendom, those who are at the heart of each division are all closer to one another than those who are at the fringes. I would even carry this beyond the borders of Christianity: how much more one has in common with a *real* Jew or Muslim than with a wretched liberalising, occidentalised specimen of the same categories. Let us by all means pray for one another: it is perhaps the only form of "work for re-union" which never does anything but good. God bless you.

Yours most sincerely
C. S. Lewis

---

[1]She had left the Episcopal Church to become a Roman Catholic.

As from Magdalen College,
Cambridge
20/2/55

Dear Mary

Thanks for your letter of 14th. But why on earth didn't you write it a day later and tell me the result of the examination? I don't think we ought to try to keep up our normal prayers when we are ill and over-tired. I would not say this to a beginner who still has the habit to form. But you are past that stage. One mustn't make the Christian life into a punctilious system of *law*, like the Jewish [for] two reasons (1) It raises scruples when we don't keep the routine (2) It raises presumption when we do. Nothing gives one a more spuriously good conscience than keeping rules, even if there has been a total absence of all real charity and faith. And people who stay away from Mass with the approval of their director and at the bidding of their doctor are just as obedient as those who go. Check all these points with your confessor: I bet he'll say just the same. And of course the presence of God is not the same as the *sense* of the presence of God. The latter may be due to imagination; the former may be attended with no "sensible consolation". The Father was not *really* absent from the Son when He said "Why hast thou forsaken me?" You see God Himself, as man, submitted to man's sense of being abandoned. The real parallel on the natural level is one which seems odd for a bachelor to write to a lady, but too illuminating not to be used. The act which engenders a child ought to be, and usually is attended by pleasure. But it is not the pleasure that produces the child. Where there is pleasure there may be sterility: where there is no pleasure the act may be fertile. And in the spiritual marriage of God and the soul it is the same. It is the actual presence, not the *sensation* of the presence, of the Holy Ghost which begets Christ in us. The *sense* of the presence is a super-added gift for which we give thanks when it comes, and that's all about it. I am very sorry you are so overworked. Thanks for the review of Griffiths' book which I have of course read and enjoyed already. And I'm so pleased about the *Abolition of Man*, for it is almost my favourite among my books but in general has been almost totally ignored by the public. Give my love to Fanda. I am very "cat-minded". And always, let us pray for one another.

Yours
Jack

The Kilns,
Headington Quarry,
Oxford
19/3/56

Dear Mary

A line in haste about the bits underlined in your letter (which I enclose for reference). Don't be too easily convinced that God really wants you to do all sorts of work you needn't do. Each must do his duty "in that state of life to which God has called him". Remember that a belief in the virtues of doing for doing's sake is characteristically feminine, characteristically American, and characteristically modern: so that *three* veils may divide you from the correct view! There can be intemperance in work just as in drink. What feels like zeal may be only fidgets or even the flattering of one's self-importance. As MacDonald says "In holy things may be unholy greed". And by doing what "one's station and its duties" does not demand, one can make oneself less fit for the duties it *does* demand and so commit some injustice. Just you give Mary a little chance as well as Martha!

Yours
Jack

The Kilns,
Headington Quarry,
Oxford.
31/3/58

Dear Mary

Thank you for your letter of the 26th. I am very sorry to hear about the earache. It is a horrid thing, much worse than toothache. We all go through periods of dryness in our prayers, don't we? I doubt (but ask your *directeur*) whether they are necessarily a bad symptom. I sometimes suspect that what we *feel* to be our best prayers are really our worst; that what we are enjoying is the satisfaction of apparent success, as in executing a dance or reciting a poem. Do our prayers sometimes go wrong because we insist on trying to talk to God when He wants to talk to us. Joy tells me that once, years ago, she was haunted one morning by a feeling that God wanted something of her, a persistent pressure like the nag of a neglected duty. And till mid-morning she kept on wondering what it was. But the moment she stopped worrying, the answer came through as plain as a spoken voice. It was "I don't want you to *do* anything. I want to *give* you something"; and immediately her heart was full of peace and delight. St. Augustine says "God gives where He finds empty hands". A man whose hands are full of parcels can't receive a gift. Perhaps these parcels are not always sins or earthly cares, but sometimes our own fussy attempts to worship Him in *our* way. Incidentally, what most often interrupts my own prayers is not great distractions but tiny ones—things one will have to do or avoid in the course of the next hour.

We are all well, but tired of the refusal of spring to arrive. I've never known a colder, wetter, darker March. This is pretty early in the morning and Joy is still asleep: otherwise she would join me in our love to you.

Yours
Jack

The Kilns,
Headington Quarry,
Oxford
July 21st 1958

Dear Mary

(1.) Remember what St. John says "If our *heart* condemn us, God is stronger than our heart". The *feeling* of being, or not being, forgiven and loved, is not what matters. One must come down to brass tacks. If there is a particular sin on your conscience, repent and confess it. If there isn't, tell the despondent devil not to be silly. You can't help *hearing* his voice (the odious inner radio) but you must treat it merely like a buzzing in your ears or any other irrational nuisance. (2.) Remember the story in the *Imitation,* how the Christ on the crucifix suddenly spoke to the monk who was so anxious about his salvation and said "If you knew that all was well, what would you, to-day, do, or stop doing?" When you have found the answer, do it or stop doing it. You see, one must always get back to the practical and definite. What the devil loves is that vague cloud of unspecified guilt feeling or unspecified virtue by which he lures us into despair or presumption. "Details, please?" is the answer. (3.) The sense of dereliction cannot be a bad symptom for Our Lord Himself experienced it in its depth—"Why hast thou forsaken me?"

Of course we will continue to pray for you.

A *tripos* at Cambridge is an examination: so called for the *tripos* (compare *tripod*) or 3-legged stool on which the candidate used to sit when the exam. was still, not written work, but a disputation.

Joy and I have just been for a lovely fortnight in Ireland. She, and my brother, are both well. We send our loves and blessings.

Yours
Jack

FROM *Letters to Children*

The Kilns, Kiln Lane,
Headington Quarry,
Oxford.
26th October 1963.

Dear Ruth . . . ,

Many thanks for your kind letter, and it was very good of you to write and tell me that you like my books; and what a very good letter you write for your age!

If you continue to love Jesus, nothing much can go wrong with you, and I hope you may always do so. I'm so thankful that you realized [the] "hidden story" in the Narnian books. It is odd, children nearly *always* do, grown-ups hardly ever.

I'm afraid the Narnian series has come to an end, and am sorry to tell you that you can expect no more.

God bless you.

yours sincerely,
C. S. Lewis

SELECTED BIBLIOGRAPHY

I. Books Written by C. S. Lewis

A. AUTOBIOGRAPHY

A Grief Observed (1961)
Surprised by Joy: The Shape of My Early Life (1955)

B. CHILDREN'S FICTION

The Horse and His Boy (1954)
The Last Battle: A Story for Children (1956)
The Lion, the Witch and the Wardrobe: A Story for Children (1950)
The Magician's Nephew (1955)
Prince Caspian: The Return to Narnia (1951)
The Silver Chair (1953)
The Voyage of the "Dawn Treader" (1952)

C. ADULT FICTION

"The Dark Tower" and Other Stories (1977), ed. by Walter Hooper
The Great Divorce: A Drama (1945)
Out of the Silent Planet (1938)
Perelandra: A Novel (1943)
The Pilgrim's Regress: An Allegorical Apology for Christianity, Reason and Romanticism (1933)
The Screwtape Letters (1942) [with *Screwtape Proposes a Toast* (1961)]
That Hideous Strength: A Modern Fairy-Tale for Grown-Ups (1945)
Till We Have Faces: A Myth Retold (1956)

D. NONFICTION

The Abolition of Man; or, Reflections on Education with Special Reference to the Teaching of English in the Upper Forms of Schools (1943)
The Allegory of Love: A Study in Medieval Tradition (1936)
Beyond Personality: The Christian Idea of God (1944)
Broadcast Talks [in America *The Case for Christianity*] (1942)
Christian Behaviour: A Further Series of Broadcast Talks (1943)
The Discarded Image: An Introduction to Medieval and Renaissance Literature (1964)
English Literature in the Sixteenth Century, Excluding Drama (1954)
An Experiment in Criticism (1961)

The Four Loves (1960)
Letters to Malcolm: Chiefly on Prayer (1964)
Mere Christianity (1952)
Miracles: A Preliminary Study (1947) [Chapter Three revised in 1960]
The Personal Heresy: A Controversy (1939), with E. M. W. Tillyard
A Preface to "Paradise Lost" (1942)
The Problem of Pain (1940)
Reflections on the Psalms (1958)
Spenser's Images of Life (1967), ed. by Alastair Fowler
Studies in Words (1960)

E. BOOKS OF ESSAYS WRITTEN BY C. S. LEWIS

Christian Reflections (1967), ed. by Walter Hooper
Fern-Seed and Elephants and Other Essays on Christianity (1975), ed. by Walter Hooper
God in the Dock: Essays on Theology and Ethics (1970) [*Undeceptions* in England] ed. by Walter Hooper
Of Other Worlds: Essays and Stories (1966), ed. by Walter Hooper
Present Concerns (1986), ed. by Walter Hooper
Rehabilitations and Other Essays (1939)
Selected Literary Essays (1969), ed. by Walter Hooper
Studies in Medieval and Renaissance Literature (1966), ed. by Walter Hooper
They Asked for a Paper: Papers and Addresses (1962)
Transposition and Other Addresses (1949) [*The Weight of Glory* in America]
The Weight of Glory and Other Addresses (1980), expanded and edited by Walter Hooper
The World's Last Night and Other Essays (1960)

F. POETRY AND VERSE

Dymer (1926) [originally published under pseudonym Clive Hamilton]
Narrative Poems (1969), ed. by Walter Hooper
Poems (1964), ed. by Walter Hooper
Spirits in Bondage: A Cycle of Lyrics (1919) [originally published under pseudonym Clive Hamilton]

G. BOOKS EDITED BY C. S. LEWIS

Arthurian Torso (1948)
Essays Presented to Charles Williams (1947)
George MacDonald: An Anthology (1946)

H. LETTERS

Letters to an American Lady (1967), ed. by Clyde S. Kilby
Letters to Children (1985), ed. by Lyle W. Dorsett and Marjorie Lamp Mead
Letters of C. S. Lewis (1966), ed. by Warren H. Lewis
They Stand Together: The Letters of C. S. Lewis to Arthur Greeves, 1914–1963 (1979), ed. by Walter Hooper

II. Major Secondary Works

Adey, Lionel. *C. S. Lewis's "Great War" with Own Barfield* (1978)

Aeschliman, Michael D. *The Restitution of Man: C. S. Lewis and Case Against Scientism* (1983)

Arnott, Anne. *The Secret Country of C. S. Lewis* (1975)

Barratt, David. *C. S. Lewis and His World* (1987)

Beversluis, John. *C. S. Lewis and the Search for Rational Religion* (1985)

Carnell, Corbin Scott. *Bright Shadow of Reality: C. S. Lewis and the Feeling Intellect* (1974)

Carpenter, Humphrey. *The Inklings* (1979)

Christensen, Michael J. *C. S. Lewis on Scripture* (1979)

Christopher, Joe R. *C. S. Lewis* (1987)

Como, James T., ed. *C. S. Lewis at the Breakfast Table* (1979)

Cunningham, Richard B. *C. S. Lewis: Defender of the Faith* (1967)

Derrick, Christopher. *C. S. Lewis and the Church of Rome* (1981)

Dorsett, Lyle W. *And God Came In: The Extraordinary Story of Joy Davidman, Her Life and Marriage to C. S. Lewis* (1983)

Edwards, Bruce L., Jr. *A Rhetoric of Reading: C. S. Lewis's Defense of Western Literacy* (1986)

Ford, Paul F. *Companion to Narnia* (1980)

Gibb, Jocelyn, ed., *Light on C. S. Lewis* (1965)

Gibson, Evan K. *C. S. Lewis, Spinner of Tales: A Guide to His Fiction* (1980)

Glover, Donald E. *C. S. Lewis: The Art of Enchantment* (1981)

Green Roger Lancelyn, and Walter Hooper, *C. S. Lewis: A Biography* (1974)

Griffin, William. *Clive Staples Lewis: A Dramatic Life* (1986)

Hannay, Margaret Patterson. *C. S. Lewis* (1981)

Harries, Richard. *C. S. Lewis: The Man and His God* (1987)

Hart, Dabney Adams. *Through the Open Door: A New Look at C. S. Lewis* (1984)

Holmer, Paul L. *C. S. Lewis: The Shape of His Faith and Thought* (1976)

Hooper, Walter. *Past Watchful Dragons: The Narnian Chronicles of C. S. Lewis* (1979)

Howard, Thomas. *The Achievement of C. S. Lewis* (1980)

Keefe, Caroline. *C. S. Lewis: Speaker and Teacher* (1971)

Kilby, Clyde S. *The Christian World of C. S. Lewis* (1964)

———. *Images of Salvation in the Fiction of C. S. Lewis* (1978)

———. ed., *A Mind Awake: An Anthology of C. S. Lewis* (1968)

———. and Marjorie Lamp Mead, eds., *Brothers and Friends: The Diaries of Major Warren Hamilton Lewis* (1982)

———. *C. S. Lewis: Images of His World* (1973), with Douglas Gilbert

Kreeft, Peter. *C. S. Lewis: A Critical Essay* (1969)

Lindskoog, Kathryn A. *C. S. Lewis: Mere Christian* (1973) [Revised 1987]

———. *The Lion of Judah in Never-Never Land: God, Man and Nature in C. S. Lewis's Narnia Tales* (1973)

Moynihan, Martin. *The Latin Letters of C. S. Lewis* (1987)

Meilaender, Gilbert. *The Taste for the Other: The Social and Ethical Thought of C. S. Lewis* (1978)

Patrick, James. *The Magdalen Metaphysicals: Idealism and Orthodoxy in Oxford, 1901–1945* (1985)

Payne, Leanne. *Real Presence: The Holy Spirit in the Works of C. S. Lewis* (1979)
Peters, John. *C. S. Lewis: The Man and His Achievement* (1985)
Purtill, Richard. *C. S. Lewis's Case for the Christian Faith* (1981)
Sammons, Martha C. *A Guide Through C. S. Lewis's Space Trilogy* (1980)
————. *A Guide Through Narnia* (1979)
Schakel, Peter J. *Reading with a Heart: The Way into Narnia* (1979)
————. *Reason and Imagination in C. S. Lewis: A Study of Till We Have Faces* (1984)
Schofield, Stephen, ed., *In Search of C. S. Lewis* (1983)
Smith, Robert H. *Patches of Godlight: The Pattern of Thought in C. S. Lewis* (1981)
Takeno, Kazuo. *A Study of C. S. Lewis's Doctrine of God* (1984)
Walsh, Chad. *C. S. Lewis: Apostle to the Skeptics* (1949)
White, William Luther. *The Image of Man in C. S. Lewis* (1969)
Willis, John Randolph. *Pleasures Forevermore: The Theology of C. S. Lewis* (1983)